THE ANTHROPOLOGY OF WHITE SUPREMACY

The Anthropology of White Supremacy

A READER

EDITED BY
AISHA M. BELISO-DE JESÚS,
JEMIMA PIERRE, AND JUNAID RANA

PRINCETON UNIVERSITY PRESS
PRINCETON & OXFORD

Published by Princeton University Press
41 William Street, Princeton, New Jersey 08540
99 Banbury Road, Oxford OX2 6JX

press.princeton.edu

All Rights Reserved

Library of Congress Cataloging-in-Publication Data

Names: Beliso-De Jesús, Aisha M., editor. | Pierre, Jemima, 1973– editor. |
    Rana, Junaid, 1973– editor.
Title: The anthropology of white supremacy : a reader / edited by
    Aisha M. Beliso-De Jesús, Jemima Pierre, and Junaid Rana.
Description: Princeton : Princeton University Press, 2025. |
    Includes bibliographical references and index.
Identifiers: LCCN 2024040645 (print) | LCCN 2024040646 (ebook) |
    ISBN 9780691258171 (hardback) | ISBN 9780691258188 (paperback) |
    ISBN 9780691258195 (ebook)
Subjects: LCSH: Racism in anthropology—History. | White supremacy (Social structure) |
    Ethnology—Moral and ethical aspects. | BISAC: SOCIAL SCIENCE / Anthropology /
    Cultural & Social | HISTORY / Social History
Classification: LCC GN33 .A454 2025 (print) | LCC GN33 (ebook) |
    DDC 305.809—dc23/eng/20241004
LC record available at https://lccn.loc.gov/2024040645
LC ebook record available at https://lccn.loc.gov/2024040646

British Library Cataloging-in-Publication Data is available

Editorial: Fred Appel and James Collier
Production Editorial: Nathan Carr
Jacket/Cover Design: Felix Summ
Production: Lauren Reese
Publicity: William Pagdatoon
Copyeditor: Dawn Hall

THis book has been composed in Arno

10 9 8 7 6 5 4 3 2 1

CONTENTS

THE ANTHROPOLOGY OF WHITE SUPREMACY

Anthropology of White Supremacy

Jemima Pierre, Junaid Rana, and Aisha M. Beliso-De Jesús

ON JANUARY 6, 2021, a group of armed insurrectionists supporting the losing incumbent, US president Donald J. Trump, stormed the Capitol—the seat of government—to halt the certification of the election of Joseph Biden. In addition to attacking police and destroying property, some of the rioters brandished Confederate and neo-Nazi flags, along with other recognized white supremacist symbolism.[1] One New Jersey man convicted of storming the Capitol had shaved his mustache to look like Adolf Hitler. This rioter was caught on camera declaring, "The revolution will be televised!"[2] From Viking costumes to "hail Trump" signs, Auschwitz sweatshirts to a noose and galley set up outside the capitol grounds,[3] it was clear that, among the hodgepodge of rioters, many were drawing on the cultural symbolism of white supremacy even as they claimed to only be challenging the election results.

As the December 2022 congressional report on the "Attacks on the U.S. Capitol" demonstrated, a good number of participants were from white nationalist and neofascist groups, such as the Proud Boys and the Oath Keepers. Other reports show that a broad swath of the January 6 rioters—including those not specifically linked to the fringe neo-Nazi groups—were motivated by racism and white resentment.[4] But this was not white resentment and discontent borne solely of the economic malaise of the white working poor. It was clear that the riots were a cross-class event. Contemporary white discontent within the United States should not be understood as a minority position—especially as Donald Trump received more than seventy-four million votes during the elections, the great majority of the US white population. The wide-scale support for Trump and the January 6 rioters is a reflection of the current state of US race relations. In fact, scholars have pointed to the increasing popularity of the "Great Replacement" theory among US and other Western white populations as an example of how these racist sentiments are cross-cutting (Beydoun Sediqe 2023). The Great Replacement theory is a "neofascist-white supremacist belief that white Americans are in danger of 'white genocide' and becoming a minority in their own country because of demographic change and an intentional effort by liberal and Democratic leaders to 'replace' the 'real' white America with immigrants" and other people of color.[5] This theory is fueling what some would say is an already established "right-wing populism," which was tapped by Trump and his campaign.[6] We saw the invocation of the replacement theory during the shocking 2017 Charlottesville tiki march and riot where the large group of white men were chanting, "You will not replace us!" Thus, whereas earlier understandings of white supremacy depended on, dare we say "classic" examples, such as Jim Crow segregation, apartheid South Africa, or Hitler's Nazi movement, it seems that many people currently associate white supremacy with iterations of white nationalist and neo-Nazi groupings, high-profile acts of racial terrorism, and a growing right-wing ideological discourse around white population displacement.

We argue in this book, however, that white supremacy is, in the words of the late philosopher Charles W. Mills, "institutionalized white power." Of course, it is important to recognize the disturbing and dangerous resurgence of white racist hate groups, racial terror, and racist ideology. And, importantly, this resurgence of white racist hate groups is not only in the United States but also in other settler states, and especially in European countries. But to accept these as the sole representations of white supremacy is to not only exceptionalize these movements and tie them to specific times and (Western) places, but it is to also minimize the understanding of the ways our contemporary world has been organized around a racialized hierarchy in which humanity and civilization are defined by whiteness and Europeanness.

Along with many other scholars, we argue that white supremacy is a global political, economic, and cultural system in which those racialized as "white" have power and control resources. It is a system that "includes 'conscious and unconscious ideas of white superiority and entitlement,' as well 'relations of white dominance and non-white subordination' reenacted 'daily across a broad array of institutions and social settings'" (Ansley 2010). This system is a global scheme of "institutionalized white power" consolidated through the brutalities of European expansion that led to African enslavement, near indigenous extirpation, and the Western military, political, and cultural domination of the rest of the world. This expansion was then justified, in the early nineteenth century, by a racial science that promulgated the idea of white racial superiority and nonwhite racial inferiority. The idea that European, "Western" culture, and, by extension, white people, are superior, is so deeply ingrained in our world that it configures everything from international governance to beauty standards. From what is considered the highest form of culinary training (French cuisine) to the way that international finance capital operates, white supremacy is firmly entrenched in the organization of global political and cultural structures.

Recognizing that white supremacy structures the world requires the identification that, "whiteness is a metaphor for power" (Baldwin and Peck 2017) and the understanding of the various ways that this power pervades all social, political, cultural, and economic realities of nonwhite racialized peoples across the planet. By naming whiteness and analyzing white supremacy as central to local and global sociopolitical formations, this volume challenges the tendency to only see white supremacy in localized terms and in identity categories, or only as represented through specific Western white nationalist groups.

Historicizing and Theorizing White Supremacy

What, exactly, is white supremacy? How did it emerge? How is it mobilized and made so powerful? We begin with the basic claim that it is not possible to understand white supremacy—as a concept and ideology, a set of material practices, and a structure of power—without recognizing its relationship to the ideology of race, the belief in hierarchical racial difference, and the complex and uneven practices of race formation. The relations of power that scaffold white supremacy were established not only through the colonization of the Americas and dispossession of First Nations, as well as the enslavement of Africans, but also through the classification and ordering of peoples based on presumed racial difference. The global economic and political system that emerged was dependent on this difference, where the construction of race meant a hierarchical relationship to power with the category "white" on top. At the same time, it must be remembered that, at the height of its appropriation, race was a "catchall" that included physical, cultural, and linguistic elements as well as qualities of "civilization" (Stocking 1993). Race, in other words, "is always a description of a social, historical, cultural, and political position" (Pierre and Beliso-De Jesús 2021, 250); significantly, race is also, to paraphrase Stuart Hall (1994), the modality through which other structures of power, including class, gender, religion, and ethnicity, are enacted and lived. And even as racial meanings could be malleable and shifting in various contexts, the presumed "white" race (and whiteness) was constructed—and then considered—as superior in every aspect. This valorization of whiteness and the ideologies and practices that consecrate its power enable the creation of material realities of inequality, racial oppression, and hierarchies as well as the acceptance of "white-framed interpretations, "white-imposed community norms," scientific and medical categorizations, racial images and ideologies of science and popular culture, among other things (Pierre and Beliso-De Jesús 2021).

We focus on white supremacy instead of only race or racism to demonstrate the point to a centrality of whiteness—as power—to the construction of the racialized modern world. We argue that for change to occur in these relations of power it is important for us to, first, acknowledge that the frames of white supremacy produce the very hierarchies, from "savage" to "civilized," that have placed whiteness on top. These hierarchies have led to a self-fulfilling prophecy of global white governance and nonwhite subordination, but also to the maintenance of white power in places and by those not racialized-as-white. Thus, for example, relationships and conflicts within and between nonwhite communities and nations (such as internal conflicts on the continents of Asia, Africa, and Latin America) are shaped by the history of white supremacy and the world made through European colonialism, chattel slavery, and indenture. White supremacy also governs global standards and, as we will see in this book, impact capital accumulation, territoriality, notions of "good" versus "bad" governance, credit worthiness, and local economies.

We must also acknowledge anti-Blackness as a core feature of white supremacy. Blackness (and Africanness) is constructed as the extreme opposite of whiteness—from racial science where Africans were deemed as a separate species from Europeans to travelogues and literary representations of Africans as beasts or, specifically, apes (Jordan 1968)—and Black people, particularly Black Africans, as the antithesis of civilized humanity. It is also important to note that white supremacy manifests as anti-Blackness within other nonwhite communities through anti-Black views such as colorism, even within majority Black communities. White supremacy also often manifests as "white adjacency"—where some in non-Black communities align with whiteness and buy into the racial hierarchy to gain proximity to whiteness to distance themselves from Black people (and, sometimes, their own communities) presumably to have access to the privileges that whiteness affords. Moreover, understanding white supremacy as a structure with varied processes demands recognition also of structural whiteness. Structural whiteness means that racialized relations of power occur both in tandem with and in excess of the corporeal. In other words, those racialized-as-white are not the only ones that can enact white supremacy. Others, non-whites, can also invoke or participate in structural whiteness, projecting and performing its attributes with varying degrees of consciousness (Pierre 2013; see also Hesse 2007).

The essays in this reader demonstrate the various ways that white supremacy is deployed and takes its hold across the planet. White supremacy is global because it points to the *racial* dimensions of an international power system that emerges from the history of colonialism and imperialism and includes an intertwined ideology of white racial superiority and the ubiquity of capitalism as a racialized force. For example, we cannot honestly make sense of climate disasters over the last few centuries without understanding the historical and contemporary workings of white supremacy. The concept of the "Anthropocene," which refers to the geological age defined by human dominance, cannot be truly rendered without situating how European humans dominate and control the world. Global climate change, for instance, was affected by how European settlers killed fifty-six million indigenous people in the Americas and effectively changed carbon levels, cooling the atmosphere.[7] Indeed, rather than the Anthropocene, as Renya Ramirez argues in this reader, we should understand this instigation of the "capitalocene" as the ever-present, yet hidden, "Colonialocene" situated at the heart of the system of global white supremacy.

By explicitly examining how whiteness is constructed as a clear power position and establishing the role of white supremacy in both historical and contemporary structures of power, this reader offers an expansion on analyses of race, racialization, and racism.

Anthropology and the Making of White Supremacy

One of the key interventions of this reader is to demonstrate the significance of the discipline of anthropology to the construction of race and the consolidation of white supremacy. The history and ideological foundation of white supremacy can be traced to the emergence of the discipline and the study of race. But to understand this history, we must, even if briefly, historicize race and racism. The racial colonial order that established white, European ethnocentrism as the epitome of civilization solidified over a very long period from the 1400s (Sanjek 1994). What emerged from European conquest, indigenous dispossession, and African enslavement was the naturalization of the social status of the conquered as biological difference. By the early eighteenth century, this naturalization was codified in what would become Western "science." At this point, race emerged as a concept to make sense of the diversity of human phenotypes and behavior along the lines of hierarchical difference. With the early works of European scientists such as the Swede Carolus Linnaeus and the German Johann Friedrich Blumenbach, biological variation was "used to develop universal taxonomies for classifying human populations" (Harrison 2024). As Faye Harrison notes, these "differences were linked to social and moral characteristics that stereotyped and rank-ordered the world's population in a global hierarchy" (Harrison 2024). This was the high point of racial science, where human groups were divided into five racial groupings—Caucasian, Mongolian, Ethiopian, American, and Malayan—all based on the material relationships that defined the conquerors and the conquered and enslaved. This would lead to further refinements of racial science, particularly with the rise of the use of anthropometric measurements.

What is called the "American School of Anthropology" would soon emerge through the work of Samuel Morton, who deployed anthropometric measurements of brain size to consolidate the idea of biological differences between humans that justified European cultural and racial supremacy. Morton focused on measuring skull capacity for his ranking of races, "with the Caucasoid at the top, the Mongoloid in the middle, and the Negroid at the bottom" (Harrison 2022). One of the most popular of the polygenists, Morton believed that human races were separate species. At the time, the polygenists were in a debate with monogenists, who believed that because of divine creation by God, all humans were united by a single origin. Polygenists, on the other hand, believed in multiple species origin for humans, which for them crystallized in a presumed racial order. Significantly, both groups were wedded to the idea of European superiority and the inferiority of all other beings, especially Africans. Morton was joined by the likes of anatomist Louis Agassiz, J. C. Nott, and G. R. Gliddon, and other leaders in the professionalization of anthropology in the United States, such as physical anthropologist Aleš Hrdlička (Blakey 1987).

Racial science was not only limited to the United States. The racializing consequences of African enslavement and the near-genocidal disenfranchisement of indigenous populations in Africa, the Americas, and Asia were global. Even as specific European national traditions arose in the classification of human difference in anthropology, by the early nineteenth century, all early anthropological traditions subscribed to the idea of race as a natural difference that determined a racial hierarchy of humans (Pels 2000). As we have demonstrated elsewhere, "anthropology's scientific racism had tremendous impact around the world, not only influencing the eugenics movement of the early twentieth century, but also in helping to entrench the view of African and Indigenous inferiority, as well as the inferiority of others" (Beliso-De Jesús, Pierre, and Rana 2023, 420). The dehumanization of people through the construction of racial categories within a hierarchy cannot be overstated.

Of course, anthropology's racial science was challenged from the beginning by many. Scholars of African descent, such as Haitian anthropologist Anténor Firmin (2002) and US abolitionist Frederick Douglass (1854), argued against polygenism and the hierarchization of race. Yet, the challenges these Black scholar-activists made to racial science are not as well documented within the discipline as the interventions of Franz Boas, who is considered the "father" of US anthropology. Boas is understood to have provided a radical break with anthropology's racialist assumptions with his theoretical shift from "race" to "culture." Boas critiqued the entrenched legacy of evolutionism in the discipline advocating for the study of culture. By developing an anthropological method that focused on internal cultural change in different groups, Boas argued for an embrace of cultural relativism, the idea that all cultures have inherent value and should be examined on their own terms (Stocking 1968). However, Boas's move away from explicit racial science did not necessarily mean the disavowal of the concept of race as biology (Visweswaran 1998). Rather, as Stocking has argued, it was mostly a shift in terms where "culture" replaced "race" or "race temperament" in analysis (Stocking 1968). The Boasian separation of race, language, and culture resulted in the various subfields of anthropology: biological/archaeology, linguistic, cultural/social fields within the broader discipline of anthropology. Boas's shift of anthropological analysis of human difference from biology to culture produced what has been seen as a US (antiracist) cultural approach. These methods propagated by Boas's students, including Margaret Mead, Ruth Benedict, and Ashley Montagu, insisted that the race concept (biological approaches) was not adequate for understanding societies. Instead, they argued, the focus ought to be on understanding internal patterns of cultural change over time (Mead 1934).

European anthropological traditions also moved away from earlier evolutionism. By the early twentieth century, the categories of European anthropological analysis were not specifically about culture but instead emphasized social structures. In these traditions, the focus shifted to society as a structured whole, made up of related elements that functioned together. French ethnology as well as British social anthropology stressed the relations of social structures, where the likes of Émile Durkheim pushed for an understanding of the integral nature of social structure (structuralism) and those of Bronislaw Malinowski and A. R. Radcliffe-Brown on "structural-functionalism," where societies were treated as living organisms. While the European traditions seemed counter to the cultural emphasis of US anthropology, the two traditions were nevertheless mutually reinforcing, particularly in the disavowal (or the diminishing) of the evolutionism that marked the racialized hierarchization of world populations.

Both the Boasians and the European liberal anthropologists of the early to middle twentieth century articulated—if not in word, but sentiment—a cultural relativism, a theory and method that advocated both the jettisoning of the ranking of cultures and the valorization of non-Western cultures. This "antiracist" cultural relativism, however, also reentrenched racial difference such that the theory and method of relativism continued to depend on a racialized and racializing hierarchy of races and cultures, with the white European, at the top (Baker 2021). This can be seen from Boas's "salvage" ethnographies of Indigenous cultural practices to Malinowski's "functionalism" that worked in tandem with British indirect rule and colonial knowledge formation.

The Boasian intervention has had far-reaching influence in anthropology, particularly its North American articulations, and beyond. We must remember here the critiques of Kamala Visweswaran (1998) and Michel-Rolph Trouillot (2003) who argued separately that the use of culture as a replacement for race was more of a political, rather than a theoretical, move, as it was merely a shift in terms and not a result of rigorous analysis and discussion. Visweswaran argues that this shift emerged out of an antiracist liberalism that advocated the study and preservation of culture, while reifying race and white racial domination (Visweswaran 1998; 2010). Indeed, Lee Baker (2021, 128) also demonstrates how, in his promotion of biological assimilation as a solution to US race relations, Boas also supported an Americanization movement that "fueled the hegemony of white supremacy." As a result, mainstream anthropology's continued inability to address race is linked to the Boasian assignment of race to biology and defining culture as "not race."

The critique of this Boasian shift to culture remains, however contentious, even today (Trouillot 2003). Boasian paradigms of examining culture instead of race is deeply entrenched in current anthropological approaches. For example, renewed calls for a return to the Boasian concept of culture in contradistinction to analyses of race and racism are part of this legacy (Bashkow 2004). It is important to map the discipline's epistemic attachments to ideas of "culture" as a substitute to tackling difficult conversations on its origins in racism and racial science, and the consolidation of white supremacy. The concepts of "ethnicity" or even the designation of "ethnic group" as tools of and categories of analysis, for example, remain a steadfast part of the terminology and structures of engagement used in (North American) anthropological research. In this process, an obscuring of an analysis of race and white supremacy happens through the deployment of culture. There is an implicit disavowal of race that does not allow room to explore how the deployment of culture is itself often racialized. It would not be an exaggeration to say that, "ethnicity" is often used as a stand-in for "race," confirming Brackette William's (1989) classic point that such concepts as "tribe" and "ethnicity" are only labels for the different aspect of the same historical and sociopolitical process through which the world is structured. There is a trained inability to understand the role of race and white supremacy as core features of anthropology's methods and theory. This reader reveals how race, processes of racialization, and white supremacy are constitutive of all modern relations, and, therefore, also, disciplinary formations. To understand the current intensification of explicitly white supremacist acts of violence and discourses from an anthropological perspective then means to not exceptionalize these cases. Instead, this reader demonstrates how we must highlight how the *long durée* of white supremacy is a structuring component of all these political, economic, cultural, and social relations.

Faye Harrison (2024) reminds us that the Boasian agenda was "not the only antiracist trajectory to influence anthropology." W. E. B. DuBois, for example, challenged racial determinism from the beginning of the twentieth century, producing critical antiracist analysis in the Black "vindicationist" tradition (Foster 1997). The first generation of African diaspora anthropologists, such as W. Montague Cobb, Caroline Bond Day, and W. Allison Davis, used anthropological tools as well as other interdisciplinary frameworks against rampant biological determinism and racism. And, over the years, against mainstream an-thropology's reluctance to engage race as a category of analysis, it has been primarily schol-ars of color who challenged early racial science *and* advocated the need to understand the significance and workings of race. We cannot forget, therefore, William Willis Jr.'s famous indictment in the essay, "Skeletons in the Anthropological Closet," that argued that an-thropology is the "social science that studies dominated colored people—and their ancestors—living outside the boundaries of modern white societies" (Willis Jr. 1972, 123). The main point is that anthropology, despite (or, perhaps, because of) its claims of liberal-ism, actually "essentialized difference across the color line, misrecognized the pervasive-ness of racism, and perpetuated white imperial power" (Anderson 2019, 164). These schol-ars have called for anthropology to not only understand global structures of race and power but to address its role in the construction and maintenance of white supremacy (Allen and Jobson 2016; Harrison 1995, 1998, 2012; Costa Vargas 2004; Mullings 2004; Spears 2014; Pierre 2020, 2013). Yet, we must acknowledge that much of the work on white supremacy has been cultivated outside of anthropology, principally by Black studies, In-digenous studies, and critical and race and ethnic studies (e.g., DuBois 1899; Frederickson 1981; Higginbotham 1992; hooks 2000; Jung 2015; Jung and Vargas 2011; Koshy et al. 2022; Lipsitz 2006; Leonardo 2004; Marable 2000; Mills 1998; Moreton-Robinson 2015; Omi and Winant 2015; Rodriguez 2021; Silva 2007; Warren and Twine 2008). Sociology has also made significant contributions to the analysis of white supremacy (Bonilla-Silva 2001; Doane and Bonilla-Silva 2003; Ferber 2007). It is long overdue for anthropology to include in its critical examination how white supremacy structures the world.

Anthropology of White Supremacy

In the summer of 2023, the membership of the American Anthropological Association over-whelmingly voted to join the boycott of Israeli academic institutions, joining the call by Palestinians for international solidarity in their struggle for liberation.[8] Following signifi-cant debate within the organization and informed by decades of scholarship and political advocacy, the position of boycott is an important direction toward decolonizing anthropol-ogy and taking a principled stance against settler colonialism, genocide, and apartheid.[9]

Shortly thereafter on October 7, 2023, a joint attack by Palestinian resistance groups in Israeli-settled towns across the border from Gaza led to the killing of 1,200 and the abduction of more than 200 Israelis as hostages.[10] This was followed by an unrelenting barrage by the Israeli military in Gaza that through June 2024 led to the deaths of over 40,000 civilians, injured nearly 90,000, with thousands missing (including 21,000 children),[11] displacing nearly two million inhabitants of Gaza, and the abduction and imprisonment more than 9,000 Palestinians from the West Bank and an unknown number from Gaza.[12] The basic infrastructural damage includes over 60 percent resi-dential, 80 percent commercial, and 88 percent of educational buildings.[13] All twelve universities in Gaza were bombed and destroyed, depriving almost 90,000 students of their rights to education and inflicting catastrophic damage to Palestinian culture and knowledge.[14] Access to water and basic food has been denied, not only by the Israeli government, but also the active disruption of supplies by Israeli settlers, which is leading to the condition of famine.[15]

Despite the claims by Israeli officials to self-defense, on December 29, 2023, South Africa filed an application in the International Court of Justice charging Israel with committing genocide against Palestinians in Gaza.[16] In accordance with international law and the conventions of protection of occupied people of Palestine, the Israeli government has been charged with intentional and deliberate use of genocide to punish the civilian population of Gaza. The intervention of a postapartheid South Africa is an indictment on the history of settler colonialism and the use of genocidal violence by Israel on the Palestinian people. For anthropologists who have advocated for Palestinians and witnessed this brutal catastrophe, this devastation by the Israeli military in Gaza should be considered, in the words of the International Court of Justice, "plausible genocide."[17]

Israel has carried out land seizure and the annihilation of the Palestinian people as part of its logic of becoming a modern nation-state (Khalidi 2020; Masalha 2021; Pappé 2007; Wiezman 2007), which is part of the longer continuation of European settler colonialism across the world (Wolfe 2016). That the Israeli settler colonialism, occupation, and practices of apartheid are uneasily connected to white supremacy is part of how Israeli nationalism has undone critical thinking and dissent.[18] Indeed, years ago, Edward Said described Palestine as America's last "taboo" (2000).[19] Structural white supremacy is at the heart of modern projects of settler colonialism (Inwood and Bonds 2016), which are defined through a liberal racialized white privilege that provides certain states with the right to practice genocide, apartheid, and the dispossession of indigenous people's land (Wolfe 2006).

As this recent example demonstrates, an anthropology of white supremacy must, first, take the history of European expansion and the political, intellectual, cultural, and ideological sedimentation of presumed white superiority as given and recognize the impact of that history on the political positions and social practices of the communities with which we work.

Second, and consequent to the recognition of this history, is the understanding of white supremacy as global. In this sense, we can see how the persistent investment, privilege, and power of whiteness is central to the world as we know it, and how white supremacy is structural, pervasive, and, indeed, mundane. This means that the history and structures of white supremacy inform institutions, habits, laws, policies, representations, pleasures, desires, and so on.

Third, considering its global history, white supremacy cannot be examined solely as narrow forms of identity formation and a focus only on local extremist groups. To be sure, there are extremist white nationalist and fascist groupings advocating white supremacy (and as we have seen, even the localized white nationalist groupings are part of transnational white supremacist movements), but these groups must be examined as just one of white supremacy's many manifestations.

Fourth, we must also remember that white supremacy is the modality through which many social and political relationships are lived. It is clear, for example, that racism, patriarchy, settler colonialism, and capitalism differentially affect nonwhite and white people.

Even gender and race subordination are experienced differently by varied groups because they are uniquely positioned within structures of white supremacy. Relationships of class, ethnicity/nationality, sexuality, among other factors, are necessarily altered by the overarching reality in their different manifestations of white domination (Mills 2007).

Fifth, anthropology must reckon with its role in the development of white supremacy. Anthropology is the discipline that gave us racial science and which was foundational to the consolidation of global white supremacy. We insist, therefore, that anthropology has a specific responsibility to address the consequences of this history through the examination of, not only the realities of global hierarchical relations, but also the ways that our institutions, theoretical models, and research practices continue to be shaped by racial logics and the privileges of whiteness. This means that an anthropology of white supremacy must come with a commitment to dismantling global structures of race and power.

Finally, we argue that a key part of this commitment to dismantling white supremacy must be a stance against Western imperialism and capitalist domination—both shaped by and through white supremacy. In other words, an anthropology of white supremacy must have the aim of "moving further toward an anthropology of liberation" (Harrison [1991] 1997).

We believe that the discipline of anthropology is primed for the careful study of the legacies and realities of white supremacy. Despite the troubling history and development of anthropology, radical anthropologists—especially those from communities who made up and continue to make up the bulk of the anthropology's subjects—have been at the forefront of critical analysis of the discipline as well as the development of new methodological and theoretical innovations within the discipline. In this way, scholars can then draw on these innovations as well as some key trends within the discipline, from the focus on the mundane, the daily practices and cultural rituals, the linguistic and semiotic, the historical and archaeological, to critical social and political analysis. Anthropologists, as theorist ethnographers of everyday forms of power, can offer much to the project of dismantling racial inequality. Indeed, anthropology has a long history of public engagement that sought to intervene in the problems of racism and white supremacy. Yet, it is notable that anthropologists have receded from the public critique of racism and white supremacy in recent times due to several complex factors (Andersen 2019; Baker 2010; Price 2004, 2008), while critical race scholars and historians have continued to play an important role.[20]

The *Anthropology of White Supremacy* reader situates white supremacy historically and analytically. The reader brings together anthropologists from across the world to examine white supremacy in local, national, and transnational contexts. From Okinawa to Senegal, Norway to Mexico, US to Palestine, the research in this reader examines the different forms, shapes, and contours of white supremacy as a core feature of the world in which we live. Challenging the Northern/Western/White epistemic hold on anthropological scholarship, we feature analysis of white supremacy that crosses different regions, areas, and subfields. Through an engaged practice, the scholars explore a range of approaches to the problem of white supremacy and its attendant ideological systems, making the case that a critique of white supremacy is also a critique of capitalism, imperialism, and patriarchy. Contributions to this reader examine an anthropology of white supremacy that addresses questions of indigeneity, anti-Black racism, imperialism and coloniality, sovereignty, xenophobia, homo- and transphobia, racism/antiracism, anti-Muslim racism, feminism, sexism, and patriarchy globally.

This reader expands the anthropological project by, first, expanding the breadth and scope of analysis to address global white supremacy. Second, featuring non-US/non-Western anthropologists, and third, emphasizing work that is committed to action-oriented and transformative agendas. In doing so, *Anthropology of White Supremacy* does not simply analyze white supremacy but aims to dismantle it. We make no claims that this reader is exhaustive. We feature a series of theoretical and methodological interventions along with ethnographic and methodological techniques that demonstrate the usefulness of different anthropological tools to understand and undo white supremacy. In this vein, several of our chapters shift away from a traditional ethnographic approach to explore the historical and discursive sites that structure white supremacy both in and outside of the discipline.

An overreliance on theoretical knowledge produced from the United States and Europe is also part of the maintenance of white supremacy and follows what Harrison (2016, 162) has described as an *epistemological apartheid*. This "theory-forming landscape" restricts knowledge production to imperialist, racial, and national spaces. And, even when that scholarship is produced by scholars of color, they too are situated from global centers of power. The Global South becomes a place of extraction used as a site of raw data and is not seen as a site from which theory is *made*. This form of "imperial globality," grounded in "modernity, development practices, and white supremacy" is integral to the logics of academia dominated by the Global North (Harrison 2016, 172). Part of the work to undo white supremacy then, must also "desediment" this epistemological apartheid (Chandler 2013). To practice a decolonial anthropology we must read, teach, cite, and engage with the vast canon of global scholarship produced outside of North American and European power centers (Harrison 2016). Recognizing the various marginalized anthropologies that exist can begin to unravel concentric sites of oppression. However, even with a new generation of anthropologists who acknowledge that race matters, there are still many who will not recognize the structural system of white supremacy.

The Anthropology of White Supremacy reader is organized around thematic sections. In Section I, "Anthropology as White Supremacy," we begin with the role of the discipline in the making and consolidation of white supremacy through examinations of Western science (Blakey), liberal philosophies (Rana), epistemologies (Pierre), and the upholding of whiteness as a position of power (Halvorson and Reno). Section II, "Empire, Colonialism, and White Supremacy," draws on ethnographic work to examine historical and contemporary forms of imperial and colonial formations that continue the project of white supremacy. From how US settler capitalism structures the lives of Indigenous migrant women from Mexico and Central America (Speed), the strategic deployment of mestizaje and anti-Blackness in Mexico (Jerry), the deployment of whiteness in South Asia (Channa) and Senegal (de Sá), to how European feminism served colonialism in Africa (Rahier), this section examines how white supremacy operates through empire, colonialism, and imperialism.

We continue expanding our global approach in Section III, "White Supremacy as Global Currency," which reveals how anthropological analysis can provide insight into the profitability and economies of white supremacy transnationally. For example, the essays demonstrate how the mining industry and finance capital in South Africa is reliant on anti-Black racial hierarchies and white supremacist forms of accumulation (Styve), as well as how extractivism in itself allows the construction and affirmation of whiteness in Nigeria through crude oil enclaves (Adunbi). The global currency of American multicultural advertising, how it is concerned with white consumers in the deployment of the term "diversity" (Shankar), or the ways institutional racism embeds white supremacy in Hollywood industries (Rosa and Díaz). The section also explores how whiteness is commodified globally by Nordic countries (Loftsdóttir), and how "white supremacist ways of knowing" operate in development discourses in Mali (Rahman).

In Section IV, "Militarized Geographies of White Supremacy," anthropologists examine white supremacy as Western state power. We examine how fascist intimacies are molded into US police cadets (Beliso-De Jesús), the role of white supremacy in militarized Okinawa (Carter), the plight of asylum seekers in US immigration courts (Loperena), the war on terror in Kenya (Al-Bulushi), along with the relationship between the criminal justice system, military power, and police torture between Guantánamo and Chicago (Ralph), and the role of Muslim racialization in global constructions of violence (Li).

Lastly, an anthropology of white supremacy must develop new strategies and ethics for writing, research, and data collection. In our final Section V, "Toward an Anthropology of Liberation," we draw on the well-developed tools in Black, Arab, and Indigenous feminist anthropology to assist us in undoing white supremacy. We are inspired by the Black feminist struggle for democracy in Brazil (Perry), and the new methods of love and care by Palestinian feminist abolition movements (Ihmoud). This section also looks at how Indigenous anthropologists can undo the white supremacy of settler-colonialism (Ramirez) toward an ethics of liberation. The reader concludes with an interview with Black feminist anthropologist of empire, Faye V. Harrison, who inspires anthropologists to push for transformation both within and outside of the discipline.

Throughout this reader we provide historically based ethnographies and research that demonstrate how an analysis of white supremacy is a necessary endeavor if the discipline is ever to decolonize. This reader, we hope, will serve as an inspiration for students and scholars who wish to engage in an anthropology (and a social science) that is committed to liberation and transformation.

Notes

1. Associated Press, "White Supremacist Images Culminate at Capitol Riot," YouTube, January 15, 2021. www.youtube.com/watch?v=pfxagX_TEpI.

2. Bruce Golding, "Jan. 6 Rioter with 'Hitler Mustache' Claims Ignorance about Capitol, Convicted Anyway," *New York Post*, May 30, 2022. https://nypost.com/2022/05/30/hitler-mustache-jan-6-rioter-claims-ignorance-about-capitol-convicted-anyway/.

3. Mallory Simon and Sara Sidner, "Decoding the Extremist Symbols and Groups at the Capitol Hill Insurrection," CNN, January 11, 2021. www.cnn.com/2021/01/09/us/capitol-hill-insurrection-extremist-flags-soh/index.html.

4. Char Adams, "'Vintage White Rage': Why the Riots Were about the Perceived Loss of White Power," NBCNews.com, January 7, 2021. www.nbcnews.com/news/nbcblk/vintage-white-rage-why-riots-were-about-perceived-loss-white-n1253292. Thomas B. Edsall, "White Riot," *New York Times,* January 13, 2021. www.nytimes.com/2021/01/13/opinion/capitol-riot-white-grievance.html.

5. Anthony DiMaggio, "White Supremacy and January 6: What's Missing from the Congressional Report," Counter Punch, December 20, 2022. www.counterpunch.org/2022/12/30/white-supremacy-and-january-6-whats-missing-from-the-congressional-report/.

6. Jason Wilson and Aaron Flanagan, "The Racist 'Great Replacement' Conspiracy Theory Explained," Southern Poverty Law Center, May 17, 2022. www.splcenter.org/hatewatch/2022/05/17/racist-great-replacement-conspiracy-theory-explained.

7. Lauren Kent, "European Colonizers Killed So Many Native Americans That It Changed the Global Climate," CNN, February 2, 2019. www.cnn.com/2019/02/01/world/european-colonization-climate-change-trnd.

8. "AAA membership endorses academic boycott resolution." *American Anthropological Association.* November 7, 2023. https://americananthro.org/news/aaa-membership-endorses-academic-boycott-resolution/.

9. In 2016, the first AAA member vote was held to consider the academic boycott of Israeli academic institutions in solidarity with the Palestinian struggle for self-determination. This call was to challenge the seventy-five-year settler-colonial apartheid system across historic Palestine that included racialized violence and ethnic cleansing of the Palestinian population. The campaign, spearheaded by AnthroBoycott, first suffered a narrow defeat in 2016. But in 2023, the boycott resolution was passed with an overwhelming majority. AnthroBoycott took on the difficult task of advocating both for the recognition of and dismantling of settler colonialism in historic Palestine. AnthroBoycott organizers do the important anti-imperial work that links the prevailing systems of white supremacy and racial settler capitalism. We see this scholarly work as part of this tradition, which understands that our futures are connected through our collective labor.

10. Aaron Boxerman, "What We Know about the Death Toll in Israel from the Hamas-Led Attacks," *New York Times,* November 12, 2023. www.nytimes.com/2023/11/12/world/middleeast/israel-death-toll-hamas-attack.html. The 1200 number has since been disputed by the Israeli newspaper, *Haaretz:* https://www.politifact.com/factchecks/2023/oct/31/instagram-posts-haaretz-rebuts-claims-about-its-reporting-on-israe/.

11. "Gaza's Missing Children: Over 20,000 Children Estimated to Be Lost, Disappeared, Detained, Buried under the Rubble or in Mass Graves," *Save the Children International,* June 24, 2024. www.savethechildren.net/news/gazas-missing-children-over-20000-children-estimated-be-lost-disappeared-detained-buried-under.

12. "Israel has arrested 9,170 Palestinians in West Bank Since Oct. 7: PPC," Muslim Mirror, June 13, 2024. https://muslimmirror.com/eng/israel-has-arrested-9170-palestinians-in-west-bank-since-oct-7-ppc/.

13. AJLabs. June 26, 2024, Israel-Gaza War in Maps and Charts: Live Tracker. *Al Jazeera.* www.aljazeera.com/news/longform/2023/10/9/israel-hamas-war-in-maps-and-charts-live-tracker.

14. "How Israel Has Destroyed Gaza's Schools and Universities," *Al Jazeera,* June 10, 2024. www.aljazeera.com/news/2024/1/24/how-israel-has-destroyed-gazas-schools-and-universities.

15. WFP Editorial Team, "Gaza Updates: WFP Responds to Hunger Crisis as Rafah Incursion Cuts Access to Warehouse: World Food Programme," May 17, 2024, *UN World Food Programme.* www.wfp.org/stories/gaza-updates-wfp-responds-hunger-crisis-rafah-incursion-cuts-access-warehouse.

16. International Court of Justice, *Application of the Convention on the Prevention and Punishment of the Crime of Genocide in the Gaza Strip (South Africa v. Israel),* June 28, 2024. https://www.icj-cij.org/case/192.

17. International Court of Justice, *Application of the Convention on the Prevention and Punishment of the Crime of Genocide in the Gaza Strip (South Africa v. Israel),* June 28, 2024. https://www.icj-cij.org/case/192.

18. See Abraham Gutman, "Supporting Palestinian Rights Is Antisemitic Because Israel Wants It to Be," NBCNews.com, May 27, 2021. www.nbcnews.com/think/opinion/how-jews-can-support-palestinian-rights-condemn-antisemitism-ncna1268680. Indeed, the Jewish activists in Germany, many of whom are themselves Israelis, "make up a disproportionate percentage of those detained for protesting against Tel Aviv's warpath." Maximilian Hess, "Criticism of Israel's War and Occupation Is Not Anti-Semitism," *Al Jazeera*, March 13, 2024. www.aljazeera.com/opinions/2024/3/13/criticism-of-israels-war-and-occupation-is-not-anti-semitism. Also, Jemima Pierre, "Zionism, Anti-Blackness, and the Struggle for Palestine," Savage minds, November 10, 2015. https://savageminds.org/2015/11/10/zionism-anti-blackness-and-the-struggle-for-palestine/.

19. Danica Kirka, Menelaos Hadjicostis, and Fatima Hussein, "A Global Day of Protests Draws Thousands in Washington and Other Cities in Pro-Palestinian Marches," AP News, January 13, 2024. https://apnews.com/article/protest-gaza-israel-palestinians-london-29d5cd664c81654283344d1874691a4f. See also Willem Marx, "Campus Protests over the War in Gaza Have Gone International," NPR, May 3, 2024. www.npr.org/2024/05/03/1248661834/student-protests-gaza-universities-international. Also, Al Jazeera, "Calls to End Gaza 'Bloodbath' after Israeli Attack Kills 274 Palestinians," *Al Jazeera*, June 9, 2024. www.aljazeera.com/news/2024/6/9/bloodbath-israels-central-gaza-raids-condemned-as-274-palestinians-die.

20. It is important to note the work of American studies scholar and historian Kathleen Belew (2018) and their role in the congressional hearings on "Confronting White Supremacy" and the problematic theme of "Addressing the Transnational Terrorist Threat" that adopts the troubling language of the War on Terror that racializes Muslims while comparing this to white supremacist violence. US Congress, House of Representatives, Confronting Violent White Supremacy (Part III): Addressing the Transnational Terrorist Threat, 116th Cong., 1st sess., September 20, 2019. www.govinfo.gov/app/details/CHRG-116hhrg37975/CHRG-116hhrg37975. Contrary to the insinuations of "terrorism," Belew's work connects the violence of white supremacists to the US military and the mobilization of a white power social movement that draws on conservative Christianity and a militant masculinity constructed in the last half century of US imperial wars.

References

Allen, Jafari and Ryan C. Jobson. 2016. "The Decolonizing Generation: (Race and) Theory in Anthropology since the Eighties." *Current Anthropology* 57, no. 2: 129–48.

Ansley, Frances L. 2010. "White Supremacy (and What We Should Do About It)." In *Critical White Studies*, edited by Richard Delgado and Jean Stefancic, 592. Philadelphia: Temple University Press.

Baker, Lee. 2010. *Anthropology and the Racial Politics of Culture.* Durham, NC: Duke University Press.

———. 2021. "The Racist Anti-Racism of American Anthropology." *Transforming Anthropology* 29, no. 2: 127–42.

Baldwin, James. 2017. *I Am Not Your Negro: A Major Motion Picture Directed by Raoul Peck.* First Vintage international ed.). New York: Vintage Books.

Battle-Baptiste, Whitney. 2011. *Black Feminist Archaeology.* New York: Routledge.

Beydoun, K. A., and N. A. Sediqe. 2023. "The Great Replacement: White Supremacy as Terrorism?" *Harvard Civil Rights–Civil Liberties Law Review* 58, no. 1: 69–116.

Bonds, Anne, and Joshua Inwood. 2016. "Beyond White Privilege: Geographies of White Supremacy and Settler Colonialism." *Progress in Human Geography* 40, no. 6: 715–33.

Bouie, Jamelle. 2018. "The Enlightenment's Dark Sides: How the Enlightenment Created Modern Race Thinking, and Why We Should Confront It." *Slate*, June 5.

Brodkin, Karen, Sandra Morgen, and Janis Hutchinson. 2011. "Anthropology as White Public Space?" *American Anthropologist* 113, no. 4: 545–56.

Brown, Jacqueline Nassy. 2005. *Dropping Anchor, Setting Sail: Geographies of Race in Black Liverpool.* Princeton, NJ: Princeton University Press.

Chandler, Nahum. 2013. *X-The Problem of the Negro as a Problem for Thought*. New York: Fordham University Press.

Cobb, Montague. 1936. "Race and Runners." *Journal of Health and Physical Education* 7, no. 1: 3–56.

Daniels, Jesse. 2009. *Cyber Racism: White Supremacy Online and the New Attack on Civil Rights*. New York: Rowman and Littlefield.

Dávila, Arlene. 2006. "The Disciplined Boundary." *Transforming Anthropology* 14, no. 1: 35–43.

Davis, Allison, Burleigh Gardner, and Mary R. Gardner. 1941. *Deep South: A Social Anthropological Study of Caste and Class*. Chicago: University of Chicago Press.

Drake, St. Clair, and Horace R. Cayton. 1945. *Black Metropolis: A Study of Negro Life in a Northern City*. Chicago: University of Chicago Press.

DuBois, W. E. B. 1933. *Black Reconstruction*. New York: Harcourt, Brace.

Feagin, Joe, and Sean Elias. 2013. "Rethinking Racial Formation Theory: A Systemic Racism Critique." *Ethnic and Racial Studies* 36, no. 6: 931–60.

Firmin, Anténor. 2002. *The Equality of the Human Races*. Urbana-Champaign: University of Illinois Press.

Foster, K. M. 1997. "Vindicationist Politics: A Foundation and Point of Departure for an African Diaspora Studies Program." *Transforming Anthropology* 6, no. 1–2, 2–9.

Goett, Jennifer. 2016. *Black Autonomy: Race, Gender, and Afro-Nicaraguan Activism*. Palo Alto, CA: Stanford University Press.

Hale, Charles R. 2006. *Más Que Un Indio (More Than an Indian): Racial Ambivalence and Neoliberal Multiculturalism*. Santa Fe, NM: School for Advanced Research Press.

Hall, Stuart. 1980. "Race, Articulation, and Societies Structured in Dominance." In *Sociological Theories: Race and Colonialism*, edited by UNESCO. Paris: UNESCO.

Harrison, Faye. 1995. "The Persistent Power of 'Race' in the Cultural and Political Economy of Racism." *Annual Review of Anthropology* 24: 47–74.

———. 1997. *Decolonizing Anthropology: Moving Further Toward an Anthropology for Liberation*. The Association of Black Anthropologists.

———. 1998. "Introduction: Expanding the Discourse on Race." *American Anthropologist* 100, no. 3: 609–31.

———. 2012. "Racism in the Academy: Toward a Multi-Methodological Agenda for Anthropological Engagement." In *Racism in the Academy: The New Millennium*, edited by Audrey Smedley and Janice Hutchinson, 13–32. Arlington, VA: American Anthropological Association.

———. 2016. "Theorizing in Ex-Centric Sites." *Anthropological Theory* 16, no. 2–3: 160–76.

———. 2024. "Race and Anthropology." Encyclopedia.com. www.encyclopedia.com/social-sciences/applied-and-social-sciences-magazines/race-and-anthropology.

Jackson, John. 2005. *Real Black: Adventures in Racial Sincerity*. Chicago: University of Chicago Press.

Khalidi, R. 2020. *The Hundred Years' War on Palestine: A History of Settler Colonialism and Resistance, 1917–2017*. New York: Metropolitan Books; Henry Holt.

Lake, Marilyn, and Henry Reynolds. 2008. *Drawing the Global Colour Line: White Men's Countries and the International Challenge of Racial Equality*. Cambridge: Cambridge University Press.

Lowe, Lisa. 2015. *The Intimacies of Four Continents*. Durham, NC: Duke University Press.

Magubane, Bernard. 1979. *The Political Economy of Race and Class in South Africa*. New York: Monthly Review Press.

Mamdani, Mahmood. 1996. *Citizen and Subject: Contemporary Africa and the Legacy of Late Colonialism*. Princeton, NJ: Princeton University Press.

Masalha, N. 2021. *The Palestine Nakba: Decolonising History, Narrating the Subaltern, Reclaiming Memory*. London: Zed Books.

Mills, Charles W. 1998. *Blackness Visible: Essays on Philosophy and Race*. Ithaca: Cornell University Press.

———. 2003. *From Class to Race: Essays in White Marxism and Black Radicalism*. New York: Rowman and Littlefield.

———. 2007. "Racial Liberalism." *PMLA* 123, no. 5: 1380–97.

Mullings, Leith. 2005. "Interrogating Racism: Toward and Antiracist Anthropology." *Annual Review of Anthropology* 34: 667–93.

Orser, Charles E. 2007. *The Archaeology of Race and Racialization in Historic America*. Gainesville: University Press of Florida.

Pappé, I. 2007. *The Ethnic Cleansing of Palestine*. Oxford: Oneworld.

Perry, Keisha-Khan. 2013. *Black Women against the Land Grab: The Fight for Racial Justice in Brazil*. Minneapolis: University of Minnesota Press.

Pierre, Jemima. 2013. *The Predicament of Blackness: Postcolonial Ghana and the Politics of Race*. Chicago: University of Chicago Press.

Rana, Junaid. 2011. *Terrifying Muslims: Race and Labor in the South Asian Diaspora*. Durham, NC: Duke University Press.

Rosa, Jonathan, and Yarimar Bonilla. 2017. "Deprovincializing Trump, Decolonizing Diversity, and Unsettling Anthropology." *American Ethnologist* 44, no. 2: 201–8.

Rosa, Jonathan, and Nelson Flores. 2017. "Unsettling Race and Language: Toward a Raciolinguistic Perspective." *Language in Society* 46, no. 5: 621–47.

Said, Edward. 2000. "America's Last Taboo." *New Left Review* 6: 45–53.

Smith, Christen. 2016. *Afro-Paradise: Blackness, Violence, and Performance in Brazil*. Urbana-Champaign: University of Illinois Press.

Thomas, Deborah, and Kamari Clarke. 2013. "Globalization and Race: Structures of Inequality, New Sovereignties, and Citizenship in a Neoliberal Era." *Annual Review of Anthropology* 42: 305–25.

Weizman, E. 2007. *Hollow Land: Israel's Architecture of Occupation*. London: Verso.

Wolfe, P. 2016. *Traces of History: Elementary Structures of Race*. London: Verso.

SECTION I

Anthropology as White Supremacy

THE VERY FOUNDATONS of the anthropological project were grounded in racist conceptualizations that emerged in late nineteenth-century notions of hierarchical difference and twentieth-century antiracist cultural relativism. From the late nineteenth to the middle of the twentieth century, research by anthropologists informed the broad consensus on constructions of racial categories (and racial Others) in the effort to justify the wide-scale and destructive expansion of Europeans throughout the world. Anthropology emerged as a discipline through "race science," itself a direct response to the abolition movement against the European trade in Africans. This led to a discipline focused on the naturalization and hierarchization of difference, and a variety of methodological and theoretical tools—history, ethnography, phrenology, archaeology, and linguistics. Over the years, however, the discipline's contradictory relationship with the concept of race has yielded different trajectories in research and methodology. One of the immediate results of the critiques of nineteenth-century evolutionary anthropology—and especially the notion that race was a social and not a biological construction—was a shift away, in the early twentieth century, from engaging with race and the concomitant ideologies and practices of racism (ideologies and practices that had given the concept of race its raison d'être in the first place). Another result, consequently, was the deployment of the concept of ethnicity that, while a significant substitute for addressing cultural differences, nevertheless unwittingly biologized culture.

Beginning with the assumption that race fundamentally shapes the discipline's epistemology, theory, and methodology, this section engages with the epistemological foundations of anthropology, a set of foundations structured through imperialist white racial superiority. From the emergence of the discipline through its consolidation and current articulations, the essays demonstrate how race (and the implicit and, at times, explicit valorization of whiteness) pervades all anthropological knowledge production.

1

The Blinding Light of Race
and the Nature Politic

Michael L. Blakey

RACE IS THE CENTERPIECE of a worldview that joins "Western" science and White society in a conceit. The obvious conceit of White supremacy against the subhumanity of "others" is a powerful tool of moral cover for otherwise immoral conquest, enslavement, and a long inequitable "White" occupation of now modern societies, stratified by race, class, and gender. Racism continues to soak the US social fabric and that of its sciences, too. I will set a historical understanding of racism, born in US slavery of likely parents in another era, to make its current manifestations, hidden in plain sight, more obvious. I call the broad set of assumptions of a worldview in which racism is lodged, the nature politic.

The Marshy Watershed

Racism, social and scientific, did not develop unaided by the ancillary philosophical assumptions that make sense of it. As a *biological* unit, an idea of the European Enlightenment, race stands as an example of the Enlightenment's debt to previous, Christian philosophy of which it was born (Jennings 2010; Keel 2019). The scientific concept of race, while claiming to be in opposition to religious ways of knowing, exists in unity (shares much in common) with its ideological root, even so. One broad idea at the dialectical nexus of science and religious ideology of which race is part is the philosophical notion of "nature." Nature is not simply the observable geology and biomass of Earth. As an idea, philosophy, or theory—nature constitutes the meanings attributed to the relationships of the objects of our universe—meanings with the same power Christians saw in their God. It is generally employed to externalize human responsibility, attributed to a ubiquitous "nature" (human and ecological) as though more powerful than humanity's capacity for choice.

The idea of nature, of which race is part, existed prior to its Enlightenment synthesis of the religious and secular. Moorish translations of Aristotle (384–322 BCE) placed it on the palate of the "europenses" as they first formed Christendom (Lewis 2008). Once loosed upon the world in the fifteenth century, the idea of nature was used by these Europeans similarly to Aristotle's intent of relinquishing moral responsibility for enslaving and dehumanizing others. That the relations of master to slave, Athenian to Barbarian in the age of Alexander's colonial expansion, were "natural" made nature the resolution of contradictions between slavery and Greek virtue or justice, of which contemporary philosophers had been critical in Aristotle's *Politics*. After his nonempirical and circular reasoning, Aristotle essentially concludes that "nature" is simply the way things are and, therefore, should be.

While he does represent, through fallacious twists of logic, the apologetic use of nature, Aristotle did not give us race. He is an originator of natural science, particularly for those who stick a pin in Europe on the continuous thread of ideas (Spencer 1997, 107–9). Generally, the Greeks, as the Egyptians before them, recognized human biological variation did not essentialize and reduce the diverse peoples with whom they were familiar to "populations that differ from others in the frequency of one or more biological traits." They were deeply ethnocentric, prizing their own cultural, religious, and even physiognomic traits, but the latter did not cause the former in their philosophies. The atmosphere and geography (heat, cold, and the proximity of rivers) comprised environments acting on all traits. And these Mediterranean peoples—in the middle as they saw it—could argue their perfection as balance, over the relative extremity of Africans from whom they knew their civilization first derived and the Scythians and other northerners to whom they owed little (Snowden 1970; Bernal 1987, 1991). Still, Greek mythology (as Snowden 1970 shows) is full of admiration for the African societies whom they fought alongside and against, who they were among and who were among them. Aristotle, in argument with both Classical predecessors and near-Hellenic contemporaries, was an outlier in his belief that Greeks were natural "masters" of slaves. One should not overlook the irony of the ultimate material refutation of the naturalness of Greek mastery in their defeat and enslavement by Roman barbarians (outsiders) at the pinnacle of Hellenic arrogance.

Here I set the stage for an idea of nature as the inevitable or fated universe, leaving human responsibility and morality unscathed, whose time had not yet come for more than a fleeting moment. The conditions of moral consternation were present around imperialism and enslavement in this, the nature politics', first, still birth as Greeks argued with Aristotle's intended use of nature to serve as moral cover for Alexander. Alexander might have benefited from that newly imagined "natural" order to oppose the idea that slavery, or his wealth of captives, was unjust.

In the wake of the fall of Rome, most Medieval peoples in the northern and western parts of what would first be surmised as the europenses were pagans and crudely organized into polities whose political successions tended to patricide and fratricide. The Norse (Hedenstierna-Jonson, Ljungkvist, and Price 2018) and the Visigoths looted and enslaved for gain. Christianity, marching onward under the Franks and Byzantium from its remnants in Rome, would not begin to achieve world dominance as a European "Christendom" for nearly a millennium after the fall (Lewis 2008).

Islam, Saracens, the Moors were the rightful heirs to the Roman Empire. Their five-hundred-year occupation of all (and a three-hundred-year continued occupation of part) of Iberia, taken from the Visigoths, put them in the once-developed home of three Caesars they would call al Andalus. From here to Damascus (the metropole) they translated, innovated, and carried forward the intellectual legacy of the ancients of the Mediterranean. A multicultural society, al Andalus skillfully incorporated Christians, Jews, Berbers (indigenous African Amazigh, as discussed by Keïta 2010), other African Muslims and Arabs into one society dominated by Islamic rulers. Slavs (captured from the Visigoths who had also enslaved them) and other non-Muslims were enslaved by Muslims in wars abroad. Yet Christians and Jews who paid a special tax and swore loyalty to the Moors could remain in the Iberian state as near equals, though rarely achieving high office (Lewis 2008).

Those whom we call, "Black," like the people of Mali, living free within the bounds of Islam were admired for their lawfulness and studious faith, but were ethnocentrically admonished for their indigenous-Muslim cultural syncretism (ibn Battuta 1304–ca. 1370) (Killingrey 1873). When Arab slave trade expanded into the non-Muslim center of Africa, the armchair narrator, Ibn Khaldun, began to use the biblical myth of Ham to morally justify it, in argument with the empiricist Ibn Battuta (Kendi 2016). For most of the history of al Andalus, the word "tolerance" is perhaps a more appropriate description of the institutional ethnic and religious relations among Iberia's peoples. It is certainly more appropriate for that time than it is as a current aspiration. Not full equality, but interethnic tolerance (Lewis 2008). Let al Andalus serve as the counterpoint for appreciating the subsequent development of intolerance in Europe.

Christian kingdoms in Iberia became successful in their "Reconquista" on much of that peninsula by the thirteenth century, completing the removal of Islamic control in the south with the fall of Granada in 1492. A remarkable year. In this moment of simultaneous reconsolidation of domestic authority with one hand and the effort to expand, loot, and consolidate "the New World" with the other, major ideological changes occurred in Iberian Christianity that affect the story of race. Rather than incorporate loyal unconverted others on the basis of special taxation as the Moors had done, Spain and Portugal required Christian conversion, expulsion, or death of the others with whom they had lived for centuries under the Moors.

By 1444, according to Jennings (2010), the obvious debasement of Africans, now being enslaved in chains in crude markets on the beaches of Lisbon, required Zurara's and Valignano's construction of slavery as *Christian charity*. This was an answer to the problem of an obvious brutalization of men, women, and children who "too are of the generation of the sons of Adam" (Zurara 1444 in Jennings 2010, 17), thus, to dry the royal court's "tears." At the same time, "whiteness," an emblem of Christian purity and goodness, he explains, fills the residual void of Christian election left by the removal of "the chosen people," Jews, from the Judeo-Christian identity then being cleaved at its hyphen. This spiritual whiteness and physical Europeanness would merge, as in the body of Christ commonly depicted in Renaissance art. These "white," most Christian and charitable conquistadors and enslavers invade much of the world as though to bless it.

Iberia's domestic consolidation as Christendom was difficult, showing its contradictions from the beginning, as loyalty to the faith of ostensibly converted Jews and Muslims (*conversos* and *moriscos*) was doubted. A reasonable doubt, if evinced by supernatural signs, since a claim to Christian conversion was the only avenue remaining for those who wanted to stay in their homes.

The Pope agreed pagan bodies and lands belonged to Christian rulers, facilitated by the idea, if not fully resolved, that their souls could be "saved" (Patterson 1995; Jennings 2010). In essence, true humanity with its reciprocal rights and obligations, would be defined under Christian ideology as possession of an immaterial "saved soul." Now, Christian membership would also be materially marked by color, if still more aesthetic than biological. In deep dogmatism, defined by the ardor of the Inquisition, only Christians—and in time, a white Christendom—were deserving of moral obligations.

Enter Protestantism. A new form of Christianity for the consolidation of power by northwest Europe (most exclusively and profoundly for Britain) now competing with Catholic Spain, France, and Portugal for control of an ever-expanding New World. This is just as Catholicism had served as the ideological and ethnic banner for the usurpation of the Moors in Iberia (though largely failing in the Levant). Through a series of sixteenth-century Protestant reforms, Western Christianity became at once more monotheistic and individualistic, even personal, in its religious interpretations and motivations. The Protestant work ethic emerged from the idea that God worked through human hands, yet there were some sects (Lutherans) in which an individual's belief (what is in one's heart), not actions, became the principle criterion of faith and moral goodness.

Protestantism became more bound to individual biblical interpretation (for example, by Puritans and others on the colonial frontier) than to institutionalized and highly ritualized practices (Smedley and Smedley 2012). Eventually, disestablishmentarians like Thomas Jefferson argued not only for the decoupling of church and state but for the simultaneous synthesis of a moral belief in God with a secular worldview, still bound to government ("in God we trust"). Thus, believers would marginalize the formal interference of religious institutions with governance. I view this seventeenth- and eighteenth-century development as not only the secularization of Western government but the reframing of fundamentally religious beliefs, like "nature," for use in secular institutions. This is where Enlightenment science begins in discussions of God as nature as God (see Marks 2018, 20–38, for an abundant interest in theological implications of nature by Enlightenment biologists and natural theology). For many other reasons, Keel (2018) explains the advent of racial science as yet another supersession (the theological version of an evolutionary speciation event) of Judeo-Christian religion. I focus on philosophical nature, which only plausibly derives from Europe's hegemonic Christian theology, not inexplicable pure reason.

While the ideas of Western science must carry forward fundamental tenets of Christianity, what seems most important is that both share ideological messages. These include being an epistemic capable of: (a) the authority of universal and neutral truth, and (b) explanations that externalize morally unacceptable behavior to that over which humans have little control (acts of God, the Devil, or consequences of original sin, are Christian examples; natural causes, "human nature," and racial or genetic reductionism, are scientific examples).

Natural science emerged under conditions that fostered brutal injustices of enslavement and greed at the expense of humanistic morality and virtue. In British colonial North America and its consequent United States, conditions were ripe for a return of the Aristotelian moral cover of nature. Science was more than divination, of course, with its reliance on material evidence and increasing (ostensible) disregard for deity. Yet it retains a reductionist episteme and externalization (including its claim to methods capable of neutral, extrahuman authority and universal truth) from its monotheistic root. Consider, that neither a scientist's sociocultural neutrality, nor the universal witness required to materially prove the existence of a universal truth, are possible. These ideas are based in belief.

The Rising Tide of Race

Race (a universalized, essentialized, biological category) would be applied to categorize Europeans as belonging to the normal rights of humans (as for Christians with souls). Demonstrably, the first Virginia law (an antimiscegenation law in 1691) to use the term "white" in describing a people, replaces "Christian" identity (Epperson 1999). I, therefore, capitalize "White people" from this point on to demark the legally and socially established group it has become. Race is centered in the ideological transition from religion to science, God to nature.

Note that initially White people's institutional Church will have the authority to assign full humanity by baptism. But baptism was an opportunity for the manumission claims of enslaved Africans in the Americas (see, for example, Jea 1810, in New York). The muddiness of the contradictions of Christian slave-holding (see Koo 2007, in seventeenth to early eighteenth-century colonial Boston) are profound: the "charity" of proselytization that justified slavery as moral also extinguished its justification as the enslaved obtained by it the saved souls of true Christian humans. This is the same dilemma Iberians faced during the Inquisition. Conversion was often a matter of individual choice and, therefore, so would be human rights. This equivocal authority over one's own rights was inconvenient for those with socially structured power who wished to justify their own privilege and restrict the empowerment of others.

Predictably, therefore, racial science (anthropology) emerged in the social context of the pervasive Christianization of enslaved Americans that followed the illegalization of the Anglophone transatlantic slave trade (1807/8) and the employment of Christian empathy by abolitionists. Then the convenient emergence of natural (biological) distinctions of humanity, increasingly beyond the equivocations of the Church, stepped into the ideological breach. The criteria of humanity were increasingly referenced in "nature." Whether or not they had converted to Christianity, "Afer," "Americanus," and "Asiaticus" were classified as irrational stereotypes created by Genesis to be ruled by a reasoning and lawful "Europaeus" (Linnaeus 1758) or were naturalized as "degenerate" descendants of Adamic Caucasians (Blumenbach's monogenesis, 1781). Non-Caucasians would then be reimagined as separate, nonhuman species under the polygenesis of Samuel Morton's American School (see Gould [1981] 1996) in the anxious years between Nat Turner's rebellion in 1831 and the Civil War. The contradictory fact that enslaved Africans could do all of the things other people were capable of (right down to their genitalia, as Thomas Jefferson knew well) was the entire value of slavery, if their ideological dehumanization would allow White people to make them do so for nothing. Nonetheless, these leading White scientists adhered their wishful thinking to the idea of *fixity* in common with biblical special creation and ranked races on a Christian Great Chain of Being that replaced Aristotle's *Scala naturae*.

The late nineteenth-century rise of Herbert Spencer's social Darwinism (Spencer 1898, 1978), rooted in the naturalizing assumptions of royalist (Hobbes 1651) and Anglican (Malthus 1798) apologists, dismissed all social responsibility for the effects of inequities, including those suffered by the White poor Charles Dickens described. These ideas also embodied the dialectical Christian perception of nature as "sin" or what today is called "secular humanism"—the Devil's work unredeemed by grace—yet always present in struggle with higher authority. Christianity (or, humankind, their followers might say) is defined by the unity of these opposites that it manages. An uncivilized human nature (Hobbes's every man against every man) or a natural inclination toward reproductive excess (contradictory to Malthus's good Protestant practice) produced social and economic inequality according to these Enlightenment scientists. These theorists conclude that working-class "misery" (Malthus's term) is necessitated by nature (excessive child-bearing and competition) and redeemed by the coexistence of a civilizing powerful elite, which also exists by nature. Charity becomes not only a waste of effort but an investment in sin as nature requires a Malthusian "struggle for existence." Charles Darwin (1859) will of course adopt this dispassionate concept from Malthus's interpretation of early capitalism for an analysis of organic change, made more apologetic with every new Darwinist application to modern society by others. The same Christian dialectic relates "civilized" Europeans and the "primitive races" or "tribes" (see Pierre 2020) their scholars construct. The point made here is that the presumed naturalness of races or classes serves to blind society to the unjust and immoral corruption White and elite privileges afford by making these inequitable divisions seem acceptable, even a redemptive blessing.

The many rational contradictions and inconsistencies within Christian apology and the nature politic are perhaps understandable given the deeply hypocritical morality of colonialism, chattel slavery, and capitalist class exploitation. The racial and class elites of these regimes sought to justify the unjustifiable. Perhaps what mattered most was their user's authority to claim the reasonableness of their authority over "others," as though they remained good and moral people despite their barbarism toward the fellow human beings they conveniently redefined for the taking. The "others" were inclined, nonetheless, to observe the moral and rational faults of the convoluted arguments White scientists waged against human decency. Douglass and Firmin describe these anthropologist's pomposity explicitly in the later nineteenth century. By the turn of the next century the social Darwinist trope will rise (and at times, fall) against the alternative Marxian explanation of working-class misery caused by capitalist elite's (industrial owners) unjust extraction of surplus value from worker's wages (Marx 1867) and the resources of the colonized world.

Complementing the rapid pace of change in industrial capitalism, evolutionism provided more dynamic ideas of life than had been allowed by its scientific predecessors influenced by a belief in the fixity of species. The same inequities the European and European American elite created on the ground continued, however, to be spun as natural—racial, class, and gender—inequalities, now in motion but never ending (Blakey 1987, 1996, 2020a and b; see Stepan 1993 on the metaphorical artistry connecting scientific interpretations of race and gender inequalities).

Eugenical (applied evolutionary theory) tropes for a natural ranking of societal groups or racially determined behaviors were fallacious and free. For example, social Darwinists, past and present, often confounded intraspecific differences (like large and small families) with interspecific differences (like r and K selection). They have been at pains to make the genetic inheritance of the elite (with typically the fewest children) those whose highly adaptive traits are selected for when the genes of poor and working-class children are always the most abundant in the next generation (Blakey 2020b). And never has a single gene been *observed* to cause any normally distributed social behavior in the human species.

Emptied to the Sea

This *biological determinism* that begins in slavery under a long, naturalizing gaze, will continue into the twentieth century after a brief pause for the immediate post–Civil War Reconstruction (see Hrdlička 1918 on the pause in craniometry). The slicing and dicing of the human population with the opportunity of any perceivable biological difference takes off in the laboratories of the skull doctors (as physical anthropology's twentieth-century founder, Aleš Hrdlička, was named by native Mexicans whose graves he raided). Let Ripley's *Races of Europe* (1899) stand to epitomize the mainstream industry of human biology in the West, splitting and splitting again races on the basis of the abundance of randomly accruing human diversity (see Gould 2002 for a developed appreciation of random or stochastic change); lumping an increasingly small and exclusive White self (Nordics and Aryans) from the other, by any degree, now even across Europe.

During this time, tens of thousands of human skeletons were collected by American museums (most prominently the National Museum of Natural History, Smithsonian Institution) and universities beginning in the early nineteenth century and continuing still. Although such "materials" were important for methods of sex and age assessment of the skeleton, these were organized by race, as was their initial inspiration. By the 1980s Native Americans mounted efforts to take control of their ancestral remains and sacred objects, won by NAGPRA in 1990. The First African Baptist Church (see Rankin-Hill 2016) and New York African Burial Ground (Blakey and Rankin-Hill 2009), in which Black biological anthropologists were among the leadership, set new standards of reburial and informed consent for remains considered sacred by African Americans.

Generally, anatomical collections (from dissected cadavers of institutionalized persons), like the 4,000 at the Smithsonian and Cleveland Museum of Natural History, evince the objectification of "the other," destitute White and Black people. Only very recently has the disempathetic handling of African American children's remains at the universities of Pennsylvania and Princeton brought public outcry (Ed Pilkington, "Bones of Black Children Killed in Police Bombing Used in Ivy League Anthropology Course," April 23, 2021). These collections constitute the cumulative material objectification of the "other" and the poor throughout the history of American science. Exceptionally, a protocol was forwarded to honor individual descendant's claims for burial of skeletons from Howard University's Cobb Collection (Watkins 2020) of approximately 600 remains of unclaimed dead whose cadavers were dissected in the anatomy laboratory. Ironically, the collection had been assembled during Jim Crow to defend Black people from scientific racism (Rankin-Hill and Blakey 1994; Watkins 2020).

Biological variants, physiognomic and serological, were assumed to relate to the causes of social behavioral variation according to the reductionist assumptions of post-Enlightenment scientists. The biodeterministic imagination spread by scientific authority, not "pseudoscience" as is often reported. These leading scholars used scientific methods, but their racist and apologetic theoretical interpretations of the material evidence were simply found wrong. Albert Einstein said as much about Aristotle's biased interpretation of natural slavery: "It is clear that he was enmeshed in a traditional prejudice from which, despite his extraordinary intellect, he could not free himself" (Jerome and Taylor 2005, 141, from "The Negro Question," *Pageant*, January 1946).

In our time following a Second World War, human and civil rights movements, racial analysis will be tainted by its abject technical failure (eugenics did not work to improve anything) and moral failure (societies built on racial supremacy were deemed morally evil by many conventions and declarations of the United Nations). Therefore, the moral shield of race and racism was itself sanctioned against. The focus on natural biological variation, however, continued though altered, most obviously by relinquishing explicit racial categories. Population geneticists like Frank Livingstone (1962) discovered the nonracial discordant and clinal variation of human genes led more directly than race to explanations of their adaptations. Ironically, one stood to understand the natural world best by disregarding race, which, therefore, does not exist in nature.[1] It remains, however, a powerfully effective, culturally constructed category of social difference.

The late twentieth-century Human Adaptability Programme in Britain and the United States stopped using the term "race" but initially only viewed culture as a control variable for understanding the relationship between the natural ecology and biological variation (Baker 1962). They sought to reconcile retaining the focus on nature with a then-popular liberal, "antiracist" postwar Boasianism in which culture operated on human biological plasticity (Boas 1911, 1912). But they incorporated culture into schema of natural Darwinian adaptation, which is counter to Boas's actual dismissal of evolutionary grand theory (Stocking 1968). At any rate, by the end of the twentieth century, biological anthropology faculty and graduate students at the University of Massachusetts Amherst (see Goodman and Leatherman 1998; Zuckerman and Martin 2016) will begin to employ culture seriously, as the chief independent or dialectical variable influencing important human biological variation and change.

This "biocultural anthropology" might have been fostered earlier had the intellectual innovations of those being characterized as not fully human (African diasporic scholars) been followed by the White academy. Douglass (1854), Firmin (1885), DuBois (1906), and Cobb (see Blakey and Watkins 2021) began the nurture argument against polygenesis and slavery and innovated a biocultural approach to public health during Jim Crow. That tradition continued, however, in synthesis with the biocuturalism of UMass by an Afro-Latina and African American scholars on projects they led (Rankin-Hill 1997, 2016; Blakey 1988; Blakey et al. 1994; Blakey and Rankin-Hill 2009; Blakey 2020c). The African diasporic perspective, however, had always offered a sharper political critique of the role of racism in American society and health (the only important biological variant) than had the liberal White groundings of Boasian cultural plasticity.

Efforts toward true antiracism (not just an antiracialism, which ignores or denies the massive societal import of White racialized privilege) might continue with new syntheses of biocultural anthropology. The dominant mainstream, however, continues to seek to wed human biological variation to "natural" causes, with (as per the failed Human Genome Diversity Project) or without (the Human Genome Project) race. Biological anthropology seems stalled with the still-incessant culling of, now molecular, genetic data for natural explanations without practical application. Still defining the field (and "hard" science) by its near-exclusive reliance on natural stories, the subdiscipline remains either stuck to the stage props of ecologies very distant from the urban industrial life most people live, or to reductionist (genetic or racial) variables still producing apologetic ideology and not much more (Blakey 1996, 2020a and b). What, may I ask, has the study of intraspecific variation in human genetics done for you lately?

Race and its visible differences had been analyzed as a primitive surrogate for what we now consider to be genetic variation. Today, without the use of the R-word, an overemphasis on the now-presumed *possible* implications of genetic variation often becomes a surrogate for the implications previously believed of race as the nature politic continues.

Audrey Smedley (1999) helped us understand that a worldview consists partly of an assortment of ideologies—assumed and unquestioned beliefs. The exaggerated Western attribution to nature (the nature politic) is one such ideology, mutually reinforcing and undergirding that of White supremacy. White people's alarming defensiveness to accusations of racist injustices today (DiAngelo 2018) demonstrates how well they have been buffered from the guilt and shame of their responsibility for harms of unjust privilege. A significant reason for this dissonance is their belief, without evidence, that inequality is "natural."

Note

1. Livingstone's work to discover the correlation of the histories of malaria and sickle cell trait remains the most profound and solid evidence for adaptive human variation. I will note, however, that of the hundred or so other human polymorphisms discovered by the end of the twentieth century, few have (yet, they might say) revealed their adaptations as sickle cell had. Sickle cell, furthermore, is at least as well understood as the result of human agriculture (the epitome of "culture") as of natural forces, since the ecological changes that elevated the breeding of vector's and their human hosts, precipitating selection, are principally caused by human agriculture and its civilizing momentum.

References

Baker, Paul. 1962. "The Application of Ecological Theory to Anthropology." *American Anthropologist* 64: 15–21.

Bernal, Martin. 1987. *Black Athena: The Afroasiatic Roots of Classical Civilization (The Fabrication of Ancient Greece, 1785–1985, vol. 1).* New Brunswick, NJ: Rutgers University Press.

———. 1991. *Black Athena: The Afroasiatic Roots of Classical Civilization (The Archaeological and Documentary Evidence, vol. 2).* London: Free Association Books.

Blakey, Michael L. 1987. "Skull Doctors: Intrinsic Social and Political Bias in the History of American Physical Anthropology; with Special Reference to the Work of Aleš Hrdlička." *Critique of Anthropology* 7: 7–35.

———. 1988. "Social Policy, Economics, and Demographic Change in Nanticoke-Moor Ethnohistory." *American Journal of Physical Anthropology* 75: 493–502.

———. 1996. "Skull Doctors Revisited: Intrinsic Social and Political Bias in the History of American Physical Anthropology; with Special Reference to the Work of Aleš Hrdlička." In *Race and Other Misadventures: Essays in Honor of Ashley Montagu in His Ninetieth Year,* edited by Larry T. Reynolds and Leonard Lieberman, 64–95. Dix Hills, NY: General Hall.

———. 2020a. "On the Biodeterministic Imagination." *Archaeological Dialogues* 27, no. 1: 1–16.

———. 2020b. "Understanding Racism in Physical (Biological) Anthropology." *American Journal of Physical Anthropology,* December: 1–10.

———. 2020c. "Archaeology under the Blinding Light of Race." In "Atlantic Slavery and the Making of the Modern World," supplement, *Current Anthropology* 61, S22: 184–97. doi:10.1086/710357.

Blakey, Michael L., T. E. Leslie, and J. P. Reidy. 1994. "Frequency and Chronological Distribution of Dental Enamel Hypoplasia in Enslaved African Americans: A Test of the Weaning Hypothesis." *American Journal of Physical Anthropology* 95: 371–84.

Blakey, Michael L. and Lesley Rankin-Hill, eds. 2009. *The New York African Burial Ground: Unearthing the African Presence in Colonial New York,* vol. 1: *Skeletal Biology of the New York African Burial Ground.* Washington, DC: Howard University Press.

Blakey, Michael L., and Rachel Watkins. 2021 (under review). "W. Montague Cobb: Near the Origins of Activist and Biocultural Anthropology." *Anatomical Record.*

Blumenbach, J. F. 1781. *De generis humani varietate nativa* (On the Natural Variety of Mankind) with 5 Races, Adding to 4 Races Following Linnaeus in the First Edition (1775) and as Retained in the Third and Final Edition, see (1795) in Gould 1996, 401–12.

Boas, Franz. (1911) 1912. *Changes in Bodily Form in Descendants of Immigrants.* The Immigration Commission, Washington, DC: Government Printing Office; New York: Columbia University Press.

Darwin, Charles. 1859. *Origin of Species by Means of Natural Selection, or the Preservation of Favoured Races in the Struggle for Life.* London: John Murray.

DiAngelo, Robin. 2018. *White Fragility: Why It's So Hard for White People to Talk about Racism.* Boston: Beacon Press.

Douglass, Frederick. (1854) 1950. "The Claims of the Negro Ethnographically Considered." In *The Life and Writings of Frederick Douglass,* edited by Philip S. Foner, 289–309. New York: International Publishers.

DuBois, W. E. B. 1906. "The Health and Physique of the Negro American." Proceedings of the Eleventh Conference for the Study of the Negro Problems, Atlanta University. See abstracted in "The Health and Physique of the Negro American," "Voices of the Past," *American Journal of Public Health* 93, no. 2 (2003): 272–76. https://doi.org/10.2105/AJPH.93.2.272.

Epperson, Terrence W. 1999. "Constructing Difference: The Social and Special Order of the Chesapeake Plantation." In *I, Too, Am America: Archaeological Studies of African-American Life,* edited by Theresa A. Singleton, 159–72. Charlottesville: University of Virginia Press.

Firmin, Anténor. (1885) 2002. *The Equality of the Human Races.* Translated by Asselin Charles. Introduction by Carolyn Fluehr-Lobban. Urbana: University of Illinois Press.

Goodman, Alan H., and Thomas L. Leatherman. 1998. "Traversing the Chasm between Biology and Culture: An Introduction." In *Building a New Biocultural Synthesis: Political-Economic Perspectives on Human Biology*, edited by Alan H. Goodman and Thomas L. Leatherman, 3–42. Ann Arbor: University of Michigan Press.

Gould, Stephen Jay. (1981) 1996. *The Mismeasure of Man*, 472. London: W. W. Norton.

———. 2002. *The Structure of Evolutionary Theory*. Cambridge, MA: Belknap Press of Harvard University Press.

Hedenstierna-Jonson, Charlotte, John Ljungkvist, and Neil Price. 2018. *The Vikings Begin: Treasures from Uppsala University*. Uppsala, Sweden: Uppsala University Museum.

Hobbes, Thomas. (1651) 2017. *Leviathan*. Introduction by Christopher Brooke, editor. London: Penguin Classics.

Hrdlička, Aleš. 1918. "Physical Anthropology: Its Scope and Aims; Its History and Present Status in America." *American Journal of Physical Anthropology* 1: 3–34.

Jea, John. (1810) 1998. "The Life, History, and Unparalleled Sufferings of John Jea, the African Preacher, Compiled and Written by Himself." In *Pioneers of the Black Atlantic: Five Slave Narratives from the Enlightenment, 1772–1815*, edited by Henry Louis Gates Jr. and William L. Andrews, 367–439. Washington, DC: Counterpoint. Citations refer to the 1998 edition.

Jennings, Willie James. 2010. *The Christian Imagination: Theology and the Origins of Race*. New Haven, CT: Yale University Press.

Jerome, Fred, and Roger Taylor. 2005. *Einstein on Race and Racism*. New Brunswick, NJ: Rutgers University Press.

Keel, Terence. 2019. "The Religious Preconditions for the Race Concept in Modern Science." *Zygon* 54, no. 1: 225–29.

Keita, S. O. Y. 2010. "Biocultural Emergence of the Amazigh (Berbers) in Africa: Comment on Frigi et al. 2010." *Human Biology* 82, no. 4: 385–93.

Kendi, Ibram X. 2016. *Stamped from the Beginning: The Definitive History of Racist Ideas in America*. New York: Nation Books.

Killingray, David. 1973. *A Plague of Europeans: Westerners in Africa since the Fifteenth Century*. New York: Penguin Press.

Koo, Katheryn S. 2007. "Strangers in the House of God: Cotton Mather, Onesimus, and an Experiment in Christian Slaveholding." *Proceedings of the American Antiquarian Society* 117, no. 1: 143–76.

Lewis, David Levering. 2008. *God's Crucible: Islam and the Making of Europe, 570–1215*. New York: W. W. Norton.

Linnaeus, Carolus. 1758. *Systema Naturae*. Nieuwkoop: B. de Graaf.

Malthus, Thomas Robert. 1798. *An Essay on the Principle of Population*. London: J. Johnson.

Marks, Jonathan. 2018. *The Alternative Introduction to Biological Anthropology*. 2nd ed. New York: Oxford University Press.

Marx, Karl. 1867. *Das Kapital*. Hamburg: Verlag von Otto Meissner; New York: L. W. Schmidt.

Patterson, Thomas C. 1995. "Archaeology, History, *Indigenismo*, and the State in Peru and Mexico." In *Making Alternative Histories: The Practice of Archaeology and History in Non-Western Settings*, edited by Peter Schmidt and Thomas C. Patterson, 69–86. Santa Fe, NM: School of American Research Press.

Rankin-Hill, Lesley M. 1997. *A Biohistory of 19th-Century Afro-Americans: The Burial Remains of a Philadelphia Cemetery*. South Hadley, MA: Bergin and Garvey.

———. 2016. "Identifying the First African Baptist Church: Searching for Historically Invisible People." In *New Directions in Biocultural Anthropology*, edited by Molly K. Zuckerman and Debra L. Martin, 133–56. Hoboken, NJ: Wiley Blackwell.

Rankin-Hill, Lesley M., and Michael L. Blakey. 1994. "W. Montague Cobb (1904–1990): Physical Anthropologist, Anatomist, and Activist." *American Anthropologist* 96, no. 1: 74–96.

Ripley, William Z. 1899. *Races of Europe: A Sociological Study*. New York: D. Appleton.

Smedley, Audrey. 1999. *Race in North America: Origin and Evolution of a Worldview*. 2nd ed. Boulder, CO: Westview Press.

Smedley, Audrey, and Brian D. Smedley. 2012. *Race in North America: Origin and Evolution of a Worldview*. 4th ed. Boulder, CO: Westview Press.

Snowden, Frank M., Jr. 1970. *Blacks in Antiquity: Ethiopians in the Greco-Roman Experience*. Cambridge, MA: Belknap Press of Harvard University Press.

Spencer, Frank. 1997. *History of Physical Anthropology: An Encyclopedia*. New York: Garland.

Spencer, Herbert. 1898. *The Principles of Sociology*. Vol. 1. New York: D. Appleton.

———. (1897–98) 1978. *The Principles of Ethics*. 2 vols. Reprint, Indianapolis: Liberty Fund.

Stepan, Nancy Leys. 1993. "Race and Gender: The Role of Analogy in Science." In *The "Racial" Economy of Science: Toward a Democratic Future*, edited by Sandra Harding, 359–76. Bloomington: Indiana University Press.

Stocking, George W., Jr. 1968. *Race, Culture, and Evolution: Essays in the History of Anthropology*. Chicago: University of Chicago Press.

Thomas, R. Brooke. 1998. "The Evolution of Human Adaptability Paradigms: Toward a Biology of Poverty." In *Building a New Biocultural Synthesis: Political-Economic Perspectives on Human Biology*, edited by Alan H. Goodman and Thomas L. Leatherman, 43–74. Ann Arbor: University of Michigan Press.

Watkins, Rachel J. 2020. "An Alter(ed)native Perspective on Historical Bioarchaeology." *Historical Archaeology* 54: 17–33.

Zuckerman, Molly K., Jonathan R. Belanich, and George J. Armelagos. 2016. "The Hygiene Hypothesis and the Second Epidemiologic Transition: Using Biocultural, Epidemiological, and Evolutionary Theory to Inform Practice in Clinical Medicine and Public Health." In *New Directions in Biocultural Anthropology*, edited by Molly K. Zuckerman and Debra L. Martin, 363–84. Hoboken, NJ: Wiley Blackwell.

2

Africanist Ethnography

RACE, POWER, AND THE POLITICS OF OTHERNESS

Jemima Pierre

I love the Nuer. They were our case study in anthropology.
—VICTOR WILLIAMSON, 2009[1]

THE LEGACY—AND BURDEN—OF ANTHROPOLOGY in Africa is its historical construction of African Otherness that has served to mark the continent in ways that are unparalleled elsewhere (Hickey and Wylie 1993). Contemporary critiques of ethnographic constructions of its objects notwithstanding, Africa continues to exist within a particular context of an anthropologically specific kind of "difference." The unrelenting attack from African scholars both within and beyond the anthropological and "Africanist" enterprise speaks to this. In *The Invention of Africa*, V. Y. Mudimbe (1988) argued that Africa is invented through "gnosis," the imperial trope of authentic alterity. He explained how anthropology contributes greatly to the "invention of primitive Africa" with its continued "search for primitiveness" (1988). Mudimbe further assailed the "epistemological determinism" within the discipline that testifies—even to this day—to its general "ethnocentrism" (Mudimbe 1988). Similarly, Ebere Onwudiwe asserted that the minds of Western anthropologists are "still filled with malicious notions of Africa and Africans," notions of the continent that are unintelligible—and untranslatable—outside of an explicitly, racially, "Black" African context (Onwudiwe 2001, 217). As an instrument of colonialism, Onwudiwe argues, anthropology cannot be objective "in the application of descriptive terms to Africa." "The adopted Western vernacular for an alien Africa," he continues, at worst perpetuates "the idea that African identities and conflicts are in some way more 'primitive' than those in other parts of the world" (Onwudiwe 2001, 217)

The strength of these critiques lies in both their frequency and consistency. They are certainly not new, and they continue (see Murunga 2008; Nyamnjoh 2012). Africanist anthropologists, perhaps because of the obvious dubious history of their discipline, have often acknowledged, and at times addressed, the critiques, however marginally

(Moore 1998; Guyer 1999; Apter 1999). South African anthropologist Archie Mafeje (1997) castigated the anthropological study of Africa as linked to racism and imperialism. Jane Guyer (2004, 510) called for these issues to be "brought into new philosophical and macrohistorical/comparative perspective." Andrew Apter (1999), responding to Mafeje and Mudimbe, explained that, though anthropology's "imperial subtexts" cannot be negated, they must be acknowledged.

In this chapter,[2] I make the case for understanding the way that white supremacy continues to shape disciplinary formations through an analysis of the anthropological construction of African Otherness. To do so, I argue that this construction of African "Otherness" can only be understood through the discipline's relationship to race and the processes of racialization through which it emerged and continues to be practiced. Race structures both the historical and contemporary anthropological project, fundamentally shaping the discipline's epistemology, methodology, and analysis. Within Africanist anthropology scholarship, these racialization processes are often not self-evident as they are (1) hidden behind ambiguous articulations and implications of cultural difference that continue to have racial underpinnings, and (2) depend on these same articulations of cultural difference to naturalize African otherness. In other words, the seeming acceptance of cultural difference as given without the acknowledgment of the subtleties of race implied in this difference, authorize ethnographic practice that reinforces Africa's global marking as the site of racial otherness. A related argument is that the Africanist "culturalist" frame works to disallow discussions both about the relationships of anthropology and white supremacy to Africa and about the workings of white supremacy on the African continent.[3]

In what follows, I demonstrate in detail how the continued essentialization of culture in current anthropological research and practice contributes to the persistent racial marking of Africans. I do so through a critical re-reading of some "classic" Africanist anthropological texts, with some comparison to some current analysis. This is an attempt to affirm the continuous critiques of African scholars by demonstrating that race and racializing processes are at the core of anthropological engagement with African communities. Race and racialization processes are expressed in articulations and representations of African cultural difference reifying the white supremacist logics upon which the discipline is founded. My goal here is not to provide a comprehensive review of all Africanist ethnographic texts, nor is it to broadly condemn all Africanist texts as engaging in this racializing process. Rather, I chose a few texts to show how, even in the most minute and unintentional ways, Africanist ethnography continues to Other African people. I am particularly interested in how the terms of Africanist engagement with African societies become some of the most powerful sites of racialization. These terms consist not only of various categorizations of African peoples but also the way anthropologists conceive and construct their research projects and describe African phenomena.

––––––––

The three "classics" that are particularly relevant for this discussion are: *The Nuer: A Description of the Modes of Livelihood and Political Institutions of a Nilotic People* by E. E. Evans-Pritchard

(1940); *The Forest People* by Colin Turnbull (1961); and *Nisa: The Life and Words of a !Kung Woman* by Marjorie Shostak (1981). These ethnographic studies have been lauded for their specific theoretical innovation and methodological contribution to anthropology. *The Nuer* is considered a landmark study, a classic of British social anthropology, and indeed can be considered one of the most important ethnographic case studies in the history of anthropology. The people under study, "The Nuer," are presumably well known to all anthropology students and "have been one of the best-known peoples in Africa, thanks to the pioneering cultural studies of British social anthropologist E. E. Evans-Pritchard" (Jok 2018). A student of Charles Seligman and Bronislaw Malinowski, Evans-Pritchard is one of the first trained professional anthropologists to conduct fieldwork in Africa; his work in East Africa remains foundational for Africanist anthropology. *The Nuer* has been lauded for providing an understanding of the group's political and economic functions and the paradigmatic model of "segmentary lineage" systems. Colin Turnbull's *The Forest People* is recognized for popularizing anthropological accounts and for presenting a study of the harmonious life of the so-called Mbiti Pygmies with their environment (the "forest"). Shostak's *Nisa* is known as a "proto-feminist" text and one of the first ethnographic monographs about Africa that focused primarily on women and uses their voices. Though not trained as an anthropologist, Shostak's book became one of the most widely read life histories in anthropology and is often used as a foundation text for feminist anthropology. The book was a best seller and continues to have wide acclaim.

All three texts are not only "timeless classics" but also texts that, at least in the case of Evans-Pritchard and Turnbull, were presented as challenges to anthropology's "evolutionism." Furthermore, they continue to be favored texts for contemporary introductory courses in anthropology.

That these Africanist texts remain so extremely popular despite years of varying sets of critiques is remarkable. More remarkable, I suggest, is the benign nature of such critiques and the silences they continue to foster. *The Nuer*, for example, has been critiqued on every aspect from its rhetorical style (especially questions about its ethnographic "authority") to its theoretical models (particularly Evans-Pritchard's characterization of "Nuer" society as egalitarian and patrilineal). Turnbull's idyllic image of the "Mbiti" has often been described as crossing the boundary between ethnography and fiction. In the context of revisionist studies of populations of the Kalahari Desert as well as those against cultural determinism, *Nisa* has received particular scrutiny for its presentation of !Kung San life as bounded and ideal. Yet, I argue, little attention is given to the racial subtext of the representation of Africans in these "classics."

Despite their entrenchment within anthropological teaching and the production of theory, all three texts use a particular set of techniques that work to racialize and pathologize the African communities under study, even when there is not explicit use of race as an explanation of cultural difference. I demonstrate how the three text Other (through racialization) Africans in three specific ways: (1) by locating the community under scrutiny within "nature" and, often, in symbiotic relation to animals and inanimate objects; (2) what I call moments of "differentiating distancing," where, at a specific point in the text, the author explicitly distinguishes themselves as the extreme cultural (racial) opposite of those under study; (3) by both generalized and explicitly racial distinctions of the ethnographer and subjects.

In *The Nuer* and *The Forest People*, respectively, we find two arresting passages:

> [The] symbiotic relationship [between "Nuer" and cattle] is one of close physical contact . . . No high barriers of culture divide men from beast in their common home, but the stark nakedness of Nuer amid their cattle and the intimacy of their contact with them present a classic picture of savagery. (Evans-Pritchard [1940] 1969, 40)
>
> They reappeared, announcing their presence with low whistles that sounded like the call of a night bird. They were two pairs, each pair carrying between them, over their shoulders, a long slender object. Even at that moment I wondered if they would veer off into the complete blackness of the forest. (Turnbull 1961, 75)

In these descriptions, it is difficult to distinguish between the people being studied and their environments. The "Nuer" are one with their cattle; the two species are caught up in a relationship so close that it is difficult to separate out humans from animals. Relatedly, the Mbiti "pygmies" are one with the forest—particularly the "blackness" of the forest—and are so connected to it that they can potentially fade into it. In these descriptions we find a direct link to late nineteenth-century images of the dark-skinned savage as well as attendant racialist assumptions about Africans' relationship to nature, their bio moral characteristics, and their primitiveness. The sentiments reflected in the quoted passages are not unique moments in the texts. In fact, Evans-Pritchard's photographic representations of the "Nuer" have a similarly disturbing effect. They depict what he calls the "crudity" and "savagery" of the "Nuer" life as well as close physical contact between "man and beast" ([1940] 1969, 40). And Turnbull's account is replete with similar descriptions of Mbuti oneness with the forest.

Turnbull's *The Forest People* also racializes its subjects by employing the technique of what I call, "differentiating distancing." Despite the author's utopian and liberal claims of universal humanity and empathy toward the Mbiti, there is a moment in the text where he nevertheless openly acknowledges his extreme distance from them. Amazingly, Shostak has an identical moment. Here is Turnbull describing the hunt and capture of a sindula (water chevorian):

> The youngster . . . had speared it with his first thrust, pinning the animal to the ground through the fleshy part of the stomach. But the animal was still very much alive, fighting for freedom. . . . Maipe put another spear into its neck, but it still writhed and fought. Not until a third spear pierced its heart did he give up the struggle. *It was at times like this that I found myself furthest removed from the Pygmies.* (1961, 101, my emphasis)

Compare Shostak's moment:

> [Nisa] planted the stick, with the skewered insect at the top, upright in the ground and tapped it gently with her fingers. The insect's wings burst into motion . . . then it stopped. Nisa tapped the stick again . . .

I watched horrified . . . what Nisa was doing was different. It seemed like inexcusable torture . . .

My gaze was drawn once again toward Nisa. Her head and the upper parts of her body had begun to move rhythmically . . . as the insect held itself erect, Nisa's body also became erect; when the insect circled, drooped, and strained, Nisa's body did the same . . . the incident . . . reminded me of the cultural gulf between Nisa and me . . .

The differences in our backgrounds, though I sometimes tried to deny them, would always be there. (1981, 312–22, my emphasis)

This process of differentiation reinforces African racial distinction through a double strategy. First, both scenes depict the person's intimate relationship to the animal she or he is in the process of killing. Nisa's body, for example, is in harmony with the insect; when it moves, she moves; as well, her face and torso echoed the insect's plight (Shostak 1981, 321). Second, and probably most revealing, is the author's explicit and unapologetic personal distancing from her or his interlocutors. At each of the moments described, African humanity is questioned, both in its proximity to the animals and in its distance from the human (European) anthropologist.

The racio-cultural differentiation between European/Western the anthropologist and her or his African subject in all three texts is the third racializing technique. Done particularly through the juxtaposition of "Europeans" or "Westerners" and the (tribal?) group under study, each text engages in this differentiation. For example, in *The Nuer*, Evans-Pritchard makes direct contrasts between "Nuer" and "Europeans," and between all "white men'" and the "Nuer":

From a European's point of view, Nuerland has not favourable qualities. . . . It is throughout hard on man and beast. Turnbull takes it a step further and differentiates through ongoing and brute physical descriptions of various members of the group under study. ([1940] 1969, 51)

Furthermore, he takes liberties of using racial identifiers in his description of subjects. Thus, he describes Ekianga, a member of the community, as "hairy, broad-chested, and powerful almost to the point of ugliness" (Turnbull 1961, 35). Or there is "Cephu's handsome nephew . . . a very light-skinned youth who had two children lighter than he," and "Masisi's children had finer features, with longer faces and straight noses, and they were slimmer and less stocky" (33). It should go without saying, of course, that the "colorism" (the valorization of the lighter skin, which is also linked with presumed European physical "finer" features such as a narrower nose) is a key aspect of white supremacy.

But how is it possible for contemporary anthropologists to read, teach, theorize with these texts so exhaustively and not provide a satisfactory treatment of their specifically racializing aspects? My aim in reviewing these "classic" texts is not only to provide specific detail on the racializing techniques of Africanist ethnographies but also to demonstrate that we cannot relegate them to discussions of late nineteenth-century evolutionism. Nor should we relegate this discussion only to issues of negative and problematic representations of African ethnographic subjects. It is also not enough to justify them by rendering such representations to the context of the time. (*Nisa*, for example, was written in 1981—*after* the first of the postcolonial critiques. And, in *Return to Nisa* [2000], Shostak details her return to the community years later using very similar racialized tropes.) Rather, these texts should show us that even theoretical innovation marked by the idealism of political liberalism continues to be mapped onto the racial palimpsest of nineteenth-century evolutionism.

In his response to critics (who condemned his call for an end to anthropology), Mafeje (1998) argued that his critique of European constructions of African "alterity" goes beyond the challenge to Eurocentrism. He stated that he should have been more forceful in his argument that, "while liberal Euro-American anthropologists and their kith and kin in the ex-colonies can consciously deconstruct colonial anthropology, it is doubtful if they can *deracialize the original idea of anthropology* as the study of 'other,'" (my emphasis). This point is important in helping to contextualize the nature of the critiques leveled at African-ist anthropology, particularly by African scholars. Even as the discipline diligently works to change the theoretical and methodological orientation of work dealing with African communities, there are codes, symbols, signs, words, and concepts that continue to dictate the terms of engagement. They reflect the political reality of Africa's entrenched historical position in the global racial order. In fact, in "Anthropology in Post-Independence Africa," Mafeje (1998) reviewed the more recent "anti-colonial texts" that aimed at a liberal decon-struction of anthropology but still found them wanting in ideas for a radical transformation of anthropological practice. Andrew Apter (1999), in a review article titled "Africa, Empire, and Anthropologists," engaged the African scholars' critiques of anthropology by acknowl-edging the discipline's "imperial subtexts" while providing evidence of the contemporary dialogical production of ethnographic texts, especially those from the "anthropology of colonial spectacle." He demanded that African scholars recognize how "imperial centers and colonial peripheries developed in reciprocal determination," and ended by stating that (white) Africanists should nevertheless not forget the imperial subtexts.

But what does "not forgetting" entail?

There has been another set of responses to Mafeje's blistering critiques of Africanist anthropology. It is to challenge static representations of African phenomenon by taking, as a point of departure, the coevalness of Africa with the rest of the world and attempt to treat the sociocultural practices of the people as unexceptional. Thus, in some anthropo-logical studies, the phenomenon under discussion and the analysis of the phenomenon is said to not depend on context as much as process, "less our locus than our focus" (Coma-roff and Comaroff 1992, as quoted in Mafeje 1998). For example, in the introduction to their edited text, *Modernity and Its Malcontents: Ritual and Power in Postcolonial Africa*, John and Jean Comaroff explained why their focus on ritual was not intended to further exoticize Africa:

> Let us remind ourselves of contemporary forms of Western witchcraft, witchcraft that addresses the contradictions of advanced capitalist societies. A clutch of images in the

recent popular culture of North America are especially revealing in this respect: the "Fatal Attraction of the corporate harridan who would use sexual and professional wiles to destroy home, husband, and family; the dangerous market woman of Wall Street, a trader in the vortex of voodoo economics . . . , the standardized nightmare of child abuse, embodied in the callous babyminder, whose 'Hand . . . Rocks the Cradle'" . . . (1993, xxviii)

If we put aside, for a moment, the issue we might have with the comparison of movie plots with the real situations of ritual and witchcraft practices that the essays in the book analyze, and if we also put aside the extremely exoticized and racialized subtext of the terms "voodoo economics" and "market woman," we are still able to ask if a book with a title of "Modernity and Its Malcontents," and with the subjects of "ritual" and "witchcraft" could really be about Europe or North America. Do the stories about ritual, witchcraft, and the malcontents of modernity work (especially as anthropological texts) if they are not in Africa? Or, more importantly, if they are not in rural Africa? And if the stories were not to be about (rural) Africa, would they elicit the same response, the same acceptance? These questions, though seemingly simple, are extremely important for this discussion. In making the comparisons between witchcraft in African societies and images that may or may not) be associated with witchcraft in North America, the Comaroffs make a preemptive (and defensive) move against the potential well-worn critiques of exoticization. Why else would this comparison be needed if "witchcraft," "ritual," and "Africa" did not, together, already invoke a complex set of images—a set of images that has everything to do with the very processes of racialization that enable the invocation of such images in the first place? My point here is not to say that the analyses in the text, on their own, are necessarily problematic. Rather it is to demonstrate that, regardless of intentions or theoretical program, anthropology's racializing effect on Africa remains salient. Because deep within the heart of Africanist anthropology is its association with race, the Comaroffs do not—and cannot—work outside of its "imperial subtexts" (Apter 1999). Indeed, they acknowledge that Africa's "modern" witches are part of the economic and cultural processes of globalization and that they "embody all the contradictions of the experience of modernity itself." At the same time, however, ideas about "witchcraft," "ritual"—as well as other "savage slot" (Trouillot 1991) topics—emerge and exist in the metaphoric and racialized spaces of Africa.

What has Africanist anthropology done to address this issue? And are all research projects in and about African phenomena always already "indexed ultimately to race"? (Guyer 2004). I briefly turn here to Apter's own efforts at complicating the research, theory, and analysis of African phenomena. In "The Pan-African Nation: Oil-Money and the Spectacle of Culture in Nigeria" (a 1996 article that prefigures his 2005 monograph with a similar title), Apter provides a historical ethnographic examination of the 1977 "Second World Black and African Festival of Arts and Culture" (Festac '77) hosted by the then-military regime of Lieutenant General Olusegun Obasanjo. Placing Nigeria's "oil wealth" at the center of his analysis, Apter explores the ways the state used newly found riches to forge a new nation through the commodification of culture and the construction of expansive notions of Blackness. We then see how Nigeria's current postcolonial predicament of crises—on all levels—are directly related to the ways the "money-magic" of the state's oil wealth worked to bind culture to politics and ultimately informed governance failures. Apter wants to know how Festac's "utopian dream" turned into such a "dystopian night-mare" (1996, 444). Festac '77, according to him, proved to be a "grand illusion since the modern Nigeria envisioned by the state did not materialize." As a result, today's Nigeria is not in good shape:

> What was once a monument to a booming oil-economy is now crumbling and cracking at the seams, like the *morally* and economically bankrupt nation-state so thoroughly plundered by its ruling military clique. . . . Oil, once the demi-god of national rebirth, now stands for national pollution and decay. . . . After years of rapacious looting of oil revenues, today Nigeria is a mess. (Apter 1996, 443, my emphasis)

As a result, corruption (a new form of "money-magic") abounds and acts as a contagion, even migrating from the structures of the state to individuals as foreign businesses and "businessmen" continue to be victimized by unscrupulous Nigerians.

This is certainly not a "traditional" ethnographic representation of Africa and Africans—there are no thick descriptions of ritualistic practices, of witchcraft (modern or not); no detailed esoteric discussions of "gift-exchange" economies; no analysis of lineage seg-ments. It is a study, not necessarily of a people, but of a state and its structures (of politics and culture). Nevertheless, both Apter's tone and analytical bent reflect a "culturalising of corruption of sorts that seem to work to make Nigeria (Africa?) exceptional and to make us forget the universality of corrupt state practices" (Amselle 2003). The content and ve-racity of the analysis aside, there is no denying that the way the essay attributes this type of abuse of power—one that, like a disease, later seeps through state facade into the general population—to a specific geographic and cultural entity does a particular kind of work outside the intellectual frame of an anthropological study of money, culture, and politics. Given that in the late twentieth century specialists in African politics "focused on corrup-tion . . . as a fundamental cultural characteristic of the African continent, it should cause little surprise when some wonder if corruption" (linked, of course, to state and governance failures) is not the "new racial stereotype" for Africans (De Figuereido 2005; Pierre 2020). What is fascinating about the study is the presentation of the Nigerian predicament as particularly *insular*. There is no discussion that explores the economic and political struc-tures in the movement between colonial and postcolonial moments, the broader political economy of oil production and the marginal role of Nigeria, or the role of the United States in establishing the "petrodollar" as global currency. Instead, from Festac '77 onward, the Nigerian state acted like a "vampire state" (Akpan 2005) that deploys culture (even mim-icking colonial cultural practices) to feed on the blood of its own people. Even the foreign white oil businessmen become victims to Nigerian avarice!

My point here is not to argue that the subjects of state decay, corruption, or commodity fetishism are not permissible topics of study for contemporary Africanists. There seems to be, however, a way in which scholarly excitement over particular topics—and the terms of engagement with them as well as the lively debates among Africanists—"masks the deeper question of Western representations of Africa as a continent of absolute horror, a theatre of primordial savagery only temporarily interrupted by European colonization" (Amselle 2003). The inherently racialized nature of such representations of Africans makes the "excessive anthropologizing" (Akpan 2005) of their cultural practices even more significant.

The racializing impact of Africanist ethnographic analysis continues apace in the current, more modern analysis—from the excessive focus on African waste and infrastructure as uniquely representative of modern African urban citizenship to the large-scale depictions of African (racial) "lack" in the scholarship on development. The long and established legacy of the anthropology of development needs to be taken to task, as I have done elsewhere (Pierre 2020), for the ways that it deploys and sustains notions of presumed African inferiority through the deployment of a "racial vernacular"—using problematic terms such as "capacity building," "corruption," "resource curse," "(bad) governance," among others—that index racial meanings, prescribe social practices, and, in effect, uphold white supremacy. The scholarship on development often depends on certain assumptions, including the overall goodness of western institutions, aid projects, and ideals (such as "democracy") as well as the "assumption of the cultural/civilization/racial binary oppositions between Africans and the rest" (Pierre 2020). These assumptions are embedded in the structure of global white supremacy.

The notion of "racial vernaculars" can be extended to explore the specific ways Akpan's point of "excessive anthropologizing" is made even more potent, more damaging. Toni Morrison once lamented that, as a Black writer, she has struggled with the deployment of language that works to both evoke hidden signs of racial superiority and to other people in dismissive ways (1992, x). She recognizes the embedded assumptions of language and its often-singular power in constructing and calcifying hierarchies. Africanist anthropology is no stranger to this kind of linguistic and conceptual othering. Terms such as "tribe," "primitive," "savage," "premodern," and concepts such as "ritual" and "witchcraft" all continue to have explicit racial coding. There are also the thick and lively descriptions of animalistic and "predatory" practices—be they in the form of the failed state, or "soul-eating" witches. Coupled with the examples given, Alan Barnard's review of Africanist texts, where he contrasts Joy Hendry's relativist comparison of English and Amba (Uganda) witchcraft, is instructive:

> Witches, in an Amba view, exhibit an inversion of physical and moral qualities of human beings. They hang upside down, eat human flesh, quench their thirst with salt, go about naked, and . . . shake their victims from their own villages and share them with witches in other villages . . .
>
> It is difficult to say whether current witchcraft practices in England are related to any kind of crisis or social change, or, indeed, whether they have ever really abated in the intervening years. It is certainly true, however, that magic and witchcraft continue to intrigue members of the wider society, and practising witches are found among the most apparently staid and middle-class professions. (2001, 163)

Note the animal-like, predatory description of the Amba witches and the nonspecific, generalized language used to talk about the English witches.

Ultimately, what this discussion suggests is that, at the very least, the racial inflections that undergird researching, theorizing, and writing about Africa demand rigorous analysis. What seems most stark in our current anthropological enterprise is the continued "desire to understand better other cultures so as to preserve more effectively the differences" (Malik 1996, 150). Yet, in a world shaped through global white supremacy, the failure to acknowledge the racialized epistemologies that continue to shape Africanist anthropology is itself a racial act.

———

The construction of African Otherness is not reducible only to a politics of representation. More significant is what Trouillot refers to as the "referential value of ethnographies in the wider field within which anthropology operates and upon whose existence it is premised" (1991). The Africanist ethnographic project, along with its constructions of African cultural and racial difference, operates within this field of power. That Africa has been a totalized vision of Otherness since the discipline's founding is given. That this Otherness has been conferred in terms of race is also evident, but this fact needs explicit—and particular—articulation. David Goldberg correctly asserts that:

> An epistemology so basically driven by difference will "naturally" find racialized thinking comfortable; it will uncritically (come to) assume racial knowledge as given. . . . Production of social knowledge about the racialized Other, then, establishes a library or archive of information, a set of guiding ideas and principles about Otherness: a mind, characteristic behavior or habits. (1993, 150)

The very practices of anthropology are deployed in real contexts and, as such, racialization occurs in many sites, on many levels: in the field, in the relationship between the anthropologists and the subject of study; in ethnographic texts (and in the language of these texts); in the dynamics of anthropology departments.

Although the main context of anthropological practice is academia, the ultimate context of its relevance is the world outside. Thus, this current discussion must be understood as part of a universal struggle against white supremacy. The reality is, we do not need to single out anthropology and treat it in isolation from "bourgeois" social sciences that were also implicated in the imperialist project. Indeed, anthropology was not the *only* child of imperialism. The problem of Africanist anthropology is more universal than specifically colonial, more general than exceptional. But it is anthropology that began the science of race and, since then, has been inadequate in exorcising its past in the current constructions of Africa. Africa's historic and contemporary marginalization within the global racial capitalist system is not by accident. Full appreciation of this history will open a space for us to better understand the ways that our work is in a field of power relations that inform, in concrete ways, notions of (Western) intellectual, social, and political superiority, global notions of social justice, IMF/World Bank policies, and even refugee resettlement schemes—in a world of turmoil and unequal distribution of resources.

Africanist anthropologists should also understand that racism is one of the fundamental constituent elements of the rise of capitalism, bourgeois culture, and alienated science, and is still necessary for their reproduction. To do so would be to: (1) relinquish the ideological and epistemological belief in, and practice of, constructing African exceptionalism; (2) accept responsibility for the construction and maintenance of this exceptionalism; and (3) consciously and actively construct decolonized counterpractices that challenge rather than affirm white supremacy.

Notes

1. Comment from a viewer of a documentary on "The Nuer" uploaded to a YouTube channel: www.youtube.com/watch?v=J0VBnrIkAtA (retrieved April 20, 2021).

2. This chapter is an abridged and updated version of what first appeared as Jemima Pierre, "Anthropology and the Race Of/For Africa." 2006. In *The Study of Africa*, Vol. 1: *Disciplinary and Interdisciplinary Encounters*, edited by Paul Tiyambe Zeleza, 39–61. Dakar, Senegal: Council for the Development of Social Science Research in Africa.

3. I thank anonymous Reader #1 for helping me to better articulate this argument.

References

Akpan, W. 2005. Review of *The Pan-African Nation: Oil and the Spectacle of Culture in Nigeria*, by Andrew Apter. *African Sociological Review* 8, no. 2: 185–88.

Amselle, J.-L. 2003. "Africa: A Theme(s) Park." *Anthropoetics* 9, no. 1.

———. 1998. *Mestizo Logics: Anthropology of Identity in Africa and Elsewhere*. Translated by Claudia Royal. Stanford, CA: Stanford University Press.

Apter, A. 1997. "Africa, Empire, and Anthropology: A Philological Exploration of Anthropology's Heart of Darkness." *Annual Review of Anthropology* 28: 577–98.

Barnard, A. 2001. "Africa and the Anthropologist." *Africa* 71, no. 1: 162–70.

Comaroff, J., and J. Comaroff. 1998. "Occult Economics and the Violence of Abstraction: Notes from the South African Postcolony." *American Ethnologist* 26, no. 2: 279–303.

———. 1993. *Modernity and Its Malcontents: Ritual and Power in Postcolonial Africa*. Chicago: University of Chicago Press.

De Figueiredo, A. 2005. "Is Corruption a New Racial Stereotype?" *New African*, July.

Evans-Pritchard, E. E. 1940. *The Nuer: A Description of the Modes of Livelihood and Political Institutions of a Nilotic People*. New York: Oxford University Press.

Goldberg, D. T. 1993. *Racist Culture: Philosophy and the Politics of Meaning*. Oxford: Blackwell.

Guyer, J. 2004. "Anthropology in Area Studies." *Annual Review of Anthropology* 33: 499–523.

Hickey, D., and K. C. Wylie. 1993. *An Enchanting Darkness: The American Vision of Africa in the Twentieth Century*. East Lansing: Michigan State University Press.

Jok, Jok Madut. 2018. "Nuer." *Worldmark Encyclopedia of Cultures and Daily Life*. Encyclopedia.com. September 18, 2023. www.encyclopedia.com.

Kanneh, K. 1998. *African Identities: Race, Nation, and Culture in Ethnography, Pan-Africanism and Black Literatures*. London: Routledge.

Mafeje, A. 1976. "The Problem of Anthropology in Historical Perspective: An Inquiry into the Growth of the Social Sciences." *Canadian Journal of African Studies* 10, no. 2: 307–33.

———. 1998a. "Anthropology in Post-Independence Africa: End of an Era and the Problem of Self-Redefinition." *African Sociological Review* 2, no. 1: 1–43.

———. 1998b. "Conversations and Confrontations with My Reviewers." *African Sociological Review* 2, no. 2: 95–107.

Malik, K. 1996. *The Meaning of Race: Race, History and Culture in Western Society.* New York: New York University Press.

Mudimbe, Y. V. 1988. *The Invention of Africa: Gnosis, Philosophy, and the Order of Knowledge.* Bloomington: Indiana University Press.

Onwudiwe, E. 2001. "A Critique of Recent Writings on Ethnicity and Nationalism." *Research in African Literatures* 32, no. 3: 213–28.

Pierre, Jemima. 2020. "The Racial Vernaculars of Development: A View from West Africa." *American Anthropologist* 122, no. 1: 86–98.

Shostak, M. 1981. *Nisa: The Life and Words of a !Kung Woman.* Cambridge, MA: Harvard University Press.

———. 2000. *Return to Nisa.* Cambridge, MA: Harvard University Press.

Trouillot, M.-R. 1991. "Anthropology and the Savage Slot: The Poetics and Politics of Otherness." In *Recapturing Anthropology: Working in the Present*, edited by Richard Fox. Santa Fe, NM: School of American Research Press.

———. 2003. *Global Transformations: Anthropology and the Modern World.* New York: Palgrave Macmillan.

3

Anthropology and the Riddle of White Supremacy, Making It Plain

Junaid Rana

Anthropology's White Supremacy Problem

When I first began drafting this article, it was in the midst of what seemed like a James Baldwin renaissance. Baldwin was being cited to put the racism of police brutality and killings in the context of the long struggle for Black liberation, to think of the social condition of whiteness and white supremacy in the United States, and to add poetic defiance to the global reach of US empire. In all of this, I kept wondering why Baldwin's little book with the iconic anthropologist Margaret Mead was not part of the discussion. As much as I cherish Baldwin's writings, I've always admired his verbal jousting just as much. In this moment where the possibilities of an anthropology otherwise constructed as anticolonial, anti-imperial, and radically antiracist would shake up the discipline's foundations and epistemological aims, Baldwin is a breath of fresh air. Calling white supremacy a riddle, in *A Rap on Race* (1971) Baldwin thinks with Mead about the violence and catastrophe wrought on Black life and as a global and international system that racializes around the world. In our contemporary setting, there has been a long-standing anthropological engagement with the concepts and problems of racism and white supremacy, yet the discipline has not undone the structures and systems of white supremacy embedded in its foundation (Beliso-De Jesús, Pierre, and Rana 2023).

To make it plain, there has always been a blind spot for the discipline of anthropology regarding white supremacy. More explicitly the issue of anthropology's colonial foundations is a part of the self-criticism of the discipline. Yet European and North American anthropology have had a hard time acknowledging the profound reaches and depth of white supremacy and the complicity in ongoing colonialism and racism. Over a half century ago, these two thinkers, the anthropologist Margaret Mead and the writer James Baldwin, met to discuss the problem of racism and how in their time it led to a world on fire. And yet this fire continues and has been configured in different ways in the aftermath of the Ferguson uprising, the George Floyd protests, and a worldwide pandemic. For some, the fact that white supremacy has become a keyword again in the 2020s is a shock. There are certainly many more who are in denial of white supremacy because of their consent to the politics of such a racial order. It should not come as a surprise that in what follows is an argument based on a system of white supremacy that is at the core foundation of the American way of life. This is not an argument that white supremacy is marginal or based on violent and grisly actors of specific groups. Instead, this is a theorization of white supremacy in the Baldwinian mode that sees it as a systemic way of being, thinking, and doing that is everywhere throughout social life. In Baldwin's critique, this applies directly to Mead and her approach to anthropology, and I would add, Mead's legacy in the discipline.

While it is easy to peg the conversation between Mead and Baldwin as a meeting of two opposing views, liberal racist and radical antiracist, the dynamic is far more constitutive of positions that challenge the transformational possibility of knowing, thinking, and acting. While Mead has often been considered as a problematic yet liberal stand-in for anthropological thought and its unbearable whiteness of being, this exploration of the exchange between Mead and Baldwin contemplates the possibility of bringing Baldwin the poet to bear as an ethnographic witness and critic. The call for a Baldwin skewered anthropology is to ask for a dwelling in accountability and commitment that goes beyond the empirical fact of white supremacy. To take the language and precision of Baldwin the poet seriously is to question the discipline of anthropology as it has been, and to ask what it can be. An anthropology of white supremacy calls for an anthropology of liberation, anticolonialism, and social transformation beyond observation of the present. Speculating about a Baldwinian anthropology as an antidote and condemnation of the social fact of white supremacy is to linger in the metaphorical and poetic possibilities of undoing, being undone, and thinking anew.

In the summer of 1970 Margaret Mead and James Baldwin met in New York City over a two-day period to record a conversation subsequently published in book form as *A Rap on Race* (1971).[1] The following year an edited version was released as a double vinyl LP.[2] In a surprisingly accessible conversation meant to intervene in the public discourse regarding race and racism, it is easy to miss their discussion of white supremacy. Early on, Baldwin refers to what he calls "the riddle of white supremacy" (RR, 32) to frame their conversation, and perhaps to set the terms of the problem. In a self-reflexive mode, Mead describes her experience of white supremacy growing up in Pennsylvania. Both bring up how white supremacy persists as a problem with a global scale. Their differences revolve around how they interpret white supremacy, the relationship of racism and capitalism in what Cedric Robinson would later call racial capitalism (Robinson 1983; Melamed 2015),[3] and ultimately how to struggle against white supremacy. In their exchange, I am interested in two strands of their conversation that appear secondary to their analysis of racism. First, that the problem of white supremacy is global as opposed to simply confined to the United States, North America, or Europe. While racism and white supremacy are often thought of as conceptually related, it is important to make clear their differences, and specifically expand the theoretical discussion of global white supremacy. Second, I draw on the reference Mead and Baldwin make to religion, morality, and theology to characterize the scope of racism and white supremacy. In what is an underappreciated aspect of the theoretical analysis of white supremacy, religion and theology present a number of insights and contradictions to conceptualize white supremacy. In this chapter, I draw on the exchange between Baldwin and Mead to theorize these two components, the global and the theological, in relationship to white supremacy. By conceptualizing global white supremacy as intimately tied to religion and theological discourse, anthropological theory can address the ongoing forms of racialization, such as anti-Muslim racism, and better understand struggles against white supremacy. In their discussion of race, religion, and white supremacy, for Mead and Baldwin Islam and Muslims are lurking close to the surface, something that is telling in the ongoing shifts of global racial formations and the social protest movements that have responded to them.

Racism and white supremacy are not often considered in relationship to theology and religion. The scholar of theology J. Kameron Carter has shed light on how race and religion are connected to white supremacy, and in the role of liberation theology as a site of struggle. In the modern period of European history, the concept of race emerged through an ethnological transformation in which Christianity biologized notions of religiosity in contrast to Judaism (Carter 2008). In a twofold process, Jews were first made into a racial group distinct from Christianity and European Christian culture. Second, Judaism was deemed inferior, creating a racialized anti-Judaic sentiment of white supremacy, and more succinctly, white Christian supremacy (Carter 2008, 4). This theological perspective provides an account for how race and white supremacy are related to Christian ideas of religion and being, which also led to the historical emergence of the racialization of Islam and Muslims (Bayoumi 2006; Medovoi 2012; Rana 2007; Razack 2008).

With these Christian theological origins of white supremacy, Carter does not dismiss religion as racist but instead turns to liberation theology and the work of James Cone to confront whiteness and white supremacy as theological problems of racism (Carter 2008, 157–58). Cone was one of the first theologians to connect liberation in the Christian tradition to the Black Power struggle. He importantly argued that the position of political Blackness is an antioppression stance that regards dispossession and the dispossessed as positions within the hierarchies of racial capitalism (Cone 1969; 1970). The quintessential icons of the civil rights movement Martin Luther King Jr. and Malcolm X, or Malik el-Shabazz, were both political figures as much as they are religious ones, and both fundamentally engaged in a political praxis that drew from theological reasoning and liberation struggles in the Black radical tradition (Cone 1991; Curtis 2015; Robinson 1983). Black liberation theology provides insight into the complex ways that social justice movements offer a substantive critique of politics, religion, racism, and antiracism, from both the Christian and Islamic tradition (Jackson 2005; 2009). In other words, religion and theology play a role in upholding white supremacy, and in struggling against it. As there are theologies that uphold white supremacy, there are also theologies of liberation that work to upset white supremacy.

Anthropologists and social scientists have not fully elaborated a theory of white supremacy. The work of Faye Harrison (1991; 1995; 1999; 2008), who importantly called for the decolonization of anthropology through the study of racism, is an important parallel to the anthropological theorization of white supremacy. What Leith Mullings calls an antiracist anthropology (2005; 2015), and what both allude to as the challenge of global apartheid (Harrison 2002; Mullings 2009), provides an agenda of how race and racism are implicated in social structures, systems of hierarchy, and antiracist struggles. The difficulty is in distinguishing white supremacy from racism, since the assumption is that white supremacy is the ideological machinery that propels and defines the objects of racism. In the most recent edition of their influential study of racial formation, Michael Omi and Howard Winant allude to white supremacy as structural and ideological (2015, 94–95) in terms of establishing a racial order based in hierarchy (Omi and Winant 2015, 107, 130). More specifically, they conceptualize it as "an evolving hegemonic racial project that has taken different forms from the colonial era to the present" (Omi and Winant 2015, 127). This line of argument follows what George Lipsitz calls the "possessive investment in whiteness" in which white supremacy is a mechanism of accumulating profit (Lipsitz 1998), and the innovative work of legal scholar Cheryl Harris in her well-known definition of "whiteness as property" (Harris 1993). In this theoretical genealogy one can trace a number of influences and related concepts that invoke white supremacy as, for example, hegemony, structure and superstructure, process, system, and racial capitalism. White supremacy is often thought of as ideological, a constellation of ideas and values that explain social practices and boundaries, or as a system, something far more encompassing than social practice that is institutionalized and maintained throughout social life.

The anthropological theorization of race significantly discusses culture. In a significant critique of the discipline of anthropology, Kamala Visweswaran argues that race and culture are placed in tension with each other despite the purported disavowal of the former over the supposedly progressive victory of the latter (1998; 2010). As culture has been imbued with racial ideas, so too has religion. With this ongoing race-ing of religion in the legacy of white supremacy, theological debates and popular discourses are critical to how Islam and Muslims become figures of racialization in the present and in the past. Drawing on the exchange between Mead and Baldwin, I argue that anthropological theory can give rise to ethnographic examples to understand everyday encounters and struggles against white supremacy. Theorizing white supremacy from these vantage points opens up new vistas from which anthropology can approach and encounter the problem of white supremacy and racial violence.

Racial Liberalism and the Race Rebel

In the conversation between Mead and Baldwin, the discipline of anthropology has much to reckon with. Foremost is the public engagement and intellectual debate of the concepts, values, and struggles associated with racism and white supremacy. Their interaction is a lesson in disentangling the viewpoint of a liberal, secularist, view of the world that might be called the white world, or what the philosopher Charles Mills refers to as the racial contract and as racial liberalism (Mills 1997; 2017).[4] This ability to see through this viewpoint, to renounce it, and then to work against it is the point of the confrontation in *A Rap on Race*. In what Mead recognizes as her difference with Baldwin is based in this racial contract that both are living through.

Right away, Mead and Baldwin establish a rapport taking on specific roles. Mead in her characteristically plain language is often trying to convince Baldwin, to sway him to her position. As an anthropologist, one who insists on a broader public impact, Mead is the teacher, the analyst, and the optimist. Baldwin, on the other hand, is not interested in winning a debate outright. Instead, he disavows the role that white supremacy has forced him into, claiming the status of an exile to the American way, and insisting on the role of the poet-philosopher to renounce unexamined convention.

The conflict between their positions escalates when Baldwin claims culpability in the Birmingham church bombing of 1963 that resulted in the death of four Black girls. Asked if he bombed those little girls, he responds, "I'm responsible for it. I didn't stop it" (RR, 223). Mead accuses him of thinking like a member of the Russian Orthodox Church where everyone is guilty of all human suffering. To which Baldwin-the-poet responds "that blood is also on my hands . . . everybody's suffering is mine" (RR, 224). As they continue to parse what this means, Baldwin interjects: "you are identified with the angels, and I'm identified with the devil. We are living in a kind of theology" (RR, 228), a harsh retort to a point Mead had made earlier with associations of racial innocence and sin. Living out this theology they turn to experiences of power, capitalism, and colonialism. Mead provides examples of similar kinds of oppression, as Baldwin consistently applies an analysis of race to capitalism. Mead admonishes Baldwin by raising her voice and banging the table on the audio recording: "it isn't the same principle as long as you are going to continue to make it racial." Baldwin denies he is "being racial." In the text, Mead is given emphasis through italics: "you *are* being racial. I present you with human situations and you make them racial" (RR, 233). Audio excised from the text records Mead saying, "we are not having a rational conversation anymore" (8:26, 2:2). Without missing a beat, or becoming rankled, Baldwin quickly quips, "We are talking about the profit motive" (RR, 233), a point he mentioned earlier as a critique of capitalism (RR, 163–64). Again, Mead is edited out of the text when she responds, "we weren't." In reply to this, audio of Baldwin can be heard edgily laughing, directing the recording technician to "cut it off." Yet, they continued.

In short, this interaction summarizes their theoretical and political differences. Mead is frustrated by what she deems an elusive Baldwin who is basically not making sense for her pragmatic approach to problem-solving. Baldwin, on the other hand, is quite aware of Mead's ideas and pushes for more complexity, a kind of radical resolution to the problem of white supremacy. While it is easy to dismiss some of the race and culture thinking of Mead as anachronistic and offensive,[5] it is far more representative of a political ethos from which anthropology has inherited a particular language of critique and advocacy. Mead, and in general the notion of liberal anthropology, displays what might be called the position of racial liberalism. Critical race philosopher Charles Mills describes racial liberalism as "the actual liberalism that has been historically dominant since modernity: a liberal theory whose terms originally restricted full personhood to whites (or, more accurately, white men) and relegated nonwhites to an inferior category, so that its schedule of rights and prescriptions for justice were all color-coded" (2017, 31). In an earlier work, Mills relates this general philosophy as the "racial contract" in which white supremacy is the "unnamed political system" (1997, 1) in which exploitation and dominance continues into the present. Racial liberalism is premised in the notions of a rights-based framework accorded by the racial contract in which global white supremacy extends its social and political framework, and it might be added, was constructed in relation to theological debates and ideas of religious difference.

The idea of racial liberalism is pervasive to a kind of transformative politics within modernity and capitalism. Scholars have typically assigned this to a double-edged meaning in which the idea of expanding liberal ideas of rights and resources is a kind of force and dominance in which social hierarchies are produced, replicated, and diffused in a system of racism and white supremacy.[6] In this estimation, Mead is a racial liberal who espouses a left-liberal antiracism of her time. Baldwin is not exactly a counter to this as much as a disrupter of the entire system. More than just a witness to the crime of white supremacy, Baldwin is a race-radical who seeks to upend the racial thinking that is systematically configured through racial capitalism. Jodi Melamed uses the term "race radicalism" for figures like Baldwin to draw attention to the "genealogy of a persistent opposition to liberal anti-racisms" (2011, xvii).[7] Racial liberalism itself presupposes a kind of liberal antiracism that is the response to the problem of white supremacy. Thinking of this dialectic as a move between racial liberalism and race radicalism is an explanation of the genuine philosophical and ethical dialogue between Mead and Baldwin that also demonstrates their incommensurability. It is this distinction that is the problematic of liberal anthropology, and what an anthropology of white supremacy must fully address. Because of Mead's adherence to racial liberalism, the anthropologist has trouble fully comprehending Baldwin, the writer-poet.

The Theological Problem of White Supremacy

Both Mead and Baldwin are convinced that the problem of white supremacy and racism must be confronted. From the first minutes of their conversation, they refer to religion to address the values, beliefs, and morals associated with race thinking. Baldwin refers to a younger generation that is "repudiating the entire theology . . . which has afflicted and destroyed—really, literally destroyed—Black people in this country for so long." He continues with a specific diagnosis:

> they realize, that you, the white people, white Americans, have always attempted to murder them. Not merely burning them or castrating them or hanging them from trees, murdering them in the mind, in the heart. By teaching a black child that he is worthless, that he can never contribute to anything in civilization, you're teaching him how to hate his mother, his father, and his brothers. Everyone in my generation has seen the wreckage that this has caused. And what black kids are doing now, no matter how excessively,

is right. They are refusing this entire frame of reference and they are saying to the Republic: This is your bill, this is your bloody bill written in my *blood*, and you are going to have to pay it. (RR, 11, italics in original)

From "theology" to "frame of reference," Baldwin refers to an entire cosmology organized by the "wreckage" of white supremacy in religious terms. Mead responds, quoting Frantz Fanon's *Black Skin, White Masks* (1952) to say "what the black man is offered as civilization is *white* civilization" (RR, 12, italics in original), a reference that appears to understand the workings of racial liberalism.

Soon after, Mead describes the problem of whiteness in which "white skin is a terrible temptation." Resorting to functionalism to explain the disparities of skin color with a religious twist of Christian ontology, Mead states: "we look like angels, you know that?" (RR, 29). By this, she is referring to a kind of godlike existence and relationship in which whiteness is associated with light, fairness, and identification with angels. Baldwin responds that there is a deeper problem, to which Mead claims they are already "terribly deep." Baldwin, in a rapid-response, says, "deeper than churches" (RR, 30). Darkness, Mead maintains through her ethnological reasoning, is identified with danger. It is with this thinking regarding lightness and darkness that Baldwin addresses what he refers to the "riddle of white supremacy" as not only "historical and theological" (RR, 32) but something more profoundly structural and systematic. In this muddled interaction, both are finally at the crux of the issue—the difficulty of explaining white supremacy—and the connected frameworks of a profound relationship to religion and theology.

As they move toward the influence of white domination through colonialism and the expansion of Christianity, Baldwin and Mead tussle over the place of morals and the role of religion. In one passage, Baldwin condemns the "white man's religion" to "accuse the white Christian world of nothing but a tissue of lies, nothing but an excuse for power, as being removed from any sense of worship and, still more, from any sense of love" (RR, 86). Mead pushes for a shared morality in which there might be some sort of universality of secular enlightenment ideals, to which Baldwin responds, "what I am dealing with is the morality beneath all this" (RR, 87), that is to say that Christianity and colonialism blended with white supremacy to normalize racial hierarchy. As they jostle between their respective origin stories, they follow with this exchange:

MEAD: I am not trying to call you a Christian. What I am talking about is that one gets from the Christian tradition—

BALDWIN: I'll accept the term because I am not a Muslim.

MEAD: —everything. That the good things that we have, the good things you are insisting on—that people should love each other and recognize each other as brothers—is a Christian idea.

BALDWIN: But it isn't a Christian idea. Isn't it also a Muslim idea?

MEAD: No. Because Muslims don't believe in loving everybody as brothers. They only love Muslims as brothers. They don't really have an idea of universal brotherhood. (RR, 89)

At this point, Baldwin does not argue. He claims he was not fully versed in the religious claims Mead was making. Despite his well-known association with Malcolm X and his writings on the Nation of Islam,[8] and the mention in their exchange of his extensive travels to Turkey and Palestine, Baldwin refrains from a direct response in the moment. The mention of Islam and Muslims is curious as a counterpoint to the white settler colonial logic.

Mead's odd assertion that Islam is devoid of a conception of universal brotherhood in contrast to Christianity requires some further interpretation. From this passage it is not clear whether she is referring to the Nation of Islam, traditional Islam, or both.[9] What does this animus with Islam say about Mead, or more generally the provocation she might be eliciting? Why make the distinction between Christianity and Islam, if not in the context of the militancy of the Nation of Islam, or more broadly as competing Abrahamic traditions as a provocation of white Christian supremacy? In other parts of the text that follow, Baldwin refers to Malcolm X in what appears as a counter to the universalisms of Mead's racial liberalism. Indeed, Baldwin's initial point of mentioning "Muslim" appears to be a counterpoint to Mead's notion of "Christian." Perhaps as a belated rebuttal to Mead's comment of Islam's nonuniversality, Baldwin quotes Malcolm to say "white is a state of mind" to explain his "role in the *present*" (RR, 169), or what might be thought of as a description of the moral stakes of being trapped by white supremacy. Soon after, in a theological discussion of "guilt" and "responsibility" (RR, 174), Baldwin refers to Malcolm again to claim that "sin demands atonement" (RR, 175) as a kind of reconciliation of historical wrongs, and as a theological condemnation of white supremacy as sin from an Islamic point of view. From these quotes, and Baldwin's own admissions, his attraction to Malcolm's politics were for his opposition to the universality of white supremacy and in some sense to the practice of Christianity as the "white man's religion." Taking these points of both Mead and Baldwin, the undercurrent of religious morality and theological discourse is apparent in racialization, and to how race as a historical concept has jostled between the secular and scientific, and the religious and the unknown. How else might the obsession of white supremacist ideas regarding Christian religious others be understood, why are Islam, Jews, and even Communists the quintessential racial object of white supremacy?

Taking what Karen and Barbara Fields refer to as the concept of racecraft (2012),[10] I am interested in theorizing how Islam and Muslims are conjured as an object of white supremacy. As an epistemological process of racialization that denotes the inexplicable and magical, and simultaneously a structure, system, and ideology, the racecraft that conjures anti-Muslim racism can appear on the scene, yet not (Rana 2016). Whether Mead meant this in her comment regarding the differences between Islam and Christianity is not exactly the issue. Rather, in thinking through the relationship of religion to white supremacy, it is a question of how Christianity and Islam are differently situated as religious *and* racial discourses. Simultaneously, racial capitalism and settler colonialism are systems of power and hierarchy from which white supremacy constructs Islam and Muslims—what might be properly called the figure of the Muslim.[11] Following this reasoning, Islam and Muslims are made into racial objects of white supremacy. Yet, more than racialization, religion is also positioned in ways to offer other possibilities—what Mead is alluding to in terms of

Enlightenment values and Christianity, and to what Baldwin sees in the aspirations of Malcolm X and his critique of white supremacy that signal aspects of struggle and resistance.

To think of the racecraft that conjures anti-Muslim racism is to take seriously both the Islamic theology of liberation that Malcolm X espoused, and to make sense of the claims that the Nation of Islam are a hate group that are reverse racists to white people, particularly Jewish people (Felber 2020). These lingering debates are about the confrontation with the system of white supremacy that seeks to racialize Muslims as a multiracial group, defying the common sense of the phenotypic homogenizing of racialization. Claims such as those Mead makes with Baldwin, denigrate Islam and Muslims as outside modernity, liberalism, and perhaps even capitalism, in other words, white supremacy. While such claims are far more complex on the global stage, it is worth accentuating Baldwin's commitment and attraction to Malcolm X's ideas of Islamic liberation theology and the condemnation of white supremacy. Malcolm X, and his legacy as Malik el-Shabazz, sought a way out of the system of white supremacy *and* the American way of life parallel to Baldwin's ideas of exile and responsibility. It is in this sense that racecraft is simultaneously about racializing Muslim's and Islam and demonizing liberation, anticolonialism, and calls for the end of white supremacy.

The Riddle of Anthropology

The challenge that the discipline of anthropology faces is how to confront the issue of white supremacy and racism. One task for the anthropologist is to return to works such as *A Rap on Race*, first, as a teaching text to critique white supremacy and racism and, second, to think of racial capitalism as a system in which white supremacy continues to expand as a flexible and ever-changing form of dominance. As anthropologists have pointed out, when the United States is thought of as a settler society that structures social life, it requires a different orientation toward indigeneity, racial capitalism, and white supremacy (Cattelino 2010; Simpson 2014). Finally, to return to the impetus and force of Mead and Baldwin's dialogue, they propose ways of understanding suffering and morality that require a necessary involvement in the politics of the world. Regardless of what one makes of the content of the conversation between Margaret Mead and James Baldwin, the anthropologist and the writer, it was a remarkable experiment. In a few days, and seemingly with little preparation, they were able to engage in a wide-ranging discussion that should be revisited for its insights into the contemporary, and toward the future, but also as a form from which anthropologists should engage the world at large. The epistemological problem of white supremacy can be summarized as such: as ideology it is very specific, as a system it depends on the beginning point of analysis that requires seeing the United States within a global system of racial capitalism. In other words, white supremacy is real, material, and has effects.

At the close of the conversation the last word in *A Rap on Race* is left to Baldwin. The cadences of Baldwin's speech are paced only by what is the perfect conclusion:

I have to talk out of my beginnings, and I did begin here auctioned like a mule, bred as though I were a stallion. I was in my country, which I paid for and I'm paying for. Treated as not even as a beast is treated. Died in ditches not even as a mule is murdered. And I have to remember that. I have to redeem that. I cannot let it go for nothing. The only reason I'm here is to bear witness.

I don't *really* like my life, you know. I don't really want a drink. I've seen enough of the world's cities to make me vomit forever. But I've got something to do. It has nothing in it any longer for me. What I wanted is what everybody wanted. You wanted it, too. Everybody wanted it. It will come. It comes in different shapes and forms. It is not de-spair, and the price one pay's is everybody's price.

But on top of that particular price, which is universal, there is something gratuitous which I will not forgive, you know. It's difficult to be born, difficult to learn to walk, difficult to grow old, difficult to die and difficult to live for everybody, everywhere, forever. But no one has a right to put on top of that another burden, another price which nobody can pay, and a burden which really nobody can bear. I know it's universal, Margaret, but the fact that it is universal doesn't mean that I'll accept it.

With this elegant closing and Baldwin's lyrical denouncement of the universality of white supremacy and racial capitalism as a system, barely audible in the recording, Mead can be heard saying in a droll voice, "cut it off."

Notes

1. This chapter is an abridged and revised version of what first appeared as Junaid Rana, 2020. "Anthropology and the Riddle of White Supremacy." *American Anthropologist* 122, no. 1: 99–111. doi: https://doi.org/10.1111/aman.13355. Mead and Baldwin (1971), hereafter referenced as RR.

2. The digital version of this audio recording is available through the Yale University Library and can be listened to here: https://brbl-dl.library.yale.edu/vufind/Record/3749231. Mead and Baldwin (1972).

3. Cedric Robinson argues that capitalism is simply racial capitalism as it emerged out of European history and into an American form: "In contradistinction to Marx and Engel's expectations that bourgeois society would rationalize social relations and demystify social consciousness, the obverse occurred. The development, organization, and expansion of capitalist society pursued essentially racial directions, so too did social ideology. As a material force, then, it could be expected that racialism would inevitably permeate the social structures emergent from capitalism. I have used the term 'racial capitalism' to refer to this development and the subsequent structure as a historical agency" (1983, 2). In Melamed's astute elaboration of racial capitalism she argues that "we often associate racial capitalism with the central features of white supremacist capitalist development, including slavery, colonialism, genocide, incarceration regimes, migrant exploitation, and contemporary racial warfare. Yet we also increasingly recognize that contemporary racial capitalism deploys liberal and multicultural terms of inclusion to value and devalue forms of humanity differentially to fit the needs of reigning state-capital orders" (Melamed 2015, 77).

4. The critiques of secularism in the work of Talal Asad (1993; 2003), and in particular the collection of essays between Asad, Wendy Brown, Judith Butler, and Saba Mahmood (2013), are particularly relevant here.

5. For example, Mead uses the racist word "wetback" to describe Mexican immigrants (RR, 150).

6. Literary scholar Jodi Melamed periodizes racial liberalism as a state antiracism in the United States that emerged in the 1940s to 1960s, giving way to other antiracisms such as liberal multiculturalism and neoliberal

multiculturalism (Melamed 2011). Similarly, historian Nikhil Singh identifies racial liberalism in the oft-cited work of sociologists Michael Omi and Howard Winant (2015) in the emergence of racial formation and the "great transformation" that takes place from World War II to the 1960s and its subsequent normalization (Singh 2017, 125–26).

7. Melamed defines race radicalism as the "attempt to rupture how race as a sign has been consolidated with the cultural, ideological, political, and material forces of official antiracisms and to reconsolidate race as a sign with the cultural, ideological, political, and material forces of [a] worldly and radical antiracist movement, which have crucially analyzed race within the genealogy of global capitalism" (2011, 49).

8. Baldwin's play based on Malcolm X is titled *One Day When I Was Lost* (1972). In addition, he discusses his visits to Elijah Muhammad and his thoughts of the Nation of Islam in *The Fire Next Time* (1963) and shortly after this conversation in *No Name in the Street* (1972).

9. To clarify, what Mead describes as universal brotherhood for Christians under Christianity is parallel to Islamic tenets with the caveat that in Islam the Abrahamic religions are given special status as shared traditions. The Nation of Islam and the Black nationalist teachings of Elijah Muhammad were often considered "black racist" and "black supremacist" by the mainstream US media. For example, the documentary *The Hate That Hate Produced* (1959).

10. "Distinct from *race* and *racism*, *racecraft* does not refer to groups or to ideas about groups' traits, however odd both may appear in close-up. It refers instead to mental terrain and to pervasive belief. Like physical terrain, racecraft exists objectively; it has topographical features that Americans regularly navigate, and we cannot readily stop traversing it. Unlike physical terrain, racecraft originates not in nature but in human action and imagination; it can exist in no other way. The action and imagining are collective yet individual, day-to-day yet historical, and consequential even though nested in mundane routine. The action and imagining emerge as part of moment-to-moment practicality, that is, thinking about and executing every purpose under the sun. Do not look for racecraft, therefore, only where it might be said to 'belong.' Finally, *racecraft* is not a euphemistic substitute for *racism*. It is a kind of fingerprint evidence that *racism* has been on the scene" (Fields and Fields 2012, 18–19).

11. Here I am referring to Muslims as people of faith and people of color, and as Muslim-looking (Grewal 2005; Naber 2006; Rana 2011; Volpp 2002), both categories of racialization. Recently Khabeer has theorized Muslim racialization through ethnographic examples that are comparative and gendered (2017; cf. Cainkar 2009). I have theorized this paradox of race and religion as Muslim racial becoming in which race is mobilized in increasingly flexible practices of racism and white supremacy (Rana 2016).

References

Abdullah, Zain. 2010. *Black Mecca: The African Muslims of Harlem*. New York: Oxford University Press.

Asad, Talal. 1993. *Genealogies of Religion: Discipline and Reasons of Power in Christianity and Islam*. Baltimore: Johns Hopkins University Press.

———. 2003. *Formations of the Secular: Christianity, Islam, Modernity*. Stanford, CA: Stanford University Press.

Asad, Talal, et al. 2013. *Is Critique Secular?: Blasphemy, Injury, and Free Speech*. New York: Fordham University Press.

Baldwin, James. 1963. *The Fire Next Time*. New York: Dial Press.

———. 1972. *No Name in the Street*. New York: Dial Press.

Baldwin, James. (2007) 1972. *One Day When I Was Lost: A Scenario Based on Alex Haley's* The Autobiography of Malcolm X. New York: Vintage International.

Bayoumi, Moustafa. 2006. "Racing Religion." *New Centennial Review* 6, no. 2: 267–93.

Beliso-De Jesús, Aisha M., Jemima Pierre, and Junaid Rana. 2023. "White Supremacy and the Making of Anthropology." *Annual Review of Anthropology* 52, no. 1: 417–35.

Cainkar, Louise. 2009. *Homeland Insecurity: The Arab American and Muslim American Experience after 9/11*. New York: Russell Sage Foundation.

Carter, J. Kameron. 2008. *Race: A Theological Account*. New York: Oxford University Press.

Cattelino, Jessica. 2010. "Anthropologies of the United States." *Annual Review of Anthropology* 39: 275–92.

Cone, James H. 1969. *Black Theology and Black Power*. New York: Seabury Press.

———. 1970. *A Black Theology of Liberation*. Philadelphia: Lippincott.

———. 1991. *Martin and Malcolm and America: A Dream or a Nightmare*. Maryknoll, NY: Orbis Books.

Curtis, Edward E. 2006. *Black Muslim Religion in the Nation of Islam, 1960–1975*. Chapel Hill: University of North Carolina Press.

———. 2015. "'My Heart Is in Cairo': Malcolm X, the Arab Cold War, and the Making of Islamic Liberation Ethics." *Journal of American History* 102, no. 3: 775–98.

Elman, Richard. 1971. "A Rap on Race." *New York Times*, June 27, BR5.

Felber, Garrett. 2020. *Those Who Know Don't Say: The Nation of Islam, the Black Freedom Movement, and the Carceral State*. Chapel Hill: University of North Carolina Press.

Fields, Karen E., and Barbara J. Fields. 2012. *Racecraft: The Soul of Inequality in American Life*. New York: Verso.

Grewal, Inderpal. 2005. *Transnational America: Feminisms, Diasporas, Neoliberalisms*. Durham, NC: Duke University Press.

Grewal, Zareena. 2014. *Islam Is a Foreign Country: American Muslims and the Global Crisis of Authority*. New York: New York University Press.

Harris, Cheryl I. 1995. "Whiteness as Property." In *Critical Race Theory: The Key Writings That Formed the Movement*, edited by Kimberlé Crenshaw, Neil Gotanda, Gary Peller, and Kendall Thomas. New York: New Press.

Harrison, Faye V. 1991. *Decolonizing Anthropology: Moving Further Toward an Anthropology for Liberation*. Washington, DC: Association of Black Anthropologists; American Anthropological Association.

———. 1995. "The Persistent Power of 'Race' in the Cultural and Political Economy of Racism." *Annual Review of Anthropology* 24: 47–74.

———. 1999. "Introduction: Expanding the Discourse on "Race." *American Anthropologist* 100, no. 3: 609–31.

———. 2002. "Global Apartheid, Foreign Policy, and Human Rights." *Souls: A Critical Journal of Black Politics, Culture, and Society* 4, no. 3: 48–68.

———. 2008. *Outsider Within: Reworking Anthropology in the Global Age*. Urbana: University of Illinois Press.

Jackson, John L. 2001. *Harlem World: Doing Race and Class in Contemporary Black America*. Chicago: University of Chicago Press.

Jackson, Sherman A. 2005. *Islam and the Blackamerican: Looking toward the Third Resurrection*. New York: Oxford University Press.

———. 2009. *Islam and the Problem of Black Suffering*. New York: Oxford University Press.

Kashani, Maryam. 2018a. "The Audience Is Still Present: Invocations of El-Hajj Malik El-Shabazz by Muslims in the United States." In *With Stones in Our Hands: Writings on Muslims, Racism, and Empire*, edited by Sohail Daulatzai and Junaid Rana. Minneapolis: University of Minnesota Press.

———. 2018b. "Habib in the Hood: Mobilizing History and Prayer towards Anti-Racist Praxis." *Amerasia Journal* 44, no. 1: 61–84.

Khabeer, Su'ad Abdul. 2016. *Muslim Cool: Race, Religion, and Hip Hop in the United States*. New York: New York University Press.

———. 2017. "Citizens and Suspects: Race, Gender, and the Making of American Muslim Citizenship." *Transforming Anthropology* 25, no. 2: 103–19.

Lipsitz, George. 1998. *The Possessive Investment in Whiteness: How White People Profit from Identity Politics*. Philadelphia: Temple University Press.

Maira, Sunaina. 2016. *The 9/11 Generation: Youth, Rights, and Solidarity in the War on Terror*. New York: New York University Press.

Mandler, Peter. 2013. *Return from the Natives: How Margaret Mead Won the Second World War and Lost the Cold War*. New Haven, CT: Yale University Press.

Mead, Margaret, and James Baldwin. 1971. *A Rap on Race*. Philadelphia: Lippincott.

———. 1972. *A Rap on Race! A Recorded Conversation between Margaret Mead and James Baldwin*. [n.p.]: CMS 641–42. Sound recording.

Medovoi, Leerom. 2012. "Dogma-Line Racism: Islamophobia and the Second Axis of Race." *Social Text* 30, no. 2: 43–74.

Melamed, Jodi. 2011. *Represent and Destroy: Rationalizing Violence in the New Racial Capitalism*. Minneapolis: University of Minnesota Press.

———. 2015. "Racial Capitalism." *Critical Ethnic Studies* 1, no. 1: 76–85.

Mills, Charles W. 1997. *The Racial Contract*. Ithaca, NY: Cornell University Press.

———. 2017. *Black Rights/White Wrongs: The Critique of Racial Liberalism*. New York: Oxford University Press.

Mullings, Leith. 2005. "Interrogating Racism: Toward an Antiracist Anthropology." *Annual Review of Anthropology*. 34: 667–93.

———. 2015. "Presidential Address: Anthropology Matters." *American Anthropologist* 117, no. 1: 4–6.

Mullings, Leith, ed. 2009. *New Social Movements in the African Diaspora: Challenging Global Apartheid*. New York: Palgrave Macmillan.

Naber, Nadine C. 2006. "The Rules of Forced Engagement: Race, Gender, and the Culture of Fear among Arab Immigrants in San Francisco Post-9/11." *Cultural Dynamics* 18, no. 3: 269–92.

———. 2012. *Arab America: Gender, Cultural Politics, and Activism*. New York: New York University Press.

Omi, Michael, and Howard Winant. 2015. *Racial Formation in the United States*. 3rd ed. New York: Routledge.

Price, David H. 2000 "Anthropologists as Spies." *The Nation* 271, no. 16: 24–27.

———. 2004. *Threatening Anthropology: McCarthyism and the FBI's Surveillance of Activist Anthropologists*. Durham, NC: Duke University Press.

———. 2008. *Anthropological Intelligence: The Deployment and Neglect of American Anthropology in the Second World War*. Durham, NC: Duke University Press.

Rana, Aziz. 2010. *The Two Faces of American Freedom*. Cambridge, MA: Harvard University Press.

Rana, Junaid. 2007. "The Story of Islamophobia." *Souls: A Critical Journal of Black Politics, Culture, and Society* 9, no. 2: 148–61.

———. 2011. *Terrifying Muslims: Race and Labor in the South Asian Diaspora*. Durham, NC: Duke University Press.

———. 2016. "The Racial Infrastructure of the Terror-Industrial Complex." *Social Text* 34, no. 4: 111–38.

Razack, Sherene. 2008. *Casting Out: The Eviction of Muslims from Western Law and Politics*. Toronto: University of Toronto Press.

Robinson, Cedric J. 1983. *Black Marxism: The Making of the Black Radical Tradition*. London: Zed Books.

Simpson, Audra. 2014. *Mohawk Interruptus: Political Life across the Borders of Settler States*. Durham, NC: Duke University Press.

Singh, Nikhil Pal. 2017. *Race and America's Long War*. Oakland: University of California Press.

Visweswaran, Kamala. 1998. "Race and the Culture of Anthropology." *American Anthropologist* 100, no. 1: 70–83.

———. 2010. *Un/common Cultures: Racism and the Rearticulation of Cultural Difference*. Durham, NC: Duke University Press.

Volpp, Leti. 2002. "The Citizen and the Terrorist." *UCLA Law Review* 49: 1575–600.

4

Racial Flyover Zones

WHITE SUPREMACY AND THE POLITICS
OF FIELD RESEARCH

Britt Halvorson and Joshua Reno

WE EXPLORE THE RACIAL GEOGRAPHY of field research, one area where the anthropology of white supremacy meets the historically shaped institutional whiteness of anthropological knowledge production. We are interested in how certain field sites become "racial flyover zones," that is, locations largely thought of as lacking in viable possibilities or professional prestige.[1] Such racialized places have much to tell us about white supremacy in the discipline, beginning with the geopolitical categories we inherit and the kind of field research upheld as an example to follow. More than that, understanding racial flyover zones helps demonstrate the subtle ways in which academic knowledge (like whiteness itself) can serve as a form of valued property (Harris 1993). Following scholars of empire (Said 1978; Coronil 2019; Chakrabarty 2000), we argue that exploring the racial politics of location opens up for examination the geohistorical categories and epistemological "vacant lots" (Harootunian and Miyoshi 2002, 7) marshaled to further global market and political interests. But, expanding on this earlier work, these globalized forms of power—in which anthropology has long been uneasily situated—fundamentally rely on white supremacy as a central logic or on "the structural, material, and corporeal production of white racial hegemony" (Bonds and Inwood 2016, 720; see also Mills 2003; Robinson 2000). While considerable work has examined the colonial and racial history of anthropology (see e.g., Harrison [1991] 2010; Gupta and Ferguson 1997; Anderson 2019), we turn our attention in this chapter to the connections between preferred and overlooked sites of research. These hidden linkages and, in particular, the flyover zones of anthropological fieldwork, are surprisingly central to white supremacist thought and practice, furthering forms of racialized power through a "connected set of relations and logics" (Beliso-De Jesús and Pierre 2019, 4), even as they may seem outside it.

We come to these questions as anthropologists who have worked in a place that is not highly valued as a site of anthropological knowledge production—the American Midwest region. Some places lack such value, we argue, due to associations they have with histories of race in the United States and beyond. Over the last decade we wrote a book on the history and ongoing imagining of white supremacy through public images of the Midwest United States (Halvorson and Reno 2022). This work led us to reflect on two long-recognized features of ethnographic research: That field sites—like all physical places in the world, from neighborhood blocks to towns to regions—are overtly and covertly racialized and placed in a hierarchy of relative prestige and desirability, with consequences for individual scholars' ability to access valued professional trajectories and jobs. And, even more, that how scholars have tended to "race" toward, or away from, these "raced fields" is deeply informed by how white supremacy shapes logics of world mapping and knowledge production specific to colonial rule and area studies. Here, we argue that one step toward decolonizing field research is recognizing in a more thoroughgoing way how white supremacy takes shape through specific histories of place-making, including the kind performed, even if unknowingly, by researchers. The colonial and imperial history of fieldwork in anthropology has left, we suggest, blind spots as some areas still seem off limits for research—or lacking in forms of legitimacy, earned prestige, and professional credit—but which actually make visible the structuring logics of white supremacy in the field in new ways.

The Midwest United States is a fascinating location for exploring this exact process. As we discuss in the book we wrote, the region has long operated in the American public imagination as a canvas or stage for articulating the value and desirability of whiteness, including by identifying forms of white deplorability, at different points in US history. For instance, widespread references to the insularity and whiteness of the Midwest around the 2016 election, a time when whiteness was being reimagined as a force in US national politics, were neither coincidental nor new. Though the term *Middle West* was initially used by the settler state to survey and seize land from Native American communities, it was not until the late nineteenth and early twentieth centuries that the Midwest regional label took on nationalist sentiments associated with the farming livelihood of white European settlers, as a counterpoint to the perceived changes of rapid industrialization and as a property claim to forestall indigenous land reclamation. Dominant representations of the pastoral Midwest, from Grant Wood's *Fall Plowing* to *The Wizard of Oz*, were in keeping with this selective "invented tradition" of white midwestern farming, as a foil to the modernity of industrial labor as well as its toil, pollution, inequalities, workers of color, and forms of alienation. In remarkably parallel ways to today's uses of this trope, it began to function in the early twentieth century as an idealized representation of an imagined earlier form of economic production and social relations coded as white. Popular imagery and narratives of the Midwest have long bundled together whiteness, labor, and property—or a particular kind of racial capitalism—in ways that helped underwrite white political and economic interests.

Yet even with and perhaps because of this history of reinforcing white supremacist views of property, labor, and settlement, it is safe to say that few cultural anthropologists have identified their area of specialization as the Midwest, even if they did long-term field research in Chicago or Minneapolis, for example. The Midwest is a broad and vague regional designation to be sure, but it has long seemed too familiar and insulated to be worthy of anthropological research. To many anthropologists, it is still a no-site, not an "area" where one can suitably do long-term research, let alone build a career. These very reactions to the region are place-making effects of whiteness, nationalism, and class. They form a complex, mutually reinforcing relationship with the racial identities of individual researchers, who are themselves thought to embody varying kinds of proximity and distance from racialized field locations, a fact long recognized by feminist scholars of color (see, e.g., Abu-Lughod 1991; Narayan 1993; Harrison 2008). As white researchers who have each done fieldwork in primarily white communities in the Midwest, fellow anthropologists have tended to respond to us in a few recognizable ways. Some suggested that it would be better for our careers if we worked with identifiable ethnic and racial minorities. Others chuckled when the word "Midwest" came up, because it seemed oddly provincial. Still others have indicated some comfort with the idea that "our white folks" are somehow different, marginalized by class or labor positions, or actually quite global through their ties overseas. And, more recently as we worked on our book, some reviewers tried to add technical rigor to the idea of the region by dividing it into finer and finer appellations, such as the "Great Lakes" or the "Ohio River Valley."

Underlying each of these moves is a white racialization of the field—of fieldwork, fieldworkers, field sites, and the field of anthropology itself—that requires further exploration. Looking into the politics of white supremacy in fieldwork should encompass places and histories of place-making that seem too (unmarkedly) white and familiar for field research as much as more distant, "exotic" sites elevated for the most prestigious research. As we will show, such banal places are in fact deeply intertwined with more attractive, distant sites through colonial tactics of racial power.[2] Even though the Midwest has not carried professional prestige for cultural anthropologists, its popularly imagined white homogeneity and banality have been crucial ideological pillars for the form of democratic order, land-holding, and agricultural labor thought characteristic of the region. These features have emerged in complex dialogue with global racio-political hierarchies that could, in turn, cast both colonized spaces overseas and domestic communities of color as lacking in those desirable qualities of democracy and development (see Pierre this volume). In anthropology, it's long been remarked in exchanges between colleagues, in graduate training, peer reviewing, job searches, in the halls of the annual meeting, teach-ins, and other kinds of political organizing against US imperialism that colonially rooted area studies designations troublingly map the world through a US-based lens. What has been less discussed is how the discipline's historical orientation to the United States and especially the Midwest feeds this logic and, specifically, how it furthers globalized forms of white supremacy (but see di Leonardo 1998). That the arguable discursive center of white nationalism in US history—the Midwest—is typically not seen as legitimately anthropological speaks to how the discipline has struggled to interrogate *proximate* forms of political and economic power and racial logics in which academics and academia have long participated. In what follows, we place the Midwest in a necessarily brief discussion of the history and ongoing structuring logics of white supremacy in field research, from the place of the "field" in colonial knowledge construction to the world mapping of area studies. One of our goals is to therefore think imaginatively, with the Midwest United States, about what it would mean to recognize that racialization and place-making are already thoroughly interwoven with all research fields, in order to better trace their connecting logics of race, labor, and empire.

The Whiteness of Overlapping Fields: Colonization Meets Area Studies

We can begin to assess the awkward role of racial flyover zones in anthropological research through a brief look at area studies. Many regard area studies as a decidedly American Cold War construction, which partly accounts for the telling absence of the Midwest United States or any other American places from this global mapping. Historically, the Midwest is the region most emblematic of Jeffersonian democratic values and small-scale white private property bearing. As such it plays an underrecognized role as both an assured "safe space" and a hidden model for places around the globe where values conjoining race and labor in a recognizable sociopolitical order are either perceived to be threatened or in need of development (Harootunian and Miyoshi 2002). In other words, such overtly racialized places and the imagined Midwest were shaped in tandem; this happened not only conceptually but also practically as geopolitical categories mediated the rollout of distinct projects of neoliberalism, including when specific places and people were targeted for capital accumulation and dispossession over the course of the twentieth century (Harvey 2007). This conceptual and practical interrelation can be understood better by looking further into the geo-imperial mapping of area studies and its colonial origins. These imperial geographies had a direct role in cultivating specific fields of academic and intellectual labor that still shape anthropology today.

If these imperial projects were partly carried out in the name of race and labor, they demanded other new forms of knowledge work in turn, including academic jobs. Indeed, substantial post–World War II funding from the State Department and Rockefeller, Carnegie, and Ford Foundations fed an area studies agenda—with a new focus on shifting global zones, such as "Southeast Asia" and "the Middle East"—that helped found departments, programs, and PhD training at universities. All too often these global zones were also potential or actual war zones.[3] We can see this shift, for instance, in the career of Ruth Benedict. While she had focused on Native American communities for her dissertation and for her first book, Benedict's *Chrysanthemum and the Sword* (1946) was commissioned by the Office of War Information, whose "purpose was to better understand the behavior of the enemy the United States was fighting" (Harootunian 2002, 155). If support for democratic values ostensibly motivates such academic labors, less obvious is the way they turn known places into new kinds of intellectual property (TallBear 2013). The added value of this kind of academic labor is the way it underwrites national political and economic interests, including the identification of "emerging markets," while concealing them in a seemingly benign mapping of global regions, such as the "Asian Pacific" (Dirlik 1992) and

"Inner Asia" (Gupta and Ferguson 1997). Perhaps above all, in these mappings, the United States is the nerve center from which the area studies gaze emanates and, at the same time, the gaze negates the United States—except as an occasional outlier and comparative site—as a legitimately "global" focal point.

Yet, a fuller, more global lens is necessary to see area studies as not only a national project of the US security state alone, but also as co-created by animating historical logics of white supremacy, labor, and colonialism. Several connections are worth tracing to this end. In the first place, area studies clearly bears ties to the "massive information retrieval" and colonial creation of specialists and bodies of knowledge on non-Western people (Chow 2002, 107), which involved nineteenth- and twentieth-century anthropologists, economists, and political scientists.[4] The concept of the field was an orienting, mobile metalogic of labor, race, and knowledge production essential to this project that wove together people and places in ways that complemented imperial power and overlapped with the global color line, a problematic racial orientation to fieldwork that remains to this day. Moreover, this structure could be applied to a variety of sites and relations while excluding other configurations completely. Even when early Boasians and English functionalists worked in the northern half of the Western Hemisphere, they focused almost exclusively on documenting cultural practices among Native Americans and Black communities. And yet, if research on "culture" focused on what made these communities seemingly different (whether folklore, kinship, religion, language . . .), the webs of capital and power that embraced researcher and researched alike were arguably of less immediate concern in early studies. When ethnographic work on Black communities in the Americas did highlight how cultural lifeworlds existed in the midst of centuries of diaspora, slavery, and revolution, they were less widely read by contemporaries (James [1938] 1989) or only published posthumously (Hurston [1927] 2018). The commodification of land and labor in all of these places provides one basic set of connections that link researchers and researched, in a sense, regardless of race but also very much as a consequence of the work of empire and white supremacy.

We can take this further to point out how these racial labor and place-making practices of field research also relied on and supported a set of less obvious, connecting logics that underpinned the broader racial labor practices of colonization. This can be seen in the complex, influential dialogue between the transatlantic movement to abolish slavery and the emerging language of colonial administration, within which field research initially took shape, but that has arguably continued to exert influence in other, more contemporary forms. By identifying unfree, constrained, and indentured labor, eighteenth-century reformers and abolitionists, for example, established the conditions for "free" colonial and working-class industrial labor forces. Historian Thomas Haskell (1985, 346) points to how this new moral discourse on labor was taken up as a disciplining force both "at home" and in colonial projects around the globe when he writes, quoting David Brion Davis,

> As members of an entrepreneurial class confronted by an "unruly labor force" prone to "uninhibited violence" and not yet "disciplined to the factory system," late eighteenth-century reformers had strong incentives to formulate an ideology that

would "isolate specific forms of human misery, allowing issues of freedom and discipline to be faced in a relatively simplified model."

Humanitarian reformers supplied a language of free/unfree labor that was always racialized in dialogue with the history of transatlantic slavery. It also created the conditions for the development and expansion of colonial market enterprises and for an interest in knowledge that would help in furthering those projects. Though post–World War II area studies may seem far distant from these eighteen- and nineteenth-century humanitarian debates, they inherited and transmuted into other forms the white supremacist contours and political-economic interests of earlier anxieties concerning administering and governing the land and labor of "populations" around the world.

Before area studies became ascendant as a geopolitical mapping of the world, some scholarly fields openly focused on white supremacist problems of colonial administration, including labor control, and even viewed their work as one of "race management." In *White World Order, Black Power Politics*, political scientist Robert Vitalis (2015) reveals that the flagship *Journal of International Relations* was originally titled the *Journal of Race Development* before it was renamed in 1919. W. E. B. DuBois contributed articles to the *Journal of Race Development* in its early years, giving a clear sense of the global reach of DuBois's work on race before it was mostly omitted from the commonly taught canon of international relations. This striking fact, Vitalis shows, opens up a long, ongoing division of international relations from the open consideration of matters of race while tacitly tethering the field to a predominantly white, American center. Prior to that time, problems of imperialism and global development were fundamentally—and more openly—considered matters of race. In the late nineteenth century, as well as through Teddy Roosevelt's "imperial turn" that involved annexing Puerto Rico, Hawaii, the Philippines, and Guam, an influential white American intelligentsia, including political scientists like Alleyne Ireland (1871–1951) and sociologists like Edward Ross (1866–1951), were framing American empire-building in a racialist language of maintaining white supremacy. This American interpretation of the "white man's burden" was informed not only by Reconstruction-era eugenicist fears about racial stock, but also by much wider Anglo imperial conversations on race and colonial administration that extended from Australia and New Zealand to South Africa's Natal Colony to India to the American South (Lake and Reynolds 2008).[5]

White politicians' and scholars' shared discussions of colonial self-government and the imperial administration of colonized places built, in turn, on earlier social evolutionary theories and burgeoning scientific racism on the hierarchical "backwardness" of individual Black and brown *people*, not only places or "societies." In other words, there was always a connection between how the essence of places were imagined and mapped and how the internal essence of people was hierarchically imagined, even if the latter was concealed over time. As Jemima Pierre (2006, 43–44) writes,

> In other words, the racialization of people from "Africa" into "Black" and "tribal" had everything to do with the link between identity and place. Race, then, was not just about cultural/behavioral and mental difference; it was also about geographic and time distance/difference.

Though these ideas were never uncontested, social evolutionary theories and eugenicist forms of scientific racism were open considerations in some of the social science research on colonial administration, which formed one of several antecedents to area studies. For example, the political scientist John W. Burgess advanced in his writing in 1890 the idea that only Aryans had developed the capacity for state government, while the sociologist Ross was convinced of superior white eugenicist vigor and energy (Vitalis 2015, 35, 31). To these writers, colonial administration was fundamentally a problem of race management.

Why should it matter today that scholarly fields were thoroughly shaped by colonial tactics of labor and interventionist logics of place-making and used to devote considerable energy to openly white supremacist views of global development? It is clear that the racialist language of the earlier colonial era went underground, only to reappear in other, seemingly more benign forms, severed from their original intent and meanings. Clear examples include "dependency theory," "emerging democracies," "development," "culture," and so on, but many more could be identified. This has permeated many familiar theoretical and geopolitical categories, such that colonial tactics of racial power continue to exert an untold but no less significant influence in another guise. Appreciating how field research links together race, place, and labor is no simple task but requires in the first instance more consideration of global histories through which prospective field sites become legible and attractive or are dismissed as already known and unilluminating. Casting renewed attention on how "fields" are made (or ignored) as racial assets can help shine light on important links between the proximate and distant workings of white supremacy.

Returning to the Midwest: The Racialized Hierarchy of Fields

Our basic argument is that what counts as "fieldwork" has been and continues to be inescapably a form of "racial knowledge production" (Goldberg 1993), and this is so regardless of the ends toward which such knowledge is put. In other words, individual ethnographers may espouse an antiracist practice, and the consumption of their research may be guided by a progressive and enlightened critical approach, as it is read in classrooms or taken up and championed by social movements, for instance. Yet the prevailing conditions that produce a hierarchy of "fields" worthy of research in the first place (see Gupta and Ferguson 1997), which then circulate as abstracted "sites" or "areas," remain tied to global projects of white supremacy.

To return to the Midwest United States, we propose that this region is actually a critical part of the colonially shaped area studies system, rather than outside it, as it may first appear. This is the case, moreover, not only because funding for global area studies has in part come from institutions with ties to "the Midwest" like the Sloan and Ford Foundations. Because the Midwest region's imagined whiteness in public discourse has been assured, though not often openly discussed, it feels fully outside of, even estranged from, the international, global, and cosmopolitan focus of area studies. But this tells us something about how the Midwest has an ongoing influence on whitened and exclusionary conceptions of American national identity. It also raises interesting questions about how the imagined insularity of the Midwest and its banal and supposed homogeneous qualities feeds into the reproduction of whiteness, labor, nationalism, and empire. Put another way, insisting on the Midwest's insularity and closed-off qualities ironically compels, rather than curtails, American imperialism because it creates the image of a national racial core to protect or, in what amounts to the same thing, to leave alone untouched or divest from. Decolonizing the field means in some ways deprovincializing the areas that historically seemed too proximate, too close, and too homespun to be worthy of attention.

These place-making characteristics of the Midwest region are not merely about a quality of whiteness but are shaped by, and power, specific political economic stakes. However, tracing the precise mechanisms through which banal forms of white supremacy further interconnecting global logics of race, labor, and empire requires specific methodological strategies and creative approaches to the "field" of analysis. We suggest much can be gained in this respect by linking theories of global white supremacy to scholarship on empire. In his essay on Cuban anthropologist Fernando Ortiz's book *Cuban Counterpoint* ([1940] 1995), Fernando Coronil (2019, 74) uses the term "contrapuntal," building also on Edward Said's later (1993) use, to describe how Ortiz "shows the play of illusion and power in the making and unmaking of cultural formations."[6] For both Ortiz and Said, a contrapuntal analysis requires showing how colonial oppositions quietly animate and link places together through what Coronil calls a kind of "imperial alchemy" (75). That is, it examines cultural formations as a product of ongoing historical dialogue that complicates the imagined divides between geopolitical actors and categories that the idea of origin presumes. Such an analysis can work toward revealing the influence of the colonial and imperial encounter while not, in Coronil's words, "imprison[ing] an emancipatory politics in [those terms]" (74).

Building on these insights, the central idea for our analysis of place-making and race is that, just as Cuban tobacco and sugar are social creations for Ortiz that "illuminate the society that gave rise to them" (86), so too is the imagined Midwest a mutable form that bears the stamp of its shifting relations with global imperial forces and political values conjoining the region to places elsewhere. In our book, for instance, we examine the shifting meanings of the Midwest in media reporting of Trump's election and in paintings like Grant Wood's 1930 *American Gothic* as well as in popular fantasy films like *Superman* (1978), *Children of the Corn* (1984), and *Field of Dreams* (1989). In each case, distinct figurations of the Midwest put the imagined trope to work in different ways, yet each betrays linkages to white supremacy, and to fantasies of virtuous white labor in particular; these demonstrate the broader social and political-economic origins of the construction of the region, in Coronil's and Ortiz's sense. Not only has the dominant pastoral image of the region furthered ideas of white productivity and control of land with deep and far-reaching Anglo imperial origins, it has even been considered a positive model of white settlement to be exported and applied in other world regions, such as Colombia's Cauca Valley in the 1940s (Lorek 2013). Looking at the Midwest through a contrapuntal analysis reveals the variety of imperial processes that produce regional tropes and other fields of analysis and the opposing elements and power dynamics that further white supremacy.

The tendency to imagine some field sites (like the American Midwest) as uninteresting and somehow not truly anthropological, relies on "the uncritical mapping of 'difference' onto exotic sites (as if 'home,' however defined, were not also a site of difference) as well as the implicit presumption that 'Otherness' means difference from an unmarked, white Western 'self'" (Gupta and Ferguson 1997, 14–15). This has been connected to the historical propensity to abstract "local community" in field research from global histories of power and capital (Gupta and Ferguson 1997, 24–25). In the process, places become congealed and beguiling value forms, not unlike tobacco or sugar, the products of academic labors that not only rely on imperial and white supremacist histories but also help reconstitute such webs of geo-imperial connection anew.

Conclusion: Locating White Supremacy in the Field

With this chapter we make a small contribution to a broader, collective project of uncovering the "racializing tendencies and techniques" (Pierre 2006, 51) of white supremacy that underlie familiar representations and rankings of location and place. To be sure, what happens in the domains of anthropology and area studies make up only one, relatively small slice of such tendencies and techniques. Yet, in many ways, what happens in these fields of study has arguably had an outsized impact on the racial logic and inflections that mediate both elite and ordinary imaginations and engagements with global difference. Location has only become a shorthand for race, as many have shown, due in part to the work that many scholars performed as part of white supremacist projects of (mis)-measuring humankind. Whatever the origins, though, it cannot be denied that today many people only can *place* themselves and others, cultivate valuable expertise, or move about the world because of racial orderings that are presupposed and reproduced by their having done so. The result is inevitably partial and privileged representations that often seem deracialized and depoliticized as part of the rhetorical politics of multiculturalism. But as Rey Chow puts it, "If indeed multiculturalism is intent on promoting a liberalist politics of recognition, recognition is still largely a one-way street—in the form, for instance, of *white culture recognizing non-white cultures only*" (Chow 2002, 113, italics in original).

What this means is that, to really understand how the field (or rather, fields) has and have been racialized means examining the racial qualities of places. However, in many cases these qualities have long been considered too familiar to be worthy of analysis. We certainly encountered this belief when we first attempted to publish an article in anthropological journals on how the Midwest is imagined and were informed, in several early reviews, that we were not depicting the Midwest that reviewers thought they knew. These reviewers' skepticism was not premised on having done or read fieldwork from seemingly "midwestern" places but on notions they had that they already knew midwestern places and people. This shows that peer reviewers, like all people, carry their social immersion into dominant geopolitical categories and their cultural positioning into their work, sometimes in ways that remain to them opaque or imperceptible. If, empirically "being there" in "the field" has become the sine qua non of anthropological and area studies expertise, then this secret ingredient is premised on feeling like one knows *where not to go* to make authoritative and valuable place-claims.

Racial flyover zones exist everywhere, not only in the middle of the United States. What these all-too-familiar places and people share in common, we suggest, is that they fall outside of prestige notions about "others," those who are worth studying and whose alterity contributes to worthwhile knowledge production. However inadvertently or advertently, this process maintains an untouched core of white supremacy in the field. Deprovincializing such places (Rosa and Bonilla 2017) would mean critically reengaging with how white supremacy has shaped the fields scholars work in, including what ideas are produced by and through their labors. When it comes to the seeming banality of the Midwest, the problem as we see it is not that people are uninterested in the region. Rather, it is that they fail to wonder why they think they know so much about places they readily fly over in the first place and how that taken-for-granted imbalance between banality and interest might bespeak systemic processes that have already shaped the ready-made places and people, the fields, they're headed toward.

Notes

1. We refer here to the problematic idea of the Midwest or middle United States as a flyover zone, uninteresting and bypassable. For an in-depth discussion of flight and racialized space, see Chandra Bhimull's *Empire in the Air* (2017). Bhimull points out that air travel was—and is—a central feature of imperial expansion as well as anthropological fieldwork (21). Yet, as Bhimull argues, the complex racialization of mobility itself, air spaces, travel routes, and the places imagined as travel destinations, has received less scrutiny overall.

2. We thank an anonymous reviewer for encouraging us to highlight this point.

3. We would like to thank Junaid Rana for helping us to clarify this point.

4. In *Orientalism*, Edward Said called area studies programs a contemporary example of "how orientalist knowledge has been recoded," an argument that H. D. Harootunian (2002, 152) says was largely "ignored and forgotten" as Said's work was taken up in postcolonial studies.

5. British novelist Rudyard Kipling's original 1899 poem, "The White Man's Burden," focused in fact on the annexation of the Philippines by the United States.

6. Said (1993) famously repurposed the musical term "contrapuntal" to read colonial literature as involved in making the inextricable, though often hidden, relationships between colonizing and colonized places. As one example, Said examines the Bertram family of Jane Austen's *Mansfield Park* (1814) and their financial reliance on a sugar plantation in Antigua. Ortiz's use of counterpoint (*contrapunto*), which he developed independently of Said, was brought into conversation with Said's use of the term through Coronil's reading of both. In that sense, Coronil is arguably presenting a contrapuntal understanding of the very term "contrapuntal" itself.

References

Abu-Lughod, Lila. 1991. "Writing against Culture." In *Recapturing Anthropology: Working in the Present*, edited by Richard Fox, 137–62. Santa Fe, NM: School of American Research Press.

Anderson, Mark. 2019. *From Boas to Black Power: Racism, Liberalism, and American Anthropology*. Stanford, CA: Stanford University Press.

Beliso-De Jesús, Aisha, and Jemima Pierre. 2019. "Introduction: Anthropology of White Supremacy." *American Anthropologist* 122, no. 1: 1–11.

Bhimull, Chandra D. 2017. *Empire in the Air: Airline Travel and the African Diaspora*. New York: New York University Press.

Bonds, Anne, and Joshua Inwood. 2016. "Beyond White Privilege: Geographies of White Supremacy and Settler Colonialism." *Progress in Human Geography* 40, no. 6: 715–33.

Chakrabarty, Dipesh. 2000. *Provincializing Europe: Postcolonial Thought and Historical Difference*. Princeton, NJ: Princeton University Press.

Chow, Rey. 2002. "Theory, Area Studies, Cultural Studies: Issues of Pedagogy in Multiculturalism." In *Learning Places: The Afterlives of Area Studies*, edited by Masao Miyoshi and H. D. Harootunian, 103–18. Durham, NC: Duke University Press.

Coronil, Fernando. 2019. *The Fernando Coronil Reader: The Struggle for Life Is the Matter*. Durham, NC: Duke University Press.

Di Leonardo, Micaela. 1998. *Exotics at Home: Anthropologies, Others, American Modernity*. Chicago: University of Chicago Press.

Dirlik, Arif. 1992. "The Asia-Pacific Idea: Reality and Representation in the Invention of a Regional Structure." *Journal of World History* 3, no. 1: 55–79.

Goldberg, Theo. 1993. *Racist Culture: Philosophy and the Politics of Meaning*. Wiley-Blackwell.

Gupta, Akhil, and James Ferguson. 1997. *Anthropological Locations: Boundaries and Grounds of a Field Science*. Berkeley: University of California Press.

Halvorson, Britt, and Joshua Reno. 2022. *Imagining the Heartland: White Supremacy and the American Midwest*. Oakland: University of California Press.

Harootunian, H. D. 2002. "Postcoloniality's Unconscious/Area Studies' Desire." In *Learning Places: The Afterlives of Area Studies*, edited by Masao Miyoshi and H. D. Harootunian, 150–74. Durham, NC: Duke University Press.

Harootunian, H. D. and Masao Miyoshi. 2002. "Introduction: The 'Afterlife' of Area Studies." In *Learning Places: The Afterlives of Area Studies*, edited by Masao Miyoshi and H. D. Harootunian, 1–18. Durham, NC: Duke University Press.

Harris, Cheryl I. 1993. "Whiteness as Property." *Harvard Law Review* 106, no. 8: 1707–91.

Harrison, Faye. 2008. *Outsider Within: Reworking Anthropology in the Global Age*. Champaign-Urbana: University of Illinois Press.

———. (1991) 2010. *Decolonizing Anthropology: Moving Further Toward an Anthropology for Liberation*. 3rd ed. Arlington, VA: Association of Black Anthropologists, American Anthropological Association.

Harvey, David. 2007. "Neoliberalism as Creative Destruction." *Annals of the American Academy of Political and Social Science*. 610: 22–44.

Haskell, T. L. 1985. "Capitalism and the Origins of the Humanitarian Sensibility." *American Historical Review* 90, no. 2: 339–61.

Hurston, Zora Neale. (1927) 2018. *Barracoon: The Story of the Last "Black Cargo."* New York: HarperCollins.

James, C. L. R. 1938 [1989]. *The Black Jacobins*. New York: Vintage.

Lake, Marilyn, and Henry Reynolds. 2008. *Drawing the Global Color Line: White Men's Countries and the International Challenge of Racial Equality*. Cambridge: Cambridge University Press.

Lorek, Timothy W. 2013. "Imagining the Midwest in Latin America: U.S. Advisors and the Envisioning of an Agricultural Middle Class in Colombia's Cauca Valley, 1943–1946." *The Historian* 75, no. 2: 283–305.

Mills, Charles W. 2003. *From Class to Race: Essays in White Marxism and Black Radicalism*. Lanham, MD: Rowman and Littlefield.

Narayan, Kirin. 1993. "How 'Native' Is a Native Anthropologist?" *American Anthropologist* 95, no. 3: 671–86.

Pierre, Jemima. 2006. "Anthropology and the Race of/for Africa." In *The Study of Africa*, Vol. 1: *Disciplinary and Interdisciplinary Encounters*, edited by Paul Tiyambe Zeleza, 39–61. Dakar, Senegal: Council for the Development of Social Science Research in Africa.

Robinson, Cedric. 2000. *Black Marxism: The Making of the Black Radical Tradition*. 2nd ed. Chapel Hill: University of North Carolina Press.

Rosa, Jonathan, and Yarimar Bonilla. 2017. "Deprovincializing Trump, Decolonizing Diversity, and Unsettling Anthropology." *American Ethnologist* 44, no. 2: 201–8.

Said, Edward. 1978. *Orientalism*. New York: Vintage.

———. 1993. *Culture and Imperialism*. London: Vintage.

TallBear, Kim. 2013. *Native American DNA: Tribal Belonging and the False Promise of Genetic Science*. Minneapolis: University of Minnesota Press.

Vitalis, Robert. 2015. *White World Order, Black Power Politics: The Birth of American International Relations*. Ithaca, NY: Cornell University Press.

SECTION II

Empire, Colonialism, and White Supremacy

THE CURRENT international power system emerged through European expansion across the world. The terms of this expansion, anthropologist Michel-Rolph Trouillot (1991, 32) reminds us, were violent "conquest, colonization, and universal legitimacy of European—and racialized white—power." Keeping in view the long history of European conquest and the establishment of white supremacy as the organizing logic of the modern world, this section addresses contemporary and historical formations of empire and its entanglements with white supremacy.

Combining historical analysis with ethnographies of the present, the essays demonstrate how the "colonial" remains crucial for understanding the violent material production of the hegemony of whiteness. But this colonial legacy is often naturalized, hidden through articulations of progress, liberalism, and rationality of history. The essays present the multiple imperial and colonial registers of white supremacy, including structures of settler-capitalism, religious and philosophical systems, global extractive techniques, and competing forms of whiteness.

5

The Persistence of White Supremacy

INDIGENOUS WOMEN MIGRANTS AND
THE STRUCTURES OF SETTLER CAPITALISM

Shannon Speed

SINCE 2016, there has been a resurgence of openly white supremacist discourse and action in the United States. The key word in the preceding sentence is "openly," not "resurgence." Prior to Donald Trump's election, the idea that the United States was a "postracial" society enjoyed significant popularity. The public debate following the election often seemed to suggest that Trump and his followers represented a backlash against this assumed progress, particularly the previous election of the country's first Black president. However, the unexamined assumption inherent in this perspective that white supremacy can be elected out or voted back in is deeply problematic. As I will argue, the United States, indeed power throughout the modern world since the advent of European colonialism, is founded on and structured by the interrelationship of settler colonialism and capitalism, and their attendant logics of race and gender—or more specifically, white supremacy and patriarchy. Because the United States is structured on white supremacy, shifts in public discourse and policy, while significant, do not change the fundamental structures of power. While the forms that these structural logics take over time are historically contingent, they remain as persistently present today as they have been for hundreds of years.[1]

In this chapter, based on research with Indigenous women migrants from Mexico and Central America, I apply an analytic of settler colonialism in order to explore how white supremacy is structured into our institutions and everyday social relations as well as transnational processes. In particular, I consider the intersection of capitalism and the settler state, and how the changing needs of capitalism shape discourses of race differently over time, yet remain fundamentally underwritten by white supremacist premises. Examining the shift from neoliberal multiculturalism to what I call "neoliberal multicriminalism," I argue that the neoliberal multicultural moment, with its accompanying discourses of tolerance and rights that allowed for such notions as "postracial society" to arise, has reached its limits, and that the resurgence of open white supremacy in public discourse and action since Trump's election is a response to the changing needs of white settler capitalist power.

The Enduring Racial Structure of the Settler Capitalist State

A settler colonial analytic has rarely been applied to the study of white supremacy. One of the primary insights of settler colonial theory is that some of the states formed by European colonial expansion are characterized by colonial occupation as an *enduring structure* (Wolfe 2006, emphasis mine). The difference between settler colonialism and other kinds of colonialism is that the settlers come to stay, and thus by necessity must eliminate the Indigenous population of the lands to be "settled" by invading white Europeans. Wolfe's ubiquitous statement that "settler invasion is a structure, not an event," is so often cited because it succinctly captures the enduring nature of occupation and dispossession (1998, 2). Further, because "indigeneity itself is enduring . . . Indigenous peoples exist, resist, and persist" (Kaahumanu 2016, 1), settler colonial structures require constant maintenance in an effort to eradicate them (Wolfe 2006). Settler colonialism thus entails an ongoing structural violence of dispossession and elimination.

In order to justify that dispossession and elimination, elaborate racial logics have been deployed, rendering the Native as nonhuman, uncivilized, and unsuited for civilization, and thus inevitably ceding to white liberal progress by disappearing (Barker 2011; Berkhofer 2011; Goeman 2013; Grande 1999; Lowe 2015; Morgenson 2010). White settler identity is premised on this foundational relationship to Indigenous people. The "uncivilized" and "savage" Native comes into existence only as the racialized Other of the "civilized" white settler. Regarding the United States in particular, Moreton-Robinson ties whiteness to Native dispossession:

> The USA as a White nation state cannot exist without land and clearly defined borders, it is the legally defined and asserted territorial sovereignty that provides the context for national identification of Whiteness. In this way . . . Native American dispossession indelibly marks configurations of White national identity. (2008, 85, cited in Glenn 2015, 59)

These racial logics were fundamentally premised on white supremacy: they invoked social hierarchies in which white, European men were understood as superior to all Others and thus by definition had a right to possess and control the land and the labor of Others. As Bonds and Inwood framed it, these settler "imaginations valorized whiteness and sanctioned the violence of white domination, enslavement, and genocide while bolstering Eurocentric understandings of land use, private property, and wealth accumulation," a framing that usefully forefronts not only white supremacy's dispossessive and eliminatory capacities but its foundational role in the formation of capitalist modernity (Bonds and Inwood 2016, 720; see also Lowe 2015; Trouillot 2003).

The intimate relationship between colonialism, capitalism, and white supremacy is not incidental. As European colonial expansion facilitated the development and spread of capitalism, it brought white supremacy along with it. Robin D. G. Kelley recently highlighted Cedric Robinson's work regarding how racism emerged with capitalism out of the feudal order in Europe, and this codevelopment rendered them fundamentally one system: racial capitalism (2017). Importantly, Kelley underscored Robinson's argument that racial capitalism was the product of a colonial process within Europe:

> [For Robinson,] the first European proletarians were racial subjects (Irish, Jews, Roma, or Gypsies, Slavs, etc.) and they were victims of dispossession (enclosure), colonialism, and slavery within Europe. Indeed, Robinson suggested that racialization within Europe was very much a colonial process involving invasion, settlement, expropriation, and racial hierarchy. (Kelley 2017, paragraph 5)

Thus, the relationship between European colonization, capitalism, and racialization is foundational and co-constitutive. Settler colonial capitalism necessitates the eradication of Indigenous populations, the seizure and privatization of their lands, and the exploitation of marginalized peoples in a system of capitalism established by and reinforced through racism (Bonds and Inwood 2016, 716). Coulthard (2014) has highlighted the continuity of the ongoing relationship between settler colonialism and capitalism in his theorization of primitive accumulation. Coulthard argues that primitive accumulation (the process in which the producer is divorced from the means of production), rather than being the historical point of departure for capitalism or the "pre-history of capital," as Marx theorized, is instead an ongoing process, deeply imbricated in the violence of capitalism's continuing dispossession of land and resources.[2] Following on Coulthard, Brown emphasizes the "points of intersection between primitive accumulation and settler colonialism as *ongoing processes*" in what he terms "settler accumulation" (2013, 4, italics in the original). Because settler capitalist dispossession is ongoing, white-supremacist-based racialization is as well. The racial logics that underpin Native dispossession, slavery, and successive waves of capitalist labor exploitation are structuring logics, inherent to the settler capitalist state.

These racial logics are not static, but rather have been molded and applied to Indigenous people in different forms over time, alternatively justifying genocidal violence, removal, assimilation, termination, and relocation, all policies designed to eliminate, either through direct killing, physical removal, or biocultural assimilation. The same white supremacist logics have been extended to successive waves of arrivants, to use Byrd's (2011) term, who were necessary for labor but understood to similarly put at risk the privileged place of whiteness in the settler state.[3] As Indigenous people were constructed as savage and uncivilized for the purposes of dispossessing them through colonial enclosure, African and Asian arrivants were constructed as "slave" and "coolie" in forced labor systems of enslavement and indenture,[4] and various Others subject to racialized constructions in successive coercive or exploitative labor regimes. Xenophobic white supremacy in the United States is thus intimately tied to settler structures, differing over time and among differently racialized "exogenous others" in relation to evolving labor regimes of capitalism (Glenn 2015). These various racializations are distinct iterations of a common dynamic: settler capitalist societies are premised on maintaining white dominance over Indigenous people and asserting state sovereignty against the incursion of people deemed "Other" and generating them as populations to meet the labor needs of capitalism. Such racialization takes shape in the current moment in the production of the terrorist/criminal immigrant who must be detained, deported, or rendered deportable. Each of these constructions served a particular moment of capital expansion, and each leaves its ideological imprint in racial and gender formations that continue to mark contemporary political subjectivities. While the construction of immigrants as terrorist, rapists, "bad hombres," and bad parents was most virulent in the Trump administration, underpinning policies of racialized exclusion such as the Muslim ban, family separation, and maniacal pursuit of the border wall, they are in fact extreme extensions of the logics already at play under previous administrations, while the discourse of the United States as postracial flourished.

Indigenous Women Migrants and the Settler Capitalist State

It is well known that the Obama administration deported more immigrants than any prior administration, prompting immigration advocates to dub the president "deporter-in-chief" and decry the administration's "five-year deportation spree."[5] In total, more than 2.5 million people were deported during the Obama administration.[6] President Obama justified the high level of deportations by arguing that those deported were criminals. In 2014, Obama's memo on priorities for immigration enforcement emphasized this criminality: "We're going to keep focusing enforcement resources on actual threats to our security. Felons, not families. Criminals, not children. Gang members, not a mom who's working hard to provide for her kids."[7] Nevertheless, the reality is that between 2009 and 2017, half of those deported had committed no crime at all, and 60 percent of those that did had only victimless crimes (mostly immigration violations).[8] The vast majority (approximately 95 percent) of those deported in any given year were from Mexico and Central America.[9] In the racialization of brown bodies as dangerous criminals, President Obama continued down the path opened by his predecessor George W. Bush. Following the events of September 11, the Bush administration set in motion a series of actions that cast immigrants as criminals and terrorists. In 2003, the Immigration and Naturalization Service (INS) was dissolved and reformulated as Immigration and Customs Enforcement (ICE) under the Department of Homeland Security (DHS), the mission of which is defined in the Homeland Security Act as "preventing terrorist acts in the United States [and] reducing the vulnerability of the United States to terrorism."[10] In 2005, the DHS began its Secure Border Initiative (SBI), which has as its stated goal, "improving public safety by working to better identify, detain and ultimately remove dangerous criminal aliens from your community."[11] These shifts clearly constructed immigrants as terrorists and criminals. That construction was applied specifically to women and children refugees under the Obama administration, when ICE first began arguing that women and children refugees should not be freed from detention while their asylum claims were processed because they represented a "risk to our national security."[12]

Trump also racialized Central American and Mexican women and children fleeing violence as criminals and terrorists, even taking this as far as declaring their presence on the border a national emergency.[13] While numbers are difficult to obtain because the US government does not record indigenous identity, only national origin, many of these migrants are Indigenous and are not strangers to settler state racialization. This state interpolation effectively strips them of their indigeneity while constructing them as political subjects as terrorist/criminal threats. Many of the stories I gathered from Indigenous women migrants from Mexico and Central America reflect these multilayered and ongoing racialization processes. Multiply subject to power through their race and gender in their homes in Mexico and Central America, on their journeys to the United States, and in the States once they have crossed the border, their stories illustrate the permanence of colonial occupation, the impacts of shifting forms of capitalism, and the persistence of white supremacy and patriarchy.

I met Floricarmen in the T. Don Hutto immigration detention center in Central Texas in 2013.[14] Floricarmen had been in the United States for fourteen years when she was detained. She had come to the United States after many others in her southern Mexico town had departed, as their local subsistence economy shriveled under the changes wrought by the North American Free Trade Agreement (NAFTA). Implemented in 1994, NAFTA had promised to make Mexico the poster child of neoliberal globalization. Instead, the trade agreement had given rise to the forceful opposition of the Indigenous Zapatista uprising, but in spite of that opposition, undermined subsistence and small-scale economies by imposing a neoliberal market logic on what were fundamentally unequal economies in terms of production and distribution (Bacon 2016; Sealing 2003; Wise 2009). This was the neoliberal moment, Fukiyama's "end of history," in which ostensibly free market economies marched across the globe, accompanied by rights regimes and democracy. While this was in a sense a fantasy of the settler capitalist imaginary to begin with, there was arguably a neoliberal multicultural moment in Latin America in which democratization and rights recognition seemed to move in tandem with the spread of neoliberalism. As states undertook an often massive reorientation of their economies (Mexico is particularly notable), ending land reform, eliminating state subsidies for farming and industry, privatizing capital and natural resources, limiting tariffs on foreign goods, and slashing government social welfare programs, they also moved toward popularly elected governments and expanded notions of human rights and the rule of law. A number of states, including Mexico and Guatemala, reformed their constitutions to recognize Indigenous peoples and extend to them some level of collective Indigenous rights (Sieder 2002; Van Cott 2000; Yasher 1991). Often posited as the inevitable spread of neoliberal democracy on a US model (at times with an evolutionist flavor of development toward the highest state of being, naturally epitomized by the United States), these processes seemed to promise at least a minimal increase in political stability, rights, and accountability. This was the moment Charles Hale (2002; 2005) critically referred to as neoliberal multiculturalism.

The fallacy of neoliberal multiculturalism's promise of equal rights and economic trickle down are evident on Floricarmen's story, as are the continuity of racial and gendered structures. As Floricarmen's migration suggests, the real benefits of those rights gains were meaningless for many Indigenous people in Mexico, who found themselves forced to undertake difficult journeys, only to spend the next decade and a half living shadow lives as undocumented workers (by definition outside the scope of liberal rights), and always at risk of being cast eventually into the United States' detention and deportation regime. More importantly, as Floricarmen's migration reflects, the real beneficiaries of these economic and political shifts were never intended to be Indigenous peoples. Even as they were discursively written into the state, Indigenous people were economically disenfranchised to an extent that they had not been since the prior to Mexican Revolution. Their agricultural and subsistence lifeways were consciously decimated by the settler elites in power, so much so that the Indigenous Zapatista uprising, launched on the eve of the North American Trade Agreement, characterized the changes as a "death sentence for Indigenous peoples." The settler racial logics of the uncivilized Indian finally ceding to the progress of civilization and modernity were ever-present, even as Indigenous people were acknowledged as rights-bearing individuals in the nation-state (which again signaled their entry into modernity.) The superiority of white capitalist modernity over Indigenous backwardness had never been more potently asserted. White supremacy was lurking in plain sight in the neoliberal multicultural era in Mexico.

More than a decade after Floricarmen left her home in southern Mexico, Nadania departed her home on Honduras's north coast. Nadania had witnessed a murder on a bus, carried out by local gangs linked to drug cartels, whom she referred to simply as "the men who run the town." A short time later, her small store at the front of her home was open fired on. She fled the next day, certain she would be killed if she stayed. Leaving Honduras did not free her from danger, as she was held for ransom by cartel gangs in northern Mexico, and later detained for over a year in immigration detention in the United States.

Nadania's experiences of cartel-related violence reflect the shifting dynamics in Mexico and Central America in which the neoliberal multicultural moment of Floricarmen's story, even with the limitations to its promise, quickly faded into obscurity as the deregulation of the end of corporatism and the unleashing of free market logics, in the absence of solid legal and political systems, led quickly to the growth of mass-scale illegal markets. Drug, gun, and human trafficking expanded as the cartels flourished in Mexico, feeding on widespread corruption of the government and military and the deregulated money flows and reserve army of newly impoverished generated by neoliberalism (Campbell 2009; Paley 2014). In Guatemala, the exclusionary state constructed by "predatory economic and military elites" (Gavigan 2011, 99) and a culture of violence left by the thirty-year civil war that left 200,000 dead, the majority Mayan, created fertile ground for the spread of the cartels as the US-backed drug war in Mexico got underway (Briscoe and Rodríguez Pellecer 2010). In Honduras, the power vacuum produced by the US-supported 2005 coup and its aftermath, which included massive repression against protestors, opened the door for the expansion of illegal drug activity and the consolidation of power by cartel gangs and street gangs (Loperena 2017). Increasingly, authoritarian and militarized governance became the norm in this new national security era. The denationalization of resources and invitation of foreign capital fostered megadevelopment projects ranging from extraction to tourism and disproportionally affected Black and Indigenous communities seeking autonomy and territorial control (Loperena 2016). Dissent was increasingly criminalized, and there has been a rise in paramilitary violence to quash resistance, usually linked to the government and to cartel powers controlling the areas. Highlighting the role of racialization in this process, Birss notes, "This neocolonialism relies on racist attitudes against Indigenous and other tribal peoples, providing governments and companies with an excuse to behave as though the resources they encounter belong to them, regardless of the inhabitants of the area or the social and environmental consequences."[15] While Birss refers to this dynamic as "neocolonial," as Yagenova and Garcia suggest, there is nothing new about it: "the racist and ethnocentric nature of the state and its links with capital [in Guatemala are] part of a long history of dispossession and occupation" (Yagenova and Garcia 2009, 158). In short, this web of neoliberal illegality, with settler states fully enmeshed, generates new forms of dispossession and exploitation as well as swelling violence rates, making Honduras the murder capital of the world,[16] while Guatemala has competed for the record for femicide,[17] and Mexico grapples with violence so extreme it has been deemed a "crisis of civilization," with at least 250,00 dead and by official reports 37,400 disappeared in recent years (2018 alone had more than 33,000 homicides).[18] In this context, "rights rang hollow" (Hale, Calla, and Mulling 2017, 87), and the rights struggles and Indigenous autonomy claims of neoliberal multiculturalism waned in the face of obscene levels of bloodshed and massive impunity. This was neoliberal multicriminalism, and Nadania experienced the violence generated by it at home and on her journey north (Speed 2016).

In Latin America, the onset of neoliberalism necessitated fundamental shifts in the ways that states related to their population. Free market extremes could not be facilitated either by authoritarian control or by corporatist control, the two main models of governance in the region. Governments needed more democratic structures in order for the contradictions of social inequality (inevitably produced by capitalism) to be mediated by civil society (hence the concurrent rise of NGOs, as I have argued elsewhere—Speed 2008). For this type of governance to function, society needed to be composed of rights-bearing individuals, leading to the wave of constitutional reforms and rights recognition in the early 1990s. Racial regimes shifted, and Indigenous people became a positive for the nation rather than a problem, at least nominally and often folklorically.

While this kind of process was underway for most of the 1990s, in Mexico and Central America it did not achieve democratic consolidation. In the absence of checks and balances and independently functioning judiciaries, populations, particularly the most vulnerable, were left simultaneously exposed to predatory foreign capital and predacious illegal economies that operated outside the realm of any regulation and inside the realm of ostensibly legitimate government. Authoritarianism resurged, and not surprisingly the state increasingly racialized Indigenous people as criminals and terrorists in the context of escalating violence. Nadania's experience in Honduras reflects the harsh social realities of neoliberal multicriminalism, in which the racialization of Indigenous people underlies both new forms of the economic dispossession and the violent response by the settler state to any contestation of it.

Nadania, like all of the women in my research, left their homes and came to the United States seeking a safe and stable environment. At the time they entered the United States, neoliberal multiculturalism still reigned. Yet, I want to suggest that their stories of detention and deportation pointed even then to the fissures. Capitalism had expanded globally—there was nowhere left to go—and the inherent contradictions it produces, most readily visible in ever-increasing inequality, were becoming more apparent in popular discontent. The United States' inability to grapple with immigration is in part a product of these contradictions: capitalism requires the labor of the disposable migrant population, yet the presence of these racialized Others challenges white settler sovereignty and privilege. This was reflected in the massive contradictions in the Obama administrations detention and deportation policies, so incongruous with his presidency and his generally neoliberal approach to governance, in which the free market economy stood, global economic cooperation was emphasized, and individual civil rights were forefronted. In some sense, we might say that immigration detention and deportation were the canary in the coal mine, signaling the impending political crisis of multiculturalist policies that would come to fruition in the US presidential campaign and election of 2016.

But if immigration policy under Obama signaled the tensions arising within neoliberal multiculturalism, Donald Trump's election marked the end of the US multiculturalist period. Often, public commentary in the media has focused on the fact that Trump's ascent to power and the attendant resurgence of overt white supremacy was brought about in part by white people who are angry and fearful of the gains of nonwhites in the neoliberal multicultural period. However, the contradictions of capitalist expansion are also crucial to the resurgence of open white supremacy. The neoliberal expansion—what has often been referred to as globalization—with its extreme free market logics, has generated a disenfranchised population frustrated with the disappearance of working-class—and even middle-class—prosperity and well-being. Earlier forms of laissez faire capitalism took into account the need for states to mediate social inequality. Neoliberalism, the extreme version of free-market capitalism, shuns state intervention, leaving social inequality to the play of market forces. In the United States as in Latin America, this has led to previously unseen levels of social and economic inequality. During the Obama administration, even as unemployment dropped and the economy grew, people struggled to stay afloat, and people who had expected to live middle-class lives descended further and further into poverty (whether it was defined as such by decreasing federal standards or not). It was in part that anger that fueled Trump's election, embracing the idea that it was globalization (in the form of free trade agreements, outsourcing of jobs, and so on) that had brought them to this place. The embrace of Trump's assertion that he would "bring the jobs back," however untenable that claim was to anyone with even a shallow understanding of how capitalism works, nevertheless reflects the underlying contradictions of capitalism at play in the political moment. It is in that moment that white Americans felt the need to reassert their settler right to possess this land and reap the profits of economic exploitation in this country.

Conclusions on the Endurance of White Supremacy

In this chapter, I departed from the oral histories of Indigenous women migrants and applied a settler colonial analytic to examine the intersection of capitalism and the settler state in order to understand the enduring nature of white supremacy. The stories of Indigenous women illustrate larger processes at work than just a US election, or even a "state of mind" of the US population. They reflect the ongoing and enduring structures of settler capitalism, which, I have argued, is fundamentally premised on Native dispossession and white supremacy. As capitalism evolves, new racialized rationales must be provided, and old tropes are revived in new guises. Neoliberal multiculturalism was expanded out from the United States across much of the globe, and the contradictions produced in that expansion are being felt in social tensions in the United States, as in Mexico and Central America. Overt expressions of white supremacy and misogyny—always structurally present but discursively muted at a particular moment in time in order to facilitate a particular kind of capitalist expansion (neoliberal multiculturalism)—are being deployed in new and more overt ways to address capitalism's crisis. The modified "friendlier" forms associated with the multiculturalist moment have been too easily understood as progress toward elimination rather than as new iterations that would be recalibrated as the structural needs of settler capitalist power changed. Further, while the racial logics in this new phase are not the same iterations as those deployed against settler capitalist Others in distinct moments of history and across distinct geographies, they are nonetheless still logics of white supremacy, mobilized in order to justify ongoing European American "rightful" occupation and continued subjugation of nonwhite Others.

Notes

1. This chapter is an abridged and revised version of what first appeared as Shannon Speed, 2020. "The Persistence of White Supremacy: Indigenous Women Migrants and the Structures of Settler Capitalism." *American Anthropologist* 122, no. 1: 76–85. doi.org/10.1111/aman.13359.

2. For a review of the recent literature rethinking primitive accumulation, see Nichols 2015.

3. In *Transits of Empire*, Byrd argues that "racialization and colonization have worked simultaneously to other and abject entire peoples so they can be enslaved, excluded, removed, and killed in the name of progress and capitalism" (Byrd 2011, xxiii). She uses the term "arrivant" to distinguish racially subjugated non-Indigenous people inhabiting Indigenous lands from white settlers due to their distinct location in the power formations of the settler capitalist state.

4. I do not mean to conflate these two systems of forced labor. Chattel slavery is fundamentally distinct in its reduction of humans to commodities owned and sold as private property, and it entails very particular forms of racialization and dehumanization. My point is simply that all of these forms of racialization are based in white supremacy and emerge from the changing needs of the settler capitalist state. In different periods and geographic locations, Indigenous people have been subjected to both of these forms of unfree labor.

5. Alejandra Marchevsky and Beth Baker, *The Nation*, "Why Has President Obama Deported More Immigrants Than Any President in US History?: Since 9/11, Immigration Has Become Increasingly Tangled with Criminal Enforcement and National Security." Available at www.thenation.com/article/why-has-president-obama-deported-more-immigrants-any-president-us-history/. Last accessed September 2017.

6. Between 2009 when Obama took office and 2015, more than 2.5 million persons were deported, a total that exceeded that of the two terms of his predecessor, George W. Bush, in which just over 2 million people were deported, An additional 450,000 were deported in 2016, bringing the Obama administration's total close to 3 million. Department of Homeland Security, 2017. DHS Immigration Enforcement (Enforcement Priorities). Available at www.dhs.gov/immigration-statistics/enforcement-priorities. Last accessed September 2018.

7. White House Office of the Press Secretary. 2014. "Remarks by the President in Address to the Nation on Immigration." Available at https://obamawhitehouse.archives.gov/the-press-office/2014/11/20/remarks -president-address-nation-immigration. Last accessed September 2017.

8. Cato Institute, "60% of Deported 'Criminal Aliens' Committed Only Victimless Crime," by David Bier. June 6, 2018. Available at www.cato.org/blog/60-deported-criminal-aliens-committed-only-victimless-crimes -few-violent-crimes. Last accessed February 12, 2019.

9. Removal statistics by year are available at www.ice.gov/removal-statistics/. For an analysis of 2012 and 2013, see https://trac.syr.edu/immigration/reports/350/. Last accessed February 16, 2019.

10. Homeland Security Act 2002. Available at www.dhs.gov/xabout/laws/law_regulation_rule_0011.shtm . Last accessed November 2018.

11. Immigration Control and Enforcement (ICE) Secure Communities website. www.ice.gov/doclib /secure-communities/pdf/sc-brochure.pdf. Last accessed May 12, 2016.

12. ICE bond hearing documentation packet, in possession of the author.

13. In just a couple of examples: "President Trump calls caravan immigrants 'stone cold criminals.' Here's what we know." Bart Jansen and Alan Gomez, *USA Today*, November 26, 2018. www.usatoday.com/story/news /2018/11/26/president-trump-migrant-caravan-criminals/2112846002/; "Trump: Migrant Caravan 'Is an Invasion.'" Jordan Fabian, *The Hill*, October 29, 2018. https://thehill.com/homenews/administration/413624 -trump-calls-migrant-caravan-an-invasion.

14. I had entered the facility as part of the Hutto Visitation Program (HVP). The goal of the project was to visit women detainees, accompanying them during their often prolonged detention periods, and monitoring human rights conditions in the facility. "Hutto" is a former medium security prison, converted to a "residential facility" for the detention of immigrant families in 2006. It became an infamous symbol of expanded immigration policing, detention, and deportation following the September 11 attacks and eventually became the target of an ACLU lawsuit against ICE and the Department of Homeland Security on behalf of immigrant children detained at the center. The resulting settlement ended family detention at Hutto, and when I began working with the HVP, the facility housed only women. However, there were multiple reports of abuse in the facility, which has been the subject of two federal sexual abuse investigations. In 2011 a former guard pled guilty to federal charges for sexually assaulting detained women. "Sexual Abuse of Female Detainees at Hutto Highlights Ongoing Failure of Immigration Detention System, Says ACLU." Available at www.aclu.org/news/sexual-abuse -female-detainees-hutto-highlights-ongoing-failure-immigration-detention-system. Last accessed August 2017. Ryan Kocian, *Courthouse News Service*, "CCA Guard Accused of 8 Sexual Assaults," April 15, 2015. Available at www.courthousenews.com/cca-guard-accused-of-8-sexual-assaults/. Last accessed August 2017.

15. As Birss points out, the United States is no exception, as reflected in the violent repression and criminalization of protesters of the Dakota Access Pipeline on the territory of the Standing Rock Sioux (Birss 2017, 316).

16. Kuang Keng Kuek Ser, "Map: Here Are Countries with the World's Highest Murder Rates." *PRI's The World*, June 27, 2016 Available at www.pri.org/stories/2016-06-27/map-here-are-countries-worlds-highest -murder-rates; *Time*, Maya Rhodan, "Honduras Is Still the Murder Capital of The World: Decapitations and Mutilations Are on the Rise Even as the Overall Murder Rate Declines." February 17, 2014. Available at world .time.com/2014/02/17/honduras-is-still-the-murder-capital-of-the-world/.

17. Sue Branford. 2013. "Guatemala: Region's Highest Rate of Femicide." Latin America Bureau. https://lab .org.uk/guatemala-regions-highest-rate-of-femicide/. Last accessed February 2, 2019.

18. *Wall Street Journal*, "It's a Crisis of Civilization in Mexico," by José de Córdoba and Juan Montes. November 14, 2018. www.wsj.com/articles/its-a-crisis-of-civilization-in-mexico-250-000-dead-37-400-missing -1542213374. Last accessed February 26, 2019.

References

Bacon, David. 2008. "Displaced People: NAFTA's Most Important Product." *NACLA Report on the Americas* 41, no. 5: 23–27.

Barker, Joanne. 2011. *Native Acts: Law, Recognition, and Cultural Authenticity*. Durham, NC: Duke University Press.

Berkhofer, Robert F., Jr. 2011. *Images of the American Indian from Columbus to the Present*. New York: Vintage Books, Random House.

Birss, Moira. 2017. "Criminalizing Environmental Activism." *NACLA Report on the Americas* 49, no. 3: 315–22.

Bonds, Anne, and Joshua Inwood. 2016. "Beyond White Privilege: Geographies of White Supremacy and Settler Colonialism." *Progress in Human Geography* 40, no. 6: 715–33.

Briscoe, Ivan, and Martin Rodríguez Pellecer. 2010. *A State under Siege: Elites, Criminal Networks, and Institutional Reform in Guatemala*. The Hague: Netherlands Institute of International Relations.

Brown, Nicholas A. 2014. "The Logic of Settler Accumulation in a Landscape of Perpetual Vanishing." *Settler Colonial Studies* 4, no. 1: 1–26.

Byrd, Jody. 2011. *Transits of Empire: Indigenous Critiques of Colonialism*. Minneapolis: University of Minnesota Press.

Campbell, Howard. 2009. *Drug War Zone: Frontline Dispatches from the Streets of El Paso and Juarez*. Austin: University of Texas Press.

Coulthard, Glen. 2014. *Red Skin/White Masks: Rejecting the Colonial Politics of Recognition*. Minneapolis: University of Minnesota Press.

Gavigan, Patrick. 2011. "Organized Crime, Illicit Power, and Threatened Peace Process: The Case of Guatemala." In *Peace Operations and Organized Crime: Enemies of Allies?*, edited by James Cockayne and Adam Cupel, 99–115. New York: Routledge.

Glenn, Evelyn Nakano. 2015. "Settler Colonialism as Structure: A Framework for Comparative Studies of U.S. Race and Gender Formation." *Sociology of Race and Ethnicity* 1, no. 1: 52–72.

Goeman, Mishuana. 2013. *Mark My Words: Native Women Mapping Out Nations*. Minneapolis: University of Minnesota Press.

Grande, Sandy. 1999. "Beyond the Ecologically Noble Savage: Deconstructing the White Man's Indian." *Environmental Ethics* 21: 307–20.

Hale, Charles R. 2002. "Does Multiculturalism Menace?: Governance, Cultural Rights, and the Politics of Identity in Guatemala." *Journal of Latin American Studies* 34, no. 3: 485–524.

———. 2005. "Neoliberal Multiculturalism: The Remaking of Cultural Rights and Racial Dominance in Central America." *Political and Legal Anthropology Review* 28, no. 1: 10–28.

Hale, Charles R., Pamela Calla, and Leith Mullings. 2017. "Race Matters in Dangerous Times." *NACLA Report on the Americas* 49, no. 1: 81–89.

Kauanui, J. Kēhaulani. 2016. "'A Structure, Not an Event': Settler Colonialism and Enduring Indigeneity." *Lateral* 5, no. 1.

Kelley, Robin D. G. 2017. "What Did Cedric Robinson Mean by Racial Capitalism?" *Boston Review: A Political and Literary Forum*. Available at http://bostonreview.net/race/robin-d-g-kelley-what-did-cedric-robinson-mean-racial-capitalism.

Khalidi, Rashid. 2020. *The Hundred Years' War on Palestine: A History of Settler Colonialism and Resistance, 1917–2017*. New York: Metropolitan Books; Henry Holt.

Loperena, Christopher A. 2016. "Conservation by Racialized Dispossession: The Making of an Eco-Destination on Honduras's North Coast." *Geoforum* 69: 184–93.

———. 2017. "Settler Violence?: Race and Emergent Frontiers of Progress in Honduras." *American Quarterly* 69, no. 4: 801–7.

Lowe, Lisa. 2015. *The Intimacies of Four Continents*. Durham, NC: Duke University Press.

Masalha, Nur. 2021. *The Palestine Nakba: Decolonising History, Narrating the Subaltern, Reclaiming Memory*. London: Zed Books.

Moreton-Robinson, Aileen. 2008. "Writing Off Treaties: White Possessions in the United States, Critical Whiteness Studies Literature." In *Transnational Whiteness Matters*, edited by A. Moreton-Robinson, M. Casey, and F. Nicoll, 81–98. Lanham, MD: Lexington Books.

Morgensen, Scott Lauria. 2010. "Settler Homonationalism: Theorizing Settler Colonialism within Queer Modernities." *GLQ: A Journal of Lesbian and Gay Studies* 16, no. 1–2: 105–31.

Nichols, Robert. 2015. "Disaggregating Primitive Accumulation." *Radical Philosophy* 194: 18–28.

Paley, Dawn. 2014. *Drug War Capitalism*. Oakland, CA: AK Press.

Pappé, Ilan. 2007. *The Ethnic Cleansing of Palestine*. Oxford: Oneworld.

Sealing, Keith. 2003. "Indigenous Peoples, Indigenous Farmers: NAFTA's Threat to Mexican Teosinte Farmers and What Can Be Done about It." *American University International Law Review* 18: 1383–98.

Sieder, Rachel. 2002. "Recognizing Indigenous Law and the Politics of State Formation in Meso-America." In *Multiculturalism in Latin America: Indigenous Rights, Diversity, and Democracy*, edited by Rachel Sieder. New York: Palgrave.

Speed, Shannon. 2016. "States of Violence: Indigenous Women Migrants in the Era of Neoliberal Multicriminalism." *Critique of Anthropology* 36, no. 3: 280–301.

Trouillot, M. R. 2003. "Anthropology and the Savage Slot: The Poetics and Politics of Otherness." In *Global Transformations*. New York: Palgrave Macmillan.

Van Cott, Donna Lee. 2000. *The Friendly Liquidation of the Past: The Politics of Diversity in Latin America*. Pittsburgh: University of Pittsburgh Press.

Weizman, Eyal. 2007. *Hollow Land: Israel's Architecture of Occupation*. London: Verso.

Wise, Timothy. 2009. "Agricultural Dumping under NAFTA: Estimating the Costs of U.S. Agricultural Policies to Mexican Producers." *AgEcon: Research in Agricultural and Applied Economics*. https://ageconsearch.umn .edu/record/179078/. Last accessed February 26, 2019.

Wolfe, Patrick. 1998. *Settler Colonialism and the Transformation of Anthropology: The Politics and Poetics of an Ethnographic Event*. New York: Continuum Press.

———. 2006. "Settler Colonialism and the Elimination of the Native." *Journal of Genocide Research* 8, no. 4: 387–409.

———. 2016. *Traces of History: Elementary Structures of Race*. London: Verso.

Yagenova, Simona V., and Rocío Garcia. 2009. "Indigenous People's Struggles against Transnational Mining Companies in Guatemala: The Sipakapa People vs. GoldCorp Mining Company." *Socialism and Democracy* 23, no. 3: 157–66.

Yasher, Deborah. 1999. "Democracy, Indigenous Movements, and Postliberal Challenge in Latin America." *World Politics* 52, no. 1: 76–104.

6

The Obscuring Effect

WHITENESS IN THE CELEBRATION OF BLACK PERFORMANCE IN SENEGAL

Celina de Sá

IN 2018, A GROUP of martial artists traveled from France and across West Africa to participate in a week-long event commemorating the twentieth anniversary of "Africa Capoeira," Senegal's first homegrown school of an Afro-Brazilian martial art. The group's founder is Moctar Ndiaye, a Wolof man who was born on the historic former slave port Gorée Island and has lived there all his life. It is also where he first saw capoeira. He recalled seeing a child on the beach whose "legs were always in the air . . . It changed my life." He had a passion for studying Latin American independence movements in his twenties but knew little about Brazil until his encounter with capoeira: "I discovered that in Brazil, there was this art, that was also my own history. Our own history, Africans, Senegalese, and most of all us Goreeans. In all of Africa it is Gorée that holds the strongest symbol of this tragedy of the period of the Atlantic slave trade." Now in his fifties, Ndiaye has taught children and adults to skillfully display their legs in the air across Senegal, and the week-long twentieth anniversary event marked his legacy. That week, the congregation of Brazilian, French, Senegalese, and other francophone West African capoeiristas held a performance at the Place de l'Obélisque in Dakar that was broadcast by the Radiodiffusion Télévision Sénégalaise (RTS) as part of a World Cup screening event. As the performers caught their breath once the cameras left, a man stormed past in a fit of anger, shouting in Wolof. Dieudonné, a capoeirista from Dakar, translated the complaint for the mixed crowd of West Africans: "[The man] just said, 'Stop doing this monkey thing!'"

In a brutal irony, the comment echoed Jean Dard's—colonial West Africa's first French language instructor—description of Europeans' general sentiment toward the Wolof language in 1826:

> We have gone so far as to say that negros in general only speak a kind of chuckle without rules, without principles; a jargon almost similar to that of the orangutan. (Quoted in Calvet 2010)

The monkey [*sic*, ape] descriptor also resembled the depiction of James Wetherell, an Englishman visiting colonial Bahia who wrote in his subsection "The Fighting of the Blacks," referring to what we know today as capoeira, "they throw their legs about like monkeys during their quarrels. It is a ludicrous sight" (1856, 119–20). The Senegalese passerby's critique of capoeira may have stemmed from other conventions of respectability, such as an Islamic framework for indecent displays of the body in public, of gendered interactions, or of the use of secular music in a predominantly Muslim context. However, the racialized grammar (Ochonu 2019) of his critique drew on well-established racialized tropes (the inappropriate use of the body being "monkey-like"). References to animals read as subhuman behavior should be contextualized within the broader framework of what is common sense in postcolonial West Africa: comparisons to "nature," or to rurality ("bushness") are inextricably linked from the racialization of enslaved and colonized subjects (Faye and Thioub 2003; Mbembe 2001; Pierre 2020; Quijano 2007).

The passerby's affective response and word choice trigger a set of questions about the possibility of white supremacy as it operates in the context of Senegal, even without direct white actors. White supremacy rests on the surface of the everyday in urban West Africa. It lives in language ideologies, the circulation of common phrases, and in the categorization of bodily movement. Coloniality is a framework to capture the enduring logics of the colonial encounter that survive the ostensibly liberatory events of independence or abolition (Mignolo 2012; Ndlovu-Gatsheni 2013; Quijano 2007; Wynter 2003). If we take seriously that coloniality is a mechanism for white supremacy to remain normative, and germane even in contexts without a significant presence of white bodies, then we see this discourse playing out in a most pronounced way on ideas about and uses of the body. The realm of performance calls attention to the body as an important site for the production of social categories. However, the performing body's materiality can be deceiving in its reification of "culture," "tradition," or nationalism, all concepts that traffic in racialism often without doing so explicitly. What I call *the coloniality of Black performance* is an iteration of white supremacy in postcolonial African sites that thrives in a context in which beliefs of Black or African inferiority to whiteness or Europeanness intersects with multiracial artistic spaces designed to celebrate Black cultural production. Black performance has long been a fascination of Portuguese, French, and British colonial imaginaries, and therefore it is foundational to the impulse to consume and exploit the Black Other. The continuation of consuming Black performance can be a form of coloniality. Embodying Blackness through performance is bound up in white guilt that has not yet given way to addressing the reality of white supremacy that continues to structure social relations worldwide.

A few performers from the group expressed only mild annoyance at the monkey comment, seeing it as another instance of critique from someone who "doesn't understand" their practice. In Dakar, racial discourse is not linked to structural dehumanization and its accompanying precarity of the bodily integrity of its targets, as is the case in white settler colonies such as the United States (Sharpe 2016; Ticktin 2011). What is specific to the dynamics of white supremacy here, and between differently positioned Black Africans, is the fact that racialized grammars are so deeply embedded in everyday ways of thinking, perceiving, and interacting as to be ignored. The fact that the capoeiristas' reaction of mild irritation to being told they were behaving like monkeys is not proof of the insignificance of the event. Rather, it demonstrates the degree of normalcy, a common sense that racialized insults enjoy as they circulate in everyday interactions.

The relationship between globally legible racial schemas and regionally specific discourses of difference in African contexts is increasingly under investigation (e.g., Lecocq 2005). Still, the debate has created a clear divide between those who find race to be relevant to diasporic but not continental contexts—and by extension those see the root of race in Africa as predating Euro-African contact—and those working to demonstrate the interconnectivity of race as a global phenomenon that also affects *all* African postcolonial societies. Coloniality in the form of the continued privileging of whiteness and the structuring of postcolonial societies into racial hierarchies are inextricably linked to schemas of social difference often framed as narrowly contained within vectors of ethnicity, class, or caste (often perceived to be outside of or prior to European ideas of race). Autochthonous schemas of difference such as the enduring attachment to ethnicity, and race as a phenomenon rooted in the diaspora co-occur in sites like Dakar, seemingly side by side, and therefore appear as two separate and therefore unrelated phenomena. Yet their inextricable relationship is particularly evident in *the coloniality of Black performance*. Black performing arts create spaces that center racial discourse, the body, historical narratives that are often dangerously oversimplified, public spectacle, and tensions of cultural authorship.

Race is a fundamental technology of colonial and postcolonial statecraft in Africa, or what Barbara Fields and Karen Fields (2012) and Jemima Pierre (2013) have called *racecraft*. Ghana is a cosmopolitan site built with political and cultural ideologies such as Pan-Africanism that are inextricably linked to transnational capitalist development aspirations. Senegal is similarly global, yet is also a construct of Islamic statecraft, the administrative headquarters for all of French West Africa, and therefore subject to the legacy of direct *assimilation* efforts of the French civilizing mission (Conklin 1997; Cruise O'Brien and Diouf 2002). Therefore, processes of racialization are entangled with religio-political structures and Wolof cultural hegemony that often eclipses ethnic diversity in Senegal (McLaughlin 1995; Villalón 1995). I build on Jemima Pierre's argument that diaspora can sometimes act as an obstructive force that decenters postcolonial African racial realities. There are therefore two entry points from which to look at coloniality here, one is the racialized grammar and categorization normalized in Senegalese society, and two, the presence of foreign guests that are not spotlighted in discussions of whiteness because they are not directly tied to colonial rule.

Brazil has strong cultural purchase around the world, while the racial implications of its cultural exports is often radically and intentionally ambiguous. White subjects who are experts in Black cultural forms, such as the French, Brazilian, and American capoeira *mestres* that regularly visit West Africa, have been active consumers of Black cultural production for decades. Their expertise positions them as embodiments of "Black culture" for West African practitioners who are somewhat marginalized from global capoeira networks. As a result, whiteness in the postcolonial social landscape becomes flattened and depoliticized, especially in and through the realm of popular cultural production that centers racially obscured influences like Latin America. Beyond formal political systems and state-sponsored cultural events, grassroots, transnational artistic networks show how race is desired, rejected, and invisibilized in everyday life in urban West Africa through discourse and the affective experiences attached to performing bodies. I argue that the dislocation of Blackness as occurring elsewhere, and therefore needing to be borrowed from the western hemisphere, leads to a process by which the racial dynamics of access to "quintessential Black Arts" obscures how Black bodily arts are read by West African publics.

Performance, Creativity, and Making Race

Performance can elicit reactions from formal (and unintentional) audiences that reveal ideological frameworks and historical memories in the way performance is read (Apter and Derby 2010; Adelakun 2021). Capoeira is a musical martial art invented by enslaved Africans in Brazil likely in the eighteenth century to defend their honor, perpetuate Central African cultural practices, and even achieve manumission (Desch-Obi 2008). "Africa Capoeira" is a testament to the symbolic "return" of the martial art to an imagined African origin. Capoeira is a little-known but significant and generative practice in the historical trajectory of Senegal's postindependence self-image. At the First World Festival of Negro Arts, Senegal's first president Léopold Sédar Senghor's effort to paint the newly independent country as a Black, Pan-African cultural character and convener of international Black Arts, a Brazilian contingent performed capoeira, led by one of capoeira's most important twentieth-century figures, Vincente Ferreira Pastinha. This event was also the first documented instance of modern capoeira on the African continent. In Dakar, urban West African young professionals are in dialogue with Brazil, its cultural forms, artistic networks, and their imaginary of the nation (Besnier and Brownell 2012). Through expressive arts such as capoeira, postcolonial predicaments come to light, including the continuous process of constructing a nation entangled with multiple diasporic trajectories, contested representation, and grappling with the country's place in the global scheme.

Afrodiasporic spaces on the continent, as Xavier Livermon (2020) has called them, can also result in the misrecognition of postcolonial Africans' own racialization. At rehearsal for an upcoming show, Africa Capoeira rehearsed a dramatization of the capoeira song "Sinhazinha," which tells the story of a white slave master's daughter (Sinhazinha) who falls in love with a Black man her father owns, named Benedito.[1] When discussing roles, Yaya, an Ivorian law student, joked that Christopher, a master's student from the Central African Republic, should play Benedito. He commented, "He has the profile of a slave, look at him!" eliciting chuckles from the others. No one stepped up to play the slave owner and father, so the role remained unfilled in that moment. While many Africanists have argued for the centrality of domestic slavery (or "African slavery") as enduring in postcolonial sociality, all references to slavery in the Dakar-based capoeira school came from the slave trade in the Americas.

When it came time to decide on Sinhazinha, the women unanimously decided on me. I noticed that Marianne, a reserved Senegalese capoeirista of Guinea-Bissauan descent, was more motivated in practice lately. I wanted to encourage her confidence, so I recommended she fill the role instead. Marianne responded by shielding her torso with crossed arms, saying "It's better if you do it." This show required basic capoeira and dance moves that all the women present were more than capable of performing. As a light-skinned Black Brazilian American, and a confident capoeirista (even if my skills had not caught up with my confidence), I was often *trusted* to have valuable contributions for creative projects and *entrusted* with important positions. Proximity to whiteness—even stemming from diasporic Blacks—elicits "difference and deference" from West African interlocutors (Pierre 2013). In part my proximity to capoeira as the daughter of an Afro-Brazilian master made me a logical choice for a creative advisor. Yet by 2018, I had friendships with the members for nearly a decade, who well knew my capoeira skills and Portuguese proficiency to be far below the expectations that spring from those characteristics. As a Western "guest," I should likely not have had so much influence in performances and administrative decision-making in this twenty-year West African cultural institution.

My racial identification shifted depending on context. At times my status as a biracial, middle-class Black woman from the United States landed me as a *tubaab*[2] (white person/Westerner). At other times—most especially due to my Brazilian background and being a fellow capoeirista—I was seen as a diasporic Black and therefore racial kin. However, my proximity to whiteness relative to the other African woman rendered me—by the normative schema of white supremacy—more central than I deserved to be. Later on, Aziz, a Burkinabé doctoral student in physics, evoked Marianne's name as someone with the poise to play Sinhazinha. Aziz perceived Marianne as being suitable for the role of the slave master's daughter, the object of desire, femininity, and unattainability for an enslaved Black man. And yet, as a collective, we allowed for the foreign anthropologist to take the role.

Making race exclusively through the vector of "slavery" in an imagined Brazilian past misses the ways that the creative process necessarily draws on the local ideological resources of how to think, talk, joke about, and embody race. The context shapes the way race is discussed, or hidden from plain view. What other logics would come in to play in the absence of a Black Westerner? Would the national differences that were central to rifts in Africa Capoeira's past determine who could embody which racialized trope in the dramatization? What does it mean that Christopher, who was from the Central African Republic and notably lighter skinned than Yaya, is humorously read as possessing "the profile of a slave?" What are the connotations of ethnicity and nationality that become racialized in the region?

The Racial Coloniality of Social Difference in Dakar

All of us are suffering coloniality, it's just that the significant presence of white bodies in South Africa and the United States make it easier to visualize.

—PANACHE CHIGUMADZI

Njaajaan Njaay existait ... [Étymologiquement] Le Sénégal n'a jamais existé. C'est une
fabrication absolument *tubaab*.

—BIRAGO DIOP (VIEYRA 1982)

Jemima Pierre and Laura Chrisman have demonstrated how the diaspora (predominantly
in the United States) seems to possess ownership over race and slavery as cultural and
political subject positions (Pierre 2013, 2020; Chrisman 2003). What's more, Africans are
also so often portrayed as either passive imitators of Black diasporic "culture" or opportu-
nistically insincere in identifying as Black for proximity to Black diasporic access to Western modernity (Chrisman 2003). In addition to the centering of diasporic experiences in
sighting/citing/site-ing race, Latin American contexts like Brazil are automatically celebrated for their African "cultural survivals," which is often confused for Black political
consciousness, but can even be at odds (Smith 2016). The emphasis on the continuation
of "African culture" in the Brazilian national image traffics in depoliticization of the racial
hierarchy that structures Brazilian society. This self-image is then reinforced through the
global export of performance traditions like capoeira. Black/African bodily practices are
further depoliticized as up for grabs for any Westerner who can afford to join a capoeira
school or take a dance class (Robitaille 2014; Sawyer 2006). The lived reality of race for
Africans absconds even further into invisibility.

Combat forms are classed and spatialized in ways that express the racial hierarchy of
colonial logics that are foundational to those divisions. Take for example the discussion
of modernity with regard to Senegalese wrestling. On the surface, the central concern
seems to be the "neoliberal commodification" of a combat game that was considered to be
"traditional" and therefore romanticized as a marker of Senegalese cultural autochthony
before and despite colonial rule. Wrestlers are characterized by a linguistic style, *Français
mbër* that is in fact not particular to wrestlers. It is often associated with working-class,
rural, and marginalized people, particularly in urban publics like Dakar that prize linguistic
mastery of French. In one such mundane post-match interview on YouTube, the video was
titled, "You all will die of laughter: with the Français mbeur of the fighter Gouyegui,"
highlighting the wrestler's accent and grammatical deviations from metropolitan French.[3]
Some have described the phenomenon of *Français mbër* as "class snobbery" that privileges
the colonial language, without explicit mention of race (Hann, Chevé, and Wane 2021).
Yet they also write that the peripheral, poor neighborhoods from which many wrestlers
emerge in Dakar as are also called "ghettos" in English. I read this terminology alongside
the mockery of French language skill in a constellation of ways that racialization is both
transnational but also directly linked to the production of ethnicity through performance
(wrestling) and performativity (modern subjects). The reference to ghettos is not an import of racialized spatial frames that are foreign to Dakar's historical processes; rather, it is
a borrowed lexicon that provides a shortcut for speaking to similar dynamics of poor Black
masses marginalized in the once-colonial headquarters for the region.

Why does it matter then to mock wrestlers in particular? Or framed another way, why
do wrestlers come to embody the trope of a Senegalese failed modern subject? In part,

wrestlers are expected to embody "tradition," which is both revered and romanticized as Senegalese precolonial history, spirituality, and ethnic origins through recitation of Wolof poetry. And yet the Senegalese failed modern subject from the "popular neighborhoods" of Dakar—a racialized colonial trope—and the paragon of Senegalese Wolof ethnic tradition are one in the same (body). The idea that Africans become racialized as Black when they migrate or travel to the West is colloquially established as social fact. How African bodies are racialized in African contexts is an underexplored area of the processes of colonial continuity in the contemporary moment.

Performance is a key tool in the construction of ethnicity and postcolonial nationalism that privileges a particular ethnic subjectivity. Wrestling in Senegal has "contributed to reinforcing the identity of an ethnicity, of a city, in an era when territorial and social landmarks mingle and get lost," while also feeding the commercial interests of various religious and state interests as well as the search for economic opportunity by athletes (Chevé and Wane 2018). The contemporary wrestling industry represents a tension between precolonial nostalgia and neoliberal commodification that demonstrates how colonialism and capitalist globalization has affected Senegambian societies (Repinecz 2020). In the reverse scale, wrestling is also a tool for young men to battle economic precarity, and to fashion themselves as religious, ethnic, and masculine subjects (Hann, Chevé, and Wane 2021).

Senegal enjoys a "special" status as the crowning jewel of French colonial assimilationism. As the administrative headquarters for French West Africa, it served as the managing site of the civilizing mission's racial hierarchical construction for the region. The postcolonial legacy of this is evident in common phrases like Dakar's status as the "Paris of West Africa" (rivaled at times by Abidjan). The result of Senegal's special status can also extend to the "peaceful" reputation of Senegal's Islamic and decolonial movements. While the postindependence *négritude* movement centered on a celebratory rhetoric of Blackness, discussions of *whiteness* as a currency of social power after decolonization remained largely absent. Hamidou Anne even decries protofascism in Senegal rooted in turning a blind eye to the coloniality of power (2021).

Jemima Pierre has written on how West Africans approach Blackness with a complex set of distinctions and considerations, while whiteness is far less interrogated for its relationship to wealth and undoubted social status (2013). One of the few and earliest studies of whiteness in Senegal was Rita Cruise O'Brien's sociological investigation of French expatriates in Senegal directly before and after independence in 1960. Cruise O'Brien argued that the context of the newly independent West African nation resulted in "a consolidation of white identity" for the expats. Social distinctions meaningful in France dissolved in Senegal (1972). Whiteness was consolidated in large part through the construction of a racialized Senegalese Wolof Other, while pitting the trope against other ethnic groups like Sereer was considered more civilized (1972). In an updated version of Cruise O'Brien's study, Hélène Quashie argued that whiteness is a social discourse in Senegal that describes Senegalese who display characteristics normally attributed to Westernness or excelling in formal education (similarly to the racialized discourse of being "uppity" in the United States). Quashie sees this internal discourse as a double-edged sword: both a "repulsion" toward straying too far from "African origins" and a marker of sophistication, efficiency, and productivity. "Modernity is racial," and whiteness is therefore not bound to corporeality (Hesse 2007). This shifting target of whiteness reveals it as a discourse of power rather than wedded to certain bodies. Whiteness is used as a rhetorical weapon that attempts to narrativize the gaps of structural inequality in Senegal.

Popular culture depictions of whiteness contribute to the depoliticization of the *tubaab*. The *tubaab* is often a harmless or silly figure that can be teased, but ultimately incorporated or centered. For instance, a film directed and starring Lamine Mbengue called *Toubab du Woujj* (White People Aren't Polygamous) tells the story of a Senegalese man living in France with his white French girlfriend. On his visit home, the French girlfriend pays him a surprise visit in Dakar and discovers he has three Senegalese wives. The ensuing antics involve the wives dressing up as white women to combat the French girlfriend's embodiment of a Senegalese woman, which she performed through wearing local outfits and conducting household chores. The Senegalese wives, however, are made to appear ridiculous in their mocking of whiteness, while the white woman manages a "successful" racial embodiment of Black womanhood evident by cooking a delicious *ceere* (couscous) dinner. The love story ends with the man and his French girlfriend returning to Paris, strolling amorously under the Eiffel Tower.

A musical group called Toubab Krewe based in Asheville, North Carolina, provides another example of the free rein of whiteness to exercise co-optation of West African cultural traditions. The band members (all white except for one Black member), play with whiteness ("Toubab") and New Orleans Mardi Gras lingo ("Krewe") while centering the Kora, a West African instrument linked to a tradition that requires family lineage for apprenticeship. Reviews on their website feature a *New York Times* blurb that states, "Their music avoids cliché with authentic extrapolations of traditional Manding beats, percussion, and jam-band flare," while another from Blurt declares, "This is the sound of liberation." The figure of the *tubaab* is ultimately a portrayal of whiteness as the ability to take on and off Black West African cultural forms, bodies, and political subjectivities in a playful spirit, divorced from the structures of white dispossession through coloniality.

Returning to one of the performances of a capoeira *roda* (gathering) where the monkey comment occurred, Paulo Boa Vida, the Brazilian *mestre*, led the show. Meanwhile, RTS interviewed three Senegalese capoeiristas to describe the martial art to their viewers. Although African women capoeiristas were a substantial portion of the participants during the week's events, very few of them participated in the televised show. Two French women in attendance, on the other hand, played often. In the final cut of what aired, RTS played a repeating reel of the French women, spliced with scenes of three interviews, two of which were with Senegalese who were based in France and therefore spoke with metropolitan French accents. Both white subjects and the Senegalese media effectively centered whiteness in the presentation of their work to the broader public.

Boa Vida opened most of the events that week with a speech to set the tone. On one occasion, he claimed he "planted the seed" that became the group that exists today. Boa Vida had not been back to Senegal in the ensuing twenty years since his initial visit that helped spark Ndiaye's group, citing a disagreement with Ndiaye over the artistic direction of the brand-new Senegalese capoeira school. Ousmane, a Senegalese participant at the event, commented in frustration, "The seed metaphor is a bad one. Did he water the seed? Check on it? No, he just planted it and then came to harvest." Later in the speech, João stated that he "too was a child of Gorée Island." He essentially laid claim to embodying diaspora by orienting himself in relation to an African "origin," despite his positionality as a white Brazilian. He had recourse to a Brazilian racial ideology of creolization, in which all who possess Brazilian nationality are understood to carry the blend of Indigenous, European, and African heritage—a discourse that evacuates the country's deeply racist structures.

At the pinnacle event, the *batizado* (baptism) in which belts are granted to those advancing to a new level, Boa Vida banned any and all belts just hours before the ceremony. This was, as he framed it, to push the group to accept *capoeira angola*, a genre of capoeira that does not recognize the belt system. The restriction was deeply unsettling for experienced members of the West African school who took great pride in the belt they earned and for the newest members who worked all year to receive one. The reproduction of colonial dynamics operates not only through assertions of white privilege to embody Blackness and assert ownership over Black art forms and cultural institutions. Coloniality also shows up in the way that postcolonial subjects might defer to the knowledge and expertise of white authority even in Black performance traditions, and even in spaces of their own creative ownership. Therefore, it is paramount to dis-locate our gaze from the usual suspects of whiteness, such as the sentiments of racist white subjects, and to think beyond the given geographies of direct links to colonial rule as predictable sources of coloniality.

Conclusion

Without the significant presence of white bodies, and with the powerful social reality of social norms around frameworks like caste, why even bring race into the realm of possibility? I argue that forms of racialization rooted in coloniality and the landscape of other ideologies of social stratification in Senegal such as nationality are inextricably linked, sometimes operating in the space of the same interaction. I take seriously the wise caution of some Senegalese scholars not to collapse the complexities schemas of social difference (e.g., ethnicity, nationality, caste) perceived as "parallel" to race but ultimately distinct.[4] However, I take seriously that in everyday life, race and other distinct schemas of difference are often confused, conflated, and entangled in ways that require further attention. Focusing on the distinctions, and making room for the possibility of their historical connection, is also of great urgency as we enter a new moment in which there is tremendous energy building around solidarity movements on the continent with organizations like Black Lives Matter based in the United States. How can these transnational solidarity movements be generative in their dialogue around global white supremacy, but how might they also obscure the specificities of explicit racial categories (i.e., Blackness or whiteness) with implicit and localized conceptualizations of social difference and hierarchy? Additionally,

African migrants to sites like Brazil are increasingly racialized in ways that suggest we can no longer hold separate racial ideologies outside of the United States from ethnicity, religion, and regionalism endemic to African contexts (Ndiaye 2020).

Not only do we need to look at the autochthonous definitions of Blackness in dialogue with global Blackness, but also locally specific treatments of whiteness and manifestations of white supremacy, so that we can also elucidate the perhaps unexpected sites of its social reproduction in the "postcolonial." By looking at the coloniality of Black performance, discussions of Blackness, slavery, freedom, oppression, and expression are conventional, albeit imported from a diasporic context. What does not get imported, however, is an appropriate framework for understanding whiteness and Blackness(es) specific to Senegal.

In contemporary Dakar, white supremacy manifests as the upholding of whiteness as an aspiration, the protection of whiteness from political scrutiny, and the infiltration of language and ways of perceiving social difference located in the body. The global nature of whiteness is not to be ignored. If we only look to former or contemporary empires for the production of whiteness, we miss the way that racial ideologies have local specificities, but also operate through global mythologies about how the world is racialized. Brazil's rather successful propaganda campaign to perform racial mixture and racial harmony to a global audience is as popularly consumed in West Africa as it is in the United States. Black performance in Dakar is at the intersection of three key contexts: (1) Brazil's so-called racial democracy, (2) diasporic Blackness as the central tropes of race and slavery, and (3) Senegal's dual legacy of racial empowerment and the denial of the continuity of colonial logics. In the celebration of Black arts, the collision of these intersecting colonialities is on full display.

Notes

1. This reenactment is a popular trend among capoeira schools everywhere.
2. I use the Wolof spelling here. Upcoming references use the French spelling "toubab."
3. Notably, almost all the comments on the video mocking the wrestler's French are written in Wolof.
4. I keep these critiques in mind in large part by analyzing conferences in Senegal and the United States as an extension of my fieldwork.

References

Adelakun, Abimbola A. 2021. *Performing Power in Nigeria: Identity, Politics, and Pentacostalism*. Cambridge: Cambridge University Press.

Anne, Hamidou. 2021. "Le Fascisme Rampant Sénégalais." Seneplus. www.seneplus.com/opinions/le-fascisme-rampant-senegalais.

Apter, Andrew, and Lauren Derby. 2010. Introduction to *Activating the Past: History and Memory in the Black Atlantic World*, edited by Andrew Apter and Lauren Derby. Newcastle: Cambridge Scholars Publishing.

Besnier Nico, and Susan Brownell. 2012. "Sport, Modernity, and the Body." *Annual Review of Anthropology* 41, no. 1: 443–59.

Calvet, Louis-Jean. 2010. *Histoire du Français en Afrique: Une Langue en Copropriété*. Paris: Ecriture.

Chevé, Dominique, and Cheikh Tidiane Wane. 2018. "Ce Que Lutter Veut Dire? Lamb, Bëre et Monde de Vie au Sénégal." *Corps* 1, no. 6: 11–26.

Chigumadzi, Panache. 2020. "Why I'm No Longer Talking to Nigerians about Race." Africa Is a Country Blog. https://africasacountry.com/2019/04/why-im-no-longer-talking-to-nigerians-about-race.

Chrisman, Laura. 2003. *Postcolonial Contraventions: Cultural Readings of Race, Imperialism, and Transnationalism*. Manchester: Manchester University Press.

Conklin, Alice. 1997. *A Mission to Civilize: The Republican Idea of Empire in France and West Africa, 1895–1930*. Stanford, CA: Stanford University Press.

Cruise O'Brien, Rita. 1972. *White Society in Black Africa: The French of Senegal*. Evanston, IL: Northwestern University Press.

Desch-Obi, T. J. 2008. *Fighting for Honor: The History of African Martial Art Traditions in the Atlantic World*. Columbia: University of South Carolina Press.

Diouf, Mamadou, and Donal Cruise O'Brien. 2002. "La réussite politique du contrat social sénégalais." In *La construction de l'État au Sénégal*, edited by Donal Cruise O'Brien, Momar-Coumba Diop, and Mamadou Diouf, 9–15. Paris: Éditions Karthala.

Faye, Ousseynou, and Ibrahima Thioub. 2003. "Les marginaux de l'État à Dakar." *Le Mouvement Social* (204): 93–108.

Fields, Barbara J., and Karen E. Fields. 2012. *Racecraft: The Soul of Inequality in American Life*. London: Verso.

Hann, Mark, Dominique Chevé, and Cheikh T. Wane. 2021. "'Tying Your Ngemb': Negotiating Identity in Senegalese Wrestling." *Ethnography* 22, no. 3: 1–15.

Hesse, Barnor. 2007. "Racialized Modernity: An Analytics of White Mythologies." *Ethnic and Racial Studies* 30, no. 4: 643–63.

Lecocq, Baz. 2005. "The Bellah Question: Slave Emancipation, Race, and Social Categories in Late Twentieth-Century Northern Mali." *Canadian Journal of African Studies / Revue canadienne des études africaines* 39, no. 1: 42–68.

Livermon, Xavier. 2020. *Kwaito Bodies: Remastering Space and Subjectivity in Post-Apartheid South Africa*. Durham, NC: Duke University Press.

Mbembe, Achille. 2001. *On the Postcolony*. Berkeley: University of California Press.

McLaughlin, Fiona. 1995. "Haalpulaar Identity as a Response to Wolofization." *African Languages and Cultures* 8, no. 2: 153–68.

Mignolo, Walter D. 2012. *Local Histories/Global Designs: Coloniality, Subaltern Knowledges, and Border Thinking*. Princeton, NJ: Princeton University Press.

Ndiaye, Gana. 2020. "Mobility and Cultural Citizenship: The Making of a Senegalese Diaspora in Multiethnic Brazil." In *Migration and Stereotypes in Performance and Culture*, edited by Y. Meerzon, D. Dean, and D. McNeil, 157–77. Cham, Switzerland: Springer International.

Ndlovu-Gatsheni, Sabelo J. 2013. *Coloniality. of Power in Postcolonial Africa: Myths of Decolonization*. Dakar, Senegal: Codesria.

Ochonu, Moses E. 2019. "Looking for Race: Pigmented Pasts and Colonial Mentality in 'Non-Racial' Africa." In *Relating Worlds of Racism*, edited by P. Essed et al., 3-37. Cham, Switzerland: Springer International.

Pierre, Jemima. 2012. *The Predicament of Blackness: Postcolonial Ghana and the Politics of Race*. Chicago: University of Chicago Press.

———. 2020. "Slavery, Anthropological Knowledge, and the Racialization of Africans." *Current Anthropology* 61, no. S22: S220–31.

Quashie, Hélène. 2015. "La 'blanchité' au miroir de l'africanité: Migrations et constructions sociales urbaines d'une assignation identitaire peu explorée (Dakar)." *Etudes Africaines* 220: 761–86.

Quijano, A. 2007. "Coloniality and Modernity/Rationality." *Cultural Studies* 21, no. 2/3: 168–78.

Repinecz, J. 2020. "Senegalese Wrestling between Nostalgia and Neoliberalism." *African Studies Review* 63, no. 44): 906–26.

Robitaille L. 2014. "Promoting Capoeira, Branding Brazil: A Focus on the Semantic Body." *Black Music Research Journal* 34, no. 2: 229–54.

Sawyer, Lena. 2006. "Racialization, Gender, and the Negotiation of Power in Stockholm's African Dance Courses." In *Globalization and Race: Transformations in the Cultural Production of Blackness*, edited by Kamari Maxine Clarke and Deborah A. Thomas. Durham, NC: Duke University Press.

Sharpe, Christina. 2016. *In the Wake: On Blackness and Being*. Durham, NC: Duke University Press.

Smith, Christen A. 2016. *Afro-Paradise: Blackness, Violence, and Performance in Brazil*. Champaign: University of Illinois Press.

Ticktin, Miriam I. 2011. *Casualties of Care: Immigration and the Politics of Humanitarianism in France*. Berkeley: University of California Press.

Wynter S. 2003. "Unsettling the Coloniality of Being/Power/Truth/Freedom: Towards the Human, After Man, Its Overrepresentation—An Argument." *CR: The New Centennial Review* 3, no. 3: 257–337.

Villalón, Leonardo A. 1995. *Islamic Society and State Power in Senegal: Disciples and Citizens in Fatick*. Cambridge: Cambridge University Press.

7

Many Shades of White

WHITE SUPREMACY AND WHITENESS IN SOUTH ASIAN PHILOSOPHIES

Subhadra Mitra Channa

WHITE IS A COLOR that has multivocal expressions in South Asia, signifying purity as well symbolizing death and mourning. Expanding on my previous work on codifying bodies (Channa 2017), and the multifarious expressions of "whiteness" in overtly nonracial, yet "racialized" contexts, this chapter interrogates the cultural premium on "whiteness" in South Asia. Since South Asian philosophies are not necessarily dichotomous, white is not considered as an opposite of black, in the sense it is constructed in Western perspectives. Black also has its own spiritual and aesthetic symbolizations in South Asian contexts. The contemporary cultural premium on whiteness and the simultaneous marginalization of Blackness can be understood in the context of intersections of coloniality and existing forms of discrimination, the historical racialization of bodies and related social processes. Several centuries of European conquest, domination, and subordination, along with social inequalities, are reflected in the present-day color hierarchy, which is further nurtured by the neoliberal market economy and the commodification of racial body aesthetics.

This chapter analyzes white supremacy at two levels, a specific, historical, and regional level where it may exist as "racism without races" (Balibar and Wallerstein 1991, 21) or as "racialized discriminations" to include instances where culture and religion stand in for phenotypical "races"; for example, the Rohingyas in Myanmar, the Korean in Japan, and the Uyghur in China. In such cases, both invisible and imagined "differences" continue to stoke animosities that remain unresolved. Since these hidden differences are seen as being nonexistent, they are unresolvable. We can see this for instance in Northern Ireland, Kashmir, the Gaza strip, and so on. The phenomenon of "invisible racism" (Takezawa 2011, 1) works in myriads of ways globally and may become overtly "racialized" due to a political historical process, such as territorial colonization and the neocolonization of the global market. In South Asia, existing systems of inequality were "racialized" by the intervention of European scholarship and science during the period of European colonization, so that racialization can be understood as a process by which race is introduced into systems where it had not existed prior to contact with Europeans. I discuss South Asia as a specific case of racialization in this context.

At another level, as universalized "race," the hierarchies transcend variations in the regional, local, and historically specific manifestations to the essentialized dichotomous, "black" and "white" systems of coding as a global "white supremacy." Harrison (1995, 63) describes it as "white public space" that routinely privileges Euro-Americans over non-whites. From my experience, there is an unwritten, insidious, and often unconscious bias existing toward the Euro-American white social institutions, norms, and what may be understood as an esoteric "white culture," undefinable yet real, that pervades the thoughts and feelings of most people around the globe. One of its primary manifestations is linguistic. As of now the majority of accepted global languages originate from Europe. English, French, and German (occasionally Spanish) are the languages that dominate most international meetings and conferences and are seen as the "scientific languages" through which a global science dominates the realm of all knowledge and its production. Harding refers to this as the "racial economy of science" (Harding 1993, 2).

I will give a few examples of universal "white domination" from my own experience of participating in the global academic world as a woman of color. The most frequent question that I have been asked in the course of my interactions with global scholars has been, "Have you studied in the USA or abroad?" People have looked at me with questioning eyes, and often askance, when I have replied that I have been totally educated in India, and in fact had only ventured abroad at a fairly advanced age. Most academics of color from various parts of the world make no pretense of flaunting their degrees from prestigious universities of the United States, United Kingdom, or Europe, if they have them. Most conversations are gently steered toward, "I got my degree from so and so university," or that "I was a researcher at that institute and so on." Apart from one's material academic contributions, this association is taken as a hallmark of claims to superiority. Unfortunately, most academics who do this are staunch supporters of social justice and would be aghast if called "racist." In the same vein, most universities in South Asia advertise their staff as having degrees from Harvard, Columbia, Oxford, or Cambridge as an index of their own superior standards. Still, there are many homespun scholars who have excelled as teachers and academics in these very institutions.

Although seemingly diffuse and undefinable, "White cultural practices" (Hartigan 1997, 496) have become so ingrained into the global culture that people have stopped noticing them, they have become infused into the habitus in the form of "doxa" (Bourdieu 1990). Let us as an example take the culture of sitting at the dining table to eat with a knife, fork, and spoon. As a child I grew up sitting on the floor and eating with my hand. The dining table came into the household when I was quite grown up, and I learned to eat with a fork much later in life. However, almost everywhere at present, this mode of eating has become the accepted norm, as "normal," with no questions asked, but it is a fact that it came with the white colonists to most parts of the world. It was a surprise to me that in Japan, restaurants still expect patrons to sit on the floor to eat, and wells are cut into the floor for those westerners who may find it impossible to sit on the floor. However, all over South Asia, a European mode of eating has been accepted as "civilized" and to be followed as accepted public etiquette. Vestiges of cultural habits left behind by the Europeans in their mission of civilizing the "savages" has persisted and taken roots in native soils, ingrained into both public and private culture of South Asia among other European colonies. "White culture" remains the key for global acceptability and both voluntarily emulated and compulsorily learned by postcolonial subjects who go abroad, especially to the west, for education and work. In this sense, race continues to be reinvented in the process of neoliberal globalization as part of the global economic network, taking on the character of what Harrison (2008, 220) reiterates as "global apartheid."

The pervasive intrusion of race into the inner consciousness can be seen in the adherence to white culture, not only in the public domain but also followed religiously at home and in the private lives of postcolonial subjects, especially by the elite in the developing countries like India. White culture must be absorbed as part of one's personality if one aspires to access even a part of the "privileges generally associated with being white" (Hartigan 1997). This "white culture" includes proficiency in English (or another global language), also seen as an essential part of the cosmopolitanism deemed essential for being a global citizen. One encounters this culture at the international hotels, airports, conference halls, and practically all over the global publicly traversed spaces. So, one does not acquire this culture arbitrarily, or out of one's liking for it, but rather must acquire it in order to be accepted into a pervasive system of white privileges, which includes being able to travel, to work, and to be accepted as a global citizen. It is in relation to this widely spread (not universal) "white culture" that established itself as the correct way of living through centuries of European colonial domination that establishes "white supremacy" as what Harrison (1998) has called "the key site of racial domination." It is true that what is commonly recognized as "European" refers only to those who were able to establish political control and expand the boundaries of their rule over others. One may cite from a British administrator of the early nineteenth century Colonel G. Waters (1899) who gives a racial analysis highly favorable to the northern Europeans but denigrating the Irish, Welsh, Basques, and others as having a "Semitic" mixture in their blood. As Trautmann (2004) had explained, the "Aryan" myth helped justify the legitimacy of British rule over India, even as there was a nagging admiration for a civilization far more ancient than theirs. Therefore, power of controlling minds, to perpetuate and make believable myths of natural superiority, may be seen as the key factor of "racialization," invisible as it often is. However, the colonized are never perfectly "fabricated" (Sartre 1961) but tend to retain their identity, subversive yet real, as Fanon (2021, 16) puts it, minds are dominated but not domesticated.

In this form of a universal "global apartheid," white supremacy certainly derives from European roots, but we can apply it to more general forms of discrimination. This white supremacy is not just about "being white" in the literal sense. In the next section I put together some reflections on the "nonmorphological" meanings of white supremacy before I go to the specific application to South Asia.

Historicizing White Supremacy, in the Context of South Asia

Can "white supremacy" be understood as a specific temporal and spatial manifestation of "racialization," as one instance of ideological and practical technologies of "othering" that cover up for the lack of evidence, genetic, serological, psychological, and medical, to divide the human species? In an earlier essay (Channa 2017) I had elaborated on the paradox of codifying bodies as "different," high and low, pure and polluted, sacred and profane, and valued or expendable. The epoch of slavery driven by a Eurocentric white supremacist ideology provides the one instance that epitomizes white supremacy as it is commonly understood (Smedley 1999, 694). But is it the only way one can apply it analytically or can it be deconstructed to mean more "situated" modes of discrimination?

Since white supremacy is irreducibly associated with European colonization of the world, one may again ponder on, if this form of colonization is the only source for white supremacy. What kind of criteria was used for discriminations prior to European contact and how did they get racialized in white supremacist terms as in India? One can delve into history to analyze how preexisting forms of discrimination were racialized into the model of white supremacy or of "race" in its essentialized form. I concur with Smedley (1999) that "race" in the form of white supremacy was not existing in the earlier times in many parts of the world.

The Indian subcontinent has been colonized by multiple waves of foreigners, coming from Central Asia, the Middle East, and Europe, much before it became a British colony, with small domains of Portuguese and French. These invasions, if we begin from the recorded and known ones (ignoring the debate about the Aryans), can be traced to the incursion of Greek soldiers into the northwest of the Indian continent, under the leadership of Emperor Alexander. This invasion has been romanticized in Indian oral traditions and texts and ballads constructed, films made, and its fragments embellish literature and folklore. There is a popular myth (perhaps real history) that Emperor Chandragupta Maurya (Thapar 2002, 171) married the sister of Seleucus Nicator (successor to Alexander, in India), as part of a peace treaty with the Greeks, which may be one of the many marriages that took place at this time. What is interesting to note is that there is no mention of racial differences or morphology as far as marriage between Greeks and Indians were concerned.[1] Smedley (1999, 693) also mentions that there was no evidence of skin color as a mark of identity prior to the seventeenth century in Europe and America. Smedley (1999, 695) has quoted from Allen (1997), who traces the invention of a white race following the unsuccessful Bacon's Rebellion of 1676, in which servants and freed slaves took part. But the real impact of race becomes socially salient in the United States, after the Civil War, when skin color emerged as the prime political marker of identity.

In India, in accounts of the many invasions and settlers coming in from outside, there is no mention of "white skin" or any physical types. The Greeks were followed by several waves of invasions from the northwest side. The Turks and Iranians who came were presumably lighter in skin tone than the native populations of India. We have no evidence but there is a folk-based prejudice against a very light skin and especially light eyes. My mother-in-law, who came from a region far up in the salt ranges bordering Afghanistan, considered "cat eyes" or green or blue eyes, as "inauspicious" in a woman. Generally, in many parts of India, light eyes and light hair are not regarded as signs of beauty, and very white skin is considered abnormal. It is possible these colors were associated with invaders and outsiders. Linguistically, in South Asian languages and in Sanskrit, *golden-hued* describes a bright complexion but *beauty* is often described as like the blue lotus or the monsoon clouds (Chandra 1997). Only when speaking in English is the term *fair* used. In Hindi the term *Gora*, meaning "white" or light-skinned, was also used for the English men, pointing to its colonial origin.

In contemporary times, the color white in South Asia in cosmetic and aesthetics has been seen primarily in terms of the preference for a light skin, which is seen as a sign of beauty. But the concept of whiteness (not just the color) is not in any way linked to social superiority and rank of a person per se. The question that needs to be asked is, was white, both physically and metaphorically, considered superior even in antiquity as a mark of social rank and beauty? From the shadowy past of history, is it possible to retrieve some information about this?

Mythological sources and ancient literature do not provide any evidence of the superiority of "white," in terms of beauty as well as in terms of ritual purity and divinity. The Hindu caste system (Channa 2019) derives its ideological legitimacy from a hymn in the Rig Veda that describes the sacrifice of the cosmic Purusa and the creation of the four Varna, which are hierarchically arranged according to the part of the body from which they originated. The Brahmins from the head, the Kshatriyas from the arms, the Vaisyas from the thighs, and the Sudra from the feet. The term *Varna* is polysemic, meaning both color and nature or property. In the Varna system it means property or character, as each of the varna denote the property of the part of the body from which they originate. The Brahmin represent intellect and learning, the Kshatriyas valor and ability to rule/command, the Vaisyas are traders and agriculturalists also associated with household and earthly pleasures, the Sudras are servants meant to serve others. Undoubtedly these meanings are derived and attributed culturally, in other words, the way these body parts are symbolized in a particular culture only, the shared Hindu universe. However, none of these attributes make any reference to physical attributes, and there is no mention in any ancient texts about skin color or bodily characteristics, except those of strength, skill, and intelligence.

Klass (1980, 41) and Hocart (1950, 28), both serious scholars of the caste system, have been critical of the assumption of some Western scholars that Varna depicts color, giving it a racial connotation. Hindus were always concerned with inner and ritual purity associated with food, habits, and religious practices, all of which were also determined by one's Jati identity. What food one ate was always more important that how one looked. "Varna as skin colour does not tie up with the Hindu religious expression but with the European racial expression" (Klass 1980, 41). Linguistically the Sanskrit and also Hindi word *Shyam*, meaning dark or dusky, is used for descriptions of beauty rather than ugliness. Girls and boys are fondly named as Shyama or Shyam, where they are also seen as akin to the dark-complexioned gods, Rama and Krishna; both seen as incarnations (avatars) of the supreme Hindu god, Vishnu. The Hindu pantheon contains numerous gods and goddesses who come in all hues and shades, but are all shades of a single Divinity. Out of the supreme Trinity of Brahma, Vishnu, and Shiva (Smart 1969, 95); Brahma, who is not worshipped, is somewhat alabaster in representations, Vishnu is dark (like the blue lotus), and Shiva[2] is golden or dusky, depending on the mood of the artist who is creating the image. The dark color of Vishnu, the supreme preserver of the universe, also has deeper metaphysical significance, "the consciousness is said to be dark (Shyam) not as opposed to 'light,' but in the sense that it is unseen by or unknown to man as long as he remains rooted in ter-restrial experiences—The Consciousness is the pure self or Atman within" (Parthasarathy 1993, 116). Of the major goddesses, Kali, the representative of female power, or Sakti, is black like the night. There are many poetic expressions of her dark beauty, some of them penned by famous poets like Kazi Nazrul Islam of Bengal, a renowned freedom fighter and poet, who in spite of being a Muslim was a devotee of Kali; so was the guru of the famous Hindu monk Swami Vivekananda. No other goddess has her beauty described poetically like Kali, who has numerous verses devoted to her dark beauty. The others like Durga, Parvati, and Lakshmi are depicted as golden in hue, and only Saraswati, the daughter of Brahma, is alabaster in color.

From all textual and literary sources from ancient India, it is clear that there was no premium of the color white. The most famous beauty, from the epic Mahabharata, that depicts a fratricidal war of the proportions of the Homerian Iliad, Draupadi is described as a dusky beauty (Ray 1995), a woman whose beauty destroyed a civilization, like her counterpart Helen who launched a thousand ships.

The color black was neither considered inauspicious nor inferior, nor unesthetic. Unlike in the West, black animals like black dogs are actually considered more auspicious and fed on ritual occasions; apart from being preferred as house pets. Again, while in the West the bride wears white, in India it is the color of widowhood and of mourning. Mourners at a funeral and at death rituals turn out in impeccable white clothes. But white does not imply sadness or grief either. It is the color of purity and asceticism but only of a lower order. A novice monk for example may wear white, but an ordained one will wear saffron, the color of the highest form of asceticism and sacredness. But this is also only for conservative Hindus, those belonging to heretic sects like Tantrism may wear red or black, depending on their faith.

The possibility of a color bar takes on another dimension in a worldview with a circular sense of space and time and a graded and continuous mode of perception instead of the dialectical. The Jati/Varna (Inden 1976; Srinivas 1981) system, the prime signifier of hier-archy in Indian society, is a nested or step-by-step hierarchy rather than one that is "either/or." Even in this, there are many local variations of placement of caste groups in any kind of order. At the middle level, the matter of hierarchy is always contested and fluid in nature. Ibbetson, the British scholar-administrator who compiled the commendable *Punjab Castes* as part of the 1881 Punjab Census, highlighted the occupational rather than the ritual aspects of caste (Bayley 1995, 205), also showing through his data that the same groups could be referred to as belonging to different ranks, depending on their occupation, and even this was not a fixed identity, changing as the political and economic fortunes of any community changed. Hocart (1950, 52) and Inden (1990) have also been dismissive of the European view of the rigidity of caste. The myths of ahistoricity (Wolf 1982) and rigidity implied for the caste system in Western scholarship was part of Orientalism (Said 1978), a technology of justifying colonization (Smedley 1994; Malik 1996). A flexible caste system's association with race, like characters, seems dubious.

The only caste groups that suffer from pervasive and uncontested discrimination are the untouchables (Mendelsohn and Vicziany 1998), who form the bottommost layer, opposed to the upper castes or "touchables." In the Hindu worldview this appears as the relation between the "Dwija"[3] (Twice Born) and the Sudra, a relation that is not oppositional as there is ritual and economic interdependence between them. But in practice, the condition of the untouchables can be compared with the "blacks" in a racialized society (Channa 2005).

To be an untouchable is to be like any other most discriminated, most dehumanized, and most exploited community, race, or group, anywhere in the world. Yet, within the Indian worldview, even an untouchable was not assigned any physical characteristics. It was this very lack of physical visibility that made the imposition of the strictest sanctions in the form of dress code, mannerisms, and forms of consumption and display permissible to the lowest strata of the caste hierarchy (Channa 2018). Even in very recent times there are incidences of violence against those untouchables or Dalits who challenge the upper caste enforced norms of dress and demeanor. There have been incidences of people killed for daring to wear shoes, or carrying an umbrella, or riding a horse, in the presence of upper-caste people.

Given the lack of morphological ascriptions in caste society, what historical and political factors could have introduced the notion of "white" or "fair" complexion as a sign of superiority in South Asian society, where it is now pervasive.

When Caste Became Race, and When White Became Superior

According to Bayley (1999, 104), the Mughals first introduced color coding into India as an administrative measure, but they used three color codes to classify people according to their potential for criminal activities, without reference to caste or community. White is still not considered absolutely superior in Indian society and is coded in multiple ways. For example, the particular designation of "foreigner" is reserved only for white-skinned tourists, excluding those who do not fit into the "Euro-American" physical and cultural type, like the Japanese or Korean or African or even African American. But it is only an indicator that he or she can be charged exorbitantly for various services and goods or, according to the local tour and informal sectors operator's, language, "fleeced" easily. Such stereotypical "whites" become objects of deference and an overtly servile attitude, as strategies, driven by purely commercial interest.

It is doubtful that the Indians, with their entrenchment in the systems of purity, pollution, and lineage, ever accorded any real superiority to the color white. Dirks (1996, xiv) mentions Gilchrist's manual for British officers coming for the first time to serve in India, being warned to acquire enough language skills to be able to tell when their servants or local subordinates were addressing them in derogatory colloquial language. On the ritual scale the casteless foreigners are *Mleccha* (Trautmann 2004, 12) or impure, and even today many temples in the conservative southern part of India do not allow the entry of "foreigners," defined as a stereotypical "white" person. Someone not visibly white, and if wearing Indian clothes, can "pass."

Even in popular visual media "white" is not exclusively preferred. Popularity of a film star is not linked to lighter skin color. Just like the Western preoccupation with "blood," the Indian preoccupation with lineage and ritual status overrides their preference for "white." It is pertinent to mention that to the best of my knowledge, I know of no one from an untouchable caste group who has made it big in the film industry or anywhere in popular culture.

Race entered into the Indian thought process through British influence, acquisition of Western languages, and most importantly Western science. British scholars, coming from an ascriptive hierarchized society similar to India, searched diligently for ancestry and origins of populations in their colonies, thereby reinforcing the same in India. Bayley (1995) has shown how the scholar-administrators, collecting evidence and compiling data on Indian society, were applying what they thought a universal, scientific, and rational system to fit the Indian people within the "fact" of human biological, social, and psychological existence: "race." The poison that entered the Indian intellectual and political thought process was the existence in India not just of different caste groups but of "races" that actually legitimized the hierarchy of the castes. Theorization by professionals like Hunter (1898) and Risley (1908) provided a scientific basis to a mythological phenomenon.

The so-called scientific, rational, and meticulous data of anthropometry, physical measurements, and psychosocial traits compounded caste hierarchy into a typology of "racial types" that "castes were really 'races,' and the distinction between high and low caste was really a distinction between peoples of supposedly superior and inferior racial endowment" (Bayley 1994, 169). The existence of an Aryan race, with its identification with the Europeans (here read British) and their kinship with the earlier invaders and the myth of Aryan invasion (Trautmann 2004), established the legitimacy of the caste hierarchy as well as the legitimacy of British rule in India (Channa 2005). But it did much more than that, it created, for posterity, an intellectual and elitist Hindu ideology of superiority, the fountainhead of Hindu supremacist ideology, that parallels the "white supremacist ideology" and has given rise to a dominant group of upper-caste Hindus "who wish to redefine Indian nationhood as the exclusive province of a so-called Hindu race" (Bayley 1994, 185). The present populist government in India is driven by this ideology of a glorious Hindu past and the perception of Muslims as the "others" as invaders and outsiders (Thapar 2002, 21). It also created for the world the image of an "Indian White," when "white" becomes the equivalent of "the privileged" or even more importantly, the normal. Thus, whiteness and Blackness take on their historically specific, spatially localized characters when seamlessly incorporated within existing structures of inequality. This "normal" legitimizes what is called "white cultural practices" (Hartigan 1997, 496), where such practices may accrue to only a few dominant members of society.

This manner of determining normal can be exemplified by a personal experience. As a Hindu Indian, I have been asked many times and, in many countries, as to why I am a meat eater. Vegetarianism in India is found only among a few communities of upper castes in some parts of India only. Many upper castes and even Brahmins from eastern India, Kashmir, and the hills are meat eaters. India also has a fairly large population of Muslims, Christians, and Indigenous peoples who collectively outnumber the vegetarians by far. Yet, because it is a culture of the dominant few, vegetarianism has established itself as a stereotype of Hindu normality.

The one single cultural practice by which the dominant upper-caste Hindus have created what DuBois ([1940] 1980) has referred to as an invisible yet tangible glass plate, that divides the dominant Hindu majority from the "others," is the practice of beef eating. Contrary to the almost globally prevalent perception that all Indians do not eat beef, it is a fact that many do. Muslims, Christians, lower castes, Indigenous people, those in the northeast part of the country, and the left-leaning people of any caste, class, and religion do eat beef. But the dominant majority of upper-caste Hindus, the main propagators of what is "Indian culture," consider beef eating as a sin, and all beef eaters as sinners, heretics, and definitely, "others." Under the tutelage of a populist Hindutva-driven regime, there have been fringe groups of so-called cow vigilantes who have gone about lynching people on the suspicion that they were eating or carrying beef. After several such murders, the government was forced into action and had to punish the culprits. Yet in all the cases the victims were initially harassed by police who had alleged that they were actually carrying/eating beef or were in some ways actually guilty. "Beef-eating," having strong emotional, ritual, and religious significance, therefore has become a powerful and essentialized symbol of the "other" opposed to a caste Hindu, almost akin to skin color in racism in the United States and elsewhere.

This oppression of alleged "beef eaters" is an example of Takzawa's statement that the definition of race, based on physical phenotypes, "fails to identify socially oppressed groups that are not perceived to be physically different from mainstream groups, and yet are treated as different kinds of human species by the dominant majorities" (2011, 8).

The first consequence of the racial theory of caste was to justify and legitimize this division between upper and lower castes as "racial" and not just ritual. The division was concretized, so to say, by its "scientific" validity.

Another insidious consequence of the racial theory was a wedge driven between the north and south of India, by the theory of the north being populated by a light-skinned Aryan race, having affinity to the Europeans through the common root language of Sanskrit and for scholars like T. H. Huxley (1868), quite different from the dark-skinned, long-headed men of the Deccan. This fracturing of the Aryan and the Dravidian has led to the people of both these regions forever regarding each other as separate species. Time and again, and even to present times, the peoples of the south of India erupt in resentment against the north, one particular point of contention being what they feel as the "imposition" of Hindi as the national language. Because of the simmering protests against the universal use of Hindi, a three-language formula exists in India, with Hindi, English, and a third language to be taught at the school level.

A third was the identification of so-called criminal tribes as analogous to race and promulgating the Criminal Tribes Act of 1871, which treated entire communities as if they were hereditary criminals and having crime as part of their physiological (genetic was not known at that time) constitutions, incapable of any kind of possible reform. "The belief that criminals were biological degenerates was widespread during the nineteenth century, especially as it drew to its close and the writings of Darwin and Spencer reinforced such beliefs" (Fourcade 2003, 150). Although finally and quite late, the label was changed to, ironically, "Ex-Criminal Tribes," they are stigmatized and routinely harassed by the police whenever there is any crime in their neighborhood. The classifications, markings, and typologies created during the colonial period have far outlived their purpose and have become ingrained in the administrative rationale of the Indian state (Channa 2015) in a postcolonial continuity of the coercive tactics of the colonial rulers.

These typologies and their associated stereotypes have helped buttress a system of "internal colonization," where a politically and socially dominant majority has marginalized many such stigmatized categories, even when their legitimacy has expired due to advances in scientific knowledge. Thus "ex-criminal tribes" and "tribes" and "non-Aryans" remain degraded to the status of second-class citizens, and often bear the brunt of the state oppression and police brutality that has, as pointed out by Márquez and Rana (2017, 506) been "central to race/ethnic studies scholarship."

These divisions also carried with them the implicit and sometimes explicit reference to skin color and appearance. It was the British equation of Aryan (read fair and tall), with the upper castes as well as north Indians (Bayley 1999, 128), that introduced the notion of "white superiority" among Indians, who began to equate complexion with higher social ranking (Channa 2011) as well as regionality. As of now there is a well-established stereotype of fair-skinned north Indians and dark-skinned south Indians and fine-featured upper castes and coarse-looking lower castes. This caste/class equation with appearance has led to preference for lighter skins and more "refined," meaning Western type of looks, among the elite of Indian society.

When caste norms dominated, most marriages were arranged by the families through matching of horoscopes and Jati credentials (Inden 1976). The physical appearance of the bride and the groom, often married as children, was of little concern. But with modernization and globalization, there is a takeover of caste by class. It is the class-based society that has put a premium on "looks," which includes skin color, that yet remains a "desired" but not essential criteria as caste values and family ethics prevail. For example, on the flip side, the good looks and fair skin of a low-caste person does not elevate his or her social status. Skin color by itself has almost no direct relation to access to power, social resources, or any kind of preferential treatment in the public domain. It is still something that largely prevails in the private and domestic domain and in interpersonal relationships.

Skin color, however, has been reinvented to serve another purpose in neocolonization, pushing people from south to north, seeking to participate in the global economy. It is here where lighter-skinned South Asians find it easier to blend with "white," culturally and morphologically, in the global "white public space" (Page and Thomas 1994), and where, "the edifice of liberal modernity is itself racial capitalism" (Márquez and Rana 2017, 505). Skin color here becomes also part of the global economy of the beauty industry.

Interestingly, the Indians who are most preoccupied with looking "western" are the ones located in the Global North. One can rationalize it as a normal wish for acceptance in a society already pervasively "white" dominated and where one's appearance is directly related to the social, economic, and political resources accessible to one. Take for example Nikki Haley and her "passing" as a white American. I see the same phenomenon among friends and family living in white-dominated countries. But within South Asia, where a majority of people are of darker hues and skin color is not related to any kind of privilege, including in the world of glamor, "white" is to be understood in metaphoric terms (Channa 2005) rather than as a morphological actuality.

Conclusion, If At All

If we wish to recognize "white supremacy" in South Asia, it has to be in the form of "invisible" race or nonmorphological racism. But to me, that is the character of white supremacy globally. It is this racism that makes British dominate over Irish, Western Europe to dominate over Eastern Europe and the Middle East to be demonized, post 9/11. There are several views on just how race acts as a mark of divisiveness and domination. Frankenberg (1993) has characterized it as a structural position of privilege and power, but such positions accrue to multiple signifiers. In China, to be born a Han, and not a Uyghur, in India, being born into an upper caste, and in the modern world to the "state nobility" (Bourdieu 1996). Assumption of universality of white supremacy requires its deconstruction and redefinition to mean all the unmarked positions whose superiority is taken as given and "natural and/or God given" (Smedley 1998, 694). Universal white supremacy assumes that there are many shades of white, and racism manifests itself innovatively and imaginatively, allowing some groups somewhere to create and maintain dominance in historically specified locations and temporalities. "Whiteness" then becomes an empty signifier "of only emotional value" and "rhetorical significance" (Laclau 1977, 166) but drawing sustenance from historical and political antecedents—a spreading "racialscape" (Harrison 1995, 49) casting its net wide through rhetoric, mythmaking, and pseudoscience. Taking its origin from the dominant white populations of Europe, it spread through European colonization, taking its most virulent form in those situations where its application allowed the maximum economic exploitation of the human body, like in the indigo fields of colonial India. But deconstructed from morphology, it can be used in all instances of structural inequalities, as suggested by Smedley (1998, 690), who has defined "Race" by saying it "emerged as the dominant form of identity in those societies where it functions to stratify the social system."

I agree with all scholars who have reiterated that race is only a way to legitimize hierarchies, that have their roots or rationale in economic, political, and pragmatic roots. Taking recourse to historical data to describe American society in the seventeenth century,

Smedley (1998) reminds us that it was ownership of property that determined freedom. Therefore, all kinds of unequal relations justified and legitimized as "given," "natural" and "inevitable" are variants of the theme of "white supremacy," with its roots in economics and politics and not in any abstract idealism of the color white. White, as "white" was introduced globally through European colonization, and I have discussed this process of "racialization" in South Asia. However, neocolonization in the form of a global economy is playing an even more proactive role in elevating the premium placed on "white," both in the global market and in the "white cultural spaces" of the world. From colonizing specific regions, the European culture has colonized practically the entire public space in the world making "white supremacy" a reality that is ubiquitous.

Notes

1. Thapar (2002, 177) mentions that this could "have referred to the legalizing of marriages between the Hellenistic Greeks and the Indians living in the cities or as part of the garrison settlements in eastern Afghanistan."

2. Shiva is most often worshipped in the form of a black stone lingam (a penis). Like all other gods and goddesses, Hinduism professes an all-pervasive divine presence, the Paramatman, and all other beings are different aspects of this supreme essence. The Trinity is also a threefold manifestation but actually only One.

3. Dwija is a Sanskrit word that means Twice Born, referring to the ritual of wearing a sacred thread, by boys of the upper castes, that makes them into members of a caste and entitles them to the services of a Brahmin for their life-cycle rituals. The Sudra can neither wear a sacred thread nor have the Brahmin perform their rituals, meaning they remain at the margins of the Hindu fold.

References

Allen, Theodore W. (1994) 1997. *The Invention of the White Race*. Vols. 1 and 2. London: Verso.

Anderson, Elijah. 1990. *Streetwise: Race, Class, and Change in an Urban Community*. Chicago: University of Chicago Press.

Bayley, Susan. 1995. "Caste and 'Race' in the Colonial Ethnography of India." In *The Concept of Race in South Asia*, edited by Peter Robb, 165–218. Oxford: Oxford University Press.

———. 1999. *The New Cambridge History of India: Caste, Society, and Politics in India from the Eighteenth Century to the Modern Age*. Cambridge: Cambridge University Press.

Bourdieu, Pierre. 1990. *The Logic of Practice*. Cambridge: Polity Press.

———. 1996. *The State Nobility: Elite Schools in the Field of Power*. Translated by Lauretta C. Clough. Stanford, CA: Stanford University Press.

Channa, Subhadra Mitra. 2005. "Metaphors of Race and Caste-Based Discriminations against Dalits and Dalit Women in India." In *Resisting Racism and Xenophobia*, edited by Faye V. Harrison, 49–66. Walnut Creek, CA: Altamira Press.

———. 2008. "The Crafting of Human Bodies and the Racialization of Caste in India." In *Dalits in Contemporary India*, vol. 1, *Discrimination and Discontent*, edited by Nandu Ram, 157–74. New Delhi: Siddhant Publications.

———. 2011. "Global Economy and Constructed Social Imagination: Intersection of Aesthetics, Race, Gender, and Caste in South Asia." In *Keynotes in Anthropology*, edited by Peter Nas and Hao Shiyuan Zhang Xiaomin, 84–100. Book Series of the Sixteenth World Congress of IUAES, China.

———. 2015. "State Control, Political Manipulations, and the Creation of Identities: The North-East of India." Nehru Memorial Museum and Library, Occasional Paper, History and Society, New Series, No. 72.

———. 2017. "Selves and Codified Bodies." In *The Routledge Companion to Contemporary Anthropology*, edited by Simon Coleman, Susan B. Hyatt, and Ann Kingsolver, 219–33. London: Routledge.

———. 2018. "Understanding Caste through an Anthropological Lens." In *History of Ancient India*, vol. 6, *Social, Political and Judicial Ideas, Institutions, and Practices*, 1–42. New Delhi: Vivekananda International Foundation.

Chandra, Rajan. 1997. *The Complete Works of Kalidasa*. Vol. 1. New Delhi: Sahitya Academy Press.

DuBois, W. E. B. (1940) 1980. *Dusk of Dawn: An Essay towards an Autobiography of a Race Concept*. Franklin Center, PA: Franklin Library.

Fanon, Frantz. 2021. *The Wretched of the Earth*. Translated from the French by Richard Philcox. 60th anniversary ed. New York: Grove Press.

Fourcade, Marie. 2003. "The So-Called 'Criminal Tribes' of British India: Colonial Violence and Traditional Violence." In *Violence/Non-Violence: Some Hindu Perspectives*, edited by Denis Vidal and Gilles Tarabout, 132–74. Manohar: Centre de Sciences Humaines.

Frankenberg, Ruth. 1993. *White Women, Race Matters: The Social Construction of Whiteness*. Minneapolis: University of Minnesota Press.

Harding, Sandra. 1993. "Introduction: Eurocentric Scientific Illiteracy—A Challenge for the World Community." In *"Racial" Economy of Science*, edited by Sandra Harding, 1–29. Bloomington: Indiana University Press.

Harrison, Faye. 1995. "The Persistent Power of 'Race' in the Cultural and Political Economy of Racism." *Annual Review of Anthropology* 24: 47–74.

———. 2008. *Outsider Within*. Urbana: University of Illinois Press.

Hartigan, John, Jr. 1997. "Establishing the Fact of Whiteness." *American Anthropologist* 99, no. 3: 495–504.

Hocart, A. M. 1950. *Caste: A Comparative Study*. London: Methuen.

Hunter, W. W. 1897. *Annals of Rural Bengal*. London.

Huxley, T. H. 1868–69. "Opening Address." *Journal of the Ethnological Society of London*, new series 1: 89–93.

Ibbetson, Denzil. 1916. *Punjab Castes*. Lahore.

Inden, Ronald B. 1976. *Marriage and Rank in Bengali Culture*. Berkeley: University of California Press.

———. 1990. *Imagining India*. Oxford: Oxford University Press.

Klass, Morton. 1980. *Caste: The Emergence of the South Asian Social System*. Philadelphia: A Publication of the Institute for the Study of Human Issues.

Laclau, Ernesto. 1977. *Politics and Ideology in Marxist Theory*. London: Verso.

Malik, Keenan. 1996. *The Meaning of Race: Race, History, and Culture in Western Society*. London: Macmillan.

Márquez, John D., and Junaid Rana. 2017. "Black Radical Possibility and the Decolonial International." *South Atlantic Quarterly* 116, no. 3: 505–28.

Mendelsohn, Oliver, and Marika Vicziany. 1998. *The Untouchables*. Cambridge: Cambridge University Press.

Page, Helán E., and R. Brooke Thomas. 1994. "White Public Space and the Construction of White Privilege in U.S. Health Care: Fresh Concepts and a New Model of Analysis." *Medical Anthropology Quarterly* 8, no. 1: 109–16.

Parthasarathy, A. 1993. "Krishna." In *Symbolism in Hinduism*, edited by Swami Nityananda, 116–22. Bombay: Central Chinmaya Mission Trust.

Ray, Pratibha. 1995. *Yagnaseni: The Story of Draupadi*. Translated by Pradip Bhattacharay from original Oriya. New Delhi: Rupa.

Risely, H. H. 1908. *The People of India*. Calcutta: Thacker, Spink.

Said, Edward. 1978. *Orientalism*. London: Penguin Books.

Sartre, Jean Paul. 1961. Preface to *The Wretched of the Earth* by Frantz Fanon. Translated by Constance Farrington. New York: Grove Weidenfeld.

Smart, Ninian. 1969. *The Religious Experience of Mankind*. Englewood Cliffs, NJ: Prentice Hall.

Smedley, Audrey. 1999. "'Race' and the Construction of Human Identity." *American Anthropologist* 100, no. 3: 690–99.

————. 2003. "Race Ideology North America." In *Is Race a Universal Idea? Colonialism, Nation-States, and a Myth Invented*, edited by Yasuko Takezawa, 167–86. Kyoto: Institute for Research in Humanities, Kyoto University.

Srinivas, M. N. 1991. *India: Social Structure*. Delhi: Hindustan Publishing.

Thapar, Romilla. 2002. *The Penguin History of Early India: From the Origins to AD 1300*. London: Penguin Books.

Trautmann, Thomas R. 2004. *Aryans and the British in India: New Perspectives on Indian Past*. Delhi: Yoda Press. First published in 1997 by the University of California Press.

Waters, G. 1899. "Ethnographical Survey: India and England." *Journal of the Anthropological Society of Bombay* 5, no. 5: 283–93. Reprinted in Subhadra Mitra Channa and Lancy Lobo, eds. *Colonial Anthropology: Technologies and Discourses of Dominance*. London: Routledge (in press).

Wolf, Eric. 1982. *Europe and the People without History*. Berkeley: University of California Press.

8

Early European Feminism at the Service of Colonialism in the Belgian Congo

Jean Muteba Rahier

Women will know that white feminist activists have begun to confront racism in a serious and revolutionary manner when they are not simply acknowledging racism in feminist movement or calling attention to personal prejudice, but are actively struggling to resist racist oppression in our society. Women will know they have made a political commitment to eliminating racism when they help change the direction of feminist movement, when they work to unlearn racist socialization prior to assuming positions of leadership or shaping theory or making contact with women of color so that they will not perpetuate and maintain racial oppression or, unconsciously or consciously, abuse and hurt non-white women. These are the truly radical gestures that create a foundation for the experience of political solidarity between white women and women of color.

(BELL HOOKS, FROM "SISTERHOOD: POLITICAL SOLIDARITY
BETWEEN WOMEN," 1986)

VERY FEW BELGIAN OR EUROPEAN WOMEN were involved in Leopold II's Congo Free State (CFS, 1885–1908), which formally emerged out of the negotiations of the Berlin Conference (1884–85). The early Belgian colonial population in the CFS was almost entirely composed of men. It remained so in the first years of the Belgian Congo (1908–60), after the CFS was transformed from Leopold II's "private property" into a colony of the Belgian state. Both the CFS and colonial medical science feared the impact the tropical climate could have on white women's bodies and "reason" (see Habig 1948; Jeurissen 2003; Lauro 2013). Additionally, the cost of moving a "nonproductive" person to accompany her husband to Congo for the standard three-year duration of his contract remained expensive for both Belgian state agencies and private companies.

The situation changed somewhat in the 1920s following colonial authorities' growing anxiety about the widespread practice of colonials' interracial sex with Congolese women and girls. The Belgian colonial state began considering Belgian women's potential role as "civilizers" and adopted a policy of encouraging the departure of Belgian couples instead of single men, who could—if unchecked by a "moral values-laden white woman"—behave in ways that could endanger white prestige and supremacy, the backbone of the colonial enterprise. In 1923, with the backing of various Belgian state officials, a small group of Belgian women created the association Union des Femmes Coloniales (UFC)—Union of Colonial Women—to provide support to Belgian women before, during, and after their departure to Congo, and to attempt a coordination of their "civilizing roles and initiatives" once in the colony. The UFC members, as self-described "European feminists" (Jacques and Piette 2004a, 2004b) were enthusiastically convinced of the fundamental goodness of their objective to help African women go up the unilineal evolutionist ladder to reach civilization, from where they—white European women—were looking at things. In 1924, the UFC began publishing the *Bulletin de l'Union des Femmes Coloniales* (BUFC, "Union of Colonial Women's Bulletin").

This chapter is based on a systematic examination of the thirty-eight years of publication of the BUFC.[1] It is part of a larger critical reading of the BUFC's colonial discourse until 1961, when it ceased operations (the Congo-DRC reached independence on June 30, 1960). The research aims to discuss how the articles and advertisements published in the BUFC represented Black/African women over almost four decades. It shows how much the BUFC's objective of "helping" Congolese women "reach civilization" was in fact part of an early European feminist approach that invoked "global sisterhood" at the same time that it blatantly reproduced a system of racialized difference interwoven with the ideology of white supremacy. This chapter aims to illustrate how much imbued by that ideology early European feminists were when they engaged in "solidarity" with African and other colonized women, particularly before independences. In Belgium, early feminists disagreed with and "fought" against the male-only hiring policies of the Belgian colonial authorities on the ground of gender equality. They wanted to increase the number of white European women in the colony. At the same time, they unequivocally shared with male colonials the fundamental premise that the colonial mission of Belgium was indeed to bring Congolese "primitives" of all sexes up to civilization (see Jacques and Piette 2004a, 2004b; Jacques 2009; Jeurissen 2003; Gérin 1969; Mianda 2009). The historians of European feminisms Catherine Jacques and Valérie Piette, who worked on Belgium's UFC, emphasized both the UFC's attachment to (nonradical) feminist movements in the early twentieth century and its determination to be useful to the Belgian colonial project:

> Since its creation, the UFC was clearly committed to the moderate Belgian and international feminist movement, embodied respectively by the National Council of Belgian Women (CNFB) and the International Council of Women (CIF). The Bulletin informed colonial women about feminist advances, in the metropole and elsewhere. However, the UFC never distanced itself from the interests of the colonial world: it remained above all an association of colonials' wives or women agents of the colonial government. The Union worked for the development of the colony in the interest of

the metropole. If it called loud and clear for a European female presence in the Congo and was interested in the fate of indigenous women and children, it was always in the name of the economic and social interests of the metropole. The UFC never distanced itself from colonial discourse. (Jacque and Piette 2004a, 113)

The Belgian colonial discourse reproduced in the BUFC transformed, following the redirections of the ideological mood of each time period considered. In the 1920s, the BUFC represented African men and women as ineluctably inferior beings who have— or not, depending on the political orientation of the speaker/writer—the ability to learn and reach civilization. In the late 1950s—when independence began to be seen as inevitable—the BUFC's articles relayed a quasi-utopian discourse underlining the pos-sibility of the making of a Belgian-Congolese (and therefore multiracial) community in the Congo (see Mianda 2009). That ideological shift pushed in the background (without erasing them) notions of Congolese inferiority. And while *métissage* (Belgian-Congolese race mixing) resulting mostly from white colonial men's sexual intimacy with Congolese women, was treated in the BUFC as a biological aberration in the late 1920s and 1930s, it was represented somewhat less negatively in the late 1950s.

The BUFC was read both in the Belgian Congo and in Belgium. It could be found in medical doctors', hospitals', and state organ offices' waiting rooms, and in many colonials' houses. It was one of the rare publications with relatively wide circulation that was dedi-cated to life in the Congo.

White Supremacy and Early European Feminism in the 1920s

A recently published section of the *American Anthropologist* on the anthropology of white supremacy (Beliso-De Jesús and Pierre 2020) has served as a source of inspiration to com-plete this short piece. This chapter reveals how unsurprising and blatantly obvious, right-up-in-your-face, ordinary manifestations of white supremacy unfolded in the pages of the BUFC, issue after issue from 1924 to 1961. The BUFC provides an excellent point of entry into the ordinary, commonsensical, and profoundly racist imaginaries of European citi-zens, and colonials—both men and women—in the Belgian Congo, and in other European colonies in Africa from the 1920s to the early 1960s. By extension, it illustrates well how "naturalized," taken as an unquestioned given, the colonial racial order was, how it was upheld and reproduced in a multitude of small and big acts, situations, interactions, and representations. It uncovers the profound sense of superiority, of the "ineluctability" of white supremacy, Belgian and European colonials of both sexes shared—including those who self-identified as "feminists" (see Gérin 1969). With its numerous references to the BUFC articles, the chapter uncovers the affective disposition—their shared "empowering affect"—of white, feminist, European women as they engaged in the reproduction of white supremacy while interacting with African women, and thinking and writing about them. All racial orderings implicate the engagement of, and impacts on, affects. Ulla Berg and Ana Ramos-Zayas (2015, 662) theorized "racialized affect" and distinguished between

Black and brown people's "liable affect" and white people's "empowering affect," as they refer to Blacks' and whites' positionings vis-à-vis race, racialization, and the racial ordering of peoples and things anywhere in the world, in contexts impregnated by white supremacy:

> "Liable affect" [refers to] the affective practices that serve to racialize, contain, and sustain conditions of vulnerability and a constitutive element of subject formation for poor, migrant, and socially marginalized populations. . . . "Empowering affect" [points to] the affect associated with privilege and always-already perceived as complex, nuanced, and beyond essentialism. While a conception of "liable affect" results in a simplified and essentialized "inner world" that undermines the complexity and subjectivity of populations racialized as Other, a conception of "empowering affect" perpetuates the privileged and nuanced subjectivity frequently reserved for [whites] and . . . self-styled whitened elites. . . .
>
> "Liable affects" and "empowering affect" . . . operate in multiple, shifting, and complex configurations. . . . There is a relational and mutually constitutive aspect to these affective modes. (Berg and Ramos-Zayas 2015, 662–63)

I have found Berg's and Ramos-Zayas's two notions of "liable affects" (in relation to references to Congolese individuals) and "empowering affect" (in relation to white European men and women) very useful for the reading of the BUFC. Indeed, white supremacy is maintained and reproduced through the edification of an "affective structure" that informs all interactions between individuals and groups in society, and their representations.

After World War I, feminist movements in Europe reorganized to fight against the many occurrences of gender inequality. In the Global North in general, women did not have the right to vote, could not access certain professions, and were subjected to the authority of their husbands for most of the important matters in their lives (Jacques 2009). In Belgium, many of the women assuming positions of leadership in feminist movements at that time had gone through university education (they were medical doctors, attorneys, and other professionals), which was out of the ordinary and a notable difference with the level of education of feminist leaders before World War I (Jacques and Piette 2004b). They regrouped in various organizations, such as the Belgian Federation of Women with University Degrees founded in 1921, which was itself affiliated with the National Council of Belgian Women (CNFB)—founded in 1905—and with the International Council of Women (ICW)—founded in 1888 (Jacques and Piette 2004b; Jacques 2007, 2009; Di Tillio 1998; Offen 2007).

The founding members of the UFC were very much immersed in these Belgian and international feminist circles. Indeed, in addition to the individual engagement in feminist activism of its members, the UFC was affiliated since its foundation with the CNFB, which automatically gave access to the influential International Council of Women (Jacques and Piette 2004). Beginning in 1937, a UFC member sat in all commissions in existence in the CNFB to represent the interests of colonial women in all discussions of interest in this early Belgian feminist organization.[2]

At the time, Belgian feminist associations were very much concerned with breaking up the glass ceiling and opening-up to (white) women professional job opportunities in the Belgian Congo. That concern corresponded to their—contemporary, then—political fight for women's right to work (Jacques and Piette 2004a, 79). However, while they had the highest expectation for the recognition of their (white and educated) women's rights, they had a different position toward the emancipation of African women, which they undoubtedly saw as inferior to them, less civilized, less refined, infant-like, in need of supervision.

The reading of the BUFC uncovers how important race, racial hierarchy, and unilineal evolutionism were in early Belgian feminist conceptions of women's rights, in the way they saw the world's populations, and in the design and formulation of the actions they should engage in as feminists "to help Congolese women." Between the two world wars, the UFC and other feminist organizations had three major objectives in their strategy to prepare Congolese and African women to progress toward a stage where they could become fully emancipated: "prove that African women are human beings worthy of interest and consideration, civilize them through education, and moralize them through their work" (Jacques and Piette 2004a, 81).[3]

In the 1920s, the BUFC was published once a trimester, and its articles habitually dealt with issues supposed to be of interest to Belgian colonial women. The number 2 issue, of March 1924, for example, was dedicated to the problems European colonial women faced during the travel to, and arrival in, Congo. The number 3 issue of May 1924 published, among other articles, a piece on the alimentation of newly born babies. It criticized the argument defended by some who were opposed to the presence of white women in the colony because of the negative effect on the level of productivity of their husbands it would have, while also representing a considerable cost.

There were articles on "The Progress of Congolese Women," or "The Women in Primitive Peoples," in which references to African peoples located them closer to nature than culture, unlike Europeans. African women were consistently portrayed as being in dire need of education and exposure to civilization and high morality so that they could acquire proper female behaviors and take care of their families and children using basic rules of hygiene, and the like (Hunt 1988).

An article, signed by Rustica, published in the BUFC's number 10 issue of July 1925 titled "La Femme Noire" ("The Black Woman"), which occupied the issue's entire first page, denotes well the Belgian-initiated interracial feminist solidarity of the time, in its intertwining of basic feminist solidarity between Belgian and Congolese women with the racist ideology that provided a spinal foundation to the European colonial enterprise in Africa. The article does not radically reject patriarchal values, or what bell hooks has called "white supremacist, capitalist patriarchy" (2000, 118). Instead, it proclaimed the civilizing mission of the colonialism UFC members wanted to serve. However, the article's female author, following the more moderate general political line of the BUFC in the 1920s, rejected the most racist of colonials' positions according to which the "Negro" is not perfectible and the "Negress" is barely a woman to speak of. The article is in that sense directly opposed to views widely shared at the time that said that "it is more difficult to educate a negress than a negro [because] a longer enslavement hampered the development of her mental faculties and because social conditions have made it virtually impossible for her to be educated" (cited in Jacques and Piette 2004, 80).

That article claimed that African women were deserving to be educated, to learn proper moral values, and become civilized. The author made references to the male French intellectual and traveler Louis Huot who claimed that if we consider intelligence, character, and feelings, the Black woman is far from superior to the man of her race. The article concludes that, in fact, in the entire species women have been far superior to men, before asserting about Congolese women:

> The most beautiful trait of their character for Dr. Huot is certainly the pride they have in their race, the attachment they feel for that collectivity that oppresses them so mercilessly and from which, nevertheless, they extract the influence they sometimes have on certain white men . . . [this is a direct reference to interracial sex]
>
> The sensitivity of the indigenous woman is equated by her intelligence, and this is so when the primitive negro remains most of the time incapable of any feeling. It is not necessary to insist on the power of her maternal instinct, so developed since childhood . . . But, and this is a more curious remark, the notion of beauty, as we understand it, radically absent from the negro, is accessible to the negress . . .
>
> . . . we must contribute, by all means at our disposal, to the good will activities, the missions, the Red Cross, the Organization *l'Enfance Noire* (Black Childhood), that will hopefully lighten progressively their burden and clear up, for the greatest profit of civilization, the fertile terrain of the feminine intelligence in Central Africa. (Rustica 1925, 1)[4]

Other articles focused on butterflies, West African midwives, culinary recipes, African art, medicinal plants, the fact that the UFC was opening what was called in French *ouvroirs*, which were education centers for African women to learn about hygiene, sewing, and other such activities, so that they could become, as good domestic employees as men (called "boys") were, and adequately "responsible" mothers.

Brief essays called for proper behaviors for single white women who moved to the Congo, criticizing those who are sometimes found in the burgeoning urban areas and who behave as *poupées* ("barbies") and who think about nothing more than to have fun in bars and parties, who sometimes have affairs with Belgian men to whom they are not married, and the like. It reminded white women in Congo to respect "their mission" as colonial women: social work to civilize the Natives ("Women and Barbies").

The BUFC in the 1930s

In the 1930s, the BUFC became a bimonthly periodical.

Of particular interest in this decade was, in the number 37 issue of January–February 1930, an article on an ouvroir created by the UFC at Elisabethville (today's Lubumbashi) and that could not illustrate better the early European feminist conviction in focus here, of "the undeniability" of white supremacy, of these women's own

individually lived sense of racial superiority, and of what they saw as the "obviously beneficial" outcome of their own "well-intentioned" actions. In that article came an explanation
of what the Elisabethville ouvroir attempted to accomplish:

> extract the highest number of indigenous women from an inaction that often leads
> them to unhealthy pleasures and prostitution, to bring them to work and make a healthy
> living in sewing shops.
>
> Their principal objective is the social work through the influence that the European
> women can have on the general education of the Congolese women, who are also
> receptive to the lessons given occasionally about hygiene, *puericulture*, nursery, and
> everything that is necessary for the practical knowledge useful to proper household
> management. (BUFC 1930a, 10)

The assumption here, quite blatantly, was that prior to the arrival of Belgians, Congolese
people did not have household management practices and practically lived as disorganized
savages. As if to assert that point more straightforwardly, later that year (number 42
November–December, 1930) an article written by a BUFC staff member and titled *élégance
nègre* ("Negro Elegance") begins with a paragraph that says:

> It might appear reckless and daring to associate the word "elegance," which evokes the
> admirable creations of the *grands couturiers* and of the related industries, with the sub-
> stantive "negro," which for most of us evokes savage and naked men. (BUFC 1930b, 2)

Another article of interest printed in 1931 and titled "The Problem of the Races," was
authored by the UFC founding president, Mme. E. Dardenne (1931a, 1931b), an ardent
feminist (see Jacques and Piette 2004a, 2004b). The article was published over two numbers of the bulletin.[5] Undoubtedly, Dardenne's argument shows to have been very much
influenced by scientific racism and Nazi theories. The article presented a study conducted
by a certain Professor Nolf and began with this paragraph:

> Among the numerous problems posed by colonization, one of the most important
> for sure is the nature of the relations that should be established between the individu-
> als of both sexes of the colonizing people and of the indigenous population in the
> lands colonized. Since the old Antiquity, this question was relevant for the migrating
> peoples who had understood the danger for a conquering race when it establishes
> itself in small numbers in the midst of an abundant conquered population to be ab-
> sorbed by it and to dissolve itself like a crystal of salt would dissolve in a glass of water.
> (Dardenne 1931, 2)

Then, the author goes on to comment on Professor Nolf's explanation of Gregor Mendel's
discoveries about the existence of dominant and recessive characters inherited from one's
parents. The article's discussion moved from the vegetal domain to the world of animals and
finally to human beings who, as the article emphasized, were not that much different from
the rest of living species because they were submitted to the exact same biological rules.
Then, the article's author, the UFC founding president, concluded by writing:

What takes place to the individual born from two parents from the same race also happens to the hybrid. But with the latter, the characters received from the father and from the mother are not equivalents. A *mulâtre* (mulatto) is the depositary of juxtaposed white and black characters, but none of those actually fusions with the others. His paternal chromosomes only have a neighboring relation with those of his mother. Those and these conserve unaltered their individuality, not only in him, but also in all the line of his descendants throughout the centuries.

. . .

It is nothing but illusions to imagine that an inferior race is capable, thanks to an effort of adaptation or through the prolonged influence of the environment, to climb up to the point of becoming equal to a superior race. . . . The inferior race will be able to give, through hybridization, a mestizo race (*une race métisse*) of a level in average intermediary, and it will happen that some of these *métis*, thanks to a happy segregation of characters, will exceptionally possess at a high-degree certain qualities of the superior race.

Then the author wrote, in italics as to underscore her statement:

It is the unending infiltrations of white blood into the black population of the U.S. more than the educative influence of the environment that has lifted it to an average intellectual level clearly superior to the level of the negros of Africa . . .

It can therefore be advantageous for the inferior race to be allowed to be watered by the source of life from the superior race, but who doesn't see immediately that this advantage for the former is a danger for the second? (Dardenne 1931a, 2)

Quite obviously, the argument echoed the Nazi ideas that were circulating across Europe at the time.[6]

The BUFC number 48 of November–December 1931 came with an article on Ms. Suzanne Sylvain, a Haitian erudite woman who was about to complete a doctorate at the Université de la Sorbonne in Paris, France. This provided the BUFC writing staff with an excellent example of what they wanted to achieve, in the long run, with Congolese women (BUFC 1931, 11).

The BUFC in the 1940s and 1950s

World War II interrupted the regular publication of the BUFC. However, the few published issues reveal a first half a decade influenced by Nazi political ideology, pseudoscience, and scientific racism. This was a continuation of what was already happening in the BUFC in the 1930s. Obviously, the subsequent defeat of the Nazis and of what they stood for brought about after World War II a questioning of what was taking place in European colonies in Africa, where race and white supremacy had been so fundamentally sustaining the colonial ordering of peoples since the late nineteenth century. The consequences of the defeat of Nazism (and the ideas and values it stood for) for the colonizing nations of Europe began to be felt right after the war. Africans, particularly the most educated among them, were hungry for freedom, liberation, and independence. This was of course looked at by European nations, and particularly by colonials, as a calamity that would bring the end of their colonial projects.

An article titled "La Femme au Congo Belge" ("Women in the Belgian Congo") published in February 1940 (number 112: 27–29) summarizes a lecture given by Paul Coppens, a professor at the Belgian Université de Louvain, at the occasion of the opening of the Marie Haps school for girls in Brussels. In that lecture, as reported by the BUFC staff writer-author of the article, Coppens insisted, rightfully so, on "the dangers that the white woman will have to face once she arrives in Congo": the boredom that results from the fact that the maintenance of the household is taken care of by Congolese domestics, the sexual propositions made by Belgian single men, the relationships she will need to establish with her Congolese domestics.

As was the case in preceding decades, one can find in the BUFC of the 1940s a multitude of reassertions/reproductions of stereotypical representations of Africans, who are constantly constructed as existing in direct opposition to Europeans, as in the opposition of "emotional and primitive" versus "cold and cerebral," or "social solidarity" (and being imprisoned by a clan) versus "individualist ethics." And this happens as the articles deal with organizations of (white and European) girl scouts in Elisabethville; advice about how a family should move from one assignment in a given town to another situated in another region of the colony; advice on how to be happy about one's day activities instead of complaining of boredom; advice on how to take care of one's physical appearance and health, how to protect oneself and employees against leprosy, tricks to be elegant when you go back to Belgium, what to do to have a beautiful neck and attractive face; how to take care of your hair.

An article published in January 1947 (number 116) and signed by Betty Barzin, projects Belgians' and Belgian colonials' anxieties about independence. In her "*billet international*" published in that issue, Barzin writes, among other things, about what were at the time "recent debates" at the United Nations where, in the Commission de Tutelle, a call had been made to "the nations that do not govern themselves" to send representatives to the UN so that the commission could listen to their demands. As Barzin wrote: "all the colonizing nations felt threatened" (Barzin 1947, 8). She then hoped that certain nations would think twice before voting and prayed that they could see the grave consequences that their votes could fatally bring: the end of European colonies!

The period after World War II saw a notable increase of advertisements in black and white, which in fact denotes the postwar economic boom in the Congo.

The BUFC in the 1950s

That article by Barzin, which projected the growing colonial anxiety, announced what was about to come in the 1950s: an increased preoccupation with the idea of independence, which was becoming ever more popular in colonized populations across Africa. The BUFC of the 1950s saw a multiplication of traces of such colonial anxiety along with the emergence of a sort of colonial utopia: the making of a *communauté belgo-congolaise* (a Belgian-Congolese community). The pressing and repetitive appearance of that utopic (even-though-still-colonial) project in the BUFC pages remained linked to a surviving white supremacist discourse.

In 1954, the BUFC published an article by Odette Buysschaert Blanjean titled "Blanches et Noires" ("White Women and Black Women"), with the subtitle "What Should the Interactions between European and Indigenous Women Be?" The piece expands on all the benefits European women can bring to their "Congolese sisters." And after celebrating the abilities of African women to improve themselves by following white women's advice and progress towards civilization, the author then concludes the article with:

> But European women can help them a lot in this civilizing role and their influence can be enormous! They have no commercial responsibilities and time is not lacking (what has not been said about the idleness, the boredom of white, inactive women in the Congo). In addition, white women have the means. And this civilizing role, is it diffi-cult? But no, not at all, it is about a woman in front of another woman, of a mother in front of another mother. . . . And every European woman must want to succeed in this humanitarian task. (Buysschaert Blanjean 1954, 10)

The same year, another article titled "The Progress of Native Women," written by Vicomte Terlinden, professor at the University of Louvain in Belgium, about his several trips to Congo in the then recent past, celebrated the obvious "progress" that Congolese women had accomplished in their quest for civilization. Terlinden concluded with:

> Women will thus become in Africa what, since the Middle Ages they have been among us, a permanent element of civilization.
>
> The task is immense, it will take generations to complete it, but the results achieved in just a few short years make it possible to look to the future with confidence. (Terlin-den 1954, 12)

An article of 1955 titled "Reflections on the Role of Indigenous Women in the Congo," authored by Arthur Doucy, a professor at the Université Libre de Bruxelles, Belgium, deplored Congolese women's ignorance about feeding their husbands the proper alimen-tation so that they can sustain the physical efforts needed when working for European colonials. The author also lamented the continued pressure from their kin groups Congo-lese women remain under. Belgian colonials valued as a mark of progress the emergence among the Congolese of a family unit composed of a couple and their children instead of the extended kin group (Doucy 1955).

In 1956, the article "The Modern Black Woman" (BUFC 1956, 16–17) is entirely dedi-cated to the wives of Congolese *évolués*—which literally means "evolved." "Évolué" was the status Congolese who demonstrably met a number of criteria (including education, good table manners, proper way of dressing, and such) received through the award of a card (an évolué ID) that opened the door to certain social spaces reserved for Europeans and Évolués. The évolués were usually Congolese men. Most Congolese women could not meet all the criteria. These spaces of interracial social interactions multiplied in the 1950s.

After complaining that although they have benefited from the formation given in ouvroirs and taken other courses to learn good manners and sewing techniques, the BUFC staff writer affirmed that for the most part the wives of évolués do not meet the demand for distinction and proper behavior; they remain far behind their husbands. In a move that already evoked the notion of a still-colonial Belgian-Congolese community that was circulating at the time, the writer concluded in a statement that reaffirmed Congolese inferiority while also calling for a dialogue . . . "among equals":

> The *évolués'* wives must attend the *Foyers Sociaux*, they must know how to knit, sew, cook, etc. But the social situation of their husbands demands more. And this "more" we would be illogical with ourselves if we did not go out of our way to give it to them. Let's create a "mutual aid" between white and black women. Let's make the effort to give our black sisters the "good manners" they need. . . .
>
> Let us establish a dialogue between the white woman and the black woman, but a dialogue not marred by this somewhat condescending, often unacknowledged indulgence of those who believe themselves to be superior; lets establish a dialogue among equals. (BUFC 1956, 17)

In 1957 (Fisher 1957, 2–5), the BUFC invited M. Fischer, an attorney who served as administrative counsel to the Union Minière du Haut-Katanga, a major Belgian mining company active in the Congo's southwest, to comment on a speech on "the Belgian-Congolese Community" given by the then governor general of the Belgian Congo . . ., Léon Pétillon, at the opening ceremony of a Government Council session in 1955. The address marked a clear new policy designed to attempt to, if not avoid independence entirely, delay it as much as possible through the creation of something that had never existed before: a "Belgian-Congolese community."

Fischer began by summarizing the new Belgian policy toward the Congo announced by Pétillon. It consisted in two principles aimed at edifying a harmonious Belgian-Congolese community:

– Association of the two racial elements to form a Belgian-Congolese community.
– possibility for the most advanced Congolese to integrate into the European element of the community by assimilating into it. (Fischer 1957, 2)

Fischer then went on to elaborate, briefly, on the changes that needed to be implemented to reduce social, economic, and political inequalities so that everyone, including the Congolese, would participate and contribute to that community without rancor or otherwise ill feelings. The picture he drew was nothing less than a multiracial utopia that did not correspond at all to anything in the social structure of the preceding decades of Belgian colonialism, and its quite visible separation—at all levels—between Congolese and Belgians. He listed some of the reforms that will need to take place, including plans to develop the colony's education system to increase the levels of education of the

Congolese; the creation of a Congolese elite coming out of higher education institutions who would also be admitted (as évolués) in the social circles frequented by Belgians. Fisher reported that Pétillon added that as the level of education of the Congolese improved, the authorities would need to begin considering the principle of equal pay for equal labor. The "Belgian-Congolese community" the Governor General Pétillon, the author of the piece—Fisher—and the BUFC were calling for was nothing but—quite obviously—a reformulation of white supremacy. That is to say that the "community" they were envisaging was simply a somewhat reformed version of the then current colonial situation that would now provide more avenues for upward social mobility and "better integration" of the Congolese into the colonial project.

Conclusion

UFC members and BUFC staff writers were attached to a naturalized notion of white supremacy. Jacques and Piette noted that the articulation of the Conseil National des Femmes Belges' (CNFB) feminist struggle for women's right to work in Belgium with the struggle of other international feminist movements led the CNFB to advocate an equality between women of any race that the members of the UFC were not ready to accept. They were emotionally unable to abandon what they saw as their "maternalistic role" in the colony:

> While the UFC seem[ed] to have difficulty in conceiving that the African women can be seen as autonomous women who do not require paternalistic or maternalist supervision, the CNFB [was] increasingly committed to an egalitarian perspective. (Jacques and Piette 2004a, 91)

Considering the contents of this essay, it is indeed surprising how little the expression "white supremacy" is used in scholarship about European colonialisms in Africa in general, and Belgian colonialism in Congo in particular. And this happens as if white supremacy had not been absolutely fundamental and instrumental as it has been, permeating all aspects of colonialism in Africa.

Notes

1. This was done in the archives of the Department of History of the Royal Museum for Central Africa at Tervuren, Belgium, and of the Royal Library of Belgium in Brussels.

2. See the BUFC of July 1937, 6.

3. In this chapter, I have translated to English all texts published in French that I quote.

4. Every time I refer to a BUFC article without naming its author, that is because the article was not signed and was written by a BUFC staff writer. When the reference does not have a title, that is because the article was published untitled.

5. Number 46 of July–August 1931, 1–2; and number 47 of September–October 1931, 2–5.

6. This article by UFC president Mrs. Dardenne, evokes the work of Nazi sympathizer and French intellectual René Martial (1942) in which *métissage* is nothing but a biological aberration.

References

Accapadi, Mamta Motwani. 2007. "When White Women Cry: How White Women's Tears Oppress Women of Color." *College Student Affairs Journal* 26, no. 2: 208–15.

Barzin, Betty. 1947. "Billet International." *Bulletin de l'Union des Femmes Coloniales* (BUFC), no. 116, 8.

Beliso-De Jesús, Aisha M., and Jemima Pierre. 2020. "Introduction, Special Section: Anthropology of White Supremacy." *American Anthropologist* 122, no. 1: 65–75.

Berg, Ulla D., and Ana Y. Ramos-Zayas. 2015. "Racializing Affect: A Theoretical Proposition." *Current Anthropology* 56, no. 5: 654–77.

Bulletin de l'Union des Femmes Coloniales (BUFC). 1930a. "L'Ouvroir d'Elisabethville." *Bulletin de l'Union des Femmes Coloniales* (BUFC), no. 37, 10.

———. 1930b. "Élégance Nègre." *Bulletin de l'Union des Femmes Coloniales* (BUFC), November–December, no. 42, 10.

———. 1931. "Melle. Suzanne Sylvain, erudite haitienne." *Bulletin de l'Union des Femmes Coloniales* (BUFC), November–December, no. 48, 11.

———. 1940. "La Femme au Congo Belge." *Bulletin de l'Union des Femmes Coloniales* (BUFC), February, no. 112, 27–29.

———. 1956. "La Femme Noire Moderne." *Bulletin de l'Union des Femmes Coloniales* (BUFC), no. 154, 16–17.

Buysschaert Blanjean, Odette. 1954. "Blanches et Noires." *Bulletin de l'Union des Femmes Coloniales* (BUFC), February, no. 146, 9–10.

Dardenne, E. 1931a. "Le Problème des Races." *Bulletin de l'Union des Femmes Coloniales* (BUFC), July–August, no. 46, 1–2.

———. 1931b. "Le Problème des Races." *Bulletin de l'Union des Femmes Coloniales* (BUFC), September–October, no. 47, 2–5.

de Broux, Pierre-Olivier, and Bérengère Piret. 2019. "Le Congo Était Fondé dans l'Intérêt de la Civilisation et de la Belgique: La Notion de Civilisation dans la Charte Coloniale." *Revue interdisciplinaire d'études juridiques*, February, 83, 51–80. DOI 10.3917/riej.083.0051.

Di Tillio, Viviane. 1998. "La Fédération belge des Femmes universitaires: Naissance et essor." *Sextant: Revue du Groupe interdisciplinaire d'Etudes sur les Femmes* (Belgium), 83–114.

Doucy, Arthur. 1955. "Réflexions sur le Rôle de la Femme Indigène au Congo Belge." *Bulletin de l'Union des Femmes Coloniales* (BUFC), September, no. 150, 4–5.

Fischer, M. 1957. "Réflexions sur la communauté belgo-congolaise." *Bulletin de l'Union des Femmes Coloniales* (BUFC), no. 156, 2–5.

Gérin, Paul. 1969. "Louise Van den Plas et les débuts du 'Féminisme chrétien de Belgique.'" *Revue Belge d'Histoire Contemporaine*, no. 2, 254–75.

Habig, Jean-Marie. 1948. *Initiation à l'Afrique*, vol. 2. Brussels: L'Édition Universelle.

hooks, bell. 1986. "SISTERHOOD: Political Solidarity between Women." *Feminist Review* no. 23, June: 125–38.

———. 2000. *Feminist Theory: From Margin to Center*. 2nd ed. London: Pluto Press.

Hunt, Nancy Rose. 1988. "'Le Bébé en Brousse': European Women, African Birth Spacing, and Colonial Intervention in Breast Feeding in the Belgian Congo." *International Journal of African Historical Studies* 21, no. 3: 401–32.

Jacques, Catherine. 2007. "Le CIF face aux enjeux géopolitiques." *Sextant: Revue publiée par le Groupe interdisciplinaire d'Etudes sur les Femmes* (GIEF), no. 23–24, 39–56.

———. 2009. "Le Féminisme en Belgique de la Fin du 19ᵉ Siècle aux Années 1970s." *Courrier hebdomadaire du CRISP* (Belgium), 7, no. 2012–2013: 5–54.

Jacques, Catherine, and Valérie Piette. 2004a. "L'Union des femmes coloniales (1923–1940): Une association au service de la colonisation." In *Histoire des femmes en situation coloniale: Afrique et Asie, XXᵉ siècle*, edited by A. Hugon, 95–117. Paris: Karthala.

———. 2004b. "Féminisme et société coloniale au Congo Belge (1918–1960)." In *Femmes d'Afrique dans une société en mutation*, 77–98. Louvain-la-Neuve, Belgium: Bruylant Academia.

Jeurissen, Lissia. 2003. *Quand le métis s'appelait "mulâtre": Société, droit et pouvoir coloniaux face à la descendance des couples eurafricains dans l'ancien Congo belge*. Louvain-la-Neuve, Belgium: Academia Bruylant.

Lauro, Amandine. 2013. "De la puberté féminine dans les 'zones torrides': Expertise médicale et régulations du corps des jeunes filles dans le Congo colonial." *Sextant: Revue du groupe interdisciplinaire d'études sur les femmes et le genre*, no. 30, 33–45.

Mianda, Gertrude. 2009. "L'état, le genre et l'iconographie: L'image de la femme au Congo belge." In *Images, mémoires et savoirs*, edited by Ndaywel è Nziem et al., 515–37. Paris: Karthala.

Offen, Karen. 2007. "Thinking Historically about the International Women's Movement." *Sextant: Revue publiée par le Groupe interdisciplinaire d'Etudes sur les Femmes* (GIEF), no. 23–24, 9–38.

Rustica. 1925. "La Femme Noire." *Bulletin de l'Union des Femmes Coloniales* (BUFC), July, 1.

Terlinden, Vicomte. 1954. "Le Relèvement de la Femme Indigène." *Bulletin de l'Union des Femmes Coloniales* (BUFC), no. 146, 11–12.

9

Recognizing Blackness and Mestizaje as a Methodology for White Supremacy in Mexico

Anthony R. Jerry

IN 2011, DEEMED THE INTERNATIONAL YEAR for People of African Descent by the UN General Assembly,[1] the Mexican government began to ramp up its efforts for the constitutional recognition of Black Mexicans. That summer, through the federal office of the Comisión Nacional para el Desarrollo de Pueblos Indigenas/National Commission for the Development of Indigenous Communities (CDI) and local branches of the Secretaría de Asuntos Indigenas/Secretary for Indigenous Affairs (SAI),[2] the Mexican government would hold a series of consultations (*consultas*) in order to inform the Black Mexican communities in the Costa Chica of their efforts. Throughout the year, the CDI and SAI hosted their consultations in the small communities throughout the region, explaining the Mexican government's interests in Black recognition as well as the methodology that the CDI had devised in order to systematically document the "unique culture" of Black Mexicans in the region. Later that year, small teams of researchers, including local Mexican anthropologists and government employees, arrived at the small towns in order to collect information based on a previously developed survey focused on the specificities of Black cultural life in the region.

Many activists that I spoke with felt that the effort for constitutional recognition was partly motivated by the Mexican government's need to be recognized by the global community as a modern nation that was serious about supporting the civil rights of its minority communities. The Black Mexican activists were also aware of the potential pitfalls associated with multicultural recognition efforts and schemes and had therefore been strategizing on how to create a unified front between local activists as well as how best to educate local Black Mexicans about what recognition might mean for Black communities at the local level. While Black activists in the Costa Chica had been organizing around issues of racial discrimination and lack of resources since the mid-1990s, the government's efforts in 2011 marked a serious turn in the popular conversation about Black communities in Mexico and the potential for these communities to become internationally visible.

The point of visibility and representation created a serious tension between activists and the government, as represented by the employees of the CDI and SAI. For example, at one of the first planning meetings between activists and the Mexican government in the town of Santiago Jamiltepec, Oaxaca, the CDI unveiled its plan for the official government recognition of the "Afro-Mexican" communities of the Costa Chica. Almost immediately after seeing the term "Afro-Mexican" on the screen on which the CDI employees were projecting their PowerPoint presentation, Black activists began talking among themselves about the CDI's preference for the use of "Afro" as a categorical description for the Black communities of the Costa Chica. One Black woman then spoke up to the CDI representatives and explained that the term did not accurately describe the identities of Black Mexicans in the region. The woman continued, "somos negros" (we are Black), and therefore explained the woman, "we prefer to use the term 'Negro' rather than 'Afro'" as an official term for the communities and people of the region.

The rejection of the term *Afro* by the Black activists was met with surprise by the exclusively non-Black government panel. The term *Afro* had been incorporated into the language of the government employees and the official documents without consultation with the Black communities of the region. The reason for this, explained the white mestiza heading the effort, was simple. She explained to the group that the term "Negro" had a negative connotation and was also in poor taste. Therefore, this term was simply not acceptable as a term for the official recognition of Mexico's Black communities. However, this woman was quickly reminded by the Black activists in attendance that the term "Negro" was only seen to have a negative connotation by non-Black Mexicans, and in fact, Black Mexicans in the region used the term regularly among themselves to describe each other and their towns.

The tension between activists and government officials/academics created by the issue of naming and Black Mexican identity demonstrates the investments that both Black and non-Black Mexicans have in Blackness and the project for Black recognition in Mexico. For Black Mexicans, the issue of naming, literally an issue of self-representation, is about the ability for Black Mexicans to represent themselves to the broader nation in a way that speaks to the contemporary existence of Black communities as a historic consequence of the social relations around race and Blackness within Mexico. Therefore, for Black Mexicans in 2011, Black recognition was partly about recognizing the role that Blackness had historically played in the development of the Mexican nation. For non-Black Mexicans, the stakes of Black recognition are equally as high. For non-Black Mexicans, the issue of officially identifying Black Mexicans is about being able to control the contemporary narrative around Blackness in Mexico in a way that creates historical continuity between an imagined past and the present and does not threaten a historical understanding of the Mexican mestizo, and the mestizo nation, as non-Black. As I sat listening to the conceptual argument between the Black activists and the government employees of the CDI that day in Jamiltepec, I realized just how many non-Black Mexicans were involved in the process of Black recognition. I also realized that Black recognition in Mexico is not simply about producing Mexico's newest multicultural group. Rather, the project for Black recognition in Mexico is part of a practical methodology that supports the broader ideology of whitening and white supremacy inherent in the ideology of mestizaje that has historically been used to produce the non-Black mestizo as the archetypal Mexican citizen (Sue 2013; Telles 2004; Vasquez 2010; Hernández Cuevas 2004; Wade 2001; Jones 2013).

In this chapter I focus on the methodology employed by the Mexican government in 2011 to recognize Black Mexicans as a unique cultural group within Mexico. I argue that while the process of Black recognition is informed by the broader ideology of mestizaje in Mexico, the strategy by which the government actually went about this process should be perceived as one of the direct methodologies of mestizaje. Focusing on mestizaje as a methodology allows for the recognition of the sites, both formal and informal, at which ideology is reproduced and around which the mestizo is perpetually reproduced as the "norm subject" (Wynter 2003) in Mexico. I argue that by focusing on mestizaje as methodology it becomes clear that Black recognition in Mexico is less about a project of equality for Black Mexicans and more about managing the potential crisis of Mexican identity that is a practical outcome of contemporary Black Mexican's demands for recognition within a social and political environment in which they were imagined not to exist. In this way, mestizaje is employed as a practical methodology for reproducing the white supremacy that is inherent within the broader Mexican ideology of mestizaje.

Black Recognition as a Method for Reproducing the Non-Black Mestizo

Christina Sue (2013) argues that there is a tendency to look at ideology as already crafted and always after the fact. This tendency overlooks the fact that ideology must be continually reproduced, not only through the mundane practices that are outcomes of ideologies but also more directly through the specifically crafted programs and state projects that allow for ideology to be hegemonically set into practice within social and political systems (Wade 2001, 847). Much of the work on Blackness in Mexico demonstrates how practices are informed by ideologies and unconsciously enacted on a quotidian level by both state and nonstate actors. For example, many discuss the ways in which Black Mexicans often reject the label of "negro" in the presence of non-Blacks (Sue 2010, 2013; Hoffman 2014; Lewis 2000, 2001) and regularly seek social strategies that allow them to distance themselves from Blackness and embrace what have been perceived as non-Black identities such as *moreno* (Lewis 2000, 2001), which are intended to allow access to the mestizo ideal. Through the practice of "racial distancing" or the "displacement of blackness" (Godreau 2006; Sue 2010, 2013), many Black Mexicans, most often in the presence of non-Black Mexicans, reject the "black/negro" label for themselves and place the "black" label on others (Sue 2010, 275).

The practice of racial distancing can be seen as one of the mundane side effects of the embracing of whiteness that is inherent to the Mexican brand of mestizaje (Sue 2013; Telles 2004; Vasquez 2010; Hernández Cuevas 2004; Jones 2013). Focusing on such practices of racial discrimination, whether from within or without, has allowed for analyses that force Black Mexicans to carry the burdens of society's racial pathologies rather than focusing on where and how these pathologies are overtly reproduced within Mexican society. Within these analyses, *the mestizo* is regularly retheorized (and reproduced) as the archetypal citizen within Mexican society, leaving the existence of the norm subject (the mestizo) as a simple matter of fact rather than a conscious reproduction. By contrast, this chapter demonstrates how the reproduction of the "other" is actually a practical methodology for the reproduction of the norm subject in Mexico; the Mexican mestizo. By focusing on mestizaje as a methodology, we can avoid the a priori assumption and acceptance of the mestizo as the natural Mexican citizen to which all others are compared and aspire, and rather focus more sharply on the conditions under which the mestizo itself comes into being as an active or inactive subject (Kazanjian 2003, 15), and the formal and informal practices by which this subject reproduces itself as the ideal within Mexican society.

I argue that we can see Black recognition in Mexico as a continuation of the process of the actual production of the mestizo as the norm subject that began in the nineteenth-century postindependence period. This is not to argue that Blackness is an epiphenomenon of Mexicanness. Rather, within the ideology of mestizaje Black and Mexican are dialectically articulated, and to say Mexican is to automatically conceptualize Blackness (in its negative form as dialectically opposed—not Black) and vice versa. In this way, Black and Mexican are perceived as mutually exclusive (Jones 2013; Sue 2010; Jones 2018) yet always mutually constitutive (Wade 2010). The historic acceptance and utilization of mestizaje as an ideology by which to define the nation in Mexico (see Wade 2010) has made the actual processes by which Black people are imagined out of the nation and by which the mestizo has been embraced as the norm subject within Mexico invisible. As I demonstrate here, Black demands for recognition in Mexico make this process painfully visible. Within this political climate for recognition and acknowledgment, this chapter explores how the ideology of mestizaje is once again manifested as a methodology that actually reproduces the mestizo norm of the Mexican nation. As we see next, the Mexican government has been using this methodology as a way to maintain its monopoly over the means of representation of Mexicanness and to produce the multicultural Black Mexican subject in a way that reinforces the white supremacy inherent to the Mexican mestizaje ideology.

The Methodology for Recognition

The Carta Descriptiva (Descriptive Charter) was one of the instruments used by the CDI in 2011 to organize the community gatherings and facilitate the collection of data for the official recognition of African descendants in the Costa Chica. The actual title for the document is "Talleres para la Identificación de Comunidades Afrodescendientes de Mexico" (Workshops for the Identification of the Afro-Descendant Communities of Mexico). The

Carta Descriptiva (CD) used a "primordial" approach to ethnicity that perceives the Black Mexican as a "stable group of people who have in common relatively enduring characteristics of culture (including language) and psychology, as well as a unity of conscience" (Eisenstadt 2006, 109). Scholars have noted that the classic cultural indicators used for identifying Indigenous ethnic communities such as language, clothing, or "traditional social organization" do not work for Blackness in Mexico (Hoffman 2014, 94). Even still, the CDI document implicitly takes cultural indigeneity as the foundational form of acceptable difference within Mexico. It focuses mainly on the anthropologically informed characteristics of indigenous communities and applies them to Black Mexicans.

The Carta Descriptiva lists several thematic areas, each with its own set of specific questions, enabling a systemic way to categorize Blackness and Black culture as well as demarcating the cultural and regional boundaries associated with the African descendant communities of the Pacific coast. These thematic categories included "Demography"; "Economy"; "Identity, Language, Native/Traditional Dress, Culture, Culinary Practices, Art, and Collective History"; "Festival Cycles and Ritual Life"; "Territorial Dispersion"; "Authority or Forms of Governance and Our Own Legal Systems"; "Social Attributes or Characteristics"; "Geographic and Social Connections to Region"; and "Invisibility, Racism, and Discrimination." All but the last thematic category appear to be conceived of as ways to link the communities to cultural traditions and authenticity rather than modern Mexicanness. By situating Black Mexicans within the realm of culture and tradition rather than the social and economic contexts of the modern nation, this strategy intuitively reinforces the non-Black mestizo as the inheritor of the modern nation and therefore the rightful manager of cultural difference within the country. Attempting to distinguish Black Mexicans as one of the traditional cultural roots of Mexico, rather than an active racial root, adds to the cultural repertoire available to mestizos without threatening the racial character of the modern mestizo. Furthermore, by using conceptualizations of the rural peasantry, the Descriptive Charter supports a logic that perceives Blackness as existing outside the modern nation (Ranger 1983; Trouillot 1984) and overlooks the historic economic, social, and political relations that have produced both Black Mexicans and the modern mestizo.

Ultimately, the CD sought to establish specific forms of organization, whether material or symbolic, that differentiate African descendant communities from other local and nationally recognized groups. Questions within the demography objective include: "Which locations, ranches, and places can be linked to us within our municipality"; "With which other localities, ranches, and municipalities beyond our own municipality do we have relations"; "Are there indigenous and Whites in our locality"; and "Are there Blacks living in the municipal seat?" These questions support the broader intention of the section in attempting to officially situate the African descendant communities of the Costa Chica into some systematic organizational and geographical framework. The questions attempt to recognize symbolically important places within the communities or larger municipality as well as the larger geographic and social relations that link communities in the region, therefore creating a distinct cultural/ethnic geography for Blackness in Mexico.

One core theme of the Carta Descriptiva is simply labeled "*economía.*" This long and detailed section is aimed at getting a sense of the economic activities that support the Black communities of the Costa Chica region. The main goal of the section is to understand in what ways each community can be seen as an *unidad economica* (economic unit). The subsections within this core theme of economy include "agriculture, raising of livestock, forestry, fishing, salt mining, migration, government support"; "festival cycles and seasonal production"; "economic cooperation"; and "market systems and forms of exchange." After reading the subsections of the document, it becomes clear that the intention of the core theme of economy is to outline the "traditional" ways in which the communities of the Costa Chica sustain themselves. The CD contextualizes these practices through the understanding of traditions in the same ways that Indigenous communities are seen to employ traditional trade and subsistence activities.

The location of a "Black Mexican economy" within the context of tradition situates the African descendant population outside of the context of modernity, or at least modern capitalist production, and places Black communities within the realm of cultural authenticity and tradition. Questions for the communities in the subsections of the CD are interested in understanding issues such as the traditional forms of cultivation used in the Black communities and whether the introduction of new types of agricultural products have modified these traditional forms. The government methodology employed for identifying Black communities approached Black Mexicans as if they had remained untouched and left to their own cultural and material production within their supposed social and cultural isolation. However, the architects of the CD overlook how African descendants arrived in the region in the first place, as part of the colonial project and enslavement, and later as part of the machinery of postcolonial capitalist production through cattle ranching, cotton production, and broader agricultural development in the region (Vinson and Restall 2009; Guardino 1996; Chassen-López 1998). In the government methodology for Black recognition, connections to the state and the social, political, and cultural norms of the nation are sacrificed for the perception of Black communities as traditional, and therefore potentially practicing quasi-African (read Indigenous) forms of economic production. A convenient forgetting of the history of Black labor within the region allows for the large-scale reinvention of the African descendant population in the Costa Chica region through the lens of tradition and culture rather than the more realistic context of the broader social and physical relations that have historically informed production throughout the nation. In this way, Blackness in Mexico is conceived as a cultural phenomenon rather than the outcome of the sociopolitical relations around race in Mexico that have historically facilitated Black Mexican exploitation, exclusion, and invisibility.

One of the longer sections of the Carta Descriptiva discusses the theme of "Identity, Language/Dialect, Dress, Culinary Culture, Art, and Collective History." According to the document, the point of this section is "To define how common cultural practices, uses of language, collective historical and present memories, culinary practices, common dress, and shared health knowledge and practices, form a framework for a collective sense that distinguishes the community from other collectives . . . so the community can then be seen as a cultural unit." The question is designed according to an intuitive logic of "us" and "them." The first question of the core theme focusing on culture and identity asks, "What cultural characteristics distinguish us?" This question sets the stage for the recognition of a series of traditional and authentic elements for the cultural demarcation of Mexican Blackness in the future. Following this general inquiry is a series of questions on language meant to identify local vocabulary and common oral expressions.

Language continues to be one of the most widely accepted markers of racial and ethnic difference in Mexico, obeying a seemingly simple Spanish/Indigenous binary (Saldívar and Walsh 2014, 457; Telles 2014, 31). One key question—What unique words do we think form part of our "way of being?"—is meant to identify a vocabulary unique to Black Mexicans in the Costa Chica. While the communities of the Costa Chica have been forgotten by the broader nation-state, they do not live in total geographic and social isolation. Lacking this isolation, the African descendant communities of the Costa Chica, unlike the indigenous groups of the region, do not speak an "ancient dialect," or even a dialect much different from the Spanish dialect spoken generally throughout the nation. In 2011 and on subsequent research trips, I worked with a local activist to also try and identify words that might be specific to Black Mexican communities in the region. Ultimately, it became clear that while there may arguably be a few words unique to the region, the use of these words was not restricted to Black Mexicans. Moreover, these words were used to differentiate Black Mexicans from other non-Black Mexicans based on biological characteristics such as skin color and hair texture. This demonstrates that while there is a language associated with Blackness in the region (a language of race), there is no Black Mexican language per se.

Another question within the core theme of identity has to do with the preparation, consumption, and the meaning of food: *cultura culinaria* (culinary culture). The questions in the subsection ask: (1) "what typical food dishes represent us in the community, (2) what ingredients do we use to prepare these dishes, and (3) in what moments do we prepare these dishes?" According to Joén Brett, the very act of codification makes food appear exotic (2012, 161). Oaxaca, as a cultural region and longtime tourist destination, has a tradition of incorporating indigenous flavors into the popular regional diet. In the summers of 2014 and 2015, I collected several recipes and remedies (some thirty culinary and another twenty or so medicinal recipes) that are part of the culinary repertoire of the Costa Chica region. Interestingly, many of the Mexican American students helping with the project recognized the recipes as like those commonly prepared by their own families. For the most part, the dishes of the Costa Chica represent tastes and habits common throughout Mexico and the US-Mexico border region. And differences in regional preparation were not due to specific culinary practices or the uniquely exotic pallet of the African descendants who prepared them. Rather, differences in preparation were due mostly to the preference and availability of regional herbs and spices. Rather than highlighting Black culture as constitutive of Mexicanness and the contributions that African descendants have made to the national palate (Hernández Cuevas 2004), the process of Black recognition further obscures African descendants' contributions to the broader nation's culinary traditions.

The question of *indumentaria* (dress) asks a series of subquestions including, "How do we like to dress?" "What colors do we prefer to dress in?" "In what ways does our form of dress distinguish us from others"? In asking these questions, the CDI is attempting to recognize the cultural uniform associated with traditional forms of Blackness within the region. The preferred uniform for many of the men in the region is a pair of board shorts and flip-flops that seem to represent their time spent fishing, whether from small motorboats in the open ocean or from the shoreline with nets made from heavyweight fishing line. Apart from this, men commonly wear jeans and lightweight button-down shirts in order to keep cool in the hot weather. Women seem to be most comfortable in lightweight store-bought dresses, while younger men and women wear any number of fashionable items, such as knock-off designer jeans, t-shirts, and miniskirts. However, as the cultural movement has gained steam in the region, some of the activists have turned to performing a more "traditional" appearance and have adopted cultural styles in a manner similar to the Jarocho style of Veracruz. However, unlike some Indigenous communities, these "cultural costumes" are not a part of the everyday dress of Black Mexicans in the region. In fact, it is entirely plausible that these costumes are an actual outcome of the recent recognition process.

Lastly, the question of origins plays a key role in the process of contemporary cultural invention. A subsection within the core theme of identity and culture is the question of "local history—formation of the community and founding events." The first question asks whether participants remember the origin of their community. Many Indigenous communities in the region continue to relate origin myths of the specific communities and the ethnic groups associated with these communities. Several of the Mixteco activists and language teachers with whom I have worked and studied, for example, share a common narrative of the town of Apoala as being the home of the first Mixtecos (see Troike 1978). According to the narrative, the mountains around Apoala are the site for the first Mixtecos, who descended from the clouds. A narrative focusing on Blackness and Black origins in the Costa Chica has yet to develop and does not appear to frame Black Mexicans' understandings of their own existence in the region. Many of the people with whom I spoke shared the sense that African descendants had always occupied the communities in the Costa Chica. Others reference the remains of a capsized ship in the region that was responsible for bringing the first Africans to the shores of the Costa Chica (see Lewis 2001). Historians of the region, however, are convinced that African descendants were brought to the region from other areas of the country in order to work in agricultural production and as ranch hands who eventually fled these farms and ranches to make their own settlements within the region (Lewis 2012; Castañeda 2012; Vinson 2001).

In 2011, the CDI used the Carta Descriptiva as an instrument to help establish the Costa Chica as a nationally recognized Black cultural geography, much in the way in which Veracruz is recognized as Mexico's Black Caribbean cultural region (Sue 2010, 277–80; Hoffman and Rinaudo 2014, 143; Castañeda 2012). The production of an official "Black geography" is the first step in the process of establishing citizenship, however conditional, for Black Mexicans in the Costa Chica. As the nation has long been accepted as the rightful domain of the mestizo, and in general a Latin American mode of whiteness, the production of racial geographies is an important strategy for anchoring "others'" claims to citizenship in real geographic space without threatening claims to the broader nation as a mestizo property. This can be clearly seen by the ways that Indigenous culture and history in Mexico have long coincided with official geographies of indigeneity. It is within this geography that indigenous history and culture are allowed to be reproduced. A key difference here is that unlike Blackness, indigeneity in Mexico has been long used as one of the foundational building blocks of the national origin myth. Therefore, Indigenous culture and history are whitened and cross the sanctioned borders of indigeneity through cultural forms that have been appropriated or employed for the sake of nourishing the conceptualization of the nation and the mestizo (Wade 2001, 855). This is clearly demonstrated by the ways that indigenous culture has historically been used to attract tourism to many of the rural and urban tourist destinations of Mexico. By creating an official geography of Blackness, the Mexican government is attempting to set this same process into motion for Black communities.

Mestizaje as a Method for Reproducing White Supremacy

At first glance, the project to recognize Black Mexicans may appear to be a departure from the ideology of mestizaje. However, I argue that it is important to focus on the multiple by-products of the actual process of Black recognition in Mexico. The making and sustaining of our identities is a dialogic and dialectic process (Taylor 1994, 32; Appiah 1994, 154). The power dynamic inherent in this process also creates the need to produce others in order to reproduce the position and identity of the norm subject. For the norm subject, maintaining power seems to be partly about having control over this process—the production of the other for the sake of reproducing the self (see Jerry 2018). The power to represent and reproduce the other, through any number of ideological and practical strategies, is part of the property associated with whiteness (Mullen 1994; Harris 1993). I argue that this is what is at stake for non-Black Mexicans in the process for Black recognition in Mexico.

Sue (2013) argues that the role of the mestizo in the Mexican story of race remains largely untold (5). One consequence of the exclusion of the mestizo from the racial narrative of Mexico is that by normalizing the position itself we overlook the sites and methodologies for the everyday reproduction of the mestizo. In this way, we focus on the other and forget that the production of the other is a key strategy for the reproduction of the norm subject, or the Mexican mestizo. Recognizing this allows us to ask deeper questions about race in Mexico, especially about the project of official Black recognition in Mexico and the actual work that this recognition accomplishes in reproducing non-Black mestizos as a consequence of the recognition of the contemporary Black Mexican. Wade argues that "Indigenous and black minorities' growing consciousness of their own identity and position does not take place only from the bottom up." Rather, this process is mediated by a number of non-Black and non-Indigenous actors (Wade 2010, 115). It is important to ask what investment these non-Black actors have in the recognition and reproduction of Blackness through the project of Black recognition in Mexico. As Wade argues, the mestizo nation needs the image of "los negros" (2005, 243). While Indigenous and Black communities physically exist on the margins of society in Mexico, as well as most nations in Latin America, the conceptualization of these communities is central to the conceptualization of the nation and provides nourishment to the mestizo nation (Wade 2001) in the form of providing a baseline for difference by which the norm subject is always measured and reproduced. In this way, Blackness in Mexico continues to be constitutive of Mexican Mestizoness (Wade 2005). The key to this process for Black Mexicans is that the non-Black monopoly over Mestizoness limits the ability for Black Mexicans to capture the value that they provide in the production of the mestizo and the mestizo nation, as Black Mexicans are never allowed to embody that which they are used to produce, the archetypal mestizo citizen and the mestizo nation.

Mestizaje is not just a nation-building ideology but is also a "lived process that operates within the embodied person and within networks of family and kinship relationships" (Wade 2005, 239). I argue that this process also extends to the broader relationships between communities that define the nation. That is, mestizaje sets the possibility for allowing the mestizo to act as a metonym for the nation by physically embodying the nation (Williams 1989). While this relationship between the mestizo and the nation, and by extension the mestizo and communities of "others" within the nation, has been normalized, the reproduction of this relationship takes real structural work. In this way, the ideology of mestizaje is turned into methodology through structural practices that are consciously employed in order to bring about the desired outcomes of the mestizaje ideology. A prime example here is the ways in which the Mexican government has approached education and the incorporation of indigeneity into a curriculum that reinforces and reproduces the ideology of mestizaje, and the role that indigeneity is expected to play within that ideology. Because of the embracing of whiteness within the ideology of mestizaje (Sue 2013; Telles 2004; Vasquez 2010; Hernández Cuevas 2004; Wade 2001; Jones 2013), the exclusion of Blackness within this curriculum has also been an active part of this methodology for the quotidian reproduction of the mestizo nation and the archetypal Mexican citizen. By valuing whiteness and actively promoting whitening, even while valuing the conceptualization of indigeneity, mestizaje as an ideology is practically manifested as a methodology for white supremacy. The government project for Black recognition in Mexico does not challenge this methodology. Rather, by recognizing Black Mexicans as a group apart, the project for Black recognition leaves the classic conceptualization of the mestizo untouched. In this way, the project for Black recognition in Mexico is one of the actual methodologies by which the non-Black mestizo, by way of recognizing that which is not the mestizo, is perpetually reproduced.

Notes

1. The proclamation of the International Year for People of African Descent was made with resolution 64/169—www.un.org/en/events/iypad2011/global.shtml.

2. The SAI has recently changed its official name to the Secretaría de Asuntos Indigenas y Afromexicanos.

References

Appiah, K. Anthony. 1994. "Identity, Authenticity, Survival: Multicultural Societies and Social Reproduction." In *Multiculturalism: Examining the Politics of Recognition*, edited by Amy Gutman and Charles Taylor, 149–64. Princeton, NJ: Princeton University Press.

Brett, Joén. 2012. "Conclusions: Culture, Tradition, and Political Economy." In *Reimagining Marginalized Foods*, edited by Elizabeth Finnis, 156–66. Tucson: University of Arizona Press.

Castañeda, Angela N. 2012. "Performing the African Diaspora in Mexico." In *Comparative Perspectives on Afro-Latin America*, edited by Kwame Dixon and John Burdick, 93–113. Gainesville: University Press of Florida.

Chassen-López, Francie R. 1998. "Maderismo or Mixtec Empire: Class and Ethnicity in the Mexican Revolution, Costa Chica of Oaxaca 1911." *The Americas* 55, no. 1: 91–127.

Eisenstadt, Todd A. 2006. "Indigenous Attitudes and Ethnic Identity Construction in Mexico." *Mexican Studies/Estudios Mexicanos* 22, no. 1: 107–30.

Godreau, Isar P. 2006. "'Folkloric Others': Blanqueamiento and the Celebration of Blackness as an Exception in Puerto Rico." In *Globalization and Race*, edited by Kamari Maxine Clarke and Deborah A. Thomas, 171–87. Durham, NC: Duke University Press.

Guardino, Peter F. 1996. *Peasants, Politics, and the Formation of Mexico's National State: Guerrero, 1800–1857*. Stanford, CA: Stanford University Press.

Hernández Cuevas, Marco Polo. 2004. *African Mexicans and the Discourse on Modern Nation*. Lanham, MD: University Press of America.

Hoffman, Odile. 2014. "The Renaissance of Afro-Mexican Studies." In *Blackness and Mestizaje in Mexico and Central America*, Elisabeth Cunin and Odile Hoffman, 81–116. Trenton, NJ: Africa World Press.

Hoffman, Odile, and Christian Rinaudo. 2014. "The Issue of Blackness and Mestizaje in Two Distinct Mexican Contexts: Veracruz and Costa Chica." *Latin American and Caribbean Ethnic Studies* 9, no. 2: 138–55.

Jerry, Anthony Russell. 2018. "The First Time I Heard the Word: The 'N-Word' as a Present and Persistent Racial Epithet." *Transforming Anthropology* 26, no. 1: 36–49.

Jones, Jennifer Anne Meri. 2013. "'Mexicans Will Take the Jobs That Even Blacks Won't Do': An Analysis of Blackness, Regionalism, and Invisibility in Contemporary Mexico." *Ethnic and Racial Studies* 36, no. 10: 1564–81.

———. 2018. "Afro-Latinos: Speaking through Silences and Rethinking the Geographies of Blackness." In *Afro-Latin American Studies: An Introduction*, edited by Alejandro de la Fuente and George Reid Andrews, 569–614. Cambridge: Cambridge University Press.

Kazanjian, David. 2003. *The Colonizing Trick: National Culture and Imperial Citizenship in Early America*. Minneapolis: University of Minnesota Press.

Lewis, L. A. 2000. "Blacks, Black Indians, Afromexicans: The Dynamics of Race, Nation, and Identity in a Mexican Moreno Community (Guerrero)." *American Ethnologist: The Journal of the American Ethnological Society* 27, no. 4: 898–926.

———. 2001. "Of Ships and Saints: History, Memory, and Place in the Making of Moreno Mexican Identity." *Cultural Anthropology* 16, no. 1: 62–82.

Lewis, Laura A. 2012. *Chocolate and Corn Flour: History, Race, and Place in the Making of "Black" Mexico*. Durham, NC: Duke University Press.

Ranger, Terrence. 1983. "The Invention of Tradition in Colonial Africa." In *The Invention of Tradition*, edited by Eric Hobsbawm and Terrence Ranger, 211–62. Cambridge: Cambridge University Press.

Saldívar, Emiko, and Casey Walsh. 2014. "Racial and Ethnic Identities in Mexican Statistics." *Journal of Iberian and Latin American Research* 20, no. 3: 455–75.

Sue, Christina A. 2010. "Racial Ideologies, Racial-Group Boundaries, and Racial Identity in Veracruz, Mexico." *Latin American and Caribbean Ethnic Studies* 5, no. 3: 273–99.

———. 2013. *Land of the Cosmic Race: Race Mixture, Racism, and Blackness in Mexico*. New York: Oxford University Press.

Taylor, Charles. 1994. "The Politics of Recognition." In *Multiculturalism: Examining the Politics of Recognition*, edited by Amy Gutman and Charles Taylor, 25–74. Princeton, NJ: Princeton University Press.

Telles, Edward E. 2004. *Race in Another America: The Significance of Skin Color in Brazil*. Princeton, NJ: Princeton University Press.

Troike, Nancy, P. 1978. *Fundamental Changes in the Interpretation of Mixtec Codices. American Antiquity* 43, no. 4: 553–68.

Trouillot, Michel-Rolph. 1984. "Caribbean Peasantries and World Capitalism: An Approach to Micro-Level Studies." *New West Indian Guide* 58, no. 1/2: 37–59.

Vasquez, Irene A. 2010. "The Long Durée of Africans in Mexico: The Historiography of Racialization, Acculturation, and Afro-Mexican Subjectivity." *Journal of African American History* 95, no. 2: 183–201.

Vinson, B. 2001. *Bearing Arms for His Majesty: The Free-Colored Militia in Colonial Mexico*. Stanford, CA: Stanford University Press.

Vinson, B., III, and M. Restall. 2009. *Black Mexico: Race and Society from Colonial to Modern Times*. Albuquerque: University of New Mexico Press.

Wade, Peter. 2001. "Racial Identity and Nationalism: A Theoretical View from Latin America." *Ethnic and Racial Studies* 24, no. 5: 845–65.

———. 2005. "Rethinking 'Mestizaje': Ideology and Lived Experience." *Journal of Latin American Studies* 37, no. 2: 239–57.

———. 2010. *Race and Ethnicity in Latin America*. London: Pluto Press.

Williams, Brackette F. 1989. "A Class Act: Anthropology and the Race to Nation across Ethnic Terrain." *Annual Review of Anthropology* 18: 401–44.

Wynter, Sylvia. 2003. "Unsettling the Coloniality of Being/Power/Truth/Freedom: Towards the Human, After Man, Its Overrepresentation—An Argument." *New Centennial Review* 3, no. 3: 257–337.

SECTION III

White Supremacy as Global Currency

IN JULY 2022, there were widely shared pictures and videos showing Moroccan police subjecting Black migrants to cruel, inhumane, and degrading treatment. Videos circulated of hundreds of migrants hogtied, thrown on top of one another, and being beaten with batons by the police. As part of a deal between Spain and Morocco, Moroccan police work on behalf of Spain to keep migrants from Africa from reaching Melilla, a Spanish enclave and military base located in the northern coast of Morocco. This horrendous incident is but a continuation of mistreatment of nonwhite migrants and refugees attempting to enter "Fortress Europe."

The treatment of Black and other migrants at the borders of Europe, however, is in sharp contrast to the open access given to Ukrainian migrants fleeing war. And European politicians and media pundits quickly explained that whiteness was the reason for disparate treatment of refugees. For example, the prime minister of Bulgaria, referring to Ukrainian migrants, stated, "These are not the refugees we are used to. . . . These people are Europeans."[1] In another example of the global currency of whiteness, David Sakvarelidze, former deputy general prosecutor of Ukraine, told people about how difficult it was to witness the death of white people. "It's very emotional for me," Sakvarelidze, referencing the war in Ukraine, "because I see European people with blond hair and blue eyes being killed every day."[2] Echoing these sentiments about how whiteness and Europeanness make certain places worthy of an emotional reaction, Charlie D'Agata, a CBS senior correspondent in Kyiv, Ukraine, stated, "This isn't a place . . . like Iraq or Afghanistan that has seen conflict raging for decades. This is a relatively civilized, relatively European [city]."[3]

As we will explore in this section, whiteness is the global currency of white supremacy. This section provides evidence to this, revealing how white supremacy is a broad global system that includes widespread "conscious and unconscious" ideas that reinforce how white superiority and white entitlement are foundational elements to global relations of power. Here, we can see how white dominance and nonwhite subordination are constantly reproduced across a broad array of institutions, social settings, cultural practices, and beliefs.

Notes

1. "Bulgaria takes first steps to welcome those fleeing Ukraine." European Website on Integration. March 10, 2022. https://migrant-integration.ec.europa.eu/news/bulgaria-takes-first-steps-welcome-those-fleeing-ukraine _en.

2. M'Bha Kamara. "Humanitarian intervention." Noli Me Tangere (Touch Me Not). Last accessed on August 20, 2024. https://touchmenot.indiana.edu/gallery/kamara-essay.html

3. Annabel Nugent. "CBS News Reporter Apologises for Saying Ukraine Is More 'civilised' than Afghanistan." *The Independent*, February 27, 2022. https://www.independent.co.uk/arts-entertainment/tv/news/charlie-dagata-cbs-apology-ukraine-iraq-b2024265.html.

10

The White Supremacy of Mining Finance in South Africa

Maria Dyveke Styve

Finance capital offers its suitors a choice: either create a favourable context for the seeking of profits, or forego the chance of significant loans and investments. Finance capital would be bored with the very idea of running a country: it is blind to race, ethnicity, and personality; blind to everything, in fact, other than security and percentage return.

—DAVID YUDELMAN (1982, 268).

DESPITE WHAT HISTORIAN David Yudelman states, finance capital in South Africa has not been "blind" to race and ethnicity. Yudelman is describing the relationship between the Transvaal government and finance capital in the early twentieth century just before the unification of South Africa in 1910. However, the description could nonetheless very well apply to the self-perception of actors within the field of contemporary mining finance. Covering any type of financing for mining projects and mining companies, the mining finance industry in South Africa tends to follow the boom-and-bust cycles of the mining industry itself.[1] When deciding on investments, mining finance professionals will tell you that what they consider most is the level of "security and percentage return" that investors can expect. Mining finance professionals care about a so-called favorable context, and whether this is ensured by government policies. Concerns about the certainty and predictability of South African government policies were reiterated consistently by the mining finance professionals I met during my fieldwork in London, Johannesburg, and Cape Town between 2016 and 2017.[2] As we will examine, the assertion that finance capital is "blind to race, ethnicity, and personality" is both ahistorical and inaccurate.

The chapter will first provide historical contextualization of how financial investments into the mining industry in South Africa since its early beginnings in the late nineteenth century were fundamentally reliant on anti-Black racial hierarchies that sustained capital accumulation on the mines. Second, by offering a depiction of how white mining finance professionals respond to potential political challenges to the economic status quo in South Africa, the chapter will aim to show how contemporary mining finance reinforces and perpetuates anti-Black extraction within a system of white supremacy. It concludes that while mining finance professionals perceive themselves to be "blind to race," when making investment decisions and speaking about political risk climates they nonetheless operate the field of mining finance in a way that reproduces the historical patterns of racialized capital accumulation in South Africa. Understanding how mining finance is located within a system of white supremacy requires thinking in historical terms and interrogating how economic relations today are premised on colonial and apartheid structures that have not been upended.

Because History

The early decades of the development of the mining industry toward the end of the nineteenth century were important in structuring South Africa's integration into the world economy and played a crucial role in shaping the social, political, and economic formations within the country. The imperial context of financial expansion in this early period had particular and devastating consequences, creating massive ruptures within the Southern African region with the establishment of the mining industry. The vast dispossession of land, first through imperial conquest and wars that lasted over the whole nineteenth century, and then through the 1913 Land Act that eventually dispossessed Africans of 87 percent of the land in South Africa, contributed toward the proletarianization of Black mine workers (Ncube 1985, 14–16; Magubane 2007, 203; Terreblanche 2002, 259, 396–97). The compromises made between the nascent South African state, capital, and white labor in this early period were all at the expense of Black workers. The migrant labor system that was established included the entire region, with many mine workers coming from Mozambique, Lesotho, and other areas within South Africa, especially from the Eastern Cape. The rapidity of the growth of the mining industry in practice meant that the industry needed the state to create a proletariat for it (Marks and Trapido 1979, 64).

Using such migrant labor was a way for the mining industry to keep wages at an extremely low level, make organizing resistance more difficult and for the industry to attract or dismiss workers in accordance with fluctuating labor needs (First 1983, 30; Wolpe 1972). The closed compound for African labor, which had first been introduced at the diamond mines in Kimberley in 1885, was soon copied by the gold-mining companies. The compounds were made to accommodate single Black mine workers and allowed for the total control of the labor force (Ncube 1985, 17–18; Turrell 1986, 48). The combination of having a monopoly on the recruitment of labor, the closed compound system, and the imposition of maximum wage rates eventually enabled the mining industry, in collaboration with the state, to keep African wages at an extremely low level, with real wages in fact declining over time (Feinstein 2005, 67).

The racialization of capital accumulation on the Rand was a strong feature very early on, and the system that was instituted was in many ways a precursor to the much later apartheid system. African workers were restricted to what was defined as "unskilled" manual work, while "skilled" work was reserved for whites (Ncube 1985, 20), although in practice African workers often had to teach and train their white supervisors (Feinstein 2005, 78). The mine compounds, the migrant labor system and pass laws, combined with entrenched imperial racism, contributed to an extremely racialized pattern of capital accumulation in the mines.

While the British had been established on the Cape long before any mineral discoveries were made in the Transvaal, the link between finance and imperial expansion became stronger toward the end of the nineteenth century. After gold was "discovered" in 1886, British interests in the mining industry grew, and by 1899 between 60 and 80 percent of foreign investments on the Rand came from British investors (Cain and Hopkins 1980, 487). Gold reserves were also essential to Britain's ability to finance free trade globally and maintain the trust in the gold standard (Cain and Hopkins 1980, 487; Van Helten 1980, 234). The profits made on investments channeled through London to the South African mining industry were fundamentally dependent on the anti-Black nature of extraction on the mines, as the development of the gold industry would not have been possible without the superexploitation of Black workers (Rodney 1972, 152).

This early period of the development of the mining industry, and the implications that it had for the social, economic, and political relations in South Africa, became a key part of historical debates in the 1970s on the relationship between racism and capitalism (Saunders 1988). Martin Legassick and David Hemson (1976, 4), for instance, describe how racial differentiation was used to ensure the profit rates of the mining industry from its inception in the late nineteenth century. The term *racial capitalism* was used by a range of radical South African scholars in the 1970s to describe how racial segregation was central to the capitalist system in South Africa, in opposition to liberal views that claimed that job reservations functioned as an impediment to economic growth (Wolpe 1972; Johnstone 1976; Legassick 1975; Marks and Rathbone 1982).

The economic model of capitalist development in South Africa, which relied so heavily on the use of cheap Black labor and state violence to sustain it, came under pressure from a number of angles from the 1970s. The racially segregated labor market based on job reservations, combined with the low quality of the apartheid education system, resulted in increasing shortages of skilled labor (Hart and Padayachee 2013, 71). While the real wages of mine workers did not increase even once from 1911 to 1969 (Wilson 2001, 103), there was an upsurge in worker strike action from the early 1970s, starting with the 1973 Durban strikers. This marked a turning point, with Black resistance increasing in intensity throughout the 1970s and 1980s, forcing the recognition of trade unions and the right to strike (Terreblanche 2002, 378, 380). The position of mine workers became much stronger after the unionization of Black workers became legalized in the 1980s. At the forefront of this was the militant National Union of Mineworkers, then headed by current president Cyril Ramaphosa. Black resistance in the period became increasingly radical, with the rise of the Black Consciousness Movement led by Steve Biko in the 1970s, armed resistance, and the township uprisings throughout the 1980s.

Black resistance from the 1970s onward ultimately contributed to the demise of the apartheid regime in 1994, but while overt white political domination ended, the structure of the economy continued to produce intractable unemployment and large inequalities, and there has not been any substantive land redistribution.[3] Sampie Terreblanche (2002, 378–80) makes the argument that from a longer historical perspective, from the 1840s until 1970, Africans were forced into an unfree labor market and had their freedom and economic independence consistently undermined in order to satisfy the demands of white employers for cheap and unskilled labor. However, by 1970 when this process had been completed, the economy was structurally transformed to replace labor with an increased mechanization of production, which became more capital-intensive. The outcome was a rise in unemployment among Black workers, and Black poverty worsened dramatically after 1970. Terreblanche thus shows that after 130 years of subjugation owing to colonial wars, land theft, and the oppression of apartheid, the economic independence that Africans had had was destroyed, so that when jobs became scarcer after 1970 there were very few alternative economic avenues available. With increasing Black political resistance and labor militancy from the 1970s, the response of the white entrepreneurial class and white bureaucracy was to marginalize the Black labor force to safeguard their economic interests (Terreblanche 2002, 380).

The Now of History

So in a sense, we just wanted to bring history back into the contemporary. Part of the 1994 project was to make us forget, reconciliation without justice essentially meant forgetting history, and forgetting how the cycle of accumulation by political elites was created prior to this moment. . . . Because of the power of historical white capital to control the narrative, quickly the politics of, if you like, good governance, corruption, and so on, meant black people. So we wanted to disrupt this narrative, because we as a movement are interested in addressing the historical injustices. . . . And also, to reveal the power of white capital. In Black First, Land First we say, the urgent task of black consciousness today is to make visible the invisible hand of white capital, because it has made itself completely invisible.

—ANDILE MNGXITAMA, PRESIDENT OF BLACK FIRST, LAND FIRST

I met Andile Mngxitama, president of the political party Black First, Land First, in Johannesburg in January 2017. At that time, the public debates on white monopoly capital in South Africa were heated. Mngxitama raises several important points central to thinking about the role of white supremacy in mining finance. First, the key role played by the historical relationship between white capital and the South African state in creating an anti-Black pattern of capital accumulation. In the mining sector in particular, the relationship between white capital and the state dates back to the establishment of the industry itself in the 1870s. Second, Mngxitama points out how particular terms, such as "corruption" and the need for "good governance," were placed within a narrative that associated these negative stereotypes with Black people (rather than, for example, with the operations of South African mining companies). Third, the historical injustices brought about through colonization and the apartheid regime have not been addressed, and as Mngxitama points out, the power of white capital has been made invisible in the post-1994 period.

The debate on white monopoly capital, and the explosive power that the debate had, cannot be divorced from the enduring racial inequalities of both income and wealth distribution in South Africa. The expanded unemployment rate stands at 42 percent nationally (Statistics South Africa 2023b, 8). The more restricted definition of unemployment (excluding those who no longer actively search for work) stands at 33 percent nationally, and with this more restricted definition, the unemployment rate for Black Africans is 37 percent, where the equivalent for white South Africans is 7.5 percent in 2023 (Statistics South Africa 2023b, 23–24). With a very formalized economy, the high level of unemployment should also be seen in connection with a high proportion of South Africans living in poverty, with a poverty headcount of 57 percent of the population (Statistics South Africa 2023a). While the post-1994 period has seen an increase in the share of Black South Africans in middle-income and high-income groups, they remain overrepresented in the low-income group (Statistics South Africa 2015, 22–23), and Black South Africans earn much less on average than white South Africans (World Bank 2018b, 86).

An alarming feature of the post-1994 period has been the increase in inequality levels, with a Gini coefficient at a staggering level of 0.68 in 2015 (Statistics South Africa 2017), and at 0.70 in 2023 (Statistics South Africa 2023a). While this is slightly lower than the 2006 level of 0.72, it is much higher than the estimate for 1993 of a coefficient of 0.59 made by the World Bank (2018a).[4] Going beyond income to also look at wealth, the top 10 percent of South Africans holds a staggering level of 86 percent of all wealth (Chatterjee, Czajka, and Gethin 2020). Other estimates have also shown that within the top 1–5 percent bracket, about 80 percent are white.[5] The makeup of inequality in South Africa shows a serious lack of structural transformation, with racial inequalities persisting.

The mining industry, as a whole, employs about 394,000 people (Department of Labour 2020, 63). African men represent about 69 percent of so-called unskilled workers (a problematic term in itself in terms of what kind of labor is deemed "skilled" or "unskilled," see Pierre [2020]), while white men hold about 50 percent of top management positions (Department of Labour 2020, 34, 17). While the distribution has improved compared to previous years, it is still extremely far from representing the demographic makeup of South Africa. The remnants of the migrant labor system established in the late nineteenth century can still be seen within the industry, with many workers still being migrants from across the region or from the Eastern Cape within South Africa (Chinguno 2013, 640–41). The legacies of the past are also visible in the lack of mechanization in the mines, meaning that rock drillers are still using handheld machine drills, which have barely changed over the past century (Stewart 2013, 49); this contributes to the continued special status of rock drillers in the industry, but also to the particularly excruciating nature of their work. Many workers live in informal settlements close to the mine, often in corrugated iron shacks, without proper sanitation, running water, or electricity.[6] Within the platinum industry as a whole, over one-third of workers are employed through third parties, that is, subcontractors and labor brokers, making work more precarious with fewer permanent positions (Chinguno 2013, 640).

The lack of jobs in South Africa, and continued political calls to increase productive investment, make it a paradox that what can be termed "apartheid-infused" capital has been allowed to push toward global expansion rather than be invested in South Africa.[7] The reintegration of South Africa into the global economy since 1994 has rehashed some of the core contradictions and problems with the extroversion of the economy, which have structural roots in the colonial exploitation of mineral resources from the late nineteenth century (Styve 2019). The period of intense financial expansion in the late nineteenth century is also echoed, albeit on a much larger scale, in the global reach and massive growth of financial capital over the last few decades. The mining magnates and family dynasties of the late nineteenth and early twentieth centuries within mining have now been replaced by large, impersonal, transnational corporations, as can be seen in the transformation of the now global mining company Anglo American.

When discussed in concrete ownership terms, the form of white monopoly capital that dominated the South African economy in the 1980s was a particular form of large conglomerates and state-owned companies, where both the terms *white* and *monopoly capital* were quite unambiguous. The large size and well-developed nature of the financial sector is an outcome of the historical role of British imperial capital, and later Afrikaner finance capital, which had produced a specific conglomerate structure of ownership of the major corporations and finance houses (Ashman and Fine 2013, 146). In 1990, the South African mining industry was dominated by six major mining houses that all had their headquarters in Johannesburg (Robinson 2016), epitomizing the notion of white monopoly capital. After 1994, the large conglomerate structures were broken up, with Anglo American being the prime example. The opening up of the South African economy has led to a large increase of foreign ownership of companies and shares on the Johannesburg Stock Exchange, while the major South African players like Anglo American have internationalized using London as a base for global expansion. Apartheid-infused mining capital has thus expanded globally from South Africa through the City of London, instead of finance capital being channeled to South Africa as in the early period when the mining industry was established.

The City of London, which was so central to the early financing of the South African mining industry, is now rather a conduit for the internationalization of formerly South African companies (Robinson 2016; Styve 2019). For the African continent as a whole however, the City of London remains the major hub for mining finance. The fact that the City of London has kept its central position within the global economic system should be understood in the context of the imperial history of the City. When measured in terms of international lending and deposits, London is the largest international financial center, followed by New York. However, this dominance becomes even stronger when including British jurisdictions like Jersey, Guernsey, and the Cayman Islands, which, all put together, account for about one-third of loans and deposits, compared to about 10 percent going through the United States (Palan and Stern-Weiner 2012; Palan 2015, 1–2). Describing what he calls a "British imperial pole," Palan (2012, 4) argues that at the core of global financial markets today is "a second British Empire." While many financial transactions are registered in tax havens like the Cayman Islands, in fact the important decisions are very often made in London (Palan and Stern-Weiner 2012, 4). Having worked extensively on tax evasion by large multinational corporations, Eva Joly describes the process as a continued plunder of developing countries, having taken the place of direct occupation during colonial rule (Joly quoted in Oswald 2017). Illicit capital flows that leave the African continent have been estimated at about $50 billion every year, with a large proportion of this being due to trade mis-invoicing by multinational companies (Readhead 2016, 4; UNECA 2014, 13). The global economic structures of white supremacy can be seen in this plunder, while the narrative concerning the need for "good governance" and reducing corruption is used to refer to African government officials rather than multinational mining companies (Pierre 2020). Within a South African context, capital flight has been concentrated in the mining industry, through the use of systematic trade mis-invoicing (Ashman, Fine, and Newman 2011, 22).

Despite postapartheid policies to redistribute control and ownership in the mining industry, the racial divisions are still evident. Black equity in mining companies listed on the Johannesburg Stock Exchange (SJE) only represented 7.4 percent of market capitalization in 2011 (Kilambo 2021, 9).[8] The Minerals Council of South Africa (formerly the Chamber of Mines) claims that meaningful Black economic empowerment in the mining industry has been achieved at an average of 38 percent, exceeding the target of 26 percent by 2014 (Senkhane 2015). The discrepancy appears to lie in the fact that Black economic empowerment reporting allows for the inclusion of historical transactions, even if the Black Economic Empowerment (BEE) partner no longer owns the share (Minerals Council 2019). The South African mining industry still has a strong concentration of ownership, with a high degree of foreign dominance in certain metals and minerals, as well as a high degree of export orientation (Malikane 2021).

While the breaking up of conglomerates has created some space for Black capitalists, that does not mean that the dominance of white capital has necessarily ended, although it has shifted in form. One of the key counterarguments to the notion of white monopoly capital has been that the Public Investment Corporation (PIC), the pension fund for state employees, is now a large investor in South Africa, and this is, arguably, mainly Black capital. This argument was also part of the response of Charles,[9] one of my informants who worked within mining finance in Cape Town:

It just plays on that sentimental thing about you're extracting value from the earth, and we own the earth and it is white monopolistic capital that's exploiting, whereas actually if you look at who is investing, [this is] the discussion I had with the Minister of Mines. I said, listen, you talk to me and you say I'm white, monopolistic capital, [but] I'm here representing pension funds, government pension funds, so there is still this view of "It's white capital," if you look at who is really there, it's the pensioners, so the face of capital has changed quite dramatically inside of South Africa as well. . . . I'm a capitalist by heart, and I think as long as there is free flow of capital, capital will be correctly allocated, and there will be returns generated that will benefit everyone. . . . [Y]ou still have capital apartheid [through BEE], you still have different classes of capital, by definition, . . . there is still labelling of capital as being black or non-black, so that can't be the end game.

Here, Charles argues that because large pension funds are investing money on behalf of Black pensioners it means that the concept of "white monopoly capital" is not applicable. However, those maintaining that white monopoly capital continues to dominate in South Africa, like professor Chris Malikane (2017) at Wits University, argue that even during apartheid the pension funds for Black workers were used as investment vehicles, without meaning that there was no dominance of white capital. His statement that "I'm a capitalist by heart" is also echoed in his belief in the potential of the market to benefit everyone, if it is only allowed to function effectively, but letting the market operate "freely" serves to re-entrench a highly racialized system of accumulation. The idea that the current situation can be described as "capital apartheid," because capital is branded and counted according to the skin color of its owners, excludes any understanding or analysis of the continued legacies of the apartheid system. The twist on reading BEE policies as somehow a form of "capital apartheid" because capital is labeled as being Black or white, is quite a provocative choice of words, given the violent history of apartheid. His "capitalist by heart" approach interestingly yields much less of a recognition of the historical patterns of capital accumulation in South Africa than the mining finance panel of South Africans at the MineAfrica panel in London in 2017. There, it was recognized that the historical legacies of mining in South Africa inform current debates on radical economic transformation, and some of the debates there showed that in certain ways parts of the mining finance community in London and South Africa, and the radical Black left groups like Black First, Land First, agree on what is at stake, for instance regarding nationalization. While people within mining finance praise the judiciary, the media and institutions like the Reserve Banks, from Mngxitama's point of view, these same institutions are protecting the status quo, white monopoly capital and hindering radical economic transformation.

Mngxitama places the argument about white capital in South Africa in a longer historical context and argues that the relationship between the state and capital still favors white interests. Thinking in historical terms here would mean interrogating the way that cycles of accumulation in South Africa were premised on colonial and apartheid structures that have not been upended. Part of the explosive power of the term *white monopoly capital* is that it has to be approached through the continued significance of the historical influence of white capital in South Africa, the lack of substantial structural transformation since 1994, and how the new dispensation has been seen to leave white privileges intact (Phiri 2013; Anwar 2017).

Responses to Demands for Change

When I began my fieldwork, I anticipated that professionals within mining finance would express concerns about political demands for nationalization. This expectation came from the fact that only a few years previously, a new political party, the Economic Freedom Fighters (EFF), had been established, which had nationalization of the mines as a clear objective in their political program. I was therefore surprised that almost no one I met took the demands for nationalization seriously, but instead brushed them off as populist demands. One of my white informants told me that he did not think that even Julius Malema himself, president of the EFF, believed that it would be feasible to nationalize the mines. Instead, what did concern everyone I met who worked on mining finance related to South Africa were the government regulations regarding transformation of ownership and employment patterns in the mining sector. Black Economic Empowerment (BEE) policies in the mining sector have been one of the tools used by the ANC government to attempt to increase Black ownership and representation in management structures within the industry (Kilambo 2016).

Alfred was one of the white bankers I met in Johannesburg who was working on mining deals and who had previously started his own mining company. He expressed a lot of dissatisfaction with the policies to promote transformation in the industry. Claiming that the legislation and regulations are "bad law, applied by activist officials," he complained that the requirements kept changing and were unpredictable. His tone was disparaging when he stated that "all these activist officials believe that they must encourage transformation," and he went on to explain how government officials would come up with new demands without it being clearly laid out in the relevant legislation. Talking about these problems at length, he did not express any recognition of the need for transformation stemming from the historical racialization of the mining industry.

Similar frustrations with government regulations in the mining industry were echoed by many of my informants, including Daniel, one of the investment bankers I met during the Mining Indaba in Cape Town in 2017. Having been in mining finance for over twenty years, he argued that it would not be hard to invest in South Africa if it was not "regulated to death." Describing the regulations that require a minimum level of Black ownership as having to "give away 26 per cent on day one," he was of the opinion that regulators make it "impossible to manage your business." Stating that a company has to "give away" 26 percent refers to the fact that the government requires a minimum of 26 percent Black ownership for large companies to qualify as compliant with its Broad-Based Black Economic Empowerment regulations (Kilambo 2016). The ownership shares are always paid for, thus by no means "given away," although in many cases large mining companies provide loans for people or Black-owned businesses wishing to buy shares, and dividends made on these shares are then used to pay back the loans. Margaret, one of the investment bankers in London who was working for a South African bank, echoed similar sentiments but also said that she sees it as an opportunity to provide funding for BEE structures. For banks, the regulations are thus providing business opportunities.

Charles, the white mining portfolio asset manager I met while the Mining Indaba in Cape Town in 2017 was taking place, described the transformation policies as a "cappuccino," with what he called "black sprinkles on top, white cream and black coffee." The "cappuccino" image is one that can be heard often in South Africa with respect to BEE policies. In response to criticism of the first round of BEE policies being too elitist, a new set of policies was instituted in 2003 and given the name "Broad-Based Black Economic Empowerment." The different rounds of changes to both the BEE policy framework and the laws governing mineral extraction have led to tension and conflict between the major mining companies and the ANC government. The frustration in mining finance circles is a reflection of this line of confrontation; the mining companies claim that regulatory uncertainty is hampering their business, while the government is saying that the industry has not achieved sufficient transformation.

References made by my informants to "government regulating the hell out of everything" and it being "bad law implemented by activist officials," imply a desire for less government regulation and interference but also function within a larger discourse of demonizing African states (Pierre 2020). As Mngxitama pointed out, in the post-1994 dispensation the complaints about corrupt government officials have been taken to "mean black people," while the large illicit capital flight out of the country by large multinationals is not framed as a question of corruption or a problem of "good governance." As Pierre (2020, 95) shows, the assumptions of "African lack" are part of the structure of global white supremacy and are reflected in the way mining finance professionals relate to and describe government regulations and policies.

Conclusion

While perceiving themselves to be "blind to race" when making investment decisions or speaking about political risk climates, fund managers, mining bankers, and mining analysts nonetheless operate the field of mining finance in a way that reproduces racialized patterns of capital accumulation. This can be seen in the perceived lack of feasibility of demands for nationalization and more fundamental redistribution in the mining industry, the perception that Black economic empowerment represents a form of "capital apartheid" by "activist officials," and the fear of any political changes that would disturb the status quo. Concerns about "security and percentage return" are then not blind to race but function within a structure of anti-Blackness as technocratic terms that ward off possibly emancipatory politics and contribute to sustaining white supremacy.

In this chapter I have aimed to show that this happens both through the continued legacies of the historical role that mining finance from London played in instituting an anti-Black economic system in the South African mines from the late nineteenth century onward, and through how mining finance professionals reinforce a deeply racialized status quo and power structures that sustain white supremacy today.

Notes

1. From the phase of exploration to the development of a mine and eventual production stage, there can be different companies involved at different stages, and there are several entry points into investing in the mining industry with varying degrees of risks involved. Compared to other industries, the mining industry has a particularly long time lag between when investments are made into the exploration and development of a resource, and when production actually starts to supply the market. There tends to be overinvestment and overcapacity during boom times and the opposite during downturns (Jacks [2013] 2018; Mining Journal 2018; PwC 2016, 2018).

2. Most of my key informants were either responsible for mining investments at large banks or they were managers at large investment funds. In London, Cape Town, and Johannesburg, the majority of my informants were white and male.

3. As per the government land audit of 2017, out of the total area of farms and agricultural holdings held by individual landowners (hence excluding land held by companies, trusts, or state-owned land that also make up a large part of South African land), 72 percent of this land is owned by white people, 15 percent by colored people, 5 percent by Indians, and a meager 4 percent is owned by Africans (South African Government 2021).

4. A note of caution, these statistics are not necessarily directly comparable as they depend on the underlying dataset used, which might not be the same in the estimates of the World Bank and Statistics South Africa.

5. Thomas Piketty quoted in Simon Allison, "'Black Economic Empowerment Has Failed': Piketty on South African Inequality," *The Guardian*, October 6, 2015, www.theguardian.com/world/2015/oct/06/piketty -south-africa-inequality-nelson-mandela-lecture.

6. Muleya Mwananyanda, "Marikana: Shame on You, Lying Lonmin—Houses Promised to Workers Still Not Reality," *Mail and Guardian*, August 12, 2016, https://mg.co.za/article/2016-08-12-00-marikana-shame -on-you-lying-lonmin-houses-promised-to-workers-still-not-reality.

7. I have borrowed and adapted the concept "apartheid-infused capital" from Andy Higginbottom who uses the term "apartheid-enriched capital" (interview with Higginbottom in Styve 2018).

8. Looking at the entire JSE, another study found that 41 percent of the ownership of the top 100 companies on the JSE was held by foreign investors, and that direct Black ownership of these top 100 companies stood at a mere 10 percent in 2013 (Thomas 2017, 20). White ownership on the JSE accounted for 22 percent in 2017 (Culverwell and Culverwell 2017).

9. Real names have been anonymized.

References

Anwar, Mohammad Amir. 2017. "White People in South Africa Still Hold the Lion's Share of All Forms of Capital." Accessed October 15, 2021. https://theconversation.com/white-people-in-south-africa-still-hold -the-lions-share-of-all-forms-of-capital-75510.

Ashman, Sam, and Ben Fine. 2013. "Neo-Liberalism, Varieties of Capitalism, and the Shifting Contours of South Africa's Financial System." *Transformation: Critical Perspectives on Southern Africa* 81/82: 144–78.

Ashman, Sam, Ben Fine, and Susan Newman. 2011. "Amnesty International? The Nature, Scale, and Impact of Capital Flight from South Africa." *Journal of Southern African Studies* 37, no. 1: 7–25.

Cain, P. J., and A. G. Hopkins. 1980. "The Political Economy of British Expansion Overseas." *Economic History Review* 33, no. 4: 463–90.

Chatterjee, Aroop, Léo Czajka, and Amory Gethin. 2020. "Estimating the Distribution of Household Wealth in South Africa." Southern Centre for Inequality Studies and the World Inequality Lab wid.world Working Paper 6.

Chinguno, Crispen. 2013. "Marikana: Fragmentation, Precariousness, Strike Violence, and Solidarity." *Review of African Political Economy* 40, no. 138: 639–46.

Culverwell, Sonya, and John Culverwell. 2017. "'The JSE is 23% black-owned and 22% white-owned': Interview with Nicky Newton-King CEO of JSE." Moneyweb. www.moneyweb.co.za/in-depth/fnb-business -leadership/the-jse-is-23-owned-by-black-people-22-by-white-people/.

Department of Labour. 2020. *20th Commission for Employment Equity Annual Report 2019/2020.*

Feinstein, Charles H. 2005. *An Economic History of South Africa: Conquest, Discrimination and Development.* Cambridge: Cambridge University Press.

First, Ruth. 1983. *Black Gold: The Mozambican Miner, Proletarian and Peasant.* Sussex: Harvester Press.

Hart, Keith, and Vishnu Padayachee. 2013. "A History of South African Capitalism in National and Global Perspective." *Transformation: Critical Perspectives on Southern Africa* 81/82: 55–85.

Jacks, David S. (2013) 2018. "From Boom to Bust: A Typology of Real Commodity Prices in the Long Run." NBER Working Paper 18874. National Bureau of Economic Research. Accessed October 9, 2018. www.nber .org/papers/w18874.

Johnstone, Frederick A. 1976. *Class, Race and Gold: A Study of Class Relations and Racial Discrimination in South Africa*. Edited by John E. Flint and David Fashole Luke. The Dalhousie African Studies Series 6. Lanham, MD: University Press of America.

Kilambo, Sixta R. 2016. "Black Economic Empowerment and Changes in Ownership and Control in South Africa's Mining Industry." PhD diss., University of Edinburgh.

———. 2021. "Black Economic Empowerment Policy and the Transfer of Equity and Mine Assets to Black People in South Africa's Mining Industry." *South African Journal of Economic and Management Sciences* 24, no. 1: 1–14.

Legassick, Martin. 1975. "South Africa: Forced Labor, Industrialization, and Racial Differentiation." In *The Political Economy of Africa*, edited by Richard Harris, 229–70. Cambridge, MA: Schenkman.

Legassick, Martin, and David Hemson. 1976. "Foreign Investment and the Reproduction of Racial Capitalism in South Africa." In *Foreign Investment in South Africa*. A discussion series No. 2. London: Anti-Apartheid Movement.

Magubane, Bernard M. 2007. *Race and the Construction of the Dispensable Other*. Pretoria: Unisa Press.

Malikane, Christopher. 2017. "Concerning the Current Situation." Accessed July 20, 2018. http://khanyajournal .org.za/wp-content/uploads/2017/05/Concerning-the-Current-Situation-Chris-Malikane.pdf.

———. 2021. "Transformation of the Mining Industry to Serve the People." SACP Eastern Cape. www.youtube .com/watch?v=-YB7bQpOmdE.

Marks, Shula, and Richard Rathbone. 1982. Introduction to *Industrialisation and Social Change in South Africa: African Class Formation, Culture, and Consciousness, 1870–1930*, edited by Shula Marks and Richard Rathbone. London: Longman.

Marks, Shula, and Stanley Trapido. 1979. "Lord Milner and the South African State." *History Workshop* 8: 50–80.

Minerals Council. 2019. "Transformation: Frequently Asked Questions." Accessed October 15, 2021. www .mineralscouncil.org.za/downloads/send/25-downloads/852-transformation-faqs.

Mining Journal. 2018. "Global Finance Report." Accessed October 8, 2018. www.mining-journal.com/capital -markets/special-report/1317652/global-finance-report-2017.

Ncube, Don. 1985. *Black Trade Unions in South Africa*. Johannesburg: Skotaville Publishers.

Oswald, Michael. 2017. "The Spider's Web: Britain's Second Empire (documentary)." http://spiderswebfilm .com/.

Palan, Ronen. 2015. "The Second British Empire and the Re-Emergence of Global Finance." In *Legacies of Empire: The Imperial Roots of the Contemporary Global Order*, edited by Sandra Halperin and Ronan Palan, 50–68. Cambridge: Cambridge University Press.

Palan, Ronen, and Jamie Stern-Weiner. 2012. "Britain's Second Empire." Accessed March 5, 2018. www .newleftproject.org/index.php/site/article_comments/britains_second_empire.

Phiri, Aretha. 2013. "Kopano Matlwa's Coconut and the Dialectics of Race in South Africa: Interrogating Images of Whiteness and Blackness in Black Literature and Culture." *Safundi* 14, no. 2: 161–74.

Pierre, Jemima. 2020. "The Racial Vernaculars of Development: A View from West Africa." *American Anthropologist* 122, no 1: 86–98.

PwC. 2016. "Platinum on a Knife-Edge: PwC's Perspectives on Trends in the Platinum Industry." Accessed October 8, 2018. www.pwc.co.za/en/assets/pdf/platinum-perspectives-brochure.pdf.

———. 2018. "Mine: Tempting Times." Accessed October 8, 2018. www.pwc.com/gx/en/mining/assets/pwc -mine-report-2018.pdf.

Readhead, Alexandra. 2016. "Preventing Tax Base Erosion in Africa: A Regional Study of Transfer Pricing Challenges in the Mining Industry." Natural Resource Governance Institute. Accessed March 6, 2018. https://resourcegovernance.org/sites/default/files/documents/nrgi_transfer-pricing-study.pdf.

Robinson, I. 2016. "The Globalization of the South African Mining Industry." *Journal of the Southern African Institute of Mining and Metallurgy* 116: 769–75.

Rodney, Walter. 1972. *How Europe Underdeveloped Africa*. Dar es Salaam: Tanzania Publishing House.

Saunders, Christopher. 1988. *The Making of the South African Past: Major Historians on Race and Class*. Cape Town: David Philip Publishers.

Senkhane, Mpinane. 2015. "Chamber Research Report on Progress on Ownership." Accessed October 15, 2021. https://miningnews.co.za/2015/05/15/chamber-research-report-on-progress-on-ownership/.

South African Government. 2021. "Land Reform." Accessed October 15, 2021. www.gov.za/issues/land-reform.

Statistics South Africa. 2015. *Census 2011: Income Dynamics and Poverty Status of Households in South Africa*. Pretoria: Statistics South Africa.

———. 2017. "Media Release 22 August 2017: Poverty Trends in South Africa; An Examination of Absolute Poverty between 2006 & 2015." Accessed December 9, 2018. www.statssa.gov.za/?p=10341.

———. 2023a. "Poverty." Accessed July 16, 2023. www.statssa.gov.za/?page_id=739&id=1.

———. 2023b. *Quarterly Labour Force Survey Quarter 1: 2023*. Republic of South Africa.

Stewart, Paul. 2013. "'Kings of the Mine': Rock Drill Operators and the 2012 Strike Wave on South African Mines." *South African Review of Sociology* 44, no. 3: 42–63.

Styve, Maria Dyveke. 2018. "The Informal Empire of London: An Interview with Andy Higginbottom." In *Dialogues on Development*, Vol. 1, *Dependency*, edited by Ushehwedu Kufakurinani, Ingrid Harvold Kvangraven, Frutuoso Santana, and Maria Dyveke Styve, 53–60. Harare: University of Zimbabwe Press.

———. 2019. "From Marikana to London: The Anti-Blackness of Mining Finance." PhD diss., University of Bergen. http://bora.uib.no/handle/1956/20832.

Terreblanche, Sampie. 2002. *A History of Inequality in South Africa, 1652–2002*. Scottsville: University of KwaZulu-Natal Press.

Thomas, Lynne. 2017. "Ownership of JSE-Listed Companies: Research Report for National Treasury." Pretoria: National Treasury. www.treasury.gov.za/comm_media/press/2017/2017100301%20Ownership%20monitor%20-%20Sept%202017.pdf.

Turrell, Rob. 1986. "Diamonds and Mining Labour in South Africa, 1869–1910." *History Today* 35, no. 5: 45–49.

UNECA. 2014. "Illicit Financial Flows: Report of the High Level Panel on Illicit Financial Flows from Africa." United Nations High Level Panel of the Economic Commission for Africa. Accessed December 9, 2018. www.uneca.org/sites/default/files/PublicationFiles/iff_main_report_26feb_en.pdf.

Van Helten, Jean Jacques. 1980. "Review Article: Mining and Imperialism." *Journal of Southern African Studies* 6, no. 2: 230–35.

Wilson, Francis. 2001. "Minerals and Migrants: How the Mining Industry Has Shaped South Africa." *Daedalus* 130, no. 1: 99–121.

Wolpe, Harold. 1972. "Capitalism and Cheap Labour-Power in South Africa: From Segregation to Apartheid." *Economy and Society* 1, no. 4: 425–56.

World Bank. 2018a. "GINI Index (World Bank Estimate)." Accessed December 9, 2018. https://data.worldbank.org/indicator/SI.POV.GINI?locations=ZA.

———. 2018b. *Overcoming Poverty and Inequality in South Africa*. World Bank, Washington, DC.

Yudelman, David. 1982. "Lord Rothschild, Afrikaner Scabs, and the 1907 Strike: A State-Capital Daguerreotype." *African Affairs* 81, no. 323: 257–69.

11

Extractivism as Whiteness

THE RACIAL CONSTRUCTION
OF OIL ENCLAVES IN NIGERIA

Omolade Adunbi

IN A FACEBOOK POST by Orugbo News Drop, an online platform, in response to worldwide protests over the death of George Floyd and broader issues of police brutality and racism including the demand for racist monuments to be pulled down across the United States, a former aide to ex-president Goodluck Ebele Jonathan of Nigeria, Reno Omokri, was said to have tweeted on Wednesday, June 10, 2020, asking why Nigerians were not on the streets protesting against racist and colonial monuments. In the tweet, Omokri said: "In America and Europe, they are pulling down statues of slave traders, and Nigerians applaud them. Meanwhile, in Nigeria, we have a town named Escravos, meaning slave in Portuguese, and another named Forcados, which means forced labourer. Are we serious, people?"[1] Many Nigerians responded to the tweet with some supporting comments while others claimed there were many other pressing issues such as high rates of unemployment, incompetent government, corruption, and nepotism in high places that Nigerians needed to focus on, rather than monuments. The tweet did not generate the kind of mass protests that the author had envisaged—Nigerians did not start demanding colonial relics be pulled down—however, the message was not lost on the communities who live in the Niger Delta region. Those communities have been waging the battle to remove these monuments since long before the global protests against George Floyd's murder. Indeed, this battle has been ongoing and, one could argue, began when the Portuguese first disembarked in the region in the early 1400s looking for Africans to be purchased for enslavement in the New World.

Although slavery and colonialism ended many years ago, some of the relics of slavery have been inherited by a new form of commodification—in the extractive practices of oil production on the continent. As many of my interlocutors told me, the relics of slavery remain, and have been specifically retained in the naming practices of multinational oil corporations. Even as Western extraction of Nigeria was epitomized in the oppression and subjugation that began during the era of slavery, it was further cemented during colonialism and continues today with the discovery of oil in the region over sixty years ago. The history of European encounter in the area has, many told me, always been a history of one form of extraction or another, beginning with extraction of humans as commodities, continuing with extraction of agricultural produce, and culminating in another devastating extraction—oil. The Portuguese, British, and their European allies benefited from all these extractive practices, and postcolonial Nigeria with its corporate allies who are mainly American and European multinational oil corporations are the major beneficiaries of this historical continuum of white supremacist extractionism.

Nigeria runs an economy that is highly dependent on fossil fuel. Since its discovery in commercial quantities in 1956 and its eventual shipment to the international market in 1958—two years before Nigeria's independence from Britain in 1960—oil has continued to play a significant role in shaping socioeconomic life, politics, and policy in Nigeria. While the importance of oil to Nigeria's economic development over the past half century cannot be overemphasized, the devastating impact of the extractive industry on the lived experiences of the people and landscape of the Niger Delta where the oil is extracted is enormous. Prior to the emergence of oil extraction, Nigeria had witnessed other forms of extraction over the last few centuries. Extractive practices predate independence in 1960. Some of the extractive practices include the transatlantic slave trade and trading in palm produce, cocoa, and other agricultural products (Adunbi 2022). Thus, the entity that became Nigeria in 1960 has always been an enclave for different extractive practices by Euro-American capitalist enterprises. This Euro-American capitalist enterprise entrenched itself through different business concerns beginning in the early nineteenth century. For example, the Royal Niger Company—a business enterprise chartered by the British government—claimed ownership of the Lower Niger region of Nigeria (Okonta and Douglas 2001), and Shell Da'Archy who started initial search for oil in the region in the first quarter of the twentieth century (Adunbi 2015) began the entrenchment of oil extraction in the region. The people, the entire landscape, and all natural resources in the region were considered the properties of these businesses until those "properties" were transferred to the British in the early twentieth century when the South became Southern Protectorate and the North became Northern Protectorate, and eventually, in 1914, both protectorates amalgamated to become Nigeria (Adunbi 2015; Okonta and Douglas 2001). Nigeria thus became a site for the entrenchment of white supremacy through the extraction of its natural resources.

In this chapter, I pay particular attention to how these extractive practices are shaped by a form of capitalism that situates race at the center of its trading practices. I ethnographically map these practices by looking specifically at two Niger Delta communities that are hosts to multinational oil corporations. My interest is to show how these communities have always been at the center of a form of racial capitalism that started during the transatlantic slave trade, consolidated through colonialism, and continues in the era of fossil fuel extraction. More importantly, I show how the particular history of these Niger Delta communities is indicative of a form of capitalism that interacts actively with race and racial discrimination. The chapter examines the relationship between race and oil extraction in Nigeria by paying particular attention to the ways in which oil shapes a form of racial hierarchy that places Black people and resources in countries with predominantly Black people as disposable properties in what I call the crudity of extraction. It suggests that in Nigeria's history of oil extraction, race and racial injustice has always been a constant marker of extraction in the oil creeks of the Niger Delta. I situate my analysis within a particular history that constructs Nigeria as an enclave of resource production and extraction. I look specifically into the ways in which oil enclaves are enclosed in the lexicon of race and racial injustice. Using the example of Escravos—a Portuguese name for slaves—an oil export terminal operated by Chevron, and Forcados, one of the largest and oldest oil export terminals in Nigeria, I argue that race and white supremacy have always been a major marker in how resources are produced, extracted, and used in Nigeria. Forcados was a slave port operated by the Portuguese in Nigeria's Niger Delta but became an oil export terminal after the discovery of oil in 1956. The history of extractive practices in Nigeria is intricately connected to race and racial subjugation of Black people and resources. Oil as a global commodity is engrained in particular practices that are entrenched in racial capitalism and white supremacy, especially in Nigeria, Africa's largest oil producer. I argue that race and racial injustice are crucial in understanding the properties of oil and the practice of extractivism and the affordances of capitalism in Nigeria.

This chapter is organized into three sections. The first section relies on ethnographic mapping in tracing how extraction is embedded in the history of two communities rich in oil resources. The section suggests that the retention of relics of slavery as part of the communities' names are indicative of a white supremacist practice that sees Black people and resources owned by Black communities as disposable commodities. The second section interrogates the relationship between white supremacy, colonialism, and the subjugation of Black people. The section argues that colonialism helped consolidate a form of rule that privileges racial segregation in an oil-rich Niger Delta region of Nigeria. This form of racial segregation, the section suggests, is imbued in the particular ways in which colonialism cemented a particular practice that gives credence to white supremacy in Nigeria. The final section locates racial capitalism and its affordances within the particular history of resource extraction in Nigeria, suggesting that the history of extraction in the Niger Delta in particular and Nigeria in general can only be properly understood if we look at the development of oil capitalism as a form of racial capitalism that is entrenched in natural resource extraction in enclaves that are considered usable.

What's in a Name?

In the summer of 2018, I visited Warri, one of the cities in Delta state in the oil rich Niger Delta region of Nigeria. Warri is second home to many who are from other towns and villages around the many creeks where oil is extracted by different multinational corporations (MNCs). While in Warri, I also visited some of the communities where the infrastructures of the MNCs are located to interview community members. During my stay in the area, I became interested in why some of the communities are referred to as Forcados and Escravos. As I ponder the names, I am reminded of Ryder's (1959) piece about how the Portuguese named the river known as Forcados today as Rio dos Forcados, from the swallow-tailed birds they saw there. I am also reminded of how that name came from João II of Portugal who was said to have decreed the rivers Mahin, Benin, Escravos, Forcados, and Ramos as the "five slave rivers." The Ugborodo River, formerly Escravos River, is a distributary of the Niger River, which flows for 56 kilometers along a westerly course before ending in the Bight of Benin of the Gulf of Guinea where it flows into the Atlantic Ocean. The river is connected through a series of interconnected waterways and creeks to the Forcados, Warri, Benin, and Ethiope Rivers.[2] Joseph is from Ugborodo community. Joseph[3] is a fifty-eight-year-old fisherman who has lived most of his life in Ugborodo with occasional visits to Warri. When I met Joseph in the summer of 2018, he had just returned from the river where he went to fish. As we sat down that evening to talk about extractive practices in his community, he beckoned to one of his sons to bring out a drink for us. The son quickly ran inside and returned with a bottle of locally brewed ogogoro (gin), which Joseph and his family brew in their backyard to supplement their income. Joseph's wife had prepared a meal of starch and banga soup (made from ripe palm fruits), one of the most important cuisines in the region. Joseph quickly invited me to join him for a meal, to which I responded in the affirmative. It is considered disrespectful when a guest is offered a meal and the guest turns it down. As soon as we finished the meal (I only took a few bites), Joseph popped open the ogogoro bottle, pour a little in his cup, and immediately emptied it on the ground saying, "that belongs to our ancestors because they were here before us and may they continue to protect us," to which I responded "Ashee!!" He poured the drink in my cup before his because guests are expected to be served first. As we took the first sip, Joseph once again welcomed me to the community. He looked at me and asked, "what's in a name?"

Joseph's question is not just about what's in a name but also about the ways in which the name of his community was changed to reflect racial oppression. The name of Joseph's community is Ugborodo, one of the oil-bearing communities in the Niger Delta and host to some of Chevron's oil infrastructure in the region. While many community members refer to the town by its name, Ugborodo, the same cannot be said for the oil infrastructures in the community. The oil infrastructures are named Escravos. In 1964, Chevron leased the land from the Ugborodo people to build their oil terminal and airstrip after large deposits of oil were found off the Ugborodo shores. Chevron dubbed the property Escravos Terminal and Airstrip rather than Ugborodo Terminal and Airstrip.[4] Many in the community told of how they woke up one morning and saw the name of their community completely changed without any consultation. While many did not exactly know how Chevron decided to name the terminal Escravos, they also told me that Chevron plead ignorance of the meaning of the name since they are a global conglomerate with tentacles spread across the world. As one of the elders of the community told me, "Chevron cannot feign ignorance of how damaging this name is to the entire community. If they didn't know then, how about now?"[5] Asking about now is not just a rhetorical question but an affirmation of how Chevron, based on its reach and access to resources, should have known that the name connotes slaves. Naming the terminal Escravos by Chevron is not accidental since slavery ended several years before the discovery of oil in the region. With its main Nigerian oil production facility at the mouth of the Ugborodo River, the oil terminal pumps approximately 460,000 bbl/d (barrels a day), and serves a submarine oil field 18 kilometers offshore. To many members of the community, naming the terminal Escravos basically confirms the ways in which Chevron views the site, just another extractive enclave that is not in any way different from the previous purpose that it served—slavery. As I (2022) point out in *Enclaves of Exception*, oil is a form of energy that can be crudely captured through an extractive practice that is entrenched in rendering enclaves where the resource is located as disposable. There is a parallel that can be deciphered here. Slaves were considered commodities that were captured and sold into the new world as non-human expendable products. In the same vein, crude is captured today as a form of energy that is also sold to the new world, the Global North, extracted from the Global South as a consumable good. Hence, enclaves where these commodities are captured, in the case of Nigeria the Niger Delta, become a site where the practice of bodies and natural resources as commodities have a shared history. It is this shared history that defines Escravos. The Escravos is also home to Chevron's gas to liquids plant, which converts natural gas to liquid petroleum products. Developed in partnerships with Chevron Nigeria Limited (75 percent) and the Nigerian National Petroleum Company (15 percent), Chevron began operations the summer of 2014;[6] many residents of the community told me Chevron is not oblivious of the dark history associated with the name. Continuing to use the name is a further confirmation of how they see the community and its rich oil resources as slaves to the multinational corporation and its partner, the Nigerian state. The area called Escravos has always been known locally as Ugborodo after the largest and oldest village in the area. It was said to have been founded by Ijebu fishermen from Ijebu-Ode, a Yoruba city in the southwest of Nigeria. The fishermen were said to have come down through River Niger. The story tells that two brothers and their five sons spread out to form the various communities of Ugborodo, and thus the people of the region referred to themselves as "Ikpere ale meje," Ikpere (Ugborodo) or seven sections. The Escravos was also a key area of commerce for the Gbaramatu settlement of Oproza. In 1588, the Portuguese built settlements both at Warri and on the island of Ugborodo. Several centuries later, in the late nineteenth century, the French built a salt factory in Ugborodo (Alagoa 1969, 151–56).

Escravos is a Portuguese word meaning "slaves," and the area was one of the main conduits for the slave trade between Nigeria and the new world in the eighteenth century. Another history of the naming of the river according to the account of Pereira is that the Portuguese, the first Europeans to visit the area in the sixteenth and seventeenth centuries, named the estuary and the river Escravos as "two slaves were obtained by barter there when it was discovered" (Alagoa 1969, 151–56). In a scathing opinion piece against the name of the River Escravos, Dr. Oritsegbemi Omatete argues that the region, formerly known locally as Ugborodo after the largest and oldest village on the river, had existed long before the Europeans arrived. However, after the Portuguese dubbed the river

Escravos—slaves—the other European colonizers continued to use these term. As Omatete writes, "the title is not new nor is the sentiment. But the humiliation is excruciating and continuous. Ugborodo and its communities are being reduced to Escravos, the SLAVES [capitalization in original]." He also wrote, "the misery, the poverty, the bombed-out houses, school and hospital, the erosion of the land, finally the lost identity—Ugborodo is now Escravos, the Slaves. Even sons and daughters of Ugborodo now refer to it as Escravos! Tears formed in my eyes. I cried for Ugborodo. In another generation Ugborodo will be forgotten, replaced by Escravos."[7] Omatete further notes that even the Nigerian National Petroleum Corporation (NNPC) uses the moniker Escravos in all its reports on the activities in the Ugborodo axis. He further highlights that in the fifty years that Chevron has been active in the Ugborodo area, its company policies encouraged workers from the Ugborodo area to move to the larger towns of Warri and Sapele, ferrying employees by air or sea to their fenced off properties.[8]

As it is with Escravos so it is with Forcados, another oil rich community in the region. The area known as the village of Forcados and neighboring Burutu on the Forcados River were key slave trading centers. The Portuguese built a slave dungeon in 1475 where slaves were kept before they were exported to Europe and the Americas. The Forcados slave wharf was also the longest in Africa, built in 1472 by the Portuguese.[9] The Bight of Benin specifically was the site of extensive slave trading between the sixteenth and nineteenth centuries with the region of coastal lagoons west of the Niger Delta being dubbed the Slave Coast.[10] For over twenty years, the Forcados was the scene of trade for the Portuguese Crown who traded for slaves and cowries there. The Portuguese took an indirect approach to the Focardos, making landfall at the Benin River, due to the challenges of recognizing the Forcados River from the sea. The principal identification that was used was two particularly tall trees on the southern point, which often meant that the Ramos River was mistaken for the Forcados where ships were regularly wrecked on the shallow bar (Ryder 1965). The Portuguese regarded the Ijaw people on the southern bank of the river as warlike people, accused of cannibalism, but with whom they could trade slaves and ivory.

Ryder (1959) notes that the Dutch ousted the Portuguese from the Benin, Ijebu, and Forcados Rivers by the early 1600s but, at that time, were uninterested in buying slaves, instead preferring to trade for ivory and peppers. A Dutch merchant, de Marees, remarked that "other than the plentitude of slaves for whom the Dutch had then no use . . . in this river nothing else of any importance is found, save some blue green and black stones which are cut into beads." However, Ryder argues that, because these stones—cowries—could be found in the Benin River, it was unlikely that the Dutch ships frequently sailed the Forcados River to purchase them (Ryder 1959). The British, Dutch, Portuguese, and other Europeans turned the river into access to human commodities found in many of the villages, towns, and cities around the area. Since the river provided easy access to the Atlantic Ocean, the river became a convenient location for a port that could transport human cargoes across the Atlantic Ocean to the new world. The use of the river for this form of assemblage of humans as cargoes was to later give way to a new form of assemblage by the early twentieth century when oil was discovered in the region. The oil companies, particularly Chevron, known then as Gulf Oil, transformed the former slave port into an oil port, thereby continuing in the same tradition of extractive practices that shapes racial capitalism in Nigeria and elsewhere. As Joseph reiterated to me, "many people were shipped as slaves from our community here. Slavery ended, we thought our community will know peace but as soon as oil was discovered in our area, the little graveyard peace we experienced after slavery came to an abrupt end. Now we are at the mercy of these oyinbos (white people) who come to take our resources every day and leave us to suffer."[11] Joseph is not alone, as many other interlocutors such as Debby, James, and Dorcas corroborated his story while I was in the field collecting this data. Debby considers herself an activist, and she, in concert with many others in her community, has organized several protests in the past not just about the name but also about environmental pollution and loss of liveli-hood as a result of oil spills in the region. As Debby told me, "if I have my way, I will shut down the oil operations in this region so that we can have our life back. We all knew how devastating slavery was but how can we still be subjected to another form of slavery after one ended? Oil extraction is a form of slavery because it subjugates our land, resources, and livelihood to oppression. Can you imagine living in a community named *slaves* in this day and age? That is what Chevron, Shell, and others have turned us into, slaves who live in slave community."[12] Contextualizing Debby's analysis would involve understanding colonialism, the postcolonial state, corporate allies, and how these three are intercon-nected in ways that places land, resources, and people at the disposal of extractive prac-tices. Slavery produced a system that turns humans into commodities, a system that got replaced with a form of colonial project that also turns communities into sites of extraction where all lands, resources, and people were considered properties and subjects of the Crown. It is this particular practice of seeing Black people, land, and resources as dispos-ables that continues in the postcolonial state. As the next section shows, this form of ex-tractive practice where all resources were/are considered properties of the Crown and state is entrenched in a colonial legal system that is carried forward into the postcolonial state. A legal system crafted by white males who were the major beneficiaries of the re-sources is at the heart of how white supremacy is illustrative of a form of dominance that constructs oil enclaves as enclaves of domination. This form of white supremacy, as I show in the next section, uses the instrumentality of the law to institutionalize a process of capture that turns people, land, and other natural resources into properties of the Crown during the colonial and postcolonial period.

Replacing the Crown with the State

At the end of the horrendous transatlantic slave trade that saw many Black people shipped from the coast of Nigeria to the new world, a new scramble for natural resources by European powers in Africa had emerged. In the early 1900s, a German company named Nigerian Bitumen Corporations, registered as a British company and listed in the West African section of the London Stock Exchange, had started initial oil exploration in the Araromi area of Okitipupa in the southwest part of Nigeria. This exploration was later followed by that of the Anglo-Dutch company, Shell D'Archy, a British oil prospecting company that later became Shell Petroleum Company of Nigeria (Adunbi 2015; Steyn 2009). With the prospect of striking oil imminent, the British government enacted laws that transferred all land and other natural resources to the Crown. Some of these laws included the Nigeria Oils Minerals Ordinance of 1907, 1914, 1925, and 1946. For example, Section 6(1)(a) of the 1914 ordinance stipulated that, "No lease or license shall be granted except to a British subject or to a British company registered in Great Britain or in a British colony having its principal place of business within Her Majesty's dominion, the Chairman and the Managing Director (if any) and the majority of the other directors of which are British subjects" (Ayodele-akaakar 2001, 2). Reference to British subjects in this ordinance did not include Nigerians whose land and resources had been taken by the Crown without consultation. The debate over the passage of the ordinance at the British House of Lords on May 15, 1945, is a testament to how the British saw the land, resources, and the people.[13] The British House of Lords, an arm of the British parliament constituted overwhelmingly by white males, made several references to the "natives who are inferior" while advocating for total control by the Crown of the land and other natural resources. The debate focused on how much private ownership should be allowed to control mineral resources in the colony. What is clear from the ordinance is the establishment of a practice that transfers the wealth of communities in Nigeria to the Crown. The ordinance was to later be amended in 1925 and 1946. The 1946 ordinance is incisive because section 3(1) stipulates that, "The entire property in and control of all minerals, and mineral oil in, under or upon any lands in Nigeria, and of all rivers, streams and water courses throughout Nigeria is and shall be vested in the Crown" (Ayodele-akaakar 2001, 4). While the 1914 ordinance barred non-British from mining and engaging in minerals exploration because the British were, at this time, contending with possible incursion into the territory from other European powers, the 1945 ordinance placed control and ownership of minerals, land, rivers, streams, and water in the Crown. What this ordinance did was to place absolute control of the livelihoods and people of the entire territory known as Nigeria and more specifically the people of the Niger Delta with the Crown. People whose life and livelihoods depended on water, land, and the resources were forced to become properties of the Crown. Herein lies the beginning of the entrenchment of a new form of racial capitalism in Nigeria—a form of racial capitalism that is constructed on the planks of slavery and colonialism.

In the aftermath of independence, the new government sought to foster development in a country that had been intentionally underdeveloped for so long. However, their new vision of development "was born into limitations of the old one, the colonial version of development" (Cooper 2002, 156). Under British colonialism, institutions and industrialization were the hubs of the colonial administration. Little attention was paid to the well-being and development of the colonies. Instead, those areas became the sources of raw materials for the colonial state. The colonial economy favored unprocessed commodities, which have little added economic value to the colonies. As the Nigeria Oil Minerals Ordinance of 1945 shows, Britain forced Nigeria to open itself up completely to foreign exploitation. Thus, when independence arrived, the Nigerian government should have turned inward, focusing on building their own domestic economy and infrastructure. Unfortunately, this did not happen.

With the discovery of oil in commercial quantities in 1956 and its eventual shipment into the international market in 1958, Nigeria, once again as it was during the era of slavery, became an attractive bride for the international commodity market dominated by racial capitalism. Oil was to be the catalyst of Nigerian economic growth, fostering development around the country. However, it quickly became a source of conflict, subjugation, and oppression especially for the communities where the resources were located. Nothing illustrates this better than what Johbull, who considers himself a community organizer in the Niger Delta, told me during my personal communication with him. As he says, "the Delta communities have been subjugated several times in their history, beginning with slavery and then colonialism to what we have now which we consider to be another form of colonialism."[14] Johbull believes that the subjugation of his community to different practices that take away its resources makes himself and other members of his community disposable properties. Being disposable here is anchored on the notion that lack of access to livelihood practices is tantamount to humans being seen as bodies that can be disposed of. Following the same path as the colonial administration that preceded it, the postcolonial state quickly enacted its own oil minerals law, which mirrors the colonial law. The 1969 Petroleum Act, just like the 1945 ordinance, invested ownership and control of minerals in the state and even went ahead to define land in Section 1 as including any land covered by water, which extends as far as Nigeria's continental shelf (Adunbi 2015). What the 1969 Act effectively did was to replace the Crown with the state while the major players, white Euro-American oil executives, remained the same. In this sense, the Nigerian state, at independence, basically transformed to an administrative organ of multinational oil corporations, controlled by white males with subjugated communities at the receiving end of the consequences of transfer of resources to these powerful forces. Some of the most important players include Chevron, Shell, ExxonMobil, and Agip (now known as Eni).

No community exemplifies this subjugation more than Ugborodo, whose name was changed to Escravos—slaves—by Portuguese slave traders. The same name was adopted by Chevron, an American oil corporation, for its major oil terminal in the Niger Delta. The Chevron oil terminal in Ugborodo is fenced around with what looks like electrified inner barbed wires. The entire premises are patrolled by Nigerian military personnel who are mostly drawn from the military Joint Task Force. The oil terminal functions as a state within a state with all of its own disciplinary apparatuses. Today, the oil terminal is a symbol of isolation and subjugation. A symbol of isolation because the entire Ugborodo community who owns the land and rivers on which the oil terminal is located are completely isolated from it. It is a symbol of subjugation because the premises are a stark reminder of how sites such as this served as slave depots during the era of the transatlantic slave trade. As many in the community told me, some of the employment opportunities available to community members today include clearing of overgrown grasses in and around the premises. As Jacob, one of the youths in Ugborodo who works as a grass cutter at the Chevron oil terminal narrated, "clearing grass on a land that belongs to you but have been taking away by foreigners is like being a slave in your own land. You wake up every morning looking at the well-manicured premises of Chevron a few distance from across the shacks that serves as housing to you and members of your community. As you prepare for breakfast before going to work as grass cutter, the thought that comes to your mind is your own subjugation at the hands of foreigners with the connivance of your own government. You then think about how Chevron started in your area in the early 1960s with all the promises they made to the community about development and the conclusion you come to is that, now you have been enslaved again by these white people."[15] To Jacob, being enslaved again connotes denial of access to livelihood practices, subjugation to a polluted atmosphere on a daily basis, and the trauma of having to see the entire community under military patrol. All of these symbolize a form of power that reduces Black people into mere disposable commodities, just like the oil that is extracted both onshore and offshore in the community.

Thus, Ugborodo and other communities face the consequences of a postcolonial Nigerian state, which now plays the role of a collaborator and an exploiter, a position that was once occupied by the Portuguese, British, and other European countries. Hence, we see a form of what Suberu (2013) says: "prebendalism . . . has involved the systematic use of official state resources (budgets, appointments, licenses, permits, etc.) for the private benefits of the office holders and their political or communal clienteles" (80).[16] The Nigerian state and its corporate allies—mostly MNCs dominated by white Americans and Europeans—exploits oil in the Niger Delta while the region remains one of the poorest in the country despite generating the majority of the country's revenue (Omotola 2009, 42).

The question then becomes, how did the new extractive practices by MNCs in sites such as Nigeria amplify a form of racial capitalism that is detrimental to the people of the Niger Delta in particular and Nigeria as a whole? The answer lies in the form of relationship developed between the Nigerian state and the MNCs on the one hand and that of the MNCs with communities where the oil is extracted on the other.

Oil Communities of Extraction and Racial Capitalism

In most literature, racial capitalism interrogates how racialism and capitalism are mutually constituted. Scholars point to Marx's examination of slavery as a mode of accumulation prior to the emergence of modern capitalism to re-term what he called "primitive accumulation" as racial capitalism and thus stressed the integral role that expropriation plays in shaping economic growth in capitalist systems. The idea of racial capitalism thus emerged as a way of grappling with the role of violence in the production of capital (Ralph and Singhal 2019; Rodney 2018; Loperena 2017, 2016). Many of the scholars who theorized racial capitalism follow in the footsteps of Cedric Robinson. Melamed (2015), for example, writes, "the development, organization, and expansion of capitalist society pursued essentially racial directions, so too did social ideology. As a material force . . . racialism would inevitably permeate the social structures emergent from capitalism. I have used the term 'racial capitalism' to refer . . . to the subsequent structure as historical agency" (2). As Ralph and Singhal (2019) argue, to Robinson, Marx only discusses race in passing in his critique of capitalism, with Robinson arguing that plantation economies were either irrelevant or incidental to Marx's critiques. Thus, if race is central to capitalism and Marx's accounting of race is inadequate, then the term *racial capitalism* would make up for these deficits.

Therefore, critical understandings of racial capitalism, which proceed from the recognition that racialization and capitalism are never completely separable from the other, looks to understand the "complex recursivity between material and epistemic forms of racialized violence, which are executed in and by core capitalist states with seemingly infinite creativity" (Melamed 2015, 77). To complicate this form of racial capitalism, Melamed (2015) builds on Harvey's "state-finance nexus" to advance the idea of a "state-finance-racial violence nexus" whereby the confluence of political/economic governance becomes inseparable from racial violence, which enables ongoing accumulation through dispossession by using race as a way to legitimate state violence in the interest of the financial asset-owning classes that would otherwise appear to violate social rationality. Moreover, as Melamed (2015) shows, while accumulation under capitalism entails the expropriation of labor, land, and resources, we must move to a new way of thinking about capital as a system of expropriating violence on collective life as a whole. This expropriating violence, as I have shown in this chapter, is ingrained in a form of racial capitalism that is anchored on the tripod of slavery, colonialism, and a postcolonial state that borrows heavily from the use of violence through the methods of colonialism in ways that resonate with what Mamdani (1996) calls democratic despotism. Intricate to racial capitalism is how it shaped the subjugation and turning of Black people and their resources into commodities, first through slavery and later through colonialism where both contributed in no small measure to the development of the economy of the Global North (Inikori 2020; Rodney 2018; Magubane 1979). With the end of slavery and the emergence of oil as a system of energy practice, racial capitalism that shapes oil exploration in colonial and postcolonial Nigeria is entrenched in racial prejudice against the people who inhabit enclaves where oil resources are located. In order for the oil enclaves to maximize their extractive practices, social separateness becomes an important element in its operative mechanism. Thus, following Gilmore (2002), who argues that racial capitalism is a technology of antirelationality (a technology for reducing collective life to the relations that sustain neoliberal democratic capitalism), I see the embeddedness of oil extraction in racial capitalism as an epitome of what Gilmore calls a base algorithm for capitalism that only exists according to its capacity to control. To control is to develop technologies of separateness that dichotomize extractive enclaves into areas that are usable and unusable (Adunbi 2022; Ferguson 2011). In the case of Nigeria, the Niger Delta region, home to many oil enclaves, falls into the category of usable and unusable. Usable areas are those demarcated for extractive purposes such that they host oil pipelines, flow stations, wells, and other apparatuses of oil infrastructure both onshore and offshore. Unusable areas are those where community members whose land and sources of livelihood are daily devastated by oil exploration through pollution. The life of those who live in the unusable areas, to borrow Agamben's word, becomes banal. Here lies the ecologies of abolition that produce new technologies of extraction that don't enslave in the physical sense but engage in practices that metaphorically enslave those in extraction's path.

As I described in *Enclaves of Exception* (2022), those who live in extractive enclaves suffer a form of condemnation to the social death of the environment. The environment suffers from what Heyman and Ybarra (2012) call abolition ecology, taking a page from DuBois's idea of abolition democracy, which viewed the revolution as more than just the inclusion of free Blacks into existing social structures but a transformation of those social structures through abolition ecologies that examine the role of white supremacy in the creation of uneven social power relations. Abolition ecology (Heynen and Ybarra 2021) builds on Gilmore's (2017) abolition geography to enrich the logics of political ecology and environmental justice to demonstrate how "radical consciousness in action resolves into liberated lifeways" (Gilmore 2017, 227–28). Heynen (2018) defines the goal of abolition ecology as to recognize the deeper, racialized ways that nature has always been unevenly socially produced through relations of empire, settler colonialism, and racial capitalism to understand the ways that reciprocal land relations are often synonymous with liberation struggles. This chapter builds on this notion of abolition ecology to think through how oil extraction exposes capitalism as a racializing form that dispossess, pollutes, and displaces populations to give way to profit maximization.

While some scholars of racial capitalism are specifically interested in the role of slavery in relation to capitalism (Baptist 2014; Johnson 2013; Morgan 2018), others employ the term to explain moments when capitalism deploys particular strategies for extraction and accumulation that are based on racial hierarchies (Bhattacharyya 2018; Jenkins 2018; Leon 2013; Magubane 1979). Baptist (2014), among others, highlights the important relationship between coercion and productivity in capital accumulation. Ralph and Singhal (2019), for example, draw on the work of Orlando Patterson to outline some of the limits of "racial capitalism" as a theoretical project. First, they argue that the term "racial capitalism" rarely explains what is meant by the terms "race" or "capitalism." Further, they argue that many scholars who engage with the idea of racial capitalism treat Black subjectivity as a debilitated condition, a by-product of the transatlantic slave trade and derived from an African American exceptionalism that treats slavery as a form of abject status particular to capitalism without providing adequate theoretical justification or historical explanation (Leary 2005; Wilderson 2015). Ralph and Singhal (2019) argued that scholarship around racial capitalism tends to focus on the Mississippi Valley during the height of cotton production, which overlooks how enslaved people cultivate expertise with implications for how we understand factors like race, gender, sexuality, age, and ability. They further argue that theorists of racial capitalism ignore the work of Orlando Patterson, in particular his theory of the "social death" within slavery. Ralph and Singhal thus build on Patterson's insights about the forms of "human suffering and brutalization" that define political and economic relationships to explore the role of war in the production of capital. In contrast to Robinson, Patterson (2018) combines a Marxist critique of political economy with an analysis of how this political economy creates social difference. In his analysis, Patterson (2018) illustrates how slavery can be understood as a "relation of domination" and that violence creates a platform for such domination to manifest. Patterson (2018) reminds us that, "capital does not exist as capital, because autonomous wealth as such can only exist on the basis of direct forced labor, slavery, or indirect forced labor, wage labor. Wealth confronts direct forced labor not as capital, but rather as a relation of domination" (2). Patterson's analysis resonates with the particular history of the Niger Delta region of Nigeria where transition from one form of capital domination has consistently being replaced by another. The first capital accumulation in the region was that of violent capture and sale of humans into slavery. This form of cruel and inhuman commodification of the body were to later transition to indirect forced labor where land was tilled for the purposes of producing raw materials for the newly industrialized Europe and North America. This particular transition resulted in many years of colonialism not only in Nigeria but the entire African continent with the exception of Ethiopia. The final phase of this transition coincided with an important energy transition that occurred in North America in the late eighteenth century—transition from coal as a form of energy to oil as a reliable and cheaper energy source (Mitchell 2013). The outcome of the last transition has been the domination, through violent means, of the lives, livelihood, and environment of the entire region by a form of racial capitalism that devolves into plundering the resources of one landscape for the general use of landscapes farther from where the resources are located (Adunbi 2015; Nader 2015; Mattei and Nader 2008; Mitchell 2013).

Thus, Nigeria and the extractive practices in the Niger Delta epitomize a form of racial capitalism that dispossesses, accumulates, subjugates, and transfers the wealth of one race to the other. Hence, racial capitalism in the extractive enclaves of Nigeria resonates with what Leong (2013) defines as the process of deriving social and economic value from the racial identity of another person. In the case of the Niger Delta, it is the natural resource wealth of the region that defines its identity, such that, to borrow Leong's (2013) words, a form of racial capitalism that has encouraged white individuals and predominantly white institutions to derive value from nonwhite racial identities such as in the Niger Delta. The people of the Niger Delta, rather than benefit from the oil resources they claim to own, have been at the mercy of corporations that put profit before people in ways that fashion Black people and their natural resources as disposable. This is why Pulido writes that, "this disposability allows both capital and the state to pursue policies and practices that are catastrophic to the place and its many life forms because much of the cost is borne by 'surplus: people and places'" (2016, 8). The Nigerian state and its corporate partners—multinational oil corporations—engage in extractive practices that make the Niger Delta landscape and the people that inhabit it recipients of dispossession, pollution, and disposability.

Notes

1. www.facebook.com/109595267376363/posts/report-sectionescravos-a-demeaning-identity-in-the-niger-delta-penglobalthe-word/138662427802980/.

2. www.britannica.com/place/Escravos-River.

3. To protect the identity of my interlocutors, I am using a pseudonym for all those that I interviewed while I was in the region.

4. https://guardian.ng/features/culture/ugborodo-is-not-escravos/.

5. Personal communication with some of the elders of the community, September 2021.

6. "Escravos Gas-to-Liquids Project, Niger Delta, Nigeria." Hydrocarbons Technology. SPG Media Limited. Retrieved January 6, 2021.

7. https://guardian.ng/features/culture/ugborodo-is-not-escravos/.

8. www.waado.org/environment/petrolpolution/Ugborodo_Omatete.htm.

9. www.britannica.com/place/Bight-of-Benin.

10. www.latimes.com/archives/la-xpm-1992-01-12-mn-215-story.html.

11. Interview conducted in June 2019.

12. Interview conducted in June 2019.

13. See, for example, Mines in the British Colony, *HL Deb 15 May 1945 vol 136 cc184-219*. https://api.parliament.uk/historic-hansard/lords/1945/may/15/mines-in-british-colonies. Accessed December 10, 2021.

14. Personal communication, September 15, 2021.

15. Interview conducted in Warri, June 2018.

16.

References

Adunbi, Omolade. 2011. "Oil and the Production of Competing Subjectivities in Nigeria: 'Platforms of Possibilities' and 'Pipelines of Conflict.'" *African Studies Review* 54, no. 3: 101–20.

——. 2015. *Oil Wealth and Insurgency in Nigeria*. Bloomington: Indiana University Press.

——. 2022. *Enclaves of Exception: Special Economic Zones and Extractive Practices in Nigeria*. Bloomington: Indiana University Press.

Alagoa, E. J. 1969. "Oproza and Early Trade on the Escravos: A Note on the Interpretation of the Oral Tradition of a Small Group." *Journal of the Historical Society of Nigeria*: 151–56.

Al-Bulushi, Y. 2020. "Thinking Racial Capitalism and Black Radicalism from Africa: An Intellectual Geography of Cedric Robinson's World-System." *Geoforum* 132: 252–62.

Anghie, A. 2006. "The Evolution of International Law: Colonial and Postcolonial Realities." *Third World Quarterly* 27, no. 5: 739–53.

Arvin, M., E. Tuck, and A. J. F. Morrill. 2013. "Decolonizing Feminism: Challenging Connections between Settler Colonialism and Heteropatriarchy." *Feminist Formations* 25, no. 1: 8–34.

Ayodele-Akaakar, F. O. 2001. "Appraising the Oil and Gas Laws: A Search for Enduring Legislation for the Niger Delta Region. *Journal of Sustainable Development in Africa* 3: 1–23.

Baptist, E. E. 2016. *The Half Has Never Been Told: Slavery and the Making of American Capitalism*. New York: Basic Books.

Bhandar, B. 2018. *Colonial Lives of Property*. Durham, NC: Duke University Press.

Bhattacharyya, G. 2018. *Rethinking Racial Capitalism: Questions of Reproduction and Survival*. Lanham, MD: Rowman and Littlefield.

Bledsoe, A., T. McCreary, and W. Wright. 2019. "Theorizing Diverse Economies in the Context of Racial Capitalism." *Geoforum* 132: 281–90.

Coombes, B., J. T. Johnson, and R. Howitt. 2013. "Indigenous Geographies II: The Aspirational Spaces in Postcolonial Politics—Reconciliation, Belonging, and Social Provision." *Progress in Human Geography* 37, no. 5: 691–700.

Cooper, Frederick. 2002. *Africa since 1940*. Cambridge: Cambridge University Press.

Coulthard, Glen Sean. 2014. *Red Skin, White Masks: Rejecting the Colonial Politics of Recognition*. Minneapolis: University of Minnesota Press.

Daigle, M. 2016. "Awawanenitakik: The Spatial Politics of Recognition and Relational Geographies of Indigenous Self-Determination." *Canadian Geographies/Géographies canadiennes* 60, no. 2: 259–69.

Eichen, J. 2020. "Cheapness and (Labor-)Power: The Role of Early Modern Brazilian Sugar Plantations in the Racializing Capitalocene." *Environment Planning D: Society and Space* 38, no. 1: 35–52.

Ferreira, P. 2021. "Racial Capitalism and Epistemic Injustice: Blindspots in the Theory and Practice of Solidarity Economy in Brazil." *Geoforum* 132: 229–37.

Fluri, J. L., A. Hickcox, S. Frydenlund, and R. Zackary. 2020. "Accessing Racial Privilege through Property: Geographies of Racial Capitalism." *Geoforum* 132: 238–46.

Gilmore, R. W. 2018. "Abolition Geography and the Problem of Innocence." *Tabula Rasa* 28: 57–77.

Gonzalez, C. 2021. "Racial Capitalism, Climate Justice, and Climate Displacement." *SSRN* 11, no. 1: 108–47.

Grosfoguel, R. 2006. "The Implications of Epistemic Otherness in the Redefinition of Global Capitalism." *Multitudes* 3: 51–74.

———. 2016. "What Is Racism?" *Journal of World-Systems Research* 22, no. 1: 9–15.

Grosfoguel, R., L. Oso, and A. Christou. 2015. "'Racism,' Intersectionality, and Migration Studies: Framing Some Theoretical Reflections." *Identities* 22, no. 6: 635–52.

Haley, S. 2016. *No Mercy Here: Gender, Punishment, and the Making of Jim Crow Modernity*: Chapel Hill: University of North Carolina Press.

Heynen, N. 2018. "Toward an Abolition Ecology." *Abolition: A Journal of Insurgent Politics* 1: 240–47.

Heynen, N., and M. Ybarra. 2021. "On Abolition Ecologies and Making 'Freedom as a Place.'" *Antipode* 53, no. 1: 21–35.

Hunt, S. E. 2014. "Witnessing the Colonialscape: Lighting the Intimate Fires of Indigenous Legal Pluralism." PhD diss., Simon Fraser University.

Inikori, J. E. 2020. "Atlantic Slavery and the Rise of the Capitalist Global Economy." *Current Anthropology* 61 (S22): S159–S171.

Jenkins, D., and J. Leroy. 2021. Introduction to "The Old History of Capitalism." In *Histories of Racial Capitalism*, 1–26. New York: Columbia University Press.

Johnson, W. 2013. *River of Dark Dreams*. Cambridge, MA: Harvard University Press.

———. 2018. "To Remake the World: Slavery, Racial Capitalism, and Justice." *Boston Review* 20.

Kelley, R. 2017. "What Did Cedric Robinson Mean by Racial Capitalism?" *Boston Review* 12.

King, J. E. 2015. *Dysconscious Racism, Afrocentric Praxis, and Education for Human Freedom: Through the Years I Keep on Toiling; The Selected Works of Joyce E. King*. New York: Routledge.

Leary, J. D. 2005. *Post Traumatic Slave Syndrome: America's Legacy of Enduring Injury and Healing*. Milwaukie, OR: Uptone Press.

Leong, Nancy. 2013. "Racial Capitalism." *Harvard Law Review* 126, no. 8: 2151–226.

Lewis, J. S.2020. "Subject to Labor: Racial Capitalism and Ontology in the Post-Emancipation Caribbean." *Geoforum* 132: 247–51.

Liebman, A., K. Rhiney, and R. Wallace. 2020. "To Die a Thousand Deaths: COVID-19, Racial Capitalism, and Anti-Black Violence." *Human Geography* 13, no. 3: 331–35.

Lipsitz, G. 2007. "The Racialization of Space and the Spatialization of Race: Theorizing the Hidden Architecture of Landscape." *Landscape Journal* 26, no. 1: 10–23.

Loperena, C. A. 2016. "Conservation by Racialized Dispossession: The Making of an Eco-Destination on Honduras's North Coast." *Geoforum* 69: 184–93.

———. 2017. "Honduras Is Open for Business: Extractivist Tourism as Sustainable Development in the Wake of Disaster?" *Journal of Sustainable Tourism* 25, no. 5: 618–33.

Lowe, L. 2015. *The Intimacies of Four Continents*: Durham, NC: Duke University Press.

Luke, N., and N. Heynen. 2020. "Community Solar as Energy Reparations: Abolishing Petro-Racial Capitalism in New Orleans." *American Quarterly* 72, no. 3: 603–25.

Magubane, Bernard M. 1979. *The Political Economy of Race and Class in South Africa*. New York: Monthly Review Press.

Mamdani, Mahmood. 1996. *Citizens and Subjects: Contemporary Africa and the Legacy of Late Colonialism*. Princeton, NJ: Princeton University Press.

Marx, K. 1992. *Capital*. Vol. 3. London: Penguin UK.

Mattei, U., and L. Nader. 2008. *Plunder: When the Rule of Law Is Illegal*. Malden, MA: Blackwell.

McClintock, N. 2018. "Urban Agriculture, Racial Capitalism, and Resistance in the Settler-Colonial City." *Geography Compass* 12, no. 6: e12373.

McCreary, T., and R. Milligan. 2021. "The Limits of Liberal Recognition: Racial Capitalism, Settler Colonialism, and Environmental Governance in Vancouver and Atlanta." *Antipode* 53, no. 3: 724–44.

McIntyre, M., and H. Nast. 2011. "Bio (Necro)Polis: Marx, Surplus Populations, and the Spatial Dialectics of Reproduction and 'Race.'" *Antipode* 43, no. 5: 1465–88.

McKittrick, K. 2011. "On Plantations, Prisons, and a Black Sense of Place." *Social and Cultural Geography* 12, no. 8: 947–63.

Melamed, J. 2015. "Racial Capitalism." *Critical Ethnic Studies* 1, no. 1: 76–85.

Mitchell, T. 2013. *Carbon Democracy: Political Power in the Age of Oil*. First paperback ed. London: Verso.

Moore, D. 2015. "Conflict and After: Primitive Accumulation, Hegemonic Formation, and Democratic Deepening." *Stability: International Journal of Security and Development* 4, no. 1.

Morgan, J. 2018. "Partus sequitur ventrem: Law, Race, and Reproduction in Colonial Slavery." *Small Axe: A Caribbean Journal of Criticism* 22, no. 1: 1–17.

Nader, L., ed. 2015. *What the Rest Think of the West: Since 600 AD*. Oakland: University of California Press.

Nash, A. 2019. "The Moment of Western Marxism in South Africa." In *Rethinking the Labour Movement in the "'New South Africa,"* 96–110. New York: Routledge.

Nixon, R. 2011. *Slow Violence and the Environmentalism of the Poor*. Cambridge, MA: Harvard University Press.

Okonta, Ike, and Douglas Oronto. 2001. *Where Vultures Feast: 40 Years of Shell in the Niger Delta*. San Francisco: Sierra Club Books; Ibadan, Nigeria: Kraft Books.

Omotola, J. Shola. 2009. "'Liberation Movements' and Rising Violence in the Niger Delta: The New Contentious Site of Oil and Environmental Politics." *Studies in Conflict and Terrorism* 33, no. 1: 42.

Patterson, O. 2018. *Slavery and Social Death: A Comparative Study*. With a new preface. Cambridge, MA: Harvard University Press.

Price, R. 1996. *Maroon Societies: Rebel Slave Communities in the Americas*. Baltimore: Johns Hopkins University Press.

Pulido, L. 2016. "Flint, Environmental Racism, and Racial Capitalism." *Capitalization Nature Socialism* 27.

Quijano, A. 2000. "Coloniality of Power and Eurocentrism in Latin America." *International Sociology* 15, no. 2: 215–32.

Ralph, M., and M. Singhal. 2019. "Racial Capitalism." *Theory and Society* 48, no. 6: 851–81.

Robinson, C. J. 2020. *Black Marxism: The Making of the Black Radical Tradition*. Revised and updated 3rd ed. Chapel Hill: University of North Carolina Press.

Rodney, W. 2018. *How Europe Underdeveloped Africa*. New York: Verso Trade.

Roediger, D. R. 2019. *Class, Race, and Marxism*. New York: Verso.

Ryder, A. F. C. 1959. "An Early Portuguese Trading Voyage to the Forcados River." *Journal of the Historical Society of Nigeria* 1, no. 4: 294–321.

Saldanha, A. 2020. "A Date with Destiny: Racial Capitalism and the Beginnings of the Anthropocene." *Environment Planning D: Society and Space* 38, no. 1: 12–34.

Simpson, A. 2014. *Mohawk interruptus*. Durham, NC: Duke University Press.

Steyn, P. 2009. "Oil Exploration in Colonial Nigeria, c. 1903–58." *Journal of Imperial and Commonwealth History* 37, no. 2: 249–74.

Suberu, Rotimi T. 2013. "Prebendal Politics and Federal Governance in Nigeria." In *Democracy and Prebendalism in Nigeria: Critical Interpretations*, edited by W. Adebanwi and E. Obadare, 80. New York: Palgrave Macmillan.

Tuck, E., and K. W. Yang. 2012. "Decolonization Is Not a Metaphor." *Decolonization: Indigeneity, Education and Society* 1, no. 1.

Virdee, S. 2019. "Racialized Capitalism: An Account of Its Contested Origins Consolidation." *Sociological Review* 67, no. 1: 3–27.

Wallerstein, I. 2004. *World-Systems Analysis*. Durham, NC: Duke University Press.

Wilderson, F. B. 2015. *Incognegro: A Memoir of Exile and Apartheid*. Durham, NC: Duke University Press.

Wilson, R. W. 2009. *Golden Gulag: Prisons, Surplus, Crisis, and Opposition in Globalizing California*. Berkeley: University of California Press.

Wolfe, P. 2006. "Settler Colonialism and the Elimination of the Native." *Journal of Genocide Research* 8, no. 4: 387–409.

Yates, M. 2011. "The Human-as-Waste: The Labor Theory of Value and Disposability in Contemporary Capitalism." *Antipode* 43, no. 5: 1679–95.

12

Nothing Sells Like Whiteness

WHITE SUPREMACY, DIVERSITY, AND AMERICAN ADVERTISING

Shalini Shankar

ON SATURDAY, October 7, 2017, Dove skin care marketers released a short video on Facebook for body wash. The ad features three women disrobing. A Black woman removes her shirt to become a white woman, who removes her shirt to become a Brown woman, whose undressing returns us to the first of the three models. Outrage was soon followed by calls to #BoycottDove on Twitter. The company quickly pulled the ad, but not before viewers saved versions of it. What circulated widely on the internet is a loop of images of three women, each wearing a nude-colored shirt to match the model's skin tone. Another screen grab captured a Black woman transforming into a white one. Dove offered several statements in response, expressing that it had "missed the mark" and that their ad was "tone-deaf." They additionally promised that this feedback "will help in the future." These statements did little to quell the outcry, and the ad grew to become the topic of much public consternation on social and broadcast media. Critics who labeled it as racist raised questions about skin color and representation that were familiar to proponents of post-civil-rights multiculturalism. Yet, others who reacted publicly suggested that rather than regard the ad as racist, we should see it as a commitment to diversity. But what is the nature of that commitment, and to whom is it being made?[1]

The ideal of whiteness, so casually conveyed in this Dove ad, has been the tried-and-true basis for centuries of successful American advertising. Middle-class whiteness and its lifestyle preoccupations set the agenda for all other echelons of society. The supremacy of whiteness, once openly celebrated in a pre-civil-rights United States, materialized in ads for soap and hygiene products that routinely featured white bodies as paragons of purity (Burke 1996). Some aspects of racial representation changed in the post-civil-rights era, as I have illustrated in detail elsewhere (see Shankar 2012, 2013, 2015). In the US advertising industry, the most tangible evidence of this is the growth and development of multicultural advertising (Davila 2001, 2008). This small aggregate of agencies comprises a relatively tiny subset of the advertising world and creates ads aimed at Latinos, Asian Americans, and African Americans. Following the broader tenets of multiculturalism, multicultural advertising foregrounds race, ethnicity, language, and culture. Yet multicultural advertising tends to reach small audiences through nonmainstream media outlets. By contrast, most racial representation is still created by mainstream advertising or general-market advertising, which encompasses most of American advertising. Once only concerned with white consumers, American advertising has, over several decades, become far more invested in representing the increasing diversity of the United States.

In this chapter, I examine the semiotic transformation from racial and ethnic specificities of "multiculturalism" to the more open-ended term "diversity," which indexes difference in unspecific and nonthreatening ways and pulls focus back to a white mainstream. The ontological differences between multiculturalism and diversity speak to differences in understanding human subjectivity. Ontology, the study of the nature of being, draws attention to meanings of existence and reality. It organizes basic categories of being and their relations (see, for instance, Myers 2004; Wright 2010). Ontology matters for my discussion of race because if different constituents in the advertising world have conflicting ontological views of what race is, the role it plays in society, and how it organizes reality for potential consumers, that will lead to very different ideas about what ads should look like and how people will react to them.

These differences are operationalized in the register each party uses to promote their understandings of race, as well as in the form and content of the apologies that accompany controversial ads. Register, or language used in a particular speech context, can include specialized language or jargon by experts. Significant differences are evident between the registers of multicultural and diversity advertising; their ontologic conceptions of race and ethnicity either challenge or reaffirm white supremacy. By white supremacy, I am referring to the normalization of white power, wealth, social standing, and cultural norms, and the conscious or unconscious furthering of these positions of power (Delgado and Stefancic 2017; Yosso 2005). Advertising has long acted as a vehicle for white supremacy, and by analyzing diversity register, there is much to be learned about the current work done by this medium.

After contrasting the racial ontologies of diversity and multiculturalism and exploring the language each of their practitioners uses, I'll look at some recent ad campaigns that expose the contradictions of diversity while still managing to promote particular brand agendas. The brief examples I present are drawn from ethnographic research conducted on Asian American advertising between 2009 and 2014. I observed the day-to-day creative and production work of ad executives in three Asian American ad agencies and visited five general-market ad agencies. The differences between these two types of agencies were especially apparent in how they conceived of racial categories in their work. Ultimately, both categories affirm long-standing anthropological notions of cultural and linguistic relativity as espoused by Franz Boas (1911; see Baker 2021), in that advertising's emphasis on difference does not challenge white supremacy; if anything, it strengthens this ideology through particular semiotic and rhetorical strategies (Shankar 2023).

Racial Ontologics and American Advertising

Racial representation in advertising today is strongly guided by logics of diversity or multiculturalism. More than simply differing viewpoints, these two concepts have starkly different ontologies about the significance of race and how it structures social reality. I use the term *racial ontologics* because it allows me to compare two ontologies—multiculturalism and diversity—that seem similar but are actually oppositional while also addressing the semiotic processes by which these meanings are operationalized. As an analytic, racial ontologics addresses the cosmology of race as it is institutionally produced for consumption. Such ontologics expose the instrumentalist ways corporate conceptions of race are used to supplant those that reflect racial inequality wrought by capitalism, colonialism, and imperialism. The "logic" in racial ontologics is reasoned through creative strategies to depict race and ethnicity, while it is also vital to the corporate apologies that often accompany diversity advertising. In short, racial ontologics expose the disjuncture between civil-rights-based understandings of race espoused in multiculturalism and their investigation through critical race and postcolonial theory, and those borne of institutions through the moniker of "diversity" that are purported to address the same vital issues.

The racial ontologic of diversity is rooted in Enlightenment thinking, in which all humans are thought to be rational and free. Critical race and feminist theorists have amply demonstrated that this notion of liberalism and liberal society are only possible because of slavery and patriarchy, but these are omissions in diversity discourse (Collins 2002; Hesse 2014; Mills 2008). When liberalism functions correctly, the social contract ensures liberty and equality across racial and ethnic difference. This is the kind of liberalism that underpins Jürgen Habermas's (1991) version of the public sphere. The public sphere is heterogeneous, and rational discourse assures fair participation. Critics have argued that the Habermasian public sphere is utopic, and issues of access and privilege affect who is able to enter the coffee house and who is heard in public debate (Fraser 1990). Yet the racial ontologic that the public sphere is available to all who wish to partake obscures these dynamics of power and privilege. As such, it does not acknowledge humanity's social failings based on race—slavery, segregation, colonialism, state brutality and incarceration, and even day-to-day prejudice. Philosopher Charles Mills (2014) makes this point in his foundation book *The Racial Contract*. This conception of diversity, I argue, is an ideal vehicle for white supremacy in advertising.

As I noted earlier, mainstream American advertising has, for well over a century, elevated middle-class whiteness as the ultimate consumer aspiration. The audiences for these messages were white and did not feature minorities. When minorities were featured in these early ads, they were often depicted in barbaric and demeaning ways, with Blacks as slaves or caricatured servants and Asians as ratlike creatures speaking "yellow" or broken English (Shankar 2012). Post–civil rights, minorities simply had no presence in mainstream advertising, apart from being extras, sidekicks, or the butt of white humor. Much has improved, but stereotypes and offensive portrayals have continued. Recurring stereotypes from mainstream advertising index the racial ontologic of diversity at work:

they are ads for a predominantly white audience, made by people who do not see why racial caricatures like these could be offensive. Indeed, in all of my time in ad agencies, no one set out to make an intentionally racist ad.

This approach is notably different from the racial ontologic that structures multicultural advertising, which segments consumers into categories of Black, Latino, and Asian American and creates specialized messaging for them. In the 1960s and 1970s, minority marketers lobbied to advertise directly to these consumers, arguing that specificity of ethnicity and language would increase brand identification among minority consumers otherwise bombarded with images of whiteness. Their work focuses on translation, "transcreation," and ways to maintain brand identity alongside racial specificity. With the general market largely ignoring nonwhite America, these entrepreneurs saw a great untapped market and approached it with varying degrees of integrity and thoughtfulness (Chin 2001; Davila 2008, 2012). Elsewhere I have written of the creation of aspirational Asian American stereotypes that were ethnically and linguistically specific but nonetheless elitist regarding class mobility and social integration (Shankar 2015). In all these cases, multicultural advertising lacks access to mainstream media platforms that target a general viewership. Even at its best, multicultural advertising does little to challenge white supremacy as much as offer alternative visions of difference to culturally and linguistically marginalized consumers.

Perhaps a more pressing concern is that even as multicultural advertising continues to reach consumers in this way, multiculturalism itself is over. It has been dismantled by "free speech" mongers who rail against the so-called politically correct speech register. Alongside the takedown of multiculturalism's verbal hygiene comes the virulent backlash against affirmative action. Diversity emerged as a corrective to the excesses of civil rights and multiculturalism and a reinstatement of white liberalism's core beliefs. It is multiculturalism 2.0. While multiculturalism celebrates heritage languages and cultures but offers little institutional support, diversity work champions difference as a strength in capitalist and institutional logics. It is future-looking, unwilling to get mired in a complicated past and highly attuned to where the United States is going. Diversity is often paired with "inclusion," but without any mention of the power imbalances and racial inequality that underpin exclusion (see Ahmed 2012; Ferdman 2017).

Diversity has only grown in importance and power after the results of the 2010 Census created a turning point for the mainstream ad world to pay more attention to minorities. The emphasis on diversity has elicited intensive backlash during the Trump presidency, culminating in the takeover of the US Capitol on January 6, 2021. While such acts are a reminder that any emphasis on minoritized individuals is a threat to white supremacy, they cannot disrupt the shifting demographic reality of the country. Early results from the 2020 Census confirm the increasing nonwhite population in the United States and add credence to the prediction that America will be a majority-minority nation by 2042. Such shifts lend strength and momentum to the racial ontologic of diversity, which aims to portray nonwhiteness in ways most palatable to white people. Ad executives reimagine and objectify minoritized bodies and speakers by centering whiteness and surrounding it with its opposite. This can take the form of token minorities, including those that epitomize "ethnic

ambiguity," meaning they are represented devoid of any racial, cultural, or linguistic specificity. Such differences are unimportant because only the difference from whiteness
matters here. Any representation of nonwhiteness indexes diversity.

Diversity is visibly represented in the infrastructure of many large agencies. Whenever
I contacted agencies requesting to observe their everyday work for my research project,
I was directed to the individuals who "handle" diversity. Often, but not always, they are
minority individuals who did the semiotic work of repackaging racial and ethnic difference in institutionally relevant ways for white audiences. Units formed to examine
"Culture" and undertake "Cultural Discoveries," for instance, offer their services as correc-
tives for what the rest of their agency has failed to do: acknowledge that mainstream,
general-market agencies still only see white America as its target audience. "Culture" is not
simply the opposite of whiteness, but rather, a call for unity across disparate racial categories once created for specialized consumer identification. A closer look at the semiotic
modalities through which this work happens will shed light on how this still occurs.

Diversity Register in American Advertising Production

The ontological distinction between multiculturalism and diversity manifests either as race
being a marked category of social and linguistic representation or race being an unmarked
category in which it is one of many social variables in a civil society. This split is evidenced
in the speech registers used by multicultural and diversity proponents, as well as in the ads
that feature race to construct brand. Linguistic anthropologist Bonnie Urciuoli (2009),
in her writing about higher-education settings, demonstrates how social differences are
managed through specific register items and are used to further a diversity agenda. Multicultural advertising has developed jargon that showcases specificities of language and culture, which I have analyzed in detail elsewhere (Shankar 2012). They make ads for regional
media in-language and in-culture, aiming to heighten, rather than downplay, cultural specificities (Shankar 2013; see also Cavanaugh and Shankar 2014). In contrast, diversity advertising uses "culture" to indicate the nonwhite population of the United States, but it may
also include other niche populations, such as LGBTQ or people with disabilities. Diversity
is also used to signal the global on a worldwide scale. Culture is preferable to dividing
people into Black, Latino, and Asian American "silos," meaning that these categories un-
naturally divide people rather than allowing brands to reach people across differences.

In the ad agencies I visited, terms from a diversity register were affectively performed
in a cheerful, positive manner. In a conversation with two white female ad executives
(whom I will call Lisa and Stephanie) in their Madison Avenue offices in 2013, the executives explained the racial ontologics of diversity advertising. Taking an expert stance, they
began by acknowledging that many of their advertising colleagues were concerned about
diversity, but many get it wrong because they are stuck in a multicultural past. As I set up
my audio recorder, Stephanie offhandedly remarked, "My niece is in a spot[2] for Ogilvy and
says it looks like the rainbow coalition, everyone is ethnic." Casually maligning a civil-
rights-inspired concept forwarded by the Reverend Jesse Jackson resonated well with her

colleague Lisa, who nodded sympathetically. Lisa added, "The guy from Ogilvy was saying that they need to do something different, but it's going to be messy for a while." Both women then trained their gaze on me, smilingly. Lisa began by telling me her origin story on what race means: "People used to identify with very specific groups. Now peoples' identities are a little more complicated." In a calm, soothing voice, she continued that people share more similarities than differences and suggested that an identity steeped in ethnicity was a relic of an older generation. Noting the change between the earlier era of multiculturalism and our current moment, she elaborated that consumers and ad executives alike have been slow to adopt a diversity approach: "They feel like if they let go of a little, they'll lose a lot." This futuristic version of diversity signaled hope and promise rather than the anger and bitterness of unfulfilled civil-rights promises.

Cautioning strongly against "siloing," she remarked, "multicultural marketing is funny because it just, it tries to focus on the *differences* only based on culture or language, as opposed to *similarities*." Presenting a panacea to a divided society, the diversity approach could offer salvation from a backward multicultural past and deliverance into a modern present and future. To do this, Lisa explained, they would simply cast diverse talent in the form of a "diverse person" who could speak English. Aiming to connect with me as a "diverse" person, they gently reminded me, "People are in the world together and are buying the same brands." This vision of diversity entails consumers of different races finding sameness through brand identification rather than racial identification. Bringing people out of a multicultural past into a racially utopic future means supplanting multiculturalism's cultural and linguistic specificities with diversity's assurances that racial sameness is the way forward. Such sameness bolsters white supremacy by erasing myriad political economic and historical differences in America's vast nonwhite population.

Such a diversity approach confirms that mainstream advertising's core objective is to make racial and ethnic difference palatable to white consumers. As ready vehicles for white supremacy, such ads retain whiteness as the normative and normal center, around which minoritized individuals arrange themselves. By advocating for egalitarian consumer participation and the notion that all consumers are equal, the whiteness of liberalism is retained as the core of diversity, with all other difference grouped around it.

The most skillful executions of this racial ontologic exploit the elasticity of diversity by organizing racial and ethnic differences into a tableau. Consider, for instance, a 2018 Toyota ad that aired at Super Bowl LLII. In it, a rabbi, a priest, an imam, and a Buddhist monk pack into a Toyota truck, meet up with nuns at a football game, and enjoy interfaith sports fandom. "When we are free to move, anything is possible," says the voiceover of the ad. In this futuristic vision of diversity, everyone speaks American-accented English and is loyal to the American sport of football. Conflicts of settler colonialism in the Middle East and trauma created by the Muslim travel ban exist in a parallel universe from the postracial utopia offered by this pickup truck.

In a similar fashion, Coca-Cola has successfully circulated ads of this nature, wedding individuality and diversity in such concepts as "The Wonder of Us," their 2018 Super Bowl ad that acknowledged the non-gender-conforming pronoun "they." The ad showcases differences, with a voiceover in American-accented English, saying there is a Coke for each of us. We can contrast this to a Coke ad from the 2014 Super Bowl, in which the song "America the Beautiful" sung in several languages served as the backdrop of a multicultural tableau. That ad experienced major backlash from white supremacists for not following the racial ontologics of diversity, in that it acknowledged the existence of languages other than English. And rather than simply including ambiguous brown and Black people, they chose individuals from identifiable ethnic groups, like the hijab-clad woman. The ad worked favorably for Coca-Cola and was praised for its treatment of diversity, but it drew the ire of conservative viewers and potentially lost them as consumers. Few ads are able to successfully render race in this way, though many try. What is far more common are ads that push the limits of diversity in ways that incite criticism from minoritized people, which generally leads to apologies.

The apology is a key feature of diversity register, as it seems to do the ideological exposition of how an idea for an ad came to be. The apology allows for a statement of intentionality, also very important in proving that a corporation did not "intend" to be racist, even though that is how some people perceived it. If the intention of an ad was good, then an imperfect execution should be readily forgiven. This is perfectly sensible in the racial ontologic of diversity—that is, if white liberalism is an agreed-on social fact, then any offense people feel is their own shortcoming. These apologies take the form of "We are sorry that people were offended." It's a "sorry-not-sorry," as some might call it. A few more examples will further demonstrate how diversity register, including the apology, furthers the racial ontologic of diversity by keeping whiteness at its core.

Racial Ontologics of Diversity in Ads

In April 2017, Pepsi released a long-form ad featuring Kendall Jenner. In it, Jenner plays a model, which is her profession in real life. The ad features a social justice protest modeled after Black Lives Matter protests, but with only young people. We see numerous individuals of color holding signs meant to be progressive but that do not espouse any specific politics (i.e., "Join our conversation"). Jenner is compelled to join the protest when a boy beckons, and she hands her blond wig to an attendant—a Black woman who looks none too pleased with this move—and begins walking with the crowd. Another major character is an angry Muslim photographer woman in a headscarf, whose artistic frustration only abates when she can photograph Jenner handing a police officer a can of Pepsi. The entire protest march erupts in gleeful celebration when he accepts. The ad exhibits several elements of diversity register. There are many nonwhite people, most of them quite attractive. The utopic futurity of the ad is evident in the protest party, replete with a band and celebration when the cop receives Jenner's Pepsi. The ad furthers white supremacy by elevating whiteness and trivializing a profound movement that emerged in response to racially focused police brutality.

The ad immediately came under fire and Pepsi pulled it, but it took several months for the apologies to emerge. Pepsi's apology statement highlighted intentionality: "Pepsi was trying to project a global message of unity, peace and understanding. Clearly, we missed the mark and apologize. We did not intend to make light of any serious issue." The apology features key diversity register items, including "global" and "unity." The word "apologize" is used to qualify a failed creative attempt rather than the grave judgment error in commodifying Black Lives Matter to sell soda. The apology relies heavily on white liberalism and aims to elicit consumers' understanding by focusing on the *intention* of the ad, rather than the message they created.

Meme-worthy images juxtaposed stills from the ad with actual racial struggle. Some featured Dr. Martin Luther King Jr. in protest, crediting Kendall Jenner for having the dream. @BerniceKing tweeted a photo of King being arrested with the caption, "If only Daddy would have known about the power of Pepsi." @CharlesMBlow juxtaposed Jenner with Black Lives Matter protest images, most notably of Ieshia Evans from a July 2016 demonstration in Baton Rouge, Louisiana, underscoring exceptionalism of a white interaction with the police and those of Blacks. Here we can see white supremacy in the power that Kendall holds that thousands of Black Americans don't, elevating her above the law and safe from reproach in ways that bodily endanger the lives of Black people.

There are many similarities between this ad's arc and Dove's approach to diversity discussed at the start of this chapter, in which three models of different races are essentially interchangeable, their racial differences reduced to a T-shirt hue. Like many corporate apologies, Dove's missive on Facebook attempted to explain its intent: "An image we recently posted on Facebook missed the mark in representing women of color thoughtfully. We deeply regret the offense it caused." Standing by its vision of diversity, Dove apologized for the offense caused, not the ad itself. They circulated a statement about the "the diversity of real beauty" to underscore their commitment to an antiracist agenda. On this note, it is interesting to consider that Dove frequently challenges social norms in campaigns featuring "real women," partnering with Black television producers like Shonda Rhimes. Even so, some on social media were quick to point out that this was not the first time that Dove had come under fire for depicting diversity in its ads. In 2011, the brand ran a campaign promoting body wash that showed three women of different skin colors standing in a row. Copy reading "before" appeared over the woman with darker skin color while the word "after" appeared over the lighter-skinned woman. Dove responded by claiming that all three women were meant to represent the "after."

Some critics tweeted images of the 2011 and 2017 ads next to each other, underscoring that Dove had learned little since this debacle. Even one of the models in the Dove ad was blindsided. The 2017 ad's Black model, Lola Ogunyemi, wrote in *The Guardian* that she did not want to be considered a "before" image in the ad.[3] As a Nigerian woman born in London and raised in Atlanta, she was thrilled to be offered a chance to be the next face of Dove. She expressed criticism that Dove simply pulled the ad rather than stand by their casting of a darker-skinned model. In a time when diversity advertising celebrates ethnic ambiguity, brands like Dove can get away with featuring people who simply "embody" diversity. What is unambiguous is that they are not white. Vigilant consumers took Dove to task, but there is no evidence that incidents like this affect the racial ontologics that shape their approach to diversity.

A final example epitomizes the barely concealed partnership between diversity register and white supremacy. A 2011 Nivea print-ad campaign called "Re-Civilize Yourself" featured a Black man holding a version of his own face with an afro and facial hair. In this bizarre image, the man's "before" face dangles like a Halloween mask in his hand, its negative value unequivocal. Once again, the apology proffered was eventually followed by a repeat offense. Nivea's campaign from 2017 went for it again, with "White Is Purity." The public called for apologies, and clever memes emerged when none were proffered. Disturbingly, an actual white supremacist group posted on Nivea's Facebook page: "We enthusiastically support this new direction your company is taking. I'm glad we can all agree that #WhiteIsPurity."

In all three controversies concerning Pepsi, Dove, and Nivea, diversity register bridges the racial ontologics of diversity and the circulation of the ad. The apologies offered are ripe with statements of intentionality—that positive signs were conveyed in each ad but not interpreted as intended. Misunderstandings are simply topics for public debate, not rallying cries against racism and white supremacy. Corporate apologies do the semiotic work of reminding audiences that diversity may not be perfect, but that it is the way forward. With good intentions stated, if not actually demonstrated, the racial ontologics of diversity burden the consumer to find the progressive intent of the ad, however racist and distorted.

Concluding Thoughts

In the racial ontologic of diversity, race unites rather than divides, while it also remains salient for consumer identification. Nonwhiteness is conveyed through bodies that stand for idealized racial difference. Diversity renders the racial past as conflict-free but in need of updating and projects inviting, futuristic versions of race. On a solid foundation of white supremacy and white liberalism, diversity has become synonymous with an idealized heterogeneous, harmonious mainstream US population. Advertising firms thus further the language of Boasian relativity (Baker 2021; Shankar 2023) in crafting the diversity paradigm as one in which race is no longer a relevant social fact. Such a stance absolves ad executives of their attachments to white supremacist tropes and imagery while also eliding institutionalized inequality and everyday racisms.

After decades of watching multiculturalism crack the facade of whiteness in advertising, the fissures are closing, leaving multicultural racial ontologics, like multiculturalism itself, left to wither away. For ad executives whose world is primarily white and middle class, diversity discourse renders racial differences as ambiguous, interchangeable, and nonthreatening. Whiteness supremacy is neatly reinstated, like past eras when minorities were far less numerically, politically, socially, and economically significant. What is different now is that minorities are so economically significant that it does not make sense to ignore them altogether. In 2018, I received this email from a Neilson list announcing that

"Black Dollars Matter," a clear co-option of Black Lives Matter. It's subheading, "With African-Americans spending 1.2 trillion annually, brands have a lot to lose if they don't engage black consumers," it epitomized the racial ontologic of diversity and the facility with which it reinvents race for brand growth.

Notes

1. This chapter is an abridged and revised version of what first appeared as Shalini Shankar, 2020. "Nothing Sells Like Whiteness: Race, Ontology, and American Advertising." *American Anthropologist* 122, no. 1: 112–19. doi.org/10.1111/aman.13354.

2. A "spot" is advertising parlance for a television advertisement.

3. "I Am the Woman in the 'Racist Dove Ad.' I Am Not a Victim." *The Guardian*, October 10, 2017. www .theguardian.com/commentisfree/2017/oct/10/i-am-woman-racist-dove-ad-not-a-victim.

References

Ahmed, Sara. 2012. *On Being Included: Racism and Diversity in Institutional Life*. Durham, NC: Duke University Press.

Baker, Lee. 2021. "The Racist Anti-Racism of American Anthropology." *Transforming Anthropology* 29, no. 2: 127–42.

Boas, Franz. 1911. Introduction to *Handbook of American Indian Languages*, pp. 1–84. Bureau of American Ethnology Bulletin 40. Washington, DC: Government Printing Office.

Burke, Timothy. 1996. *Lifebuoy Men, Lux Women: Commodification, Consumption, and Cleanliness in Modern Zimbabwe*. Durham, NC: Duke University Press.

Cavanaugh, Jillian, and Shalini Shankar. 2014. "Producing Authenticity in Global Capitalism: Materiality, Language, and Value." *American Anthropologist* 116, no. 1: 1–14.

Collins, Patricia Hill. 2002. *Black Feminist Thought: Knowledge, Consciousness, and the Politics of Empowerment*. New York: Routledge.

Davila, Arlene. 2001. *Latinos, Inc.: The Marketing and Making of a People*. Berkeley: University of California Press.

———. 2008. *Latino Spin: Public Image and the Whitewashing of Race*. New York: New York University Press.

Delgado, Richard, and Jean Stefancic. 2017. *Critical Race Theory: An Introduction*. New York: New York University Press.

Ferdman, Bernardo M. 2017. "Paradoxes of Inclusion: Understanding and Managing the Tensions of Diversity and Multiculturalism." *Journal of Applied Behavioral Science* 53, no. 2: 235–63.

Fraser, Nancy. 1990. "Rethinking the Public Sphere: A Contribution to the Critique of Actually Existing Democracy." *Social Text* 25/26: 56–80.

Hesse, Barnor. 2014. "Escaping Liberty: Western Hegemony, Black Fugitivity." *Political Theory* 42, no. 3: 288–313.

Mills, Charles W. 2008. "Racial Liberalism." *PMLA* 123, no. 5: 1380–97.

———. 2014. *The Racial Contract*. Ithaca, NY: Cornell University Press.

Myers, Fred R. 2004. "Ontologies of the Image and Economies of Exchange." *American Ethnologist* 31, no. 1: 5–20.

Shankar, Shalini. 2012. "Creating Model Consumers: Producing Ethnicity, Race, and Class in Asian American Advertising." *American Ethnologist* 39, no. 3: 578–91.

———. 2013. "Racial Naturalization, Advertising, and Model Consumers for a New Millennium." *Journal of Asian American Studies* 16, no. 2: 159–88.

———. 2015. *Advertising Diversity: Ad Agencies and the Creation of Asian American Consumers*. Durham, NC: Duke University Press.

———. 2023. "Language and Race: Settler Colonial Consequences and Epistemic Disruptions." *Annual Review of Anthropology* 52: 381–97.

Urciuoli, Bonnie. 2009. "Talking/Not Talking about Race: The Enregisterments of Culture in Higher Education Discourses." *Journal of Linguistic Anthropology* 19, no. 1: 21–39.

Yosso, Tara J. 2005. "Whose Culture Has Capital? A Critical Race Theory Discussion of Community Cultural Wealth." *Race Ethnicity and Education* 8, no. 1: 69–91.

13

Raciontologies

RECONCEPTUALIZING RACIALIZED ENACTMENTS AND THE REPRODUCTION OF WHITE SUPREMACY

Vanessa Díaz and Jonathan Rosa

If race is only epiphenomenal, how does it continue to ground material reality?

—VISWESWARAN (1996, 73)

IN OCTOBER 2012, Vanessa Díaz was introduced to Chris Guerra by paparazzi photographer Galo Ramirez—one of the main collaborators involved in Díaz's fieldwork, which focused on race and gender in the production of celebrity media, specifically on the work of and relationships between the predominantly Latino paparazzi photographers and predominantly white women celebrity reporters who produce content for celebrity magazines.[1] Guerra was an aspiring paparazzo who had only recently begun working on a freelance basis for the same agency for which Ramirez worked. Ramirez was instructed to mentor Guerra, and Díaz photographed one of their training sessions as they waited near Heidi Klum's mansion in Pacific Palisades, an extremely wealthy neighborhood in Los Angeles. Guerra simultaneously practiced his photography using Díaz as a subject. Her photos of his training were shown during his memorial service.

Guerra was struck by multiple cars and killed on New Year's Day in 2013 as he reportedly followed a California Highway Patrol (CHP) officer's orders to return to his car after trying to photograph pop star Justin Bieber's Ferrari in Los Angeles. Guerra was twenty-nine years old. According to witness testimony and dashcam transcriptions,[2] the Ferrari was pulled over for speeding. When the passenger of the Ferrari told the officer that Guerra was videotaping the stop, the officer focused his attention on Guerra and let the car's occupants go,[3] despite having stopped them for speeding and questioning them about the scent of marijuana in the car.[4] Mainstream news outlets reported that when the officer ordered Guerra to return to his car, he did not look both ways before crossing and was therefore hit.[5] In official statements, the officer and investigator declared that Guerra's death was his own fault. The dashcam transcription tells a more complicated story. After releasing the individuals stopped in the Ferrari, the officer asked Guerra, "What the hell are you doing?" When Guerra explained that he was a photographer and a member of the press, the officer asked, "Do you have any credentials other than you just standing there?" As the officer's tone became more aggressive, Guerra exclaimed, "OK, alright! Relax!" The officer then scolded Guerra, explaining that the paparazzi should not hassle people and demanded that he return to his car, which was parked across four lanes with no nearby crosswalk. Guerra's last words were, "All right, brother." Guerra was hit by one SUV and then by a second car as he attempted to return to his vehicle in accordance with the officer's orders.[6] The officer then stopped traffic, eventually calling for help. There was no attempt to revive Guerra, despite the CHP officer's training in CPR. The dashcam later recorded the officer talking to his partner, "Dude I was just like, I just told him he couldn't stand there. Fucking idiot, man."

Despite Guerra's position as the victim in this situation, the discourse surrounding his death—from the officer who was present at the scene, to celebrities, to the public—treated him as an ignorant nuisance, and his death as a relief. Reacting to the incident, pop star Miley Cyrus posted a series of tweets in which she called the paparazzi "fools," also stating:

Hope this paparazzi/JB[7] accident brings on some changes in '13. Paparazzi are dangerous! . . . It is unfair for anyone to put this on to Justin's conscious (sic) as well! This was bound to happen! Your mom teaches u when your (sic) a child not to play in the street! The chaos that comes with the paparazzi acting like fools makes it impossible for anyone to make safe choices.

Comments from viewers of online video reports of Guerra's death echoed many of these sentiments, declaring such things as: "It's sad when people die. Paparazzi, not so much"; "Paparazzi don't count as human beings, so it's ok to laugh when one gets flattened"; "Poor Justin. I feel so bad for him. Fuck you, paparazzi"; and "More paparazzi need to die. If I see one on the road, I will swerve to hit the mother fucker."[8]

Instead of being seen as an integral part of Hollywood and broader media industries, paparazzi work is popularly derided and framed as disposable. Still, Guerra's position as a photographer on whose labor the entertainment industry relies and yet ridicules, implicates him in fraught modes of surveillance and the reproduction of hierarchies linked to this monitoring of celebrity figures. Paparazzi photography tends to focus on white, mostly women celebrities; it renders predominantly white celebrities vulnerable and worthy of empathy and humanization, while systematically erasing people of color and dehumanizing the paparazzi of color who perpetuate this system (Díaz 2020). The gendered and racialized media patterns that led to Guerra's death are intimately linked to the broader dynamics that problematically position particular victims of racial profiling and institutional racism as more grievous than others.[9]

Guerra's story highlights the disparate treatment and (im)mobilities of particular laborers within the Hollywood-industrial complex (Díaz 2020), but such realities are not unique to these laborers or this industry; rather, they are representative of institutional structures that produce dramatically disparate and highly consequential experiences based on the racialized ways various entities come to be perceived and positioned. We are interested in exploring not only the ways institutional contexts and processes such as mass media, the criminal justice system, racialized labor (trans)formations, and gentrification function as sites or vehicles for the reproduction of white supremacy, but more specifically how institutions become endowed with the capacity to act in their own right—that is, institutions as subjects, profilers, and even killers. This view of institutions as actors *in* rather than simply sites or vehicles *for* the reproduction of white supremacy represents what we call a *raciontological* perspective that attends to the central role that race plays in constituting modern subjects and objects, including forms of embodiment and broader material realities. *Raciontolologies*—the fundamentally racialized grounding of various states of being, which sheds light on complex forms of institutional racism and white supremacy—powerfully shape how entities are endowed with the capacity to engage in particular acts while also conditioning perceptions, experiences, and material groundings of reality.

Our conceptualization of raciontologies seeks to contribute to the broader anthropology of white supremacy by offering frames for rethinking the nature of institutionalized racial violence and vulnerability. In this chapter, we engage with the killings of Guerra and other highly publicized police and public vigilante killings. Since the first version of this essay was published in 2019, we have seen countless additional examples of the perilous implications of raciontological realities. In the summer of 2020, incidents of anti-Black state violence sparked unprecedented public protests and rebellions across the United States and throughout the world. The uprisings erupted after the police murder of George Floyd, the civilian murder of Ahmaud Arbery, and the state-sanctioned police killing of Breonna Taylor. During this time of uprising, additional state-sanctioned racial violence included the police killings of Latinx youth such as Sean Monterrosa and Andrés Guardado in California as well as thirteen-year-old Adam Toledo in Chicago. Many mainstream institutions responded by superficially affirming racial diversity in ways that obscure institutional racism and frame antiracism as a matter of celebrating naturally occurring racial identities, rather than fundamentally transforming historical power structures and their ongoing realities. In contrast, to understand the central role of race in constituting modern states of being, our conceptualization of *raciontologies* combines anthropological analyses of institutional racism and ontologies beyond the human. By synthesizing insights from these literatures, it becomes possible to understand institutions as actors, on the one hand, and various ontologies' fundamental anchoring in race, on the other. That is, while institutional racism has emerged as a crucial framework for conceptualizing racism as an endemic structural phenomenon and not simply a problem at the level of interpersonal bigotry or discrimination, we emphasize the ways that institutions operate not only as sites for but also actors in the reproduction of white supremacy. Relatedly, while anthropological engagements with the ontological turn have attuned ethnographic attention to human and more-than-human actors, we point to the need to reconceptualize race as a key element in constituting modern ontologies.

We examine instances of institutional racism and racial profiling drawn from ethnographic research and broader accounts to demonstrate the potential benefits and limitations of various approaches to documenting and analyzing these phenomena; we also point to examples situated in a range of institutional and interactional settings to emphasize that racism is an endemic modern antagonism rather than a problem particular to any specific institution or individual. We illustrate part of what is at stake here by pointing to the particular instance of institutional racism tied to the death of Vanessa's research collaborator, Chris Guerra. And yet, we emphasize that it is not an unusual case. In fact, it represents the kinds of daily and deadly state-sanctioned institutional racism and white supremacy fundamental to the founding and continued reproduction of the United States as a settler-colonial project.

Rethinking Institutional Racism and the "Ontological Turn"

In 1955 (2001, 42), Caribbean philosopher Aimé Césaire declares, "My turn to state an equation: colonization = thingification." Insofar as the emergence of modern racism can be conceptualized as a justification for colonialism, we must also analyze the relationship between racialization and thingification. This relationship was illustrated during the 2013 trial of George Zimmerman for the killing of Trayvon Martin, a fifteen-year-old African American boy. During his closing arguments, Mark O'Mara, Zimmerman's defense attorney, disputed the prosecution's claim that Martin was an unarmed teenager. O'Mara carried a slab of concrete into the courtroom and displayed it before the jury. He suggested that Martin was in fact armed with the sidewalk, which he allegedly used to bludgeon Zimmerman during their altercation, thereby constituting Zimmerman's use of a firearm as a legitimate form of self-defense. Zimmerman went on to be acquitted. Seemingly objective things were fundamentally and consequentially transformed in the encounter between Zimmerman and Martin, as well as the legal recontextualization thereof. Zimmerman perceived the can of juice and pack of skittles Martin carried as potential weapons or drug paraphernalia, his hooded sweatshirt as thug wear, his slight stature as threatening; meanwhile, Zimmerman's attorney argued that Martin's very presence weaponized the sidewalk. Thus, *things*, including candy, soft drinks, sweatshirts, sidewalks, cell phones, and cameras are only constituted as such when they are inhabited and animated by—that is, indexically grounded in—normative whiteness.[10] For those who perceive the world through what DuBois (1903) formulated as a racial veil that produces experiences of double consciousness, there is significant question as to whether they are experiencing the same *things* as those who are not.

Thinking back to Césaire's equation of colonization and thingification, it is crucial to reconsider the fundamental role of racial domination in constituting the modern order of *things*. In fact, we might examine the interplay between racial thingification and anthropological empiricism—how white supremacy constitutes things without being recognized as functioning in such ways. Following Kamala Visweswaran (1996, 73), we ask, "If race is only epiphenomenal, how does it continue to ground material reality?" This is not simply an important consideration for societies rooted in histories of chattel slavery and Indigenous genocide, such as the United States, but rather across a modern world that has been profoundly shaped by the global imposition of colonial distinctions and hierarchies. In her analysis of these white supremacist configurations and contestations thereof, Christina Sharpe (2016, 21) notes that anti-Blackness is a "total climate," which she formulates as "the Weather."

In *Black Skin, White Masks*, Frantz Fanon (1967, 109) conceptualizes race as a fundamentally ontological problem.[11] He writes, "I came into the world imbued with the will to find a meaning in things, my spirit filled with the desire to attain to the source of the world, and then I found that I was an object in the midst of other objects." Fanon articulates a theory of race as ontological overdetermination. Building on Fanon's thinking, racism must be understood not in terms of a conflict that can be resolved by redistributing rights and resources in prevailing political and economic orders, but rather as an ontological problem that is the foundation of modern governance and subjectivity. That is, modern governance *is* institutional racism.

In some ways, this reframing of institutional racism can be understood in relation to the move toward an anthropology of the posthuman and the study of ontological logics that differentiate human and more-than-human entities. However, in our analysis of institutionalized forms of racial profiling, we highlight the ironic avoidance of race, racism, and racialization in recent anthropological accounts of ontology that seek to examine and expand the range of entities understood to be endowed with the capacity to act. While the "ontological turn" has received a great deal of attention in anthropological literature over the last decade (De la Cadena 2015), and while studies in Indigenous contexts are often the reference point for alternative ontological realities, race has largely been absent from these analyses. In fact, one of the most central and compelling components of race is its capacity to transform particular subjects into objects—or, in the context of institutionalized modes of profiling, targets of surveillance, measurement, management, remediation, expulsion, and extermination. How might the "ontological turn" be reconceptualized through attention to the profound role of race in structuring modern ontologies?[12]

This attention to the racial dimensions of ontology is informed by Sylvia Wynter's (1994) thinking on the institutional transformation of particular racialized persons into nonpersons. In the aftermath of the Rodney King beating, the acquittal of the officers involved, and the subsequent public rebellion, Wynter analyzed the use of the category "No Human Involved" within the City of Los Angeles's criminal justice system to refer to alleged African American and Latinx gang members who were shot or killed by police. Wynter argued that the category "No Human Involved" was part of broader institutional logics that sanctioned police officers' use of chokeholds that killed multiple young Black males. At the time, police chief Darryl Gates attributed these killings to Black males' abnormal windpipes (Wynter 1994).

In 2014, New York City police officer Daniel Pantaleo used a similar chokehold to kill Eric Garner, an unarmed African American man who was selling loose cigarettes (Goodman and Wilson 2014). Video recordings of both the Rodney King beating that prompted

Wynter's inquiry and the killing of Eric Garner prompted widespread public outrage, yet none of the officers involved were convicted of criminal charges (in the case of Garner, no criminal charges were filed; in the King case, two of the officers were eventually found guilty of violating King's civil rights). The inability of these recordings to legally delegitimate police officers' actions reflects the need for a reconsideration of a racialized semiotics of visibility. As Charles Goodwin (1994, 606) notes in his analysis of the institutionalized "professional vision" through which the King recording was interpreted, "the ability to see a meaningful event is not a transparent, psychological process but instead a socially situated activity accomplished through the deployment of a range of historically constituted discursive practices." It is now customary for police officers to wear body cameras to document their actions, and yet videos of police officers assaulting and killing unarmed and compliant individuals continue to surface regularly; thus, Goodwin's insights help us to understand the limitations of these body cameras as a check on extrajudicial police violence.

These cases demonstrate how institutionalized ways of perceiving racialized persons can transform their ontologies. Rodney King was described as a "PCP-crazed giant," even though he never tested positive for consumption and was huddled in a ball on the ground throughout the beating. This is similar to officer Darren Wilson's description of Michael Brown, the unarmed African American teenager he shot and killed in Ferguson, Missouri, in August 2014. In the grand jury hearing, Wilson referred to Brown as "it," characterized him as a "demon," and said that he "felt like a five-year-old holding onto Hulk Hogan," even though he and Brown were the same height (Bonilla and Rosa 2015). Twelve-year-old Tamir Rice was illegible as a child playing with a toy gun when Cleveland police shot and killed him within two seconds of encountering him. Institutionalized perceptions of racial difference can overdetermine what kind of a thing one is and legally authorize extreme, indeed existential, measures. The sections that follow demonstrate the implications of the co-constitution of race and ontology—raciontologies—across a range of interactional and institutional contexts.

Raciontologies and Institutionalized Disposability

Analyses of institutional racism and white supremacy must grapple with the ways various institutions—even those seemingly unrelated to one another—work in tandem to reproduce formations of power. The concept of raciontologies can provide insight into this interinstitutional coordination by drawing connections among systematic, racialized perceptions and attributions of deficiency and disposability across contexts. Díaz encountered these racialized perceptions and attributions in her fieldwork with celebrity photographers, centering on Hollywood as a major cultural and institutional force that wields larger systemic power. Over the last two decades, the demographics of the Los Angeles paparazzi photographers transitioned from a labor force of predominantly white men to one of predominantly men of color—mostly Latino. In the wake of this shift, figures across Hollywood industries characterized the new paparazzi as unprofessional and dangerous.[13] This critique was often framed in explicitly racialized terms, focused on *whose* bodies were producing this media content and how that devalued the work and potential professionalism inherent in the work itself (Díaz 2014). It quickly spread into public discourse, with news articles referring to paparazzi as "untrained," "corner-cutting" "foreigners working on . . . questionable visas,"[14] and online reader comments calling them "bottom feeders"[15] and "illegals"[16] who should "be deported."[17] The unique positions these photographers occupy, demographically and professionally, within the labor chain of celebrity media production, have made them convenient, if problematic, scapegoats for the current climate of celebrity obsession in the United States.

Raciontologies and Social Death

The story about photographer Chris Guerra's death which opens this chapter illustrates how, from a raciontological perspective, we can understand the intertwined nature of various sociohistorical, individual, material, and institutional entities and processes. When institutional racism and white supremacy are enacted, it is often presupposed that these phenomena can only be produced by racist white individuals. This logic obviates institutional culpability and recenters interpersonal interaction and embodiment. In cases such as the killing of unarmed African American Florida teenager Trayvon Martin, the self-identified mixed-race Latino man who killed him—George Zimmerman—was labeled by outlets like the *New York Times* and CNN as "white Hispanic" to enhance the narrative of interpersonal racism.[18] When Philando Castile, an African American man, was killed in Minnesota by a Latino police officer, Jeronimo Yanez, numerous articles presupposing a mutual exclusivity between Blackness and Latinidad pointed to Yanez as embodying anti-Blackness among Latinxs. Indeed, anti-Blackness is endemic in Latin America and the Caribbean, and their diasporas, as it is in the United States and throughout the modern world. However, narratives focused on interpersonal, as opposed to institutional, racism prevent us from understanding cases such as the three Black officers who were involved in the killing of Freddie Gray in Baltimore. More recently, five Black officers were charged in the 2023 police murder of Tyre Nichols. Similarly complex racial politics were at play in the death of Chris Guerra. We suggest that the *institutional* position of these officers (and those functioning as ad hoc police subsidiaries, as in the case of Zimmerman), regardless of their racial identities or interpersonal prejudices, allows them to enact white supremacy as agents of the state. Thus, simply diversifying an institution such as the criminal justice system does not eliminate racism or the broader raciontological realities through which it is enacted and reproduced.

The CHP officer who policed Guerra to death was Black. Guerra is the son of a Mexican father and an African American mother. In a conversation between Díaz and Chris's mother, Vicky, during which they collectively mourned Chris's death, she did not view his treatment as influenced by his racial positioning. Focusing instead on his economic positioning, she stated, "Nobody cares about this because Chris was poor." Vicky Guerra's emphasis on class rather than race in efforts to understand her son's killing aligns with her valorization of Chris's efforts toward upward socioeconomic mobility. While race was not something that Vicky Guerra, her husband, Juan Guerra, or their son could control, they understood class as a variable, a particular circumstance that she declared Chris was trying to get himself out of. She said Chris was doing paparazzi work for the money, but "being a paparazzi wasn't going to be a full-time forever job. Eventually he wanted to go back and do his own business. He had his own landscaping business before. He wanted to maybe open up a pizza place." Vicky suggests that Chris was simply attempting to fulfill the American dream—trying to pull himself up by his paparazzi bootstraps to improve his life. In her theorization of social death and accompanying attempts to humanize those who are not seen as human, Lisa Cacho (2012) notes that tropes of the American Dream and the "pull yourself up by the bootstraps" narrative are commonly invoked in attempts to render racialized populations worthy of empathy. However, Cacho suggests that such efforts run up against racialized populations' fundamental disposability. Vicky Guerra pondered a similar logic in a dialogue with Díaz in which she reconsidered how Chris's racialization might have affected the way his labor was policed. She explained:

> It never occurred to me how Chris looked. He usually didn't wear a hoodie on shoots but it was January and cold. He had a baseball cap under the hood also. The more I pictured what he must have looked like, the more . . . it makes even more sense that this officer thought Chris was a Hispanic nobody from the "hood," similar to Trayvon [Martin] who was perceived as trouble as he was just innocently walking home from the store. But I do think it was a power trip and rage also . . . [it] double hurts if that makes sense. Almost like he had no chance to survive even if the cop didn't lose his temper because he thought Chris was just a lowly Mexican. And that was why he never helped him in any way and had so much hate for him even after he was hit.

Vicky Guerra sought to reconcile racialized perceptions of Chris's position as a paparazzo with the notion that her son's killing was the product of an exceptional instance of police power. Cacho's analysis of this interplay between individual characteristics and institutional processes in her theorization of everyday life for people of color, specifically Black and/or Latinx identified people, echoes Vicky Guerra's sentiment: "We learn that the 'facts' of people's behaviors have little significance for determining whose deaths are tragic and whose deaths are deserved" (Cacho 2012, 150). Even if in interpersonal encounters it was possible for Guerra's racial identity to be perceived in shifting ways, his racialized structural reality left him in a state of being that Cacho characterizes as "permanently criminalized," "ineligible for personhood," and, thus, experiencing social death (Cacho 2012, 6–7).

In previous cases, the race of agents of the state in relation to those who are killed under their watch or by them has been used to assert that racism was not a factor in the targeting of particular individuals. For example, the legal defense team of a Latino US Marine successfully argued that their client, who shot and killed a Latino teenager on the teen's family property in Texas, "could not have possibly racially profiled" because the perpetrator and victim were both Latino and phenotypically similar (Márquez 2012, 498).[19] As John Márquez argues in his theorization of a racial state of expendability, examples like these serve as reminders "of how expendability is not derived from the perceptions and/or consent of white people and is also not reducible to corporeal signifiers of racial difference" (498).[20] Thus, regardless of their racial identities, agents of the state participate in the maintenance and reproduction of white supremacy. The death of Chris Guerra reflects the limitations of understanding race, racial profiling, and institutional racism exclusively in relation to the body; Guerra's body could be racially identified in different ways, but in this particular encounter, he inhabited a racialized structural position that rendered him disposable.

The importance of not limiting one's analysis of race to perceived bodily features is underscored by Barnor Hesse's (2016, viii) "colonial constitution of race thesis," which holds that "race is not in the eye of the beholder or on the body of the objectified," but instead "an inherited western, modern-colonial practice of violence, assemblage, superordination, exploitation, and segregation . . . demarcating the colonial rule of Europe over non-Europe." For Hesse, race must be understood as a historically situated, institutionalized process that creates the conditions of possibility for perceptions of bodies and the consequences thereof. These structuring, institutionalized preconditions for perception were reflected in the comments of paparazzi, who frequently told Díaz that when debating how to respond to someone chastising or harassing them, how to defend themselves, or how they might behave in a way that would appease others: "We're already hated, so it doesn't matter." When conceptualized in relation to raciontologies, it becomes clear that overdetermined processes of mattering and nonmattering are not unique to paparazzi. Even when physical death is not the outcome of systematic surveillance and policing, the disposability of the racialized underscores their social death. These racialized incidents reflect the intimate interplay between social death as an existential phenomenon and disposability as realized interactionally and institutionally. This dynamic interplay is enacted through raciontologies that constitute statuses of being and regimes of value across institutional contexts.

Beyond Anthropological Empiricism in
the Analysis of Institutional Racism

The ubiquity of cases such as those discussed in Díaz's ethnographic data and throughout this chapter points to the shortcomings and problematic nature of demanding ethnography first before theorizing everyday life regardless of whether one is engaged formally in what typically constitutes fieldwork. It is important to interrogate the tendency toward privileging anthropological empiricism, which presumes that ethnographic data are the most reliable evidence of phenomena like institutional racism, racial profiling, and white supremacy. To the extent that these phenomena are often perceived in dramatically disparate ways based on the racial positions of the actors involved, we might reconsider the limits of anthropological empiricism in relation to alternative systems of knowledge production. These include intersectional feminist conceptions of theory in the flesh, which situate embodiment as a historically mediated process that can simultaneously facilitate particular insights and obscure others. Rather than presuming that knowledge emerges primordially from marginalized identities, theory in the flesh foregrounds embodiment as one among many legitimate ways of knowing. Cherríe Moraga and Gloria Anzaldúa (1981, 23) suggest that "a theory in the flesh means one where the physical realities of our lives—our skin color, the land or concrete we grew up on, our sexual longings—all fuse to create a politic born out of necessity." Relatedly, the ability of many racially minoritized anthropologists to understand daily encounters with racism in marginalized communities emerges from necessity rather than simply ethnographic curiosity. Their lives quite literally depend on the ability to understand these realities as scholars and theorists of race, racism, and racialization regardless of whether they are situated in a stint of fieldwork. Yet mainstream disciplinary skepticism of theory in the flesh, coupled with the privileging of anthropological empiricism, too often prevents scholars of color—particularly those writing about communities close to home—from being viewed as legitimate theorists or even legitimate anthropologists and instead consistently relegates their conceptualizations to the "savage slot" (Trouillot 2003).

Anthropological empiricism and ethnographic exceptionalism must also be interrogated in relation to hegemonic notions of scholarly authority. Mainstream conceptions of intellectual expertise are rooted in institutional racism and white supremacy through which many academic institutions are built and sustained. Any attempt to develop counterhegemonic approaches to the synthesis of theory and ethnography must grapple with the anchoring of these forms of knowledge production in white supremacist institutional structures. Countless ethnographies reproduce exoticizing and stigmatizing tropes that naturalize or obscure colonial histories and racial hierarchies. More specifically, there is a long and complex history of ethnographers working with and on behalf of the state (e.g., Benedict 1946), contributing more directly to the reproduction of institutional and structural inequalities. This history further underscores the importance of challenging assumptions about ethnographic authority and anthropological empiricism (Loperena 2020).

As both the ethnographic and popularly mediatized examples of state-sanctioned violence against people of color we have examined in this chapter demonstrate, these issues do not reduce to single cases that we might observe ethnographically. Ethnographic moments are part of larger systemic patterns that are readily recognizable in sites beyond fieldwork encounters. That ethnography should inspire theory is an anthropological given. That theory grounded in everyday lived experiences, particularly the lives of racialized people, might not require a two-year stint of fieldwork is perhaps a more radical proposal.

Unsettling Raciontologies

It is remarkable that in anthropological discussions of thing theory, the posthuman, and the ontological turn, questions of race have been largely avoided or ignored altogether. However, those who study race and racialization have always been confronted with the question of what it means to be institutionally defined as a particular kind of thing endowed with the capacity to act in particular kinds of ways—faced not simply with the ontological turn as a conceptual issue, but rather the everyday consequences of having one's ontology twisted and turned, contorted in ways that produce not only Du Boisian double consciousness but also Batesonian double binds.

In an indictment of the failure to grapple with the foundational ontological status of race in widespread scholarly invocations of concepts such as bare life and biopolitics, Alexander Weheliye (2014, 3) suggests that "race, racialization, and racial identities," should be construed as:

> ongoing sets of political relations that require, through constant perpetuation via institutions, discourses, practices, desires, infrastructures, languages, technologies, sciences, economies, dreams, and cultural artifacts, the barring of nonwhite subjects from the category of the human as it is performed in the modern west.

These experiences of being positioned outside the category of the human necessitate strategies for institutionally navigating racial disembodiment and reembodiment, as Uri McMillan (2015) and Aimee Cox (2015) argue in their respective analyses of Black women's and girls' performances and presentations of self across institutional and broader societal contexts. Insofar as raciontologies involve long-standing colonial distinctions that differentiate legitimate human actors from nonhumans or subhumans, this line of thinking and critique can also be applied to the universalizing indictment of humanity associated with the theorization of the Anthropocene. This indictment obscures how that very specific modern Western political and economic mode of governance and lifeworlds, rather than humanity writ large, produced this geological period, such that it might be better framed as the raciopocene.

If, as Elizabeth Povinelli (2016) argues in her conceptualization of geontologies, we must reconsider the institutional and epistemological logics through which the life/nonlife divide is constituted, we might take our cue from race theorists who have long been grappling with such divides. This could include James Baldwin's (1963) celestial characterization of white views of racial integration as "an upheaval in the universe" that "is out of the order of nature," in which the "black man," who "has functioned in the white man's world as a fixed star" shakes heaven and earth to their foundations "as he moves out of his place"; or Christina Sharpe's (2016, 21) geological and meteorological theorization of anti-Blackness as "the ground on which we stand," "a total climate," "the weather," and the target of "an insistent Black visualsonic resistance to that imposition of non/being"; or Gloria Anzaldúa's (1987, 86) ecopolitical analysis, in which abject populations "count the days the weeks the years the centuries the eons until the white laws and commerce and customs will rot in the deserts they've created, lie bleached." Thus, the stakes of raciontological and raciopocentric perspectives, which seek to denaturalize hegemonic semiotic differentiations between being and nonbeing, are nothing short of a reimagination of alternative lifeworlds, forms of institutionality, and modes of governance.

Many critiques of US-based racial profiling focus on the need to ensure equal access to democratic processes and secure the integrity of the nation's fundamental institutions. Rather than simply seeking to secure or recuperate these institutions, we would be well served by a careful reconsideration of what, exactly, they have been doing to people like

Chris Guerra, Stephen Clark, Andrés Guardado, Philando Castile, Sandra Bland, Vanessa Marquez, Trayvon Martin, Michael Brown, Atatiana Jefferson, Eric Garner, Tamir Rice, Alton Sterling, Esequiel Hernández, Breonna Taylor, Dante Wright, Sean Monterrosa, Freddie Gray, Adam Toledo, Rodney King, and countless others.

Notes

1. This chapter is an abridged and revised version of what first appeared as Jonathan Rosa and Vanessa Díaz, 2020. "Raciontologies: Rethinking Anthropological Accounts of Institutional Racism and Enactments of White Supremacy in the United States." *American Anthropologist* 122, no. 1: 120–32. doi.org/10.1111/aman .13353.

2. Dashcam transcriptions were provided to Díaz by Guerra's family, who hired a forensic specialist to analyze and transcribe the footage.

3. Velasco, Juan. 2013. State of California, California Highway Patrol Traffic Collision Report 13-08-04052. Los Angeles. January 1.

4. Walton, Charles. 2013. State of California, California Highway Patrol Narrative/Supplemental Report 13-08-0452. Los Angeles. May 2, 2013.

5. Brumfield, Ben, and K. J. Matthews. 2013. "Paparazzo Killed by Oncoming Traffic after Photographing Justin Bieber's Ferrari." *CNN* website, January 2. www.cnn.com/2013/01/02/showbiz/california-bieber -paparazo-death/index.html.

6. The driver of the first car who hit Guerra was stopped, questioned, and sent on her way with no charges. In fact, per the police report, the CHP officer told the driver that "the accident was not her fault." The second driver was a hit and run, which is a felony, but no investigation followed.

7. "JB" refers to Justin Bieber.

8. Nicolini, Jill. 2013. "Celebrity Photographer Killed While Following Justin Bieber's Car." *Fox News* website, January 2. www.youtube.com/watch?v=yPNqmcyibU4.

9. The extrajudicial killing of Latina actress Vanessa Marquez in her own Los Angeles home during a police wellness check was reported in an ambiguous fashion that reflects racialized hierarchies of humanity and vulnerability. The arrest and subsequent death of Sandra Bland, a Black woman, under the watch of law enforcement, was treated in a similarly ambiguous fashion in media representations. Intersectional power structures position women of color in ways that deny their humanity, vulnerability, and worthiness of sympathy.

10. In the later discussion of Chris Guerra's position as a racialized paparazzo, his camera became weaponized; the officer felt the need to protect celebrities from both Chris and his camera at the expense of Chris's life. Indeed, promotional merchandise for one of the main antipaparazzi lobbying groups, the Paparazzi Reform Initiative, includes a shirt with an image of a camera and the slogan "Weapon of Mass Destruction."

11. Anthropologists, too, have taken up questions about race and ontology. Virginia Dominguez (1997, 93) suggests that "the ontology of 'race' refers to the claims, premises, habits of thought, and other socially learned cognitive operations that support and underwrite the objectification of 'race,' that is, the often unconscious learned habit of treating 'race' as a thing in the world."

12. In her work on practitioners of African diasporic religions, Aisha Beliso-De Jesús discusses the notion of racialized—and specifically "blackened"—ontologies to address the embodied racializing experiences of Santería practitioners across various modes of racial identification (2014, 508; 2015, 7, 31). While Beliso-De Jesús speaks to a set of unique realities that encompass these particular forms of racialized ontologies, her conceptualization is an important precursor to raciontologies.

13. For more on this history, see Díaz (2014).

14. Halbfinger, David M., and Allison H. Weiner. 2005. "As Paparazzi Push Harder, Stars Try to Push Back." *New York Times*, June 9, 2005.

15. Pearson, Ryan. 2008. "'Britney Beat': Paparazzi Are No Longer Faceless Pack Animals." Accessed January 10, 2011. Associated Press, April 3, 2008. www.foxnews.com/story/0,2933,346212,00.html.

16. Winton, Richard, and Tonya Alanez. 2012. "Paparazzi Flash New Audacity: As Competition Grows, Photographers Trailing L.A.'s Celebrities Become More Aggressive." *Los Angeles Times, Nation*, October 16, 2005. Accessed September 10, 2012. http://articles.latimes.com/2005/oct/16/local/me-paparazzi16.

17. See also: "Photographers Sue!: Bachelor Wedding Airs, ABC Exploits Security's Attack on Photographers." X17 online, March 8, 2010. Accessed January 10, 2011. http://www.x17online.com/celebrities/the _bachelor/photographers_sue_bachelor_wedding_airs_abc.php#mjp52AAI935IRhkH.99.

18. Bouie, Jamelle. 2014. "Will Today's Hispanics Be Tomorrow's Whites?" *Slate* website, April 15. https:// slate.com/news-and-politics/2014/04/americas-future-racial-makeup-will-todays-hispanics-be-tomorrows -whites.html.

19. US Marine Clemente Buñuelos, who killed teenager Esequiel Hernández on Hernández's family's property, was not indicted based on his defense's argument that Hernández's death could not have been a result of racial profiling (Márquez 2012, 498).

20. Referencing recent extrajudicial killings in which the names of US Border Patrol agents who killed people have been kept confidential by the state, Márquez asserts that "the namelessness of the agent reflects how he is transformed from a person who killed into a mechanism of the sovereign state, programmed to perform a duty that has been normalized as routine, just, and necessary" (Márquez 2012, 492).

References

Anzaldúa, Gloria. 1987. *Borderlands/La Frontera: The New Mestiza*. San Francisco: Aunt Lute.

Baldwin, James. 1963. *The Fire Next Time*. New York: Dial Press.

Beliso-De Jesús, Aisha. 2014. "Santería Copresence and the Making of African Diaspora Bodies." *Cultural Anthropology* 29, no. 3: 503–26.

———. 2015. *Electric Santería: Racial and Sexual Assemblages of Trans-National Religion*. New York: Columbia University Press.

Bonilla, Yarimar, and Jonathan Rosa. 2015. "#Ferguson: Digital Protest, Hashtag Ethnography, and the Racial Politics of Social Media in the United States." *American Ethnologist* 42, no. 1: 4–17.

Cacho, Lisa. 2012. *Social Death: Racialized Rightlessness and the Criminalization of the Unprotected*. New York: New York University Press.

Césaire, Aimé. (1955) 2001. *Discourse on Colonialism*. New York: Monthly Review Press.

Cox, Aimee. 2015. *Shapeshifters: Black Girls and the Choreography of Citizenship*. Durham, NC: Duke University Press.

De la Cadena, Marisol. 2015. *Earth Beings: Ecologies of Practice across Andean Worlds*. Durham, NC: Duke University Press.

Díaz, Vanessa. 2014. "Latinos at the Margins of Celebrity Culture: Image Sales and the Politics of Paparazzi." In *Contemporary Latina/o Media: Production, Circulation, Politics*, edited by Arlene Dávila and Yeidy Rivero, 125–45. New York: New York University Press.

———. 2020. *Manufacturing Celebrity: Latino Paparazzi and Women Reporters in Hollywood*. Durham, NC: Duke University Press.

Dominguez, Virginia R. 1997. "The Racist Politics of Concepts, or Is It the Racialist Concepts of Politics?" *Ethnos* 25, no. 1: 93–100.

DuBois, W. E. B. 1903. *The Souls of Black Folk*. New York: Dover Publications.

Fanon, Frantz. 1967. *Black Skin, White Masks*. New York: Grove Press.

Goodman, J. David, and Michael Wilson. 2014. "Officer Daniel Pantaleo Told Grand Jury He Meant No Harm to Eric Garner." *New York Times* website, December 3. www.nytimes.com/2014/12/04/nyregion/officer -told-grand-jury-he-meant-no-harm-to-eric-garner.html.

Goodwin, Charles. 1994. "Professional Vision." *American Anthropologist* 96, no. 3: 606–33.

Hesse, Barnor. 2016. "Counter-Racial Formation Theory." In *Conceptual Aphasia in Black: Displacing Racial Formation*, edited by P. Khalil Saucier and Tryon P. Woods, vii–x. Lanham, MD: Lexington Books.

Loperena, Christopher. 202. "Adjudicating Indigeneity: Anthropological Testimony in the Inter-American Court of Human Rights." *American Anthropologist* 122, no. 3: 595–605.

Márquez, John. 2012. "Latinos as the 'Living Dead': Raciality, Expendability, and Border Militarization." *Latino Studies* 10, no. 4: 473–98.

McMillan, Uri. 2015. *Embodied Avatars: Genealogies of Black Feminist Art and Performance*. New York: New York University Press.

Povinelli, Elizabeth. 2016. *Geontologies: A Requiem to Late Liberalism*. Durham, NC: Duke University Press.

Sharpe, Christina. 2016. *In the Wake: On Blackness and Being*. Durham, NC: Duke University Press.

Visweswaran, Kamala. 1996. "Race and the Culture of Anthropology." *American Anthropologist* 100, no. 1: 70–83.

Weheliye, Alexander G. 2014. *Habeas Viscus: Racializing Assemblages, Biopolitics, and Black Feminist Theories of the Human*. Durham, NC: Duke University Press.

Wynter, Sylvia. 1994. "No Humans Involved: An Open Letter to My Colleagues." *Forum N.H.I.: Knowledge for the 21st Century* 1, no. 1: 42–73.

14

"Experience the Wonder"

THE NORTH, THE NORDIC AND WHITE SUPREMACY

Kristín Loftsdóttir

AT ICELAND'S INTERNATIONAL AIRPORT, a television screen is positioned on the conveyor belt portraying a slim and beautiful white woman who looks out from the screen and then bends her head submissively as she turns around, smiling mysteriously. Her body is half submerged in blue water with white steam rising slowly around her. The image stands in sharp contrast with the otherwise dark entry hall full of suitcases and people and the dull sound of the conveyor belt. This is my welcome to Iceland, and I cannot help thinking once again of the strong association made between whiteness and the Nordic countries (Hübinette and Lundström 2011; McIntosh 2015). This association benefits from notions of Nordic exceptionalism that position the country as existing outside colonial history (Loftsdóttir and Jensen 2012). After the economic crash of 2008, Iceland capitalized on this claim of innocence, being promoted as a space of exceptionalism that welcomes tourists, especially those from the United Kingdom and United States, to explore the country's wilderness, while being firmly located within the safety and presumed purity of a Global North environment.

This chapter explores the utility of the concept of white supremacy in Iceland as a Nordic country. In the twenty-first century, Iceland has had several intense media debates about racism, one of the key issues having been whether particular examples constituted racism or not within the space of Iceland, and if racism was a part of Icelandic society. The refusal to acknowledge racism has long characterized the self-narration of the different Nordic countries (Rastas 2005; Hübinette 2012; Gullistad 2006), coupled with claims of cultural homogeneity as their defining feature. This has meant ignoring the historical diversity of the region and its fluid national boundaries (Keskinen et al. 2019) as well as failing to acknowledge the existence and systematic exclusion of Nordic indigenous populations (Fur 2013).

The state has had an important role in creating and maintaining white supremacy (Moreton-Robinson 2015), in addition to the role of different media such as advertising

(Shankar 2019). This chapter draws attention to white supremacy in relation to the commercial nation-branding of the 2010s, but, as Lena Sawyer and Ylva Habel stress (2014), it is necessary to focus on the brandings of Nordic peoples in conjunction with diasporic communities in the Nordic countries (2). The chapter also seeks to draw attention to emerging spaces of resistance to hegemonic notions of Iceland's innocence. One such space emerged after George Floyd's murder in the spring of 2020, which led to a global mobilization against injustice and white supremacy, when many young Icelanders stepped forward as well and testified to their experiences of racism in Iceland, grounded in their multiple and contradictory identifications as nonwhites.

I start the chapter with a brief discussion contextualizing the Nordic countries within the phenomenon of white supremacy before focusing more generally on Iceland. I then stress the entanglements of racism and innocence. These are related to particular affective historical understandings where even when racism is acknowledged in the present, it is seen as recent in Iceland, so that the history of the nation overall continues to be a history of innocence. I then focus on narratives of nation-branding in Iceland and its emphasis on unspoiled nature and whiteness and then finally briefly discuss recent destabilization of claims of innocence through personal counternarratives.

White Supremacy in the North

I see the recent call for a stronger engagement with the concept of white supremacy as an analytical tool as stressing greater recognition of the structural and institutional aspects of racism that not only privilege whiteness, but assume it as self-evident. Beliso-De Jesús and Pierre (2020) directly address the concept's usefulness in bringing out the structural and institutional production of racism and discrimination, positioning white supremacy as part of the "baseline" in the workings of the world today (Beliso-De Jesús and Pierre 2020). Similarly, Bonds and Inwood (2016) emphasize white supremacy as the underlying logic of the current system of modernization and capitalism, which is both historically constituted and relevant to the present. Thus, white supremacy can be seen as an "ongoing colonial project" (Bonds and Inwood 2016, 719) that continues to "produce social and spatial relations that frame broad understandings of difference" (720). At the core of white supremacy is, in the words of Nasar Meer (2021), how whiteness constitutes a "type of habitus and the norm in which others are judged," with whiteness becoming the "normative" identity (5). A criticism posed on the concept of white privilege also reflects the need to shift the understanding of racism as revolving around the personal views or attitudes of individuals toward a stronger focus on its structural aspects. For example, Aouragh (2019) makes the point that, when it comes to antiracist discourses, the focus on "privilege" can reduce racism to an issue that is "primarily concerned with personal obligation" (5). Bonds and Inwood (2016) see the move from "privilege" to "supremacy" as shifting the focus from particular historical moments toward the structural aspects that continue to be embedded in society (720). Bonds and Inwood's use of white supremacy is not dissimilar to the concept of coloniality, as they situate white supremacy at the heart of the modern world, thus linking past and present. Moreton-Robinson's insights (2015) into theorizing whiteness draw attention importantly to the need to take into account indigenous perspectives that often show how whiteness tends to revolve around property. White supremacy thus often works through the logic of dispossession of a different kind, for example, from land, space, or property.

The dominance of a US perspective in discussions of racism has been critically addressed with regard to the extent to which aspects of racism, such as whiteness, have taken shape differently in Europe, while being part of global discourse and imaginary (Harrison 2002). In Europe this has meant to recognize the various intersections of different forms of racism that exist alongside and intersect with racism against Black people, such as islamophobia (Abu-Lughod 2002; Khabeer 2016), class, and labor migration (Garner 2007). The issue I see at stake here does not involve denying or trivializing the existence of racism outside the United States, but rather, as Fay Harrison's (2002) work has emphasized, the need to recognize a "diversity of racial formations" while also acknowledging the global scope of racism (151). Anthropological insights have shown how the concepts of the local and the global have to be understood as "concept metaphors" for complex and entangled social formations (Moore 2004), where there are neither "in prior" locals nor where global actions are divorced from particular historical understandings. Race can thus be seen as constituting a historical transnational formation that is constantly being transplanted in diverse localities, "mutating and adapting to new realities" (Loftsdóttir 2019b). My approach therefore follows those scholars who have demonstrated the need to recognize the temporal aspects of racism and its expression in particular geographical spaces (Harrison 2002, 1995; Nowicka 2018) that exist in intensified globalized mediascapes of racism.

For the past decade, some of the critical activist and scholarly work in the Nordic countries has centered on positioning these countries as a part of the history of colonialism (Loftsdóttir and Jensen 2012; Keskinen et al. 2016; Naum and Nordin 2013). Some of this research has been historical, but a large majority of researchers have grounded their attention to history in current concerns with racism and diversity. Some of the Nordic countries were empires at specific points in history, such as Denmark, which profited from a plantation economy using slave labor (Naum and Nordin 2013). This body of research also reflects the limitations of using "colonialism" as a framework for analysis, as not all Nordic countries did have colonies, and some were under the control of other countries. These have raised theoretical concerns regarding how to theorize European countries that benefited from colonialism in multiple ways and reproduced racist metanarratives while not fitting within a narrow definitions of colonialism that only focuses on a state ruling another. Here I have found the concept of coloniality extremely useful for capturing the underlying logic of racism (Loftsdóttir 2019a). Like the concept of white supremacy, coloniality seeks to capture imperial structures of inequalities that continue to inform and shape people's lives in the present. The concept of white supremacy can similarly be said to decenter the issue of which countries had colonies and which did not toward acknowledging particular processes and structures within which people were positioned differently, and where white supremacy played a vital role. Thus, within the different Nordic countries, white supremacy was certainly at play, as all these countries were firmly incorporated into the modern world's capitalist system.

Both within the Nordic countries themselves and in their migration into other geographical spaces such as North America the logic of white supremacy was at work in facilitating and explaining their occupation of Indigenous people's land as desirable and natural (Sverdljuk et al. 2021). This point is in line with Moreton-Robinson's (2015) emphasis on the links between entitlement to land and white supremacy.

Island of Innocence

While appearing isolated and remote in the cold Atlantic Ocean, Iceland is no exception to the global dissemination of racist practices and ideas of racism and white supremacy. In the nineteenth and early twentieth centuries, racist theories were well known among Iceland's small intellectual elite, which clearly expressed their concern with Iceland's presumed misrecognition as colonial subjects, rather than their rightful place as belonging with progressive European states and civilization (Rastrick 2013; Loftsdóttir 2019a). Icelandic intellectuals tried to insert Iceland into the narrative of colonialization in particular ways, including its occupying a particular subject position within coloniality. This has to be read against the context of Iceland being under Danish rule, which was seen as increasingly problematic by Icelandic intellectuals from the nineteenth century (Loftsdóttir 2019a). Icelandic officials and intellectual elites often experienced themselves being perceived as inferior to by their Danish rulers (Jónsson 2014). Thus, while attempting to position themselves with progressive, masculine Europe, white supremacy was not questioned in Iceland. Rather, anxieties were expressed more with regard to Iceland's position within white supremacy through the country's association with nonwhite and colonized populations by other European intellectual elites. Although Iceland does not have any Indigenous populations, when Icelanders began migrating to the Americas in the late nineteenth century, they, like other people from the Nordic countries, benefited from settler colonialism and its logic of white supremacy (Loftsdóttir et al. 2021; Eyford 2006).

Iceland received full independence from Denmark in 1944. The country's continued engagement with coloniality became strikingly evident during the first years of the twenty-first century, following various neoliberal reforms in the 1990s. The discussion about "Icelandic-ness" was deeply nationalistic, engaging intensively with older nationalistic discourses from the early twentieth century, when claims to independence were being made. However, this did not constitute an attempt to rebuild a golden age, as is the case with so many populist parties today, but was rather a conversation that emphasized recognition of Iceland as a leading Western country (Loftsdóttir and Mixa 2021). The neoliberal reforms facilitated various global flows to and from Iceland, obviously constituting some of the changes that were taking place more globally through various technologies, with the high growth of labor and other migration into the country, which was considerably facilitated by Iceland joining the Schengen area. During the economic boom starting in the early twenty-first century and ending abruptly in 2008, many migrants from more economically precarious parts of Europe, especially Poland and Lithuania, came to Iceland in search of jobs. They were quickly racialized, with reference being made to older European notions of East Europeans as not "fully" European, which have become articulated in different ways in the present (Loftsdóttir 2019a). This indicates the diverse articulations of whiteness (Meer 2021, 6), which are often strongly negotiated through the positioning of certain ethnicities in the labor market (Garner 2007). While ideas of whiteness have thus been negotiated, the racialization of East Europeans in Iceland still revolves around the principle of white supremacy, with racialized populations being excluded in multiple ways as a part of society.

Claims of innocence have been important in the recent past in understanding the logic of racism in Iceland. These claims of innocence can be observed across the Nordic countries, being linked to persistent notions of exceptionalism where the Nordic countries are seen as more equal than other countries and as lacking a colonial past (Loftsdóttir and Jensen 2012). One important way in which this exceptionalism is invoked in the present has been in the refusal to acknowledge that particular actions, images, or structures can be racist (Vertelyté and Hervik 2019), as if Nordic countries are somehow innocent of the "stain" of colonialism. In Iceland, such claims have been intensified by assertions that the country was a colony too, and that the racist slurs and images Icelanders may indulge in are not themselves racist.

This is exemplified by a media event that took place early in the twenty-first century relating to the republication of a children's book, *The Negro Boys* (Negrastrákarnir) in 2007. This book had originally been published in Iceland in 1922 as a translation and adaptation of a globalized racist nursery rhyme (Pietersen 1992, 166). The images in the book are clearly based on racist caricatures of Black people, drawn by a much loved Icelandic artist. When the book was republished in 2007, after being reissued many times before without any controversy, a short news story emerged about an Icelandic woman who had a "mixed-race" child and was afraid that the book would stimulate racism. This caused an intense media storm, with a vigorous reaction leading to a debate over whether the book was racist or not. Many people claimed that it had nothing to do with racism, as it was an Icelandic book with drawings by an Icelandic artist. Many also saw the issue as a personal decision, such that everyone just needed to decide for themselves if they wanted to interpret the images as racist or not, thus reducing racism to the intentions of those consuming the images (Loftsdóttir 2012, 64). While the vocabulary of "us" and "them," referring apparently to white-Icelanders and Black-non-Icelanders, was often used, most of those taking part in the debate did not engage with their own position as white individuals speaking about Black people, nor did they seem to assume that Black people could be Icelandic. In my interviews probing into the book's republication, many Icelandic-born white Icelanders were genuinely surprised that anyone could take the book as racist, and they often linked it to their own positive childhood memories. As one person explained to me, it was a good book for pointing out that some people are Black and only some others white. Others, however, were more critical of the book, which in some cases they had not read since they were children. In the context of this debate, for the first time, they saw racism in the book that they had not noticed earlier (see Loftsdóttir 2015).

As a white scholar educated in the United States, my primary goal at this time was to demonstrate that racism was part of Iceland's history and present, though the concept of white supremacy was not part of my intellectual tool kit at the time. I saw the refusal to acknowledge racism as part of creation of spaces of whiteness where racist statements can be uttered shielded by claims of innocence. I also suggested that one aspect that was at stake in defending the book was to secure a particular vision of Iceland's past that was not associated with racism, nor where plurality was acknowledged as part of Iceland's past (Loftsdóttir 2013). I now consider that, in this space of whiteness I identified, white supremacy can equally be seen as present, while racism and the experiences of Black and other marked racialized populations were dismissed and rendered trivial. In addition, whiteness was normalized as natural in that space. Again, thinking this through by means of the concept of white supremacy, it can be said that this vision of Iceland's supposedly nonracist past further strengthens the neutralization of racism in the country. Here, white supremacy and Iceland's innocence are ensured by denying that Iceland was ever a part of colonial and imperial history.

What is also salient here is that at this time, the population of Iceland was becoming more diversified, with the debate about the Negroboys' book coexisting within other debates framed around thinking of Iceland as a "multicultural" society (Skaptadóttir and Loftsdóttir 2009). In 1996 those defined as immigrants constituted 2 percent of the population,[1] but were, in 2023, 16.3 percent of the population, and so-called first- and second-generation immigrants 18 percent (Statistics Iceland 2023). The composition of the migrant population had also changed. In the past, most of those migrating to Iceland came from other Nordic countries, while in 2020 two-thirds of the migrant population consisted of migrants from non-Nordic European countries (especially Poland) and almost 13 percent came from Asia. These waves of migration in many cases count as chain migration, with migrants working in low-income jobs (Skaptadóttir and Garðarsdóttir 2020).

Branding Icelandic as White

I will now return to Iceland's airport and the Blue Lagoon advertisement, as well as the international branding of Iceland as a destination in the recent past. The focus on racism exclusively in relation to immigration can perpetuate the notion that racism is only an issue in relation to immigration, almost as if it only appeared with the first immigrants and was never embedded in Icelandic society's structure and history, to which the concept of white supremacy draws attention. It is necessary to focus on how particular spaces are racialized; in particular, as Shankar (2019, 113) reminds us, advertising has historically been important in strengthening white supremacy in its normalization of white power. Furthermore, as mentioned earlier, land and space have been an essential part of white supremacy.

The screen at the airport was linked to a massive campaign initiated in 2010 in Iceland in the aftermath of the 2008 economic crash. In particular, the campaign aimed to rebuild Iceland's tarnished reputation following the collapse of its banking system. The government of Iceland teamed up with various private and corporate partners, a "Promote

Iceland" office was established, and a campaign was launched under the name "Inspired by Iceland." The goal was to create an umbrella brand for Iceland for various financial benefits, such as increasing foreign investment, increasing the demand for Icelandic products, and stimulating the notion of Iceland as a destination (Pálsdóttir et al. 2011; Íslandsstofa 2013). The effects were enormous, placing Iceland firmly on the map as a tourism destination. Elsewhere I have described this campaign in more detail (see Loftsdóttir 2019a; 2023); here I will just tease out a few aspects relevant for the present discussion.

In my critical evaluation of this campaign, I focused on how it is based on ideas of Iceland's coloniality and past marginalization. As discourses of race were entangled with notions of civilization and the rejection of coevalness, European populations were often positioned alongside racialized others in the nineteenth century. As I suggested earlier, this was also the case with Iceland, even though the country was never racialized in the same sense as many other populations under foreign rule. The campaign, however, uses the lingering notion of Iceland as different and somewhat exotic, thus mobilizing tropes of coloniality and exoticism that are embedded in the period of imperialism and colonialism. This is reflected in the branding of Iceland as an almost empty land waiting to be discovered by tourists. Simultaneously, the branding presents Iceland as a white country, almost fusing together its strange, exotic, and pure landscape with its inhabitants, who are presented as somewhat strange, unique, and unspoiled. Iceland itself as a space appears as a wild territory, but also as a land of safety and comfort, where the visitor can enjoy these colonial tropes without being confronted by signs of racial inequality or memories of colonial violence, genocide, or historical injustice (Loftsdóttir 2019a).

The emphasis on Iceland as a white feminine space is clearly reflected in the Blue Lagoon advertisements and its images at the airport baggage claim. The Blue Lagoon has been one of most popular tourism destinations in Iceland and is often branded as such. In 2017, for example, it was estimated that over 1.3 million guests visited the Blue Lagoon, or on average 3,000 guests per day.[2] In the annual report where this information is found, tourists are not broken down based on gender or nationality. However, the majority of tourists to Iceland come from the United States (30 percent in 2018), with the United Kingdom coming second with 12 percent.[3] To gain access to the lagoon, it is necessary to prebook tickets in advance, making the Blue Lagoon's website highly influential in framing itself as a destination.[4] Blue Lagoon promotional material is visible in other forums too, such as magazine advertisements and in public spaces, including where one picks up one's luggage.

Navigating through the website, it quickly becomes clear that the great majority of the images are of white women's bodies. Counting and classifying images on the randomly picked dates of September 14 and 15 in 2018, showed that, of the forty-four website images that featured people, thirty-two showed white women's bodies, while only three showed men and none showed nonwhite bodies. In the images we see relaxed bodies rather passively enjoying the luxuries that the Blue Lagoon has to offer. The opening of the Blue Lagoon web page at the time showed a moving image slowly surrounded by mist, similar to the one I saw in the baggage section. The accompanying slogan, "Experience the wonder," frames the image. The woman smiles as if she knows something the viewer does not know and then looks shyly away. The Blue Lagoon thus becomes a highly gendered and racialized space, intensifying the sense of Iceland as space of whiteness (see further discussion in Loftsdóttir 2023). Notably, moreover, it is not only on the Blue Lagoon website where whiteness is strongly emphasized but more generally in promotional material of government and private partnerships, where white Icelandic bodies were stressed as involving a particular "we-ness," distinct and unique. The experiences of Black Icelandic youth with tourists reflect this cementing of Iceland as a white space, as tourists always assume that nonwhite people are foreigners or migrants and often have difficulties in acknowledging that they are not (Loftsdóttir and Mörtudóttir 2022).

In my analysis of Iceland's promotional material, I have been inspired by Ben Pitcher's observation (2014) that, for white people in Britain, part of the appeal of consuming items and experiences associated with the Nordic countries is the clear relationship that is made between geography and culture, providing a "model for white culture" (71). This comment draws attention to how the North has often been linked to purity and exploration (Kjartansdóttir and Schram 2020). We have to ask what kind of "wonder" is experienced by the overwhelmingly UK and US tourists? While there exists no data on the racial identifications of these visitors, one can ask whether or not they come to Iceland to experience guilt-free memories of white supremacy in a space of whiteness where colonialism did not happen?

Making Racism Visible

George Floyd's murder on May 25, 2020, caused intense uproar internationally as evidence of the persistence of structural racism. The historical moment of Floyd's murder, which took place at the beginning of the COVID-19 pandemic, made protest against police brutality and systematic racism coincide with a piling up of data reaffirming race as a key social determinant of health, including the disproportional effects of COVID-19 (Godlee 2020; also Tan and Umamaheswar 2021), leading some to talk of "twin pandemics" (see Nguyen et al. 2021). Across Europe these events provided a much-needed spark for protests against different kinds of institutionalized racism (Kennedy-McFoy and Zarkov 2020). The cry for social justice and acknowledgments of racism that became evident in Iceland at this time can possibly be seen as reflecting a paradigm shift in discussions about racism in Iceland, in particular with regard to the long-held notion that racism was external to Iceland.

One of the most salient challenges to this view was posed by the many Icelanders who came forward to state that racism and racialization was part of their everyday lives in Iceland. These individuals had in common to be socially identified as nonwhite. What can have made this shocking to the majority population was that these were mostly young people—thus could be perceived as having an aura of innocence—and especially that most of them were Icelandic, having been born and brought up in the country, so that the prejudice they experienced could not be excused as being due to the fact that they did not speak Icelandic, or that they spoke differently or lacked an understanding of Icelandic culture or humor. Iceland's main newspapers reported such narratives in the months after

Floyd's murder. Some of these news stories consisted of interviews after having been posted on Instagram or other social media outlets, and yet others consisted of news about social media posts, all where people had decided to recount their experiences of racism. In some cases, these narratives also overlapped with narratives or interviews referring to events that took place in Iceland related to the Floyd protests in America. Taken together, the experiences of these individuals showed that verbal abuse containing various racist slurs was part of the everyday existence of many Icelanders, coupled with the constant assumptions that they could not be Icelandic. In one interview, for example, Anna Jia explained that she was telling her story because she wanted to keep the conversation "going in this country and to raise awareness of how behind we are," referring to discussions about racism and structural inequalities. She also pointed out that she recognized very many of the prejudices that others had reported against women who would be identified as looking "Asian," but she hoped that this was just her own experience (Sigfúsdóttir 2020). These experiences are not surprising and are confirmed by earlier research on racism as a part of Icelandic society (Loftsdóttir 2013); features of racism in Iceland have become that being Icelandic means being white. If you are dark, you can still be Icelandic, but your presence has to be explained and contextualized as an exception (Loftsdóttir and Mörtudóttir 2022).

The intersections of different events have to be seen as particularly important, given the larger global atmosphere of narratives showing the endurance of systematic racism in other countries, coupled with a number of testaments of racism in Iceland. These make it clearly evident that racism is a part of the everyday experiences of people seen as nonwhite in Iceland, just as is the case elsewhere in the world. As scholars have stressed, the power of whiteness rests in its ability to normalize certain bodies (see the discussions in Hartigan 1997). Together, these narratives uncovered the experience of living in a country where you are always presumed to be an outsider. Some individuals experienced hateful racism as well, but one of the most salient issues was how these individuals were constantly and systematically assumed to be non-Icelandic. The more hateful remarks, along with more innocent questions of "where are you from?," invoked the idea of "matter out of place," to cite N. Puwar's (2004) statement (see also Loftsdóttir and Mörtudóttir 2022). How can these stories be anything other than expressions of a society that is characterized by white supremacy, one in which white bodies are the norm in multiple senses?

Some of the responses to these personal accounts of racism from the everyday reality in Iceland were certainly hateful and judgmental, and that was also the case with some of the media and politicians. The leader of the Centre Party (Miðflokkurinn), for example, talked about the "Black Lives Matter" (MLN) movement as a part of the "new cultural revolution," with the Cultural Revolution in China in mind, while also claiming that the BLM movement encouraged racism (Gunnlaugsson 2020).

These personal accounts were coupled with other activist or media stories that put inequalities and racism in the spotlight. At Austurvöllur on June 3, 2020, a solidarity meeting was held with the main goal to protest against police brutality in the United States, while also stressing it as an opportunity to emphasize that racism existed in Iceland as well (Höskuldsdóttir 2020). In September 2020, the Living Art Museum (Nýlistasafnið) hired Chanel Björk Sturludóttir to assist in changing the museum from a space of white privilege

(Ingilínardóttir 2020). Along with Elínborg Kolbeinsdóttir, Sturludóttir headed the platform Hervoice, formed in 2018, in order to create venues to make women from migrant backgrounds more visible in Icelandic society and allow their voices to be better heard. In 2001 the Anti-Rasistarnir (anti-racist) Initiative was launched on Instagram by three Black Icelandic women. Their reason for doing so, as one of them stated in an interview, was that they were "fed up with people getting away with all kinds of shit"[5] (Arnardóttir 2021).

The point of these few examples is not that there were no groups or individuals fighting against racism earlier, but that these attempts became more intensified after the spring of 2020, and they seem to have been given more visibility by the media and different institutions. However, as argued by Nguyen and colleagues (2021) in the context of the United States, it was at the time of writing too early to tell if and how these constitute lasting changes. Nonetheless, it is important to stress that these events were crucial in making white supremacy more visual as part of Icelandic society and thus facilitating the mobilization against it. These spaces of resistance to white supremacy are especially important at a time (2023) when we are seeing the rise of right-wing populism across Europe and the Nordic countries (Keskinen, Skaptadóttir, and Toivanen 2019; Sawyer and Habel 2014).

Conclusion

The concept of white supremacy is useful in understanding racialization processes in Iceland, while simultaneously taking into account the historical particularities that have shaped how racism has been expressed and justified in the country. As I have shown, in Iceland nineteenth- and early twentieth-century intellectuals tried to insert themselves more strongly into wider Global North ideas of white supremacy, rather than questioning its basic premises.

More recently, the experiences of nonwhite people living in Iceland show that white supremacy is a reality, for example, as expressed in how individuals constantly have to justify their existence as Black or nonwhite Icelanders. Analysis of promotional material regarding the marketing of Iceland as a destination also indicates that the country has been created as a space of whiteness, thus intensifying the sense that Black and other nonwhite people do not belong in that space. Here Moreton-Robinson's (2015) works with regard to how white supremacy often works through entitlement to land can be seen as relevant in the sense that partly government-sponsored materials promoting Iceland have strongly emphasized a particular materiality to the country as land and have emphasized Iceland as a space inhabited by a particular racialized population (Loftsdóttir 2023). The promotional material has changed in recent years, with the body of the Icelander disappearing and that of the tourist taking its place, but the idea of the white Icelander has already been cemented, fitting with the idea of the white north.

Notes

1. Statistics Iceland. "Innflytjendum Heldur Áfram að Fjölga." Accessed June 18, 2023, https://hagstofa.is /utgafur/frettasafn/mannfjoldi/mannfjoldi-eftir-bakgrunni-2018/.

2. Blue Lagoon Iceland. "Baðstaðir." Accessed June 19, 2023, https://arsskyrsla2017.bluelagoon.is/badstadir/.

3. Icelandic Tourist Board. "Tourism in Iceland in Figures—January 2019." Accessed June 19, 2023, www .ferdamalastofa.is/static/files/ferdamalastofa/tolur_utgafur/january-2019.pdf.

4. "919,000 Visited Iceland's Blue Lagoon in 2015." *MBL*, May 26, 2016, https://icelandmonitor.mbl.is/news /nature_and_travel/2016/05/26/919_000_visited_iceland_s_blue_lagoon_in_2015./

5. In Icelandic: "við vorum bara komnar með upp í kok af fólki að komast upp með alls konar skit."

References

Abu-Lughod, Lila. 2002. "Do Muslim Women Really Need Saving? Anthropological Reflections on Cultural Relativism and Its Others." *American Anthropologist* 104, no. 3: 783–90. https://doi.org/10.1525/aa.2002 .104.3.783.

Aouragh, Miriyam. 2019. "'White Privilege' and Shortcuts to Anti-Racism." *Race and Class* 61, no. 2: 3–26. https://doi.org/10.1177/0306396819874629.

Arnardóttir, Lovísa. 2021. "Vilja ræða um rasisma." www.frettabladid.is/frettir/vilja-raeda-um-rasisma.

Beliso-De Jesús, Aisha M., and Jemima Pierre. 2020. "Anthropology of White Supremacy." *American Anthropologist* 122, no. 1: 65–75. https://doi.org/10.1111/aman.13351.

Bonds, Anne, and Joshua Inwood. 2016. "Beyond White Privilege: Geographies of White Supremacy and Settler Colonialism." *Progress in Human Geography* 40, no. 6: 715–33. https://doi.org/10.1177/0309132 515613166.

Eyford, Ryan C. 2006. "Quarantined within a New Colonial Order: The 1876–1877 Lake Winnipeg Smallpox Epidemic." *Journal of the Canadian Historical Association* 17, no. 1: 55–78. https://doi.org/10.7202/016102ar.

Fur, Gunlög. 2013. "Colonialism and Swedish History? Unthinkable Connections." In *Scandinavian Colonialism and the Rise of Modernity: Small-Time Agents in a Global Arena*, edited by Magdalena Naum and Jonas M. Nordin, 17–36. New York: Springer.

Garner, Steve. 2007. "Atlantic Crossing: Whiteness as a Transatlantic Experience." *Atlantic Studies* 4, no. 1: 117–32. https://doi.org/10.1080/14788810601179485.

Godlee, Fiona. 2020. "Racism: The Other Pandemic." *BMJ: British Medical Journal* (online) 369. https:// doi:https://doi.org/10.1136/bmj.m2303.

Gullestad, Marianne. 2006. "Imagined Kinship: The Role of Descent in the Rearticulation of Norwegian Ethno-Nationalism." In *Neo-Nationalism in Europe and Beyond: Perspectives from Social Anthropology*, edited by Andre Gingrich and Marcus Banks, 69–91. Oxford: Berghahn Books.

Gunnlaugsson, Sigmund Davíð. 2020. "Sumarið 2020 og Nýja Menningarbyltingin." *Morgunblaðið*, July 25. www.mbl.is/greinasafn/innskraning/?redirect=%2Fgreinasafn%2Fgrein%2F1757793%2F%3Ft%3D441 804748&page_name=article&grein_id=1757793.

Harrison, Faye V. 1995. "The Persistent Power of 'Race' in the Cultural and Political Economy of Racism." *Annual Review of Anthropology* 24, no. 1: 47–74. https://doi.org/10.1146/annurev.an.24.100195.000403.

Harrison, Faye V. 2002. "Unraveling 'Race' for the Twenty-First Century." In *Exotic No More: Anthropology on the Front Lines*, edited by Jeremy MacClancy, 145–66. Chicago: University of Chicago Press.

Hartigan, John, Jr. 1997. "Establishing the Fact of Whiteness." *American Anthropologist* 99, no. 3: 495–505. https://doi.org/10.1525/aa.1997.99.3.495.

Höskuldsdóttir, Helga Margrét. 2020. "Vandamál að Ísland telji sig fullkomið en sé það ekki." RÚV, June 3. www.ruv.is/frett/2020/06/03/vandamal-ad-island-telji-sig-fullkomid-en-se-thad-ekki.

Hübinette, Tobias. 2012. "'Words That Wound': Swedish Whiteness and Its Inability to Accommodate Minority Experiences." In *Whiteness and Postcolonialism in the Nordic Region: Exceptionalism, Migrant Others, and National Identities*, edited by Kristín Loftsdóttir and Lars Jensen, 43–56. Farnham: Ashgate.

Hübinette, Tobias, and Catrin Lundström. 2011. "Sweden after the Recent Election: The Double-Binding Power of Swedish Whiteness through the Mourning of the Loss of 'Old Sweden' and the Passing of 'Good Sweden.'" *NORA—Nordic Journal of Feminist and Gender Research* 19, no. 1: 42–52. https://doi.org/10.1080 /08038740.2010.547835.

Ingilínardóttir, Kristlín Dís. 2020. "Listasafnið í Naflaskoðun: Varast Forréttindablindu og Hlut-drægni." Frét-tablaðið, September 26. www.frettabladid.is/lifid/nylistasafnid-i-naflaskodun-varast-forrettindablindu-og -hlutdraegni/.

Íslandsstofa. 2013. "Ísland-Allt árið: Áfangaskýrsla 2012–2013." www.ferdamalastofa.is/is/gogn/utgafur/utgefid -efni/imynd-og-markadsmal/island-allt-arid-afangaskyrsla-veturinn-2012-2013.

Jónsson, Kristján Jóhann. 2014. Grímur Thomsen: Þjóðerni, skáldskapur, þversagnir og vald. Bókmennta-og list-fræðastofnun Háskóla Íslands.

Kennedy-Macfoy, Madeleine, and Dubravka Zarkov. 2020. "Black Lives Matter in Europe—EJWS Special Open Forum: Introduction." European Journal of Women's Studies. https://doi.org/10.1177 /1350506820984691.

Keskinen, Suvi, Salla Tuori, Sara Irni, and Diana Mulinari, eds. 2016. Complying with Colonialism: Gender, Race, and Ethnicity in the Nordic Region. New York: Routledge

Keskinen, Suvi, Unnur Dís Skaptadóttir, and Mari Toivanen. 2019. "Narrations of Homogeneity, Waning Wel-fare States, and the Politics of Solidarity." In Undoing Homogeneity in the Nordic Region, 1–17. New York: Routledge. http://dx.doi.org/10.4324/9781315122328-1.

Khabeer, Su'ad Abdul. 2016. Muslim Cool: Race, Religion, and Hip Hop in the United States. New York: New York University Press.

Kjartansdóttir, Katla, and Kristinn Schram. 2020. "Mobilizing the Arctic: Polar Bears and Puffins in Transnational Interplay." In Mobility and Transnational Iceland: Current Transformations and Global Entanglements, edited by Kristín Loftsdóttir, Unnur Dís Skaptadóttir, and Sigurjón Baldur Hafsteinsson, 209–29. Reykjavik: University of Iceland Press. https://opinvisindi.is/bitstream/handle/20.500.11815/2333/Mobility _09022021_TOTAL.pdf?sequence=3.

Loftsdóttir, Kristín. 2013. "Republishing 'the Ten Little Negros': Exploring Nationalism and 'Whiteness' in Iceland." Ethnicities 13, no. 3: 295–315. https://doi.org/10.1177/1468796812472854.

———. 2015. 'Útlendingar, Negrastrákar og Hryðjuverkamenn: Kynþáttafordómar í Íslenskum Samtíma; Kynþáttafordómar í Íslenskum Samtíma. Ritið 15, no. 1: 157–79.

———. 2019a. Crisis and Coloniality at Europe's Margins: Creating Exotic Iceland. New York: Taylor and Francis.

———. 2019b. "Dualistic Colonial Experiences and the Ruins of Coloniality." Scandinavian Studies 91, no. 12: 31–52. http://dx.doi.org/10.5406/scanstud.91.1-2.0031.

———. 2023. "Marketing Marginality: Creating Iceland as a White Privileged Destination." In Creating Europe from the Margins, edited by Kristín Loftsdóttir, Brigitte Hipfl, and Sandra Ponzanesi. New York: Routledge.

Loftsdóttir, Kristín, Eyrún Eyþórsdóttir, and Margaret Willson. 2021. "Becoming Nordic in Brazil." Nordic Journal of Migration Research 11, no. 1: 80–94. http://dx.doi.org/https://doi.org/10.33134/njmr.403.

Loftsdóttir, Kristín, and Lars Jensen, eds. 2016. Whiteness and Postcolonialism in the Nordic Region: Exceptional-ism, Migrant Others, and National Identities. New York: Routledge.

Loftsdóttir, Kristín, and Már Wolfgang Mixa. 2021. "Nations of Bankers and Brexiteers? Nationalism and Hid-den Money." Race and Class 63, no. 2: 58–75. https://doi.org/10.1177/03063968211033525.

Loftsdóttir, Kristín, and Sanna Magdalena Mörtudóttir. 2022. "'Where Are You From?': Racism and the Nor-malization of Whiteness in Iceland." Journal of Critical Mixed Race Studies 1, no. 2: 215–32. https://doi.org /10.5070/C81258340.

Loftsdóttir, Kristín, Unnur Dís Skaptadóttir, and Sigurjón Baldur Hafsteinsson. 2020. Mobility and Transna-tional Iceland: Current Transformations and Global Entanglements. Háskólaútgáfan. https://opinvisindi.is /bitstream/handle/20.500.11815/2333/Mobility_09022021_TOTAL.pdf?sequence=3.

McIntosh, Laurie. 2015. "Impossible Presence: Race, Nation, and the Cultural Politics of 'Being Norwegian.'" Ethnic and Racial Studies 38, no. 2: 309–25. https://doi.org/10.1080/01419870.2013.868017.

Meer, Nasar. 2020. "Introduction: The Wreckage of White Supremacy." In Whiteness and Nationalism, 1–9. New York: Routledge.

Moore, Henrietta L. 2004. "Global Anxieties: Concept-Metaphors and Pre-Theoretical Commitments in Anthropology." *Anthropological Theory* 4, no. 1: 71–88. https://doi.org/10.1177/1463499604040848.

Moreton-Robinson, Aileen. 2015. *The White Possessive: Property, Power, and Indigenous Sovereignty.* Minneapolis: University of Minnesota Press.

Naum, Magdalena, and Jonas M. Nordin, eds. 2013. *Scandinavian Colonialism and the Rise of Modernity: Small Time Agents in a Global Arena.* New York: Springer Science and Business Media.

Nguyen, Thu T., Shaniece Criss, Eli K. Michaels, Rebekah I. Cross, Jackson S. Michaels, Pallavi Dwivedi, Dina Huang et al. 2021. "Progress and Push-Back: How the Killings of Ahmaud Arbery, Breonna Taylor, and George Floyd Impacted Public Discourse on Race and Racism on Twitter." *SSM-Population Health* 15: 100922. https://doi.org/10.1016/j.ssmph.2021.100922.

Nowicka, Magdalena. 2018. "'I Don't Mean to Sound Racist but . . .' Transforming Racism in Transnational Europe." *Ethnic and Racial Studies* 41, no. 5: 824–41. https://doi.org/10.1080/01419870.2017.1302093.

Pálsdóttir, Inga Hlín, and Einar Karl Haraldsson. 2011. *Come and Be Inspired by Iceland: Skýrsla samstarfsaðila.* Reykjavik: Íslandsstofa.

Pietersen J. N. 1992. *White on Black: Images of Africa and Blacks in Western Popular Culture.* New Haven, CT: Yale University Press.

Pitcher, Ben. 2014. *Consuming Race.* London: Routledge.

Puwar, Nirmal. 2004. *Space Invaders: Race, Gender, and Bodies Out of Place.* Oxford: Berg Publishers.

Rastas, Anna. 2005. "Racializing Categorization among Young People in Finland." *Young* 13, no. 2: 147–66. https://doi.org/10.1177/1103308805051319.

Rastrick, Ólafur. 2013. *Háborgin.* Reykjavik: Háskólaútgáfan.

Sawyer, Lena, and Ylva Habel. 2014. "Refracting African and Black Diaspora through the Nordic Region." *African and Black Diaspora: An International Journal* 7, no. 1: 1–6. https://doi.org/10.1080/17528631.2013 .861235.

Shankar, Shalini. 2019. "Nothing Sells Like Whiteness: Race, Ontology, and American Advertising." *American Anthropologist* 122, no. 1: 112–19. https://doi.org/10.1111/aman.13354.

Sigfúsdóttir, Sylvia Rut. 2020. "Tegund Ofbeldis Sem Þrífst í þögninni: "Kölluð Grjón og Núðla."" *Vísir,* June 28. www.visir.is/g/20201985789d/tegund-ofbeldis-sem-thrifst-ithogninni-kollud-grjon-og-nudla.

Skaptadóttir, Unnur Dís, and Kristín Loftsdóttir. 2009. "Cultivating Culture? Images of Iceland, Globalization, and Multicultural Society." In *Images of the North,* 205–16. Leiden: Brill. https://doi.org/10.1163 /9789042029064_020.

———. 2020. "Becoming an Immigration Country: The Case of Iceland, 1990–2019." In *Mobility and Transnational Iceland: Current Transformations and Global Entanglements,* edited by Kristín Loftsdóttir, Unnur Dís Skaptadóttir, and Sigurjón Baldur Hafsteinsson, 23–38. Reykjavik: University of Iceland Press. https:// opinvisindi.is/bitstream/handle/20.500.11815/2333/Mobility_09022021_TOTAL.pdf?sequence=3.

Social Statistics. 2023. Innflytjendur 16,3% íbúa landsins, November 24, 2022, 24. https://hagstofa.is/utgafur /frettasafn/mannfjoldi/mannfjoldi-eftir-bakgrunni-2022/.

Sverdljuk, Jana, Terje Mikael Hasle Joranger, Erika K. Jackson, and Peter Kivisto, eds. 2020. *Nordic Whiteness and Migration to the USA: A Historical Exploration of Identity.* New York: Routledge.

Tan, Catherine, and Janani Umamaheswar. 2022. "Structural Racism and the Experience of 'Tightness' during the COVID-19 Pandemic." *Ethnic and Racial Studies* 45, no. 9: 1649–70. https://doi.org/10.1080/01419870 .2021.1959625.

Vertelytė, Mantė, and Peter Hervik. 2019. "The Vices of Debating Racial Epithets in Danish News Media Discourse." In *Racialization, Racism, and Anti-Racism in the Nordic Countries,* edited by Peter Hervik, 163–81. London: Palgrave Macmillan.

15

White Supremacist Ways of Knowing Africa

ANTHROPOLOGY AND MUSLIM DEVELOPMENT IN MALI

Rhea Rahman

IN 1997 THE NGO ISLAMIC RELIEF began operating in the northern Mali town of Gourma Rharous. The UK-based global organization contracted with the UN High Commissioner for Refugees to facilitate the return of Tuaregs who had fled during the "Tuareg Rebellion" that began in 1990 and ceremonially concluded in 1996 (Benthall 2006, 19). Due to the success of their operations, Islamic Relief–Mali established a national head office in the capital of Bamako in 2005 and later opened a third office and base for development projects in the southern town of Oulessebougou. When I started research with the organization in 2012, Islamic Relief–Mali had established a number of development projects, including an orphan sponsorship program, multiple women's economic empowerment groups, and several microdam projects to "green the desert." Given the achievements of their programs, Islamic Relief–Mali received consistent funding from international aid agencies.

I had initially planned to conduct research with a more recently established Islamic Relief office in Chad. However, just days before I was to board a flight to N'Djamena in October 2011, I received an email from an administrator in the organization's global headquarters in Birmingham, UK, explaining that due to rising security concerns in Chad, administrators felt the organization could not guarantee my safety and consequently would not be able offer me a letter of affiliation, which I needed to obtain an entry visa. Graciously, they suggested I visit their office in Bamako, Mali, instead. At the time, Mali was considered the safest and most stable country of all those that Islamic Relief operated in throughout West Africa. I arrived in Bamako in February 2012. Over the course of the next six weeks, I reviewed archival documents, worked with local staff on funding applications and reports to donors, visited development projects around Bamako and

Oulessebougou, and met with administrators and fundraisers visiting the Mali office from the organization's headquarters in the United Kingdom.

On Tuesday, March 21, 2012, while working toward an urgent deadline with local staff on a multi-million-euro funding proposal, staff members began receiving calls and started frantically collecting their things. Sensing my confusion at what was happening, an office manager explained to me that everyone was told to go home immediately. Overhearing the conversation, another staff member held up trigger fingers and made gunshot noises. As would eventually become widely known, a group of low-ranking officers conducted what was referred to as the "accidental coup."[1] In the days, weeks, and months that followed, armed groups—alternately named as either Tuareg, or Islamist "rebels" in Western media—took control of up to a third of the country's northern territory.

While I had planned to remain in Mali for one year, due to the political instability following the coup I had to leave and was only able to return in 2019. When I did, an administrator I had met on my initial trip in 2012 told me that it was no longer the same Mali. Before the coup, Mali was regarded as a model of multiparty democracy in the region and considered a favored recipient of donations from the Western aid industry. However, by 2019, Western-based international policy and development "experts" deemed Mali the epicenter of multiple crises: analysts bemoaned the country's descent into extremist Islamist violence, regarding the Sahel region as the latest front for the Global War on Terror, and narrated violence in central Mali as the effect of centuries old ethnic tensions that erupted into a crisis of ethnic cleansing.

This way of understanding Mali—as subject to localized crises instigated by "Islamic terrorism" and "ethnic" conflict—is what I describe as *white supremacist ways of knowing Africa*. I argue that white supremacy conditions how both the international aid industry, and "mainstream" Africanist anthropology,[2] "know" Africa. To counter these analyses that, in denying global political and historical context, rely on what I will elucidate here are implicitly racist "cultural" explanations, I bring to light obscured legacies of colonial racial science and the material conditions of racial capitalism that I maintain are at the root of the so-called Mali crisis. I highlight the increase of violence and political insecurity throughout the country that follows American, French, and European military intervention. Attempts to contain supposed Islamist extremism have exacerbated tensions between local groups. Rather than the result of local influences, I affirm that the increase of violence in Mali is a result of increased Western military interventions intersecting with extreme climate change that has drastically reduced resources for survival in the region. By confining analysis to local causes, *white supremacist ways of knowing Africa* eschew the role of global processes of American imperialism, European neocolonialism, climate colonialism,[3] and racial capitalism in creating and sustaining catastrophic conditions in Mali.

As the editors of this volume have defined elsewhere, white supremacy designates "a structuring logic that serves as the baseline for modernity and its cognates of liberalism, democracy, progress, and rationality" (Beliso-De Jesús and Pierre 2020, 3). Correspondingly, the logic of white supremacy undergirds the international aid industry's efforts toward development, humanitarianism, and "peace." Mainstream anthropology, on the other hand, has provided the categories of analysis used by the international aid industry to make sense of African "crises." While thoroughgoing discussion of all the factors contributing to violent unrest in Mali is beyond the scope of this chapter, I show how the discursive field of anthropology and development promote racialized analysis of three aspects of the Mali crises: first, the distinction between "white" North Africa and "Black" sub-Saharan Africa that shapes analysis of the Tuareg rebellions; second, global anti-Muslim racism that structures the move of the Global War on Terror to the Sahel; and third, racialized use of the language and logic of "ethnic cleansing" to theorize conflict in central Mali. I conclude with an analysis of first Malian president Modibo Keïta's Islamic socialist vision for a newly independent Mali. I offer this account to provide an alternative conception of "Islamic development" that challenges the inevitability of Mali's dependency on foreign aid and its subordinated position within global racial capitalism.

The theorization of the whiteness of the international aid industry, and its use of anthropological categories of analysis, is illuminated by an examination of a Muslim development and humanitarian NGO such as Islamic Relief. As a Muslim NGO, Islamic Relief is also subject to the anti-Muslim racism that frames the ongoing Global War on Terror.[4] As Muslim actors in the international aid industry, Islamic Relief is subject to surveillance, suspicion, and designations of terrorism that are not extended to their non-Muslim counterparts.[5] However, as the tenets of international development are structured according to a logic of white supremacy, in order to successfully operate as a UK-based global NGO, Islamic Relief must concede to and operate within a foundational logic of white supremacy.

As I elaborate below, "development" can offer solutions that operate within a system that sees "problems" only in terms of what "development" can fix. As both development and anthropology epistemologically approach African realities in isolation from global processes,[6] and therefore take the aforementioned "crises" in Mali as due to local causes, the "solutions" offered within these frameworks are similarly localized. This way of engaging sites of development, more specifically development sites in Africa, and even more specifically within "Black" Africa, does not allow for a deep engagement of the historical and political contextualization of the conditions to which they respond.[7] The systemic logic of white supremacy prevents Islamic Relief from addressing and upending the global power structures that maintain Black Africa's marginalized position in the global economy—in other words, the conditions that make and sustain Mali's "poverty," and a subject to violent "crisis" in the first place. As long as "development"—even "Islamic development"—is unable to address root, global causes, I maintain that it remains limited in its stated goals "to save and transform the lives of some of the world's most vulnerable people" (Islamic Relief Worldwide 2023).

White Supremacist Africanist Anthropology

In February 2012, just weeks before the "accidental coup," a group of Islamic Relief fundraisers came to Mali to visit development projects and collect stories and marketing materials to promote and fund-raise back in the United Kingdom. On their first day, one of the fundraisers—composed of a group of young men from England, mostly of Pakistani descent—asked local staff about the situation in the north. They had heard that there were security issues that prevented them from visiting Islamic Relief's projects there. He asked for the background regarding the conflict: "Just give us the context, what are the deliverables, what are the needs?" Seemingly amused by the question, a local staff member said that there were three related problems: "Fighting, famine, and the crisis in Libya, with [Tuareg] fighters coming back into Mali." Addressing these root causes of conflict could not translate to the deliverables the fundraisers were looking for. As reflected in this exchange, development solutions require the reduction of complexity and nuance in order to offer "deliverable" solutions.

The elimination of context relegates development initiatives to what Mahmood Mamdani refers to as "culture talk," which he describes as the use of cultural explanations in place of political and historical analysis (Mamdani 2002). As Pierre argues in her analysis of the racial vernaculars of development (2020a), development in and of Africa relies on implicit racialized assumptions of African cultural/racialized inferiority, which serves to obscure a politicized historical analysis that could instead foreground "the continent's long history of unequal and exploitive experiences with colonial control, global capitalism, and neocolonialism" (2020, 90). Further, Africanist anthropology's emphasis on African realities through the categories of "ethnicity" is an effect of colonial racial politics that continues to influence emic and etic interpretations of identity, difference, and conflict on the continent (Pierre 2013, 35–36, 204). The lasting effects of colonial concepts of identity and difference condition the ways conflict and violence in Africa are understood and "managed."

Anthropology and international development belong to the same discursive field that anthropologist Michel-Rolph Trouillot has referred to as a "geography of imagination of the West" (2003). Trouillot notes, "this framework has always assumed the centrality of the North Atlantic not only as the site from which world history is made but also as the site whence that story can be told" (2003, 12). This discursive field separates "the West" from "the Rest," in effect, differentiating the people and places of the world who "know," from those that "are known." In West Africa, some of the earliest European studies of African society and culture came from the so-called scholar-administrators of the colonial era. In the second half of the nineteenth century armchair theorists from colonizing countries compared and ranked data about "primitive" peoples on an evolutionary scale from primitive to civilized. The basis of this comparison was "race." Scholars produced and specialized in distinct aspects of race from physical types, stages of evolution in human prehistory, and universal laws of cultural evolution (Conklin 2013).

Whereas the earliest anthropology was committed to a biological basis for racial hierarchy, in the mid-twentieth century, the cultural turn led in the United States by Franz Boas, in Britain with structural functionalism, and in France with ethnology, signaled a departure from the biological, racial supremacist logic of earlier anthropology. For his part, for example, Boas played an essential role in the development of a theory of cultural relativism, which was in part an effort to move away from the racial superiority of scientific racism. However, the replacement with the use of the category of "culture," and for Africanist anthropology in particular, "kinship," and later, "ethnicity" (Pierre 2020b), simply served as placeholders for "race" (Visweswaran 1998; Trouillot 2003). Hence, this liberal turn only maintained the foundational epistemological logic of racial superiority (Rana 2020). As Pierre has argued, the focus in African studies on ethnicity, as opposed to race and racialization, limits analysis of African realities to African-African relations, as opposed to African-European relations, and thereby obscures a broader analysis of racial hierarchies constituted through the global political economy (Pierre 2020).

Moreover, the underlying racial logic that undergirds the categorization of difference within Africanist anthropology is a legacy of colonial political classification. In West Africa, and contemporary Mali more specifically, a colonial legacy endures in the geographical and racial distinction between North and Sub-Saharan Africa (Lydon 2015), which separates Arab and Berber peoples from Black Africans. In French West Africa, this divide materialized through distinct perceptions of Islam's influence. As one of the earliest ethnologists to establish this distinction, Maurice Delafosse (1926) differentiates the Negro races of Africa from the non-Negro peoples of North Africa. To counter a perceived threat from the influence of Islam—and the geopolitical alliances Islam potentially posed to French colonial interests in the North and West Africa—Delafosse points out the merit of highlighting traditional African culture that was outside the influence of Islam (Delafosse 1926).

French concern with the perceived threat of "Arab" or "orthodox" Islam brought about an idea of "African" Islam as a source of possible allyship (Seesemann 2011, 12). As effective armed resistance against colonial conquest had been organized in North Africa, "Arab" Islam was perceived to be orthodox, based in scripture, and ultimately legalistic—and fanatic—in nature. "Black" Islam, as practiced in sub-Saharan Africa, was seen as syncretic, infused with magical praxis, more tolerant—and less fanatic. This colonial interest in dividing North African (white) and sub-Saharan (Black) Islam constructed racialized distinctions as newly solidified political identities.

This colonial constructed geographical/racial divide is expressed in a Western academic disciplinary divide. Following Delafosse, the disciplinary commitments of anthropology left the study of "proper" Islam, as practiced by non-Black Muslims in North Africa, to Orientalists and historians, whereas anthropologists were concerned with the study of an "authentic" African culture, untouched by "outside" influence (Launay 2006; Soares 2014). The French school of ethnology was particularly influential and characterized early anthropological study of West Africa. Marcel Griaule, one of the first anthropologists to undertake extensive field research in West Africa, was primarily concerned with African cosmologies as holistic and worthy of study on their own terms. His was a humanist project to validate African systems of thought—in essence, to affirm that Black Africans were not primitive or illogical. Yet to do so, he had to present these systems as "authentically African" and thereby uncontaminated by European or Islamic influences (Launay 2006). Yet the effort to focus on "authentic" African culture, and the resulting exclusive focus on ethnicity within Africanist anthropology, is to study African realities in isolation from broader political economic conditions. I now look at how Tuareg rebellions in Mali have been conceptualized in terms of this produced racialized distinction of "white" Tuaregs refusing to be ruled by their Black southern counterparts. In its place, I make the case for analyzing these tensions in terms of the effects of racial capitalism.

The North—A History of Tuareg Rebellions

The assimilation of the Tuareg people—who, according to anthropological categories of analysis are considered a "Berber ethnic group"—into the Malian nation-state has been in dispute since independence in 1960. Scholars have described their rebellions and resistance to join the Malian state in racialized terms.[8] This distinction operated through the French colonial concept of *Islam noir*, which distinguished those the French perceived as practicing a more militant practice of Islam who were racialized as "white" Arab-Berbers, versus the moderate, more Sufi-inspired Islam practiced by Black African Muslims. Significantly, scholars have also engaged an important debate concerning whether racial categories of "white" and "Black" are the product of European colonial intercessions, or whether these racial markers are a "distant and refracted borrowing from the Arabo-African past" (Lecocq 2010, 94).

Questions regarding the origins of whiteness and anti-Black racism in relation to Muslim Africa is significant for this analysis of a Muslim relief organization run by predominantly non-Black Muslims, operating in the majority Black Muslim African country of Mali. In his widely cited *Race and Color in Islam* (1971) Bernard Lewis associates anti-Blackness and slavery with Islam and the so-called Arab or Islamic slave trade that predates European trans-atlantic slavery. A number of scholars have acknowledged the Islamophobia and Orientalism that founds this position (McDougall 2002; Aidi 2005; Ware 2011; Miller 2017; Bashir 2019). In opposition to Lewis, the works of Mamdani argue that modern racism was a product of *Euro-American* slavery (2018) and colonialism (1996b; 2004; 2012).

In their examination of the place of race in the historical study of Africa and its relevance for Muslim Africa in particular, Young and Weitzberg (2021) make the case for a global framing to questions of race and racism. Significantly, they note the distinction between race thinking and racism. With regard to the question of anti-Blackness in Islam, they write that while "Antiblack discourses as well as rhetoric valorizing Blackness can be found in Islamic texts for most time periods, dating as far back as antiquity . . . the presence of racial discourse is not synonymous with racism as a structural condition" (Young and Weitzberg 2021, 20). Thus, while scholars have highlighted the role of racial thinking in narratives surrounding Tuareg rebellions—in terms of "white" Berbers refusing to be ruled by "Black" Sudanese counterparts—my interest here is on noting the effects of racism as a structural condition and its place in a global political economy. Thus, I situate the Tuareg rebellions in a global context and in terms of racial capitalism to highlight the effects of European-American entanglement in fashioning the "local" conditions of the rebellions.

Whereas in 1946 France authorized the creation of political parties in its African colonies, "the discovery of mineral riches in the Sahara in the mid-1950s made many in France reluctant to grant full independence to the Saharan possessions" (Lecocq 2010, 23). However, a newly independent Moroccan Sultanate claimed large parts of the Sahara as part of the historical sultanate, which Lecocq suggests are the first seeds of a burgeoning Saharan nationalism, as opposed to a slowly evolving Malian nationalism (Lecocq 2010, 23). Thus, by the time of the 1963 rebellion, three years after Malian independence, while Tuareg elites engaged racial thinking highlighting the influence and internalization of colonial hierarchies of the "natural order" of whites ruling Blacks, this racialized discourse of the rebellion conceals conditions of increasingly fraught competition over access to material resources—not only valuable mineral riches but necessities for survival such as pasture and water.

Of the second uprising that began in 1990, scholars have pointed to the role of international aid provision as a source of conflict. Some have suggested that the encouragement of sedentarization severed pastoralists from their own social and spatial networks, deemed key for surviving droughts and conflict, and that perhaps ultimately the "allocation and withdrawal of emergency aid has become the currency that regulates mobility, conflict and peace" (Giuffrida 2005, 541). While Tuareg uprisings are discussed as racial in nature, racial thinking takes on significant meaning when it conditions competition over resources. In other words, racialized categories of difference become meaningful political identities to manage competition over resources given geopolitical economic realities conditioned by global capitalism.

Islamic Relief began relief work in Mali at the end of the second uprising to help rehabilitate returning Tuareg refugees to northern Mali. At the time, Islamic NGOs were exerting a growing influence in the region, attempting to "fill gaps in economic assistance left in the wake of IMF and World Bank restructuring policies" (Rasmussen 2007, 189). However, this period also overlaps, not uncoincidentally, with growing US militarism in the region. As director of the African Security Research Project Daniel Volman notes, US foreign policy makers perceived two major reasons for American involvement in the region in the late 1990s: (1) the United States was becoming increasingly dependent on resources, particularly oil, from Africa, and (2) mounting activity of armed Islamic groups in Africa, particularly with the bombings of US embassies in Kenya and Tanzania in 1998 (Volman 2010). However, as already noted regarding the unintended effect of foreign aid in exacerbating and contributing to conflict in northern Mali, David Gutelius warned in 2007 of the destabilizing effects *not* of growing religious extremism, but rather a US-government-led promotion of a Global War on Terror in the Sahel (Gutelius 2007).[9]

We see how through growing American militarization in the region, the Global War on Terror intersects with the 2012 Tuareg uprising. In the weeks following the coup in March 2012, numerous so-called rebel groups seized all major towns in northern Mali, bringing approximately two-thirds of the country under their control. However, a split developed between the secular National Movement for the Liberation of Azawad (MNLA), who declared a new Tuareg state of Azawad, and the "Islamist" Ansar Dine and their allies, including Al Qaeda in the Islamic Maghreb (AQIM) and the Movement for Oneness and Jihad in West Africa (MUJAO). The groups Ansar Dine, AQIM, and MUJAO destroyed mausoleums and other historical and sacred Islamic sites, acts described as a war on Mali's "moderate Islam" (Sandner 2015).

While much has been written about the shifting domains of religious and political Islamic authority in Mali (Brenner 2001; Soares 2005; Schulz 2011), I seek to highlight the global context and material conditions of racial capitalism that undergird "local" articulations of religious, political, and social difference and how they shape conflict in Mali. For example, Mali's economy remains one of the poorest on earth, with major sections of the north economically disenfranchised. Despite holding reserves of valuable resources such as cotton, gold, and uranium, the majority of profits from these resources are exported abroad and not invested in Mali itself. Whereas Tuareg rebellions have been discussed in terms of racialized tensions between "white" Tuareg and Black Africans, such analyses lack a global contextualization of racial capitalism. While racialized categories of white and Black in Mali also have local histories and meanings, their articulations take place within broader global orders that reflect unequal relations between Malians (white or Black) and foreign (Euro-American) domination and exploitation of resources. However, in addition to foreign exploitation of resources, Western militarization in Mali plays a related and significant role in localized conflict. As Gutelius notes, the US-led Pan-Sahel Initiative was seen by many within Mali as "yet another attack on Islam" (Gutelius 2007, 67). In order to situate the racialized context of the spread of the Global War on Terror to the Sahel, I turn now to an account of foreign military intervention following the 2012 coup.

French Intervention and the Global War on Terror

Following a UN Security Council resolution in December 2012, and an official request by the Malian interim government, warfare in the north led to French military intervention in January 2013. Under the name Operation Serval, this effort brought more than 4,000 French troops to stop armed groups from advancing further southward in Mali (Moctar 2022). In 2014, this French military intervention was renamed Operation Barkhane and entailed a more expansive and ambitious counterinsurgency effort in former French colonies across the Sahel. Operation Barkhane sought to support military forces fighting armed insurgents in the region. By 2017, five years into France's military intervention in Mali, some commentators suggested that Mali had become France's Afghanistan (Ayad 2017; Pezard and Shurkin 2017).

Security concerns regarding the Sahel were not limited to France: in 2011 the European Union launched a Strategy for Security and Development in Sahel and deployed military and civilian missions to train armed forces in counterterrorism tactics and strategies (Larivé 2014). In a policy brief, the Sahel is pronounced "Europe's African border"; mention is made of multidimensional crises, such as poor governance, corruption, structural weaknesses, underdevelopment, drought, famine, criminality, illicit trafficking, and the rise of Jihadism (Ghanem-Yazbeck 2018). Significantly, not only are there concerns over how to stop the flow of people from the Sahel into Europe, in addition, the EU has substantial economic interests in the region, with the EU's top ore and mineral supplies coming from Mauritania, and Niger providing uranium for France's nuclear reactors, which generate 75 percent of France's electricity (Ghanem-Yazbeck 2018).

While EU efforts toward securitizing the Sahel could be traced to protecting European interests, the failure of these efforts to contain armed groups—or to keep civilians safe—in the Sahel, has further destabilized the region. Following EU and French military interventions, the Malian army staged two more coups, first in August 2020, and again in May 2021. Whereas in 2013, many Malians celebrated the arrival of French troops (Whitehouse 2013), since 2020 mass demonstrations called for the removal of French troops from Mali (Kulkarni 2022). Demonstrations evidence that Malians not only hold their civilian governments accountable but also the European powers and governmental bodies that have led the counterinsurgency operations (Moctar 2022). Escalating tensions between Malian and French governments following the August 2020 coup led to the expulsion of France's ambassador to Mali on February 1 (Al-Jazeera 2022), and ultimately, on February 17, 2022, French president Emmanuel Macron's announcement of the withdrawal of all French troops from the region.

Despite increasing international counterterrorism forces and military operations, violent attacks and reprisal killings increased throughout 2021. As the Council on Foreign Relations warns, "major terrorist networks and other militant groups remain a threat in Mali" ("Destabilization of Mali" 2022). Another report notes that the number of violent incidents increased from 115 events in 2014 to 1,007 in 2021 (Kulkarni 2022). The violence and conflict in northern Mali spread to the country's central region of Mopti. As the International Crisis Group reports, since 2016, the central Mali area of Mopti has witnessed unprecedented violence, referred to as "Mali's Descent into Communal Violence" (2020) between Fulani and Dogon civilians.

"Mali's Descent into Communal Violence"

On March 23, 2019, more than 150 Fulani/Peule[10] herders were killed in one of the deadliest such attacks in the Mopti region of central Mali. Attacks were described as taking place between rival ethnic communities of Fulani herders and Dogon farmers. Whereas land disputes and tensions between these groups have been noted from the earliest Western accounts of the Sahel, many reports stated that the violence between these groups in 2019 was unprecedented and had reached levels that qualified as ethnic cleansing (International Crisis Group 2019).

When I returned to Mali in July 2019, staff were involved in the emergency response to support thousands of internally displaced people (IDPs) fleeing violence in central Mali. One staff member I interviewed had just returned from the town of Segou in which Islamic Relief–Mali distributed cash to Fulani refugees. At a management meeting in Bamako, staff discussed growing security concerns and risk assessment for their field operations, such as the cash distribution in Segou. Ongoing security concerns since the coup in 2012 included abduction of staff, hijacking, and the theft of assets. One non-Malian staff member asked if they should send one Peule and one Dogon security guard to monitor distributions. However, the Malian staff member who facilitated the cash distribution program in Segou affirmed that the situation on the ground was complicated and that even attempting to distinguish Peule from Dogon was problematic at best, if not impossible in practice. Whereas non-Malian staff bought into Western-based analyses of the crisis as one of straightforward "ethnic" tensions between distinct groups, Malian staff knew and understood that these divisions were nuanced, malleable, and complex.

While conducting research at an Islamic Relief site in southern Mali in 2019, I asked villagers about the violence in the central region. Village elders affirmed that the ethnic groups now supposed to be fighting each other—the Peule/Fulani and Dogon—despite having conflict over resources, had also coexisted peacefully for centuries. A few villagers affirmed to me their suspicion of ongoing neocolonial aspirations and the extent to which French economic interests could be served by ongoing regional insecurity. One asked, "how did these poor farmers suddenly get all these weapons and ammunition"?

European-led counterinsurgency initiatives have brought more instability and arms to the region. One of the consequences of the racialized Global War on Terror is that the Peule/Fulani people have increasingly become associated with so-called Islamist militants and characterized as supporters of Jihadists groups. In the absence of state protection from increased insecurity and violence from armed Islamic groups in the region, vigilante squads supposedly led by Dogon and Bambara factions have steered attacks on Fulani villages.[11] As political scientist Alex Thurston notes, "The ethnicization of violence in central Mali became both an effect of escalation and a cause for it; whatever government support existed for anti-Peul militias created dynamics that the government could not control" (2020, 178). Meanwhile, Konaré suggests that the Fulani have felt abandoned and attacked by European-led counterinsurgency initiatives such as the G5 Sahel Joint Force, which they recognized as coming to eliminate Fula societies and "forever stain them with false hypothesis of their collaboration with jihadists" (Konaré 2021, 57).

A transitional Malian government communiqué from 2022 holds Europeans accountable for its role in creating conditions of instability in Mali:

> The Government of Mali reminds that (it) [European intervention in the fight against terrorism] . . . would not have been necessary if the NATO had not intervened in Libya in 2011. This intervention, which fundamentally changed the security situation in the region and in which France played an active role . . . is the root of the security problems in Mali in particular, and in the Sahel in general. (Cited in Kulkarni 2022)

And while international policy reports recognize increased competition over resources due to climate change as some of the root causes of "ethnic" or communal violence (Thibaud 2005; Ursu 2018), the Global North's responsibility for creating climate change is not addressed. Thus, despite recognizing the global political context that produces land conflict as the root causes of ethnic violence, "culture talk" (Mamdani 2002) places responsibility for violence on so-called ethnic African groups. Many reports describe the attacks as ethnic violence, the rising of age-old tensions between Dogon and Fulani, pastoralists and agriculturalists. This perspective obscures broader global forces that provide instigation and context for the conflict. Escalation of violence from a Global War on Terror is reduced to localized ethnic violence. The violence and conditions of crisis to which

Islamic Relief, and the development industry more broadly, responds to, are political, not ethnic. "Development" and humanitarianism would look quite different if instead we addressed the global political conditions at the root of conflict and crisis. By way of conclusion, I turn now to an alternative vision of Islamic development. I explore first president of Mali Modibo Keïta's vision for Islamic socialism and the global political constraints that impeded that vision.

A Future Foreclosed: Keïta's Islamic Socialist Visions

The political origins of the state of Mali did not begin with a conception of the nation-state, but rather in the short-lived union between the territories of the Sudanese Republic and Senegal, known as the Mali Federation. The Union Sudanaise–Rassemblement Démocratique Africain (US-RDA)—an interterritorial coalition of anticolonial political parties in French West Africa—formed in 1945 and was the primary force shaping a socialist federation of regional integration. The federation achieved independence on June 20, 1960; however, due to conflicts over its political course, within just two months, it dissolved. On September 22,1960, the federation became the independent Republic of Mali, with Modibo Keïta as its first president, and the US-RDA as the only legal party.

For Keïta, the collapse of the federation and the formation of an independent nation-state was a compromise of his ideals of Islamic socialism and was seen by socialist politicians in French West Africa as a form of political divide and rule (Lecocq 2010, 33). As with other African socialist leaders such as Kwame Nkrumah and Patrice Lumumba, Keïta sought to take aspects from Western Marxism and specify them for an African context. For Keïta this involved the conjoining of Islam and Malian history. In a speech delivered in Algiers in 1964, Keïta states, "Mali and her leaders draw their inspiration for socialist construction from the theory of Marxism-Leninism. But we do not adopt its materialist philosophy, and we do not adopt its atheism, because we are believers" (cited in Snyder 1967, 86). He specifies, "There is no religion more socialist than the Moslem religion, because it teaches among its principles that the rich must give to the poor, must divide their goods in order to relieve the suffering of others" (cited in Hazard 1967, 33).

Recognizing that political independence was futile without economic independence, Keïta proposed severing Mali currency from its tether to the French franc. In a speech to the National Assembly on June 30, 1962, Keïta announced, "However far back in time we may go, history teaches us that political power is always and necessarily accompanied by the sovereign right of minting money, that monetary power is inseparable from national sovereignty, that it is its necessary complement, its attribute" (cited in Snyder 1967, 85). On July 1, 1962, Keïta abandoned the CFA franc and created the Malian franc—a nonconvertible currency—the creation of which entailed Mali's exit from the West African Monetary Union. However, after sixty-eight years (1892–1960) of formal colonial exploitation through the establishment of agricultural plantations, mining operations, and forced labor, by the time of political independence Mali did not have the resources to implement the US-RDA's plans for national economic development. The party turned to human investment, implementing programs that required the population to work voluntarily on construction sites in their spare time (Lecocq 2010, 80). With so few resources to develop the nation self-sufficiently,[12] the US-RDA implemented policies such as demanding free labor or curtailing labor migration, which "resembled colonial practices it had helped abolish a decade earlier" (Lecocq 2010, 81). And despite Keïta's insistence to not rely on European aid,[13] with growing debt and a weak nonconvertible currency that threatened the country's export-driven economic plan, by 1967 Keïta appealed to France for reintegration into the CFA zone. The Malian franc was devalued by 50 percent, "resulting in increased foreign debt, rising crop prices and more budget shortfalls" (Skinner 2012, 518).

Whereas political-economic analyses of Keïta's socialist vision of development for Mali often fault fraud, corruption, and unrealistic socialist economic policies as primary causes for Keïta's eventual overthrow in a coup d'état headed by Lieutenant Moussa Traore in November 1968, an analysis situated in the context of global racial capitalism provides an alternative understanding of the failures of Keïta and the US-RDA party to enact their anticolonial vision of self-sufficient development. The economic oppression entailed by French colonial and neocolonial policies forestalled opportunities for Malian (or more broadly West African) political and economic self-sufficiency. While a thorough analysis of France's role in the continued extraction of Malian resources (Becker 2001; Tadei 2018) is beyond the scope of this chapter, I offer this account of a foreclosed vision and gesture to an alternative future in order to question the inevitability of Mali's dependency on foreign aid. Yet it is Mali's dependency on foreign aid that conditions the possibility for Islamic Relief's development and humanitarian work in the region. In an imagining of alternative possibilities, I ask, how might Islamic Relief respond differently if it was able to engage this other history of Mali's potential vision of Islamic socialism, instead of operating within the limits of white supremacist "development"?

Conclusion

In Mali today, the crises that are cause for Islamic Relief's presence are not the effects of "ethnic" or "local" disputes. The violence and insecurity that has affected the country since 2012 are the result of global political conflicts and point to two global logics of racialization. The first is a global logic of anti-Muslim racism that undergirds the movement of the Global War on Terror to the Sahel. In addition, anti-Muslim racism undergirds French colonial fear of Islam as a particular threat to European civilization. This logic of racism continues to manifest both the fear and creation of, militant Islamism. Second, the effects of Western military counterinsurgency have exacerbated what is being described as communal or ethnic violence in central Mali. This violence can be understood in terms of a global logic of anti-Black racism that condemns Africans as inherently "primitive," and as such, prone to violence. As just one example, justifying the exploitation of Mali's natural resources by former colonial powers, for example, shows how these interpretive networks serve to uphold racial capitalism and the maintenance of Mali as one of the world's poorest countries.

Despite critical work to dispel the colonial legacy of ethnicity in Africa (Amselle and M'Bokolo 2005), static and implicitly racist ideas about identity continue to inform anthropological knowledge production. Trouillot notes that, "anthropology belongs to a discursive field that is an inherent part of the West's geography of imagination," and that "any critique of anthropology requires a historicization of that larger discursive field—and thus an exploration of the relations between anthropology and the geography of imagination indispensable to the West" (2003, 8). As long as anthropologists do not question the founding premises of the discipline's discourse, anthropological critique remains within the discursive field it claims to challenge. As I've shown in this chapter, one example of this is the anthropological use of local "ethnic" categories to explain social issues with global causes.

Whereas historians have recently debated the extent to which precolonial categorizations of social difference should be understood as racial (Mamdani 2018; Young and Weitzberg 2021), as the work of Mamdani has argued (Mamdani 1996a; 2012; 2020), the solidified and political nature of ethnic and racial categorizations are a product of the modern world, colonialism, and global racial capitalism. While categorizations of difference may be related to preexisting local categorizations of difference, the inflexibility and antagonism between these identity groups that is produced by race and racism, and by colonialist legacies, is distinct to the modern world. Colonial categories of racial difference effectively turned local categorizations of social difference into political identities (Mamdani 2020). It obscures the effects of global white supremacy as evidenced by enduring epistemological legacies of colonial racial science and the material conditions of global racial capitalism.

Furthermore, it is not only anthropology, but the Western development industry that also belongs to this discursive field and its Western geography of imagination. Thus, despite Islamic Relief operating as an Islamic humanitarian NGO, the broader conditions of white supremacy and the discursive field to which both anthropology and development belong constrains Islamic Relief to also operate within this discursive field. This discursive field forces localized analyses of crises that do not allow for politicized, historicized analyses, which could—and likely would—reveal root global causes of the conditions of crisis that affect Malians.

When I began research with Islamic Relief, I did so with the question of what it meant to "do good." I wondered if Islamically situated conceptions of development and humanitarianism would prove distinct and thereby challenge the universality of such concepts. As I argue elsewhere (Rahman 2021), Islamic Relief contains multitudes, and cannot be reduced to any singular conception. Nonetheless, I did come to recognize certain constraints imposed by global white supremacy, including the different global logics of racialization that have influenced and constrained Islamic Relief's initiatives and practices. In this chapter I have attempted to counter the reductive understandings allowed for within the epistemological constraints of the West's geography of imagination—a geography in which history and the "good" are defined by whiteness. Moving beyond "culture talk," I call for anthropological analysis grounded in a global political economy that foregrounds the constraints within which racialized "others" must contend.

Notes

1. The coup was dubbed "accidental" because army officers won control of the government before realizing it (McConnell 2012). Whereas frustrated soldiers initially planned to march to the palace to reprimand President Amadou Toumani Toure, instead, the president fled. Soldiers inadvertently found themselves inside the seat of government (Associated Press 2012).

2. I borrow this phrasing from Beliso-De Jesús and Pierre (2020) so as to distinguish mainstream anthropology from a critical tradition that has and continues to confront and challenge the ideological premises of white supremacy within the discipline.

3. While I do not go into detail on the theory of "climate colonialism," it is significant to call attention to the ways colonial histories are constitutive of climate change and the global power imbalance between root causes and effects (Bhambra and Newell 2022).

4. Elsewhere I have shown how at an administrative level, Islamic Relief is subject to soft power tactics compelling assimilation to white supremacist norms of gender and sexuality (Rahman 2021).

5. The website NGO-Monitor has collected a list of accusations and condemnations of the organization, including a subsection on its "Ties to Terrorism" (NGO Monitor 2021).

6. Beliso-De Jesús and Pierre recognize this aspect of white supremacy in anthropology through the "fetishization of a particular kind of ethnographic localization (a trained disciplinary compulsion to focus on 'the particular,' the small-scale experience-based analysis) that tends to eschew broader structures of power" (2020, 1).

7. Elsewhere I have argued that it's operationalization within a logic of development and humanitarian aid withholds Islamic Relief's ability to engage their Muslim counterparts in Black Africa (Rahman 2023).

8. In his historicized analysis of the Tuareg rebellions, historian Baz Lecocq writes, "preconceived stereotyped images of each other, most of which were of a particular racial nature, effectively shaped political and social interaction between the Malian state and the Kel Tamasheq between the 1940s and 1960s" (Lecocq 2010, 22).

9. In 2002, the United States launched the Pan-Sahel Initiative (PSI) to provide training and equipment to regional militaries and to develop military relationships with key regional commanders in Mali, Niger, Chad, and Mauritania (Gutelius 2007, 65).

10. The Peule—as they are known in French, based on the Wolof name, but more commonly known in English as the Foula or Fulani—are a pastoral people spread throughout West and North Africa.

11. In 2018, Human Rights Watch reported 202 civilians killed in forty-two incidents of communal violence in Mali's Mopti region (*BBC News* 2019).

12. As just one example, French colonial policy in the Soudan promoted the production of cotton, reducing the cultivation of food grains such as rice, millet, and sorghum. However, the global market for cotton in the first half of the twentieth century was very volatile. As authors of "Exploring Africa" note, "revenues from cotton were not sufficient to support the social and economic expectations of a newly independent nation. . . . No economic system can grow and develop if it is dependent on a single product that in turn is subject to continued price changes in the global market" ("Exploring Africa" 2023).

13. In a speech on the foreign policy of Mali, Keïta states, "Moreover, we have come to the conclusion that when certain European countries afford help to the developing countries they often make such aid conditional, even if only by implication, on political option in their favour. Let me explain. When certain nations grant aid, whether to countries of Africa, Asia, or America, they are surprised that the receiving countries do not follow their policy in international affairs" (Keïta 1961).

References

Aidi, Hisham. 2005. "Slavery, Genocide, and the Politics of Outrage: Understanding the New Racial Olympics." MERIP. March 6, 2005. https://merip.org/2005/03/slavery-genocide-and-the-politics-of-outrage/.

Al-Jazeera. 2022. "Tensions Mount between Mali and France: How Did We Get Here?" *Al-Jazeera*, February 1, 2022. www.aljazeera.com/news/2022/2/1/mali-france-timeline-mounting-tensions.

Amselle, Jean-Loup, and Elikia M'Bokolo. 2005. *Au coeur de l'ethnie—ethnies, tribalisme et État en afrique*. Poche Sc.Humaines&Sociales edition. Paris: La Decouverte.

Associated Press. 2012. "Mali's Accidental Coup." *Denver Post* (blog). July 7, 2012. www.denverpost.com/2012 /07/07/malis-accidental-coup/.

Ayad, Christophe. 2017. "Le Mali Est Notre Afghanistan." *Le Monde*, November 16, 2017. www.lemonde.fr/idees /article/2017/11/16/le-mali-est-notre-afghanistan_5215799_3232.html.

Bashir, Haroon. 2019. "Black Excellence and the Curse of Ham: Debating Race and Slavery in the Islamic Tradition." *ReOrient*, September: 92–117.

BBC News. 2019. "Mali Attack: Behind the Dogon-Fulani Violence in Mopti." March 25, sec. Africa. www.bbc .com/news/world-africa-47694445.

Becker, Laurence C. 2001. "Seeing Green in Mali's Woods: Colonial Legacy, Forest Use, and Local Control." *Annals of the Association of American Geographers* 91, no. 3: 504–26. https://doi.org/10.1111/0004-5608 .00256.

Beliso-De Jesús, Aisha M., and Jemima Pierre. 2020. "Special Section: Anthropology of White Supremacy." *American Anthropologist* 122, no. 1: 65–75. https://doi.org/10.1111/aman.13351.

Benthall, Jonathan. 2006. "Islamic Aid in a North Malian Enclave." *Anthropology Today* 22, no. 4: 19–21.

Bhambra, Gurminder K., and Peter Newell. 2022. "More Than a Metaphor: 'Climate Colonialism' in Perspective." *Global Social Challenges Journal* 2, no. 2: 179–87. https://doi.org/10.1332/EIEM6688.

Brenner, Louis. 2001. *Controlling Knowledge: Religion, Power, and Schooling in a West African Muslim Society*. Bloomington: Indiana University Press.

Conklin, Alice L. 2013. *In the Museum of Man: Race, Anthropology, and Empire in France, 1850–1950*. Ithaca, NY: Cornell University Press. www.cornellpress.cornell.edu/book/9780801437557/in-the-museum-of-man/.

Delafosse, Maurice. 1926. "Islam in Africa." *International Review of Mission* 15, no. 3: 533–46. https://doi.org/10 .1111/j.1758-6631.1926.tb04716.x.

"Destabilization of Mali." 2022. Council on Foreign Relations. Global Conflict Tracker. April 15. https://cfr.org /global-conflict-tracker/conflict/destabilization-mali.

Exploring Africa. 2023. "What the French Did." African Studies Center, Michigan State University. *Exploring Africa* (blog). 2023. http://exploringafrica.matrix.msu.edu/what-the-french-did/.

Ghanem-Yazbeck, D. 2018. "The Sahel: Europe's African Borders." European Institute of the Mediterranean. www.iemed.org/publication/the-sahel-europes-african-borders/.

Giuffrida, Alessandra. 2005. "Clerics, Rebels, and Refugees: Mobility Strategies and Networks among the Kel Antessar." *Journal of North African Studies* 10, no. 3–4: 529–43. https://doi.org/10.1080/13629380 500344452.

Gutelius, David. 2007. "Islam in Northern Mali and the War on Terror." *Journal of Contemporary African Studies* 25, no. 1: 59–76. https://doi.org/10.1080/02589000601157063.

Hazard, John N. 1967. "Mali's Socialism and the Soviet Legal Model." *Yale Law Journal* 77, no. 1: 28–69. https:// doi.org/10.2307/795070.

International Crisis Group. 2019. "Central Mali: Putting a Stop to Ethnic Cleansing." March 25. www.crisisgroup .org/africa/sahel/mali/centre-du-mali-enrayer-le-nettoyage-ethnique.

———. 2020. "Reversing Central Mali's Descent into Communal Violence." Africa. International Crisis Group. www.crisisgroup.org/africa/sahel/mali/293-enrayer-la-communautarisation-de-la-violence-au-centre -du-mali.

Islamic Relief Worldwide. 2023. "About Us." *Islamic Relief Worldwide* (blog). https://islamic-relief.org /about-us/.

Keïta, Modibo. 1961. "The Foreign Policy of Mali." *International Affairs (Royal Institute of International Affairs 1944–)* 37, no. 4: 432–39.

Konaré, Dougoukolo Alpha Oumar Ba. 2021. *National Narratives of Mali: Fula Communities in Times of Crisis*. London: Lexington Books. https://rowman.com/ISBN/9781793602664/National-Narratives-of-Mali -Fula-Communities-in-Times-of-Crisis.

Kulkarni, Pavan. 2022. "Withdrawal of French Troops from Mali Is a Historic, Anti-Imperialist Victory." *Peoples Dispatch* (blog). February 22, 2022. https://peoplesdispatch.org/2022/02/22/withdrawal-of-french -troops-from-mali-is-a-historic-anti-imperialist-victory/.

Larivé, Maxime H. A. 2014. "Welcome to France's New War on Terror in Africa: Operation Barkhane." Center for the National Interest. August 7. https://nationalinterest.org/feature/welcome-frances-new-war-terror -africa-operation-barkhane-11029.

Launay, Robert. 2006. "An Invisible Religion? Anthropology's Avoidance of Islam in Africa." In *African Anthropologies: History, Critique, and Practice*, edited by Mwenda Ntarangwi, 188–203. New York: Zed Books.

Lecocq, Baz. 2010. *Disputed Desert: Decolonisation, Competing Nationalisms, and Tuareg Rebellions in Northern Mali*. Leiden: Brill.

Lewis, Bernard. 1971. *Race and Color in Islam*. New York: Harper Torchbooks. www.jstor.org/stable/164300.

Lydon, Ghislaine. 2015. "Saharan Oceans and Bridges, Barriers, and Divides in Africa's Historiographical Landscape." *Journal of African History* 56, no. 1: 3–22.

Mamdani, Mahmood. 1996a. *Citizen and Subject: Contemporary Africa and the Legacy of Late Colonialism*. Princeton, NJ: Princeton University Press.

———. 1996b. "Indirect Rule, Civil Society, and Ethnicity: The African Dilemma." *Social Justice* 23, no. 1/2 (63–64): 145–50.

———. 2002. "Good Muslim, Bad Muslim: A Political Perspective on Culture and Terrorism." *American Anthropologist* 104, no. 3: 766–75.

———. 2004. *Good Muslim, Bad Muslim: America, the Cold War, and the Roots of Terror*. New York: Three Leaves Press.

———. 2012. *Define and Rule: Native as Political Identity*. Cambridge, MA: Harvard University Press. www .hup.harvard.edu/catalog.php?isbn=9780674050525.

———. 2018. "Introduction: Trans-African Slaveries Thinking Historically." *Comparative Studies of South Asia, Africa, and the Middle East* 38, no. 2: 185–210. https://doi.org/10.1215/1089201x-6981996.

———. 2020. *Neither Settler nor Native: The Making and Unmaking of Permanent Minorities*. Cambridge, MA: Belknap Press of Harvard University Press. www.hup.harvard.edu/catalog.php?isbn=9780674987326.

McConnell, Tristan. 2012. "Mali Coup Backfires." GlobalPost. April 2. https://theworld.org/stories/2012-04 -02/mali-coup-backfires.

McDougall, E. Ann. 2002. "Discourse and Distortion: Critical Reflections on Studying the Saharan Slave Trade." *Outre-Mers. Revue d'histoire* 89, no. 336: 195–227. https://doi.org/10.3406/outre.2002.3990.

Miller, Rasul. 2017. "Is Islam an Anti-Black Religion?" *Sapelo Square* (blog). April 25, 2017. https://sapelosquare .com/2017/04/25/is-islam-an-anti-black-religion/.

Moctar, Hassan Ould. 2022. "It Is Time for Europe to Learn from Its Mistakes in the Sahel." *Al-Jazeera*, February 15, sec. Opinion. www.aljazeera.com/opinions/2022/2/15/it-is-time-for-for-europe-to-learn-from-its -mistakes-in-the-sahel.

NGO Monitor. 2021. "Islamic Relief Worldwide (IRW)." Ngo Monitor. January 21. www.ngo-monitor.org/ngos /islamic_relief_worldwide_irw_/.

Pezard, Stephanie, and Michael Shurkin. 2017. "Mali Is France's Afghanistan, but with a Difference." *War on the Rocks*, December 1. https://warontherocks.com/2017/12/mali-is-frances-afghanistan-but-with-a -difference/.

Pierre, Jemima. 2013. *The Predicament of Blackness: Postcolonial Ghana and the Politics of Race*. Chicago: University of Chicago Press.

———. 2020a. "The Racial Vernaculars of Development: A View from West Africa." *American Anthropologist* 122 (1): 86–98. https://doi.org/10.1111/aman.13352.

———. 2020b. "Slavery, Anthropological Knowledge, and the Racialization of Africans | Current Anthropology: Vol. 61, No. S22." *Current Anthropology*, Atlantic Slavery and the Making of the Modern World 61 (S22): S220–31. https://doi.org/10.1086/709844.

Rahman, Rhea. 2021. "Racializing the Good Muslim: Muslim White Adjacency and Black Muslim Activism in South Africa." *Religions* 12, no. 1: 58. https://doi.org/10.3390/rel12010058.

———. 2023. "White-Adjacent Muslim Development: Racializing British Muslim Aid in Mali." *Africa: The Journal of the International African Institute* 93, no. 2: 256–72.

Rana, Junaid. 2020. "Anthropology and the Riddle of White Supremacy." *American Anthropologist* 122, no. 1: 99–111. https://doi.org/10.1111/aman.13355.

Rasmussen, Susan. 2007. "Re-Formations of the Sacred, the Secular, and Modernity: Nuances of Religious Experience among the Tuareg (Kel Tamajaq)." *Ethnology* 46, no. 3: 185–203.

Sandner, Phillipp. 2015. "Timeline of the Crisis in Mali | DW | 15.05.2015." *Deutsche Welle World News*, May 15, 2015. https://p.dw.com/p/1FQTI.

Schulz, Dorothea E. 2011. *Muslims and New Media in West Africa: Pathways to God.* Illustrated ed. Bloomington: Indiana University Press.

Seesemann, Rudiger. 2011. *The Divine Flood: Ibrahim Niasse and the Roots of a Twentieth-Century Sufi Revival.* Oxford: Oxford University Press.

Skinner, Ryan Thomas. 2012. "Cultural Politics in the Post-Colony: Music, Nationalism, and Statism in Mali, 1964–75." *Africa* 82, no. 4: 511–34. https://doi-org.libproxy.newschool.edu/10.1017/S0001972012000484.

Snyder, Francis G. 1967. "The Political Thought of Modibo Keita." *Journal of Modern African Studies* 5, no. 1: 79–106.

Soares, Benjamin. 2005. *Islam and the Prayer Economy.* Ann Arbor: University of Michigan Press. www.press.umich.edu/175501/islam_and_the_prayer_economy.

———. 2014. "The Historiography of Islam in West Africa: An Anthropologist's View." *Journal of African History* 55, no. 1: 27–36. https://doi.org/10.1017/S0021853713000819.

Tadei, Federico. 2018. "The Long-Term Effects of Extractive Institutions: Evidence from Trade Policies in Colonial French Africa." *Economic History of Developing Regions* 33, no. 3: 183–208. https://doi.org/10.1080/20780389.2018.1527685.

Thibaud, Bénédicte. 2005. "Land Use Issues in Mondoro Mali: Peul Herders and Dogon Farmers." *Science et Changements Planétaires / Sécheresse* 16, no. 3: 165–74.

Thurston, Alexander. 2020. *Jihadists of North Africa and the Sahel: Local Politics and Rebel Groups.* Cambridge: Cambridge University Press. https://doi.org/10.1017/9781108771160.

Trouillot, Michel-Rolph. 2003. *Global Transformations: Anthropology and the Modern World.* New York: Palgrave Macmillan.

Ursu, Anca-Elena. 2018. "Resource Conflict and Radical Armed Governance in Central Mali." Under the Gun Resource Conflicts and Embattled Traditional Authorities in Central Mali. Clingandael. www.clingendael.org/pub/2018/under-the-gun/3-resource-conflict-and-rebel-governance-in-central-mali/.

Visweswaran, Kamala. 1998. "Race and the Culture of Anthropology." *American Anthropologist* 100, no. 1: 70–83. https://doi.org/10.1525/aa.1998.100.1.70.

Volman, Daniel. 2010. "The Origins of AFRICOM: The Obama Administration, the Sahara-Sahel, and US Militarization of Africa (Part Two)." *Modern Ghana.* www.modernghana.com/news/279135/the-origins-of-africom-the-obama-administration-the-sahara.html.

Ware, Rudolph T. 2011. "Slavery in Islamic Africa, 1400–1800." In *The Cambridge World History of Slavery*, Part 1, *Slavery in Africa and Asia Minor*, edited by David Eltis and Stanley L. Engerman, 47–80. Cambridge: Cambridge University Press. www-cambridge-org.libproxy.newschool.edu/core/books/cambridge-world-history-of-slavery/slavery-in-islamic-africa-14001800/F1FBBD944B3B0FB4A2CEED3434ECB213.

Whitehouse, Bruce. 2013. "Merci François!" Bridges from Bamako. January 14. https://bridgesfrombamako.com/2013/01/13/merci-francois/.

Young, Alden, and Keren Weitzberg. 2021. "Globalizing Racism and De-Provincializing Muslim Africa." *Modern Intellectual History*, May, 1–22. https://doi.org/10.1017/S1479244321000196.

SECTION IV

Militarized Geographies of White Supremacy

TO UNDERSTAND HOW WHITE SUPREMACY is reproduced through militarized violence, we must chart forms of spatial and social exclusion. People are located in material sites, mapped through networks of belonging, and come into being within complex geopolitical arrangements. This section geographically follows what Charles Mills describes as the "racial contract," where white supremacy operates as a political system simultaneously at the global, local, and national levels. These chapters trace the role of the United States as a racial-state, an imperial-state, and a settler-state, showing how white supremacy operates at the nexus of global militarized and police power. Indeed, national structures of white supremacy regularly depend on the deployment of military power outside of the nation-state territory to maintain the power of the state. Such imperial relationships circulate, where we see networks of state violence as "geographies" of white supremacy—that is, how space and race coalesce through the making of national boundaries and practices of exclusion. This section explores the occupation of lands, capital, and territories, the control of racialized populations, and the consolidation of white supremacist state power through police and military practices. It examines the role of immigration courts as part of the reproduction of racialized state violence, unraveling how the war on terror is really an unofficial war on immigrants. For anthropology to take seriously an approach to white supremacy, an anti-imperial stance is necessary to theorize the militarization and imperial geographies of the racial contract.

16

Molding White Fascist Intimacies into American Police Cadet Bodies

Aisha M. Beliso-De Jesús

"MORNIN' MA'AM." POLICE CADETS GREET ME, standing on edge against an invisible wall, arms straight at their sides as I pass them in the halls of the academy. The cadets model a militarized Southern-gentleman-style courtesy (regardless of their gender) as I maneuver the halls. Walking into a gymnasium, I see a diverse group of about fifty cadets doing push-ups. Although the majority are white, the group also includes a good number of visible Asian and Latino males, several women (including three white women), two Black women, three Latinas, and several Black male cadets, all apparently cis-gender and under thirty. The newly updated facilities are lined with thick exercise mats. Officer Nakamura, the Asian American physical fitness trainer, tells me that the entire group is being punished with push-ups because one of the new cadets had forgotten to submit a required paper. "It teaches camaraderie and accountability," he says as he screams at the class, "C'mon. Quicker. Get it done!" Officer Nakamura discusses the practice of group discipline and punishment as a way to instill both peer pressure and mutual responsibility between officers. "When they're out there on the street they need to know that everything they do impacts each other. They got to have each other's back."[1]

During another tactical combat training I observed, cadets were paired up and had to wrestle each other to the ground. As the cadets threw each other on the mats, struggling, lifting, and slamming each other's bodies, Officer Nakamura told me how this prevents them from using guns. "It's important they get out their aggression in other ways," he said. "They're fit when they leave us here [from the academy], but they become so fat a few years later, they can't chase anyone." "How are they going to catch twenty-something basketball players [on the streets]," Nakamura told me, laughing.

The suggestion that fleeing suspects are imagined as young basketball players is a not-so-thinly-veiled euphemism for Black male youth who police imagine as the naturalized criminals in "the jungle," running through the streets (see Beliso-De Jesús 2020). The fast-running Black (male) youth, endowed with superior strength, height, ability, and speed, are the racialized criminals that the "tactical athletes" are being trained offensively to fight. Nakamura's allusion to criminal Black runners ("basketball players") is not an anomaly but in fact a core white supremacist part of the molding of police-recruit bodies into tactical athletes. It also references the pliability and molding of police bodies at different stages in their careers.

This chapter draws on ethnography of the police academy to examine how white supremacy is embedded and also made invisible in the molding, crafting, and training of police-recruit bodies. I use the term *molding* to describe the process of manufactured sculpting through the manipulable material of police cadets as "tactical athletes." Drawing on ethnographic research of police academies in several different cities in the United States, I create a composite police academy. Situated in scholarship on embodiment, race, and the state, this chapter demonstrates how an anthropology of white supremacy provides insight into how white governance is intimately tied to the embodiment of the state through the institution of the police. White supremacy, I argue, is ordered, maintained, infused, and embodied in the active reshaping of everyday young citizens into police through the recruit process. Officers do not have to be white males in order to embody white supremacy. Through the practice of producing new officers in the police academy, fascist intimacies are physically, emotionally, and mentally molded into police recruit bodies.

Tactical Athletes

The need to mold recruit bodies into hard police who then could turn "soft" again without continued physical training was a recurring theme across different agencies where I conducted research. Officer Puett, a tactical trainer who runs the "force options simulator," was bothered by the low fitness levels of incoming cadets, calling them "weak." He described the "ideal officer" as "a decathlete with anaerobic strength," claiming that their weakness contributes to more serious use-of-force incidents, such as the deployment of batons, Tasers, and guns. "Every time an officer shows up at a scene, it's a gun call" because the "cop has a gun." "Cops must win every time," otherwise there could be a "maniac with a gun." He told me:

> You gotta be able to chase the bad guys for three blocks. Fight them for three minutes. . . . That's why we do partner exercises, so, people can develop timing. It's like dancing. You need to have a neurological encoding. Muscle memory is colloquial, nervous system training is in your brain. The win is that you're alive.

To ensure this neurological encoding, cadets are measured through "physical fitness qualifiers" (PFQs): four events designed to assess the athletic capacity of their bodies. They must successfully complete 80 percent of the thirty-six physical conditioning sessions (each session is one hour long). PFQs are made up of four to five "events," which include push-ups, sit-ups, pull-ups, and a one-and-a-half-mile flat run. For the second and third PFQs, a timed obstacle course is added. Recruits are scored on the speed at which they complete the event, with faster cadets given more points and a higher score. All cadets must achieve a minimum score to pass. Injuries sustained during academy fitness training are a big issue.

Police cadets are encouraged to begin training four months prior to entering the police academy, and in some cities I observed, there is even a preacademy training program to help cadets get in shape. The preacademy workout instruction includes a guidebook on how to prepare for the academy. There is a log to track daily fitness activities in the four months prior to entering the academy, and cadets must bring this to their first interview.

The front cover of the fitness log features a healthy-looking white male officer in uniform running as if in pursuit of a suspect. This image, which is repeated on a subsequent page, indicates the type of ideal police body to which cadets are expected to conform: large white athletic male. Officer Puett, a muscular white male who stands over six feet tall, complained that his (urban) police academy didn't "look like NFL teams." Lamenting the debilitation of the force, Puett told me, "It is important that departments represent the city . . . but we also have to balance that with fitness for the job." In his opinion, new recruit classes, which include an increase in women, minorities, and other "formerly excluded" people's bodies, just can't hold up to the past. This nostalgia for a past when police were large white men was a theme of the expectations of recruit physicality.

Along with the image of the large white male officer running, the guide tells cadets that "calisthenics," or "the ability to squat, reach, twist, lunge, jump, land, push, and get up and down," is an important part of the actions demanded of police officers when on patrol. The guide suggests that an attention to the exercise regime that calisthenics demands also "conveys physical readiness and discipline" needed to be a law enforcement officer. Indeed, this gendered conditioning output is even naturalized in social scientific research on police bodies. In a 2016 athletic research article, "The Use of 2 Conditioning Programs and the Fitness Characteristics of Police Academy Recruits," conducted in Australia and the United States, researchers concerned with injuries sustained on the bodies of ill-prepared cadets argued that any type of physical training program can improve the fitness of tactical athletes. What is striking is that in the results section, the authors stated that they "cleaned" the results of female recruit data due to the "heterogeneity in the numbers of female participants" (Cocke, Dawes, and Orr 2016, 889–90). They then presented their standardized findings based only on the sixty-one male police-recruit bodies measured for anthropometric and metabolic fitness.

The researchers tested two CrossFit conditioning programs, a branded fitness regime and hardcore philosophy based on Olympic-style weightlifting, interval training, plyometrics (jump training), and other "strongmen"-style exercises. CrossFit markets itself to "Cops and Soldiers" who they describe as "professional athletes," stating: "we argue that the physical preparedness required of the Law Enforcement Officer matches and regularly surpasses that required of Olympic athletes."[2] They continue, "In the sport of Protection and Service, physical fitness may indeed be the most important asset the Officer has at their disposal. CrossFit's mission is to forge a level of physical fitness and mental toughness that will allow the Officer to triumph against any challenge they face."[3]

CrossFit's envisioning of law enforcement as a "sport of Protection and Service" through Olympic-inspired athleticism mirrors Officer Puett's officer-as-decathlete comment. Officer Puett described how cops are expected "to chase the bad guys for three blocks" and then "fight them for three minutes" until backup arrives. When they are appropriately repatterned into "tactical athletes," police bodies are expected to wield weapons with expertise, strike at a moment's notice, make life-and-death decisions, and rush into dangerous situations, even though recent research has found that the everyday job of police is in fact extremely sedentary and mental (sitting in offices, filling out paperwork, driving vehicles, testifying in court). Officer Puett linked the demand for combat-style training to a "kinetic neuro repatterning" that would turn "soft" police cadets into Rambo-like warriors ready to initiate action at a moment's notice. This impossible embodied ideal is embedded in the state's expectations where, in addition to the academy's internal PFQs, cadets must also pass the state's physical fitness examination, consisting of:

- A ninety-nine-yard obstacle course that includes simulated curbs, weaving course ways of right and left turns, a wooden horse jump, and forty-yard sprint
- A 165-pound body drag for thirty-two feet on a flat surface
- A six-foot chain-link fence climb
- A six-foot solid-wall climb
- A five-hundred-yard run on a flat track

We can see how physical fitness is about the politics of embodiment, race, and the state, where white logics and norms are woven and molded into the bodies of police cadets. Indeed, white governance is intimately tied to the embodiment of the state. We will see how the ideal decathlete body is, historically, a white supremacist construction linking grandiose police physicality to Greek civilization discourses and Aryan-inspired body logics.

Fascist Intimacies

Decathletes, male Olympians who must train incessantly to outperform in ten track and field events, are considered the "world's greatest athletes." The decathlete hails a Western civilization supremacy, which has long reinforced the mythology of white origin stories and their manifest destiny to rule. The glory of the tactical athlete modeled after Olympian superheroes is yet another naturalized reinforcement of the inevitability of white governance.

As we saw in the previous section, the physicality thought to be needed by police to properly pacify the savages of the urban jungle references the "sport" of policing as an embodied regime inspired by the decathlete. A fascist intimacy can be seen here in how Nazi race theory aesthetics celebrated the "Aryan body," which was modeled after the mythical virility, power, strength, and dynamisms of classical Greece decathletes (Beamish 2011, 30). For example, at the 1936 Olympics in Berlin, Hitler used the opportunity to portray the Germans as the "rightful heir" of Aryan classical antiquity through powerful imagery of ancient Greece, such as the *Decathlete* (*Zehnkämpfer*) statue, which still stands in Olympia Park in front of the House of German Sports in Berlin. David Clay Large (2007, 157) describes the "heroic monumentalism" in the piece as "pure 'Aryan man,' an icon of buffed-up brutality."

Nazis prioritized the body as part of their anti-intellectual centering of the racial state (Plunka 2009, 34). The health and hygiene of the physical body was the guiding principle of the social body, where Nazi masculinity focused on producing an "elite force of warriors" in service of the state (34). The SS (*Schutzstaffel*) or "Protective Echelon," paramilitary corps that protected Hitler and directed policing and enforced Nazi racial policy, were modeled after the decathlete (Pine 2010, 89). Officers underwent a six-month basic training and were given exams at four and ten months broken down into tactics, political education, weapons training, military affairs, practical training, physical education, combat engineering, and automotive mechanics (Weale 2012, 140).

We cannot divorce the fascist intimacies that reinforce the creation of the perfect, able-bodied human from white supremacy, capitalism, and hetero-patriarchy (Campbell 2009; Slater 2016). Deviant and unwanted bodies are removed, isolated, incarcerated, and even executed through dis-ableing processes in systems of white supremacy (Annamma 2017). Ableism is a "network of beliefs, processes and practices that produces a particular kind of self and body (the corporeal standard) that is projected as perfect, species-typical and therefore essential and fully human" (Campbell 2009, 44). This "mythical norm" is part of what Mia Mingus (2011) has described as an ideological system where "an able-bodied standard of white supremacy, heterosexism, sexism, economic exploitation, moral/religious beliefs, age and ability" set the stage for humanity.[4] We see this used historically in white supremacist discourses that locate both homosexuality and mixed-race bodies as deviant, mentally pathological, and, hence, a disability (Somerville 2000). As J. Rohrer (2014, 65) argues, the violence of state management reveals "the coercive side of the complex workings of blood logics, compulsory heterosexuality, white supremacy and ableism to produce the normative citizen of the state's desire."

I situate the hetero-masculinities molded into police as *intimacies* of the hypermasculinity espoused in global white fascisms (Harris 2000, 798–99). Here, I see intimacies as a relatedness produced through "bodily effects"—not just physical but also imagined contact between bodies (Parreñas 2016, 120). Fascist intimacies are thus white supremacist norms produced through the relatedness that emerges through the *effects* of embodied white racialized copresence and contact with bodies of color. Officer-recruit trainings—the touching, cuffing, tackling, and arresting of subjects, the imagined encounters with bodies—bring about intimacies' bodily effects. Intimacy helps us to expand from notions of just physical proximity between bodies to the embodied effects of such contact. The entanglements of white fascist and police bodies are linked through fascist intimacies—they are copresences of each other—embodiments of white supremacist state violence. The bodily effects of white supremacy can thus be revealed in the processing of police cadets' bodies into mythical decathletes.

Fascist intimacies are riddled with the social Darwinist "law of the jungle" ideology, which situates the white race as destined to rule (Goodrick-Clarke 2003, 202–3). The "jungle" metaphor is a "be conquered or conquer" mentality linked to anti-Semitic tropes that envisioned Jews as "savage" threats to the Aryan race who must be destroyed (Carroll 1998, 188–89). "Social Darwinists took the law of the jungle and applied it to industrial capitalism and the urban jungle, but Darwin had already taken the law of industrial capitalism and the urban jungle and applied it to the tropical rainforest," thus the trope returned full circle (Giblett 2011, 256). Indeed, fascist jungle logics operate in embodied police practice, as Didier Fassin (2013, 52) notes, the same is seen in both France and the United States:

> The police who work in the [suburban ghettos] are therefore mainly white men who have been given the task of pacifying neighborhoods described as a "jungle," inhabited mainly by people of African origin who have been represented to them as "savages"— two terms which also recur frequently in the officers' own comments about the projects and their residents. Remarkably, almost exactly the same terms were used by the Chicago police in William Westley's study, "The Negro is a savage just out of the jungle."

These social Darwinisms imbue global fascist intimacies into embodied police practice. As I next discuss, the uniformed body of police and cadets forms part of the embodiment and discomfort of the white supremacy of the state.

Diversifying Whiteness

The shared demographics between police and white fascist groups have been well documented, as both are committed to the hierarchy of the established social order and the maintenance of a white-dominated society (Novick 1999, 83; Perry 2009, 30).[5] The most common image of American white supremacy is the Jim Crow South, where Ku Klux Klan patrols and police collaborated to maintain white social dominance during Reconstruction (Jenkins 1970). Throughout the United States, police recruited Klansmen as early as the 1920s, and in some places whole Klaverns were deputized (Williams 2015, 128–29).[6] In many of these cities, the Klan controlled fire and police departments, local commissions, and had deputized members among prominent businessmen, senators, and state representatives. In addition to violently attacking racial minorities, police/white fascists targeted left-leaning political groups, using beatings, murder, bombings, and arson to maintain their hold on local power structures (Williams 2015, 242).[7] During the late 1960s, "the Legion of Justice conducted a series of burglaries, beatings, and arson attacks on behalf of the Chicago Police," and "in San Diego, the Secret Army Organization—a group led by an FBI informant and armed with $10,000 worth of Bureau-supplied weaponry—was busy beating up Chicano activists, trashing the offices of radical newspapers, and attempting to assassinate anti-war organizers" (242). In his memoir, former chief of police of Atlanta Herbert Jenkins (1970, 4) recounted that throughout the South, "it was helpful to join the Ku Klux Klan to be an accepted member of the force." He describes it as "your ID card" and "badge of honor with the in-group," and it was considered an allegiance that was "stronger than the policeman's oath to society" (4).

The fight to diversify police departments was hardly easy. It was not until August 8, 1969, that Richard Nixon issued Executive Order 11478b to end discrimination in federal service based on race, color, religion, sex, national origin, or disability, and allow women to carry firearms, make arrests, and execute search warrants. Subsequently, a number of lawsuits across the country during the 1970s and 1980s were filed against police departments to end discrimination in the hiring of law enforcement and increase the number of women and minorities (Bolton and Faegan 2004). Prior to these hard-fought efforts to diversify police forces, it was taken as a given that law enforcement officers were large white males. In the 1970s, the Hispanic Society of New York noted that department height requirements were a way to exclude Latinos from law enforcement, and in 1972, the Civil Rights Act was amended to include law enforcement height requirements as discriminatory.

However, police agencies have been slow to hire outside of the "six-foot white male" sameness described by the trainer. It wasn't until the Obama administration that active attention was placed on hiring practices as part of changing policing cultures. The Obama administration's President's Task Force on 21st Century Policing emphasized that hiring was a crucial component to transforming policing into a more "just" practice. On September 13, 2016, a day-long forum was organized by the US Department of Justice's Office of Community Oriented Policing Services (COPS) and the Police Executive Research Forum (PERF) that brought together approximately fifty practitioners from state agencies, police labor organizations, police psychology, academia, and "professional associations representing police chiefs, sheriffs, women in law enforcement, Hispanic command officers, mayors, the transgender community, and police trainers" to explore the role of effective hiring in twenty-first-century policing.[8] They found that whereas previously police-hiring practices were designed to exclude candidates, "weed out criminals," and identify unsuitable applicants, it is more important to identify cadets who exhibit more positive traits that are necessary for the twenty-first-century law enforcement officer.

The workshop participants advocated moving away from the hiring of "warrior"-type individuals toward recruiting candidates who would exhibit the empathetic "guardian" approach to policing (see also Balko 2013). They reasoned that whereas the warrior elements of law enforcement could be taught, the guardian qualities needed to be in place prior to hiring. Necessary guardian qualities include empathy, a service orientation, integrity, human-relations skills, team orientation, and problem-solving skills.[9] Throughout the country, departments have shifted their hiring practices to produce more diverse cadets who better represent the cities they serve. However, this has not been without resistance.[10]

Across the country, there is stagnation in the recruitment of new officers, and while often attributed to low pay and the dangers involved in policing, for many, the toxic culture of policing is to blame. This is a serious concern for officials who have pledged hundreds of thousands of dollars to recruitment and pay raises. The stagnant growth of police departments in high-crime cities speaks to other, more systemic problems. Black and brown officers I've spoken to describe their time at the academy as "toxic" and "hostile." They discussed being treated like children or made fun of through macho hazing. In one city where I researched, treatment in the academy was given as the main reason for quitting law enforcement early in officers' careers. In this case, over sixty officers resigned in 2017, including a dozen new cadets. Although they hired over one hundred new cadets, they only netted twenty-five new officers. While these cadets enjoyed working with the public, they reported toxic treatment, such as being belittled, publicly scolded, and bullied. They mentioned a disorganized academy with rushed training that contributed to an unhealthy department. They described the boot-camp-style instruction that focused more on producing "tough guys" than ensuring lessons were properly learned.

Recruits are trained to expect submission or deploy violence. The question isn't whether they will use force but rather how much and what type of force they should use. Conversations in police training, practice, and procedure are always tactical in the sense that engagement with people is always seen as combative and dangerous. However, it is often difficult for people interested in police reform to pin down just what about the academy, and policing in general, is so toxic. The unnamed culprit of white supremacy is often left out of the equation—with the discussion instead revolving around a move from warrior to guardian. What is often left unstated is that the so-called warrior-guardian is actually an embodied white supremacist social arrangement. Indeed, even the benevolent guardian is a white male protector—a good-soldier white-savior figure. This "tactical athlete," as I will examine, is infused with Aryan-inspired body logics and fascist intimacies.

Uniformed Assholes

Sergeant Hansen, a trainer I interviewed, described police as "assholes" with an "alpha-male mentality" that doesn't allow them to admit to any faults and so "they try to maintain that facade that they are mentally better and stronger." This "asshole" posture is cultivated and enhanced through the academy. Recruits are taught they must "command respect" (recall the group in the training had put this as one of their rules). They engage with each other in a curt and tough manner modeled in the interactions of the trainer, who demonstrated that ultimate respect is obtained by control and submission. This exertion of control and submission is later deployed on the streets in what Moskos (2008, 104) describes as "eye fucking":

> If a group of suspects does not disperse when an officer "rolls up," the officer will stop the car and stare at the group. A group may ignore the officer's look or engage the officer in a stare-off, known in police parlance as "eye fucking." This officer's stare serves the dual purpose of scanning for contraband and weapons and simultaneously declaring dominance over turf.

Moskos describes how policing "requires a certain amount of aggressiveness" for officers to save "face" and not be "punked" (104). This aggressive embodied territoriality first begins in the academy around the language of "respect for the uniform." A recurring theme is officers' need to deploy violence to curb perceived disrespect. However, cadets have described feeling disrespect from the lack of resources in the academy itself. For instance, many city agencies cannot afford to provide much of cadets' gear, which can be quite costly. A Black female recruit lamented the high initial costs, discussing how she had to borrow money from family. "Police hold fundraisers for uniforms," she told me, pointing to her shirt, "pitiful."

In addition to uniforms, tactical clothing, boots, running shoes, and other fitness and training clothing, cadets must purchase their own duty gear, such as batons, Tasers, holsters, magazine carriers, mace, handcuffs, and flashlights, and in many cases, they must purchase their own handguns, ammunition, and firearms cleaning kits. They may also need to purchase safety equipment like goggles, ear protection, and a ballistics vest. More recently, tattoo sleeves have become mandatory, as agencies across the country are adopting rules prohibiting the display of tattoos. Recruits must keep their boots shiny at all times, and so polish kits are a necessity. Some cadets expressed excitement about acquiring and using these items, discussing them with care and love as if speaking about a new toy or collector's item. Guns are an important part of the tools of trade, and loving gun talk was also common.

The embodied burden of the uniforms themselves can make people assholes. Recruits and new officers describe having to become accustomed to the sheer weight of the uniform and its required gear as an additional stressor of the job. Police gear can add up to thirty pounds of weight on a person's body. The belt alone can weigh up to twenty pounds. Some have described it as like carrying several gallons of milk on their waist. Because of this heavy gear, many officers describe relief when sitting at a desk or riding in a car. Descriptions of gear include it being hot, irritable, uncomfortable, painful, and a burden. One white female officer told me that it was harder learning to carry her police load than being pregnant because the awkward way the belt fits on her hips. "They're not made for [women's] hips." Another Latina female recruit discussed how ballistic vests were not made for women's bodies, telling me it was difficult for her to find a bulletproof vest that could fit her petite frame.

Hot and burdened by uncomfortable uniforms, cadets and new police display a lot of pent-up stress and anxiety. This is heightened by training that encourages and instills fear in the communities they will work in. During trainings, senior officers discuss their "war wounds" from the streets and provide examples that reinforce jungle logics. During an introductory "Police Sciences" course, designed to give cadets an overview of the knowledge, concepts, and understandings and skills that would be needed to prevent crime, maintain law and order, and protect the public, the discussion by the trainer quickly became grim. He started talking about officers being killed on duty and how the job was "life-and-death," "yours or theirs."

For women and people of color, no amount of training can produce the white masculine body expected of the uniformed tactical athlete. During World War I, the drafting of Black and brown soldiers caused an uproar because of the concern around Black men in uniform.[11] A local Mississippi newspaper argued that "drafting Negroes as soldiers is a gross travesty and contradiction of the color line creed" (Harris 2001, 227). "The sight of Black men in official uniforms bothered many, and the fear that black soldiers might meet white women in France as social equals bothered some even more" (227). Violence against Black soldiers was so bad in Vicksburg, Mississippi, that whites would not allow Black soldiers to walk on the streets. When Black soldiers complained to local businessmen, they were told "they should not wear their uniforms" in town (227).

Uniforms demonstrate a sense of pride for white (and white adjacent) bodies, and when nonwhite bodies wear uniforms, their sense of being out of place makes them seem exceptional. Military and police uniforms serve to further naturalize the white male body as the *proper* body for these uniforms (Plunka 2009, 36). Indeed, neo-Nazi and fascist protestors are known to show up in military or police clothing and with weaponry to assert the white heritage of global dominance.[12] However, the macho masculinity of white supremacy has never been happenstance, but rather has always been carefully crafted, molded, trained, and nurtured into youth (Armengol 2014; Ferber 1999; Rose 2015). White boys and men in the South, for instance, performed rituals of attack and violence against Black people to prove their masculinity. White boys were trained and taught racial violence through the "watchful eye" of parents, community members, and other observing adults (Du Rocher 2010, 59):

> For white male adolescents, the lynching ritual offered a public venue in which to prove their readiness for manhood. Male adolescents understood that white female sexuality required aggressive protection, and their direct participation in the violent ritual proved their masculinity. Public displays of masculinity at lynching rituals offered white men a space in which to demonstrate their ability to uphold the tenets of white Southern masculinity, as well as perpetuate white supremacy to the next generation.

Under the watchful eye of trainers and superiors, police cadets (male and female) are molded to conform to aggressive masculinity and must perform demonstrations of loyalty to the blue "brotherhood." To become "one of the boys," female cadets assert how they are sometimes tougher than their male counterparts. A Black female recruit told me she was tired of being "better," mentioning her gender was constantly brought up. A white female officer who had just finished the academy told me how she was admired by her crew for being "tougher" and "harder" on "criminals" than the male officers she worked with.

White alpha-male masculinity is crucial to what Kraska and Cubellis (1997, 625) describe as the state's "violence industry." They discuss the "seductive powers of paramilitary unit subculture as promoted by for-profit industry. The techno-warrior garb, heavy weaponry, sophisticated technology, hypermasculinity, and 'real-work' functions are nothing less than intoxicating for paramilitary unit participants and those who aspire to work in such units" (625). Also alluring is the professionalizing of state-administered force through the creation of "violence specialists" (625).

Sergeant Hansen trains cadets to understand that as police they are the only profession entrusted both to police themselves and to deprive other people of their rights, and that this should be a solemn oath. However, what is not taught at the academy is how the power of violence without consequence is at the core of white supremacy itself. We can see this in the general conditions of impunity toward people of color by the state across an array of institutions—such as the poisoning of water in Flint, Michigan; the military defense of the Dakota Access Pipeline; the weaponization of schools; mass incarceration; the detention of immigrant families; and the school-to-prison pipeline—which all demonstrate systemic violence and targeted abuse by the state toward people of color even prior to the Trump administration's blatant racist acts and policies. The police's engagement with people of color is not an exception to the violence industry's white supremacy of the state; rather, police are simply its everyday enforcers.

Conclusion

The militaristic structure of the police academy enhances the performance of militarized uniformity. Military culture emphasizes a cohesive group, where expressions of stoic depersonalization are preferred. These expressions are assumed to model the expectation that the unit's goals are placed ahead of personal goals. In militaristic structurations, the superior is understood as having ultimate authority over all aspects of the officer's/soldier's life through commands that must be obeyed. As we've seen in this chapter, such approaches to police training are part of the mundane molding techniques that instill such militarized uniformity in young, new police officers. As I have shown elsewhere, cadets are taught that stereotypes and bias are seemingly ingrained and unsurmountable—unavoidable and ahistorical—and that violating someone's civil rights isn't necessarily wrong, but "expensive" (Beliso-De Jesús 2020).

If anthropologists could reframe the police academy, we might suggest that educating cadets on histories of structural racism might be helpful to produce empathy between police and impoverished communities. To promote more positive forms of cultural diversity, the academy might offer courses on the systematic impact of racial policies on communities of color since slavery. Recruits might learn how for-profit prisons have incentivized mass incarceration, where increased fines and court fees contribute to spiraling debt (Davis 2006). They could be shown that the attack and loss of affirmative action programs have enabled the resegregation of schools, or how "urban redevelopment" through gentrification has caused displacement that further increases inequality along racial lines (Chang 2016). However, police, who are disproportionately on the front lines of recruiting for the prison-industrial complex, are not taught about displacement and segregation. They are not given context about the unequal access to services, white flight, the redlining of districts, and overall disinvestment in Black and brown communities that impact the communities they will serve (Kurashige 2017).

Instead, they are trained to aggressively pursue "dangerous criminals" through a militarized logic that reinforces a police quota infrastructure intended to supplement shrinking city budgets (Opotow 2016). Recruits are trained to fear "cultural diversity" on the streets. During a training, a retired commanding officer described the communities that cadets should expect to encounter: "There's violence. Language barriers. The community fears us and they're overrun by gangs. . . . [You're thinking], 'I'm over my head. I'm scared.' . . . It's the incremental steps that can take you to the dark side."

The retired commander describes the danger of turning to "the dark side," where impressionable officers in gang-infested environments can become "incrementally" corrupted through exposure to these neighborhoods and people. Akin to the colonial language used by Europeans to describe physical and mental deterioration of whites who "went native" and spent too much time in "the tropics" (Benz 1997, 51), the retired commander produces a similar racialized topography. This type of "tropicalization" of urban poor communities by police can be seen in the oft-cited "jungle" metaphor that officers use to describe the streets they patrol (Aparicio and Chávez-Silverman 1997). Peter Moskos (2008, 39), who enlisted in the Baltimore police academy and became an officer for a year, says the "real" training begins in "the ghetto"—described by officers as a hopeless "jungle":

> One black officer said, "It's hard not to think that this is a jungle here. People running around in the street at all hours. Getting high, acting like fools. . . . They ought to tear everything down. All of it!" A white officer echoed this belief: "I'd like to napalm the whole area. Wouldn't that be beautiful?"

Recruits are trained to subscribe to a uniform group mentality as they encounter the excursionist fantasy of patrolling the "urban jungle." I see this as a *jungle logic,* a subsidiary of what Eduardo Bonilla-Silva and Tufuku Zuberi (2008, 17–20) call "White logic," which is how "White supremacy has defined the techniques and processes of reasoning about social facts." In this, white logic "grants eternal objectivity to the views of elite Whites" and "is the anchor of the Western imagination" (17). These jungle logics, or implicit notions that racial others are inherently "primitive," "backwards," and "dangerous," are foundational to overarching white logics. Jungle logics also provide for the adventurous thrill of white supremacy, the lure of excursions into racial otherness and criminality that reinforces the presumption of white superiority. Jungle logics support the dehumanization of Black and brown life. The jungle logic subsidiary of white logic is thus a crucial element in the predatory trajectory of policing as a career.

Notes

1. This chapter is an abridged and revised version of what first appeared as Aisha Beliso-De Jesús, 2020. "The Jungle Academy: Molding White Supremacy in American Police Recruits." *American Anthropologist* 122, no. 1: 143–56. doi.org/10.1111/aman.13357.

2. See www.in.gov/isp/crossfit/213.htm.

3. See www.in.gov/isp/crossfit/213.htm.

4. Mia Mingus's 2011 keynote speech, "Moving towards the Ugly: A Politic beyond Desireability," at the Femmes of Color Symposium in Oakland, California. https://leavingevidence.wordpress.com/2011/08/22/moving-toward-the-ugly-a-politic-beyond-desirability/.

5. Johnpeter Horst Grill and Robert L. Jenkins (1992, 668) show how Nazis looked to the "long established system of white supremacy" in the American South "to work out their own system of Aryan supremacy."

6. Klan recruitment into police forces was not limited to the South. In 1922, when the Los Angeles district attorney raided the local headquarters, he found that the LA chief of police, sheriff, the US attorney, the Bakersfield chief of police and police judge, seven police officers from Fresno, and twenty-five officers from San

Francisco—along with "about a tenth of the public officials and police in the rest of California's cities"—were all Klan members (Williams 2015, 129).

7. In northern cities like New York and Detroit, police refused to protect Black victims during race riots. Thurgood Marshall described the police in Detroit as "Gestapo" who "against Negroes they used the ultimate in force: night sticks, revolvers, riot guns, sub-machine guns, and deer guns" (Williams 2015, 242).

8. From COPS recruitment pamphlet, "Hiring for the 21st Century Law Enforcement Officer." https://ric-zai-inc.com/Publications/cops-w0831-pub.pdf.

9. From COPS recruitment pamphlet, "Hiring for the 21st Century Law Enforcement Officer." https://ric-zai-inc.com/Publications/cops-w0831-pub.pdf.

10. The Advance Diversity in Law Enforcement initiative was an interagency research initiative of the US Department of Justice's Civil Rights Division and the US Equal Employment Opportunity Commission (EEOC) launched in December 2015 to "help law enforcement agencies recruit, hire, retain, and promote officers that reflect the diversity of the communities they serve." www.eeoc.gov/eeoc/interagency/police-diversity-report.cfm.

11. The drafting of Black and brown soldiers to fight in World War I offered new challenges to racial oppression. With the 1917 entry of the United States into the Great War, at least 18,000 Puerto Ricans and 367,000 African American men were drafted into the armed forces (Harris 2001, 227).

12. During the deadly August 2017 "Unite the Right" rally in Charlottesville, Virginia, white fascists with camouflage clothing and armed with high-powered assault rifles, helmets, telescopic sights, tactical gear, batons, and bulletproof vests marched through the streets carrying Confederate flags while chanting Nazi-inspired slogans like "blood and soil," "Jews will not replace us," and "Heil Trump." www.independent.co.uk/news/world/americas/militia-assault-rifles-unite-the-right-rally-charlottesville-virginia-white-supremacy-latest-a7890081.html.

References

Annamma, Subini Ancy. 2017. "Disrupting Cartographies of Inequity: Education Journey Mapping as a Qualitative Methodology." In *Critical Race Spatial Analysis: Mapping to Understand and Address Educational Inequity*, edited by Deb Morrison, Subini Ancy Annamma, and Darrell D. Jackson, 35–50. Sterling, VA: Stylus Publishing.

Antón, Susan. 2012. "Commentary: A Discussion of Ethical Issues in Skeletal Biology." In *Biological Anthropology and Ethics: From Repatriation to Genetic Identity*, edited by Trudy R. Turner, 133–38. Albany: State University of New York Press.

Aparicio, Frances R., and Susana Chávez-Silverman, eds. 1997. *Tropicalizations: Transcultural Representations of Latinidad*. Lebanon, NH: University Press of New England.

Armengol, Josep M. 2014. *Masculinities in Black and White: Manliness and Whiteness in (African) American Literature*. New York: Palgrave Macmillan.

Balko, Radley. 2013. *Rise of the Warrior Cop: The Militarization of America's Police Forces*. New York: PublicAffairs.

Beamish, Rob. 2011. *Steroids: A New Look at Performance-Enhancing Drugs*. Santa Barbara, CA: ABC-CLIO.

Benedict, Ruth. (1934) 2013. *Patterns of Culture*. Boston: Houghton Mifflin Harcourt.

Benz, Stephen. 1997. "Through the Tropical Looking Glass: The Motif of Resistance in US Literature on Central America." In *Tropicalizations: Transcultural Representations of Latinidad*, edited by F. Aparicio and S. Chávez-Silverman, 51–66. Hanover: University Press of New England.

Bonilla-Silva, Eduardo, and Tukufu Zuberi. 2008. "Towards a Definition of White Logic and White Methods." In *White Logic, White Methods: Racism and Methodology*, edited by Tukufu Zuber and Eduardo Bonilla-Silva, 3–30. New York: Rowman and Littlefield.

Bolton, Kenneth, and Joe Feagin. 2004. *Black in Blue: African-American Police Officers and Racism*. New York: Routledge.

Burton, Orisanmi. 2015. "To Protect and Serve Whiteness." *North American Dialogue* 18, no. 2: 38–50.

Campbell, Fiona. 2009. *Contours of Ableism: The Production of Disability and Abledness*. New York: Springer.

Carroll, David. 1998. *French Literary Fascism: Nationalism, Anti-Semitism, and the Ideology of Culture*. Princeton, NJ: Princeton University Press.

Chang, Jeff. 2016. *We gon'be alright: Notes on Race and Resegregation*. New York: Macmillan.

Cocke, Charles, Jay Dawes, and Robin Marc Orr. 2016. "The Use of 2 Conditioning Programs and the Fitness Characteristics of Police Academy Cadets." *Journal of Athletic Training* 51, no. 11: 887–96.

Davis, Angela Y. 2006 "Racialized Punishment and Prison Abolition." In *A Companion to African-American Philosophy*, edited by Tommy Lott and John Pittman, 360–69. New York: Wiley.

Du Rocher, Kris. 2010. "Violent Masculinity." In *Southern Masculinity: Perspectives on Manhood in the South since Reconstruction*, edited by Craig Thompson Friend, 46–64. Athens: University of Georgia Press.

Fanon, Frantz. (1952) 1970. *Black Skin, White Masks*. London: Paladin.

Fassin, Didier. 2013. *Enforcing Order: An Ethnography of Urban Policing*. Malden, MA: Polity.

Ferber, Abby. 1999. *White Man Falling: Race, Gender, and White Supremacy*. Lanham, MD: Rowan and Littlefield.

Giblett, Rodney James. 2011. *People and Places of Nature and Culture*. Bristol, UK: Intellect Books.

Goodrick-Clarke, Nicholas. 2003. *Black Sun: Aryan Cults, Esoteric Nazism, and the Politics of Identity*. New York: New York University Press.

Harris, Angela P. 2000. "Gender, Violence, Race, and Criminal Justice." *Stanford Law Review* 52: 777–806.

Harris, William. 2001. *Deep Souths: Delta, Piedmont, and Sea Island Society in the Age of Segregation*. Baltimore: Johns Hopkins University Press.

Harrison, Faye V. 1995. "The Persistent Power of 'Race' in the Cultural and Political Economy of Racism." *Annual Review of Anthropology* 24: 47–74.

Jenkins, Herbert. 1970. *Keeping the Peace: A Police Chief Looks at His Job*. New York: Harper and Row.

Kraska, Peter B., and Louis J. Cubellis. 1997. "Militarizing Mayberry and Beyond: Making Sense of American Paramilitary Policing." *Justice Quarterly* 14, no. 4: 607–29.

Kurashige, Scott. 2017. *The Fifty-Year Rebellion: How the US Political Crisis Began in Detroit*. Berkeley: University of California Press.

Martinot, Steve. 2010. *The Machinery of Whiteness: Studies in the Structure of Racialization*. Philadelphia: Temple University Press.

McIntosh, Peggy. 1997. "White Privilege and Male Privilege: A Personal Account of Coming to See Correspondences through Work in Women's Studies." In *Critical White Studies: Looking behind the Mirror*, edited by R. Delgado and J. Stefancic, 291–99. Philadelphia: Temple University Press.

Moskos, Peter. 2008. *Cop in the Hood: My Year Policing Baltimore's Eastern District*. Princeton, NJ: Princeton University Press.

Novick, Peter. 1999. *The Holocaust in American Life*. Boston: Houghton Mifflin.

Opotow, Susan. 2016. "Protest and Policing: Conflict, Justice, and History in Ferguson, Missouri." In *Leading through Conflict*, 155–78. New York: Palgrave Macmillan.

Parreñas, Juno. "Producing Affect: Transnational Volunteerism in a Malaysian Orangutan Rehabilitation Center." *American Ethnologist* 39, no. 4: 673–87.

Perry, Barbara. 2009. *In the Name of Hate: Understanding Hate Crimes*. New York: Routledge.

Pine, Lisa. 2010. *Education in Nazi Germany*. Oxford: Berg.

Plunka, Gene. 2009. *Holocaust Drama: The Theatre of Atrocity*. Cambridge: Cambridge University Press.

Rodriguez, Dylan. 2010. *Suspended Apocalypse: White Supremacy, Genocide, and the Filipino Condition*. Minneapolis: University of Minnesota Press.

Rohrer, Judy. 2014. *Queering the Biopolitics of Citizenship in the Age of Obama*. New York: Palgrave Macmillan.

Rose, Stephany. 2015. *Abolishing White Masculinity from Mark Twain to Hiphop: Crises in Whiteness*. New York: Lexington.

Slater, Jenny. 2016. *Youth and Disability: A Challenge to Mr. Reasonable.* New York: Routledge.

Smith, Christen A. 2016. *Afro-Paradise: Blackness, Violence, and Performance in Brazil.* Urbana: University of Illinois Press.

Somerville, Siobhan B. 2000. *Queering the Color Line: Race and the Invention of Homosexuality in American Culture.* Durham, NC: Duke University Press.

Stubblefield, Anna. 2005. "Meditations on Postsupremacist Philosophy." In *White on White/Black on Black,* edited by George Yancy, 71–81. New York: Rowman and Littlefield.

Weale, Adrian. 2012. *Army of Evil: A History of the SS.* New York: Penguin.

Williams, Kristian. 2015. *Our Enemies in Blue: Police and Power in America.* Oakland, CA: AK Press.

Wynter, Sylvia. 1994. "No Humans Involved: An Open Letter to My Colleagues." *Institute N.H.I.* 1, no. 1: 42–73.

17

Militarized White Supremacy and Black GI Solidarity in Okinawa

Mitzi Uehara Carter

I TURNED BACK to look at the lone Black US Marine sitting a few seats behind me on the packed military tour bus moving through the southern part of Okinawa, Japan. His gaze was firmly fixed ahead, but his eyebrows were pinched and raised indicating he was also frustrated by what we had just been told on the tour. The tour guide, a captivating, well-rehearsed storyteller, had just told our bus of mostly buzzed-cut US Marines about the infamous "capture" of Shuri castle, where members of a southern white Marine regiment planted the Confederate "Stars and Bars" flag on its grounds. The story claims that that no one had the US flag on hand and the only one available was this Confederate flag, which had been gifted to the company commander by the Daughters of the Revolution. The commander who led this group of white Marines had carried the Confederate flag with him across the Pacific during the Battle of Okinawa in World War II. With a slight tinge of pride in his voice, the tour guide noted that this "rebel flag" flew over Shuri for two days before it was replaced with the official "Stars and Stripes" flag.[1] The tour guide left a deliberate heavy pause waiting for the expected reaction, which I imagine occurred repeatedly on other tours when he told this story. Several men behind me on the bus erupted into excited and loud communal "oorahs!" The tour guide smiled expectedly on cue.[2]

My ethnographic antennas prickled but my anthropological hat felt slightly askew, truly disturbed by this symbolic and literal unfolding and grounding of white supremacy in my mother's homeland. My mother is a survivor of the Battle of Okinawa, and it continues to haunt her today. This disastrous battle, which the tour commemorated, led to nearly one-third of the Okinawan population being killed. There are still approximately 55,000 military personnel and their families stationed in Okinawa. The US bases in Okinawa account for approximately 75 percent of all US military facilities in Japan even though Okinawa is only 0.6 percent of the Japanese state. Most Okinawans consider this to be an unfair burden, and yet protests, elections, global attention, and national and international lawsuits have not made any significant movement of US presence on the island to other

Japanese prefectures. This kind of consolidated military presence on such a small island, considered to be so strategically important to the US-Japan security arrangement, is dependent on the discursive shaping of Okinawa, which is done through a careful crafting of Okinawa as a military heritage site. The tour that the Black GI and me were on was part of this discursive shaping of miliary heritage. Importantly, the formation of military heritage that is produced through a culture of militarization involves a mobilization of Orientalism, the racist gaze of Asian people by the West, along with the implicit logics of a militarized white supremacy.

The academic literature detailing how places like Okinawa become militarized is plentiful; however, there is very little analysis on how ideologies of white supremacy are enacted in Asian-US militarization. In the case of Okinawa, scholars have failed to directly address the discourse of white supremacy. In doing so, Okinawa has been rendered a liminal, inert, and passive space that in turn fails to recognize the surreptitiously crafted interruptions and creative challenges by Okinawans and also US military personnel of color, like the Black GI on the tour. By focusing on the postwar practices of anti-Blackness, pre-reversion Jim-Crow-like protocols in off-base establishments and the briefly lived moments of Okinawan and Black GI solidarity, I will showcase how white supremacy has been unevenly rooted and sustained but also interrupted in the heavily militarized borderlands of Okinawa. This analysis also contributes to understanding how militarized white supremacy is central to the framing of Okinawa as a strategically necessary site for US empire.

Inscribing Race

While doing research in Okinawa, I encountered several elderly Okinawan women who wanted to know my mother's departure story. Curious about my Black Okinawan background, they would unabashedly ask what compelled her to leave Okinawa and never return permanently. By their framing, I knew they were often cynical of the overly romanticized stories of international love and keen to know how affective transactions were saturated with social and political decisions. As a result, their questions often seemed rhetorical, perhaps gathering a broader body of common stories to pass on in their conversations with family, neighbors, or friends of what might already be in circulation. These tales of quiet diasporic routes shaped by a large military presence and the specter of racialized violence are known to every Okinawan family. "She left," I often explained, "because she thought it would be too difficult for my older sister in off-base Okinawa, pre-reversion." The time stamp and the indexical racial tag of being disconnected from the privileges of a US base, would often be enough for the nod of understanding to transpire. It instantly meant she had considered making the choice of being independent from my father's military access and all it might confer, but she chose safety for my sister in that moment. Black Okinawans have suffered in ways that were more acute than other racially mixed Okinawans. Throughout my life I have wondered why there was such a devaluation of Blackness on this island and how it was connected to forms of white supremacy operating in Okinawa. I also wondered if there were other stories of Blackness that might challenge this feeling, stories that might circulate more intimately and locally and may not be as prevalent to someone like me who grew up outside the island? What I learned as a researcher is that the questions I was asking were far too simplistic and that at almost every turn, the answers led me back to how white supremacy has a far more pervasive impact on life in Okinawa in shaping the complicated palimpsest of racial memories in this militarized landscape.

In her discussion of the Katsuyama Cave incident, Rebecca Forgash (2020) illustrated how early postwar memories of Black soldiers are renarrativized within a broader economy of violence of white supremacy. The remains of three Black marines from an early postwar segregated Marine unit were found in a small Okinawan village, inside a cave locally named Kurombo Gama (Cave of the Negroes). The bones had been a hidden secret for decades, some villagers passing along the story in a hushed manner only to a handful of people. The men were apparently killed in a vigilante-type justice enacted by some of the villagers who believed they were responsible for the repeated abductions and rapes of women living there in those early postwar years. When the story first broke, the residents were initially resistant to any exploration and coverage of this incident along with other past sexual victimization of women in the village fearing it would taint the village's reputation (Forgash 2020, 57–58). In addition, Forgash suggested the US military scurried away from the news because the story would renew critiques of its systemic problem of sexual violence and usher unwelcome attention its way, especially just before the 2000 G8 Summit in Okinawa. However, once this racialized story went public, it became a useful way for local residents to articulate their subjectivity in a new and potent way, but it also offered a set of readily available scripts to contest or judge Okinawan women's involvement with Black men, Forgash argues.

This kind of narrative is given new life force, however, when it is coupled with transnational eugenic thinking to explain and compartmentalize the larger institutionalized force of military violence onto Black bodies. Forgash (2020) and Sarita See (1998, 73) have argued that racial narratives of crimes in Okinawa have been shaped by racist military historians and clumsily mesh with other locally formed racial discourses and within military communities at large. Statistics detailing military violence in Okinawa, especially data that are produced by the Okinawan prefecture, are often contested by those with Status of Force Agreement (SOFA) status and dismissed as manipulated or politically doctored to legitimize antibase positions. For example, some prominent military historians have deflected high crime rates of occupation-era US soldiers onto segregated Black troops or the later segregated Filipino units, naturalizing the eugenic idea that there was a seamless proclivity toward criminal behavior because of their poorly underresourced environment or that they were innately criminal because they were Black or Filipino (Forgash 2020, 70–73). When those segregated troops left and White troops remained, the crime rates did not subside, nor was there any discussion of the intrinsic relationship between militarization and violence outside these narratives of race. It was left as a taken-for-granted, uncontested explanation to exorcise all "bad apple"-type behaviors onto Black and brown men.[3]

Upon first glance, this analysis seems to provide scholars with a neat bite-sized answer of how white supremacy and anti-Blackness operates in militarized zones, but it is more complex given Okinawa's racialized triangulated position between Japan and the United

States. In my ethnographic research with Okinawans living around the US bases, multiple interviewees provided delicate descriptions of how they saw practices of racialization in base borderlands, as being an uneasy practice of survival within a larger economic and social system of power of white supremacy. The performative and repeated marking of the outlines of these nonsovereign spaces can only be understood by understanding how Japan is a racial state (Goldberg 2002).

Racial States

Just a few years after Japan accepted defeat in World War II, Cold War tensions rose in East Asia. Japan quickly moved from being a previous enemy state to a new ally against communism. The two nations agreed to a controversial security treaty in 1951 that effectively turned Okinawa into an even more ambiguous territory with mere "residual sovereignty" all the while restoring sovereignty to Japan in 1952. The sense of betrayal was palpable across Okinawa. Okinawa was the site of the only land battle in Japan, and the losses were devastating for Okinawa. Many Okinawans believe Japan strategically drew US forces to the island in a war of attrition, creating a buffer to the other islands, and that the specific acts of removing the majority of the US military from the mainland onto Okinawa and then giving up Okinawa indefinitely to the United States after it had already been sacrificed during the war was more of a testament that they were never fully considered complete citizens.

Tensions on the island rose to new heights after the renewal of this security treaty in 1960, which left Okinawa under more entrenched colonial conditions. After Okinawa reverted back to Japan in 1972, Japan continued to pay the United States to host its forces primarily in Okinawa. In fact, it pays a staggering 74 percent of the costs to maintain the military bases there, larger than any other country than anywhere US bases are located overseas. When Japan gambled to secure its postwar sovereignty by stripping Okinawa of its own, it had to simultaneously use an Orientalist framework that marked Okinawa as outside of modernity and distance itself from this space to create a refraction of itself as closer to whiteness.[4] (Anthropologist Masamichi Inoue has posited that as Japan became more financially secure, the United States increasingly put pressure on Japan to remilitarize in these years, and the demise of the peace constitution and the sacrifice of Okinawa was precisely possible because of Japan's patriarchal and "century-old desire" to mirror much of the values inherent in white supremacy [Inoue 2007, 64]).

Okinawans, quite accustomed to being positioned as the constitutive outside of the nation symbolically and geographically since Japan forcibly took over the once-independent kingdom in 1879, have repeatedly carved out flexible ways to reposition themselves in the face of extreme violence. The US Civil Authority of the Ryukyus (USCAR) easily adopted the language of the Japanese state, especially from wartime documents that categorized Okinawans as nonideological Japanese (Koshiro 1999) in order to justify a separate rule over Okinawa in negotiations with Japan, but the new prioritized attention to the management of women's bodies for sex for the flood of soldiers arriving on the island and the segregation of troops marked Okinawans in new ways.

In a matter of a few years, there were suddenly new technologies of panoptic surveillance, mass displacement of Okinawans from their homes to create new bases, golf courses, parking lots. The lack of any legal or effective means to contest human rights abuses, land usurpation, along with the censorship and blocking of Okinawan calls for democracy that did not benefit the USCAR plan meant Okinawans could barely contest this new form of totalizing occupation. In this newly militarized landscape a new racial and political subject was being formed on the island. Annmaria Shimabuku has painstakingly analyzed this new "petitioning subject"[5] who "must ask for things because it has little to nothing" (Shimabuku 2018, 61). In this new biopolitical order, Okinawans were forced to "petition" themselves to the United States (Shimabuku 2018), requesting previously restricted off-limit zones to be opened up, even if was to be largely sex work, sometimes fully engaging in the performative discursive work of soft power[6] masked as hegemonic notions of "friendship" and "democratization" and modernization vis-à-vis more militarized contact.

Jim-Crow-like protocols existed off-base (Onishi 2013; Ueunten 2010) and were practiced by Okinawan business owners as they also learned to practice and self-police their own movement around new fence lines that carved out former farmlands, fishing villages, or neighborhoods. Not only were Okinawans taught how to approach the contained spaces of the newly constructed military facilities as "Off-Limits," but they were taught how to recognize their own hailing as outsiders from their own lands. This production of a new geography of on/off base spaces required a new mode of Orientalist interpellation, that which rendered Okinawans as trespassers at the fence lines, between two racial states.

In an interview with me, an Okinawan woman explained that as a former sex worker in the Koza area during the early 1970s, the pimp who abused and hustled her would not allow her to be out publicly with Black men because he wanted to appease any white servicemen's racist sensibilities during a time when racial segregation was enacted in certain off-base spaces. Within an economy of violence, some Okinawan business owners, or those who thrived off the shadow economies, participated in this kind of racial hierarchy without fully consuming the discourse of white supremacy.

In other interviews, several Okinawan men and women who came of age in the pre-reversion period described the yearning for colonial shake-ups. Black military personnel in particular were viewed as possible allies, as soulful spirits in the fight against violent and systemic inequalities implemented under US security arrangements with Japan. For example, an antibase community organizer in Sunabe, Mr. Matsuda, revealed in an interview with me how he began to notice an increasing number of drafted Black men in the Vietnam War years. Through the barbed-wire fences, he could see their laboring bodies and he felt somewhat despondent about what he perceived as a shared condition of being fragmented beings in the racial state. Okinawans often saw and heard stories of discrimination against Black people on the bases and saw reports of racist incidents off base. Matsuda's sadness slipped into anger because the hope of liberation, the spirit of rebellion he had transposed onto Black bodies never happened. In his dreams, they were supposed to help fully challenge, from the inside, the colonial forms of modernity that had racialized Okinawans as "Orientals" and also as second-class Japanese citizens. When I asked what kind of resistance he imagined would materialize, he said he hoped for an organic mass to resistance to a government that drafted and put them in precarious positions in the war.[7] He read enough about the United States to know that they could not reap the full benefits of US citizenship on the base or back home. His anger and what he assumed to be Black men's complicit stance led to his hasty conclusion that Black men in uniform were more readily militarizable, embodying more of a "green identity" than a supposedly authentic politically resistant one. In this case, Matsuda wanted a somewhat objectified Black masculine form of uprising to be the catalyst for change.[8]

This was not a singular case. Okinawan antibase pre-reversion activists yearned for and directly attempted to create strategic alliances with politicized anti-imperialist Black servicemen stationed in Okinawa, some of whom they met in racially segregated off-base spaces while others circulated new imaginaries where these alliances would materialize (Onishi 2013). This type of futurism echoed in Okinawan poetry, fiction, and even shaped the actions in protests.

For example, Okinawan writer Matayoshi Eiki was acutely aware of how transnational practices of racialization and white supremacy operated along the militarized fence lines in Okinawa. He captured this brilliantly in his short story "The Wild Boar That George Gunned Down." It depicts the madness of incessant violence in an Okinawan base town in the Vietnam War era, where the energy of one Orientalized warscape transferred to a site of sexualized and gendered "rest and recreation" in the racially segregated zones in Okinawa. The story is based in the town of Koza, a real site that cropped up around Kadena Air Force Base and was known for a pocket of space called "The Bush" where Black military personnel could socialize safely, get their hair cut, and eat Southern soul food prepared by Okinawans. White GI's were not readily welcomed here.[9] In his story, the Okinawan and Black characters along the fence line found uncanny ways to resist the main character, George, a white soldier with intense racist ideas he attached to Okinawan and Black "primitive" bodies. Eiki consciously highlights George's notions of civility and modernity, which for George are rooted in his own whiteness. His white supremacist ideas are heightened against the stark darkness (of both the Okinawan and Black military personnel) and the objects connected to them. What is striking about Eiki's story is his decision to align Blacks and Okinawans against George, who perceives them literally as piglike animals, especially in these off-base militarized zones. It is a potent story that illustrates the types of jagged connections some Okinawans imagined to be possible, even with the kinds of racial hierarchies that proliferated in these military landscapes.

In my own interviews with US military personnel stationed in Okinawa in this period, including my own father, all pointed to their shared experiences of oppression they felt with Okinawans. But the possibilities to translate that energy, to create a politically disruptive opening, never materialized in a significant enough way to generate a structural shift. The US military closely monitored any Black service members who they deemed to be "political," surveilled their wives' actions, and ultimately mirrored the tactics for squashing political uprising in the United States. One interviewee, a wife of a Black Marine, explained to me how she and her husband were kicked out of Okinawa in the late 1960s because she

FIGURE 17.1. Photo provided to author by interviewee. Black radical servicemen in Okinawa in the early 1970s.

was caught joining Okinawans in an antibase protest. She had been followed, and they had found her photos she had taken of a Black Panther gathering among the Black GIs in an off-base site in Okinawa and presented them to her husband as proof of his infractions.

On December 20, 1970, after a drunk American soldier hit an Okinawan pedestrian, a brief yet powerful moment of solidarity and alliance between Okinawans and Black soldiers emerged much to the embarrassment of the US military authorities. When the civilian police tried to remove the offender's car, a crowd gathered around to stop the removal of evidence, as had happened just a few months earlier in a case where a drunken soldier had run over an Okinawan pedestrian and who was declared not guilty by a US military court (Ueunten 2010, 94–95). A large crowd gathered to upwards of five hundred people, eventually toppling and burning cars with military tags, but interestingly, neither African American soldiers nor their property were harmed, it was, according to Inoue, an "unspoken code" (Inoue 2007, 54). A day after the riot, a group of politically active Black soldiers, perhaps privy to this display of solidarity, distributed a flyer in Japanese and English announcing their solidarity with Okinawans in their fight for justice (Onishi 2013, 21–22).

The ways in which in which contemporary US military service is framed to absorb Black bodies into the nation, as a citizen-soldier, is not new. But it is interesting to think how anticolonial or settler discourses are articulated as polar valences in Okinawa. For example, a former buffalo soldier, Norman "Pop" Craft, opened a BBQ restaurant catering to the transient, mostly Black young military crowd in central Okinawa. At the age of seventy-one, he gave a talk to the III Marine Expeditionary Force recalling his time battling Native Americans on the side of settlers and patrolling borders, and yet he was not afforded the full guarantees of citizenship. Nor was he part of a lineage of people thought to be legally colonized (i.e., Native Americans). In his speech, he said, "I felt ashamed of my feelings toward the U.S., but here [in Okinawa] I was accepted and color did not matter." Being a settler in Okinawa, he noted, was a form of exile (Hottle 1994), and yet his critique was not unbound as evidenced in his comments to the Marines. As if to soften his embedded critique of nonbelonging to the nation for which he fought, he deradicalized Martin Luther King's message with his statement, "My belief was like Dr. King's, not to fight about oppression, but just to know about it, remember it and build ourselves upon it" (Hottle 1994). With that expression, perhaps as a keen businessman he knew that his words mattered in a militarized landscape, his challenge to anticolonial discourse weakened.

Chuuto hanpa Praxis

The modern forms of racism that were transplanted to Okinawa were so slippery that Okinawans had to find new ways to resist and dismantle them. Ann Stoler has noted that this type of racism has a "polyvalent mobility" (Stoler 2006, 69, 89) and is able to draw its power from a multitude of representations and imaginaries in its quest to provide a definitive truth claims about past or present inequalities not just from a singular crisis point (Stoler 2006, 91).

Chuuto hanpa-ness is a particular Okinawan praxis that has been accessed by many Okinawans to counter modern forms of racism in Okinawa. *Chuuto hanpa* is a Japanese term that broadly means neither here nor there, incomplete, or in the process of becoming. I argue it is a way Okinawans insecurely situated along the fence lines can chip away at the logics of white supremacy. It is a strategic but also mundane, everyday process that exists in the hybrid borderlands along the bases.[10]

In such a hybrid place, many Okinawans are aware of how contact with militarized entities may look like amicable relations but then realize they are a government-planned technique used to manage populations. "Friendship" in most colonial situations is managed as way to superficially monitor moments of contact with those deemed Other as a sign of proof that there is some form of agreement between those thought of as either host or guest.[11] In Okinawa, the propaganda of Okinawa-US Friendship is limited to a militarily approved form, one that ultimately supports US-Japan interests. A hip-hop artist I met in Okinawa is one specific example I will use of how young Okinawans are attempting to challenge white supremacy and the powerful discourses of military friendship.

Akiko is a young Okinawan woman, born and raised in Okinawa but who left after high school to study in the United States, where she promptly enrolled in an African American studies course. She told me that once her professor asked her why she was there, and she responded, "Because Africa is the original, the source of all things." The professor, stunned by her answer, replied that she had never met a Japanese like Akiko, to which she scoffed, "I'm not Japanese. I'm Okinawan!" The idea of connecting to other people of color, to a Global South outside the full reins of the nation-state, was appealing to her and felt freeing. Global Blackness was a concept that she found could shape her own organizing activities and inform her approach to styling her career as an independent hip-hop artist.

Akiko founded Flow Manifesto, a space for Okinawans and US Black military personnel to come together to create something radical and hybrid that could not be found in Tokyo. About three times a year, she would host a fully bilingual and curated open-mic night in a central off-base location. Her broad networks on and off base, in Black and Okinawan communities, brought a truly diverse audience of Blacks and Okinawans. Some were transient military personnel and others had long-term roots on the island; some Okinawan artists were apolitical while others firmly held vocal opinions about the US base presence. I asked her why she began that series, and she explained, "Black people are always creating something dope. I was like, why can't we do that? I don't want to be Black but I want to be more like putting ourselves on the map—like, hey, 'We are Okinawans!' These gatherings, as well as her TV show "Shikina TV" were a way to block the co-option of "friendship discourse" and to embrace forms of multiplicity that can bypass orientalist frameworks. She continued: "The military don't know Okinawans outside of lectures, hearsay and through fake-ass friendship base tournaments. There is a lack of information. All these Okinawan girls on the street messing with these military guys have more information than the politicians. I bet you they don't understand PCS—what season it is, the "Green Line," the pay scales, the cultural life of military." She was ultimately frustrated by the lack of a "planetary humanism"[12] that could emerge with a new form of contact, a different form of friendship. Some of her Okinawan attendees or viewers of her TV show would often comment that she was a prime model of "internationalism." This bothered her and she explained that these same commenters did not consider that they are also from a long history of laboring bodies who were sent to work on Japan's colonies across Southeast Asia and that they could not see themselves as the cosmopolitan people they were, having acquired long rich experiences of contact with colonizers and their Others, having absorbed the multiple narratives and cultural frameworks that have forced them to code-switch in their dynamic Okinawan *chuuto hanpa*. This reframing, she would often say, should be used as a vantage point to position themselves differently in a militarized landscape. This stance, when internalized, can be empowering in juxtaposition to the linear models of modernity that often position Okinawa as a space still lacking in the progressive economic, cultural, and political skills and resources to be independent or make its own decisions to be heard by Tokyo or Washington DC. It could help reframe their own *chuuto hanpa* praxis not as a manipulative tactic as one State Department director in Japan claimed (Vine 2001), but as a powerful, modern tool.

Her Flow Manifesto events then were intended to bring a form of "global blackness" not in its corporate neoliberal glossy appeal, but in its gritty uneven hybrid, polyvalent circulation to form new possible ways of seeing and hearing each other. It positions Okinawans and Black attendees as future-oriented, outside of the good savage/cosmopolitan binary. Her hope was for Black artists to disrupt canned ideas of Blackness that sometimes circulate in hip-hop fan clubs in Okinawa and the other islands of Japan but also make room for the Black artists to push back against the truth claims about the multiple reasons for enlisting and to give them space to absorb and connect with anticolonial feelings some Okinawan artists might raise. It would also give some participants the flexibility to make cross-cultural, public critiques of the military or directly share memories of economic or social injustices as an impetus for enlisting without fear of being chastised by a superior. It offered Okinawans a way to observe and/or interact with those artists and audience members and find meaningful ways to think about solidarity through the shared memories of incomplete citizenship and strategies to maneuver between modernities.

An Okinawan mixed media artist whose work was being featured at the site where the Flow Manifesto event was being held approached me after I read my poem on colonial in-betweenness. She whispered that too often, it is considered taboo to talk about this space of flow because it can be mistakenly, and dangerously, aligned with being simply pro-base. Her artwork, she explained, tried to touch on this space of finding future-oriented alignment, especially with a transnational Black consciousness in mind.

Thinking about how white supremacy is challenged outside of pro/anti-base logics especially with an eye toward scholars of the Black Pacific, a burgeoning field of scholarship that analyzes circulating concepts of anti-Blackness, capitalism, and Orientalism on the same analytical field, will bring a more useful framework to the understanding of transnational, hybrid forms of racism.

Notes

1. Several military history texts that focus on the battle explain that when the 77th Division complained to Lieutenant General Simon Bolivar Buckner Jr., he was not upset and is quoted as saying, "How can I be sore? My father fought under that flag!" Buckner, after all, was the son of the infamous Confederate General Simon Bolivar Buckner Sr., who surrendered to Ulysses S. Grant at Fort Donaldson during the Civil War. Buckner Jr., was also a well-known racist and openly made comments about Black troops, and Japanese, interracial mixing (social and intimate).

2. See E. B. Sledge's memoir (1981) of his recollection hearing the flag had been hoisted over the castle. "All of us Southerners cheered loudly, the Yankees among us grumbled . . ." (275).

3. See Muhammad (2010) for a more nuanced history of the ways crime statistics were used to institutionalize Black inferiority.

4. This was not just a wartime incident. Historians of Okinawa have documented the ways Okinawans became increasingly important as a temporal and spatial marker of Otherness as Japan tried to gain a foothold in the racial ordering of global nations. At the St. Louis World Expo in 1904 (Louisiana Purchase Exposition), for example, Japan lobbied to be removed from the "non-Western" category in the anthropological display of races (Koshiro 1999). Instead, the Ainu were showcased as Japan's formerly primitive subjects along with the West's internal Others, Native Americans (Koshiro 1999, 93). Ainu and Okinawans (at an earlier expo in 1903) became the necessary Other to juxtapose "pure" and "authentic" Japanese who had departed from that temporal space to join "Western" nations and distance themselves from the racial sphere of China, which was increasingly seen as further from modernity.

5. Shimabuku expands on Ichirō Tomiyama's coined concept of the petitioning subject. In her reading of his work, Shimabuku argues that this new technique of petitioning was not to produce goods and services to gain middle-class status like on the mainland, rather to produce "themselves as subjects before the law" (61). For Shimabuku, simply casting blame on Okinawan elites for being complicit in the actions is too simplistic.

6. Donna Alvah (2007) has documented the specific ways in which US military spouses were largely brought to overseas bases from the 1940s to 1960s as a form of "soft power" to "present a more humane side of the U.S. occupation and control" (Alvah 2007, 177). The policies pressured these women and children to

maintain "compliance with military goals and encouraged them to view their interests as separate from those of local women, thus defusing the potential for women's united protest" (179).

7. See Ismay (2020) for a report on how Black US Marines who were subject to racial bias on assessment tests and cast into infantry jobs and low level, mundane jobs on the bases, and how the military justice system in Okinawa was so racially charged, Black men could never be represented well during the Vietnam War years.

8. See Onishi's (2013) rich discussion of soulfulness and the hopes of Black Radicalism as a political and poetic aesthetic for survival in Okinawa.

9. Bruce Leiber, a former MP and Jewish White American who regularly patrolled Koza, recalled in an interview with me that this was not a place for whites to get caught alone and that if he had to venture into this area, he was required to go with a Black MP. He recalled rumors of Okinawan taxi drivers purposefully taking white GIs there and dropping them off.

10. Lisa Lowe's conceptualization of hybridity is particularly useful in Okinawa. Lowe defines hybridity as "the formation of cultural objects and practices that are produced by the histories of uneven and unsynthetic power relations . . . it marks the history of survival within relationships of unequal power and domination" (67). Lisa Lowe (1996) conceptualizes hybridization in immigrant communities in the United States as not simply being "the 'free' oscillation between or among chosen identities" (82) but steeped in layers of inequality that have forced particular routes on which people can move to assert their identities. Like Lowe, I argue that beyond the "material traces" of transnational movement and social/economic displacements, the Okinawan praxis of *chuuto hanpa* should be analyzed as an active process of negotiation of Okinawan multiple positionings against US-Japan security arrangements, including the past hauntings and existing forms of white supremacy.

11. See, for instance, Ann Stoler's (1997) very clear examples on colonialism in Southeast Asia on the forms of governmentality, which to some degree produced, managed, and directed "friendship" through colonial discourses of desire.

12. Paul Gilroy describes this form of humanism as future-oriented because doing so directly counters the logic of white supremacy that blocks that occupation of the temporal space. It allows for alterity outside a neoliberal encampment of race (Gilroy 2000, 337).

References

Alvah, Donna. 2007. *Unofficial Ambassadors: American Military Families Overseas and the Cold War, 1946–1965.* New York: New York University Press.

Eiki, Matayoshi. 2011. "The Wild Boar That George Shot." In *Living Spirit: Literature and Resurgence in Okinawa,* edited by Frank Stewart and Katsunori Yamazato. Honolulu: University of Hawai'i Press.

Forgash, Rebecca. 2020. *Intimacy across the Fencelines.* Ithaca, NY: Cornell University Press.

Goldberg, David Theo. 2002. *The Racial State.* Malden, MA: Blackwell.

Haines, Joe. 2006. "Rebel Yelling over Shuri Castle: How the Confederate Stars and Bars Made Its Way to Okinawa." *Okinawa Marine,* November, 3. https://media-cdn.dvidshub.net/pubs/pdf_1529.pdf.

Inoue, Masamichi S. 2007. *Okinawa and the U.S. Military.* New York: Columbia University Press.

Koshiro, Yukiko. 1999. *Trans-Pacific Racisms and the U.S. Occupation of Japan.* New York: Columbia University Press.

Lutz, Catherine. 2001. *Homefront: A Military City and the American Twentieth Century.* Boston: Beacon.

Molasky, Michael S. 2005. *The American Occupation of Japan and Okinawa.* New York: Routledge.

Muhammad, Khalil Gibran. 2011. *The Condemnation of Blackness: Race, Crime, and the Making of Modern Urban America.* Cambridge, MA: Harvard University Press.

Onishi, Yuichiro. 2014. *Transpacific Antiracism: Afro-Asian Solidarity in Twentieth-Century Black America, Japan, and Okinawa.* New York: New York University Press.

Ōta, Masahide. 1984. *The Battle of Okinawa.* Kume Publishing.

See, Sarita. 1998. "Trying Whiteness: Media Representations of the 1996 Okinawa Rape Trial." *Hitting Critical Mass: A Journal of Asian American Cultural Criticism* 5, no. 2.

Shimabuku, Annmaria M. 2018. *Alegal*. New York: Fordham University Press.

Sledge, E. B. 2007. *With the Old Breed: At Peleliu and Okinawa*. New York: Presidio Press.

Stoler, Ann Laura. 2006. *Race and the Education of Desire: Foucault's History of Sexuality and the Colonial Order of Things*. Durham, NC: Duke University Press.

Ueunten, Wesley. 2010. "Rising Up from a Sea of Discontent: The 1970 Koza Uprising in U.S.-Occupied Okinawa." In *Militarized Currents: Toward a Decolonized Future in Asia and the Pacific*, edited by Setsu Shigematsu and Keith L. Camacho. Minneapolis: University of Minnesota Press.

Vine, David. 2011. "Smearing Japan." Foreign Policy in Focus. April 20, 2011. https://fpif.org/smearing_japan/.

18

American Supremacy

REFLECTIONS ON THE RACIAL LOGICS OF ASYLUM IN US IMMIGRATION COURT

Christopher A. Loperena

> We believe in American exceptionalism. We believe the United States of America is
> unlike any other nation on Earth. We believe America is exceptional because of our historic
> role—first as refuge, then as defender, and now as exemplar of liberty for the world to see.
>
> —PREAMBLE, 2016 REPUBLICAN PARTY PLATFORM

ON OCTOBER 18, 2020, Enrique Tarrio, leader of the Proud Boys, was photographed wearing a T-shirt with the words "American Supremacist" emblazoned across his chest in bold white letters. He was attending a "Latinos for Trump" demonstration in Miami, Florida. The Trump administration's policies toward migrants from Latin America, including the separation of children from their parents, would seem reason enough to diminish his support among Latinx voters, and yet Trumpism continues to recruit Latinos into its ranks.[1] This chapter grapples with the ideology of American supremacy—a twenty-first-century brand of ostensibly "postracial" racism—and how specifically it filters into US immigration court proceedings involving asylum seekers from Central America.[2]

The ideology of American supremacy is intimately tethered to the notion of American exceptionalism—the belief that the United States is and will always be a pillar of democratic freedoms and opportunities.[3] Indeed, the Preamble to the 2016 Republican Party Platform states: "We believe in American exceptionalism. We believe the United States of America is unlike any other nation on Earth. We believe America is exceptional because of our historic role—first as refuge, then as defender, and now as exemplar of liberty for the world to see."[4] The power of American exceptionalism lies in its ability to uphold the mythological origins of the United States as an exceptional space of freedom and at the same time deflect the foundational violence on which the country was founded; it is thus complicit with white supremacy.

The claim that the United States is a defender and exemplar of liberty not only erases histories of Indigenous genocide but also centuries of institutionalized slavery and systemic racism, both before and after the Declaration of Independence. American exceptionalism has further served as a justification for US military interventions in Latin America, often carried out in the name of defending free market democracy and, subsequently, for emergent border security regimes.

As a practice of citizenship, American supremacy makes it possible for someone like Enrique Tarrio to be the visible nonwhite leader of a white nationalist group—the Proud Boys—at the same time that it structures humanitarian debates on how to handle the recent arrival of "migrant caravans" at the US southern border. With increasing fervor, far right movements and allied politicians have mobilized against migrants from Mexico and Central America, including refugees and asylum seekers, painting them as "criminals" and "invaders" who pose a menace to the country's economy and society.[5]

Anti-immigrant rhetoric in combination with draconian reforms of the immigration system have served to redouble nativist sentiment among whites and the Republican Party's growing Latino base, for whom Trump's "law and order" rhetoric has proven persuasive.[6] This demonstrates the ideological dexterity of American supremacy, which in one moment upholds racist beliefs about the threat of immigrants coming from Central America and in another celebrates the growing demographic diversity of right-wing political movements and their conservative values. None of this is new, of course, as many scholars have documented previously (Beltran 2020; Cadava 2020; Rosas 2019). That said, relatively little scholarly attention has been paid to the arrival of Black and Indigenous migrants from Latin America and how specifically claims of anti-Black and/or anti-Indigenous racism factor into the work of seeking asylum.[7] In this chapter, I demonstrate how entrenched racial attitudes and beliefs about Central Americans and Black people more generally get folded into the legal reasoning at play in US immigration court. I further consider how the asylum system conspires with the dogma of American supremacy. In short, proving an individual asylum claimant is worthy of rights serves to reinforce the larger system of racialized criminalization, in which failure to prove your innocence before the law results in imprisonment, deportation, and, in some cases, death. Lastly, I interrogate the role of expert witnesses, like myself, in this broader political drama.

Since 2016, I have worked as a country expert on over a dozen asylum cases involving undocumented immigrants from Honduras, mostly Black identified. These individuals are not merely escaping poverty and gang violence, as prominently reported by the corporate media. Rather, they are fleeing a predatory political economic system that is premised on life-annihilating resource extraction within their territories, which social movement activists have referred to as the *sistema de la muerte* (the death system). In my expert declaration, I am asked to provide evidence that the claimant has a credible fear of persecution either on the basis of their race, religion, nationality, political opinion, or membership within a persecuted social group. This emphasis of course elides some of the larger structural violences that make life in Honduras so deadly. In this chapter, I will focus my attention on the case of a woman asylum seeker who, after many years of severe sexual and emotional abuse, fled Honduras for the United States. The claimant was perceived to be of African descent but self-identified as non-Black. In my affidavit, I argued that in order to make sense of the gender- and race-based persecution she suffered it was necessary to understand anti-Black racism as a historically rooted structuring force, which targets people of African descent—or people with features deemed to be African in origin. One might assume that a structural analysis of racism would be out of place in US immigration court, but I have found the opposite to be true. Indeed, in this case, the court granted asylum. I contend that the court's willingness to grant asylum is not due to a larger cultural shift within US society, but in fact rooted in the pernicious logics of American supremacy.

I begin with a brief discussion of the Central American migration "crisis," tracing its contemporary origins to US military and economic intervention in the region. I then analyze the Trump administration's legal maneuvers to stem the flow of migrants coming from Central America, which were initially carried out in the name of protecting US jobs and security, and then the health and well-being of the population in the face of the COVID-19 pandemic. Trump-era public health restrictions were carried forth by the current president, Joseph Biden. This leads into an overview of the claimant's case, and how my work as an expert articulated with entrenched racial thinking about Honduras. Next I discuss the moral underpinnings of US asylum law and how it is used to render individual migrants into innocent victims or criminals. Lastly, I reflect on how granting asylum on the basis of race furthers the aims of American supremacy and the racist carceral logics underpinning notions of who is and is not worthy of staying.

When Did the "Crisis" Begin?

The number of adult migrants crossing the US-Mexico border has ebbed and flowed in recent years, with peaks in migrant apprehensions in 2014, 2019, and 2021.[8] Many of these migrants hailed from Honduras, Guatemala, and El Salvador—the so called Northern Triangle. However, the "crisis" of unaccompanied minors immigrating from Central America to the United States and the much maligned "migrant caravans" that followed did not spontaneously erupt in 2014, as some media pundits claimed; rather, their roots lie in a deeper history of economic exploitation aided by US military and imperial interventions in the region.[9] The very notion of a migration "crisis" tends to ignore the US government's long-standing role in fomenting the conditions that have impelled migration in the first place (Burrell and Moodie 2015; 2019).

The US State Department has wielded tremendous power throughout Latin America, in some cases colluding directly with antidemocratic forces to back the private interests of US multinational corporations, such as the United Fruit Company, in toppling governments that threatened their vast land holdings. This is precisely what happened in the 1954 coup d'état against Jacobo Arbenz of Guatemala. Military interventions in the region peaked during the revolutionary wars of El Salvador and Nicaragua, which during the 1980s and 1990s incited large flows of migration to the United States. Honduras was a key outpost for US military operations at that time, home to several US bases and the launching site for large contra operatives.[10]

This shameful history of US government support for antidemocratic forces was reiterated in June 2009 when the State Department, then under the leadership of Hillary Clinton, tacitly supported the coup d'état against Honduran president Manuel Zelaya. Zelaya was demonized by Honduras's powerful oligarchy for his increasingly left-leaning political ambitions, which the State Department also deemed to be a threat to its interests in the region.[11] His ousting only exacerbated the problems that have made life in Honduras unlivable for many of its most vulnerable inhabitants. Following the coup d'état, the Honduran per capita murder rate surged to 86.5 per 100,000 people—at that time one of the highest in the world—and in 2017, Honduras was named the most deadly country in the world for land and environmental activists.[12] Organized crime stemming from the drug trade and weakening democratic infrastructure under the administrations of Porfirio Lobo and his predecessor Juan Orlando Hernandez, in addition to extreme weather events, and a general climate of economic insecurity have forced many Hondurans to flee their homes.

Understanding the ways in which these "push and pull" factors undergird migration to the United States is crucial. However, we must also contend with how political-economic forces and concomitant processes of environmental plunder disproportionately affect historically racialized populations, not just once they resettle in the United States but also in their home communities (Blackwell et al. 2017).[13] Conditions of precarity are aggravated along racial lines, with Black and Indigenous peoples suffering the heaviest losses from the onset of neoliberal policies and free-market economic restructuring, backed by the United States, and the related expansion of extractivist economic activities into their territories (Speed 2019; Loperena 2017a). For Garifuna—a Black Indigenous people who lay claim to large expanses of land along the Caribbean coastline—tourism and agribusiness are the primary industries driving them off their ancestral lands.[14]

Country conditions for Black and Indigenous Hondurans have declined steadily since the 2009 coup d'état, which was marked by a significant weakening in democratic processes, including the elections of 2017, in which Juan Orlando Hernandez was reelected to a four-year term as president in spite of widespread condemnation among international election observers. The elections were followed by mass protests and heavy-handed state repression of social movement activists. Even so, the US government chose to aid and abet Honduras's political leaders while turning a blind eye to the glaring human rights abuses unfolding in nearly every corner of the country. It was only after an extended investigation by the Drug Enforcement Administration, and after the election of Xiomara Castro in 2021, that the United States called for the extradition of Honduran president Juan Orlando Hernandez, who is currently in US custody for drug trafficking charges.[15]

US government apathy for the plight of the Honduran people was laid bare by increasingly restrictive immigration policies and a rollback of asylum protections under Trump. On the cusp of the 2020 presidential elections, the Trump administration instated a drastic cut in the number of refugees who would be permitted to legally enter the country—15,000. He also proceeded aggressively with his plans to build a wall along the entire southwest border, from California to Texas. These policies were designed to strengthen his base of support, principally in rural regions of the country, which had for decades endured a hollowing out of their economies via neoliberal deindustrialization. Ironically, it was these same structural conditions that had decimated local economies throughout Central America, leaving many rural communities there more vulnerable to the vagaries of global commodity markets, which dictate not only what is to be produced and consumed, but the types of labor regimes that are necessary to be competitive in the global market. Dispossession and ecological degradation followed.

When coupled with a surge in racist and xenophobic rhetoric, the Trump administration's immigration policy agenda was very clearly a white nationalist project that had dire consequences for migrants of color attempting to reach the United States and for those who have entered the country as asylum seekers (see Wallace and Zepeda Millan 2020). Predictably, Trump represented migrants from Mexico, Guatemala, El Salvador, and Honduras as threatening to the job security of US citizens. But, perhaps more importantly, he used fear-mongering tactics, rooted in white supremacist discourse, to position Central American migrants as a threat to the country's safety and health.[16] He referred to them as rapists, criminals, and potential vectors for the spread of disease. In short, the perceived racial and moral inferiority of Hondurans, Central Americans, Haitians, and other migrants of non-white origin posed an existential threat to global American supremacy and thus necessitated strict immigration laws and policies to keep migrants from crossing the border.

The Biden administration kept in place many of Trump's most controversial immigration policies, including holding children in detention camps at the US-Mexico border and using the Centers for Disease Control and Prevention Title 42 authority to keep refugees in Mexico—presumably an attempt to protect US citizens from COVID-19.[17] Indeed, many chaotic and disturbing incidents involving migrant abuse have taken place under Biden's watch, including one in which Border Control agents violently corralled Haitian immigrants on horseback in scenes that were reminiscent of the US Antebellum South.

The Asylum Seeker

The asylum claimants I have worked with all suffered physical and/or sexual violence on account of their race and gender. In most of these cases, the claimant has also petitioned for protected status on account of their political opinion. Garifuna land rights activists, self-described "land defenders," have faced violent persecution from tourism developers, private investors, and even state authorities for opposing the imposition of extractivist development projects within territories.

The case I will discuss was striking for its atypical characteristics: (1) The claim was premised on domestic violence, which the claimant, whom I refer to as Suani, believed was racially motivated, and (2), the claimant was not Black identified. However, after reviewing the client's declaration, it was clear that her perceived Blackness was a crucial factor in the violence she suffered. I accepted the invitation to work on Suani's case because, in my opinion, it demonstrated the systemic nature of anti-Black racism in Honduras.

Suani was born in a small inland village about 150 kilometers south of the coastal city of La Ceiba. In Honduras the majority of the country's Black population is concentrated along the Caribbean coast in dozens of small Garifuna communities, in the Honduran Mosquitia, and in the cities of La Ceiba, Tela, and Trujillo. There is also a large Garifuna presence in San Pedro Sula, Honduras's industrial capital, and in Tegucigalpa. The interior of the country, particularly within rural areas, is notable for the demographic absence of Black people. Indeed, Suani's birthplace—a town of about 6,000 inhabitants—is majority mestizo, or Ladino. Mestizo is a term used to categorize people of mixed Indigenous and European heritage, which, in the Honduran context, excludes Blackness. Tracing this racial geography was an important component of my expert declaration in support of her case, since, as Suani argued, her darker skin tone and curly hair made her a subject of ridicule among her schoolmates and even members of her own family, who were ashamed of her "African" features. In school and around town she was called names such as "morenita" (little Black girl), "Garifuna," "negra fea" (ugly Black woman), and other racial epithets. All Suani's immediate relatives were, according to her, "light skinned."

After her mother migrated to the United States, Suani went to live with her grandparents. The modest two bedroom house was occupied by multiple members of her extended family, including her aunt and uncle. At the age of eight, Suani's uncle began to sexually abuse her. The abuse began with inappropriate touching and progressed to forced oral sex and eventually forced vaginal penetration. When Suani reported the rape to her grandparents, her aunt accused her of fabricating the story for attention and then beat her. Afraid to speak out again, she endured almost daily sexual violence for years. When Suani turned nineteen, she left her grandmother's home to start a relationship with the father of her firstborn child, but the relationship did not last, and shortly thereafter she returned to her family home where she was subjected to further sexual abuse. Suani refrained from filing charges against her uncle because she believed her family would fail to corroborate her claims, choosing to protect him instead of her.

In 2010, Suani's mother, who was still living and working in the United States, purchased a home for Suani and her two children. Suani visited her grandparents infrequently in an attempt to minimize contact with her uncle. However, he continued to torment her with verbal threats and insisted that her young daughter would be his next victim. Terrified, she retreated back to her mother's house where she lived alone and in fear of further violence from her uncle or from area gang members. She no longer felt capable of protecting herself or her children, so she fled for the United States.

In her declaration, Suani claimed she was targeted by her uncle because she was dark skinned. This, she contended, was also the reason why her extended family failed to intervene on her behalf. She believed her "African" racial features made her uniquely vulnerable to his sexual predations. In short, because her features were deemed to be Black adjacent, her body and her personal well-being was not deemed as valuable as that of the other women in her family.

The legal team representing Suani's case first contacted me in May 2016. The three principal grounds for her petition included:

(1) Membership within a discrete and protected social group consisting of young women in Honduras who are sexually abused by male family members with impunity because the country conditions are such in Honduras that women are considered the property of their husbands;

(2) The police and political institutions do not protect girls and women from family sexual abuse;

(3) The race discrimination she suffered was a result of her dark skin color and curly hair.

In my declaration, I situated the racial violence that Suani experienced within a broader engagement with the history and contemporary practices of anti-Blackness in Honduras. Although she did not identify as Garifuna or Black, I drew on research that documents the history of racial animosity toward Garifuna, including repeated attempts on the part of the state to expropriate Garifuna lands for extractivist developments in tourism and agribusiness. The dispossession of Garifuna lands is rooted in a much longer history of pillage that views Black and Indigenous territories as development frontiers, and which positions Blackness as external to the nation (Loperena 2017b; 2022). In detailing this history, I sought to establish a general pattern of violence to which Suani was also susceptible as someone who was perceived as Black, or Garifuna.

Racial discrimination was a crucial aspect of Suani's petition, as was her claim to gender-based violence. Prior to 2018, women asylum seekers were able to obtain legal protection in the United States by demonstrating that they were the victims of domestic violence. In my declaration, I demonstrated how her status as a woman of color within the context of Honduras made her uniquely vulnerable to gender violence, and even less likely to obtain adequate protections or other forms of legal recourse. Women of African descent face particular forms of discrimination that intersect other forms of oppression based on their race, sexual orientation, and so forth.

Gender-based violence has become increasingly pervasive throughout the "Northern Triangle" as drug cartels, street gangs, and paramilitary groups jockey for control over trade routes and territory, in which women's bodies become sites of control and femicidal violence (Segato 2014; Speed 2016; Briggs and Saldaña-Portillo 2021). Indeed, documented cases of femicide—the murder of women on the basis of their gender identity—has increased dramatically since the 2009 coup d'état. According to the human rights organization Centro de Estudios de la Mujer—Honduras (CEM-H), between 2003 and 2009, a total of 1,597 women were killed. From 2010 to 2017 the number of women killed shot up to 3,993.[18] Although the abuse Suani suffered can be classified as domestic violence, it fits within this larger pattern of violence against women, which has been aggravated by structural shifts in the economy and a surge in narco-activity throughout rural regions of the country.

In general, violence against women in Honduras is underreported, and the perpetrators of this violence go mostly unprosecuted. According to a 2002 report, the Office of the

Public Prosecutor for Women received 22,248 complaints for domestic violence in the previous two years, of which only 2.1 percent were adjudicated, and of these only 36 percent received a judgment (cited in CDM Report 2005, 17). In 2015, the Inter-American Commission on Human Rights reported that impunity for crimes against women surpasses 95 percent (IACHR 2015, para. 117). These rates are almost certainly higher for Afro-descendant women. A 2011 study on access to justice for women victims of sexual violence asserts, "[Afro-descendant women] are frequently affected by forms of social exclusion, racism and poverty, and their needs tend to be invisible from the public agenda of their countries; a reality which results in a limited and deficient access to justice when they are victims of sexual violence" (IACHR 2011, para. 315).

I concur with Shannon Speed (2016) and Lynn Stephen (2018) that violence against women, including domestic violence, rape, and torture, must be understood as part and parcel of the racialized gendered violence of the international political economy. Demonstrating how Black and Indigenous lives are made disposable within this context, and how specifically Black and Indigenous women get positioned as objects of sex or as socially expendable is a crucial component of the work of witnessing.

Anthropological Witnessing and Its Discontents

Today, anthropologists are increasingly called on to serve as country experts in cases involving the rights of Indigenous and Afro-descendant peoples. Training in ethnographic methods in combination with sustained field research makes us uniquely well situated to witness the conditions of social inequality, political persecution, and race- and gender-based violence that structure everyday life in our field sites; doing this work is necessary but also heavy with contradictions that expose the political limitations of translating ethnographic data into evidence within the court (Loperena, Mora, and Castillo 2020).

Miriam Ticktin argues asylum is both legal and moral, and the distinction that determines who is or is not deserving of protection is fundamentally a moral one (Ticktin 2016; 2017). Ticktin's work raises important questions regarding which narratives are capable of generating the type of moral sympathy required to obtain asylum (Ticktin 2006), and how these narratives dovetail with the racial logics that are always operative when a judge is hearing a case pertaining to Black and brown lives. We are confronted with a moral system that presents itself as just and merciful, but which is complicit in the forms of violence asylum seekers face, not just in their countries of origin, but also in the process of applying for asylum and during resettlement. Upon entry into the United States, migrants racialized as nonwhite enter into a social context in which their lives are systematically devalued. For women migrants of color, this reality is often much more acute.

As anthropologist Lynn Stephen points out, it was the case of a Guatemalan woman by the name of Rody Alvarado that eventually led the United States to recognize victims of domestic violence as a persecuted social group and thus as a basis of asylum (Stephen 2019, 243). This legal precedent, however, was overturned by Jeff Sessions, the Trump appointed US Attorney General, in 2018. Sessions argued that neither women survivors of domestic violence nor survivors of gang violence "perpetrated by non-governmental organizations" constitute a protected social group under US asylum law. Stephen demonstrates how Sessions's ruling attempted to separate private gender-based violence from public violence against women's bodies, which is an impossible task since domestic violence is often sanctioned by what Stephen calls "gendered embodied structures of violence." That is to say, individual acts of gendered violence are conjoined with historical structures of violence against women and their bodies (Stephen 2019, 231). Sessions's 2018 ruling raised many issues for women asylum seekers but also pushed experts to rely on intersectional approaches to writing their reports. Being a woman and victim of domestic abuse was no longer sufficient to qualify for asylum, but being a Black or Indigenous women who was also a victim of sexual violence in a country were women's rights are severely restricted might be adequate legal reasoning to garner protection.[19]

As experts, making structural racism and intersectional modalities of oppression visible to the court is part of the labor we must do, but doing so may also contribute to entrenched racial thinking about Latin American peoples and societies—corrupt, racist, distinctly *machista*. Gilberto Rosas refers to this as "necro-subjection," which he links to racial liberalism. To garner asylum or relief from deportation, he argues, "increasingly demands accounts of deep victimization on behalf of individuals and collectivities, playing to a deeply ingrained paternalism found in liberalisms of today" (Rosas 2019, 305). Although anthropologists have labored to undo our discipline's past complicity with scientific racism and modes of othering, our entrée into the legal arena as experts, and into the arena of asylum law in particular, entails partially submitting ourselves to racial liberalism's rule book. In other words, anthropologists can provide evidence that aids an individual in obtaining asylum, but doing this work often reinforces the moral and political precepts of liberalism, which—as the late Charles Mills reminds us—was always racial insofar as it denies equal personhood to people of color (Mills 2008).

How is it that the United States, a country that is globally derided for its racist treatment of Black and brown people, can be a sanctuary for individuals seeking asylum on the basis of racial persecution? It is because granting asylum to an individual on the basis of demonstrated racial persecution (or a credible fear of) fulfills the mandate of American supremacy, of the United States as a rights-respecting and virtuous nation that is fundamentally distinct from our southern neighbors. In this way, serving as an expert witness can also enable what Murakawa calls "our collective unwitnessing of carceral devastation" (Murakawa 2019, 474). By witnessing the violence of gendered anti-Black racism in Honduras, my declaration helps to secure asylum for an individual—a worthy goal—and at the same time it renders the system of criminal (in)justice in the United States and its inherent bias against historically racialized peoples a little more just.

For Suani, who ultimately won her case, anti-Black racism was driving the violence she endured while living in Honduras and a factor in her ability to receive protected status, but not because the court was suddenly attuned to the systemic character of racism. If anything, the court's decision to grant asylum is demonstrative of how white supremacy "serves as the baseline for modernity and its cognates of liberalism, democracy, progress, and nationality" (Beliso-De Jesús and Pierre 2020, 67). As such, we must also contend with the coarticulations of anthropological witnessing and the law and how the meeting of these presumably distinct ways of knowing buttress the overarching forces of racial liberalism (see Loperena 2020). This insight is particularly poignant in cases involving Black women asylum claimants. Their experiences with race- and gender-based violence in their countries of origin become the evidential basis for obtaining protection under the label "particular social group." Yet the court's decision conceals the ways the larger judicial system engenders and expands spaces of carcerality, as well as the racist presuppositions that undergird tropes of criminality and illegality for racially minoritized populations.

Final Reflections

The notion that some people are deserving of the rights and protections of citizenship and some are not is a crucial element of all nationalist ideologies, but it takes on unique racial connotations within the context of asylum proceedings in US immigration court. In this arena, the court determines who is legitimately fleeing persecution on account of their membership within a protected social group, and thusly who is worthy of our mercy. This, as I have suggested, makes it possible for the United States to continue upholding the mythology of American supremacy, and the wider belief that this country is an exceptional space of liberty and equality for all.

Suani's experiences of gendered racialization, which transcended her own self-identity, allowed me to draw attention to the pervasiveness of anti-Black racism as structuring logic with severe consequences for Black people. In other words, the abuse levied on her body could only be articulated as anti-Black racism if and when we look beyond the individual acts and instances of violence. Proving this, however, does little to undo the structural inequities that are endemic to the criminal justice system in the United States, and which continue to deny the vast majority of asylum petitioners. Individual asylum seekers who are denied, many of whom have been forced to leave Honduras under conditions of great duress, including children fleeing gang violence, women victims of domestic violence, and environmental displacement, are rendered criminal trespassers. They are then sent back to Honduras where they face dire odds and even death.

When an US immigration court grants asylum to an individual fleeing anti-Black racial persecution, white-dominated institutions of the US racial state appear to be more virtuous and more capable of protecting Black life—a glaring contradiction given the systemic character of racism in the United States. This reveals the ways in which American supremacy functions as a brand of racism that holds weight, not only among far right groups, like the Proud Boys, but also within court proceedings in which asylum is decided. Moreover, granting asylum protection on the basis of individual persecution allows us to ignore the enduring role of US military and economic policy in fomenting structural racism on both sides of the border.

Addressing how American supremacy factors in to the work of asylum is not to deny the real problems of state-sanctioned violence against Black and Indigenous people in

Honduras, and which I document in detail in my expert work. However, by highlighting this contradiction, I believe we are better able to grasp the particular position of Blackness within these juridico-moral configurations of power. We must grapple with the how and why of asylum. This requires that we attend to the racial logics at play in the court, and which require individuals to prove their innocence in order to obtain legally protected status in the United States. Reflecting on this contradiction and the political imperatives for abolition, Ruth Wilson Gilmore states: "Getting rid of the rules that require people to prove their relative innocence in order to have some kind of protection from systems of oppression—whether it's *Sistema de la Muerte* or other kinds of not necessarily mortal danger, but danger that accumulates as vulnerability to premature death—is part of what abolition must be" (Estes, Gilmore, and Loperena 2021). Until then, anthropologists will continue to use the tools available to us to advocate on behalf of migrants and their rights.

Carole McGranahan argues that witnessing is an exercise in compassion and privilege: "As privilege, it is to use one's status and knowledge to serve another. And as compassion it is . . . a recognition of suffering and an attempt to relieve it" (McGranahan 2020, 107). Perhaps it is for this reason we continue to do the work of witnessing, because it opens space for hope in dark times, as McGranahan suggests, not just for the future, but for our collective present. Doing this work, in spite of the contradictions I have highlighted in this chapter, is necessary.

Notes

1. According to the Pew Research Center, Biden won Hispanic voters by 21 points, 59 percent to Trump's 38 percent, but this still represents a significant shift from the previous election in which Clinton held a 38 point lead over Trump. www.pewresearch.org/politics/2021/06/30/behind-bidens-2020-victory/.

2. Anthropologist Jeff Mascovsky argues Trump's policies and populist appeal are rooted in a new form of racial politics he terms "white nationalist postracialism," and which is rooted in two contradictory objectives: "reclaiming the nation for white Americans while also denying an ideological investment in white supremacy" (Maskovsky 2017, 434). My understanding of American supremacy demonstrates how postracial racism manifests within US immigration court.

3. The putative liberties enjoyed by US citizens are of course belied by history's Indigenous genocide and over 240 years of institutionalized slavery.

4. https://prod-cdn-static.gop.com/docs/Resolution_Platform_2020.pdf. Accessed August 19, 2021.

5. Patrick J. Buchanan's *Death of the West: How Dying Populations and Immigrant Invasions Imperil Our Country and Civilization* is just one iteration of the anti-immigrant discourse that has flourished in the post-9/11 world, and which is of course bound up with anti-Muslim racism (see Rana 2007).

6. In her analysis of Latinx support for anti-immigrant policies, Christina Beltran argues that white supremacy in the United States is oriented toward a uniquely multiracial vision of the nation that is premised on white domination (Beltran 2020, 180). She says Latinx people embrace the "politics of white democracy" to ensure their own rights and standing within the political system.

7. María Josefina Saldaña-Portillo (2017) highlights the experience of Garifuna women asylum seekers, who are both Black and Indigenous, in order to push against and across the "identitarian boundaries" that circumscribe research on migration, prisons, and settler colonial studies, and which tend to conspire in the invisibilization of the Indian.

8. www.pewresearch.org/fact-tank/2021/08/13/migrant-encounters-at-u-s-mexico-border-are-at-a-21-year-high/ft_21-03-10_borderapprehensions_2/. Accessed August 10, 2021.

9. See also "A Crisis Foretold: On the Origins of the Migrant Caravan." Hot Spots, *Fieldsights*, January 23. https://culanth.org/fieldsights/a-crisis-foretold-on-the-origins-of-the-migrant-caravan.

10. Historian Suyapa Portillo (2021) demonstrates how dominant academic narratives about this historical period tend to erase the long tradition of Honduran social movement activism and resistance to US imperialism, which she traces back to organized labor movements that arose in opposition to the US multinational fruit corporations in the mid-twentieth century.

11. For a fuller discussion, see "Radicalize Multiculturalism: Garifuna Resistance and the Double-Bind of Participation in Post-Coup Honduras" (Loperena 2016).

12. www.globalwitness.org/en/campaigns/environmental-activists/honduras-deadliest-country-world-environmental-activism/. Accessed August 28, 2021.

13. Blackwell, Boj Lopez, and Luis Urrieta Jr. argue that upon arrival in the US, Indigenous migrants from Latin America confront not only the racism and prejudice of their mestizo counterparts, but also deeply entrenched racial hierarchies and violence within US society (Blackwell et al. 2017, 128).

14. Garifuna identify as both Black and Indigenous, but the racism they face in Honduras is most often predicated on their Blackness.

15. www.justice.gov/opa/pr/juan-orlando-hernández-former-president-honduras-indicted-drug-trafficking. Accessed July 5, 2023.

16. Speed (2019) has drawn our attention to the long history of racialized immigration policies and the white supremacist logics that undergird the United States' deportation regime, including those carried out by the Obama administration, and which emphasized the purported criminality of migrants.

17. In June 2021, the American Civil Rights Union together with immigrant rights organizations from around the country filed suit against the Biden administration for authorizing the use of Title 42 to expel migrant families and single adults immediately on apprehension, which they argue violates the rights of migrants to seek protection in the United States. Title 42 remained in place until May 2023 when the United States declared an end to the national emergency spawned by the COVID-19 pandemic, but the Biden administration has since introduced a policy that would place even stricter limits on who can apply for asylum.

18. www.cemh.org.hn/femicidios-2018/. Accessed March 2, 2021.

19. Sherene Razack's work on native women victims of sexual violence demonstrates how culture and essentialist understandings of difference can be used in ways that further victimize women or that conceal the present-day legacies of colonization (Razack 1998). These concerns make it all the more urgent to foreground not only how racism and sexism intersect in the lives of women asylum seekers, but also how histories of racial and sexual violence render women of color less valuable.

References

Beliso-De Jesús, Aisha, and Jemima Pierre. 2019. Introduction to "Anthropology of White Supremacy," edited by Aisha Beliso-De Jesús and Jemima Pierre. *American Anthropologist* 122, no. 1.

Beltran, Cristina. 2020. *Cruelty as Citizenship: How Migrant Suffering Sustains White Democracy*. Minneapolis: University of Minnesota Press.

Blackwell, Maylei, Floridalma Boj Lopez, and Luis Urrieta Jr. 2017. Special issue, Critical Latinx Indigeneities. *Latino Studies* 15.

Briggs, Laura, and María Josefina Saldaña Portillo. 2021. *The Crisis for Asylum-Seekers Is Gender-Based Violence*. Public Books.

Burrell, Jennifer, and Ellen Moodie. 2015. "The Post-Cold War Anthropology of Central America." *Annual Review of Anthropology*.

————. 2019. Introduction to "Behind the Migrant Caravan." Hot Spots, *Fieldsights*, January 23. https://culanth .org/fieldsights/introduction-behind-the-migrant-caravan.

Cadava, Geraldo. 2020. "The Deep Origins of Latino Support for Trump." *New Yorker*, December 29.

Copeland, Nicholas. 2020. "A New Deal for Central America." *NACLA Report on the Americas* 52, no. 1.

Estes, Nick, R. W. Gilmore, and C. Loperena. 2021. "United in Struggle." *NACLA Report on the Americas* 53, no. 3.

IACHR. 2015. "Inter-American Commission on Human Rights Report on Situation of Human Rights in Honduras." Accessed June 6, 2016. ISBN: 978-0-8270-5722-7.

Loperena, Christopher. 2017a. "Honduras Is Open for Business: Extractivist Tourism as Sustainable Development in the Wake of Disaster." *Journal of Sustainable Tourism*.

————. 2017b. "Settler Violence? Race and Emergent Frontiers of Progress in Honduras." *American Quarterly* 69, no. 4.

————. 2020. "Adjudicating Indigeneity: Anthropologist as Witness in the Inter-American Court of Human Rights." *American Anthropologist* 122, no. 3.

————. 2022. *The Ends of Paradise: Race, Extraction, and the Struggle for Black Life in Honduras*. Stanford, CA: Stanford University Press.

Loperena, C., M. Mora, and A. Hernandez Castillo. 2020. "Cultural Expertise." *American Anthropologist* 122, no. 3.

Maskovsky, Jeff. 2017. "Toward the Anthropology of White National Postracialism." *HAU: Journal of Ethnographic Theory* 7, no. 1.

McGranahan, Carole. 2020. "Ethnographic Witnessing; Or, Hope Is the First Anthropological Emotion." *Journal of Legal Anthropology* 4, no. 1.

Murakawa, Naomi. 2019. "Racial Innocence: Law, Social Science, and the Unknowing of Racism in the United States." *Annual Review of Law and Social Science*.

Portillo, Suyapa. 2021. *Roots of Resistance: A Story of Gender, Race, and Labor on the North Coast of Honduras*. Austin: University of Texas Press.

Rana, Junaid. 2007. "The Story of Islamophobia." *Souls: A Critical Journal of Black Politics, Culture, and Society* 9, no. 2.

Razack, Sherene H. 1998. *Looking White People in the Eye: Gender, Race, and Culture in Courtrooms and Classrooms*. Toronto: University of Toronto Press.

Rosas, Gilberto. 2019. "Necro-subjection: On Borders, Asylum, and Making Dead to Let Live." *Theory and Event* 22, no. 2.

Saldaña-Portillo, Josefina Maria. 2017. "Critical Latinx Indigeneities: A Paradigm Drift." *Latino Studies* 15.

Speed, Shannon. 2016. "States of Violence: Indigenous Women Migrants in the Era of Neoliberal Multicriminalism." *Critique of Anthropology*.

————. 2019. "The Persistence of White Supremacy: Indigenous Women Migrants and the Structures of Settler Capitalism." *American Anthropologist*.

Stephen, Lynn. 2018. "Gendered Violence and Indigenous Mexican Asylum Seekers: Expert Witnessing as Ethnographic Engagement." *Anthropological Quarterly* 91, no. 1.

————. 2019. "Fleeing Rural Violence: Mam Women Seeking Gendered Justice in Guatemala and the U.S." *Journal of Peasant Studies* 46, no. 2.

Ticktin, Miriam. 2006. "Where Ethics and Politics Meet: The Violence of Humanitarianism in France." *American Ethnologist* 33, no. 1.

————. 2016. "What's Wrong with Innocence." Hot Spots. Cultural Anthropology website, June 28, 2016. https://culanth.org/fieldsights/whats-wrong-with-innocence.

————. 2017. "A World without Innocence." *American Ethnologist* 44, no. 4.

Wallace, Sophia, and Chris Zepeda Millan. 2020. *Walls Cages and Family Separation: Race and Immigration Policy in the Trump Era*. Cambridge: Cambridge University Press.

19

Securing Paradise

COLONIAL WHITENESS AND THE GEOPOLITICS OF NATION-BRANDING IN THE AGE OF "TERROR"

Samar Al-Bulushi

IN EARLY OCTOBER 2011, a French tourist was kidnapped from her beach house in the Kenyan northeastern island town of Lamu. The incident occurred just two weeks after a British woman farther up the coast was similarly abducted by a group with ties to the Somali militant group Al-Shabaab. In the wake of these kidnappings, the British and American governments issued travel advisories discouraging their citizens from travel to Lamu. "At a stroke," declared *The Guardian*, "the tourism sector here was shattered." Referring nostalgically to the once serene "paradise" of Lamu island, the British news outlet wrote that, "It has always been one of the most peaceful places in Kenya, and perhaps the most beautiful too—a Swahili island paradise of warm, deep-blue water, golden sands and ancient, narrow streets where cars are banned and donkeys rule."[1]

Kenya's tourism industry is an integral component of the national economy and relies heavily on foreign visitors.[2] Contemporary depictions of Kenya, and the Swahili coast in particular, as a "paradise" rely on colonial metaphors of conquest that conjure images of virgin territory ripe for exploration. The tourism industry is structured by a careful calibration of similarity and difference—it works to project Kenya as exotic enough to stimulate intrigue but familiar enough to connote comfort and security. In this regard, the timing of the 2011 kidnappings was particularly devastating: the incidents occurred just when the industry had begun to recuperate from the aftereffects of the deadly 2007–8 postelection violence, when, as NBC News reported, "photos of angry men roaming the streets with machetes forced waves of vacation cancellations."[3] The kidnappings inaugurated a new phase of surveillance and policing, as anxious hotel owners and tour operators were quick to call on the Kenyan security apparatus to "flex its muscles." When two Spanish aid workers were abducted the following week, the government took its boldest step yet, dispatching two thousand troops across the border into Somalia.

What was initially framed as a short-term operation soon morphed into a protracted military occupation of southern Somalia. Since then, Al-Shabaab has retaliated with large-scale attacks inside Kenya. In the aftermath of these attacks, state officials and media outlets have fueled anxieties that the "terrorist threat" emanates from within Kenya's Muslim minority population. The question of indigeneity is at the heart of racialized constructions of threat, with the notion of a "local," "African" Islam juxtaposed against "foreign," "Arab/ Somali" Islam.[4] Yet what it means to be Muslim in Kenya today is shaped by a shared subjection to surveillance and criminalization that links cross-cutting experiences of racialization. While the specific context of the so-called war on terror is one that has reinscribed colonial-era ideas about Arab and Somali "foreigners" in Kenya, racial dynamics in Kenya must be situated within a consideration of wider processes and histories of race and racialization—including structures of white supremacy—in this former settler colony.[5]

This chapter grapples with the range of processes (historical, cultural, political, economic) that have naturalized the presence of white populations in Kenya. Drawing on ethnographic research focused on the war on terror in the region, I argue that the figure of the terrorist serves as the condition of possibility for the (re-)production of colonial whiteness in Kenya. Specifically, I am interested in the Kenyan state's growing preoccupation with branding as a strategy to market Kenya as exceptional, unlike the "typical" African country plagued by violence—and thereby (still) suitable for white visitors.[6] As an affective technique for crafting a favorable common sense about a particular country, nation-branding enables Global South states to geopolitically refashion themselves in a global economy structured by racial logics, including fear of so-called terrorists.

Kenyan elite preoccupations with security are enmeshed with anxieties about its Muslim minority population becoming a symbol of African barbarity and violence. This points to the ways in which the racialized figure of the threatening Muslim (one that is informed by an amalgamation of racial, religious, gendered, geographic, and cultural bases for alterity)[7] intersects with equally racialized information economies about "unstable" Africa (see especially Rana 2011; Fernando 2014; Maira 2016; Li 2020, 2022). In wrestling with these intersecting modes of racialization, I situate the racialized figure of the Muslim within the broader domain of anti-Blackness that has marked Africa as the quintessential other in the global order of nation-states (Mudimbe 1988; Grovogui 2001; Clarke 2011; Pierre 2012). I take seriously the analysis of Jemima Pierre, who argues that Africa's otherness requires explicit articulation.[8] "The very production of 'Africa,' she writes, occurs through ideas of race" (2012, 5). With this in mind, we cannot contend with policy narratives about governance and security "without recognizing the ways they are refracted through processes of racialization" (2012, 5). While not explicitly invoking race, the language of "failed" states is informed by and produces racialized ideas about place and space, functioning as a proxy for (anti-)Blackness (Grovogui 2001; Gruffydd Jones 2015; Wai 2012). With the onset of the war on terror, travel advisories constitute a mode of valuation and risk that racializes African geographies and their inhabitants as threatening, reinforcing long-standing ideas about the "dark continent."

In what follows, I briefly recount British colonial efforts to recruit white settlers to Kenya in order to trace the interlocking of past and present in the construction of Kenya as white man's paradise. I approach race and white supremacy not as fixed but as contingent and subject to a range of social meanings that are simultaneously produced and subject to everyday interaction and contestation (see especially Omi and Winant 1994; Goldberg 1992; Visweswaran 1998; Rana 2020). Returning to the present day, I observe that nation-branding entails the commodification of colonial nostalgia as the state works to project an image of tranquility and stability in which Europeans are at home in a foreign land. But as Kenyans reckon with histories of colonial violence, and with present-day abuses sanctioned in the name of "security," I demonstrate that nation-branding requires considerable *work*. The ruling-class project of cultivating an image of paradise seemingly untouched by these violent histories remains an aspirational one, as Kenyans increasingly challenge the logics underlying it. Here, ethnographic research has the potential to demonstrate the ways in which ideologies of white supremacy become a site of contestation, requiring substantial effort to maintain.

Land and the Construction of White Man's Country

In *The Predicament of Blackness*, Jemima Pierre productively builds on the work of Mahmood Mamdani (1996), who outlines the ways in which colonial rule configured racial and ethnic (or tribal) identities, distinguishing between "natives" (subjects) and "nonnatives" (citizens).[9] As Pierre observes, this citizen/subject binary was only *one* side of the racializing colonial process, the other side being "the homogenization of European groupings and the making of colonial Whiteness" (Pierre 2012, 12). In Kenya, the making of colonial whiteness is an important entry point from which to explore the construction of Kenya as white man's paradise.[10] From the recruitment of white settlers in the 1890s to contemporary branding campaigns that feature idyllic sandy beaches along the coast, the idea of Kenya as a paradise evokes racialized and gendered notions of passivity and penetrability, of a landscape ripe for exploitation and discovery. Approaching "paradise"—and the broader notion of uninhabited landscape—as a fiction that has been conjured (see especially Gonzalez 2013 and Jackson 2011), we have an opportunity to reflect on the co-construction of whiteness as a claim to civilization and modernity.

In a 1953 essay on the rise of the Kenyan Land and Freedom Army, George Padmore characterized colonial Kenya as a "white man's paradise" where British settlers lived like royalty on expropriated land (Padmore 1953, 357). Settlers first arrived in the 1890s and grew in number in the early 1900s as the British colonial government initiated a series of land-grabbing ordinances to facilitate white settlement. The 1902 Crown Lands Ordinance became the precursor for large-scale dispossession, followed by subsequent laws that privileged individual ownership and dismissed long-standing practices of communal land use (see Berman 2017; Okoth Ogendo 1976). The establishment of native reserves—allegedly intended to "protect" African rights to land—sanctioned the displacement of Africans from areas that settlers desired, even as it expanded colonial control over the spaces in which the African population lived. In 1908, East African Estates Ltd., one of the largest colonial companies operating in Kenya at the time, acquired 260,000 acres of land south of Mombasa on the coast (Berman 2017).

The colonial government's power to control ownership of prime land was legitimized by white supremacist discourses about "proper" land use (see Musila 2015; McIntosh 2016). As Grace Musila observes, the process of land alienation "was discursively mediated by the (e)vacuation of the land as large expanses of empty space without owners, inadvertent or feigned ignorance of local land use and ownership cultures, which gave the impression of 'unoccupied land'" (Musila 2015, 151). African landscapes were constructed, she writes, "as Edenic wildernesses endowed with a certain savage innocence and beauty for which the fast-modernizing West yearned as a rejuvenating breath of primordial purity and tranquility" (Musila 2015, 159–60). Guided by narratives that equated English common law concepts of property with civilized life, colonial officials and settlers alike *believed* that Kenya demanded white settlers.[11] At the same time, British farmers and ranchers could reinvent themselves, drawing on their white skin to become "somebody" (Shadle 2015, 17). Ngugi wa Thiong'o vividly captures the nature of this transformation in *Wrestling with the Devil*, reminding us that whiteness is an identity that is *constructed*, with "all too real consequences for the distribution of wealth, prestige, and opportunity" (Lipsitz 2006, vii):

> Coming ashore into Kenya meant literally riding on the backs of black workers into a white tropical paradise, and this was true for the titled and untitled alike. By setting foot on Kenyan soil in Mombasa, every European, even those soldiers resettled on stolen lands after the First World War, was instantly transformed into a blue-blooded aristocrat. An attractive welcome: before him, stretching beyond the ken of his eyes, lay a vast valley garden of endless physical leisure and pleasure that he must have once read about in the *Arabian Nights* stories. The dream in fairy tales was now his in practice. No work, no winter, no physical or mental exertion. Here he would set up his own fiefdom. (Ngugi 2018, 46)

White rule—and the attendant privileges that had come to be associated with whiteness—came under threat with the rise of the Land and Freedom Army in the early 1950's. Colonial officials concluded that the insurgency was the product of witchcraft, a psycho-pathological phenomenon rather than a political response to the violence and dispossession that characterized colonial rule (Luongo 2006; Sahle 2012). In doing so, they maintained their claim to normativity against which non-whites were measured (see Dyer 1997). Referring to the resistance derisively as "Mau Mau," the British instituted a state of emergency in 1952, launching a campaign of forced removals and detaining up to 1.5 million Kikuyu in purported "rehabilitation" camps. It was, in Ngugi's words, a "calculated act of psychological terror against the struggling millions" (Ngugi 2018, 20).

Despite the eventual demise of colonial rule, this psychological terror left a durable mark (Fanon 1963; Stoler 2018). In the debris of what Ngugi refers to as the "cultural bomb," the colonized lost "belief in their names, their languages, in their environment, in their heritage of struggle, in their unity, in their capacities and ultimately in themselves"

(Ngugi 1986, 3). The protracted quality of this decimation, writes Ngugi, "makes them see their past as one wasteland of non-achievement and it makes them want to distance themselves from that wasteland. It makes them want to identify with that which is furthest removed from themselves; for instance, with other peoples' languages rather than their own. It makes them identify with that which is decadent and reactionary, all those forces which would stop their own springs of life" (Ngugi 1986, 3).

Ngugi's observations push us to reflect on colonialism's enduring presence in the so-called postcolonial world, as an independent Black nation like Kenya looks outside of itself for validation and rejects the value of its own history, language, and culture. Even as the ruling elite that assumed power spoke in the language of rights and recognition, whiteness lingered as an aspirational ideal and symbol of modernity. As Wandiya Njoya (2021) elucidates drawing on the work of Gideon Mutiso (1975), appointments to key leadership positions were made largely on the basis of Western education. Because the educated elite deemed themselves to be superior to their uneducated counterparts, the language of "qualifications" functioned to mask what in effect was an investment in whiteness. British nationals remained civil servants in major positions even a decade into independence, under the pretext that they were more qualified. Here it is important to look beyond actual racialized white bodies to contend with whiteness as ideology (Hesse 2007; Pierre 2012), as whiteness in Kenya has been normalized so thoroughly "as not to need white bodies to enact it" (Mungai 2021).

When he assumed power in 1963, Jomo Kenyatta ruled out the nationalization of foreign-owned assets, including European-owned land. In addition to rejecting calls for land distribution, he introduced new settlement schemes and granted select parties the right to acquire plots near or on the beach, appropriating land that villagers on the coast had used for centuries (see Berman 2017; McIntosh 2016). Meanwhile, Kenyatta embarked on an expansive global marketing campaign to promote an "idea of Kenya" that would entice Euro-American tourists. The goal was to "make Kenya a knowable and familiar space to Western audiences, corresponding to a specific gendered and racial order, and one not so distant from the colonial past" (Smart 2018, 147). As officials set out to "refashion the cultures of work and even daily life in Kenya to help promote tourism," schools incorporated tourism studies into their curricula, and the state launched a national campaign to educate Kenyans about the role of citizens "in helping the advancement of the industry" (Smart 2018, 139). White men and women featured prominently in Kenyan travel brochures, naturalizing their presence in the country (Smart 2018).

Scholars have productively traced the quotidian ways in which the tourism industry in East Africa produces whiteness through frames of colonial nostalgia (see especially Bruner and Kirshenblatt-Gimblett 1994; Bruner 2001; Jackson 2011; Musila 2014; Meiu 2017). Mayers Ranch, for example, a private tourist attraction in the Rift Valley launched by a white settler family in 1968, invited European visitors to indulge their fascination with "tribal peoples" through enactments of Maasai "dancing in their warrior compound, chanting and carrying spears, proud and aloof" (Bruner 2001, 882). As Bruner and Kirshenblatt-Gimblett observe, sites like Mayers Ranch give colonialism a second life, playing on

Western fantasies about the savage, and "re-enacting an image of the stability of the colonial order in which Europeans like themselves are in charge" (1994, 457). The industry has been integral to sustaining the myth of Kenya as "a place of loyal servants and resplendent views, of sundowners in the evenings, and journeys down roads that were dusty in the dry season and oceans of mud in the rains" (Jackson 2011, 345). The function of the myth, as Will Jackson articulates, is to sidestep the political. It is "to make what was in fact structured by relations of political and economic power appear to be something naturally or divinely ordained" (2011, 355). The myth of "paradise" relies on the complete effacement of colonial violence, and of African resistance to that violence (Bruner 2001).

The fact that the Kenyan state was eventually compelled to close Mayers Ranch in the 1980s in response to protests from the Kenyan public is instructive, as it points to the ways in which logics of white supremacy underlying the tourism sector become the source of contestation and debate. In more recent years, the rise of nation-branding has similarly generated pushback. In the immediate aftermath of the 2007 election violence, which resulted in over one thousand deaths and nearly half a million displaced, the ruling elite scrambled to maintain an image of Kenya as peaceful, turning to US lobbying and public relations firms for "damage control."[12] Wandiya Njoya observed in the online platform *The Elephant* that the priority of the country's leaders could have been to heal the nation, pursue justice and reparations, and work to address the structural inequalities that were at the heart of the political crisis. "But in the midst of such trauma and need for healing and reconciliation," she writes, "what did President Mwai Kibaki do? He set up Brand Kenya." As she elaborates, the primary preoccupation of the ruling elite

> was that Kenya remained a country in which foreigners could invest or relax. The government's target audience was not the people of Kenya but foreigners. . . . Every time Kenyans are in distress, the main worry of the government is whether the investors will notice anything, and how soon we can cover up our human weaknesses so as not to scare them away. (Njoya 2018)

Njoya reflects on the psychological effects of this fixation, echoing Fanon's (1963) observations about the violence with which the supremacy of whiteness is affirmed:

> The focus of Kenya's consciousness on foreign affirmation would explain why Kenyans experience daily life and institutional and collective processes as a form of physical, moral, emotional and intellectual violence. . . . the colonial rationale is repeatedly and deliberately reinforced in the present day. Decade after decade, regime after regime, government institutions have wired themselves, built themselves, and reproduced policy documents to remain focused on the West, and to wipe Kenyans out of the picture. . . . Kenyans will have to go through a national mental re-engineering that heals us of our inferiority complex and deals with our historical wounds, and then write an affirmation of dignity as human beings. (2018)

Here, we are compelled to look beyond the narrow construction of relations between "hosts" and "guests" to contend with the larger question of how ideologies of whiteness shape everyday life outside the tourist encounter (see especially Meiu 2017). Njoya's in-tervention is especially poignant for our analysis of the routine forms of violence that are increasingly rationalized in the name of security and the war on terror (see Al-Bulushi 2021). As Muslim "terrorists" threaten the image of Kenya as an oasis of stability, and concomitantly threaten the tourism sector itself, the ruling class has frantically worked to assure tourists that it is still safe to visit the country. Alongside police crackdowns, mass roundups, and extrajudicial killings and disappearance, this has entailed a refashioning of racial significations, such that images of African men and women in military fatigues (at airports, malls, hotels, and such) have come to signify—for white visitors—modernity and *safety*. This refashioning is predicated on the construction of an external enemy. State officials have built on colonial-era distinctions between "natives" and "nonnatives" (Mam-dani 1996) to locate "violent extremism" among "Arab" and "Somali" Muslims, populations with supranational, transregional ties. Attention to these overlapping processes of racial-ization (the refashioning of "native" Blackness on the one hand, and the demonization of the "foreign" on the other) is integral to our understanding of emergent modes of nation-branding, and of the various modes of labor it entails.

In 2015, the government announced a one million USD partnership with CNN Inter-national with the objective of connecting CNN's "premium international audience with Kenya's appeal to tourists." In part, this initiative was a response to Euro-American travel advisories that discouraged citizens of Europe and North America from unessential travel to the region in the wake of Al-Shabaab attacks. "We are fed up with these threats that we keep getting in travel advisories," declared President Kenyatta. "Kenya is as safe as any other country in the world." Armed with a supplemental budget of KSH five billion (approximately fifty million USD) the Ministry of Tourism recommitted itself to promote Kenya as an ideal tourist destination and to "counter the negative publicity occasioned by restricted travel advisories in our key source markets [Western countries]." Promotional video clips tailored to the uncertain political context featured "white bodies in the Kenyan landscape looking to assure other (white) westerners that it is 'safe' to come to Kenya" (Smart 2018, 151).

Crucially, these images are conjured through the imaginative labor of the tourism in-dustry and sustained by the racialized hierarchies that it engenders. Nation-branding in the age of "terror" is thus the condition of possibility for the reattribution of value to whiteness, and for the erasure of settler colonial violence. But again, Brand Kenya's efforts to disentangle the idea of Kenya from the ruins of colonial rule remain aspirational rather than a fait accompli, as Kenyans are quick to disrupt the narrative and to unsettle the tai-lored scenery. In a Twitter post from June 2020, writer and commentator Patrick Gathara chastised the Kenyan ruling class for its imbrication in neocolonial tourism strategies that displace Africans from their own land and sanitize histories of colonial violence. In refer-ence to the country's first president, Jomo Kenyatta, Gathara wrote: "This is what happens when a Kenyatta cuts a deal to become one of the *wakoloni* (colonists) and then goes to Nakuru and promises to forgive and forget. It is what happens when we cannot hear the crying out of the blood of the *miros* (Blacks) who died so the place could exist."

FIGURE 19.1. Mordecai Ogada, https://twitter.com/m_ogada/status/1428999758702600193.

Meanwhile, ecologist Mordecai Ogada is one of many who have protested the ways in which Kenya's tourism sector is entangled in the reproduction of white supremacy:

In the predominantly Muslim coastal city of Mombasa where I lived between 2014 and 2015, residents grappled with the growing relationship between tourism and policing. On the one hand, they were anxious about the devastating impact that travel advisories were having on the coastal economy. Once a thriving tourist attraction, coastal hotels and beaches operated much of the year at minimal occupancy, leaving thousands without work. But the fact that the state's efforts to reassure tourists came with the introduction of police and military checkpoints, arbitrary arrests, killings, and disappearances, led many of my interlocutors to question the racialized modes of value differentiation that informed state-led projects of "security."

In April 2014, I met with a delegation of Kenyan government officials led by the governor and senator of Mombasa on their tour of US cities. The main purpose of the US visit was to identify and cultivate foreign investment in the coastal economy, which had been crippled by travel advisories that cautioned tourists against visiting the coast. The stakes of this trip were multiple: the leaders hoped to report back to their constituencies about promises secured for new investments, knowing that this could translate into much needed employment opportunities. Meanwhile, as I came to learn, the Kenyan Embassy in Washington—as the formal host of this delegation—hoped that these outspoken members of Kenya's ODM opposition party could "stick to the script," maintaining a unified image of Kenya that the embassy staff worked diligently to present to the wider world.

The first stop on the tour was Washington, DC, where the Mombasa government officials appeared as guests on the Swahili-language segment of Voice of America. During the hour-long show, the themes of security and the economy dominated, as the leaders were asked on multiple occasions to confirm that they were pursuing every effort to restore security in the wake of recent attacks attributed to Al-Shabaab. While both affirmed the importance of security and discussed prospects for investment, the senator was adamant that the disappearances and extrajudicial killings at the hands of Kenya's Anti-Terror Police Unit (ATPU) needed to end. He spoke at length about the unlawful targeting of the Muslim minority population by this US- and UK-trained police unit, which made the Kenyan embassy official who had been tasked with chaperoning their US visit noticeably uncomfortable. As we sat outside the booth watching the live broadcast, "Michael" turned to me, saying, "The senator is very passionate about these issues; we have to remind him that the way he talks can scare people. He got carried away the other day and I wanted to stop him but I couldn't. But you know, he has the freedom to say what he wants."

While the Mombasa senator expressed outrage about a political system that sanctioned state terror, Michael's words indicated that this posed a problem for the image of Kenya that he and his colleagues worked diligently to cultivate and maintain. In contrast to the calm and friendly Kenyans that appear at diplomatic gatherings and in government-approved promotional material, the senator's passionate denouncements had the potential to terrify. Though Michael was careful not to explicitly articulate a connection between the senator's impassioned denouncements and Islam, his words indirectly gestured to a Christian majority sensibility that has long racialized Kenya's Muslim minority population—particularly those on the coast with ties to "foreigners"—as sources of violence and instability. The senator's expressions of outrage were entirely too proximate to the image of angry Muslims that the state sought to distance itself from. Moreover, they unsettled colonial-era notions of native hospitality. As Washington, DC, was merely the first stop on a multicity tour, Michael was clearly anxious at the prospect that the senator would jeopardize the delicately crafted image of Kenya as nonthreatening and appealing to white visitors and investors. His discomfort with the senator's intervention again points to the ways in which ideologies of white supremacy become a site of contestation, as the senator explicitly called into question colonial-era modes of value differentiation that shape understandings of life worthy of mourning.

This chapter has offered a brief exploration of the range of processes that have ascribed meaning and privilege to whiteness in Kenya over time, from colonial-era narratives about "proper" uses of the land to contemporary civilizational discourses about governance and "security." While the racialized figure of the Muslim "terrorist" has served as the condition of possibility for the reproduction of colonial whiteness, ethnography has the potential to reveal the contingencies of its making. Nation-branding emerges as an active *project* that simultaneously builds on colonial modes of value differentiation and works to attach new meanings to whiteness, Blackness, and Islam alike. Yet as I have demonstrated, this project has increasingly become the focus of quotidian contestation and debate. Attending to everyday encounters and interactions, we have an opportunity to reflect on the instability of white supremacy, and on emerging attempts to confront it as a mode of power.

Notes

1. www.theguardian.com/world/2011/oct/04/kenya-kidnap-attacks-tourism-hit.

2. In 2019, travel and tourism contributed 7.9 billion USD to Kenya's Gross Domestic Product (GDP).

3. www.nbcnews.com/id/wbna44788475.

4. I do not use these categories to refer to clear-cut realities but to denote their discursive power. Despite the fact that Africa's population is over 40 percent Muslim, Islam continues to be conceptualized as an alien, external force on the continent, reifying colonial geographic imaginaries that position Blackness and Islam, and Africa and the Arab world, as distinct from each other. See Ware (2014); and D. Li, "Geographies of Blackness," this volume.

5. See Beliso-De Jesús and Pierre (2020), and also Al-Bulushi (2020) for a discussion of xenophobia and anti-Blackness in South Africa.

6. In *Ethnicity, Inc.*, Jean Comaroff and John Comaroff observe that we are witnessing the emergent model of country-as-company, of the post-Weberian state as metabusiness that claims "a natural copyright over their heritage-as-property" (Comaroff and Comaroff 2011, 131). While the Comaroffs note this very trend in Kenya, they do not address broader questions of race and power—namely, the significance of imperialism and racial capitalism for the positioning of the Global South country-as-companies.

7. In his discussion of what he calls the "terror industrial complex," Junaid Rana observes that the racialization of Muslims is a "flexible process that incorporates the possibility of a number of race concepts such as Blackness, indigeneity, colonialism, genocide, immigration, and religion" (2016, 120). In this volume, Darryl Li observes that the war on terror's racialization of Muslims cross-cuts diverse geographies of Blackness, including in Muslim-majority societies.

8. See Pierre, "Africanist Ethnography," this volume.

9. The British colonial system in East Africa classified Arabs and Somalis as nonnative citizens. These "subject races," as Mamdani (2001) observed, enjoyed legal protections not afforded to their "native" counterparts, yet they also point to the presence of an internal African "other."

10. As Dane Kennedy (1987) has documented, the dominant element within the white population consisted of aristocrats, even if they were a numerical minority. Poor whites posed a threat to ideologies of white supremacy. See also Jackson (2011).

11. For more on the significance of property law for the historical development of racial capitalism, see Bhandar (2018).

12. In 2008, the government of Kenya hired Chlopak, Leonard, Schechter and Associates to lobby policy makers and burnish the country's reputation in Washington, New York, and other cities. See Aaron Kessler and Wanjohi Kabukuru, "Shadow Diplomacy: African Nations Bypass Embassies, Tap Lobbyists," *Huffington Post*, July 2013.

References

Al-Bulushi, Samar. 2021. "Citizen-Suspect: Navigating Surveillance and Policing in Urban Kenya." *American Anthropologist* 123, no. 4: 1–14.

Al-Bulushi, Yousuf. 2020. "The Global Threat of Race in the Decomposition of Struggle." *Safundi* 21, no. 2: 140–65.

Beliso-De Jesús, Aisha, and Jemima Pierre. 2020. "Anthropology of White Supremacy." *American Anthropologist* 122, no. 1: 65–75.

Berman, Nina. 2017. *Germans on the Kenyan Coast: Land, Charity, and Romance*. Bloomington: Indiana University Press.

Bhandar, Brenna. 2018. *Colonial Lives of Property: Law, Land, and Racial Regimes of Ownership*. Durham, NC: Duke University Press.

Bruner, Edward M. 2001. "The Maasai and the Lion King: Authenticity, Nationalism, and Globalization in African Tourism." *American Ethnologist* 28, no. 4: 881–908.

Bruner, Edward M., and Barbara Kirshenblatt-Gimblett. 1994. "Maasai on the Lawn: Tourist Realism in East Africa." *Cultural Anthropology* 9, no. 4: 435–70.

Clarke, K. M. 2011. "The Rule of Law Through Its Economies of Appearances: The Making of the African Warlord." *Indiana Journal of Global Legal Studies* 18, no. 1: 7–40.

Comaroff, John, and Jean Comaroff. 2009. *Ethnicity, Inc.* Chicago: University of Chicago Press.

Dyer, Richard. 1997. *White: Essays on Race and Culture*. London: Routledge.

Fanon, Frantz. 1963. *Wretched of the Earth*. New York: Grove Press.

Fernando, Mayanthi. 2014. *The Republic Unsettled: Muslim French and the Contradictions of Secularism*. Durham, NC: Duke University Press.

Gonzalez, Vernadette Vicuna. 2013. *Securing Paradise: Tourism and Militarism in Hawai'i and the Philippines*. Durham, NC: Duke University Press.

Grovogui, Siba N. 2001. "Come to Africa: A Hermeneutics of Race in International Theory." *Alternatives: Global, Local, Political* 26, no. 4: 425–48.

Gruffydd Jones, Branwen. 2014. "'Good Governance' and 'State Failure': The Pseudo-Science of Statesmen in Our Times." In *Race and Racism in International Relations: Confronting the Global Colour Line*, edited by Alexander Anievas et al. New York: Routledge.

Jackson, Will. 2011. "White Man's Country: Kenya Colony and the Making of a Myth." *Journal of Eastern African Studies* 5, no. 2: 344–68.

Kennedy, Dane. 1987. *Islands of White: Settler Society and Culture in Kenya and Southern Rhodesia*. Durham, NC: Duke University Press.

Kessler, Aaron, and Wanjohi Kabukuru. 2013. "Shadow Diplomacy: African Nations Bypass Embassies, Tap Lobbyists." *Huffington Post*, July.

Li, Darryl. 2020. *The Universal Enemy: Jihad, Empire, and the Challenge of Solidarity*. Stanford, CA: Stanford University Press.

———. 2022. "Captive Passages: Geographies of Blackness in Guantánamo Memoirs." *Transforming Anthropology* 30, no. 1: 20–33.

Lipsitz, George. 1998. *The Possessive Investment in Whiteness: How White People Profit from Identity Politics*. Philadelphia: Temple University Press.

Lonsdale, John M., and E. S. Atieno Odhiambo, eds. 2003. *Mau Mau and Nationhood: Arms, Authority & Narration*. Athens: Ohio University Press.

Luongo, Katherine. 2006. "If You Can't Beat Them, Join Them: Government Cleansings of Witches and Mau Mau in 1950s Kenya." *History in Africa* 33: 451–71.

Maira, Sunaina. 2016. *The 9/11 Generation: Youth, Rights, and Solidarity in the War on Terror*. New York: New York University Press.

Mamdani, Mahmood. 1996. *Citizen and Subject: Contemporary Africa and the Legacy of Late Colonialism*. Princeton, NJ: Princeton University Press.

———. 2001. "Beyond Settler and Native as Political Identities: Overcoming the Political Legacy of Colonialism." *Comparative Studies in Society and History* 43: 651–64.

McIntosh, Janet. 2016. *Unsettled: Denial and Belonging among White Kenyans*. Durham, NC: Duke University Press.

Meiu, George Paul. *Ethno-Erotic Economies: Sexuality, Money, and Belonging in Kenya*. Chicago: University of Chicago Press.

Mudimbe, V. Y. 1988. *The Invention of Africa: Gnosis, Philosophy, and the Order of Knowledge.* Bloomington: Indiana University Press.

Mungai, Christine. 2021. "The Whiteness Conference," *Adi Magazine*, winter.

Musila, Grace, ed. 2015. *A Death Retold in Truth and Rumor: Kenya, Britain, and the Julie Ward Murder.* Rochester, NY: James Currey.

Ngugi wa Thiong'o. 1986. *Decolonizing the Mind: The Politics of Language in African Literature.* London: James Currey.

———. 2018. *Wrestling with the Devil: A Prison Memoir.* New York: New Press.

Njoya, Wandiya. 2018. "Invisible Citizens" *The Elephant.*

———. 2021. "A Class That Dare Not Speak Its Name: BBI and the Tyranny of the New Middle Class." *The Elephant.*

Odhiambo, E. S. Atieno. 1987. "Democracy and the Ideology of Order in Kenya." In *The Political Economy of Kenya,* edited by Michael G. Schatzberg, 177–201. New York: Praeger.

Omi, Michael, and Howard Winant. 1994. *Racial Formation in the United States.* London: Routledge.

Padmore, George. 1953. "Behind the Mau Mau." *Phylon (1940–1956)* 14, no. 4: 355–72.

Pierre, Jemima. 2012. *The Predicament of Blackness: Postcolonial Ghana and the Politics of Race.* Chicago: University of Chicago Press.

———. 2025. "Africanist Ethnography: Race, Power, and the Politics of Otherness." In *Anthropology of White Supremacy: A Reader,* edited by Aisha M. Beliso-De Jesús, Jemima Pierre, and Junaid Rana. Princeton, NJ: Princeton University Press.

Rana, Junaid. 2016. "The Racial Infrastructure of the Terror-Industrial Complex." *Social Text* 34, no. 4: 111–38.

———. 2020. "Anthropology and the Riddle of White Supremacy." *American Anthropologist* 122, no. 1: 99–111.

Sahle, Eunice N. 2012. "Fanon and Geographies of Political Violence in the Context of Democracy in Kenya." *Black Scholar* 42, no. 3–4: 45–57.

Said, Edward. 1978. *Orientalism.* New York: Pantheon Books.

Shadle, Brett L. 2015. *The Souls of White Folk: White Settlers in Kenya, 1900s–1920s.* Manchester: Manchester University Press.

Smart, Devin. 2018. "'Safariland': Tourism, Development, and the Marketing of Kenya in the Post-Colonial World." *African Studies Review* 61, no. 2: 134–57.

Stoler, Ann. 2016. *Duress: Imperial Durabilities in Our Times.* Durham, NC: Duke University Press.

Visweswaran, Kamala. 1998. "Race and the Culture of Anthropology." *American Anthropologist* 100, no. 1: 70–83.

Wai, Zubairu. 2012. "Neo-Patrimonialism and the Discourse of State Failure in Africa." *Review of African Political Economy* 39, no. 131: 27–43.

Ware, Rudolph T. 2014. *The Walking Qur'an: Islamic Education, Embodied Knowledge, and History in West Africa.* Illustrated ed. Chapel Hill: University of North Carolina Press.

20

The US Criminal In/Justice System and the International Security State

Laurence Ralph

LAURENCE RALPH (LR): Could you have done anything to avoid what happened to you? For example, if you had the kind of understanding of guilt that you have now, and if you knew your interrogators wanted you to behave in a certain way, would it have changed anything?

MOHAMEDOU OULD SLAHI (MOS): On many levels I think so. But it's very hard for me to say. Today I know that the United States of America does not always abide by the rule of law. The elite that governs the US is not convinced that democracy is the best way to govern the people. I'm not judging the US, I'm stating fact. The US leadership has said on many occasions that the law cannot be applied to certain people. They've said that in many ways. Like, "Ah, this democracy thing is not really practical all the time." Contractors outside the US break the law. The rhetoric in the US is that they want to keep Americans safe. This is very dangerous. Americans are human beings that deserve safety. But so are Mauritanians, and the Senegalese, and the Germans, and the Danes. We cannot sacrifice a Mauritanian person to keep Americans safe. That is inhumane.

THIS ESSAY EXPLORES the commonly ignored linkages between the US criminal in/justice system and the international security state. Throughout the course of this examination I closely scrutinize a few seemingly inchoate artifacts—diary entries, an Amazon book review, newspaper articles, for example, as well as my interviews and correspondences with torture survivor Mohamedou Ould Slahi—that illuminate the life and career of Richard Zuley, a Chicago police detective turned military interrogator, who tortured criminal suspects in both the United States and Guantánamo Bay.[1]

Among the police officers and military personnel who have commented publicly on Zuley's career, there exists a consensus that his actions have undermined the integrity of both the US criminal in/justice system and the international security state. Mark Fallon, for example, the deputy commander of the now-defunct Criminal Investigative Task Force at Guantánamo, said Zuley's interrogation of Mohamedou Ould Slahi "was illegal, it was immoral, it was ineffective and it was unconstitutional."[2]

"I've never seen anyone stoop to those levels," Stuart Couch, a former Marine lieutenant colonel and military commissions prosecutor, similarly said. "It's unconscionable, from the perspective of a criminal prosecution—or an interrogation, for that matter."

The problem with these expressions of contempt is that, while acknowledging that the strategies Zuley used to interrogate Slahi were "unconstitutional" and "unconscionable," they also implicitly characterize torturers like Zuley as "bad apples," which makes them easy to scapegoat. This begs the question: how do we understand the figure of Richard Zuley in a way that does not see the torture he enacted as exceptional?[3] I am particularly interested in how Fallon and Couch attempt to distance themselves from white supremacist thinking through claims to morality.

From this vantage point, we see that witnessing how someone can so unabashedly deprive a detainee of his constitutional rights is shameful. In the previous quotations, high-level military officials express shame when faced with the revelation of state-sanctioned torture. Such expressions cover over the histories of American imperialism, making the US government's background in white supremacy harder to identify and thus root out.

The logics of white supremacy, Andrea Smith (2006) says, are often emotional and symbolic rather than merely a system of ideas and ideals. "White people in North America live in a social environment that protects and insulates them from race-based stress," Robin DiAngelo (2011) similarly states. "This insulated environment of racial protection builds white expectations for racial comfort while at the same time," she continues, "lowering the ability to tolerate racial stress, leading to white fragility."

Notice how fragility passes itself off as moral integrity, as Fallon and Couch position themselves away from Richard Zuley, a strategic move that allows them to bypass the question of how pernicious the techniques he employed actually are. It is in this sense that their stance is indicative of what Ta-Nehisi Coates (2015) calls "the obsession with the politics of personal exoneration," a broader tendency for people to dismiss race in contemporary understandings of social inequality.

To understand the fragility, fear, and anxiety that help sustain the international security state, this essay focuses on Mohamedou Ould Slahi's torture. In my analysis, the ideology of white supremacy (by which I mean the system of ideas and beliefs that presumes the superiority of white people) is a major component of a "racial caste system" (Alexander 2012) that orders groups, making those at the bottom of this hierarchy subject to a disproportionate amount of state-sanctioned violence. By now, this racial caste system, in which whiteness is positioned at the top and those at the bottom tend to be Black, is so ingrained in US institutions that it is subconsciously enacted in rationales for fighting terrorism and cannot be simply "unthought" (Jung 2015, 36). The irony is that because racial hierarchies cannot be unthought, they are naturalized and go unexamined in prevailing scholarship on governance and security.

Scholars interested in white supremacy have pointed out that contemporary theorists are not expected to take race seriously in their theories of security and governance, regardless of the fact that a number of scholars in the fields of Black and ethnic studies have already addressed these issues in ways that challenge some of their central tenets (Weheliye 2014). This important works spans topics from the criminalization of Blackness (Muhammad 2011), to police violence and the prison-industrial complex (Gilmore 2007), to the Orientalist logic that non-Black, non-Indigenous people of color are permanently foreign and threatening, justifying exclusionary immigration policies and US wars (Jung 2015).

In centering race, this chapter begins from the premise that the construction of the United States as we know it today is based on forms of cruelty, discrimination, and exclusion. It acknowledges, further, that this history of conquest is "known" but is seldom acknowledged in the US military's understanding of how and why torture persists as policy. In this regard, the literature on white supremacy is intimately linked to the work on social epistemology, which is about the construction of knowledge *and* about what people actively ignore (Mills 1997; Sullivan and Tuana 2007). Using these key insights to inform my analysis, I argue that a chief legacy of white supremacy is the way that ignorance is produced as a matter of US security.

Torture as Practice and Policy

Although Richard Zuley's career as a serial torturer dates back to the 1980s, the scandal begins much more recently, in 2015, with the publication of *Guantánamo Diary*, the first memoir written by a detainee while still incarcerated at the detention center located at the southeastern end of Cuba. In it, the author, Mohamedou Ould Slahi, a Mauritanian who was held for fourteen years without being charged with a crime, describes the intimate details of his torture at the hands of Richard Zuley.

Slahi's torture has been described as "one of the most stubborn, deliberate, and cruel interrogations in the record,"[4] and this characterization stems in part from the way Zuley befriended Slahi. Zuley seemed genuinely interested in Slahi's hobbies and family life, and he used the information Slahi shared to threaten his family members, particularly his mother, whom Zuley told Slahi he was going to arrest and bring to Guantánamo—an all-male facility—if Slahi did not confess. As if that wasn't bad enough, Zuley arranged to have Slahi kidnapped and taken off the island, where he experienced a mock execution at sea. Of all the days Slahi writes about in his diary, that one has garnered the most attention.

Media and the courts have seized on this day because in checking the veracity of his story, journalists were able to prove that powerful people in the US government engineered Slahi's torture. Slahi's torture occurred according to a "Special Plan," which outlined precisely what was going to happen to him during that day at sea, and the Defense Secretary at the time, Donald Rumsfeld, personally signed off on it. The US Senate Armed Services Committee has now said Rumsfeld also bears major responsibility for the abuses committed by US troops at another black site, Abu Ghraib, the camp where the US Army imprisoned Iraqis from 2003 to 2006, during the same time they detained Slahi. That camp is now infamous for photographs of the US military police torturing Iraqi prisoners.

Like Slahi, the detainees at Abu Ghraib had been subjected to what the US government blandly and euphemistically refers to as "enhanced interrogation methods," which were put into action after Rumsfeld signed several memos in 2002 and 2003 arguing that international humanitarian laws, such as the Geneva Conventions, did not apply to the US military while they were overseas. Rumsfeld's "enhanced" methods resulted in a host of human rights violations, including physical and sexual abuse, rape, sodomy, and murder. US Supreme Court decisions, including *Hamdan v. Rumsfeld* (2006), eventually ruled that the Geneva Conventions do, in fact, apply. But by the time that decision was handed down, it was too late to prevent Slahi's torture, which occurred three years before this decision.

When it came to Rumsfeld's authorization of Slahi's "Special Plan," nothing was left to chance. The decision to have only four soldiers involved, for example, was carefully considered. Having too many people "in the know" could compromise the mission, and perhaps give Slahi a hint as to what would happen. The use of German shepherds was deliberate, as well. The dogs were meant to frighten him, to muffle his screams, and to heighten the sense of chaos during the mock kidnapping, so that the detainee could be easily transported out of his cell and onto a boat. In his reports Rumsfeld stated that the purpose of taking Slahi on an hours-long trip on a high-speed boat was to make him think that he was being transported off of the island, quickly, to a faraway place. Once they removed him from the boat, the soldiers involved planned to take Slahi to a secluded part of Guantánamo called Camp Echo, where, according to the US Senate Armed Services report, his new cell and interrogation room was to be "modified in such a way as to reduce as much outside stimuli as possible." The doors were sealed, so they did not allow even a flicker of light. The room became closed off and contained. The darkness would weigh on Slahi, pressuring him to produce the kind of knowledge that would satisfy the US government. The government demanded Slahi's compliance through torture, and on August 25, 2003, around 4:00 p.m., they staged a mock kidnapping to prove that they had the power to end his life if he did not confess, to further terrify and isolate him—as if he hadn't already been both terrified and isolated during the course of being detained at Guantánamo Bay.

This is how Slahi describes the scene of his abduction:

> Suddenly a commando team consisting of three soldiers and a German shepherd broke into our interrogation room.
>
> Everything happened quicker than I could think about it. ▮▮▮▮▮▮ punched me violently, which made me fall face down on the floor.
>
> "Motherfucker, I told you, you're gone!" said ▮▮▮▮▮." His partner kept punching me everywhere, mainly on my face and my ribs. He, too, was masked from head to toe; he punched me the whole time without saying a word, because he didn't want to be recognized. The third man was not masked; he stayed at the door holding the dog's collar, ready to release it on me.
>
> . . . "Blindfold the Motherfucker, if he tries to look—"

One of them hit me hard across the face, and quickly put the goggles on my eyes, earmuffs on my ears, and a small bag over my head. I couldn't tell who did what. They tightened the chains around my ankles and my wrists; afterwards, I started to bleed. All I could hear was ▮▮▮▮ cursing, "F-this and F-that!" I didn't say a word, I was overwhelmingly surprised, I thought they were going to execute me . . .

After fifteen minutes, the truck stopped at the beach, and my escorting team dragged me out of the truck and put me in a high-speed boat. . . . Inside the boat, ▮▮▮▮ made me drink salt water, I believe it was directly from the ocean. It was so nasty I threw up. They would put any object in my mouth and shout, "Swallow, Motherfucker!," but I decided inside not to swallow the organ damaging salt water, which choked me when they kept pouring it in my mouth. "Swallow, you idiot!" I contemplated quickly, and decided for the nasty, damaging water rather than death.

Mohamedou Ould Slahi had learned from other detainees that the interrogators on Guantánamo would put them on planes and fly them around for hours, only to return them to the same jail where they had started. One can only assume that is why he knew his kidnappers were actually driving the boat around in circles and not taking him far off the island as they wanted him to believe. Rumsfeld's plan had failed in that respect. As Slahi writes, even though military forces tried to make him believe that they had transported him to a remote location, he knew that he was still on the island, alongside the others that the US government regarded as a threat. The nature of this threat, the US government claimed, was Slahi's association with terrorists. But the more time he spent at Guantánamo Bay, the more he was convinced that he was there because of what he believed.

The Guantánamo Bay detention camp was established in 2002 by President George W. Bush as a consequence of the September 11 attacks. Five days after these events, Bush launched what he referred to as the "war on terrorism," in which he named "a racial network of terrorists" as the enemy, thereby enlisting democratic nations across the globe to assist in defeating this new "evil."[5] This, according to Bush, was an "Us vs. Them" call to arms, and governments associated with "them" (by which he specifically meant, al Qaeda, the political organization credited with the attack) should be considered adversaries. In no time at all, al Qaeda's complex historical entanglement with the United States had been reduced to the existential threat Islamic terrorism now posed; Muslims all across the globe were a casualty of that reduction.

A critical consequence of the war on terror has been the widespread acceptance of Muslims as terrorists (Rana 2011). Of course the West's antipathy toward Islam dates as far back as the Crusades (Said 1978), which is to say that the association of Muslims with terrorism through Orientalist stereotypes was deeply ingrained in US popular culture long before 9/11 (Mandel 2001; Calvert 2007; Shaheen 2008). These events, however, fostered a resurgence of anti-Muslim racism, as the US government swiftly mobilized existing signifiers and symbols that have historically been linked to Islamic identity (such as foreignness, barbarism, inferiority, and violence) to justify military intervention against Muslim populations worldwide (Selod and Embrick 2013, 650–51).

According to scholars of anti-Muslim racism (Modood 2005; Rana 2011), Muslims are racialized through and by the ways that the cultural traits associated with their religion are subjected to "othering." The creation of the Muslim as the "other" is rooted in white supremacy because, as Selod and Embrick (2013, 647) note, it is part of the same imperialist project that "imagined racial and religious differences between populations in order to justify the genocide and colonization of Asia, Africa, and the Middle East." Birthed from histories of imperialism, today's war on terror leverages enduring racial stereotypes to construct Muslims as potential terrorists, stripping people like Slahi of the privileges historically wedded to whiteness, such as due process and the presumption of innocence.

The reason the US government presumed that Slahi was a terrorist is because of his previous association with al Qaeda. He had belonged to the organization in the 1990s when its expressed mission was to root out communism, back when the US government regarded its members as allies in that fight, offering them political and economic support to help defeat socialism and communism in the Muslim world (Gunaratna 2006). When the group gravitated toward more militant ideals—ideals that, Slahi says, he vehemently disagrees with—he quit. By the time the US government began to surveil Slahi in the early 2000s, he claims to have already renounced his allegiance.

While the Central Intelligence Agency met Slahi's claim that he no longer had ties to al Qaeda with disbelief, the fact that he was a devout Muslim when he arrived at Guantánamo Bay was never in doubt. Slahi was among the 1.8 billion followers of the monotheistic religion who believe that there is only one God (Allah), and that the prophet Muhammad is his messenger. What this meant, in practical terms, is that he adhered to The Pillars of Islam, or the five basic religious acts that are considered obligatory for all believers of the faith. There is the *shahadah*, a testimony that must be recited in prayer, which affirms that Muhammad is the messenger of God; there is the *salat*, ritual prayers intended to focus a believer's mind on God, which are recited in the direction of Mecca, Muhammad's birthplace; there is *zakat*, or charity, which entails gifting a portion of your accumulated wealth to the poor or needy; there is *Sawm*, or fasting, the purpose of which is to facilitate closeness to God; and there is the *hajj*, the obligatory religious pilgrimage to the city of Mecca that every follower who is able must take at least once in his life. Of those Pillars, the one that Slahi used to sustain himself on Camp Echo were *shahadah* (testimony), *salat* (prayer), and *sawm* (fasting), though Slahi's *Guantánamo Diary* makes clear that the US military intelligence anticipated that he would use his faith as a resource, and thus part of their strategy for interrogating him was to make him betray his beliefs. Nevertheless, Slahi would depend on his religious faith to live in the moment, and by so doing, gain knowledge of his surroundings.

This is one of the most impressive things about Slahi's diary: the way he acquires knowledge while being detained. His captors tried to strip him of his humanity by limiting what he knew about the world. They did not want him to know what day of the week it was, or what hour of the day, nor did his interrogators want him to know anything about them. But he and the other detainees would find ways to obtain this knowledge just as they stole moments of prayer, even when the US military prevented them from practicing their faith.

They would steal time by glimpsing interrogators' watches during interviews. They would steal names by eavesdropping on their interrogators' conversations. They would trade this knowledge with fellow detainees like contraband so that they could know who was tormenting them or what time to turn toward Mecca during *salat*. They hid these kernels of knowledge because detainees never knew when these pieces of intelligence would come in handy.

Slahi always knew more than his captors thought he did. More than anything, that seems to have enabled him to hold on to his humanity. In this way, he never let his torturers diminish who he was.

One passage in Slahi's diary is particularly striking. Here, he lets the world know that he has learned his torturer's name:

> He always tried to make me believe that his real name was Captain Collins, but what he didn't know was that I knew his name even before I met him: ███████.

We should scrutinize this redaction, and the role of redactions in this diary more broadly. Reading the *Guantánamo Diary*, one is struck by the black-bar redactions on almost every page, over 2,500 in total, which, despite their ubiquity, are unable to mute Slahi's voice. For our purposes, these redactions represent the US government's power to shield its personnel from responsibility for torture. They cover Slahi's words so that no government officials will ever be mentioned by name, and no identifying characteristics can be ascribed to them. We can understand the instrumentality of redactions in theoretical terms through the concept of the public secret. To understand the nature of the public secret, it is helpful to examine the role of secrecy in society, more generally.

In his groundbreaking book, *The Secret and the Secret Society*, Georg Simmel (1950, 312) tells us that secrecy is linked to the lies people tell. It is grounded in concealment, which is at the root of all social interactions, affecting individuals' decisions to share knowledge and receive it back in return. In the context of the secret societies that Simmel studied, he found that people wanted to conceal information. Doing so allowed them to retain power, and to boast about misconduct while evading sanction. Ultimately, secrecy worked to ensure group cohesion and to enable certain groups and organizations to maintain power and control in society.

The paradoxical nature of all secrets is that they depend on people's ability to keep information confidential, but the public secret differs in that it can be widely known but is not articulated. Much of the academic literature on the public secret is rooted in Elias Cannetti's (1984, 295) work, which notes that "a large part of the prestige of dictatorships is due to the fact that they are credited with the concentrated power of secrecy." Michael Taussig (1997) extends Cannetti's argument, noting that the act of revealing a public secret is often accompanied by a fall from grace, because such revelations are not considered socially acceptable. As a result, people develop elaborate ways of pretending not to know what they, in fact, do know. In this way, public secrecy revolves around power and dominance. As a consequence, people in vulnerable positions protect those who provide them with material resources, which is another way of saying that public secrecy involves substantial risks. For this reason, scholarship on public secrecy raises questions such as "How do people come to live with impunity?" and "How [do] people 'remoralize' their social worlds following lengthy periods of intimate violence?" (Theidon 2006, 98). This is also why, as Jones (2014) notes, public secrecy has been of interest to anthropologists studying violence and historical injustices (Geissler 2013; Mookherjee 2006; Penglase 2009; Roy 2008; Thomas 2017).

In this context, the public secret that the redaction represents is what people in power know, but refuse to say about torture. What they know is that military officials who torture detainees will most likely not face any form of sanction. In this sense, torture in the United States is built on a contradiction: the existence of torture is, of course, forbidden by law, and yet it occurs and is condoned by the government, nevertheless. The US government, for example, has repeatedly argued that torture cases cannot be litigated without disclosing "state secrets," claiming that the litigation itself would undermine national security interests. This has allowed the government to end entire legal proceedings before they even start. Without judicial accountability, the US government has used executive orders—consensus-based decisions by particular administrations—to shut down black sites or release detainees from places like Guantánamo Bay.[6] As a result, despite numerous lawsuits against the "architects and perpetrators of the CIA torture program" during the time Bush and Obama held office, US courts "did not consider the claims of a single torture victim," as Dror Ladin, attorney for the ACLU National Security Project, has recently noted.[7]

Given the difficulty of exposing the public secret of torture, one must keep in mind that when Slahi wrote the sentence that reveals Zuley's name, there was no way for him to know that the government officials who were supposed to redact all names for the sake of US security would let a reference to Zuley slip through in the footnotes that Slahi's editor would eventually prepare for the book. That mistake would lead to reporters digging into Richard Zuley's thirty-seven-year career as a Chicago police officer, where they discovered his history of torture. Little did Slahi know it, but by writing Zuley's name, he helped unearth another secret, something that extended beyond Guantánamo: a hitherto unknown link between the US criminal justice system and the international security state.

How the US Government Produces Torturers

It is significant that the US military looked toward Chicago when they needed help extorting a confession from Slahi. Confessions had become the hallmark of policing there, and Zuley's successful track record at extracting them kept him on the military's radar. The detective had also worked as an officer in the Navy reserve. From time to time, his superiors called him up to active duty. Fighting terrorism was a source of pride for Zuley, and it seemed to give him a sense of purpose.

In the 1980s and '90s, Zuley sought opportunities to take assignments with Naval intelligence. Even while working at Guantánamo during the years that Slahi was imprisoned there, Zuley returned to Chicago to testify at hearings, where he let the court know that he had been mobilized for the war on terror. In testimony he explained that while he had initially been assigned to a Royal Air Force base in Molesworth, his superiors then "sent me to Cuba as the liaison officer for the European Command. And that job has evolved to what I'm doing now."[8] He was describing, of course, his role on the Joint Task Force as an officer in charge of collecting intelligence in Slahi's case. All of this is to say: Zuley was eager to be a part of this mission at Guantánamo. And, by his own admission, his cameo as "Captain Collins" was the role of his life.

The world now knows Zuley's true identity because of the sloppiness of the government redactors, and also because it had earlier appeared in the footnotes of the Senate Armed Services Committee's 2008 investigation into military torture. But it is also important to note that Zuley himself revealed something about his identity in—of all things—a signed review on the Amazon website for a novel by Eric Wentz titled *Killing Sharks*.

According to the cover copy, *Killing Sharks* invites readers to "dive into the explosive world of terrorism and those fearless enough to fight it." It centers on Lieutenant Commander Grant Chisholm who "is on a mission to thwart jihadists. His latest assignment as a liaison officer to Guantánamo brings him face to face with the Taliban and al Qaeda, and their hatred of the United States." In his review of the book, Zuley wrote the following:

> Wentz's ability to generate excitement and the desire to keep reading because you need to find out what happens next is right there with Vince Flynn. . . . The author doesn't give up classified material but, like Clancy, he certainly flirts with it while describing what could be a very real scenario in a fictional setting. *Killing Sharks* . . . is fiction that could easily be fact. The enemy is real, the plot not only plausible but one we prepared for, and the characters are people we all knew. I thoroughly enjoyed *Killing Sharks* and look forward to Dr. Wentz's next book and hopefully a continuation of the exploits of LCDR Grant Chisholm!

LCDR Richard Zuley, USN (Ret)
Former EUCOM LNO, senior interrogator and Special Projects Team Chief, Joint
    Task Force—Guantánamo (2002–2004)

This review stands out for what it reveals about the military imagination. The way Zuley signs his comment suggests pride in his position as "senior interrogator," and one can only wonder what "Special Projects" he headed up! What is more, the enjoyment he seems to derive from the book conveys how exciting he finds the hunt for terrorists to be, and also his belief that the book's description of terrorism is accurate, that the terrorists it portrays are "people we all knew." He clearly means for his title as Lieutenant Commander (LCDR) and his position as a senior interrogator to give credibility to his assertion that the people and events in the book are based in reality.

Reflecting on Zuley's assertion that the terrorism plots he encountered as a military officer were identical to those in a work of fiction, the circumstances of Slahi's torture and detention make all the more sense. Books like *Killing Sharks* work alongside the popular news media, official reports, and even scholarly treatises to anticipate terrorist events before they happen, creating a mythic "terrorist" in the popular consciousness. Such leaps of the imagination amplify violence and turn people the US government suspects of being enemies into "sharks," until the war on terror becomes a self-fulfilling prophecy (Masco 2014; Douglas and Zulaica 2010).

By recruiting people who already believe that terrorists are not fully human, but animal-like enemies that need to be hunted, and constantly rewarding those cadets with opportunity, the US military reinforces white supremacy. Zuley is himself white, but he need not be in order to participate in a system of domination that enacts structural violence against Muslims, treating them as potential terrorists "based on visual attributes such as skin color and phenotype, as well as customs and costumes" (Rana 2011, 28). What is important to notice, in this case, is how white supremacist security logics position an over-eager cop, with grandiose ideas about "the enemy" that seem to be based as much on popular thrillers as on his own experience, to become an interrogator at Guantánamo Bay.

At the time Mohamedou Ould Slahi met Richard Zuley, the administration at Guantánamo was facing a crisis because the interrogators were overwhelmed with their duties. There were only twenty-six interrogators on the base, compared to three hundred detainees, who came from mostly Saudi, Afghani, Pakistani, and Yemeni backgrounds. Only four of the interrogators spoke Arabic. Two spoke Farsi. It was partly because of Zuley's enthusiasm for working in such a difficult environment that he won the favor of Major General Geoffrey Miller, the Army official in charge of the detention center at the time. But this point is worth repeating: Zuley's success at eliciting confessions in Chicago also made him an attractive candidate for leading Slahi's special interrogation.

And he delivered: at the end of many months of torture, Slahi did indeed confess—to crimes his interrogators had to tell him about since, Slahi says, he had no knowledge of them. He admitted to planning to blow up the CN Tower in Toronto, for example, despite saying that he never heard of it. Asked if he was telling the truth about his confessions, Slahi answered, "I don't care as long as you are pleased. So if you want to buy, I am selling." Although Zuley was apparently pleased with it, the confession was so clearly the product of torture that the prosecutor at Guantánamo declined to file charges against him. As the ACLU recounted, "the military lawyer originally assigned to prosecute the case against Mr. Slahi, Marine Corps Lt. Col. Stuart Couch, determined that the statements wrung from Mr. Slahi during his interrogations were so tainted by torture that they could not ethically be used against him. Ultimately, Col. Couch told his supervisors that he was "morally opposed" to Mr. Slahi's treatment, and refused to participate in the prosecution." This is why Slahi was never charged with or convicted of a crime.

Even so, when a *Guardian* report exposed Zuley's history in Chicago, many news outlets expressed astonishment at both the similarities and striking differences between the torture Slahi underwent on Guantánamo Bay and the torture that Zuley had perpetrated in Chicago.

From Chicago to the War on Terror

The main difference between Zuley's torture of suspects in Chicago and in Guantánamo Bay lay in the fact that the confessions Zuley extracted in Chicago got better results, since they did lead to convictions. Black Chicagoans who were under arrest were deprived of sleep, shackled to the floor, beaten up when they were suspected of a crime, and had their families threatened. There were complaints about these practices in Zuley's police record but they were never taken seriously until *Guantánamo Diary* exposed Zuley for what he was. Since he has been exposed, five Chicago residents—Lathierial Boyd, Anthony Garrett, Andre Griggs, Lee Harris, and Benita Johnson—have either requested that their convictions be overturned on the basis that Zuley tortured them or have already been exonerated and plan to sue him.

A few of the civilian complaints Zuley amassed in Chicago over the course of thirty-seven years as a police officer have gained international attention. One of those, the case of Lathierial Boyd, reveals striking parallels between the techniques of torture Zuley used on prisoners in the city of Chicago and in Guantánamo Bay.[9]

In 1990, Zuley came to believe that Boyd had shot two men outside Exodus, a Chicago reggae club. Despite the fact that Boyd had an alibi, and despite a lack of evidence suggesting Boyd's guilt, Zuley was determined to connect Boyd to the crime.

Initially, when he learned the police were looking for him, Boyd turned himself in, volunteering to participate in a lineup. He stood for two. In a 2015 interview with Spencer Ackerman of *The Guardian*, Boyd recalls asking Zuley after the second lineup if anybody had identified him. Zuley said "no."

To this, Boyd replied: "See, I told you. You've got the wrong guy."

Zuley smiled at him, and said: "We're charging you anyway."

Boyd was then arrested and shackled to the wall in the precinct station, where Zuley left him for hours.

Boyd claims that the police planted evidence in his case. Weeks after the shooting, when there was nothing to connect him to the murder, the police found a piece of paper with his nickname written on it strewn on the floor beside the victim's hospital bed. Without a confession, this was the only hard evidence tying Boyd to the crime.

"That little piece of paper was enough," Boyd said. "Because of that paper, the judge sentenced me to 82 years in prison. 82 years. I remember thinking that the judge had given me a life sentence. But it's not gonna hold up with the jury anyway. They are going to know that I was framed.

"I was wrong," Boyd said, "It held up. It held up. And now half my life is gone. I did 23 years in prison before I was finally exonerated. I was set free in 2013. It still doesn't seem real. It doesn't seem real that I was there and went through all of that, or that I'm free now. I'm still trying to make sense of it."

When Boyd heard about what Richard Zuley had done in Guantánamo, it seemed unbelievable, but the revelation did provide some context for why he was targeted and treated so inhumanly.

"Here this guy is, in another country, torturing people, ordering that they be tortured, and so what do you think he'd do to me—a nigger in a Chicago police station."

"I didn't have a chance," Boyd said, "faced off against somebody so sick."

In the same interview with Ackerman, Boyd brought his focus back to Chicago, reflecting on the plight of other victims:

"Now I find out that I'm not alone. I've learned that Zuley sent other suspects to prison for crimes they may not have committed. I know who some of them are. The ones who I know, I have to help get them out of there. I have to help them because somebody helped me."

When I interviewed Mohamedou Ould Slahi in May 2017, one of the topics we discussed was Richard Zuley and his career on the Chicago police force. I shared Lathierial Boyd's interview with Slahi because I wanted to think through the ways survivors become visible to each other. Though I had shared some of my writing on police torture in Chicago with Slahi prior to our interview, when we talked via Skype I was intentional in not to mentioning Richard Zuley specifically because I did not know if he would feel comfortable talking about his interrogation and torture. As it turned out, my hesitations were all for naught. Slahi was intent on drawing connections between his experience on Guantánamo Bay and Chicago through Richard Zuley. For example, during one exchange Slahi said the following:

MOS: When I read your paper about what happened in Chicago, I was shocked. One of the people who spent many years, about the same time as me, was interrogated and tortured by Richard Zuley. Zuley told him the same thing he was telling me—the same thing he was telling people in Chicago, apparently. Zuley said it did not matter to him whether this man was innocent or guilty. It didn't matter because to Zuley, this was a *bad guy.*

Again, I go back to the US philosophy on guilt. Guilty means that you are a bad person. But is it supposed to mean that? In a democratic country, guilty is supposed to mean that you did this or that crime. Does it matter from a legal perspective whether you were a good or bad guy? I don't think so. But this "bad guy" mentality is brought up over and over in interrogations . . .

This happened to me while I was being interrogated by Zuley. I wrote my confession. Just like the Black guy from Chicago that you wrote about, except my confession carried the death penalty. But at that point, I didn't care. I just wanted the torture to stop. I didn't want my family to be tortured.

Zuley's sergeant told me, "We'll give you 30 years instead of the death penalty." I was thinking, "Wow, in my heart, what generous people!" [Laughter]

At some point he knew that my confession was erroneous. But instead of trying to get at the truth, he told me, "I need you to tell me what other people were involved." I said, "Look, I can write down the names of people, but they didn't do anything." Again, his sergeant said, "We know these guys are bad, so it doesn't matter."

You see: "We already know these are bad guys, so it doesn't matter whether you lie about them." . . . This is the kind of lawlessness that is reigning in the US.

Here, I find it productive to contrast Slahi's understanding of the de facto US philosophy of guilt to the ignorance and innocence that individuals have claimed in relation to the revelations related to Slahi's torture. The reference to the archetype of a "bad guy" that Slahi mentions can help us think about how the racial caste system constructs threat through a notion of guilt. On the one hand, what happened to Slahi on Guantánamo Bay had little to do with the pursuit of truth. As he mentioned, it did not matter to his interrogators whether or not he lied about other detainees because they were already presumed to be "bad." Any detainee could stand in for the threat of Islamic terrorism. Still, it is important to notice the process through which Slahi's guilt is confirmed as he is coerced into a confession. Knowledge and innocence are juxtaposed against one another throughout Slahi's description. He continuously claims to have no knowledge of his alleged crimes, and every time he proclaims his innocence he is punished in a way that reminds him of the threat that his social group presents to society. In the end, he relents and confesses.

Later on during our conversation, Slahi explained how the transparency that used to represent legal due process in the United States slowly disappeared, transforming the way he thought about US democracy and the rule of law:

LR: How has your perspective on the US changed through this ordeal? In the diary, the reader sees it shifting, and you transforming because of everything you're going through. Can you reflect on that?

MOS: Those of us who arrived at Guantánamo Bay—nearly 800 of us—were taken from all over the world. Who's left after several years? It was me—a Mauritanian—and the Yemenis. Very poor people. And this is telling, you know, because there is nothing that we could have done differently than anyone else . . .

My problem, again, Laurence, was ignorance.

I didn't understand the concepts of guilt and innocence as they seem to exist in the US. My understanding was that if you didn't do anything wrong, then you don't have to be afraid of anyone. You don't need to cooperate. You don't need to smile at your interrogator. You don't need to do anything. You can say, "Screw you, I'm going home!" You can do whatever you want to do. I learned that attitude in Germany.

This attitude is very bad in America.

In America the philosophy is that you should be a good boy. And a good boy should be very good with the FBI and with the police. And guilt? I thought guilty meant that you did it, or didn't do it. But guilt—the philosophy of guilt—in my experience with the US is not like that.

Again, I'll come back to my main point. My ignorance of American culture got me in a lot of trouble.

Notice that Slahi describes the notion that the US government abides by the due process outlined in its own Constitution as a kind of "ignorance." The reality that he experienced was that entire populations were shrouded in guilt because of who they were presumed to be. He explained that despite the fact that individual citizens of the United States spent several years fighting to set him free, he began to think of US democracy as akin to the redaction—or black box—that covered over Zuley's name.

Earlier I said that the redaction represents knowledge that is known, but concealed by the powerful. This description suggests that people in power simply "do nothing." The concept of the black box, however, points to how concealment is an active process. Perhaps the most popular idea of "black box" in US culture is the device on an airplane that stores information in the event of a flight accident. But another, lesser known meaning of "black box" is the tacit agreement, among US government officials, to secretly conceal torture. An analogy should make the implications of this tacit agreement clear. In his essay "What Is an Instinct," Gregory Bateson (2012, 313) uses the concept of the black box to explain the idea of gravity to his daughter:

> "I can tell you what gravity is supposed to do," Bateson says, "pull objects and things towards the ground. But I can't explain exactly how it does it. It's like a Black Box."
>
> "Oh," his daughter says. "Daddy, what's a Black Box?"
>
> "A Black Box is a conventional agreement between scientists to stop trying to explain things at a certain point. I guess it's usually a temporary agreement. "But that doesn't sound like a Black Box," she replies.
>
> "No, but that's what it's called," he says. "Things often don't sound like their names."
>
> "No. They don't."
>
> "It's a word that comes from the engineers," Bateson continues. "When they draw a diagram of a complicated machine, they use a sort of shorthand. Instead of drawing all the details, they make a box to stand for a whole bunch of parts and label the box with what that bunch of parts is supposed to do."
>
> "So, a Black Box is a label for what a bunch of things are supposed to do . . ."
>
> "That's right," Bateson says. "But it's not an explanation of how the bunch works."
>
> "And gravity?" she inquires.
>
> "Is a label for what gravity is supposed to do. It's not an explanation of how it does it."

I mention Bateson's discussion because it fits so nicely with the standard definition of a black box, which *Merriam-Webster's Dictionary* defines as "a complicated electronic device whose internal mechanism is typically hidden from or mysterious to the user."[10]

As Slahi's experience illustrates, the US government actively creates conceptual black boxes that serve as an implicit agreement between National Security advisors like Rumsfeld and people like Zuley that strive to ensure that their torturous activities remain concealed. This conceptual black box—like its material instantiation: the black bar redaction—contain sweeping, unexamined stereotypes about good and evil, about where and how the evil people live, about the skin color of those evil people, and about what it is permissible to do to them. *That* Black Box is the racism that keeps torture hidden. It is the contempt for the criminal suspect that allows even those interrogators not directly involved in torture to become complicit in their grim silence. They will look the other way when confronted with those who have been raped, beaten, and kidnapped, because those people deserved what they got.

Talking to Slahi, I also came to realize that in terms of the white supremacist ideology of the United States, entire countries could be thought of as black boxes, so long as there are places on earth considered "dark." The term "dark region" describes areas unlike Western democracies—those countries, and regions, supposedly unenlightened by the rule of law. Since his release, the United States has made certain that Slahi lives in a military dictatorship, a so-called dark region of the world. According to Slahi, the United States wanted him to live in a place where there is no democratic rule of law.

The irony of the situation would be comical were it not so distressing: The United States had violated its own Constitution and Slahi's rights, and now it was sending him back to a country that did not abide by any Constitution and guaranteed its citizens no rights to speak of. In so doing, the United States denied Slahi any form of redress for his torture. He explained:

> MOS: The United States didn't want me to go to Germany. The US said it would send me back to my country in Africa. It did not want me to go anywhere I could assert my rights, or where I could seek any relief, or even live in a country where there is the rule of law.
>
> ... The irony is that in August 2016, the State Department had issued a statement urging Mauritania to "respect the rule of law, and abide by conventions that Mauritania signed." That sounds very good. But it was a joke because the US State Department did not mean what it said.
>
> How do I know that?
>
> These statements are meant as a bargaining chip. They tell my country, "If you don't violate these rights, we'll tell the world about other violations you guys commit." It's a very bad deal.

And here lies the parallel between Mohamedou Ould Slahi's story and the experience of so many African Americans, especially those who have suffered police torture in Chicago. They both belong to populations that are systematically disenfranchised in the name of US militarism and imperialism. As with the war on terror, the battle cry of law and order has been a mainstay in US politics that aggressively fashions the veil that obscures state violence. By cultivating forms of non-knowing, US institutions are producing a citizenry that can comfortably retreat into innocence because the history of racial conquest has been effectively blacked out. It follows that if non-knowing is intimately related to the subject position of the Innocent, then scholars must interrogate the intimate relationship between identity and amnesia that perpetuates state violence (Mills 2007). To do so, we must begin from the premise that torture is not an exceptional circumstance. We must see it, instead, as foundational to US systems of governance and security, and thus, as the historical extension of America's white supremacists roots.

Conclusion

Anthropology in the United States has always had to engage with the ways in which "the political" has been rendered visible in other disciplines. Although critical theorists such as Agamben offer profound analyses of how the *state of exception* eventually becomes the "new normal," even this concept reifies a notion of normativity that never existed. This is not to say that there are no political philosophers who acknowledge the historical roots of white supremacy (Spillers 1987; Wynter 1989; Mills 1997; Dawson 2003; Gooding-Williams 2010). But it is to say that this violent history is often subsumed by a teleology that relegates racism to the past, or ignores it altogether. This is why the literature on white supremacy contends that racism was not more transparent in the past and is not less lethal today (Jung 2015).

As a corrective, this chapter contributes to the literature on white supremacy, especially the strand concerned with social epistemology, by demonstrating the ways in which US institutions are replete with various components of knowing and non-knowing. When it comes to racial justice, what a citizen is compelled to know is profoundly important. Based on the issues raised in this essay, future research in this field might explore the extent to which soldiers and the public are obliged to know all there is to know about state violence, as well as the degrees of culpability society attributes to institutions that actively produce this ignorance.

To be able to address these concerns we cannot see ignorance as an absence, void, or a gap in knowledge. Rather, we must see ignorance as intentionally cultivated. The implications are clear: by cultivating forms of non-knowing, US institutions are producing a citizenry that can comfortably retreat into innocence because the history of white supremacy has been effectively redacted. And thus, it should not surprise us that a police officer went on to torture Muslim detainees at Guantánamo Bay just as he tortured African Americans in Chicago. The US government produced him and rewarded him for torture. What is rare and exceptional about this chapter in US imperialism is that in this particular instance a government redactor missed the mark.

That is the *only* reason we know Richard Zuley's name.

Notes

1. This chapter is a revised version of what first appeared as Laurence Ralph, 2020. "The Making of Richard Zuley: The Ignored Linkages between the US Criminal In/Justice System and the International Security State." *American Anthropologist* 122, no. 1: 133–42. doi.org/10.1111/aman.13356.

2. Spencer Ackerman, "Bad Lieutenant: American Police Brutality, Exported from Chicago to Guantánamo," *The Guardian (London)* 18 (2015).

3. Ackerman, "Bad Lieutenant."

4. See, for example: www.dailymail.co.uk/news/article-2914696/Inmates-Guantanamo-diary-released .html. www.latimes.com/nation/la-na-guantanamo-book-20150120-story.html.

5. Kenneth R. Bazinet, "A Fight vs. Evil, Bush and Cabinet Tell US," *New York Daily News* 17 (2001).

6. On the states secrets privilege, see Zagel (1965, 875).

7. See: "In a First, the Trump Administration Moves to Invoke Secrecy Claims in Torture Lawsuit," March 9, 2017, ACLU.org: www.aclu.org/blog/national-security/torture/first-trump-administration-moves -invoke-secrecy-claims-torture/.

8. Ackerman, "Bad Lieutenant."

9. Ackerman, "Bad Lieutenant," 18.

10. "Black box," *Merriam-Webster's 11th Collegiate Dictionary*, http://unabridged.merriam-webster.com/collegiate/black%20box.

References

Alexander, Michelle. 2012. *The New Jim Crow: Mass Incarceration in the Age of Colorblindness*. New York: New Press.

Bateson, Gregory. 2012. "Metalogue: What Is an Instinct?" *Readings in Zoosemiotics* 8313.

Calvert, John C. M. 2007. "The Striving Shaykh: Abdullah Azzam and the Revival of Jihad." *Journal of Religion and Society* 2: 83–102.

Canetti, Elias. 1984. *Crowds and Power*. New York: Macmillan.

Coates, Ta-Nehisi. 2015. *Between the World and Me*. New York: Spiegel and Grau.

Dawson, Michael C. 2003. *Black Visions: The Roots of Contemporary African-American Political Ideologies*. Chicago: University of Chicago Press.

DiAngelo, Robin. 2011. "White Fragility." *International Journal of Critical Pedagogy* 3, no. 3: 54–70.

Douglas, William, and J. Zulaica. 1996. *Terror and Taboo: The Follies, Fables, and Faces of Terrorism*. New York: Routledge.

Geissler, P. Wenzel. 2013. "Public Secrets in Public Health: Knowing Not to Know While Making Scientific Knowledge." *American Ethnologist* 40, no. 1: 13–34.

Gilmore, Ruth Wilson. 2007. *Golden Gulag: Prisons, Surplus, Crisis, and Opposition in Globalizing California*. Berkeley: University of California Press.

Gooding-Williams, Robert. 2010. *In the Shadow of DuBois*. Cambridge, MA: Harvard University Press.

Jones, Graham M. 2014. "Secrecy." *Annual Review of Anthropology* 43): 53–69.

Jung, Moon-Kie. 2015. *Beneath the Surface of White Supremacy: Denaturalizing US Racisms Past and Present*. Stanford, CA: Stanford University Press.

Lyons, Carrie Newton. 2007. "The State Secrets Privilege: Expanding Its Scope through Government Misuse." *Lewis and Clark Law Review* 11: 99–132.

Mandel, Daniel. 2001. "Muslims on the Silver Screen." *Middle East Quarterly* 8: 19–30.

Masco, Joseph. 2014. *Theater of Operations: National Security Affect from the Cold War to the War on Terror*. Durham, NC: Duke University Press.

Mills, Charles. 2007. "White Ignorance." In *Race and Epistemologies of Ignorance*, edited by Shannon Sullivan and Nancy Tuana. Albany: State University of New York Press.

Modood, Tariq. 2005. *Multicultural Politics: Racism, Ethnicity and Muslims in Britain*. Minneapolis: University of Minnesota Press.

Mookherjee, Nayanika. 2006. "'Remembering to Forget': Public Secrecy and Memory of Sexual Violence in the Bangladesh War of 1971." *Journal of the Royal Anthropological Institute* 12, no. 2: 433–50.

Muhammad, Khalil Gibran. 2011. *The Condemnation of Blackness*. Cambridge, MA: Harvard University Press.

Penglase, Ben. 2009. "States of Insecurity: Everyday Emergencies, Public Secrets, and Drug Trafficker Power in a Brazilian Favela." *PoLAR: Political and Legal Anthropology Review* 32, no. 1: 47–63.

Rana, Junaid. 2011. *Terrifying Muslims: Race and Labor in the South Asian Diaspora*. Durham, NC: Duke University Press Books.

Roy, Srila. 2008. "The Grey Zone: The 'Ordinary' Violence of Extraordinary Times." *Journal of the Royal Anthropological Institute* 14, no. 2: 316–33.

Said, Edward. 1978. *Orientalism*. New York: Pantheon.

Selod, Saher, and David G. Embrick. 2013. "Racialization and Muslims: Situating the Muslim Experience in Race Scholarship." *Sociology Compass* 7, no. 8: 644–55.

Shaheen, Jack G. 2008. *Guilty: Hollywood's Verdict on Arabs after 9/11*. New York: Olive Branch Press.

Simmel, Georg. 1950. *The Sociology of Georg Simmel*, translated and edited by K. Wolff, 345–70. London: Free Press.

Spillers, Hortense J. 1987. "Mama's Baby, Papa's Maybe: An American Grammar Book." *diacritics* 17, no. 2: 65–81.

Sullivan, Shannon, and Nancy Tuana, eds. 2007. *Race and Epistemologies of Ignorance*. Albany: State University of New York Press.

Taussig, Michael T. 1999. *Defacement: Public Secrecy and the Labor of the Negative*. Stanford, CA: Stanford University Press.

Theidon, Kimberly. 2006. "The Mask and the Mirror: Facing Up to the Past in Postwar Peru." *Anthropologica*: 87–100.

Thomas, Deborah A. 2017. "Public Secrets, Militarization, and the Cultivation of Doubt: Kingston 2010." In *Caribbean Military Encounters*, edited by Shalini Puri and Lara Putnam, 289–309. New York: Palgrave Macmillan.

Weheliye, Alexander G. 2014. *Habeas viscus: Racializing Assemblages, Biopolitics, and Black Feminist Theories of the Human*. Durham, NC: Duke University Press.

Wynter, Sylvia. 1989. "Beyond the Word of Man: Glissant and the New Discourse of the Antilles." *World Literature Today* 63, no. 4: 637–48.

Zagel, James. 1965. "The State Secrets Privilege." *Minnesota Law Review* 50: 875–910.

21

Geographies of Blackness
in Guantánamo Memoirs

Darryl Li

MOHAMMED AL-GORANI WAS FOURTEEN when he first arrived at Guantánamo Bay, in shackles. It was also the first time he was exposed to the n-word. For in the eyes of his captors, al-Gorani was racially distinct from the other Muslims: he was born in Medina, Saudi Arabia, but his family came from Chad (figure 21.1).[1] That difference could also occasion familiarity: once al-Gorani became conversant in English, some of the friendlier guards nicknamed him "Chris Tucker" due to a resemblance to the famous comedian and actor. One of them was a former boxer from Louisiana whom the captives called "Mike Tyson." Al-Gorani later recounted this exchange they had:

"Brother, look at my face!" he said. "How long you've been here with Americans?"
"Four years."
"I've been suffering 27 years, man! I know what it is. They put my brother in jail for no reason, instead of a white guy." Most of the people in jail in the United States are Blacks, he told me. "My grandfather and my great-grandfather were in the situation you're in now." He meant they were slaves, shackled like us (el Gorani and Tubiana 2011).

Al-Gorani's narration of this encounter across Blackness, between an African and an American, begins with a demand for recognition as kin grounded in a genealogy of captivity. For "Tyson," al-Gorani's incarceration at GTMO occasions reflection on his own life,[2] a point of connection as well as comparison. It is a scene of sympathy, even if not solidarity—they are, after all, still captor and captive. But the conspiratorial undertones of this exchange invoke a shared Blackness against the forces of white supremacy to which they both relate. Moreover, Tyson's interest in Islam is piqued when he notices older non-Black captives readily following al-Gorani in prayer in recognition of his superior knowledge of the Quran, which he had memorized as a child. Thus, their bond is rendered fraternal twice over when Tyson communicates his intention to accept Islam and leave the military.

This encounter is a reminder of the multitudes and slippages that may be gathered under the sign of Blackness, for the two are heirs to very different histories of race-making. Al-Gorani's grandparents were among the West African Muslim pilgrim-cum-migrants in the Arabian Peninsula whose numbers swelled in the first half of the twentieth century (Miran 2015). Like other migrants, West Africans have for generations been excluded from Saudi citizenship and its accompanying welfare benefits. Hence al-Gorani had to seek schooling in Pakistan, where he was captured by local authorities and sold off to the Americans. And while al-Gorani may not lay claim to Arabia's history of slavery, that history nonetheless marked him throughout childhood whenever he encountered the slur ʿabīd (slave) (Tubiana and Franc 2019, 9). African migrants are often racialized as Black alongside the Arabian Peninsula's comparably numerous creolized (muwallad) descendants of enslaved Africans, even if the two groups may not share a strongly developed racial consciousness.[3] Yet not all anti-Black interpolations work in the same way: the n-word operates in a settler colonial context that takes for granted a historical equation between Blackness and slavery, while the emergence of "slave" as the epithet of choice in Arabic-speaking societies implicitly recognizes the fragility of this equation and seeks to violently reassert it.[4]

This chapter focuses on the figure of the Black captive through narrations of GTMO: not only the relatively small proportion of captives held there who would be considered Black under US racial regimes,[5] but also invocations of Blackness and slavery in broader discourses around the prison. In the wake of the War on Terror, there has been much commentary on how white supremacy construes the Muslim as a racialized threat, fixating on populations attributed to the Middle East and South Asia regardless of actual religious or communal affiliation (Kazi 2018; Rana 2011). Yet the broad drive to racialize Muslimness— often an attempt to distort universalist projects that invoke Islam as idiom (Li 2020)—conscripts, collides with, and reconfigures other regimes and logics of racialization. These include diverse geographies of Blackness across Muslim-majority societies outside of the Anglophone Atlantic, where white supremacy's effects are unevenly mediated and where the salience of Blackness as a category of social organization can neither be presumed nor dismissed—where it is, as Katherine McKittrick described in a different context, "an absented presence" (Hudson 2014, 235). Ignoring this reality risks reductively positioning Muslimness and Blackness as monolithic and mutually exclusive, or even opposed, categories. Accounting for the slippages and tensions between geographies of racialization is also crucial to understanding both the apparent global ubiquity of white supremacy and the sheer diversity of its manifestations.

This chapter proposes captivity as an analytical method for untangling and relating distinct and cross-cutting forms of racialization, and specifically of Blackness, under the War on Terror. Captivity is a relation of holding, one that entails both immobilization and forced mobility together in the passage from one context to another. And captivity breeds its own forms of self-awareness and narration that deeply inflect knowledge production and theorization of captivity as it invariably proceeds from a position of exteriority; captivity is often grasped through the stories told about it. Thus, this chapter employs the rubric of captive passages to highlight this process of racialization-as-transformation through both movement and storytelling.[6]

FIGURE 21.1. Mohammed al-Gorani, as photographed for *Vanity Fair*. Photograph courtesy of Mathias Braschler. "A Guantánamo Portfolio," *Vanity Fair*, January 11, 2012, accessed October 26, 2021. www.vanityfair.com/news/photos/2012/01/guantanamo-portrait -slideshow-201201. In this chapter, I have elected not to use any mug shots or other images generated by apparatuses of captivity.

Tyson and al-Gorani's encounter helpfully brings to light so much of what has been occluded in two decades of commentary occasioned by GTMO. Critics have insisted that the War on Terror must be situated in a genealogy of colonialism and white supremacy (Bonilla 2013; Kaplan 2005), in which racialized chattel slavery plays a foundational and constitutive role. Accordingly, scholars have highlighted parallels between racialized violence in domestic US policing and prisons and in extraterritorial detention sites such as GTMO and elsewhere (Daulatzai 2007); explored the circuits of expertise, personnel, and techniques connecting them (Ralph 2020, 143–77); and drawn attention to the base's previous life as an internment camp for Haitian asylum seekers in the 1990s (Kahn 2019). All of this is welcome and necessary, especially against the broader public tendency to portray the prison as exceptional ("un-American") in ways that perversely celebrated the white supremacist carceral state on the mainland—a tendency left unchallenged by the most widely cited conscriptions of GTMO for the purposes of "theory." In contrast, this chapter proposes thinking *with* captivity—instead of the more common move of thinking *from* it, using paradigmatic sites of confinement (The Prison, The Camp) as tropes for theorizing power more broadly.[7]

Captivity can provide a useful measure of precision and care situating the War on Terror's anti-Muslim animus in relation to both histories and presence of white supremacy and anti-Black racism, from slavery to the contemporary prison. Ever looser analogies between the War on Terror and racialized chattel slavery (Rowlandson 2010; Wright 2013) risk reinscribing US-centered understandings of race that obscure crucial aspects of Washington's global hegemony while also conjuring the specter of slavery as a prop that sidelines actually existing Black struggles (Sexton and Lee 2006). Moreover, the conversation above reminds us that the categories of Blackness and Islam are constituted in very different ways across contexts—an insight key to long-standing bodies of scholarship on slavery in Muslim-majority societies in Africa (El-Hamel 2013; Hall 2011; Ware 2014); on Black Muslims in the West (Abdul Khabeer 2016; Rouse 2004); on racialization and Blackness in North Africa, Southwest Asia, and farther afield (Baghoolizadeh 2018; Curtis 2014; Troutt Powell 2012); and on internationalism and Third Worldism (Azeb 2019; Lubin 2014). The debates around GTMO thus are symptomatic of a broader challenge posed by traditions of theory that grapple with the centrality of Atlantic chattel slavery to the constitution of capitalist modernity: how can Black thought travel—and in doing so reconfigure the place of the universal—without being tokenized as a generic stand-in for all forms of racialized violence? Just as the conditions of production for (white) theory and Black thought are not equal, so too are the stakes of their (mis/ab)use. As one possible response to this challenge, this chapter begins from the proposition that slavery presupposes captivity but not all captives are slaves: this elementary principle guides the attempt here to connect diverse forms of racialization.

The turn to memoir and other public discourse represents an ethnographic response to the particularity of my own various engagements in research and activism over the past two decades. I have interviewed, corresponded with, and otherwise interacted with a half-dozen survivors of GTMO and an even greater number of victims of other US extraterritorial detention practices. Many of these conversations arose during two years as part of a team representing a man held at the base in habeas corpus proceedings (Li 2020, 19–21). I am currently an expert consultant for another captive facing capital charges before the military commissions there. This legal work is governed by multiple regimes of secrecy. As a result, those cases and the materials in them are not discussed in this chapter. Instead of undertaking to represent my own experiences concerning GTMO, I hope to process them through exploring cultural production by and around former captives.

But beyond questions of constraint are motivations shaped by racial disaffection arising from liberal advocacy spaces and their background condition of compulsory whiteness.

I have on more occasions than I can count sat in on conversations where participants decried GTMO as an aberrant aspect of US carceral practice and extolled the alternative of prosecution in regular courts on the mainland as the "gold standard" for justice, thereby erasing the deeply racialized violence of the domestic legal system.[8] And yet, my attempts to speak about the War on Terror's underpinnings in white supremacy generally went unheard or, better yet, *unattended to*. As a middle-class person of East Asian origin, I enjoy neither the presumptive authority of whiteness (despite benefiting from proximity to it in other ways) nor the fraught and highly conditional deference afforded to categories officially recognized as aggrieved under the logic of liberalism (here, those racialized as Muslim) (Lee 2021). Being "in the room" but not necessarily "at the table" thus afforded a peculiar vantage point on racialization in the War on Terror that this chapter attempts to share.

The Muse (or Ruse) of GTMO

Some twenty years after it opened as a spectacle intended to intimidate foes abroad and placate a vengeful citizenry at home, Guantánamo arguably remains the most infamous site of captivity in the world. Indeed, GTMO is now older than some of the thirty (at the time of this writing) remaining captives were when they first arrived, older than some of the guards serving there today. The prison has stubbornly defied attempts at both closure and expansion, from Barack Obama's much-heralded 2009 executive order to shutter it "as soon as practicable, and no later than 1 year from [this] date" to Donald Trump's campaign promise to "load it up with some bad dudes" (Weigel 2016).[9] GTMO endures, zombie-like, going through motions without movement, going nowhere fast; not going away, but hardly a going concern to the outside world.

GTMO has also cast a long shadow over theorizations of state power. Perhaps most prominent has been Giorgio Agamben's notion of *the camp* as the spatialization of sovereign exception, which was particularly fashionable in the first decade of the War on Terror (Agamben 1998; Agamben 2005). Meanwhile, debates over the availability of the writ of habeas corpus (Latin, "you shall have the body") for GTMO captives also inspired Alexander Weheliye's influential coinage *habeas viscus* ("you shall have the flesh"), which retheorizes notions of biopolitics by elaborating a distinction between the categories of body and flesh (Miller and Driscoll 2015; Weheliye 2014). This formulation has been fruitful in treating processes of racialization as central to biopolitics—*contra* Foucault and Agamben—while also expanding the theorization of emancipatory and fugitive possibilities.

If GTMO was an inspiration for *Habeas Viscus*, we can circle back to thinking about this prison by discerning within it the outlines of a theory of captivity. The first step would be to interrogate that which remains common to the formulations habeas corpus and *habeas viscus*: What is the nature of this "having," of the verb *habere*? Here, the argument subtly shifts from captivity to enslavement as modalities of racialization. Weheliye observes that despite its occasional utility to the oppressed, habeas corpus nonetheless entails "accepting the codification of personhood as property, which is, in turn, based on the comparative distinction between groups" (2014, 77). To illustrate this point, he turns to the notorious

1857 US Supreme Court case *Dred Scott v. Sandford*, noting that its well-known exclusion of Black people from citizenship also relied on a contrast with Native Americans as conditionally assimilable. For Weheliye, *Dred Scott* is an example of the "racializing juridical assemblage that differentially produces both black and native subjects as aberrations from Man and thus not-quite-human" (2014, 79).

Yet notwithstanding Weheliye's gloss of the Supreme Court as having "invalidated Dred Scott's habeas corpus" (2014, 78), it is worth noting that as a matter of law, habeas corpus was not at issue in the case at all.[10] By the mid-nineteenth century, most states, especially those in the South, had *already* barred the use of habeas to challenge individual cases of "unlawful" enslavement (Kull 2004, 1279). As one Southern jurist put it, "The reason for denying slaves the benefit of *habeas corpus*, is manifest. They are property as well as persons, and if they could be discharged from bondage by a judge . . . the owner might be deprived of property without . . . trial by jury" (quoted in Westley 2016, 63). The more common approach—and the one Dred Scott and his wife Harriet used—was to file a lawsuit for trespass vi et armis ("by force of arms"), a tort whose contemporary analogues would be battery and false imprisonment (Kennington 2017, 27–28).[11] The distinction between juridical forms here is revealing: as anyone who has been made to feel they are always in the wrong place knows well, it is trespass even more than habeas that highlights the fraught entanglement between personhood and property that Weheliye ascribes to law more generally. Trespass vi et armis suits conceptualize personhood as property; the dispute in cases of enslavement was merely over whether claimants could also claim legal "ownership" over themselves and by extension their labor (the form of domination reserved mostly for white proletarians). Compared to habeas, trespass was a far more amenable juridical framework in which to inscribe the privatized power of the slave relation.

Weheliye's warning against liberal legality as a means of achieving freedom remains well placed, but his resort to habeas corpus as a lens to read *Dred Scott* inadvertently highlights the usefulness of conceptually disentangling personhood from property and, by extension, captivity from slavery as distinct modalities of racialization. As Walter Rodney observed, "Strictly speaking, the African only became a slave when he reached a society where he worked as a slave. Before that, he was first a free man and then a captive" (2011, 95). Rodney's insight that captivity is logically antecedent to enslavement is helpful for revisiting Hortense Spillers's distinction between body and flesh, to which Weheliye is openly indebted. Spillers—who repeatedly speaks of the "captive body" and "captivity" as synonyms for enslaved persons and slavery—called flesh a "zero degree of social conceptualization," or a "primary narrative" necessarily antecedent to the category of body (1987, 67). In the same spirit as the move backward from body to flesh, we can reach past the ambiguous "having" of habeas to captivity as a zero degree of social conceptualization. Thinking about captivity (from *capere*, "to seize") allows us to mark the zone of temporal and conceptual transition that often—but not always—led to slavery. As from *corpus* back to *viscus*, so too from *habere* back to *capere*.

Captivity can be thought of as a relation of *holding* and is, as of that moment, nothing more. There is no legitimacy or permanency attached, no reconfiguration of subjectivity as of yet in the potentiality of the "zero degree." Oftentimes the choice to call someone a "captive" rather than a "detainee," "prisoner," or "slave" draws attention to the mere facticity of constraint but also its unnaturalness and serves to deny any further normalization to that status. This is why a useful theory of captivity should resist becoming like discipline or sovereignty, a generalized model for power in society; captivity is not uncommon, but it is also not ubiquitous—or if it is, then there are other problems at work. Similarly, captivity's "commitment to contact" is a helpful counterpoint to the more general focus on precarity and abandonment in theorizations of power (O'Neill and Dua 2017, 7). Far from eschewing slavery or racialization, attending to captivity can help refine our tools for theorizing the relationships between these subjects and many others. The passage from GTMO to *Dred Scott* and back spans an enormous racial geography, including different contexts of Blackness.

Captivity implies mobility: someone is taken, often across great geographical and cultural distances, transported in the grip of another. There are echoes of this spatial sensibility in the procedural terminology of habeas corpus litigation: the captor's response to a petition, which furnishes the reasons for detention, is called a *return*. The reply from the captive's side is a *traverse*.[12] Highlighting the mobility in captivity—"the logic of the *passages themselves*" (Rodriguez 2006, 224; italics in original)—requires us to follow captives from the point of taking through their peregrinations of unfreedom, which may be difficult to distinguish from other forms of migration or movement. While liberal notions of freedom imply movement that is also strictly ordered (Kotef 2015), we can say the converse about captivity: it is a form of enforced stillness that is almost always set into motion by others. Movement is a practice of both space-making and racialization (McKittrick 2006; Gilmore 2002). Here, the history of Atlantic slavery as a paradigmatic form of captivity is illuminating—the holding of captivity becomes spatialized as "the hold" in the belly of the slave ship (Sharpe 2016, 73–75). GTMO is too often regarded in spectacular isolation, as a terminus, or for Agamben simply as fulfillment of ontological potentiality, rather than as a node in a broader global network of carceral circulation (Li 2018). Captives there arrived after spending time in other sites run by the Pentagon or the CIA, or held by client states, bounty hunters, and other actors; too many of those who have left have only moved on to new situations of unfreedom, be it prisons, house arrest, or even deportation and further pursuit.

Moreover, captivity cannot be understood apart from its contexts of narration, through the spectacle of captivation and the question of freedom. Narration produced inside of captivity posits freedom as interiority; narration from the outside, the afterward (or afterword) of captivity, presupposes freedom but also queries its own tenuous conditions. As Joy James notes, such narrations are themselves "border crossings" since "enslavement is manufactured in the 'free' world; 'freedom' is imagined and created in the slave world. Where the two worlds meet . . . there is a border crossing, an intermingling of subordinate and dominant narratives" (2005, xxxii). Such crossings also necessarily entail a "relation of appropriation and translation" structurally dominated by interlocutors outside conditions of captivity (Rodriguez 2006, 37). In this regard, letter-writing from captivity has historically been key as a "collective world-making praxis" (Burton 2021), imbued with powerful intimacies (Luk 2018). Because GTMO captives are permitted to write letters only to attorneys and family members (and even then under strict controls), this chapter attends to a more public form of narration and captivation in the form of the memoir. It is here that we must attend to the cultural production undertaken by and in the name of GTMO captives: nearly all of what has emerged in the West, be it memoir, poetry, or art, has been produced under the gaze of white liberal audiences and often by white ghostwriters, editors, and artists.[13] With such conditions in mind, I will use two captivity memoirs to trace an arc for thinking about Blackness and GTMO within the Atlantic world and then moving away from it. One is arguably the best-known memoir in the West, the other one of the least.

Slavery without Race?

Mohamedou Ould Slahi is arguably the most famous survivor of GTMO. He was held captive from 2002 to 2016 and subjected to a prolonged torture program that was individually tailored for him and personally approved by the US secretary of defense. The measures were so extreme that one of the military lawyers assigned to prosecute him resigned in protest. Ould Slahi was never charged with a crime; indeed, he even won his habeas corpus hearing in 2010, only for the decision to be overturned on appeal by the Obama administration. During his time in captivity, Ould Slahi learned English and wrote a memoir of his experiences by hand. After seven years of litigation, that manuscript was declassified in 2012—with thousands of black redaction marks, ranging from single words to whole pages—and released to the media. Larry Siems, a white American human rights activist and editor, then condensed and rearranged the text and published it in 2015 under the title *Guantánamo Diary*. Heavily promoted by the American Civil Liberties Union (ACLU), the book became an international best seller and was translated into several languages. The following year Ould Slahi was finally repatriated to his homeland, Mauritania. A lengthy 2019 profile of Ould Slahi in the *New Yorker*, which focused on his friendship with one of his guards from GTMO, won a Pulitzer Prize. His story was the basis of the 2021 Hollywood film *The Mauritanian*, starring Jodie Foster, Benedict Cumberbatch, and Tahar Rahim; the same year, Ould Slahi and Siems coauthored a young adult novel loosely based on his family's history as desert nomads. Ould Slahi has remained an eager interlocutor; he readily makes himself available to journalists and researchers and has contributed essays to academic journals and edited volumes.

After years of strenuous and exhausting public debate on the use of torture in the War on Terror, *Guantánamo Diary* arrived at a moment of renewed attention among some white publics to the emergent Movement for Black Lives after the 2014 uprising in Ferguson, Missouri. In this context, the reception of Ould Slahi's story has in some respects been reminiscent of nineteenth-century American abolitionist discourses. Ould Slahi himself invokes slavery at several points in his narrative. "I often compared myself with a slave. Slaves were taken forcibly from Africa, and so was I. Slaves were sold a couple of times on

FIGURE 21.2. Mohamedou Ould Slahi. Photograph by the ACLU. This image is taken from a video Ould Slahi recorded for the ACLU soon after returning home from GTMO. In it, he expressed forgiveness to all those who wronged him in his captivity and hoped that "the good American people will realize that holding innocent people in prison is not the way to go." ACLU, "First Video of Author Mohamedou Slahi after Release from Gitmo," YouTube video, October 28, 2016, accessed October 26, 2021, www.youtube.com/watch?v=R _KkkwlLBWY. Photograph by the ACLU.

their way to their final destination, and so was I. Slaves suddenly were assigned to some-body they didn't choose, and so was I" (Ould Slahi 2015, 314). The *New Yorker* elaborated on this comparison at length in a piece by a white editor of Harriet Jacobs's family papers (Korb 2015), and the theme has been prominent in the cottage industry of English litera-ture scholars analyzing the memoir (Coundouriotis 2020; Goyal 2017; Swanson and Moore 2021). Here, it is useful to revisit these invocations through an analytical lens of captivity that highlights shifting contexts of racialization and narration.

The specter of slavery in discussions of *Guantánamo Diary* has lurked alongside a certain disavowal of race and specifically of Blackness—or rather, one could say that it identifies racism only to situate it in an antebellum past, thereby seasoning American exceptionalism with a dose of self-critique. Indeed, it is the continuities between contemporary forms of racialized state violence in GTMO and on the US mainland that are far easier to grasp than an imaginary path back to the slave plantation. Most prominent in Ould Slahi's case was his experience at the hands of a particularly vicious interrogator, Richard Zuley, who was also a Chicago police officer notorious for torturing Black men. Several years after leaving GTMO, Ould Slahi was interviewed by the anthropologist Laurence Ralph for his book on police torture in Chicago. Ralph was interested in Zuley's story as a way to explore the connections between state violence in the domestic United States and in places like GTMO, thereby building out a richer transnational analysis of white supremacy. But there is a striking moment of disjuncture in the text, when Ralph, in an open letter ad-dressed to Ould Slahi, recounts, "You cautioned me against highlighting your religion and the race of people in Chicago as a way to contextualize torture" (2020, 164). According to Ralph, Ould Slahi opined that "such practices are human nature more than anything else. I wouldn't emphasize race or religious background. I think we humans can't handle having power as well as one might think" (164).

Locating Ould Slahi within his Mauritanian context may shed some more light on his reticence about racism. Mauritania is perhaps best known internationally as the last country to formally abolish slavery, in 1981, yet the practice endures there (and in neighboring Mali) as part of a continuum of relationships of servitude and clientelism that stand outside the model of free labor that has become hegemonic in capitalist societies. Slavery and its afterlives have been deeply racialized in Mauritania, albeit in ways very different from what emerged in the Western Hemisphere (Brhane 1997; Esseissah 2019; McDougall 2015; Wiley 2018). Phenotypical assumptions about what constitutes Blackness in North America do not readily apply. While Blackness was already stigmatized as a precondition of enslaveability throughout the western Sahara on the eve of formal colonial rule in the nineteenth century (Hall 2011),[14] the salience of Blackness as a category for social self-identification or even of institutionalized repression remains uneven at best in the face of other structuring antagonisms around lineage, language, and religion.

Nonetheless, it is fair to say that Ould Slahi does not identify as a descendant of slaves, nor is he in the Mauritanian context racially stigmatized with the mark of Blackness—he is, in local terms, white (*bīḍānī*). He hails from the Idab Lahcen, one of the prominent *zawāyā* tribes known for its Islamic learning. Ould Slahi was born in 1970 during an extended period of drought that impoverished and forcibly urbanized nomadic populations like his family. It also crippled many masters' ability to provide for and retain slaves, thus easing the way to formal abolition. As Ould Slahi told me during a Skype conversation in 2018,

> When I was young I was against slavery. A slave is someone owned by someone else. You don't have rights and you are completely subjugated to the will and whims of the master. But slavery is better than being kidnapped by the USA. Because a slave could marry, a slave could have a life, a slave could escape, a slave could have fun or could have the day off.

Here, Ould Slahi was referring not to the racialized chattel slavery that built the Western Hemisphere but rather to ideological representations of slavery as practiced in his lifetime in Mauritania. Whatever its merits as a form of generalization, it is a reminder that Western attempts to analogize Ould Slahi's experiences to those of slavery only make sense through effacing the Mauritanian context. The silences on racial categories are significant and indeed extend beyond Ould Slahi's analysis of Mauritania. When discussing slavery and GTMO, he references the United States capturing "Africans" from both sides of the Sahara, rather than Black people in particular (Ould Slahi 2015; Ould Slahi 2020). Here, "Africa stands in for race but yet, paradoxically, race does not exist in Africa" (Pierre 2012, xii–xiii).

Yet while Ould Slahi's understanding of slavery comes out of Mauritanian conversations, those conversations are themselves inflected by discourses about slavery and abolition emanating from the United States, albeit refracted in unexpected ways. After the publication of *Guantánamo Diary*, the Mauritanian historian and Islamist activist Sid'Amar Ould Cheikhna—himself a former political prisoner—wrote a newspaper article comparing Ould Slahi to Kunta Kinte, the fictionalized eighteenth-century protagonist of Alex Haley's novel *Roots*. In a not-so-subtle critique of the previous regime's cooperation with the US security apparatus, Ould Cheikhna (2015) highlighted the role of local collaborators who "stabbed Mohamedou Ould Slahi in the back, just as their forefathers did to Kunta Kinte and to thousands of tormented Africans, a tradition firmly rooted in the coasts of Africa for centuries."[15] Ould Cheikhna's narration of Kunta Kinte's life before his kidnapping by "white pirates" (*al-qarāṣina al-bīḍ*) stages racial antagonism as a purely external dynamic. He describes Kunta Kinte as the son of an Arab man and a Mandinka woman. Both of these identities are glossed in terms of tribe (*qabīla*). However, Kunta Kinte's father is further described not using the local idiom of white/*bīḍānī*, but instead anachronistically as "Mauritanian." His mother has no nationality attributed to her at all. Neither is described in racial terms. Ould Cheikhna thus casts Kunta Kinte as an icon of nationalist, multiethnic, raceless-but-non-white, anticolonial solidarity that leaves contemporary racial and gender hierarchies in Mauritanian society undisturbed.

Decontextualized readings of Ould Slahi's story through the lens of Atlantic slavery serve to obscure crucial aspects of his captivity. Among the first things dropped from most engagements with *Guantánamo Diary* are the many layers of contemporary US imperialism that do not translate easily into morality plays about torture, which depend on having white protagonists (Li 2015). Notwithstanding the book's title, nearly a third of the account covers the eight months Ould Slahi was captive in prisons other than GTMO, in Mauritania, Jordan, and Afghanistan. Even before 9/11, Ould Slahi was already caught up in various forms of transnational policing and detention: in early 2000 he was arrested while transiting through Dakar and interrogated by US agents there before being sent home to Mauritania for several additional weeks of questioning. Yet these proxy jailers—as well as Germany and Canada, where Ould Slahi lived under surveillance for years—are largely erased in discussions of *Guantánamo Diary*, to the extent that Ould Slahi even remarked on this omission in the Hollywood film (Farooq 2021).

Ould Slahi's compulsive narration—with all of the limitations and occlusions of the white liberal gaze to which it is oriented (see figure 21.2)—is also a survival strategy. When he returned home, the Mauritanian state denied Ould Slahi a passport or identity papers that would allow him to work in his native land, thanks to a secret agreement with the United States. Seeking to avoid the fate of so many other GTMO survivors who have suffered penury, further imprisonment, or worse, Ould Slahi is an active social media user who has used his contacts in the West to stay in the public eye. He is at this point arguably the most prominent Mauritanian in the world, buying himself some leverage with the government. This compulsion to narrate is itself a condition of captivity and grew out of his interrogation: the manuscript that made him so famous was written on pen and paper provided to Ould Slahi after he was tortured into providing false statements implicating fellow captives and thereby deemed "cooperative." His memoir can be read as an act of penance for harms he was forced to inflict as much as a denunciation of those who harmed him.

A Heart of Lightness

If thinking of captivity in terms of passages—both mobility and narration—helps us to read Mohamedou Ould Slahi's story against the grain of its liberal appropriation, then doing so illuminates shifting forms of racialization in narratives that circulate in very different publics. We can see this in *The Slaughter in the Fort and the Depths of Guantánamo*, the first memoir published by a GTMO survivor in what was probably the most commonly spoken language among those held at the camp, namely, Arabic.[16] Its author, Walid Muhammad al-Hajj, was imprisoned without charge from 2002 to 2008 before being repatriated to Sudan (figure 21.3).

That al-Hajj's book speaks to a very different kind of audience than memoirs published in the West is apparent even in the title, which holds GTMO equally noteworthy as "the slaughter in the fort," an episode that takes up the first—and arguably more vivid—half of the text. In November 2001, the US-aligned warlord Abdul Rashid Dostum moved some 400 prisoners of diverse nationalities to his headquarters in Qala'-i-Jangi, a nineteenth-century fortress in northern Afghanistan. The captives rose up and overpowered their guards; a CIA officer was killed in the melee, the first US casualty of the invasion. Enduring aerial bombardment, starvation, thirst, and fatigue for nearly a week, they surrendered after Dostum's men flooded the catacombs beneath the fort. Only eighty-six survived. Some of the men were later locked in shipping containers and left to die in the desert. Others, like al-Hajj, were eventually sent to GTMO.

Al-Hajj's text is sprinkled with references to the second person: "Oh reader, can you imagine," begins many a description of horrific treatment he endured. The audience is conjured as Muslim, pious, and in solidarity with other Muslims around the world—it is also not a negligible one, as his nearly 60,000 Twitter followers (twice those of Ould Slahi) suggest. The book makes no claim to innocence in the terms of liberal legality. Indeed, al-Hajj is a thoroughly illiberal subject: he portrays the United States as a country controlled by Jews and whose moral decay is symbolized by its apparent tolerance of homosexuality (Ḥājj 2009, 128–29). Al-Hajj's forms of resistance do not conform to the trope of the victim who endures their suffering with the quiet grace that asserts a shared humanity with their tormentors; rather, he writes gleefully of how he and other captives would fling their urine and feces (the latter they called "nuclear weapons") at guards (Ḥājj 2009, 146–47), employing projectiles literally abjected from processes of the flesh.

Like Ould Slahi, al-Hajj hailed from a country that was often simplistically regarded from the outside as being divided between an "Arab" north oppressing an "African" south. Unlike Ould Slahi, however, al-Hajj is racialized as Black while abroad—but the meaning of that Blackness and its relationship to Arabness shift considerably across contexts of captivity. Al-Hajj refers to himself as an Arab and to his skin as *asmar*, which means brown but is also a euphemism for black (*aswad*). He hails from Artigasha Island in the Nile River and belongs to the Danagla, a Nubian community historically settled in northern Sudan. The Ottoman-Egyptian conquest in the nineteenth century fragmented and marketized agricultural holdings and spurred the rise of new labor-intensive irrigation techniques.

FIGURE 21.3. Walid al-Hajj at a press conference in Khartoum after his return to Sudan. Photograph courtesy of the Associated Press.

These changes drove many Danagla to migrate as merchants and slave traders, selling captives taken from other parts of Sudan to work on Danaglan lands (Serels 2013, 16–22; Sikainga 1996, 13–18). Well represented in Sudan's commercial networks and state institutions since then, Danagla have historically been both agents and objects of projects of cultural Arabization (Sharkey 2007).

Al-Hajj's genealogy and biography are consistent with long-standing patterns of Danagla labor migration, which is also a rite of manhood of sorts (Khogali 1991). As a child, he "got used to the sounds of buses and lorries going to and from Khartoum with dates or

Egyptian beans, and the sounds of the souq and the shouts of selling and animals and carts" (Ḥājj 2009, 7). For most of al-Hajj's childhood, his father was also working abroad, in Egypt, Lebanon, and Kuwait. Soon after al-Hajj's father resettled in Sudan, the son migrated as well. He spent several years doing odd jobs in Saudi Arabia before joining Islamic proselytizing efforts (da'wa) in Pakistan and then Afghanistan in late 1999 during the first period of Taliban rule. There, he decided to travel for jihad after being moved by stories of rape and sexual assault of Muslim women in Chechnya. In search of basic military training, al-Hajj joined the Taliban front lines in Khwaja Ghar in the far north, the site of some of the most intense fighting with opposition factions.

By October 2001 those factions had gained the upper hand, with the assistance of US airstrikes and commandos paving the way for a full-fledged foreign occupation of Afghanistan. After several weeks of relentless bombing, al-Hajj was part of a group of fighters, including Afghans and Muslims of many other nationalities, trapped in the city of Mazar-i Sharif and surrounded by Dostum's forces. The local Taliban commander negotiated safe passage out on the condition of giving up their weapons. The terms of the agreement, however, covered only Afghans, Pakistanis, and Uzbeks—Dostum insisted on excluding Arabs, mindful that Washington was putting out bounties on them as suspected al-Qa'ida operatives (Ḥājj 2009, 28–29). The concession seemed harmless enough: the plan was simply for the Arabs to blend in by wearing Afghan garb and keeping their mouths shut.

Unfortunately, things quickly fell apart, for not all Arabs could pass as Afghan with the same ease. Al-Hajj, as the only dark-skinned (asmar) person in the group, was concerned that his racialized conspicuousness would expose not only himself but all of the other Arabs. He did his best to shroud his face in Afghan garb, to redact his appearance. But on inspection by Dostum's troops, his fears came true when they "tore off my veil [lithām] and in shock at my dark skin, started shouting 'An Arab! An Arab!'" (Ḥājj 2009, 38). The act of exposure is also an act of gendered ordering: in prevailing dress codes that sought to absent women's faces from public spaces, al-Hajj's attempt to cover his visage stands out as anomalous and attracts scrutiny. As blows rained down on him, desperate attempts to convince his captors that he was Baluchi fell on deaf ears.[17] Following Weheliye's reading of Spillers, we can mark this moment of recognition and capture as an etching of the "hieroglyphics of the flesh"—where the phenotypical signification of flesh as Black subjectivizes al-Hajj as possessing a body marked as Arab (Weheliye 2014, 39–40). In a twist on the famous "Look! A Negro!" passage in Fanon's Black Skin, White Masks (2008, 89–92), epidermalization here takes place not in the grid of defining Blackness in a relationship of inferiority to whiteness, but rather of Blackness as indexing Arabness in Afghan eyes—a more ambivalent form of alterity.[18]

On the very next page of al-Hajj's memoir, the valence of Blackness shifts dramatically. The captives are taken to Qala'-i-Jangi, and whiteness descends. A CNN camera crew swarms with fascination toward the "American Taliban," John Walker Lindh, while a towering CIA officer with a machine gun slung over his shoulder begins cataloging the men collected in the courtyard of the fort. On his knees in shackles, al-Hajj faces a barrage of questions in English: What's your name? Where are you from? Unsure about how to reply and not wanting to give away his Arabness, al-Hajj suddenly remembers that he is fluent (*ajāda*) in Nubian, "the language of my Danagla ancestors." *What's your age?* He responds with a torrent of the vilest Nubian curses he can conjure, prompting chuckles from the other captives, who understand all too well that al-Hajj is toying with the befuddled CIA man. *Are you Nigerian? From Mali? Sudanese?* More profanities. Exasperated, the American scrawls "African" in his notebook and moves on (Ḥājj 2009, 39).

However much al-Hajj may have relished this small triumph—far from the only moment of levity in his memoir—it also hinged on the persistent ambiguity that Sudanese face in global and regional regimes of racialization. For while al-Hajj and many Danagla may assert their Arabness to the exclusion of being "African" and "Black" while inside Sudan, outside of the country it is their Arabness that is often rendered suspect or precarious due to an association with those very categories. This shaped the subtext of a 2010 interview al-Hajj gave to prominent Egyptian journalist Ahmed Mansour on Al Jazeera television. As al-Hajj lightheartedly narrates the story of taunting the CIA man, Mansour's eyes widen in captivation. He invites al-Hajj to "talk to us a little in Nubian." Al-Hajj demurs with a smile—"nah, let's just drop it" (*lā lā, khalīhā shwayya*).[19] He avers that he was only stringing Nubian words together rather than speaking "as a language" and insists "I only speak Arabic," notwithstanding having just remarked that he was fluent in Nubian.

Yet Mansour persists in the demand for performance, imploring al-Hajj for just "a couple of sentences for us to see this language, to the extent possible. Never mind the insults you were saying, just a couple sentences of what you said to them, for example, when they asked for your name." After this third request, al-Hajj relents—and here, I am translating from Al Jazeera's transcript of the interview, including the bracketed text: "Maybe I would say something like [words in Nubian] or he would reply [words in Nubian] meaning, 'how are you,' 'you're good?' I was using the language fluently and the guys were laughing so hard by God! If they were going to be shot by the Americans, at least these guys were alive and smiling."

Whether al-Hajj's initial reticence stemmed from insecurity over his facility in Nubian, his modesty in not wanting to curse on television, or something else, I cannot say. But in facing a demand from an Egyptian journalist to perform his Africanness, al-Hajj could not have been unaware of the discrimination and marginalization experienced by people racialized as Black in Egypt, be they Nubian, Sudanese, or both. In Egypt, blackface performances have long been an important practice for crafting a sense of national identity as racially distinct from Africa (Troutt Powell 2003, 168–216), and much of Egyptian Nubia was quite literally flooded off the map by the Aswan High Dam (Abubakr 2021; Moll 2021). Al-Hajj's response was twofold: first, to enact a kind of redaction as care (Sharpe 2016, 118–23) in self-consciously *not* reproducing his original Nubian speech, which preempts the subsequent Arabic transcript's coding of unintelligibility with the parenthetical "[words in Nubian]." Second, al-Hajj insists on returning to the context of his original audience ("the guys" shackled around him in the courtyard of the fort), wherein the humorousness of his performance of Africanness was made possible by a shared experience of captivity *as Arabs*. There, speaking Nubian was a surplus facility arising from a complex history of multiple identities and a source of pleasant surprise, rather than a sign of incomplete Arabness as it risks becoming when performed on Al Jazeera. In the vicissitudes of capture and captivation—or of racialization in Afghan, American, and Arab eyes—al-Hajj's passage of Blackness is one from being all too Arab to being not quite Arab enough.

Notes

1. This chapter is an abridged and revised version of what first appeared as Darryl Li, 2022. "Captive Passages: Geographies of Blackness in Guantánamo Memoirs." *Transforming Anthropology* 30, no. 1: 20–33.

2. In this chapter, I follow popular usage in referring to the prison using the military designation GTMO (pronounced "Gitmo") for the US naval base in Cuba of which it is only one part. This also serves to distinguish it from Guantánamo, the adjacent Cuban city.

3. Throughout the Arabian Peninsula, enslaved *muwallads* manumitted around the time of national independence frequently took the clan names of masters and remained in relations of clientship or dependency (Hopper 2015, 208–21). In contrast to African migrants who maintain an ethnic distinctiveness (especially by taking ethnonyms such as al-Gorani, al-Hawsawi, al-Bernawi, and such as surnames), such *muwallads* often enjoy citizenship and instead seek to avoid the stigma of slavery by squarely placing themselves within Arabian tribal genealogies (Samin 2015, 147–58). This is possible because Islamic patrilineage structures enable one to claim free descent even while having some ancestors racialized as Black, unlike with the "one-drop rule" prevalent in some slaveholding societies in the New World. Such genealogical claims are of course often regarded as suspect and do not prevent racial discrimination, especially in matters of marriage.

4. When deployed by non-Black Arabs in Anglophone settler societies, however, the term serves as a functional translation for the n-word.

5. There is no publicly available racial census of the 775 captives known to have been held at GTMO. This reflects the US government's treatment of race solely as a formal category of domestic governance, one erased in logics of "international terrorism" (Husain 2020). My best estimate is that the number who would be racialized as Black is in the low dozens. There have been twenty-four captives holding the citizenship of sub-Saharan countries as well as several from Arab countries whose names, photographs, or both strongly suggest belonging to the large Afro-descended populations therein. There is some anecdotal evidence to suggest that logics of Blackness animated at least some detention decisions: for some time, al-Gorani, the Sudanese journalist Sami al-Hajj, and the Ugandan Jamal Kiyemba were all housed next to each other and subjected to anti-Black slurs (al-Ḥājj 2017, 172).

6. This formulation echoes and is indebted to Dylan Rodriguez's indispensable *Forced Passages: Imprisoned Radical Intellectuals and the U.S. Prison Regime* (2006).

7. Anthropology, too, owes unrecognized debts to captivity as concept, structure, and experience—from Radcliffe-Brown's ethnography in the shadow of the Andaman Islands penal colony to Malinowski's Trobriand fieldwork under conditions of having his movements restricted by Australian authorities as an "enemy national." Captivity is crucial but left behind, perhaps even with a hint of force, as the unnamed—and somewhat anthropologist-like—protagonist in Kafka's short story "In the Penal Colony," which uses a heavy rope to ward off the natives who attempt to board his boat as he leaves the island (Kafka 2000, 228–29).

8. This is not to deny the pragmatic arguments for seeking the federal criminal justice system as an alternative to captivity at GTMO. What is at stake here, however, is the erasure of that system's own unprecedented scale and monstrous character.

9. Executive Order 13492—Review and Disposition of Individuals Detained at the Guantánamo Bay Naval Base and Closure of Detention Facilities, 74 F.R. 4897 (January 27, 2009) § 3.

10. Habeas is only mentioned in passing in the judgment. *See* Dred Scott v. Sandford, 60 U.S. 393 (1856), 485–56, 497.

11. *See id.*, at 396.

12. The language of return and traverse is rooted in centuries-old common law usage but also preserved in contemporary federal legislation. *See* 28 U.S.C. § 2248 ("The allegations of a return to the writ of habeas corpus . . . if not traversed, shall be accepted as true except to the extent that the judge finds from the evidence that they are not true").

13. Al-Gorani was subsequently featured in an exhibit at the Park Avenue Armory museum put on by the performance artist Laurie Anderson that entailed his "telepresencing" by projecting a video feed of him speaking onto a sculpture (Feldman 2018).

14. The extent to which racialization in the western Sahara was affected by the Atlantic slave trade in earlier centuries is an altogether different question that requires its own investigation (Marsh 2018, 48).

15. All translations from Arabic in this essay are mine.

16. In 2006 a Bahraini survivor of GTMO penned a forty-two-page account of his experiences that circulated online (Kāmil 2006).

17. The Baluch people live primarily in territory presently controlled by Pakistan and Iran and overlapping slightly with Afghanistan. The coastal areas of Baluchistan include considerable Afro-descended populations due to the region's long-standing ties with East Africa, including the importation of enslaved persons.

18. The semantic association of Arabness and Blackness is not unique to Afghanistan. In contemporary Turkey, for example, the derogatory terms *siyah* (black, the color) and *zenci* (black-skinned) are also used interchangeably with *arap* (Arab) (Willoughby 2021).

19. Al Jazeera, "Walīd Muḥamad Ḥājj: Madhbaḥat qalʿat jānghī" (Walid Muhammad al-Hajj: Slaughter of Qalaʿ-i-Jangi) (part 4), *Shāhid ʿalā al-ʿaṣr*, aired November 16, 2010.

References

Abdul Khabeer, Suʾad. 2016. *Muslim Cool: Race, Religion, and Hip Hop in the United States*. New York: New York University Press.

Abubakr, Bayan. 2021. "The Contradictions of Afro-Arab Solidarity(ies): The Aswan High Dam and the Erasure of the Global Black Experience." In *Racial Formations in Africa and the Middle East: A Transregional Approach*, edited by Hisham Aidi, Marc Lynch, and Zachariah Mampilly, 73–80. Washington, DC: Project on Middle East Political Science.

Agamben, Giorgio. 1998. *Homo Sacer: Sovereign Power and Bare Life*. Translated by Daniel Heller-Roazen. Stanford, CA: Stanford University Press. First published 1995.

———. 2005. *State of Exception*. Translated by K. Attell. Chicago: University of Chicago Press. First published 2003.

al-Ḥājj, Sāmī. 2017. *Ghuwāntanāmū: qiṣṣatī* (Guantánamo: My Story). Beirut: Arab Scientific Publishers.

Azeb, Sophia. 2019. "Crossing the Saharan Boundary: *Lotus* and the Legibility of Africanness." *Research in African Literatures* 50, no. 3: 91–115.

Baghoolizadeh, Beeta. 2018. "Seeing Race and Erasing Slavery: Media and the Construction of Blackness in Iran, 1830–1960." PhD diss., University of Pennsylvania.

Bonilla, Yarimar. 2013. "Ordinary Sovereignty." *Small Axe: A Caribbean Journal of Criticism* 17, no. 2: 152–65.

Brhane, Meskerem. 1997. "Narratives of the Past, Politics of the Present: Identity, Subordination, and the Haratines of Mauritania." PhD diss., University of Chicago.

Burton, Orisanmi. 2021. "Captivity, Kinship, and Black Masculine Care Work under Domestic Warfare." *American Anthropologist* 123, no. 3: 621–32.

Coundouriotis, Eleni. 2020. "Torture and Textuality: *Guantánamo Diary* as Postcolonial Text." *Textual Practice* 34, no. 7: 1061–80.

Curtis, Edward E., IV. 2014. *The Call of Bilal: Islam in the African Diaspora*. Chapel Hill: University of North Carolina Press.

Daulatzai, Sohail. 2007. "Protect Ya Neck: Muslims and the Carceral Imagination in the Age of Guantánamo." *Souls: A Critical Journal of Black Culture, Politics, and Society* 9, no. 2: 132–47.

el Gorani, Mohammed, and Jérôme Tubiana. 2011. "Diary." *London Review of Books* 33, no. 24: 33–35.

El-Hamel, Chouki. 2013. *Black Morocco: A History of Slavery, Race, and Islam*. Cambridge: Cambridge University Press.

Esseissah, Khaled Mohamed. 2019. "'Making a Way Out of No Way': Harāṭīn Muslims' Initiatives to Gain Respectability in Post-Emancipation Mauritania." PhD diss., Indiana University.

Fanon, Frantz. 2008. *Black Skin, White Masks*. Translated by R. Philcox. New York: Grove Press. First published 1952.

Farooq, Umar A. 2021. "The Mauritanian: A Film about Surviving Guantanamo." *Middle East Eye*, March 15. Accessed October 26, 2021. www.middleeasteye.net/discover/mauritanian-guantanamo-biopic-about -prisons-most-tortured-man.

Feldman, Keith. 2018. "You (Shall) Have the Body: Patterns of Life in the Shadow of Guantánamo." *Comparatist* 42: 189–203.

Gilmore, Ruth Wilson. 2002. "Fatal Couplings of Power and Difference: Notes on Racism and Geography." *Professional Geographer* 54, no. 1: 15–24.

Goyal, Yogita. 2017. "The Genres of *Guantánamo Diary*: Postcolonial Reading and the War on Terror." *Cambridge Journal of Postcolonial Literary Inquiry* 4, no. 1: 69–87.

Ḥājj, Walīd Muḥammad. 2009. *Madhbaḥat al-qal ʿa wa-ghayāhib ghuwāntanāmū: Asrār shāhid ʿayān* (The Slaughter in the Fort and the Depths of Guantánamo: Secrets of an Eyewitness). Khartoum: Maṭābi ʿal-sūdān lil-ʿumla.

Hall, Bruce S. 2011. *A History of Race in Muslim West Africa, 1600–1960*. Cambridge: Cambridge University Press.

Hopper, Matthew S. 2015. *Slaves of One Master: Globalization and Slavery in Arabia in the Age of Empire*. New Haven, CT: Yale University Press.

Hudson, Peter James. 2014. "The Geographies of Blackness and Anti-Blackness: An Interview with Katherine McKittrick." *C.L.R. James Journal* 20, no. 1–2: 233–40.

Husain, Atiya. 2020. "Deracialization, Dissent, and Terrorism in the FBI's Most Wanted Program." *Sociology of Race and Ethnicity* 7, no. 2: 208–25.

James, Joy. 2005. "Introduction: Democracy and Captivity." In *The New Abolitionists: (Neo)Slave Narratives and Contemporary Prison Writings*, edited by Joy James, xxi–xlii. Albany: State University of New York Press.

Kafka, Franz. 2000. "In the Penal Colony." In *The Metamorphosis, In the Penal Colony, and Other Stories*, edited by Joachim Neugroschel, 191–239. New York: Scribner. First published 1919.

Kahn, Jeffrey S. 2019. *Islands of Sovereignty: Haitian Migration and the Borders of Empire*. Chicago: University of Chicago Press.

Kāmil, ʿĀdil. 2006. *Mudhakkirāt ʿĀdil Kāmil—al-Baḥraynī—al- ʿā ʾid min Ghuwāntanāmū* (Memoirs of ʿAdil Kamil, the Bahraini Returnee from Guantánamo). s.l.: s.n.

Kaplan, Amy. 2005. "Where Is Guantánamo?" *American Quarterly* 57, no. 3: 831–58.

Kazi, Nazia. 2018. *Islamophobia, Race, and Global Politics*. Lanham, MD: Rowman and Littlefield.

Kennington, Kelly. 2017. *In the Shadow of Dred Scott: St. Louis Freedom Suits and the Legal Culture of Slavery in Antebellum America*. Athens: University of Georgia Press.

Khogali, Mustafa. 1991. "The Migration of the Danagla to Port Sudan: A Case Study of the Impact of Migration on the Change of Identity." *GeoJournal* 25, no. 1: 63–71.

Korb, Scott. 2015. "'Guantánamo Diary' and the American Slave Narrative." *New Yorker*, April 16. Accessed October 6, 2021. www.newyorker.com/books/page-turner/guantanamo-diary-and-the-american-slave -narrative.

Kotef, Hagar. 2015. *Movement and the Ordering of Freedom: On Liberal Governances of Mobility*. Durham, NC: Duke University Press.

Kull, Andrew. 2004. "Restitution in Favor of Former Slaves." *Boston University Law Review* 84, no. 5: 1277–90.

Lee, Christine. 2021. "'You Don't Look American': Race and Whiteness in the Ethnographic and Disciplinary Encounter." *American Ethnologist* 48, no. 2: 206–17.

Li, Darryl. 2015. "Empire Records." *New Inquiry*, March 25. Accessed October 6, 2021. https://thenewinquiry .com/empire-records/.

———. 2018. "From Exception to Empire: Sovereignty, Carceral Circulation, and the 'Global War on Terror.'" In *Ethnographies of US Empire*, edited by C. McGranahan and J. Collins, 456–75. Durham, NC: Duke University Press.

———. 2020. *The Universal Enemy: Jihad, Empire, and the Challenge of Solidarity*. Stanford, CA: Stanford University Press.

Lubin, Alex. 2014. *Geographies of Liberation: The Making of an Afro-Arab Political Imaginary*. Chapel Hill: University of North Carolina Press.

Luk, Sharon. 2018. *The Life of Paper: Letters and a Poetics of Living beyond Captivity*. Oakland: University of California Press.

Marsh, Wendell Hassan. 2018. "Compositions of Sainthood: The Biography of Ḥājj ʿUmar Tāl by Shaykh Mūsā Kamara." PhD diss., Columbia University.

McDougall, E. Ann. 2015. "Hidden in Plain Sight: 'Hartine' in Nouakchott's 'Niche-Settlements.'" *International Journal of African Historical Studies* 48, no. 2: 251–79.

McKittrick, Katherine. 2006. *Demonic Grounds: Black Women and Cartographies of Struggle*. Minneapolis: University of Minnesota Press.

Miller, Monica, and Christopher Driscoll. 2015. "Conversations in Black: Alexander G. Weheliye." *Marginalia: Los Angeles Review of Books*, September 1. Accessed October 6, 2021. https://marginalia.lareviewofbooks .org/conversations-in-black-alexander-g-weheliye/.

Miran, Jonathan. 2015. "'Stealing the Way' to Mecca: West African Pilgrims and Illicit Red Sea Passages, 1920s–1950s." *Journal of African History* 56, no. 3: 389–408.

Moll, Yasmin. 2021. "Narrating Nubia: Between Sentimentalism and Solidarity." In *Racial Formations in Africa and the Middle East: A Transregional Approach*, edited by Hisham Aidi, Marc Lynch, and Zachariah Mampilly, 81–86. Washington, DC: Project on Middle East Political Science.

O'Neill, Kevin Lewis, and Jatin Dua. 2017. "Captivity: A Provocation." *Public Culture* 30, no. 1: 3–18.

Ould Cheikhna, Sid'Amar. 2015. "Yawmiyyāt ghuwāntanāmū judhūr al-ḥikāya" (*Guantánamo Diary*: The *Roots of a Tale*). *Al-Akhbār*, February 5. Accessed November 15, 2021. https://web.archive.org/web /20150207075545/http://alakhbar.info/opin/8065-2015-02-05-00-51-34.html (an archived version of the original page, which is no longer available).

Ould Slahi, Mohamedou. 2015. *Guantánamo Diary*. New York: Little, Brown.

———. 2020. "أضيع القياس" (Likening Can Be Misleading): Reflections on Africa and Africans in Guantánamo." *African Studies Review* 63, no. 2: 403–10.

Pierre, Jemima. 2012. *The Predicament of Blackness: Postcolonial Ghana and the Politics of Race*. Chicago: University of Chicago Press.

Ralph, Laurence. 2020. *The Torture Letters: Reckoning with Police Violence*. Chicago: University of Chicago Press.

Rana, Junaid. 2011. *Terrifying Muslims: Race and Labor in the South Asian Diaspora*. Durham, NC: Duke University Press.

Rodney, Walter. 2011. *How Europe Underdeveloped Africa*. Baltimore: Black Classic Press. First published 1972.

Rodriguez, Dylan. 2006. *Forced Passages: Imprisoned Radical Intellectuals and the U.S. Prison Regime*. Minneapolis: University of Minnesota Press.

Rouse, Carolyn. 2004. *Engaged Surrender: African American Women and Islam*. Berkeley: University of California Press.

Rowlandson, William. 2010. "Understanding Guantanamo through Its Parallel with Slavery." *International Journal of Cuban Studies* 2, no. 3–4: 217–30.

Samin, Nadav. 2015. *Of Sand or Soil: Genealogy and Tribal Belonging in Saudi Arabia*. Princeton, NJ: Princeton University Press.

Serels, Steven. 2013. *Starvation and the State: Famine, Slavery, and Power in Sudan, 1883–1956*. New York: Palgrave Macmillan.

Sexton, Jared, and Elizabeth Lee. 2006. "Figuring the Prison: Prerequisites of Torture at Abu Ghraib." *Antipode: A Radical Journal of Geography* 38, no. 5: 1005–22.

Sharkey, Heather. 2007. "Arab Identity and Ideology in Sudan: The Politics of Language, Ethnicity, and Race." *African Affairs* 107, no. 427: 21–43.

Sharpe, Christina. 2016. *In the Wake: On Blackness and Being*. Durham, NC: Duke University Press.

Sikainga, Ahmad Alawad. 1996. *Slaves into Workers: Emancipation and Labor in Colonial Sudan*. Austin: University of Texas Press.

Spillers, Hortense. 1987. "Mama's Baby, Papa's Maybe: An American Grammar Book." *Diacritics* 17, no. 2: 64–81.

Swanson, Elizabeth, and Alexandra S. Moore. 2021. "Indefinite Detention: Chronotopes of Unfreedom in Mohamedou Ould Slahi's *Guantánamo Diary*." *ARIEL: A Review of International English Literature* 52, no. 1: 33–60.

Troutt Powell, Eve. 2003. *A Different Shade of Colonialism: Egypt, Great Britain, and the Mastery of the Sudan*. Berkeley: University of California Press.

———. 2012. *Tell This in My Memory: Stories of Enslavement from Egypt, Sudan, and the Ottoman Empire*. Stanford, CA: Stanford University Press.

Tubiana, Jérôme, and Alexandre Franc. 2019. *Guantánamo Kid: The True Story of Mohammed El-Gharani*. London: SelfMadeHero.

Ware, Rudolph. 2014. *The Walking Qur'an: Islamic Education, Embodied Knowledge, and History in West Africa*. Chapel Hill: University of North Carolina Press.

Weheliye, Alexander G. 2014. *Habeas Viscus: Racializing Assemblages, Biopolitics, and Black Feminist Theories of the Human*. Durham, NC: Duke University Press.

Weigel, David. "Trump: Maybe Cuba Should Take Over Guantanamo 'and reimburse us.'" *Washington Post*, February 23, 2016. Accessed November 15, 2021. www.washingtonpost.com/news/post-politics/wp/2016/02/23/trump-maybe-cuba-should-take-over-gitmo-and-reimburse-us/.

Westley, Robert. 2016. "Restitution Claims for Wrongful Enslavement and the Doctrine of the Master's Good Faith." In *The Constitution of Whiteness: An Interdisciplinary Analysis of Race Formation and the Meaning of White Identity*, edited by S. Middleton, D. R. Roediger, and D. M. Shaffer, 44–73. Jackson: University of Mississippi Press.

Wiley, Katherine. 2018. *Work, Social Status, and Gender in Post-Slavery Mauritania*. Bloomington: Indiana University Press.

Willoughby, Bam. 2021. "Opposing a Spectacle of Blackness: Arap Baci, Baci Kalfa, Dadi, and the Invention of African Presence in Turkey." *Lateral: Journal of the Cultural Studies Association* 10, no. 1. Accessed October 27, 2021. https://csalateral.org/forum/cultural-constructions-race-racism-middle-east-north-africa-southwest-asia-mena-swana/opposing-spectacle-blackness-arap-baci-kalfa-dad-african-presence-turkey-willoughby/.

Wright, Ann. 2013. "12 Years a Slave vs. 12 Years a Prisoner . . . in Guantanamo." *Common Dreams*, December 20. Accessed October 6, 2021. www.commondreams.org/views/2013/12/20/12-years-slave-vs-12-years-prisoner-guantanamo.

Toward an Anthropology of Liberation

THIS READER'S approach to the anthropology of white supremacy does not simply analyze white supremacy but aims to undo and dismantle it. The contributions to this section take up this call to move toward what has been called an *anthropology of liberation*. For over three decades, anthropologists against imperialism, racism, and oppression have worked to undo the structural violences of white supremacy. The generations of Black, Indigenous, and other feminists and anthropologists of color have provided valuable strategies toward a liberatory praxis. Rather than simply being extractive in our research, anthropology must be in the service of the marginalized communities with whom we work. It is important to work to dismantle the structures of violence that enable white supremacy. Working with communities is one of the first steps towards an anthropology of liberation.

In many anthropology departments, conferences, and circles, if an anthropologist were to acknowledge stakes, membership in, or a commitment to the communities where we work, we might be dismissed as not conducting "serious" research. We've heard the catch-all use of the racist description that someone's research or presentation was "not sophisticated" enough, which often implies a lack of theoretical acumen. In anthropologist speak, this usually means that the person is not seen as contributing to the discipline's perpetual quest to navel gaze—theorizing the world in an exclusive language that is only intelligible and indeed useful to anthropology's small group of English-reading scholars and students situated in the ivory towers of elite Western universities.

This final section presents an anthropology of white supremacy that must strive against this type of academic imperialism and racism. We must not be complicit with an extractive approach to ethnography, and we must recognize that the people who have traditionally been seen as research subjects also are now anthropologists, aiming to use the tools of this complicated discipline in the struggle for decolonization. The chapters in this section draw on this rich tradition of Black, Indigenous, Latiné, and queer and feminist of color anthropology, to orient us toward liberation.

22

The Resurgent Far Right and the Black Feminist Struggle for Social Democracy in Brazil

Keisha-Khan Y. Perry

The most potent weapon in the hands of the oppressor is the mind of the oppressed.
—STEVE BIKO

EACH MORNING, journalist Eliane Brum and activist Monica Benicio remind us on Twitter of the number of days that have passed since the assassination of Marielle Franco. A Black queer Rio de Janeiro activist and councilwoman from the Maré neighborhood, Franco was killed along with her driver, Anderson Silva, on March 14, 2018, minutes after leaving an event for the empowerment of Black women and girls that was live streamed on Facebook. Almost two hundred (mostly left-leaning) politicians and activists (Black and Indigenous, fighting against territorial loss) were killed between 2015 and 2020 in Brazil, and many of these cases remain unsolved. On March 12, 2019, almost one year after the killing of Marielle Franco, two former police officers with direct ties to Brazilian president Jair Bolsonaro were arrested in connection with her death.[1]

Even with Lula Ignácio da Silva's defeat of Bolsonaro in the 2022 presidential election, and his appointment of Anielle Franco as minister of racial equality in Brazil, uncertainty remains around who ordered Marielle's murder and why. Much of the current political work in Brazil focuses on the radical undoing of the last four years of Bolsonaro's presidency (2019–22). However, as this chapter highlights, as important as the last four years were, there is a longer history of racial hatred that has shaped the ongoing far-right movement fighting against an intersectional approach to social transformation in the country.

In the days leading up to the Brazilian presidential elections of October 2018, Brum (2018b) published an essay in *El País* titled "*O ódio deitou no meu divã*," loosely translated as "Hate sat on my couch." She begins her essay by narrating the resurgence of hate-based threats in Brazil. She presents Silvia Bellintani, a psychoanalyst who describes threats made against his nineteen-year-old gay male client by white fascists:

> He enters without saying a word and starts to cry right away. I ask him what happened and he says, "I'm frightened," and that he was approached by a guy at the university with these words: "Hey there, faggot, have you seen the research? Take advantage of the days until the 28th [election day] to walk holding hands, because when Mito [nickname for Bolsonaro] assumes power, he'll end this nonsense and you'll be beaten until you turn into a man."[2]

Bellintani tells the story of another client, a seventeen-year-old feminist, who was also threatened just before the elections. Someone left a note in her school textbook that read, "You thought it was all about going out there screaming '#nothim' to stop Bolsomito, feminazi!!! You lost, sad old sack!!!" Brazilian women used the hashtag #nothim to register their opposition to then-candidate Bolsonaro, affectionately nicknamed "Bolsomito" by his supporters.

Brum's article describes the explosion of similar stories recounted on social media by psychologists who have revealed these private conversations (without revealing the identity of their clients) that they say point to the infiltration of hate into Brazilian society. These stories focus primarily on the loathed figure of Bolsonaro, a former army captain who is popularly described, as Brum (2018a) writes, as a "homophobic, misogynist, racist 'thing'" For many, Bolsonaro created an embodied fear and a collective neurosis that dominated conversations between psychologists and their patients. In another essay, published in *The Guardian*, Brum (2019) reminds us that this is not simply paranoia. Bolsonaro indeed articulated hatred, violence, racism, sexism, and homophobia. He stated that he is pro-torture and that he would rather his son die than be gay. His platform was won on being explicitly racist and xenophobic, and he was quoted as saying that under his leadership, "There'll be no money for NGOs. If it's up to me, every citizen will have a gun at home. Not one centimeter will be demarcated for Indigenous reserves or *quilombolas*," the descendant communities of runaway enslaved peoples (Butterworth 2018). Toward the end of his presidential tenure, a decree published in October 2022 abolished the regional committees of the National Indian Foundation (FUNAI), responsible for studying Indigenous territories for protection and demarcation.

Many also point to his sexism in his vehement support for the impeachment of former president Dilma Rousseff, the country's first female leader. (Indeed, I have argued elsewhere [Perry 2017] that misogynistic ideas about women's leadership were the root cause of her demise.) And he has been unapologetic about his support for the incarceration of President Luiz Inácio Lula da Silva, popularly known as "Lula," who was a founding member of the Workers' Party and served for two terms prior to Dilma Rousseff and began a third presidential term in 2023. Brum and others point to Bolsonaro's defense of the military regime and his investment in increased militarization of police forces in the country as manifestations of his fascism. What is most striking about Brum's analysis of the fascist hatred on full display in Brazilian society is how she situates it historically. She asserts that this president is "the monstrous product of the country's silence about the crimes committed by its former dictatorship," limiting the scope of Bolsonaro's historical precedent to the last fifty years.

While there has indeed been silence about the country's violent past and present, Black activists in Brazil have consistently reminded us that the violence of the military dictatorship (1964–80) represented only one moment in the long history of white supremacist colonial violence and the legacy of slavery in the country. As Afro-Brazilian sociologist Vera Benedito (2011) has publicly asked, "How is it that Brazil was the last country to abolish slavery in 1888, but it is still known as a racial paradise where everyone is partying and having sex with each other?" Christen Smith (2016), Ana Luiza Pinheiro Flauzina (2008), Maud Chirio (2018), Rebecca Atencio (2014), and numerous other scholars have documented that Black/brown and poor people—from the *barracoons* (stockades for the confinement of enslaved peoples in West Africa awaiting transport across the Atlantic) to the plantations, *quilombos, favelas,* and *bairros*—have borne the brunt of militarized policing, techniques of surveillance and torture, and state sponsorship of mass killings. It is impossible to maintain slavery for four centuries without rampant sexual violence and a subsequent system of racial apartheid that is always gendered and classed. The resurgence of far-right violence and politics in Brazil—specifically, the concerted attempt to repeal social gains for Blacks, women, and poor people—must be understood through this broad historical context of the ongoing enactment of white supremacy and read through an intersectional approach. As Kimberlé Crenshaw (1990) and Black feminist activists globally have shown, an intersectional approach reveals the vulnerabilities and exclusions that have further marginalized racialized and gendered populations, particularly Black women, from equal protection under laws and in policies.

What Brazilian psychologists have only recently been calling the "embodiment of hate" has thus been entrenched in the everyday and institutional lived experiences of Afro-Brazilians and Indigenous peoples. We must acknowledge that these communities have long dealt with the pervasive anti-Blackness, homophobia and misogyny, massive cuts to public universities, and military violence that some see as only recent phenomena. Critical scholar Denise Ferreira da Silva (2007) has referred to this long history of everyday violence as part of the material consequences of gendered racial subjection that has been built into the environment. For example, neighborhood segregation and separate elevators for the public and mostly Black service workers in offices and residential buildings reproduce sociospatial hierarchies and conflicts that seem unrelated to the political context (Hanchard 1994) but in fact stem directly from centuries-old racist ideas and exclusionary practices.

Thus, the right-wing desire for a return to a recent (racialist) past must be understood within longer histories of racialization and white supremacy. When Bolsonaro praises 1960s dictatorship torture chief Carlos Alberto Brilhante Ustra, stating, "We want a Brazil that is similar to the one we had 40, 50 years ago" (*O Globo* 2018), this references a longer and ongoing history of anti-Black repression and violence in the country. Indeed, the torture techniques of the military regime in Brazil and Chile during the 1960s that the president refers to had been perfected on the bodies of Black and brown people long before the (white) leftist activists. These techniques can be traced back to the violent repression of enslaved Africans kidnapped and forced into labor in Brazil.[3] Jurema Werneck (Human Rights Watch 2017), an activist of the Black women's organization Criola and head of Human Rights Watch Brazil, affirms that while most young people have no memory of the military dictatorship, they are very familiar with its aftermath, and many are still living in the *senzalas* (slave quarters) that have always existed adjacent to mansions since the slavery period.

80 Shots: A Country at War

On April 7, 2019, beloved Afro-Brazilian musician Evaldo dos Santos Rosa was driving with his family to a baptism in the Guadalupe neighborhood of Rio de Janeiro when the Brazilian military fired more than eighty rounds at his car, killing him and injuring his family, including two children. The army reported that the soldiers mistook the musician for a drug trafficker (Brum 2018a). Bolsonaro was criticized by journalists, activists, and politicians for his silence on this murder. If Bolsonaro's supporters believe that every Brazilian should own guns (although almost 70 percent of Brazilians polled in the week after the killing of dos Santos Rosa were against the right to bear arms; Ribeiro and Torres 2019), then Black and brown people, poor people, and women know precisely who and where the targets of civilian vigilantism will be. The brutal killing of capoeira *mestre* Moa do Katende in Salvador on October 17, 2018, in the hours after declaring that he had voted for Workers' Party candidate Fernando Haddad, provided an example of what was already the social reality for most Black people and what was to come. Following Evaldo dos Santos Rosa's murder, his twenty-nine-year-old son, Daniel Rosa, said, "President Jair Bolsonaro said the Army was here to protect us, not take lives" (Ribeiro and Torres 2019). In mid-February 2019, the Supreme Court denied the transfer of the case of nine military police officers on trial for a massacre in the Cabula neighborhood from Bahia to the federal court. These officers are on trial for killing twelve and seriously injuring another six young men and women between the ages of fifteen and twenty-eight, shot execution-style on February 7, 2015 (Smith 2016). Despite evidence of a massacre and cover-up and the annulment of the court's decision, as of 2022, eight of the nine officers continued to work on the streets and there was no sense of when the new trial would begin (Ribeiro 2022).

July 2018 also marked twenty-five years since the 1993 Candelaria massacre of eight homeless people, including six children, in front of the Candelária Church in Rio de Janeiro. This massacre occurred within the broader context of 1988 to 1991, during which, according to the Federal Police of Brazil, almost 6,000 street children were killed, mostly in Rio de Janeiro and São Paulo (Silva 1994).

Although these events have drawn international attention, the violent political discourses and state actions, incarceration of political opponents, and truculent military killings that have occurred in the first six months of Bolsonaro's presidency are not new. Every twenty-three minutes in Brazil, a young Black person between the ages of fifteen and twenty-nine is killed. That is, seventy-five young Black people per day, three every hour (Instituto de Pesquisa Econômica Aplicada 2022). On the night before her death, Marielle Franco (2018) tweeted about the police murder of twenty-three-year-old Matheus Melo de Castro in Rio, "How many more must die for this war to end?" Activist and founder of the anti-police-violence organization *Reaja ou Será Morta* (React or Die), Hamilton Borges, has stated that the statistics on police violence in Brazil are equivalent to those of "a country at war" (Hafiz 2016).

In 2018, the killings totaled 27,000. Between 1980 and 2014, a record one million Black people were killed (approximately 29,000 per year). Between 2009 and 2013, the Brazilian police gave the reason for killing 11,197 people as "resisting arrest." Black men and women, who make up 51 percent of the population, comprised 71 percent of the 318,000 homicide victims in Brazil between 2005 and 2015, and in 2015 police operations accounted for 3,320 murders of Blacks nationwide (Instituto de Pesquisa Econômica Aplicada 2018). Although Black women represent only 24.5 percent of the Brazilian population, 61 percent of the women murdered by the police are Black, and 144 transgender people were murdered in 2016, the majority of whom are also Black and women (Nogueira, Aquino, and Cabral 2017). In 2022, 6,430 people were killed in police operations in Brazil; 83 percent were Black. In the State of Bahia, with an 80 percent Black population, 94 percent of homicide victims were Black. The March 2022 police massacre that killed three young Black men in Gamboa de Baixo, a coastal fishing community in the center of Salvador, is understood by local residents as part of the broader process of racial genocide in the country (Perry 2022). Brazil is a country at war, and Black urban communities bear the brunt of militarized policing, technological innovation of surveillance and torture, and state sponsorship of mass killings.

Residents living on the sociospatial margins of Brazilian cities—such as Rodrigo Serrano in the Chapeu Mangueira neighborhood of Rio de Janeiro, killed when police mistook his umbrella for a gun, or as previously cited, dos Santos Rosa, mistaken for "*bandidos*," killed in front of his family on their way to a baby shower—tend to bear the brunt of militarized police violence. But as recent reports show, scholars and activists, both men and women, are not immune to violence sponsored by the state or carried out by local *milicias*, supporters of the new president.

It should not be read as a coincidence that the desire to arm the population, militarize urban neighborhoods, and implement the death penalty (legally or extrajudicially, as the case of Evaldo dos Santos Rosa shows) have appeared in the same political discourses as the urgent need to end affirmative action, eliminate the demarcation of *quilombo* and Indigenous lands, ban the teaching of gender politics in schools, and eliminate all LGBTQ+ rights. Even before Bolsonaro's presidency began, over 8,500 Cuban doctors serving over twenty-eight million people in poor and remote areas were removed from Brazil, and his government did not replace them (Darlington and Casado 2019). To reinvigorate Paul Gilroy's early ideas in *There Ain't No Black in the Union Jack* (1991), class becomes the lexicon through which race and gender are lived. Anti-Blackness and the sponsorship of racial violence (this also includes austerity measures in the form of cuts to public health care, education, housing, and cash benefits) are ever-present without ever needing to utter any explicit ideas around race, gender, and Blackness. The majority of poor people in Brazil are Black, and the majority being criminalized and incarcerated are also Black. The people described as needing the social order and control that the new government promises to implement are Black and female. This is especially clear when we consider the politicization of conservative Catholic and evangelical Christian movements, whose members continue to demonize Afro-Brazilian religions and burn down and demolish *terreiros* (houses of worship) that have strong female, lesbian, and homosexual participation and leadership as well as having more expansive practices of racial and sexual inclusion. The long-delayed extension of democratic rights to Black people, women, gays and lesbians, and poor people over the last fifteen years represents a threat to the gendered racial sociospatial order that the architects of "ordem e progresso" (order and progress) have in mind.

Gender Trouble

Even before the January 1, 2019, inauguration of Jair Bolsonaro, the most important political project on the agenda to be implemented as law was one that conservative evangelicals and Catholics had been pushing in recent years: Escola sem Partido (Schools without Politics), inspired by the US organization NoIndoctrination.org. The proposed law will prohibit the teaching of any sort of political ideology or doctrine in schools and universities, a kind of censorship unimaginable in any democratic society. This follows a similar pattern in the United States. Researcher Jeffrey Sachs tracks proposed legislation attempting to limit what can be taught in US schools for PEN America, which promotes freedom of written expression. He reported to National Public Radio in February 2022 that "since January 2021 . . . 35 states have introduced 137 bills limiting what schools can teach with regard to race, American history, politics, sexual orientation and gender identity" (NPR 2022). According to Human Rights Watch, in Brazil, "lawmakers have introduced over 200 bills at local and federal levels, since 2014, to ban 'indoctrination' or 'gender ideology' in schools. The Supreme Court struck down eight of these in 2020. Several teachers told Human Rights Watch that teaching gender and sexuality issues resulted in harassment, police requests for statements, or administrative proceedings" (Human Rights Watch 2023, 97). Judith Butler, author of the classic text *Gender Trouble* (1990), widely available in Portuguese, was aggressively verbally attacked during her November 2017 visit to Brazil. This attack was part of the political momentum of the anti-gender-discourse movement and the development of the Escola sem Partido movement. Since the 1994 United Nations Development Program conference in Cairo and the 1995 UN World Conference on Women in Beijing, the emergence of a new discourse of gender as a social construct and calls for gender-specific rights and public policies have sparked an antigender movement in education in Brazil. Schools and universities have been seen as battlegrounds for maintaining heteropatriarchy and Christian dominance.

Some feminist activists in Brazil have asserted that former president Rousseff ceded to pressure and refused to launch the Escola sem Homofobia (Schools without Homophobia) pedagogical materials, and her successor, Michel Temer, removed all references to "gender identity," "sexual orientation," and "teaching without prejudice" from the national, common core curriculum that had been taught since the 1990s (Chalhoub et al. 2017). The antigender movement has been pushing the idea of "moral education" and "Brazil for Brazilians" to resemble "America for Americans" (Lee 2019), which also has implications for the current required teaching of Afro-Brazilian and Indigenous history. In general, this represents a return to the romantic ideal of a white, heteropatriarchal Brazilian society in which women, Black, and Indigenous people "know their place." Hence, for Black activists, this political shift toward authoritarian rule is a "coup against [Black people], a coup against social rights," as Jurema Werneck stated in an interview. The election of Jair Bolsonaro was about "putting order back in the big house," rescuing old hegemonies, and "keeping the poor people in their rightful place," she continued (Chalhoub et al. 2017, 45).

In 2016, anthropologist Joanne Rappaport, then president of the Latin American Studies Association, put together a delegation to Brazil in which I participated to investigate the legitimacy of the impeachment of Dilma Rousseff. As we documented in our fact-finding report, "social movement activists were perhaps less interested in the legal technicalities that legitimated this war against social equality" (Chalhoub et al. 2017, 45). For them, the impeachment was about a white elite reclaiming power and keeping racial and class privilege intact. The impeached were, they felt, "the poor people, black people, and gays and lesbians who have been at the center of small victories gained in the last thirteen years" (Chalhoub et al. 2017, 46). The delegation report provides rich documentation of the long historical view of how we got to this political point. Several of the people we interviewed, including prominent white politicians and lawyers, asserted that affirmative action in higher education was perhaps the most effective social transformation in recent Brazilian history. Prior to the implementation of affirmative action in 2012, Black people comprised less than 10 percent of university students, although they represented 50 percent of the Brazilian population—and up to 80 percent in some regions of the country (Santos 2014). In 2023, 56.1 percent of the Brazilian population identify as Black, and now 48.3 percent of university students are Black (Alfano 2023). This is a social gain that led to a local community activist like Marielle Franco attending university and to a rise in the number of college-educated Black people and, subsequently, the shaping of a new political class.

The debates around affirmative action were an early sign leading up to the current crisis, revealing that race structured a class society in Brazil. Few whites on the left were attuned to this racial question, and as Sueli Carneiro stated, "the reaction to affirmative action, the resistance, came from the presupposition that if you open these opportunities, you would have an increase in racism in the society, of racial conflicts. And the subtext, in fact at times an explicit text, is that it was because [white elites] expected activism, violence from Blacks in defense of quotas" (Chalhoub et al. 2017, 47). However, as former president and political prisoner Lula affirmed, access to unprecedented social mobility and the public sphere by Black people, women, and poor people made the white elite uncomfortable. This is especially the case for domestic workers and their children who pursued higher education precisely at the moment when labor rights were expanded. It became increasingly difficult for the middle classes to access and afford household and childcare labor, labor often provided by poor Black women.

This emphasis on the gendered racial and class dimensions of Rousseff's impeachment—specifically, the attempts to repeal social gains for Black people, women, and poor people—could be read through an intersectional lens to understand the ongoing enactment of white supremacy. An intersectional approach allows us to analyze the structural gendered racism and state violence against which vibrant social movements in Brazilian cities have been mobilizing. For activists, the lack of abortion rights, the rise in maternal mortality stemming from inadequate public health care, and the lack of basic infrastructure, such as sewers and clean running water in neighborhoods, on the one hand, and deadly local police encounters, on the other, are two sides of the same forces of state violence. For example, it is impossible to understand the history of the militarization of policing in Brazil's northeastern city of Salvador without an understanding of the policing of Black-women-led *terreiros*, street vendors, sex workers, and activists, especially housing and land-rights activists. This approach to understanding state violence and the modern construction of the Bahian city calls for examining multiple forms of exclusion that Black and Indigenous people experience simultaneously, while being attentive to the "urgency of intersectionality," as Kimberlé Crenshaw expresses it (2016). Importantly, this approach also reminds us to not exceptionalize this moment with Bolsonaro as Brazil's elected racist and sexist president.

The Future Struggle

In October 2018, Joênia Wapichana became the first Indigenous woman elected to the national congress, and Erica Malunguinho, artist, educator, and creator of the urban *quilombo* and cultural space Aparelha Luzia, was the first trans woman elected to the São Paulo state congress. Numerous other Black women were elected to city councils and state congresses around the country, including those who had worked alongside Marielle Franco.

At an April 2018 conference on Brazil at Harvard's Afro-Latin American Research Institute, Franco was set to speak on a panel with Malunguinho that I chaired. We honored her memory, and at the moment of her scheduled speech, Erica looked into the camera that was transmitting a live stream to the world, with mostly Brazilians watching, and announced her candidacy for political office in the same party as Marielle. She expressed four key points that she considered necessary for the democratic transformation of Brazil: (1) the need to recognize Black people, Black women, and transgender people as hypervisible all over Brazilian cities (as domestic workers in apartment and office buildings, and in large numbers as prostitutes in red-light zones); (2) the hate and violence that targets these Black cis- and transgender women is in stark contrast to the demand for their labor, including sexual labor; (3) the right to education and work is key to the LGBTQ+ fight against anti-Black genocide, as Black transgender people are also killed every day; and (4) the antiracism and antisexism struggle has to be diasporic. Malunguinho recently reminded us in a Facebook post of the brutal murder of Evaldo dos Santos Rosa: "Who is mistaken 80 times? The name of this project is extermination, culture of death, genocide, necropolitics. This is the government and the legislature's public security proposal."

As we reflect on the past five years since Franco's assassination and more than one year since the defeat of Jair Balsonaro in October 2022, the Afro-futures that activists like Erica Malunguinho envision will have to be a global project as espoused by her predecessors, such as Black left feminist activists Luiza Bairros, Lélia Gonzalez, Thereza Santos, and Franco, and will have to take seriously the global anti-Black genocide taking place in communities across the Americas.

This movement against anti-Black genocide—which is also a clear movement against resurgent white supremacy—has gained momentum in Brazil, especially in the days following the violent murder of nineteen-year-old Pedro Gonzaga in a Rio supermarket on February 15, 2019, by a security guard who held him in a chokehold. Despite the centuries-old plan to eliminate the "enemies within" (abolitionists, Black and Indigenous activists, and students, for example) in Brazil and throughout Latin America (Gill 2004), I understand the role of scholars and professors to be even more urgent. I understand the classroom as being ground zero for training new generations of thinkers and doers who envision a democratic society that includes all of us. A global Black liberation project is incomplete if we do not include, in a substantive way, the specific realities of the vast majority of Black men and women living in the Americas.

Notes

1. This chapter is a revised and updated version of my previously published essay with the same title published in the Special Issue on the Anthropology of White Supremacy in *American Anthropologist* 122, no. 1 (2020): 157–62.

2. All translations are my own.

3. However, practices of violent repression can also be seen more recently, under the guise of humanitarian aid efforts. An example from a hemispheric perspective is in Brazil's leading role in the United Nations Stabilization Mission in Haiti, which consisted of a militarized humanitarianism that Frank Müller and Andrea Steinke (2018) argue was directly related to Brazil's domestic expertise with militarized urban policing. They describe how Brazil's "aid" was actually police training for use against Brazilian citizens at home: "By means of the transnational entanglements of militarisation of humanitarian work between Haiti and Rio de Janeiro and as an effect of the alleged spatial and cultural similarity between the two places, Brazil could learn from the mission to improve its operational-logistic knowledge for missions 'at home'" (Müller and Andrea Steinke 2018, 229). These hemispheric connections are crucial for our understanding of the entanglement of global racisms and how the language of humanitarianism, pacification, and peacekeeping operate to mask these networks and produce the very violence they claim to suppress.

References

Alfano, Bruno. 2023. "Proporção de negros nas universides cai pela primeira vez desde 2016." *O Globo*, June 8, 2023. https://oglobo.globo.com/brasil/educacao/noticia/2023/06/proporcao-de-universitarios-negros-cai-pela-primeira-vez-desde-2016.ghtml.

Atencio, Rebecca J. 2014. *Memory's Turn: Reckoning with Dictatorship in Brazil*. Madison: University of Wisconsin Press.

Benedito, Vera. 2011. Opening remarks in Afro-Brazil and the Brazilian Polity seminar at Brown University, Providence, Rhode Island, April 4.

Brum, Eliane. 2018a. "How a Homophobic, Misogynist, Racist 'Thing' Could Be Brazil's Next President." *The Guardian*, October 6. www.theguardian.com/commentisfree/2018/oct/06/homophobic-mismogynist -racist-brazil-jair-bolsonaro.

———. 2018b. "O ódio deitou no meu divã (Hate sat on my couch)." *El País*, October 11. https://brasil.elpais .com/brasil/2018/10/10/politica/1539207771_563062.html.

———. 2019. "He's Been President a Week—and Already Bolsonaro Is Damaging Brazil." *The Guardian*, January 10. www.theguardian.com/commentisfree/2019/jan/10/jair-bolsonaro-brazil-minorities-rainforest.

Butler, Judith. 1990. *Gender Trouble: Feminism and the Subversion of Identity*. New York: Routledge.

Butterworth, Benjamin. 2018. "Jair Bolsonaro: 17 Quotes That Explain the Views of Brazil's Fascist President-Elect." *The I.* October 29. https://inews.co.uk/news/world/jair-bolsanaro-quotes-brazil-election-2018 -result-president-elect/.

Chalhoub, Sidney, Mariana Llanos, Keisha-Khan Y. Perry, Cath Collins, and Mónica Pachón. 2017. *Report of the LASA Fact-Finding Delegation on the Impeachment of Brazilian President Dilma Rousseff*. Pittsburgh: Latin American Studies Association. www.lasaweb.org/uploads/reports/brazildelegationreport-2017.pdf.

Chirio, Maud. 2018. *Politics in Uniform: Military Officers and Dictatorship in Brazil, 1960–80*. Pittsburgh: University of Pittsburgh Press.

Crenshaw, Kimberlé. 1990. "Mapping the Margins: Intersectionality, Identity Politics, and Violence against Women of Color." *Stanford Law Review* 43, no. 1: 1241–99.

———. 2016. "The Urgency of Intersectionality." TedWomen 2016, October. www.ted.com/talks/kimberle _crenshaw_the_urgency_of_intersectionality?language=en.

Darlington, Shasta, and Leticia Casado. 2019. "Brazil Fails to Replace Cuban Doctors, Hurting Health Care of 28 Million." *New York Times*, June 11, 2019. www.nytimes.com/2019/06/11/world/americas/brazil-cuba -doctors-jair-bolsonaro.html.

Ferreira da Silva, Denise. 2007. *Toward a Global Idea of Race*. Minneapolis: University of Minnesota Press.

Flauzina, Ana Luiza Pinheiro. 2008. *Corpo Negro Caído No Chão: O Sistema Penal e o Projeto Genocida Do Estado Brasileiro (Black Body Fallen on the Floor: The Penal System and the Genocidal Project of the Brazilian State)*. Rio de Janeiro: Contraponto.

Franco, Marielle (@mariellefranco). 2018. "Mais um homicídio de um jovem que pode estar entrando para a conta da PM. Matheus Melo estava saindo da igreja. Quantos mais vão precisar morrer para que essa guerra acabe?" *Twitter*, March 12, 10:38 a.m. https://twitter.com/mariellefranco/status/973568966403731456.

Gill, Lesley. 2004. *The School of the Americas: Military Training and Political Violence in the Americas*. Durham, NC: Duke University Press.

Gilroy, Paul. 1991. *There Ain't No Black in the Union Jack*. Chicago: University of Chicago Press.

Hafiz, Jihan. 2016. "The Cabula 12: Brazil's Police War against the Black Community." *Aljazeera America*, February 25. http://america.aljazeera.com/watch/shows/america-tonight/articles/2016/2/25/the-cabula-12 -brazil-police-war-blacks.html.

Hanchard, Michael 1994. "Black Cinderella?: Race and the Public Sphere in Brazil." *Public Culture* 7, no. 1: 165–85.

Human Rights Watch. 2017. *World Report 2018: Events of 2017*. New York: Human Rights Watch. www.hrw.org /sites/default/files/world_report_download/201801world_report_web.pdf.

———. 2023. "Brazil." *World Report 2023*, 90–100. www.hrw.org/sites/default/files/media_2023/01/World _Report_2023_WEBSPREADS_0.pdf

Instituto de Pesquisa Econômica Aplicada, 2022. *Atlas da Violência*. www.ipea.gov.br/atlasviolencia /publicacoes/244/atlas-2022-infograficos.

Lee, Erika. 2019. *America for Americans: A History of Xenophobia in the United States*. New York: Basic Books.

Malunguinho, Erica. 2018. "O que eu vou dizer ao meu filho?" Facebook, April 9. www.facebook.com /ericamalunguinho50888/videos/289849225246509/.

Müller, Frank, and Andrea Steinke. 2018. "Criminalising Encounters: MINUSTAH as a Laboratory for Armed Humanitarian Pacification." *Global Crime* 19, nos. 3–4: 228–49. www.tandfonline.com/doi/full/10.1080/17440572.2018.1498336?af=R.

National Public Radio. 2022. "From Slavery to Socialism, New Legislation Restricts What Teachers Can Discuss." February 3, 2022. www.npr.org/2022/02/03/1077878538/legislation-restricts-what-teachers-can-discuss.

Nogueira, Sayonara Nadir Bonfim, Tathiane Araújo Aquino, and Euclides Afonso Cabral. 2017. "Dossiê: A Geografia Dos Corpos Das Pessoas Trans (Dossier: The Geography of the Bodies of Trans People)." Aracaju, Brazil: Rede Trans Brasil. http://redetransbrasil.org.br/wp-content/uploads/2019/01/A-Geografia-dos-Corpos-Trans.pdf.

O Globo. 2018. "Bolsonaro diz que objetivo é fazer o Brasil semelhante 'ao que tínhamos há 40, 50 anos.' (Bolsonaro said that an objective is to make Brazil similar to 'what we had 40, 50 years ago')." October 15. https://oglobo.globo.com/brasil/bolsonaro-diz-que-objetivo-fazer-brasil-semelhante-ao-que-tinhamos-ha-40-50-anos-23158680.

Perry, Keisha-Khan Y. 2017. "Ask Dilma Why Hillary Lost: Why They Both Lost." *Garnet News*, April 3. https://garnetnews.com/2017/04/03/ask-dilma-hillary.

———. 2022. "Housing Justice in the Americas: Struggle and Solidarity." *NACLA Report on the Americas*, 54, no. 3: 237–39.

Pinheiro Flauzina, Ana Luiza. 2008. *Corpo Negro Caído No Chão: O Sistema Penal e o Projeto Genocida Do Estado Brasileiro (Black Body Fallen on the Floor: The Penal System and the Genocidal Project of the Brazilian State)*. Rio de Janeiro: Contraponto.

Ribeiro, Geraldo, and Anna Carolina Torres. 2019. "'Cadê meu pai?,' repete filho de músico que o viu morrer após carro levar mais de 80 tiros de militares ('Where is my father?' Repeats son of musician who saw him die after a car got hit by military police more than 80 times)," *O Globo Rio*, April 8. https://oglobo.globo.com/rio/cade-meu-pai-repete-filho-de-musico-que-viu-morrer-apos-carro-levar-mais-de-80-tiros-de-militares-23581550?utm_source=Facebook&utm_medium=Social& utm_campaign=compartilhar.

Ribeiro, Thi. 2022. "Chacina do Cabula: Ato em memória aos 12." Agência de Notícias das Favelas, February 6. www.anf.org.br/chacina-do-cabula-ato-em-memoria-aos-12/.

Santos, Sales Augusto dos. 2014. *Educação: Um pensamento negro contemporâneo (Education: Black Contemporary Thought)*. São Paulo: Paco Editorial.

Silva, M. M. L. 1994. "Killing of 6,000 Street Kids and the Candelaria Massacre." *CJ the Americas* 7, no. 4: 1–8.

Smith, Christen. 2016. *Afro-Paradise: Blackness, Violence, and Performance in Brazil*. Urbana-Champaign: University of Illinois Press.

23

On Love, the Palestinian Way

KINSHIP, CARE, AND ABOLITION IN PALESTINIAN FEMINIST PRAXIS

Sarah Ihmoud

> From the depths of my agony, I reached out and embraced the sky of our homeland through the window of my prison cell. . . . . Worry not, my child. I stand tall and steadfast, despite the shackles and the jailer. I am a mother in sorrow, from yearning to see you one last time.
>
> —KHALIDA JARRAR TO HER DAUGHTER, SUHA,
> DAMON PRISON, HAIFA, JULY 2021

WHEN SUHA JARRAR, a bright young human rights defender, was found dead in her Ramallah home in the occupied West Bank on July 12, 2021,[1] it was a tragedy whose reverberations were felt and mourned across the *shataat*.[2] I did not know Suha personally. But I felt the depth of her loss from friends in occupied territory who had known her, and who had loved her. Suha, the daughter of Khalida Jarrar, Palestinian feminist leader and parliamentarian, and prominent representative of the Popular Front for the Liberation of Palestine, who has been held captive[3] in Israel's prisons for the better part of a decade, had borne the pain of separation from her mother multiple times throughout her brief life. She had become an impassioned and outspoken activist for Palestinian human rights, dedicating much of her youth to speaking out for her mother's release, and for the freedom of all political prisoners. At just thirty-one years old, she had died quietly and alone; Palestinian authorities named her cause of death to be a severe heart attack.

I could not help but think of Erica Garner when I first heard the news. Erica Garner, the daughter of Eric Garner, choked to death by a white police officer on Staten Island in 2014, whose final words, "I can't breathe," became a rallying call for the Black Lives Matter movement, had become an outspoken activist against police brutality. She was a mother of two young children, and had died on December 30, 2017, following a heart attack at just twenty-seven years old. "There is no video, and no villain," Melissa Harris-Perry wrote of Erica's death, "but [her story] matters all the same" (2018). That story is in part a story about how white supremacy invades the bodies and intimacies of Black women's lives in the United States and across the globe. It is a story about the deadly power of racism. While occupation forces did not directly kill Suha or Erica, systems of settler colonialism and anti-Blackness are implicated in their deaths.

I am beginning here, with Suha's story, and Erica's, too, as a way of entering the tendrils and capillaries of global white supremacy as they course through the bodies, lives, and intimacies of those living in occupied territory, from Palestine to the United States.[4] As a central organizing logic of Western modernity (Beliso-De Jesús and Pierre 2019), white supremacy energizes the racialized structures, subjectivities, and intimacies of everyday life in the settler colony. In Palestine, settler colonialism and its accompanying relations of power are manifested in the social formation known as Zionist colonialism, a racial project that has sought to colonize Palestine in order to create an exclusive Jewish national homeland, and in turn, erase the Indigenous Palestinian presence (Sayegh 1967). This genocidal project[5] is centrally organized in and through a carceral regime that attempts to fragment and rupture Palestinian intimacies and Indigenous kinship relations across occupied territory and the still expanding *shataat*.

This chapter centers the forms of diasporic kinship and care work that Palestinian women perform within and beyond the institution of the colonial prison in occupied territory through letter writing as an abolitionist feminist praxis of decolonial love. I begin by offering an overview of Zionist colonialism as a genocidal project that holds Palestinian bodies, socialities, intimacies, and subjectivities captive for eliminatory violence and removal. Here, I am analyzing the relations between Palestinian captivity and the colonial project, underscoring that Israel is a colonial formation requiring Indigenous and other forms of captivity in a state of ongoing war. I argue that the rupturing of Palestinian intimacies and kinship relations should be understood as a strategic aim of settler colonial power and a condition of genocidal elimination. This rupturing is based on a white supremacist logic that seeks to purify the white Jewish national polis and its expanding boundaries from the contaminant of Indigenous Palestinian presence.

In what follows, I explore three texts as a window onto what I term an abolitionist Palestinian feminist praxis of decolonial love: (1) The letters of Khalida Jarrar to her daughter Suha, written in the aftermath of her death; (2) A letter from Tal'at, a decolonial feminist movement in Palestine, to Muna Al-Kurd and the women of Sheikh Jarrah defending Palestinian homes and land, at the outset of what has since been called by some the "Unity Intifada"; and (3) the "Love Letter to Our People" from the US-based Palestinian Feminist Collective, a diasporic decolonial feminist movement organization, released at the height of the uprising in the Spring of 2021. Interpreted ethnographically, these epistolary texts move us across different forms of kinship relations: from the relationship between mother and daughter, to relations between Palestinian women differentially positioned across fragmented spaces in occupied territory, to kinship relations between *shataat* Palestinians and those in the homeland.

Letters expressing grief, care, and radical hope written from the space of genocidal duress are material expressions of an abolitionist praxis of decolonial love[6] that transcend colonial borders, boundaries, and fragmentation of territories and people imposed by the Zionist regime. Letter writing practices offer a material expression of the sentient life forms that suture the social fabric of the Palestinian collective, regenerating our connections to each other and to our homeland. Further, their messages evoke affective registers that mobilize what, following Ali Musleh (2022), I will call a Palestinian sensorium, an assemblage of affective and sensory methods of revolutionary praxis that assert a Palestinian *nafs* (Sheehi and Sheehi 2022) or psychic and ontological presence against "sensory genocide" (Musleh 2022, 146), the production of sensory enclosure that is central to ongoing colonial war. The letters themselves as material archives, and the Palestinian sensorium they evoke labor in service of transforming grief into radical hope, a key catalyst for emancipatory struggle against colonial violence, marking possibilities for ecologies of life and giving shape to an ethical transnational community of feminist praxes of resistance. In doing so, letters as the expression of Palestinian care and love trace the limits of the settler colonial project and map its constant unraveling. This abolitionist praxis, what I name as *Love, the Palestinian Way*,[7] performs the fracturing and collapse of the structural violence of the Israeli state, its legitimacy as a settler colonial genocidal force, and an insurgent imaginary of Palestinian futurity (e.g., Rodriguez 2019). In other words, Love the Palestinian Way is a life-affirming method that embodies and performs sovereign and communal freedom, even as it exists as a "deregulated gathering . . . that pulsates against enclosure" (Cervenak 2021, 9).

Whether authored from the space of the actual prison cell or from the prison as embodied social condition of captivity for Palestinians in occupied territory, the poetic force of the letter has a unique capacity to cultivate an abolitionist imaginary that refuses legitimacy of Zionist colonialism in Palestine, and ruptures investment in the idea that it will always exist. Rather, these letters reveal that fugitive practices of kinship and connection are happening all the time across geographies of colonialism and captivity that both survive the conditions of genocidal elimination and delegitimize and unsettle the Zionist regime. Hence, *Love, the Palestinian Way* emerges as a psychic and sensory method and praxis of communal healing and liberation that displaces the "raciontology" of white supremacy and settler colonial violence.

I focus on the ethnographic form of the letter for three primary reasons. First, in the intimacy of its address, the letter is a decidedly feminist method of writing that brings the reader into an innermost, private space, defining the reader's place and hence *bringing them into relation* with the subject, beckoning them to bear critical witness. It evokes a feminist call and response. Second, the letter is a form that enables speech to subvert and cross the carceral boundaries of the colony, whether it be the actual physical confines of the colonizer's prison cell, or the carceral geographies of occupied territory and the conditions of native captivity more broadly. Finally, as a Chicana-Palestinian anthropologist born in the space of the shataat or *ghurba* (exile), my own access to and mobility across the physical territory of Palestine is not easily incurred, due to the surveillance and violence of colonial authorities that control my entrance to the "field." These conditions, in addition to the severe censorship currently faced by Palestinian scholars in the US academy (Palestine Legal 2015), require a shift in the way we conceptualize anthropological fieldwork in Palestine, creating an imperative to write, think, and engage ethnographic praxis in Palestine in alternative ways. It is important to note here that my authorship of this essay is embedded within the knowledge and wisdom produced collectively in community with Palestinian feminists in the homeland and the diaspora, and in particular, as a member of the Palestinian Feminist Collective.

And why, dear reader, do I choose to write about love? I am choosing to write about love because I am exhausted by the quiet terror my people endure each day in occupied territory. I am writing about love because I cannot forget the face of a five-year-old girl who wouldn't speak or eat for days, and who, soon after, perished in a Jerusalem hospital after losing her home and family in a Gaza air strike in 2014. I choose to write about love because some nights I still awaken, heart racing, palms sweating, hearing the hum of helicopters overhead, as if it were only yesterday the soldiers invaded my building in the old city, dragging my neighbor away into the darkness of night. I am writing about love because I am tired of writing about death. I am exasperated, as a Palestinian woman, that the violence we must face is not only in the hands of my colonizer but also in the hands of patriarchal authorities in my community. I want to write about my sisters and their will and their struggle to survive. I am writing about love because I want to write about how we get free.

Kinship and Care Work against Captivity

Indigenous and queer feminists have long argued that the impositions of heteropatriarchy through settler colonialism as a form of sexual colonization attempts to "isolate, disperse and eliminate indigenous modes of kinship and relationship to land" (Morgenson 2013, 170). In Palestine, this critique of power not only shapes the lives of queer Palestinians but is intertwined with the sexualized racialization of all Palestinians living under Israeli rule (Alqaisiya 2018). As Dakota scholar Kim TallBear suggests, growing a white population through "biologically reproductive heterosexual marriage—in addition to encouraging immigration from some places and not others" has been a critical aspect of settler colonial nation-building since the post–World War II era, as heteronormative marriage and kinship practices forged through particular intersections of race, class, and gender have worked to increase certain populations and not others (TallBear 2018, 146). White families anchored imagined notions of safety while Otherized communities were "made available for sacrifice" (2018, 146). In short,

white bodies and white families in spaces of safety have been propagated in intimate co-constitution with the culling of Black, red and brown bodies and the wastelanding of their spaces. Who gets to have babies, and who does not? Whose babies get to live?

Whose do not? Whose relatives, including other-than-humans, will thrive and whose will be laid to waste? (2018, 147)

In Palestine, the fragmentation of Indigenous kinship networks and social relations more broadly has been a key and strategic component of Zionist colonialism since its inception, as part of what Fayez Sayegh names as the "racial exclusiveness" and "self-segregation" inherent to its ideology (1965, 213). Zionism, as a state and colonial project, absorbed the foundational racial logics of white racial and cultural hegemony (Erakat 2015; Ihmoud 2021) in attempts to transform what its intellectual architects understood as "uselessly occupied territories into a useful extension of Europe" (Seikaly 2020, 113). The racial imperative of the Zionist project is forcefully expressed through a simultaneous attempt at Jewish pronatalism and Palestinian antinatalism; that is, between the enabling of the biological reproduction of a particular aggregate of Jewish bodies on the land pinned against the restriction, containment, and elimination of Indigenous Palestinian reproduction (Ihmoud 2021). It is important to note that this politics deploys anti-Blackness through the racial and reproductive violence necessary to become part of the enlightened, European West (Ihmoud 2021; Abusneineh 2021). The carceral management of Palestinian and Israeli Jewish bodies across occupied territory (and beyond) is linked to this central imperative of Indigenous erasure and Zionist reproduction.

Policies that surveil, police, and violate Palestinian birth and marriage, energized by biopolitical imperatives that seek to limit and control Indigenous presence on the land, stand out as exemplary of such practices, though to confine an exploration of social fragmentation through the lens of the Palestinian birthing body and family as such would be limiting. Broader policies, such as the ID card and permit regimes, work to fragment and police Palestinian populations into separate and unequal territories (Gaza, 1948,[8] the Occupied West Bank, including East Jerusalem, and the shataat), limiting geographic movement, economic mobility, and intimacies through militarized surveillance, control, and the erection of checkpoints, walls, and boundaries (Hammami 2019; Shalhoub-Kevorkian 2015a; Tawil Souri 2011, 2012; Zureik 2001; Zureik et al. 2011; Shalhoub-Kevorkian and Ihmoud 2014). This fragmentation is energized by a broader logic of carceral power, which gives shape to the various modes, methods, and strategies of colonial violence. I take up Dylan Rodriguez's definition of carceral power as a "totality of state-sanctioned and extrastate relations of gendered racial-colonial dominance" (2019, 1576), a project inseparable from its roots in Western modernity and the "life-deforming algorithms of a Civilization project" wrested in the intersecting logics of enslavement and racial-colonial genocide (Rodriguez 2019, 1610) and hence, global white supremacy.

In colonized Palestine, the Israeli state prison system has devastated Palestinian society and is an issue that united Palestinians across fragmented territories. Since 1967 alone, approximately 800,000 Palestinians have been detained by Israel, an estimated 10,000 women among them, and currently 4,600 remain captive in Israeli jails (Addameer 2016, 4). The conviction rate of Palestinians in Israel's military court system stands at approximately 99 percent (Addameer 2016, 5). Palestinian women have been subjected to sexual violence and other forms of gendered coercion within the site of the prison, in addition to the same forms of repression as their male counterparts, both in the efforts to undermine Palestinian resistance and fracture traditionally cohesive social relations (Abdo 2014; Francis 2020). Scholars and activists also note how imprisoning and torturing Palestinians works to harm their families and communities by extension in gendered ways, as women bear the emotional, psychological, and financial burdens of having their loved ones incarcerated. The creation of Palestinian policing and security institutions along with the Palestinian Authority as part of the 1993 Oslo Accords has further extended this gendered carceral project, as they operate through the framework of "securitized peace," meaning in full cooperation with the Israeli regime, including in the suppression of political dissent (Hawari 2021, 2–3).

Still, the institution of the prison must be understood as but one aspect of a machinery of carceral power that holds Palestinian life and kinships captive in service of eliminatory violence. In other words, the Israeli prison system is merely one in a host of strategies for holding "native surplus," one expression of a broader geography of carceral power. Historian Rashid Khalidi notes that the entire machinery of settler colonial power and the occupation regime established after 1967, which in essence resembles policies and practices implemented in earlier stages of the colonial project from 1948, "can be seen as a carceral enterprise which is designed to control, confine, and dominate the Palestinians living in these areas" (Khalidi 2014, 7). Importantly, he notes:

> The most extreme and most perfected example of this strategy is the treatment of the Gaza Strip, which has become the world's largest open-air prison, where 1.8 million people are penned into 360 sq km, a ghetto in which most of them are confined for years. But even in the apparently more "open" circumstances of the West Bank and East Jerusalem, the same principles of control, confine, and dominate apply, as in any prison system. (Khalidi 2014, 7)

Palestine, then, stands as a space from which we can expand theorization of the relationships between captivity and colonialism. In particular, what comes into focus is the relationship between Indigeneity and captivity, also offering possibilities for expanding analysis of anticolonialism and abolition.

To further this analysis, we must consider the insights of a tradition of decolonial Palestinian feminism (Ihmoud 2022). Building on the voices of women and children in occupied territory, Palestinian feminist scholars have theorized gendered experiences navigating militarized geographies and the everyday violence of social exclusion in terms of "confinement," suffocation, and entrapment. A 2012 study by Nadera Shalhoub-Kevorkian describes how Jerusalemite youth used terms of *khan'aa* (suffocation) and *masyadeh* (trap) to "describe their lives in Jerusalem and the effects of Israeli policies of exclusion and discrimination" (2012, 7). I want to build on these key insights in theorizing colonial captivity in Palestine as an embodied and lived social condition. At the same time, attention to the intimate geographies of colonial violence as they are lived and experienced in everyday life also brings the intimate, quotidian, and embodied to the fore as spaces of gendered resistance to colonial captivity (Shalhoub-Kevorkian 2012, 7).

Despite the imposition of colonial captivity on our bodies, sexualities, and kinship relations, we are in a constant practice of persisting, reconstituting, and remembering the Palestinian body politic in response to and against the colonial regime. While feminist scholars of Palestine have situated everyday practices of marriage and "kin work" as "sites where Israeli colonialism is contested and Palestinian identity is constituted" (Johnson 2006, 53), I want to push this analysis beyond the biological family structure to explore social relations and decolonial political possibilities more broadly. If kinship matters in ways that, paraphrasing Elizabeth Freeman, "bodies matter" for Judith Butler (2007), the repetition of particular practices of building social relations or modes of belonging to each other matter in terms of what we come to imagine as thinkable for the organization and future of Palestinian social life. To extend this insight, if queerness is a "relation between rather than a sedimented end" (Shomali 2023, 5), might a queer Palestinian archive of belonging to each other, of belonging to Palestine be loved into existence through the disparate yet interconnected constellations of letters that speak out against the genocidal conditions of colonial captivity?

The three letters under examination in this chapter express a Palestinian feminist praxis of decolonial love that enables expressions of care and affect to travel beyond the prison itself and the carceral power of Zionist colonialism, examining in particular the intimate sites of rebellion that are brought to light as a method for weaving together kinship relations and the Palestinian social body. Following Orisanmi Burton, I theorize Palestinian women's letter writing as "an ethnographic and political modality" (2021, 2) that is part of a broader repertoire of Palestinian feminist praxis and the living archive of Palestinian rebellion deployed to survive within and struggle against racial gendered colonial violence and erasure. Amid the ongoing oppression Palestinian women face as a result of the intersections of settler colonial and patriarchal violence (Shalhoub-Kevorkian2015b), relations of kinship and care constitute an underexplored and undertheorized aspect of Palestinian feminist worldmaking.

Three Letters: On Decolonial Love

I. Letter from Damon Prison: On Grief and Mourning

Khalida Jarrar is writing from her cell in Damon prison, a site established by the British Mandate government in the forests of Carmel in Haifa. It reopened in 1953 as a camp for detaining Palestinian prisoners, where she is now held captive with forty other Palestinian women. She addresses the first letter to her daughter, Suha, on the day of her death. She yearns to be reunited with her daughter, but the occupation forces will not allow an early release. They will not even allow a temporary release to attend her daughter's funeral on July 13, 2021. "I am in so much pain, only because I miss you," she writes.

> This doesn't happen except in Palestine. All I wanted was to bid my daughter a final farewell, with a kiss on her forehead and to tell her I love her as much as I love Palestine. My daughter, forgive me for not attending the celebration of your life, that I was not

beside you during this heartbreaking and final moment. My heart has reached the heights of the sky yearning to see you, to caress and plant a kiss on your forehead through the small window of my prison cell.

Suha, my precious. They have stripped me from bidding you a final goodbye kiss, so I bid you farewell with a flower. Your absence is searingly painful, excruciatingly painful. But I remain steadfast and strong, like the mountains of beloved Palestine.

Jarrar's words analyze this separation, viscerally experienced as a stripping away of the power to kiss her daughter a final goodbye, as another aspect of the Zionist regime's machinery of violence. This regime attempts to sear its racialized power into the bodies and psyches of Palestinians through legalized carceral technologies of forced separation, in this case through detention in the colonial prison.[9] Lamenting her painful separation from her daughter, even in death, Jarrar provides a critique of Israel's fragmentation of Palestinian intimacies and social relations and at the same time mobilizes a decolonial praxis of *sumud* (Meari 2014).

What do we do when we are faced with being forcibly separated from and losing the people we love in ongoing conditions of genocide? Jarrar's love letters to Suha bear intimate, yet public, insights into a revolutionary Palestinian feminist politics waged from the space of captivity in the colonizer's prison: how we fight with love to maintain our humanity, in the most inhumane conditions; how this fierce commitment to loving each other is what keeps us connected to Palestine, too. Jarrar's recounting of her will to "remain steadfast and strong, like the mountains of beloved Palestine" both recognize and contest the violence of carceral separation as dynamics of the colonial encounter. As Lena Meari theorizes, the practice of *sumud*, or steadfastness, constitutes a Palestinian "relational political-psycho-affective subjectivity" that takes place outside the normalized space of formal politics (2014, 549). Under conditions of colonial violence and oppression, sumud is a "constant revolutionary becoming, opening up a possibility for an alternative regime of being, for an ethical-political relational selfhood" (2014, 549). Jarrar's own emphasis on her steadfastness in this moment of intimate encounter with the colonial regime is thus an assertion of her revolutionary subjectivity that refuses to submit to the dehumanizing conditions of Zionist colonialism.

It is important to underscore that this subjectivity is also one of a revolutionary Palestinian mothering. "Death and mourning breathe new life into revolutionary mothering toward an alternative future" (Brown and Puri 2022, 315) in which Palestinian women are not burdened with mothering in a world predicated on Palestinian death and erasure. You may confine me to the prison cell and refuse me the right to bid my child farewell, Jarrar's letter underscores. You may try to break the bonds between a mother and her child, but you will never break us apart. You will never take away my capacity to love, either my child or Palestine. In this moment, they become transposed onto one another: love for Palestine and love for her child, as a part of oneself, a part of one's body that cannot be torn away. These letters to Suha crystallize a Palestinian feminist praxis that mobilize possibilities for love as an affective force that opens space for an alternative ethical-political regime of being and revolutionary becoming. In other words, this love is not a passive "politics of the heart" (Bouteldja 2016, 140), but is intimately tied to struggle to reclaim the Palestinian homeland.

Further, as various scholars have highlighted, Israel's exercise of sovereignty extends not only over the living, but also the dead: "[settler colonial] control also rests upon disciplining Palestinian expressions of grief and mourning" (Hassan 2021, 29). In this context, preventing Jarrar from burying her daughter Suha can be read as a disruption of the "social relationship between the living and the dead" (Hassan 2021, 29), alongside an interruption of traditional networks of grief families need to cope with loss. Indeed, in a second letter addressed to her husband, daughter Yafa, and her supporters days later, Jarrar writes:

> Suha was born into this world while her father was imprisoned, and now she is departing this world while her mother is imprisoned. This is an intense and encapsulated human summary of the life of the Palestinian who loves life, hope, and freedom and hates subordination and colonialism. This occupation robs us of everything, even the oxygen we breathe. I must bid my dear Suha farewell with a rose grown in the soil of the homeland: Rest in peace, soaring bird of my heart.

This denial of mourning her daughter's death is understood as another form of assault waged by colonial forces on the Jarrar family, and by extension, the wider Palestinian collective. And yet, her public letters refuse the ungrievability of Palestinian life, while inviting the wider Palestinian collective to participate in the mourning process. This collective "wake work" (Sharpe 2017) is a feminist praxis that emphasizes the "connectivity of grief-work as a mainstay of affective kinship" (Brown and Puri 2022, 311). A call. A response. As Eman Ghanayem reminds us, "writing itself is a form of mourning" (2022), and collective grief born out of the conditions of settler colonial captivity can also form the connective tissue for radical hope. Revolutionary love the Palestinian way is about reclaiming the intimate, psycho-social, and spiritual praxes of belonging to each other that sharpen our collective vision and form the groundwork for communal action.

II. Letter to the Women of Sheikh Jarrah

On the eve of the Palestinian uprising in the spring of 2021, where the struggles of Palestinian families to protect their homes from theft by Zionist settlers in the Sheikh Jarrah neighborhood of occupied Jerusalem became a catalyst for mass organizing, Palestinians with the ability to be mobile (those with Jerusalem ID, or with citizenship from the state), cross colonial borders to join the struggle to protect the homes and families of Sheikh Jarrah with their own bodies. Many are assaulted by military forces, who enclose the neighborhood with arms and concrete blocks in an attempt to quell the resistance. Under these conditions the Tal'at movement ("rising up" in Arabic), a decolonial feminist movement established in 2019 following the murder of Israa Ghraib and organizing under the call of "no liberated homeland without the liberation of women," delivers a private letter addressed to Muna Al Kurd, one of the youth defending her home, and leading organizing efforts, and to the women of Sheikh Jarrah more broadly.

"We write this letter because we cannot go to Al-Quds [Jerusalem] and be with you, your family, and our family in Al-Quds," it begins. In asserting the relation between a collective "we" as Palestinian women in one fragmented space of occupied territory and "our family in Al-Quds," the letter asserts a social relation of kinship, a belongingness. *You are our family*. The words of the letter work as a mechanism of presence that defies the colonial orders of borders, boundaries, and captivity that fragment Palestinian life and relations across occupied territory. The letter continues,

> We felt that it was important to tell you how much pride we have in the *sumud* of our family in Sheikh Jarrah, especially that of the women. We learned of your struggle and the story of Sheikh Jarrah before these recent events, and we believe in your strength. We know you are fighting to share your story and the message across the world about the problem of Sheikh Jarrah.
>
> We are watching one of the greatest struggles that proved to us that we can stay steadfast and face and fight for that which is ours. The thought that the residents of Sheikh Jarrah are continuing their work day and night, they are giving their lives for this struggle. Our letter [addresses you] here because as women we are learning a lot from the situation of Sheikh Jarrah which women are a big part of it. You are an example that women can be a part of this fighting organization and can be on the front lines of it.

Here again, the concept of sumud is evoked as a form of anticolonial praxis. In addressing the letter to women, and centering Palestinian women's sumud as being on the front lines in the defense of home and land in Jerusalem, Tal'at's letter uplifts Jerusalemite women's critical role in the material struggle to protect Sheikh Jarrah within the history of the Palestinian freedom struggle. There is also, in this letter, an implicit critique of hegemonic androcentric and patriarchal notions of Palestinian national liberation, which has elevated men as primary revolutionary actors and peripheralized women's leadership, including revolutionary praxis in the intimate space of the home. Like their Arab sisters and other Indigenous communities who have resisted colonialism, Palestinian women have always resisted oppression and dehumanization, being primary agents of change and revolution (Ihmoud 2022).

"We thank you," the letter concludes, "because we are learning from your sumud and the sumud of the neighborhood. We are with you, although getting there is very difficult." The Tal'at movement's letter to the women of Sheikh Jarrah works as an expression of care and love extended across colonial borders in a moment of Palestinian rebellion and resurgence to assert a feminist ethos of kinship. It is important to highlight here that "borders are also social constructions of the territory, which establish that the dominant power can impose with varying degrees of "institutional right" on the lands and territories of these people" (Gruner 2018, 270).[10] Hence, the letter speaks against the carceral fragmentation of Palestinian communities imposed by Zionist colonialism to assert an intimacy and unity of Palestinians as one people. Further, in its intimate address to and centering of Palestinian women's critical role in the struggle to defend home and land in Sheikh Jarrah, the letter works against the impositions of colonial patriarchal violence, remapping how we can think about resistance outside of hegemonic Western imperialist feminist and internal patriarchal visions of national liberation. Revolutionary love the Palestinian way is about crossing borders of coloniality and claiming relations of kinship and care, while asserting women's presence and leadership in material struggles over home and homeland.

III. A Love Letter to Our People Struggling in Palestine

In the midst of mass demonstrations of Palestinian unity against Israel's occupation and settler colonial regime, in what has since been referred to by many as the "Unity Intifada," the Palestinian Feminist Collective (PFC), a recently established and intergenerational "U.S. based network of Palestinian and Arab women/feminists committed to Palestinian social and political liberation" considered how best to intervene.[11] The feeling of separation, of not being able to "be there," of watching the violence against land defenders in Palestine from afar, and of the renewed military assault on the captive Gaza strip, alongside the epistemic erasure of our voices and experiences in mainstream media coverage and the silence of international actors, felt devastating. At the same time, watching the renewed wave of mass resistance unfold was awe inspiring. As we discussed, demonstrated, mourned, and organized in conversation with our relatives, friends, and others in Palestine and across various global spaces, we considered: What might a Palestinian feminist intervention from the space of the *shataat* look like in this context?[12] What vision did we want to put out into the world in this moment? When we learned that Tal'at had shared a private letter with the women of Sheikh Jarrah, we were inspired by this act of love. We decided to write our own version of a love letter to our people with the hopes of helping re-ignite feminist organizing for Palestinian liberation in the United States and beyond.

"Your relentless will to remain on the land is a source of inspiration, perseverance, and fortitude," the letter begins.

> Once again, Palestinians from the far north to the far south of our homeland are defying settler colonialism's attempts to partition land and people. From the Galilee to Gaza you reveal the geography of Palestine, in the face of military brutality and international impunity. State and settler violence and ethnic cleansing in Sheikh Jarrah and the Al Aqsa compound are not exceptions. They are part of an ongoing Nakba that has spanned Palestinian time and space since 1948.

The letter offers a feminist analysis of Palestinian resistance to Zionist colonialism in Sheikh Jarrah, historicizing this particular struggle as part of a longer trajectory of struggle against colonial violence since the 1948 Nakba.

> To our Palestinian sisters, your steadfastness to hold ground, at the risk of injury and death, and against all odds, is our fortitude. Gendered violence is core to settler colonial practice. We stand with you as you resist this masculinized and militarized colonization. We share in your pain from this renewed assault on Palestinian life and land. We are enraged as settlers wreak havoc and call for the death of our people. We stand vigilant

as you withstand airstrikes in Gaza, and stun grenades, tear gas, skunk water, rubber bullets, and the desecration of our sacred sites in Jerusalem, no less during the month of Ramadan. We stand with you as you resist the media's violent erasure of the Palestinian struggle.

Like the letter from Tal'at, the PFC's love letter centers Palestinian women as revolutionary social actors. It offers a feminist analysis that understands gendered violence as central to Zionist colonialism and affirms and uplifts Palestinian women's experiences and labor as key to understanding life and decolonial visions of futurity.

Your labor has taught us for generations: Palestine is a feminist issue. Love guides our methodology for liberation. We affirm life and implore feminists everywhere to speak up, organize, and join the struggle for Palestinian liberation. We call for an immediate halting of the theft of homes in Sheikh Jarrah, Silwan, and beyond, and an immediate halting to the airstrikes on Gaza.

To our people throughout Palestine, we are with you. You are protecting a future where Palestinians everywhere can live without fear of colonial violence, a future where our children and our homes are safe, a future free from colonial containment and incarceration, a future where we can freely practice our spiritual worship.

We are rising up across cities in the heart of U.S. empire, that has fed the colonization and dispossession of the Palestinian people. Our vision for a radically different future is based on equality, justice, and life-affirming interconnectedness. We honor your voices, perseverance, and *sumoud*, and promise to continue our joint struggle for justice and liberation in Palestine and the *shataat*.

In reactivating the call to recognize Palestine as a feminist issue, a call issued by a long tradition of Palestinian feminist movements, the PFC both highlights the disproportionate violence and oppression that Palestinian women face in the context of Zionist colonialism and calls for open feminist solidarity with the Palestinian freedom struggle.[13] This is a vision guided by the PFC's values of love as a methodology for anticolonial resistance and liberation.

Indeed, the call from the PFC's *love letter* was amplified and answered by feminist scholars and activists in gender studies departments across the nation, who signed on to a public statement condemning the ongoing assaults on Palestinian land and life, and committing themselves to solidarity with the people of Palestine, as "proud benefactors of decades of feminist anti-racist, and anti-colonial activism that informs the foundation of our interdiscipline."[14] Even the National Women's Studies Association (NWSA) would release its own statement asserting that, "We must speak out into the wind with a loud collective voice and say that Palestinian Solidarity is a feminist issue, as the Palestinian Feminist Collective reminds us" (May 2021). While the public visibility of such acts would, in time, fade, along with the more visible aspects of political struggle on the ground, and while many of the signatories would soon come under surveillance and attack by the US-based Israel lobby, which has enhanced its assaults on anyone in US academe who dares speak up, organize, and express solidarity with the Palestinian people, I want to hold on to this moment in time and think with it as an expression of a resurgence of an ethical community through an emergent Palestinian feminist politics of decolonial love.

In its assertion of a shared but radically reenvisioned humanity, "decolonial love promotes loving as an active, intersubjective process, and in so doing articulates an anti-hegemonic, anti-imperialist affect and attitude that can guide the actions that work to dismantle oppressive regimes" (Urena 2016). Thinking with the force of the love letter as a decolonial method and praxis asks us to consider how love can be a radical and infra-structural modality of social change inspiring the reemergence of feminist solidarities between Palestinians and other Indigenous communities, but also in opening space for transforming the landscape of discourse about Palestine. Centering love as method also uplifts the value of reciprocity, as the wide response to the love letter was not just about the love that we as Palestinians received, but also a continuation of the relational forms of love we have given historically in situating our liberation as interconnected with Black, Indigenous, Third World, and queer liberation movements across the globe more broadly. Finally, what is offered here is a broader abolitionist vision for a radically different global future based on life-affirming interconnectedness between communities marginalized by the devastating intersecting structures of global white supremacy, heteropatriarchy, racial capitalism, and colonialism. Decolonial love the Palestinian way, then, which I analyze as a method that forms part of a constellation of Palestinian feminist practices of which letter writing is a part, also brings to the fore the possibility for deepening fields of intimacy and affective relations needed to create shared horizons of liberation, recognizing Palestinian liberation as part of a broader abolitionist feminist vision geared toward undoing gendered racial-colonial dominance and transforming global relations of power.

Conclusion: Decolonial Love as Method or *Love, the Palestinian Way*

What is the space between collective grief and love? How do we transform one into the other? And what does it mean to engage decolonial love as a *method* for Palestinian liberation? What is the work that love does in the space of duress, violence, and forced absenting? In revolutionary struggle? What does beginning from a space of decolonial love do to unmoor us from the political imaginaries that hold us captive to the predatory structures of settler colonialism, heteropatriarchy, anti-Blackness, and imperial power? What unnameable and ungovernable desires, what spaces of belonging—with and for each other, for the Palestinian nation—does a revolutionary love inspire us to reclaim and to imagine?

While decolonial or revolutionary love is difficult to define, traces of its alchemy can be witnessed in the letters of Palestinian women writing against colonial captivity, as letters labor toward naming and narrating the ephemeral, affective, and sensory worlds that are beyond representation. The letters that I uplift here form part of a constellation of resistance practices giving life to the enduring Palestinian freedom struggle, highlighting decolonial love as a transnational Palestinian feminist praxis of abolition. Drawing on the intimacies of letter writing, or the epistolary method, and the love letter in particular, brings to the fore a shared horizon of "affective, intellectual, and political possibility" and "world-making praxis" (Burton 2021, 5), despite the prison bars, fences, and militarized geographies that separate us as Palestinian women from each other and from Palestine. I have chosen to focus on Palestinian women's letters because they provide insights into a central aspect of liberation politics that has long been made invisible in patriarchal conceptions of what it means to "do" politics in the struggle to achieve national liberation: that of reclaiming intimate geographies of the bodily, psychic, and affective, of reconnecting the social fabric of Indigenous Palestinian relations, or kinship, that Zionist colonialism has strategically fragmented and violated through carceral politics as a precondition of genocidal elimination; and of elevating the "ephemeral and gestural archive, producing legibility in its specific moment of enactment, but with the realization that legibility is neither the end goal nor a stable, infinite state" (Shomali 2023, 5).

From a decolonial feminist perspective, writing letters has been theorized as a form that "takes risks, for it implies a close and almost intimate connection to the reader" (Acevedo-Zapata 2020, 418). In *Methodology of the Oppressed*, Chela Sandoval argues that love, accessed through poetic modes of expression, is an affective force of "differential consciousness" that has the power to rupture our everyday worlds, allowing us to "crossover" into other states of being, doing, and movement (1991, 139). "It is love," she writes," that can access and guide our theoretical and political *movidas*—revolutionary maneuvers toward decolonized being" (1991, 140). It is love that can inspire oppositional social action. Indeed, Devin Atallah writes that "decolonial love can be a passageway towards knowing and towards finding a community of resistance" (2022, 81).

Women's love letters invite a collective witnessing of Palestinian grief—invite the collective into the space of mourning and thus become an act of healing. The love letter also uplifts communal spaces, material struggles over home and homeland, and sumud that sustain longevity in this ongoing struggle. Further, the love letter invites renewed possibilities for the regeneration and strengthening of transnational constellations of feminist solidarity with the Palestinian liberation struggle, what I have referred to here as an ethical community. These letters reflect a long history and practice of letter writing among captive activist intellectuals throughout various traditions of resistance and resistance literature (e.g., Harlow 1992; James 2005; Nashif 2008).[15]

Drawing on these insights, the letters I am thinking with here illustrate a method through which Palestinians call each other into intimate relation, gathering our disparate, yet interconnected, experiments in decolonial love and amplify a Palestinian sensorium that sharpens our capacity to enact revolutionary struggle, to build communities as sanctuaries that enable survival and transformation. Whether between a mother held captive and separated from her daughter, between groups of women fragmented by the carceral geographies of colonial violence, or women based in the homeland and in the shataat, the love letter sends fugitive messages in the cracks of Zionist colonialism, writing against its domination, dehumanization, and extraction. In doing so, women invent new routes and pathways toward remembering the Palestinian social body, reimagining kinship relations with community and land, and liberating our intimacies and senses from colonial captivity.

We call out to each other across time and space, transgressing the physical, temporal, and metaphorical boundaries colonization has imposed on us. We assert a collective identity and belonging to each other as an enactment of Indigenous fugitivity and resurgence (Simpson 2017). Our presence, our insistence on being and existing, and our insistence on belonging to each other as one people, is a leap into the future in and through the ongoing spectacle of colonial terror. This is love as a method of healing, of suturing the open wound as part of an active revolutionary tradition.

Walking with a friend one afternoon and discussing this alchemic praxis of decolonial love, he wondered aloud about what he called "the preciousness of the thing." "How do we hold onto the preciousness of the thing," he asked, "in this case, decolonial love, without speaking it?" I did not have an answer in that moment. But the question lingers. In part, I read it as an invitation to consider the ethics and accountability that uplifting these methods we hold close to the heart demand of us as Palestinian scholars. I raised the question with another friend later that evening. "What if our work as Palestinian scholars in this moment is to do the work of sitting with our people, with love and care?" they replied. Can decolonial love also be imagined as a method of sitting with our people, listening deeply, leaning into vulnerability, and caring for each other; caring for the world we inhabit? What if our difficult job is to hold on to that love, amplify its power as an atmosphere, illustrating how, through modes of its assembly, we speak to the solid, embodied work of abolition?

In her writing on revolutionary love, Joy James notes that while the preciousness of the thing itself is not fully definable or knowable, we must continue to pursue it. "When we retreat from searching for it, we stagnate or stumble. On our best and worst days and nights, an elusive Revolutionary Love might be the one tangible link that holds us together as communities despite the precarity and the predatory powers arrayed against freedom in balance with all life forms" (2023, xxii). My analysis of this elusive, precious thing in this chapter has surely been imperfect, but I have pursued it nonetheless. Perhaps this is part of the urgent invitation that embracing love the Palestinian way extends to us all: that we embrace each other and chart a path collectively with all of our contradictions; that we become braver and more capable of daring to confront the predatory powers that seek to destroy our capacity to love and share in each other's loving communion. That, in the act of practicing decolonial love, in daring to embrace its vulnerability and its dangerousness, we rupture the psychic bonds to a dying colonialism, nurturing our collective healing and other ways of belonging into the world.

Acknowledgments

I thank my sisters in the Tal'at movement for trusting me with their expression of love, alongside those of the Palestinian Feminist Collective. The Palestinian Women's writing group, which includes Ashjan Ajour, Amanda Batarseh, Nayrouz Abu Hatoum, Eman Ghanayem, Jennifer Mogannam, Loubna Qutami, and Randa Wahbe, provided a nourishing space that grounded an early stage of this chapter's development. The community of scholars and activists who welcomed me to the University of Hawai'i at Mānoa as part of

"Decolonial November" 2022, especially Cynthia Franklin and Ali Musleh, further enriched my thinking about the possibilities for love as a relational praxis with the potential to transform the terms of the colonial encounter. Orisanmi Burton's friendship and our conversations over the years have been an inspiration for this piece. I am deeply grateful to Stephen Sheehi, Nadera Shalhoub-Kevorkian, two anonymous reviewers, and the editors of this volume, Junaid Rana, Aisha Beliso-De Jesús, and Jemima Pierre, for their careful engagement and support in refining its interventions. Any errors are my own.

Notes

1. This chapter is revised from an article published with the same title in *State Crime Journal* 12, no. 2 (2024): 206–224.

2. While the closest English translation of the Arabic word "shataat" is diaspora, I define it here as a still ongoing dispersal and forced exiling of Palestinians across the homeland and the globe. This distinction is a political choice that names a stake in the materiality of decolonization, including the "anticipated future of a return to a liberated homeland" (Ihmoud 2022, 13).

3. Throughout this chapter I use the term "captive" rather than "prisoner" or "detainee" following the most precise translation of the Arabic term "ة/أسير", that mobilized by Palestinians to distinguish the "capture of prisoners of war," a critical distinction that asserts the context by which prisoners are captured in settler colonialism to be one of ongoing war (Kutmah 2023).

4. My aim in raising these stories alongside each other is not to collapse differentially racialized positionalities, but to summon the interrelations between gendered anti-Blackness and Indigenous erasure, and to consider their intimate co-constitution in the United States and Israeli settler colonies.

5. Following Mohammed Abed (2015), Haifa Rashed, Damien Short, and John Docker (2014), and Nadera Shalhoub-Kevorkian (2015), I name the ongoing settler colonial expulsion and elimination of the Palestinian people as genocidal in nature. In doing so, my understanding of genocide is not reducible to the juridical category as such. In part, naming Zionist colonialism as genocidal is about the clarity of the stakes at hand—that this is a project that labors to eliminate Palestinians physically, emotionally, and spiritually. Indeed, it is this context and the political exigency it portends that is part of what makes the letters explored herein and their content both revolutionary and abolitionist.

6. I use the concepts of decolonial love and revolutionary love interchangeably throughout this chapter.

7. I thank Stephen Sheehi for suggesting the title of this piece as an allusion to the poem by Abdul Lateef A'qel, "Love, the Palestinian Way" (1982), popularized by the Palestinian folk band Sabreen.

8. Palestinians typically refer to what is recognized in broader international policy and discourse as the State of Israel as "1948," a reference to the Nakba, or the year in which 750,000 Palestinians were massacred or forcibly expelled from their homeland and the state was first recognized as such. In this way, they keep the memory of the Nakba alive, alongside claims to belonging to all of Palestine.

9. "Khalida was first detained by the Israeli occupying forces in 1989 on the occasion of a Women's Day demonstration for one month without trial. She was subsequently detained three additional times, for an accumulated period of fifty-seven months: from April 2, 2015, to June 2016; from July 2, 2018, to February 28, 2019; and since October 31, 2019. Furthermore, Khalida was issued a travel ban since 1998, which was only lifted once in 2010 to enable her to seek medical treatment in Jordan. On August 20, 2014, she was ordered by the Israeli military to forcibly transfer to Jericho for a period of six months, on the basis of a so-called security threat, finally reduced to one month. Most recently, Khalida Jarrar was detained on October 31, 2019, when twelve Israeli military vehicles surrounded her house in Al-Bireh, and around twenty armed Israeli Occupying Forces raided the house at approximately 3:00 a.m. On March 1, 2021, Ofer military court sentenced Khalida to twenty-four months in prison and a NIS 4,000 fine. During the hearing session, the military prosecutor amended Khalida's indictment, limiting it to her political role and work with the Palestinian Authority, further

declaring that there are no charges against her relating to affiliation to any "military, financial nor organizational activities." https://actionnetwork.org/letters/write-letter-to-canadian-government-unconditional-release-of-khalida-jarrar-to-attend-the-funeral-of-her-daughter-suha-jarrar/.

10. Translated from the original Spanish by the author.

11. For many of us who have faced patriarchal violence and gendered exclusion in Palestinian political spaces, the PFC has been the first place we can call a political home. Two months earlier, we had launched our first public campaign, "Palestine Is a Feminist Issue," which included organizing to reignite long-standing relations with Black, Indigenous, women of color, and queer communities within larger anticolonial, anticapitalist, and antiracist movements in the United States, and a pledge asking US women, queer, feminist, social, and racial justice organizations and people of conscience to adopt Palestinian liberation as a critical feminist issue (see Elia 2021).

12. One aspect of the conversation involved whether we should write a statement of solidarity to our people, and whether Palestinians in the *shataat* can be in solidarity with our people in the homeland—in other words, can we be in solidarity with ourselves? I thank Nada Elia for reminding me of this during a presentation of an earlier iteration of this essay presented as part of a December 2021 workshop, "Love Letters to Palestine," co-organized with Dena Al-Adeeb and Jennifer Mogannem, as part of HEKLER Assembly's "Infrastructures of Care," a series of conversations exploring the relationship between "civic engagement and collectivity through art practice and pedagogy."

13. As Palestinian feminists have argued previously, while there is a long tradition of Black, Indigenous, and third world feminist solidarity with the Palestinian liberation movement, Western liberal feminist traditions have historically colluded with Zionism in the oppression of Palestinians. While there are cases of explicitly Zionist sympathies on the part of some liberal feminists, perhaps, as other Palestinian feminist scholars and activist have noted, this is in part a consequence of the success of Israeli state-driven messaging that depicts Israel as a liberal, democratic society that is exceptional in the MENA region for its openness to women's and queer emancipation—what some have called "feminist-washing" and "pinkwashing" respectively. Embedded in this politics are Islamophobic and orientalist assumptions about Arab society: the essential incompatibility of Arab and Muslim societies with women's emancipation or queer emancipation, which again occludes the deeply heteropatriarchal homonational, violently misogynistic elements at the core of Israeli state formation.

14. See the statement titled "Gender Studies Departments in Solidarity with Palestinian Feminist Collective," http://genderstudiespalestinesolidarity.weebly.com.

15. These traditions have also been in conversation with each other, forming a radical space of kinship between captive populations and revolutionary movements. For example, Greg Thomas highlights the ways in which George Jackson, an imprisoned Black Panther and member of the Soledad Brothers, was inspired by Palestinian prisoner writings. Angela Davis notes the emotion she felt at receiving a letter from Palestinian prisoners in 1970, smuggled out of an Israeli prison and into her prison cell.

References

Abed, Mohammed. 2015. "The Concept of Genocide Reconsidered." *Social Theory and Practice* 41, no. 1: 328–56.

Abdo, Nahla. 2014. *Captive Revolution: Palestinian Women's Anti-colonial Struggle within the Israeli Prison System.* London: Pluto Press.

Abuseneineh, Bayan. 2021. "(Re)producing the Israeli (European) Body: Zionism, Anti-Black Racism, and the Depo-Provera Affair." *Feminist Review* 128, no. 1: 96–113.

Acevedo-Zapata, Diana Maria. 2020. "Letter-Writing as a Decolonial Feminist Praxis for Philosophical Writing." *Hypatia* 35, no. 3.

Addameer Prisoner Support and Human Rights Association. 2016. "Briefing Paper: Palestinian Political Prisoners in Israeli Prisons." June. www.addameer.org/sites/default/files/briefings/general_briefing_paper_-_june_2016_1.pdf.

Alqaisiya, Walaa. 2018. "Decolonial Queering: The Politics of Being Queer in Palestine." *Journal of Palestine Studies* 47, no. 3: 29–44.

Atallah, Devin G. 2022. "Reflections on Radical Love and Rebellion: Towards Decolonial Solidarity in Community Psychology Praxis." In *Decolonial Enactments in Community Psychology*, edited by S. Kessi, S. Suffla, and M. Seedat, 75–97. Cham, Switzerland: Springer Nature.

Beliso-De Jesús, Aisha M., and Jemima Pierre. 2019. "Introduction: Special Issue: Anthropology of White Supremacy." *American Anthropologist* 122, no. 1: 65–75.

Bouteldja, Houria. 2016. *Whites, Jews, and Us: Toward a Politics of Revolutionary Love*. South Pasadena, CA: Semiotext(e).

Brown, Kimberly Juanita, and Jyoti Puri. 2022. "The Uses of Mourning: An Introduction." *Meridians* 21, no. 2: 307–16.

Burton, Orisanmi. 2021. "Captivity, Kinship, and Black Masculine Care Work under Domestic Warfare." *American Anthropologist* 123, no. 3.

Cervenak, Sarah Jane. 2021. *Black Gathering: Art, Ecology, Ungiven Life*. Durham, NC: Duke University Press.

Elia, Nada. 2021. "How Palestine Is a Critical Feminist Issue." Middle East Eye. March 25. www.middleeasteye .net/opinion/how-palestine-critical-feminist-issue.

Francis, Sahar. 2020. "Gendered Violence in Israeli Detention." *Journal of Palestine Studies* 46, no. 4: 46–61.

Freeman, Elizabeth. 2007. "Queer Belongings: Kinship Theory and Queer Theory." In *A Companion to Lesbian, Gay, Bisexual, Transgender, and Queer Studies*, edited by G. E. Haggerty and M. McGarry, 295–314. Hoboken, NJ: John Wiley and Sons.

Ghanayem, Eman. 2022. "Proactive Grief: Palestinian Reflections on Death." *Meridians* 21, no. 2: 398–412.

Gruner, Sheila. 2018. "Territorio y el ser decolonial: Pervivencia de las mujeres y los pueblos en tiempos de conflicto, paz y desarrollo." In *Movimientos indígenas y autonomías en América Latina: Escenarios de disputa y horizontes de posibilidad*, edited by Pavel C. López Flores and Luciana García Guerreiro. Buenos Aires: CLACSO.

Hammami, Rema. 2019. "Destabilizing Mastery and the Machine: Palestinian Agency and Gendered Embodiment at Israeli Military Checkpoints." *Current Anthropology* 60, no. 19.

Harlow, Barbara. 1992. *Barred: Women, Writing, and Political Detention*. Middletown, CT: Wesleyan University Press.

Harris-Perry, Melissa. 2018. "Erica Garner Died of a Heart Attack; But It's Racism That's Killing Black Women." *Elle*. January 2. www.elle.com/culture/a14532058/erica-garner-death-black-women-racism/.

Hassan, Budour. 2019. "The Warmth of Our Sons: Necropolitics, Memory, and the Palestinian Quest for Closure." Report, Jerusalem Legal Aid and Human Rights Center.

Hawari, Yara. 2021. "Community Accountability in Palestine: An Alternative to Policing." Policy Brief. Alshabaka: The Palestinian Policy Network. https://al-shabaka.org/briefs/community-accountability-in -palestine-an-alternative-to-policing/.

Ihmoud, Sarah. 2021. "Born Palestinian, Born Black: Anti-Blackness and the Womb of Zionist Settler Colonialism." In *Antiblackness*, edited by João Costa Vargas and Moon-Kie Jung. Durham, NC: Duke University Press.

———. 2022. "Palestinian Feminism: Analytics, Praxes, and Decolonial Futures." *Feminist Anthropology*.

James, Joy. 2005. *The New Abolitionists: (Neo)Slave Narratives and Contemporary Prison Writings*. Albany: State University of New York Press.

———. 2023. *In Pursuit of Revolutionary Love: Precarity, Power, Communities*. London: Divided Publishing.

Jarrar, Khalida. 2021. "'Imprisoned But Free': Letter from Jailed Palestinian Leader Khalida Jarrar to Her Late Daughter, Suha." *Mondoweiss*. July 13. https://mondoweiss.net/2021/07/imprisoned-but-free-letter-from -jailed-palestinian-leader-khalida-jarrar-to-her-late-daughter-suha/.

Johnson, Penny. 2006. "Living Together in a Nation in Fragments: Dynamics of Kin, Place, and Nation." In *Living Palestine: Family Survival, Resistance, and Mobility under Occupation*, edited by Lisa Taraki. Syracuse, NY: Syracuse University Press.

Khalidi, Rashid I. 2014. "From the Editor: Israel: A Carceral State." *Journal of Palestine Studies* 43, no. 4: 5–10.

Kutmeh, Ayah. 2023. "'Prisoner' and 'Captive': Defining Positionality and Conceptualizing Carceral Regimes in the Arab World." Blog, Institute for Palestine Studies.

Meari, Lena. 2014. "Sumud: A Palestinian Philosophy of Confrontation in Colonial Prisons." *South Atlantic Quarterly* 113, no. 3: 547–78.

Morgenson, Scott L. 2012. "Queer Settler Colonialism in Canada and Israel: Articulating Two-Spirit and Palestinian Queer Critiques." *Settler Colonial Studies* 2, no. 2: 167–90.

Musleh, Ali. 2022. "To What Abyss Does This Robot Take the Earth: On the Automation of Settler Colonialism in Palestine." PhD diss., University of Hawai'i at Mānoa.

Nashif, Esmail. 2008. *Palestinian Political Prisoners: Identity and Community.* London: Routledge.

National Women's Studies Association. 2021. "Palestine Solidarity is a Feminist Issue." May. www.femst.ucsb.edu/news/announcement/770.

Palestine Legal Center for Constitutional Rights. 2015. "The Palestine Exception to Free Speech: A Movement Under Attack." Report, https://palestinelegal.org/the-palestine-exception.

Palestinian Feminist Collective. 2021. "A Love Letter to Our People Struggling in Palestine." *Jadaliyya.* May 14. www.jadaliyya.com/Details/42739.

Rashed, Haifa, Damien Short, and John Docker. 2014. "Nakba Memoricide: Genocide Studies and the Zionist/Israeli Genocide of Palestine." *Holy Land Studies* 13, no. 1: 1–23.

Rodriguez, Dylan. 2019. "Abolition as Praxis of Human Being: A Foreword." *Harvard Law Review* 132: 1575.

Sandoval, Chela. 2000. *Methodology of the Oppressed.* Minneapolis: University of Minnesota Press.

Sayegh, Fayez. 1965. *Zionist Colonialism in Palestine.* Research Center, Palestine Liberation Organization, Beirut.

Seikaly, Sherene. 2020. "The History of Israel/Palestine." In *Understanding and Teaching the Modern Middle East,* edited by Omnia El Shakry. Madison: University of Wisconsin Press.

Shalhoub-Kevorkian, Nadera. 2012. "Trapped: The Violence of Exclusion in Jerusalem." *Jerusalem Quarterly,* no. 49, 6–25.

———. 2015a. "The Politics of Birth and the Intimacies of Violence against Palestinian Women in Occupied East Jerusalem." *British Journal of Criminology* 55: 1187–206.

———. 2015b. "Stolen Childhood: Palestinian Children and the Structure of Genocidal Dispossession." *Settler Colonial Studies* 6, no. 2: 142–52.

Shalhoub-Kevorkian, Nadera, and Sarah Ihmoud. 2014. "Exiled at Home: Writing Return and the Palestinian Home." *Biography* 37, no. 2: 377–97.

Sharpe, Christina. 2016. *In the Wake: On Blackness and Being.* Durham, NC: Duke University Press.

Sheehi, Lara, and Stephen Sheehi. 2022. *Psychoanalysis under Occupation: Practicing Resistance in Palestine.* London: Routledge.

Shomali, Mejdulene Bernard. 2023. *Between Banat: Queer Arab Critique and Transnational Arab Archives.* Durham, NC: Duke University Press.

Simpson, Leanne Betasamosake. 2015. *Islands of Decolonial Love.* Winnipeg: ARP Books.

TallBear, Kim. 2018. "Making Love and Relations beyond Settler Sex and Family." In *Making Kin Not Population,* edited by Adele E. Clark and Donna Haraway. Chicago: Prickly Paradigm Press.

Tawil-Souri, Helga. 2011. "Colored Identity: The Politics and Materiality of ID Cards in Palestine/Israel." *Social Text* 29 (2), no. 107: 67–97.

———. 2012. "Uneven Borders, Coloured (Im)mobilities: ID Cards in Palestine/Israel." *Geopolitics* 17, no. 1.

Tal'at. 2021. Private Letter to Muna Al Kurd and the Women of Sheikh Jarrah. Permission to analyze and think with shared with the author by the collective November 2021. Translated from original Arabic by the author.

Urena, Carolyn. 2017. "Loving from Below: Of (De)colonial Love and Other Demons." *Hypatia* 32, no. 1: 86–102.

Zureik, Elia. 2001. "Constructing Palestine through Surveillance Practices." *British Journal of Middle Eastern Studies* 28, no. 2: 205–27.

Zureik, Elia, D. Lyon, and Y. Abu-Laban. 2011. *Surveillance and Control in Israel/Palestine: Population, Territory, and Power.* New York: Routledge.

24

Fighting White Supremacy and the Settler Colonialocene

Renya K. Ramirez

(Ho-Chunk/Ojibwe)

WHEN TRUMP WAS ELECTED as president of the United States in 2016, it was a shock for many, who could not believe that Trump was successful using openly racist and white supremacist rhetoric. For many Indigenous peoples, it was not a huge shock as white supremacy is certainly nothing new. We have suffered through white supremacy and colonization since Europeans arrived in the Americas over five hundred years ago. When I was asked to write a chapter for a book anthology about the anthropology of white supremacy, I was intrigued. As a Native anthropologist, I have always had a vexed and complicated relationship with anthropology and its colonial roots. As an undergraduate, I read Vine Deloria's pathbreaking book *Custer Died for Your Sins* (1969, 1988) and enjoyed him making fun of white anthropologists, who traveled to Native reservations to become "experts" of our cultures and communities, and thought to myself, "I will never become an anthropologist!" I eventually changed my mind. I thought about how classic anthropology—inextricably linked to both settler colonialism and white supremacy—has wreaked havoc and caused much damage, horrible pain, and sorrow for Indigenous peoples, ultimately supporting land dispossession, genocide, removal, and assimilation. I can remember talking to my anthropology colleagues at UC Santa Cruz, discussing our future plans as a department, and wondering out loud how to decolonize and transform anthropology. I said with a gleam in my eye, "Maybe we need to blow anthropology up?!" My words caused raised eyebrows and stunned looks on some of my colleagues' faces. My words, however, were merely a reflection of my strong and radical inner core as a Native studies scholar. In this essay, I argue that my identities as a Native feminist anthropologist and Native studies scholar, motivated and influenced by Indigenous activism and collaboration, encourage me to challenge settler colonialism, white supremacy, capitalism, and the Anthropocene. Unfortunately, white supremacy is often missing from anthropologists' discussion of the Anthropocene (Beliso-De Jesús and Pierre 2020). Because of the oppressive aspects of the Anthropocene concept, I provide a new definition of Settler Colonialocene, understood as the centrality of white supremacy, racism, patriarchy, settler colonialism, capitalism, and other oppressions as underlying structures that cause ecological devastation. The concept not only includes oppressive qualities but also includes colonial ecological disaster—such as Native feminist ideas, Indigenous philosophy, and intersectionality. Indeed, my use of Settler Colonialocene highlights my radical self, including my efforts to decolonize anthropology, challenge white supremacy, and express my allegiance to Native studies. My mom, Woesha Cloud North (Ho-Chunk/Ojibwe), participated in the 1969 Native occupation of Alcatraz Island that led to the creation of Native American studies at San Francisco State and the Red Power Movement, showing my militant upbringing. First, I examine the relationship between white supremacy, settler colonialism, the Anthropocene, and Settler Colonialocene. Second, I share stories about the struggles of Indigenous peoples and allies as ecowarriors and caretakers against the Settler Colonialocene.

White Supremacy, Settler Colonialism, and the Settler Colonialocene

White supremacy and settler colonialism are inextricably linked to the founding of the United States (Speed 2019). According to Speed (Chickasaw) (2019), a settler colonial lens has rarely been used to analyze white supremacy. One exception is Glenn (2015), who argues settler colonialism helps us understand gender and racial formation in the United States. In other words, white supremacy does not work alone and depends on the construction of race, gender, and ultimately patriarchy (Beliso-De Jesús and Pierre 2020). According to Wolfe (2006), settler colonialism is a structure not an event, the settler comes to stay, and the Native must be eliminated by removal, genocide, and assimilation. Whiteness becomes interchangeable with the US nation-state (Glenn 2015) and Moreton-Robinson (2008) connects whiteness to Indigenous land dispossession (Speed 2019). Settler colonialism and white supremacy are linked to private property and the stealing of Indigenous land, viewing Natives as subhuman, uncivilized, and unfit to possess property (Ramirez 2023a; Bhandar 2018). Settler colonialism includes the appropriation of Indigenous land for white settler capitalist interests (Glenn 2015) and is an ecosocial structure that violates Indigenous bodies and all life to exploit the land and resources (Ramirez 2023a, b; Bacon 2016). Settler colonialism is related to white supremacy and racist discourses that imagine Indigenous peoples as waste and our land as wastelands, justifying the contamination of Indigenous lands by dumping toxic waste and seeing Native bodies as disposable (Ramirez 2023a, b; Voyles 2015; Silko 1991; Reed 2009; Baker et al. 2020).

Unfortunately, anthropologists have too frequently left out white supremacy regarding the Anthropocene (Beliso-De Jesús and Pierre 2020). Zoe Todd (2015), a Métis anthropologist, argues that the Anthropocene is a white public space that erases the various histories and relationships that led to our current environmental crises. Todd (2015) argues that white-centered narratives of the Anthropocene emerged from colonial institutions. Thus, Todd (2015) asserts the Anthropocene needs decolonizing by bringing back and emphasizing Indigenous knowledges and perspectives about environmental struggles. The Anthropocene assumes humanity, the Anthropos, is a universal human subject and hides the global and historical inequalities between humans that caused the Anthropocene (Davis and Todd 2017; Pulido 2018). The concept fails to recognize that not all humans are equally responsible, and not everyone experiences the same negative effects of ecological damage, and climate change. Furthermore, the word, Anthropos, points to the privileging of wealthy, white, heterosexual, and male power that becomes part of a universalizing colonial discourse, leaving out tribal communities (Davis and Todd 2017). Natives do not exist as powerful subjects within settler colonial Anthropocene discourse. We are not the white man, the master of the universe, inventor of the steam engine that led to the industrial revolution and the fossil fuel industry. Indeed, many assume powerful white men will save us from our global environmental crisis, which is ultimately a result of their ingenuity (Thoresson 2021). Patriarchy encourages white men to dominate nature, women, and people of color (Henricksen 2022; Silko 1992, 1999). White men master nature and strive to progress and develop new ways to control and exploit land, women, and subordinated others (Silko 1999; Henrickson 2022). The Anthropocene as colonial discourse objectifies the natural world and nature's heterogeneity as inanimate objects to be studied, dug up, and exploited (Whyte 2017). White males' mastery of nature is not questioned, or the interdependence with nature valued (Silko 1992, 1999).

The Anthropocene is a term used in both scientific and popular discourse denoting the time when humans began influencing the climate and environment. Davis and Todd (2017) argue that the Anthropocene's beginning was Europeans' colonization of the Americas. By identifying colonization and the protocapitalist logics of extraction and accumulation through dispossession as the start of the Anthropocene, we can better understand the underlying causes of our current ecological crises (Davis and Todd 2017). Whyte (Potawatomi) (2017) asserts that colonization has intensified the negative environmental and ecological damaging effects on Indigenous peoples and has hurt our cultures, health, economies, and political self-determination. More and more scholars highlight race in what is usually seen as a race-neutral concept (Whyte 2017; Haraway 2015; Davis and Todd 2017; Vergès 2017; Pulido 2018; Baldwin and Erickson 2020).

The anthropology of white supremacy revolves around making dominant discourses visible and speaking truth to power (Beliso-De Jesús and Pierre 2020). Because of the oppressive qualities of the Anthropocene concept—such as race, patriarchy, settler colonialism, white supremacy, capitalism, and other oppressions (Whyte 2017; Haraway 2017; Henriksen 2022; Davis and Todd 2017; Pulido 2018)—I use a different term, "Settler Colonialocene" (Dutt et al. 2022). My definition of Settler Colonialocene involves making visible the consequences of structures of power such as—settler colonialism, white supremacy, racism, patriarchy, capitalism, and other oppressions—on climate change, ecological contamination, and devastation. Settler Colonialocene is influenced by Indigenous intersectionality and Native feminisms that are grounded on ancient Indigenous wisdom of All of Our Relations—a philosophy that foregrounds kinship between humans and all life (Ramirez 2023a, b; Kimmerer 2013; LaDuke 1999; Baldy and Yazzie 2018). Thus, the Settler Colonialocene highlights the colonial violence experienced by humans and more-than-humans and includes an intersectional analysis—such as race, tribal nation, gender, sovereignty, settler colonialism, white supremacy, patriarchy, and other oppressions (Ramirez 2007b, 2023a, b). Indigenous intersectionality diverges from Crenshaw's definition that concentrates on humans' oppression and leaves out more-than-humans (Crenshaw 1991; Ramirez 2023a, b). The concept not only emphasizes the structures of power that contribute to environmental and ecological devastation, but also remedies—such as Native feminist notions of love, respect, humility, caretaking, and kin-making based on Indigenous peoples' resistance, persistence, and strength—as central to fighting back against the Settler Colonialocene (Vizenor 2008; Ramirez 2023a, b; TallBear 2019; Hernandez 2021).

Next, I turn to my various research and activist projects where I challenge the Settler Colonialocene. I use the term *caretaking*—a term usually viewed from a white patriarchal and settler colonial mindset (Glenn 2010). Instead, I use the definition of TallBear (Sisseton Wahpeton) (2019) that care work moves beyond the binaries between humans and nature and includes caretaking humans and all life. The following stories are about Indigenous peoples and allies organizing as caretakers and ecowarriors (Silko's term) to fight back against the Settler Colonialocene. The narratives are about respect, love, humility, collaboration, becoming allies and kin, working toward decolonization of public school curricula, and California mission bells, and against white supremacy. Stories are powerful, and storytelling can transform settler colonial, white supremacist, and capitalistic reality and change the world for the better (Silko 1991, 1999).

Women of Color Ecowarriors and Caretakers of the Anthropocene

Recently, I joined a group of women of color anthropologists, including Janelle Baker (Métis), Paulla Ebron, Rosa Ficek, Karen Ho, Zoe Todd (Métis), Anna Tsing, and Sarah Vaughn, who came together to write an essay about people of color's experience with climate change and the Anthropocene. We organized using the term Anthropocene, so I will use the concept to recognize scholars' choice to use it for various reasons, including hoping to maintain communication with scientists, and to draw attention to environmental disasters (Matthews 2020; Tsing 2015). Our hope was to write an essay and publish it in a popular magazine to bring the negative effects of climate change and the Anthropocene on Indigenous, African American, Asian American, and Latinx communities into public awareness. We built a coalition around oppressed communities' struggles with the Anthropocene and climate change, our similar identities as feminist anthropologists, and our fight for the survival of the earth and all living things (Ramirez 2023a, b). We as women of color feminist anthropologists acted as loving caretakers of the land and all life.

We met in Davenport, a few miles north of Santa Cruz, California, for a weekend. We walked, talked, and shared our research interests about environmental justice, and discussed whether we could write an essay together. We agreed that sharing stories about ethnographic research, climate change, the Anthropocene, and the struggles of disenfranchised communities could be written about for the environmental magazine *Orion*. As I sat with women of color anthropologists, who decided to name our group, the "Slough Sayers," memories of reading Leslie Marmon Silko's novel *Almanac of the Dead* kept surfacing. Silko as a loving caretaker shares stories about the sacredness of Mother Earth, the interconnection of all species, the difficulty of ecological destruction, and the terrible harm caused by capitalism, extraction, production, and disposal of toxic waste that threatens our Indigenous peoples' right to clean air, water, and food. *Almanac of the Dead* ties these themes together and calls for Indigenous self-determination, and the return of all Indigenous lands. The end of the book describes the coming together of ecowarriors, including people of color and the homeless, to unify and heal Mother Earth. I shared my thoughts about *Almanac of the Dead* and discussed Silko's notion of ecowarriors and said, "We are ecowarriors coming together to fight for the earth and all living things."

We published an essay, "The Snarled Lines of Justice: Women Ecowarriors Map a New History of the Anthropocene," in *Orion* (2020) to fight as activists, caretakers, and feminist anthropologists for the survival of our respective marginalized communities, the earth, and all life. In our essay, Zoe Todd (Métis) as a caretaker and kin of fish writes about Alberta fish and the tragic deformities caused by the toxic effects of the settler colonial and capitalistic oil and gas companies in Canada. Canada is the biggest supplier of crude oil to the United States, showing how the Anthropocene crosses national boundaries. Alberta is the number one oil-producing region, and the Alberta oil sands are where the most oil is developed in the province. Fish are Indigenous peoples' relatives, and witnessing their suffering can be overwhelming. Fish are telling Indigenous peoples that the Anthropocene has come to the boreal forest. This is oil's slow colonial violence that hurts fish, and all life, as it oozes, disappears, and returns. Todd shares how First Nations and Métis communities eat traditional foods from the boreal forest and document environmental changes they have seen in plant, water, and animal relatives. They get involved in environmental programs that are supposed to bring their Native knowledge and science together. Their participation does not calm their fears regarding eating potentially contaminated bush food.

After meeting with women of color in Davenport, California, I began working on my chapter about Grace Thorpe (Potawatomi, Kickapoo, and Sac and Fox) and her decades-long environmental justice activism against the dumping of nuclear waste on Native reservations (Ramirez 2023a, b). Environmental justice scholars have argued western and racist capitalistic discourse links Indigenous peoples and waste and imagines our lands as wastelands (Voyles 2015; Silko 1991; Reed 2009; Baker et al. 2020; Ramirez 2023a, b). From the start of colonization to the present, white colonizers have argued that Indigenous lands are empty and undeveloped (terra nullius), and using white supremacy logics and racist discourses Indigenous peoples are less than human, savages, and ultimately disposable like waste (Anderson 2013; Reed 2009). The wasting of Indigenous peoples and lands has been continuous, according to Silko's map in *Almanac of the Dead*. Natives have constantly fought back against the colonizer stealing and taking over Indigenous lands by disease and guns in the sixteenth century to the toxic colonialism of the twenty-first century, such as throwing away toxic waste on Native lands. The euphemisms may change, such as from "national se-curity logic" to "national sacrifice zones," but the wasted lands or wastelands overlap with the boundaries of Indigenous reservations and the ghettos of people of color (Reed 2009).

Standing Rock, Indigenous Women Caretakers, and Settler Colonialocene

Native women activists as caretakers and ecowarriors continuously fight back against the Settler Colonialocene using Indigenous land to make a profit. Kim TallBear, a Native an-thropologist, uses a Native feminist lens and Indigenous intersectionality, which revolves around Native philosophy regarding All of Our Relations, developing coalitions across differences, and respect for humans and all life (Ramirez 2023a, b). TallBear (2019) wrote about Women of the Oceti Sakowin or Seven Council Fires as central to the Standing Rock movement. They join with allies from many countries to fight to protect the land, water, and all life from the white settler colonial and capitalistic interest of the Dakota Access Pipeline (DAPL). The Standing Rock movement relies on the strength and energy of the Idle No More (INM) and Black Lives Matter (BLM) movements. In 2012, three Indige-nous women, Jessica Gordon, Sylvia McAdam, and Nina Wilson, and one non-Indigenous woman, Sheelah McLean, established INM. They connected Bill C-45—legislation initi-ated by the Conservative Harper Canadian government that questioned environmental protections—to the attacks of treaties and Indigenous land in Canada. They stressed their movement is based on sovereignty and Indigenous philosophy to protect air, water, land, and all creation for future generations. They blockaded highways and railroad tracks, and round-danced in public venues to publicize oil and other fossil fuel global industry's ex-ploitation of Indigenous peoples and our lands. They as caretakers stressed that Indigenous peoples connect our lives and treaty rights to the well-being of our more-than-human rela-tives. This linkage is not only to protect Indigenous peoples' lives but humans and all life.

TallBear (2019) honors BLM, an organization African American women, Alicia Garza, Patrisse Cullors, and Opal Tometi, founded in 2013. The acquittal of George Zimmerman, who murdered Trayvon Martin in Florida, led to the organization's foundation. BLM fights police brutality against Blacks nationwide, backs vulnerable communities' rights, including queer and trans people, criminal justice reform, domestic workers, immigrant justice, and human rights. TallBear views BLM as queer and women-led governance and activism.

TallBear (2019), as a Dakota feminist and backer of BLM, connects Black women of BLM with Indigenous women leaders of Standing Rock and INM and shows how Indig-enous movements cross national borders to fight white supremacy, racism, colonialism, and capitalism. They are acting as caretakers of their relatives and kin. She clarifies the word "kin" and differentiates it from white, settler colonial, and patriarchal ideas of "kin." She not only includes human relatives, but also—similar to INM and Standing Rock movements—incorporates the earth and all living things. TallBear emphasizes that BLM members make kin too, while defending human bodies oppressed by the anti-Black, anti-trans, anti-immigrant, and antiworker world. She does not view only women as caretakers, but men are also caretakers. She honors Standing Rock Sioux Tribal Chairman Dave Archambault II, who tirelessly fought against DAPL's invasion on Oceti Sakowin territory and the young men of the #NoDAPL movement.

Furthermore, TallBear (2019) emphasizes that Two Spirit leadership has been key to both the INM and Standing Rock movements. Two Spirit scholar Alex Wilson, an INM activist, says that Two Spirit people encourage and motivate others to grow politically and personally. Melody McKiver, a Two Spirit videographer and INM member, argues that Two Spirits encourage understanding and occupy various roles. At Standing Rock, they established a Two Spirit camp as part of the Two Spirit Nation.

TallBear honors Lenca environmental justice activist Berta Caceres of Honduras. She defended Indigenous rights and the environment. Berta Caceres connected Indigenous rights, environmental justice, and LGBTQ oppression. Caceras argued that powerful interests attack both the planet and LGBTQ communities. She was murdered at home on March 3, 2016, after many threats to her life.

Standing Rock, INM, and BLM build coalitions between people from various racial, ethnic, sexual, gender, tribal, and other identities. As already mentioned, TallBear emphasizes how Standing Rock and INM have benefited from the momentum of BLM. Both Standing Rock and INM fight for humans, all life, and the planet. In this way, Standing Rock and INM movements link racial and environmental justice. INM, BLM, and Standing Rock are powerful movements that can cross national borders and generate tremendous political energy and activism, while fighting back against global white supremacy, capitalism, and the Settler Colonialocene. In sum, TallBear uses a Native feminist analysis, Indigenous intersectionality, caretaking, and kin-making to honor Indigenous women and men, Black lives, Two Spirits, LGBTQ, humans, and more-than-humans, as central to the challenge of the Settler Colonialocene. Next, I discuss our development of Critical Mission Studies (CMS), a new area of study, in collaboration with California Natives. The California missions were sites of the exploitation of Indigenous people and all living things. The Spanish disrupted Natives' ecosocial relationships by forcibly bringing them into the missions, interfering with their traditional fishing and hunting practices, and their loving relations with their land, water, plants, and all life. The Amah Mutsun Tribal Band (AMTB) continues to fight the settler colonial and capitalist gravel mining company's goal to dig up and destroy their sacred land. Our CMS collaboration uses kin-making, love, respect, humility, caretaking, and truth-telling to challenge white supremacy, settler colonialism, and capitalism of the Settler Colonialocene.

Critical Mission Studies, Decolonization, Collaboration, and Settler Colonialocene

Critical Mission Studies is a novel area of study that offers a radical revision of the history of the California missions and their legacies by centering California Indigenous perspectives. The word "critical" (Moreton-Robinson 2016) emphasizes white supremacy, settler colonialism, capitalism, and the need for collaboration with California Indigenous peoples.

354   RENYA K. RAMIREZ

I was one of the co-principal investigators of a University of California Office of the President (UCOP) 1.028 million dollar grant along with other co-PIs, Professors Charlene Villaseñor Black, Ross Frank, and Jennifer Scheper Hughes. At the start, we met with California Native leaders and community members, created a California Indian advisory board, and California tribal members elected four California Native research partners—including Dr. Yve Chavez (Gabrieleno-Tongva San Gabriel Band of Mission Indians); Dr. Jonathon Cordero (Ramytush Ohlone/Bay Miwok/Chumash); Valentin Lopez (Amah Mutsun Tribal Band (AMTB); and Dr. Stan Rodriguez (Kumeyaay-lipay, Santa Ysabel)—to work with us co-PIs. We could then administer the grant in a collaborative manner with California Natives. Our grant funded CMS research grants, including community-initiated partnerships, and UC faculty, graduate student, and humanities laboratory grants.

Our CMS editorial collective includes Cordero, Chavez, Lopez, and Rodriguez, our California Indian Research Partners, and us four co-Principal investigators, Villaseñor Black, Frank, Hughes, and myself. We worked together in collaboration to administer the grant, develop CMS, and as an editorial collective to publish a book anthology, *Critical Mission Studies*, which is under contract with the University of California Press.

Our CMS collaboration revolves around love, respect, kin-making, caretaking, and being humble so we can work to tackle white supremacy, settler colonialism, capitalism, and the colonial histories of the California missions. We non-California Indian scholars must listen, learn, and center California Native perspectives, let go of our power and privilege as university professors, and become allies (Scott et al. forthcoming). Even though I am Native, Ho-Chunk and Ojibwe, I must remember I am a guest on the land of the Uypi Tribe, the AMTB are the land stewards, and I must privilege the perspectives of California Indian scholars and leaders. It means following a California Native research protocol and checking in with California Indian scholars and leaders every step of the way. Together, we are committed to truth-telling to struggle against histories of Indigenous settler colonial oppression and white supremacy. We as Natives and non-Native caretakers and kin-makers developed close relationships and emotionally supported each other during the pandemic's challenges, including getting sick, losing loved ones, feeling anxiety and fear, receiving vaccines, and sharing deep concern about each other's welfare. We genuinely care for one another and became kin as brothers and sisters in the battle against settler colonial histories of the California missions.

I participated on a panel for our CMS UC Santa Cruz humanities lab with Valentin Lopez (Tribal Chair of AMTB), and my Education colleagues—including Judith Scott (Cherokee), Daisy Martin, and Charley Brooks—about our work to transform public school curriculum about the California missions from a Native perspective. Together, we fought white supremacy and worked toward decolonization. Our panel took place on August 27, 2021, the day before the AMTB's mission bell removal in Santa Cruz, California, on August 28, 2021. Preparing for my talk, I read about how white supremacy is linked to the colonialization of the Americas and public school curriculum. I considered how the Doctrine of Discovery established a political, spiritual, legal, and ultimately colonial justification for the stealing of Indigenous lands not occupied by Christians. The Doctrine of Discovery can be found in a series of papal bulls, or decrees, starting in the 1100s. For example, Pope Nicolas V issued Papal Bull Inter Caetera in 1493 to justify Christian colonizers' claims on land and waterways they allegedly discovered, while promoting Christian domination and superiority over Africa, Asia, Australia, and the Americas. This global colonial story of white supremacy supported the dehumanization of Indigenous peoples and the dispossession of our lands, widespread murder, and forced assimilation. The Doctrine fueled global white supremacy as European colonizers claimed they were instruments of divine authority with cultural superiority (Miller 2019).

Valentin Lopez (AMTB), CMS California Indian Research Partner, argues that the papal bulls started the historical violence against Indigenous peoples when our Native ancestors were declared as enemies of Christianity and the Vatican wanted to make sure all lands became Catholic. The Spanish killed many California Natives in the missions, including by outright murder, introduction of European diseases, and overall unhealthy conditions (Rizzo 2021). As part of white supremacy, colonizers viewed California Indigenous peoples as subhuman, primitive, savage, undeveloped, and animal-like, encouraging the Spanish and later the Americans to kill California Indigenous peoples and enslave them. Indeed, the first governor of California, Peter Burnett, a white supremacist, set aside money to arm militias and pay bounties for the genocidal murder of California Indigenous people. In 1850, he signed the Act for the Government and Protection of Indians that allowed whites to force Natives off their lands and into indentured servitude—a form of legalized slavery (Ramirez 2007a; Ramirez and Lopez 2019).

White supremacy circulates in our United States public school system. White supremacist stories, assumptions, messages, and practices are part of our educational institutions and curricula, including elementary, secondary, community college, and universities. In educational curricula, white people are overrepresented, including their values, views, and histories, while people of color, including Indigenous people, are underrepresented, including our accomplishments, histories, perspectives, and values (Mills 1994). According to the magazine *Teaching Tolerance*, in 2021, white supremacy influences every aspect of public education. In this issue, contributors highlight stories that examine the ways systems and institutions support racism and white supremacy (Dunn 2021). Bostick (2021), for example, argues that the classical world of Greece and Rome supports white supremacy. It is no wonder that President Donald Trump advocated building federal properties to make them "beautiful" again and requested architects to manufacture buildings to look like classical Greek temples. Because Rome and Greece are the bedrock of Western civilization and related to whiteness, classics in schools and whiteness become a distressing mixture.

Most children in California are taught about the California missions in the fourth grade (Miranda 2012). The problem with this curriculum is teachers present a whitewashed and colonial version of what happened in the California missions, including the Spanish fantasy that California Natives wanted to live and work in the missions, supporting white supremacy. What is missing is an Indigenous perspective of California mission history, such as Spanish soldiers kidnapping Natives, forcing them to live and work in the missions (Miranda 2012), causing over 90 percent of Natives dying in the Santa Cruz and San Juan Bautista missions (Rizzo 2021). Instead, public school teachers focus on colonial mission architecture and buildings and often encourage schoolchildren to create replicas of missions with popsicle sticks (Miranda 2012). In a 2022 talk, Deborah Miranda (Ohlone-Costanoan Esselen/Chumash) asked, "What if children were asked to build a model of a Southern plantation with people in the fields being whipped, or a concentration camp model with enslaved Jews being pushed into ovens," a similar challenge she makes in her book *Bad Indians* (Miranda 2022, 1).

Our UCSC humanities lab group members, Judith Scott (Cherokee), Valentin Lopez (AMTB), Daisy Martin, and I, hired Amah Mutsun graduate students, Alexii Segona (UCB) and Carolyn Rodriguez (UCLA), to conduct oral histories of Amah Mutsun tribal members in order to hear their truth-telling and learn their perspectives of the California missions. My education colleagues Judith Scott (Cherokee) and Daisy Martin and I conducted an independent studies undergraduate course, and students analyzed California textbooks, settler colonial and Amah Mutsun maps, and interviewed teachers. Judith Scott (Cherokee) wrote an Amah Mutsun children's story about the mission bells in collaboration with tribal chair, Valentin Lopez, including accurate endnotes from an Amah Mutsun perspective. All of this material will be placed on a website for teachers to use to develop curricula about the California missions from an Indigenous perspective.

Our CMS UCSC humanities lab members wrote an essay, "In Their Own Words: Amah Mutsun Truth-Telling, California Missions, Cultural Resurgence, and Decolonization" (Ramirez et al. forthcoming). Segona interviewed Rodriguez, and she discussed her radical resistance of the Settler Colonialocene. She, as a caretaker of Amah Mutsun land, walked with Amah Mutsun land stewards to Mount Umunhum, their sacred mountain, and joined a protest march to defend Juristac and save their sacred lands from gravel and sand companies digging up a quarry and destroying Amah Mutsun territory. The strength of marching is radical resistance that can publicize Indigenous issues (Hickey 2021). The walk to safeguard Juristac contests settler colonial histories of Indigenous elimination through highlighting Amah Mutsun presence and is labor toward decolonization. The walk moves beyond the temporal and physical boundaries of the march itself, including the media, public onlookers, and public memory. Rodriguez's protest walk defies the history of Spanish missionaries and soldiers compelling Amah Mutsun ancestors to march to the missions, and suffer horrible coerced captivity, metamorphizing this settler colonial memory into embodied forms of tribal healing, cultural revival, and decolonization. Amah Mutsun marchers strongly fought gravel and sand companies' settler colonial and capitalist intentions to dig up Mother Earth for extraction.

While working on our CMS project, I co-wrote an article with Valentin Lopez (AMTB) (2020) about decolonization and the removal of the California mission bell at UC Santa Cruz. Hundreds of mission bells dot the California landscape as a way to promote tourism of the California missions, while supporting settler colonization and white supremacy. For California Natives, mission bells evoke the colonial trauma of the widespread death and enslavement of their ancestors and are a racist symbol of white supremacy. Valentin Lopez and Amah Mutsun supporters worked with UC Santa Cruz administrators to remove the California mission bell on campus. The bell was taken down on June 21, 2019 (Ramirez and Lopez 2021). This removal occurred before activists toppled Father Serra statues in California, which was likely motivated by the widespread Black Lives Matter activism, including the removal of Confederate monuments, additional public historical symbols of white supremacy. The last California mission bell in Santa Cruz was removed on August 28, 2021, and hopefully will be placed in a museum where Amah Mutsun's perspectives can be included.

For some, Donald Trump's election as president of the United States was a shock, as he openly relied on white supremacist rhetoric and strategies. For Indigenous peoples, white supremacy is nothing new as we have experienced white supremacy from the beginning of Europeans colonizing the "New World" centuries ago. Native studies departments began based on Indigenous activism and the Red Power Movement. My research and writing as a Native feminist anthropologist to decolonize anthropology are motivated by Indigenous activism and Native studies. Unfortunately, a settler colonial lens is often missing in analysis of white supremacy (Speed 2019), and anthropologists neglect linking white supremacy and the Anthropocene. Because of this lack, I challenge the oppressive aspects of the Anthropocene, thus contributing to the anthropology of white supremacy. This essay includes a novel definition of the Settler Colonialocene that uses a settler colonial analytic to show how white supremacy, colonialism, patriarchy, capitalism, and other oppressions endanger our survival as humans, and all life. This new term also relies on Indigenous intersectionality—including tribal nation, sovereignty, capitalism, race, patriarchy, sexuality, humans, and more-than-humans—and Native feminisms, providing helpful strategies—such as caretaking, kin-making, love, and humility—to battle white supremacy and colonial ecological devastation. My scholarship also involves creating CMS, a new study area, in collaboration and alliance with California Natives, so we can fight white supremacy and support decolonization. This essay encourages optimism, rather than become stuck in despair, so that through collaboration, storytelling, and Indigenous knowledge, we can challenge the colonial histories of the California missions and the Settler Colonialocene. Indeed, we must unify as ecowarriors and caretakers to fight to heal Mother Earth for our survival as humans and all life.

Acknowledgments

I thank the editors, Junaid Rana, Aisha Beliso-De Jesús, and Jemima Pierre; the anonymous reviewers of my essay; and Sophia Reyes, Anna Tsing, Paulla Ebron, Sarah Vaughn, Rosa Ficek, Zoe Todd, Janelle Baker, Karen Ho, Valentin Lopez, Judith Scott, Daisy Martin, Charley Brooks, Amy Lonetree, Alexii Segona, Carolyn Rodriguez, and Gilbert Ramirez for feedback and discussion. I thank my mom, Woesha Cloud North, whose Red Power activism changed her and my life for the better, and Leslie Marmon Silko, Laguna Pueblo novelist, who taught me much of the theory of this chapter.

References

Anderson, Kat. 2013. *Tending to the Wild: Native American Knowledge and the Management of California's Natural Resources*. Berkeley: University of California Press.

Bacon, Jules. 2019. "Settler Colonialism as Eco-Social Structure and the Production of Colonial Ecological Violence." *Environmental Sociology* 5, no 1: 59–69.

Baker, Janelle. 2019. "Bear Stories in the Berry Patch: Caring for Boreal Forest Cycles of Respect." In *Extracting Home in the Oil Sands: Settler Colonialism and Environmental Change in Subarctic Canada*, edited by Clinton N. Westman, Tara L. Joly, and Lena Gross, 119–37. Arctic Worlds series, David Anderson and Rob Losey, editors. New York: Routledge.

Baker, Janelle, Paulla Ebron, Rosa Ficek, Karen Ho, Renya Ramirez, Zoe Todd, Anna Tsing, and Sarah E. Vaughn. 2020. "The Snarled Lines of Justice: Women Ecowarriors Map a New History of the Anthropocene." *Orion Magazine*, November 19.

Baldwin, Andrew, and Bruce Erickson. 2020. "Introduction." Race and the Anthropocene Special Issue. *Environment and Planning D: Society and Space* 38, no. 1: 3–11.

Baldy, Cutcha Risling, and Melanie Yazzie. 2018. "Introduction." *Decolonization: Indigeneity, Culture, and Society* 7, no. 1: 1–18.

Beliso-De Jesús, Aisha, and Jemima Pierre. 2020. "Introduction: Special Section, Anthropology of White Supremacy." *American Anthropologist* 122, no. 1: 65–75.

Bhandar, Brenna. 2018. *Colonial Lives of Property: Law, Land, and Racial Regime*. Durham, NC: Duke University Press.

Bostick, Dani. 2021. "The Classical Roots of White Supremacy." *Teaching Tolerance Magazine*, no. 66. https://learningforjustice.org/sites/default/files/2021-02/Teaching-Tolerance-Magazine-66-Spring-2021, accessed May 5.

Crenshaw, Kimberlé. 1991. "Mapping the Margins: Intersectionality, Identity Politics, and Violence against Women of Color." *Stanford Law Review* 43, no. 6: 1241–99.

Davis, Heather, and Zoe Todd. 2017. "On the Importance of a Date, or, Decolonizing the Anthropocene." *ACME* 16, no. 4: 761–80.

Delacroix, Julia. 2021. *Teaching Tolerance Magazine* 66, spring, online. https://learningforjustice.org/sites/default/files/2021-02/Teaching-Tolerance-Magazine-66-Spring-2021, accessed May 5.

Deloria, Vine. (1969) 1988. *Custer Died for Your Sins*. Norman: University of Oklahoma Press.

Dunn, Jalaya. 2021. "Perspectives." *Teaching Tolerance Magazine*, no. 66, Spring, online. https://learningforjustice.org/sites/default/files/2021-02/Teaching-Tolerance-Magazine-66-Spring-2021, accessed May 5.

Dutt, Priyanka, Anastasya Fateyeva, Michelle Gavereau, and Marc Higgins. 2022. "Redrawing Relationalities at the Anthropocene(s): Disrupting and Dismantling the Colonial Logics of Shared Identity through Thinking with Kim TallBear." In *Reimagining Science Education in the Anthropocene*, edited by Maria Wallace, Jesse Bazzul, Marc Higgins, and Sara Tolbert. London: Palgrave.

Glenn, Evelyn Nakano. 2010. *Forced to Care: Coercion and Caregiving in America*. Cambridge, MA: Harvard University Press.

———. 2015. "Settler Colonialism as Structure: A Framework for Comparative Studies of US Race and Gender Formation." *Sociology of Race and Ethnicity* 1, no. 1: 52–72.

Haraway, Donna. 2015. "Anthropocene, Capitalocene, Pantationocene, Chthulucene: Making Kin." *Humanities Issues* 6: 159–65.

Henricksen, Jan-Olay. 2022. "Relation and Separation: Gendered Diversity and Patriarchy in the Anthropocene." In *Theological Anthropology in the Anthropocene*, 129–37. Cham, Switzerland: Palgrave Macmillan. https://doi.org/10.10007/978-3-031-21058-7_10.

Hernandez, Krisha. 2021. "Native and Indigenous Lives and Bodies and U.S. Agricultural Technosciences." PhD diss., University of California, Santa Cruz.

Hickey, Amber. 2021. "Pathways towards Justice: Walking as Decolonial Resistance." In *Violence in Indigenous Communities*, edited by Susan Sleeper-Smith, Jess Osler, and Joshua Reid. Evanston, IL: Northwest University Press.

Kimmerer, Robin Wall. 2013. *Braiding Sweetgrass*. Minneapolis: Milkweed.

LaDuke, Winona. 1999. *All Our Relations*. Cambridge, MA: South End Press.

Matthews, Andrew. 2020. "Anthropology and the Anthropocene: Criticisms, Experiments, and Collaborations." *Annual Review of Anthropology* 49: 67–82.

Miller, Robert. 2019. "The Doctrine of Discovery: The International Law of Colonialism." *Indigenous Peoples' Journal of Law and Resistance, Culture and Resistance* 5, no.1: 35–42.

Mills, Charles. 1994. "Revisionist Ontologies: Theorizing White Supremacy." *Social and Economic Studies* 43, no. 3: 105–34.

Miranda, Deborah. 2012. *Bad Indians: A Tribal Memoir*. Berkeley, CA: Heyday Books.

———. 2022. "Bad Indians: Tribal Memoir Challenges Romanticization of California Missions." *California Report Magazine*. December 2. www.kqed.org/news/11933862/bad-indians-tribal-memoir-challenges-romanticiation-of-california-missions. Accessed May 4.

Moreton-Robinson, Aileen. 2008. "Writing Off Treaties: White Possessions in the United States Critical Whiteness Studies Literature." In *Transnational Whiteness Matters*, edited by A. Moreton-Robinson, M. Casey, and F. Nicoll, 81–98. Lanham, MD: Lexington Books.

———. 2016. *Critical Indigenous Studies: Engagements in First World Locations*. Tucson: University of Arizona Press.

Pulido, Laura. 2018. "Racism and the Anthropocene." In *Future Remains: A Cabinet of Curiosities for the Anthropocene*, edited by G. Mittman, R. Emmet, and M. Armiero, 116–28. Chicago: University of Chicago Press.

Ramirez, Renya. 2007a. *Native Hubs: Culture, Community, Identity, and Belonging in Silicon Valley and Beyond*. Durham, NC: Duke University Press.

———. 2007b. "Race, Tribal Nation, and Gender: A Native Feminist Approach to Belonging." *Meridians Journal* 7, no. 2: 22–40.

———. 2023a. "Indigeneity, Feminism, and Activism." In *Research Handbook on Intersectionality*, edited by Mary Romero. Northampton, MA: Edward Elgar Publishing.

———. 2023b. *Native Women of the Alcatraz Occupation: Woesha Cloud North, LaNada War Jack, and Grace Thorpe*. Unpublished book draft.

Ramirez, Renya, and Valentin Lopez. 2020. "Valentin Lopez, Healing and Decolonization: Contesting Mission Bells, El Camino Real, and California Governor Newsom." *Latin American and Latinx Visual Culture Journal* 2, no. 3: 91–98.

Ramirez, Renya, Valentin Lopez, Judith Scott, Daisy Martin, Alexii Segona, Carolyn Rodriguez, and Charley Brooks. Forthcoming. "In Their Own Words: Amah Mutsun Truth-Telling, California Missions, Cultural Resurgence, and Decolonization." *Critical Mission Studies*. Unpublished manuscript. Los Angeles: University of California Press.

Reed, T. V. 2009. "Toxic Colonialism, Environmental Justice, and Native Resistance in Silko's *Almanac of the Dead*." *MELUS* 34, no. 2: 25–42.

Rizzo, Martin. 2021. *We Are Not Animals: Indigenous Politics of Survival, Rebellion, and Reconstitution in Nineteenth Century California*. Lincoln: University of Nebraska Press.

Rosaldo, Renato. 1993. *Culture and Truth: The Remaking of Social Analysis*. Boston: Beacon Press.

Scott, Judith, Renya Ramirez, Daisy Martin, Valentin Lopez, and Charley Brooks. Forthcoming. "Amplifying Amah Mutsun Knowledge and Perspectives." In *Critical Mission Studies*, edited by Charlene Black, Yve Chavez, Jonathan Cordero, Ross Frank, Valentin Lopez, Renya Ramirez, and Stanley Rodriguez. Los Angeles: University of California Press.

Silko, Leslie Marmon. 1991. *Almanac of the Dead*. New York: Simon and Schuster.

———. 1999. *Gardens in the Dunes*. New York: Simon and Schuster.

Speed, Shannon. 2019. "The Persistence of White Supremacy: Indigenous Women Migrants and the Structures of Settler Capitalism." *American Anthropologist* 122, no. 1: 76–85.

St. Denis, Verna. 2007. "Feminism Is for Everybody: Aboriginal Women, Feminism, and Diversity." In *Making Space for Indigenous Feminism*. Black Point, NS: Fernwood Publishing; Zed Books.

TallBear, Kim. 2019. "Badass Indigenous Women Caretake Relations." In *Standing with Standing Rock: Voices from the #NODAPL Movement*, edited by Nick Estes and Jaskiran Dhillon. Minneapolis: University of Minnesota Press.

Thoresson, Sanna. 2021. "The Anthropocene: An Intersectional Critique; Uncovering Narratives and Forming New Subjects in a Time of Environmental Change." Master's thesis, Linköping University.

Todd, Zoe. 2015. "Indigenizing the Anthropocene." In *Art in the Anthropocene: Encounters among Aesthetics, Politics, Environments, and Epistemologies*, edited by Heather Davis and Etienne Turpin, 241–54. London: Open Humanities Press.

Tsing, Anna. 2015. *The Mushroom at the End of the World*. Princeton, NJ: Princeton University Press.

Vergès, Françoise. 2017. "Racial Capitalocene." In *Futures of Black Radicalism*, edited by T. Johnson and A. Lubin, 72–82. London: Verso.

Vizenor, Gerald, ed. 2008. *Survivance: Narratives of Native Presence*. Lincoln: University of Nebraska Press.

Voyles, Traci Brynne. 2015. *Wastelanding: Legacies of Uranium Mining in Navajo Country*. Minneapolis: University of Minnesota Press.

Whyte, Kyle. 2017. "Indigenous Climate Change Studies: Indigenizing Futures, Decolonizing the Anthropocene." *English Language Notes* 55, nos. 1–2: 152–63.

Wolfe, Patrick. 2006. "Settler Colonialism and the Elimination of the Native." *Journal of Genocide Research* 8, no. 4: 387–409.

Toward an Anthropology of Liberation

An interview with Faye V. Harrison

THIS BOOK *is indebted to the work of Professor Faye V. Harrison, a pioneer Black feminist anthropologist who has challenged white supremacy in and outside of the discipline. She is the editor of the important book* Decolonizing Anthropology: Moving Further Toward an Anthropology for Liberation *(1991) and author of* Outsider Within: Reworking Anthropology in the Global Age *(2008) in addition to many other works. Her research and writing address global political economy, power, diaspora, human rights, and the intersections of race, gender, and class. Dr. Harrison is a past president of the Association of Black Anthropologists (ABA) and the world organization, the International Union of Anthropological and Ethnological Sciences (IUAES). She is currently professor of African American studies and Anthropology at the University of Illinois, Urbana-Champaign.*

The editors had the privilege to speak with Dr. Harrison about the past and future of anthropology toward the ongoing goal of liberation. This interview features a discussion between Dr. Harrison and Aisha M. Beliso-De Jesús, the Olden Street Professor of American Studies at Princeton University, and the editor-in-chief of Transforming Anthropology, *the flagship journal for the Association of Black Anthropologists.*

———

AISHA BELISO-DE JESÚS: Thank you for all that you've given to anthropology. As anthropologists struggling for liberation, we are indebted to you. This volume is inspired by you and your work, and we are thrilled to have this opportunity to sit with you.

Our first question is: Since your field-defining and disciplinary critique in *Decolonizing Anthropology* and all of your work since then, where do you think anthropology is in terms of what you hoped to achieve through this work? Has anthropology become more connected to liberation?

FAYE HARRISON: Well, I appreciate the recognition of the intervention that the first 1991 edition of *Decolonizing Anthropology* made. We're talking about more than thirty years ago. Although there has always been an audience who welcomed the book as a resource for rethinking and teaching, it's taken this long for its impact to be acknowledged this strongly in such highly visible journals as *Current Anthropology* and *American Anthropologist*. I'm referring particularly to Jafari S. Allen and Ryan C. Jobson's provocative article "The Decolonizing Generation" (2016) and, more recently, Akhil Gupta and Jessie Stoolman's "Decolonizing U.S. Anthropology" (2022), a revision of Gupta's 2021 presidential address. It's very heartening to see that current cohorts and generations are recognizing the significance of a collaborative work that I coordinated and took the initiative to produce through desktop publishing. I raised the money so that the ABA (Association of Black Anthropologists) could fund it. I also organized external reviews with senior scholars so that we could say, "This is more than a vanity press publication or symposium proceedings. It's gone through vetting."

All that work was to make the edited collection viable as a serious piece of intellectual engagement produced under the aegis of the ABA, then a new AAA section that was more than a site of ghettoized interactions. That's the perception that some had about identity-based associations. Our stance was important, not just for the contributors (whose diversity is often not acknowledged), but also for the whole ABA, an association open to any colleagues who share and support our agenda that centers "creating scholarship that link[s] anthropological theory to struggles for social justice" (ABA website). We sought to show that we were and are more than a once-a-year forum, where Black people vent emotionally, because of how they've absorbed and struggled with the many ramifications and modalities of white supremacy, from its macrostructural to its microaggressive dimensions.

We needed a space where kindred spirits could come together to support each other and to remind ourselves that we are serious intellectuals, at a time when the significance of so much of what we did and what our predecessors had done were underestimated. As a AAA section, the ABA has a great deal of potential as a space for new knowledge production that shifts the responsibility away from conventional forces of validation and peer review, which, at least based on many minoritized and subalternized experiences in the past, very often meant that their scholarship would be rejected. Or if accepted under hegemonic terms of quality control demanding drastic revisions, the work in its final version would potentially depart from the original vision. Because of these concerns, I thought that, as a new section of the AAA, we needed to exercise relative autonomy in producing the book—for the sake of building the ABA's organizational capacity and unapologetically asserting its intellectual identity. These priorities arose due to some of our members' initial misgivings about our becoming an official part of the AAA. They were aware of alternative strategies that Black scholars had followed in other social sciences, where they established independent associations. The Association of Black Sociologists (ABS) and the National Conference of Black Political Scientists (NCOBPS) were exemplars. The existence of those bases of solidarity did not preclude Black membership and leadership in flagship associations.

When publishing *Decolonizing Anthropology* (DA) was one of the ABA's objectives, I was ABA president (1989–91) and part of the small team of officers who wore many different hats. This was reflected in the production of *Decolonizing Anthropology* and in launching the *Transforming Anthropology* (TA) journal at a time when publishing articles there was seen as a career risk. We are indebted to Arthur Spears for leading the transitioning of our newsletter, *Notes from the ABA*, into a peer-reviewed journal. The labor of love invested in getting *TA* (1990) and *DA* (1991) out were a praxis of intellectual and institutional decolonization. Among other things, those initiatives were our way of opposing white supremacy in anthropology. We understood, however, that white supremacy is more than a problem in academia. It is a global force of subjection and structural violence that anthropology had neglected and had a responsibility to interrogate and disrupt. This was a key point in the argument I made in framing the significance and purpose of *Decolonizing Anthropology* in the introduction.

Witnessing how *Decolonizing Anthropology* has become and remains a valued resource for teaching and thinking is gratifying. Of course, we all hope that our work will be taken seriously and have a lasting impact. But very often junior scholars, and sometimes more than junior scholars, don't really have the experience or aren't part of ongoing academic traditions to fully understand how this happens or doesn't happen, especially if critical scholarly trends are susceptible to being relegated to a minor stream or periphery in the field.

You asked if, over the decades, anthropology has grown more connected to liberation. Well, I would differentiate the "Anthropology" that is the hegemonic nexus of discourses, practices, and institutions, from the work of anthropologies that represent a heterogeneity of discursive practices, critical projects, and pedagogies. Included in the latter are anthropologies defined as subaltern, insurgent, fugitive, abolitionist, and decolonial. Within this context, both in the United States and around the world, there are examples of principled praxis, such as engaged inquiry and analysis aligned with progressive social movements and other struggles. I am thinking of those critical projects that are more substantive and sustainable than bandwagons and vogues. There are anthropologists who are committed to liberation, but the dominant configurations and apparatuses of the profession are still enmeshed in the "cognitive empire" (Boaventura de Sousa Santos's term) in which North Atlantic epistemologies, particularly the knowledge industry in the United States, are privileged within the world social sciences and, in many respects, get to call the shots.

The world anthropologies project addresses these problems and tries to find ways to decenter the hegemonic in the pursuit of epistemic equity. Opposition to the US cognitive empire hasn't only come from outside. There needs to be more conversation and coordination between domestic and international proponents for transforming anthropology. Minoritized and Indigenous intellectuals have long been a source of constructive vision.

AISHA BELISO-DE JESÚS: That's right. Thank you for this context. It is helpful to understand the everyday work it takes to transform the discipline and the world, and the collective action you and others have done toward a different future.

FAYE HARRISON: Michael Blakey has talked about how some of his early essays have become part of an "underground." That kind of space can be very powerful. An underground or undercommons (as Stefano Harney and Fred Moten might describe it) can be fertile soil for cultivating generative and disruptive ideas. Scholars with secure relationships to the canon are sometimes making note, whether they cite us or not. Some of the good work we do may end up being appropriated in one way or the other, while other work is subjected to erasure. If not that, it can be lost in the archive, much like how historian David Varel characterizes anthropologist Allison Davis as a "lost scholar" whose resurrection makes it possible for his oeuvre to be more broadly appreciated. A parallel case is W. E. B. DuBois, whom Aldon Morris describes as a "scholar denied" in sociology.

As I pointed out in my contribution to the #CiteBlackWomen colloquy for *Cultural Anthropology* (May 2022), in contexts in which citational practices work against the majority of Black women scholars, some of us escape invisibility by accumulating data points in the Social Science Index. However, that doesn't necessarily mean that our work is being engaged as it should be. Sometimes citations represent gestures toward inclusion, which are rituals of liberal antiracism.

I think back to Lynn Bolles's 1995 AAA paper, "Decolonizing Feminist Anthropology," which drew on the critique in *DA*. That paper was never published, but it informed her widely read "Telling the Story Straight: Black Feminist Intellectual Thought in Anthropology," published in *TA* in 2013. The paper she presented in a standing-room-only AFA (Association for Feminist Anthropology) session, was a major wake-up call on problematic citational practices. Over the years, the AFA has become more of a model of diversity and inclusion in its leadership, membership, and publications—thanks to the agency of BIPOC feminists and their white allies. Nonetheless, citations remain a problem, even with the increased visibility of Black feminists and Black women generally in professional service and leadership roles. In 2017, more than two decades after Bolles's original intervention, Christen Smith founded #CiteBlackWomen to redress the enduring problem throughout the academy, which continues to affect what is valorized as knowledge and its "unbearable whiteness."

In light of all this, I am pleased to see what appears to be an increased interest among anthropologists and other intellectuals today in decolonizing knowledge production and circulation. Important ideas from different parts of the world have played a major role in making this shift possible. At this juncture, there seems to be a greater and more positive reception to our work. I am referring to the contributions of the "decolonizing generations," from the 1980s until now, particularly those of us who work in the United States. In the case of Black scholars, we have been influenced by, among other things, the recent history of African diasporic connections and migrations that have produced an intellectual vitality shaped by the *overlapping diasporic experiences* that Blacks of nonimmigrant and immigrant backgrounds have of white supremacy, empire, and the coloniality of knowledge and being. This is the context for what has made the ABA and its allied sections and networks such compelling spaces for generating fruitful conversations about decolonizing anthropology and interrogating white supremacy. More immediately, the mass protests during the summer of 2020 created a climate conducive to some attempts at racial reckoning in the more liberal-left spheres of the academy. However, I'm not sure whether these well-intended critical engagements will be sustained or whether they are driven by the lure of an academic bandwagon.

This moment, whether a fad or a more serious commitment (and there are probably elements of both depending on the situation), is also being challenged by a right-wing backlash to the current demands for racial justice that rose to prominence in the wake of the extrajudicial killings of George Floyd, Breonna Taylor, and too many others. There is a growing imposition of a repressive regime of truth in monitoring education and critical forms of knowledge. This is exemplified in the public contestations of "Critical Race Theory" (CRT), which is interpreted as much more than the critical legal scholarship that provided the initial grounding for CRT. In the highly polarizing political debate, CRT is a broad umbrella term for many varieties of sound scholarship on race making and racism. No matter how rigorous the evidence, anything that speaks truth to power about the past and present of racism, particularly the manifestations of white supremacy in settler colonialism and slavery as well as the afterlives of slavery that persist today, is being heatedly opposed, even banned, in many parts of the United States. This logic of silencing and erasure is also being applied to the inequities that feminist and queer studies combat. Critical thinking about systemic disparities and oppressions is being discredited and penalized. Reasonable analyses of racism and its elements are being problematized as harmful indoctrination. This sentiment has begun to restrict curricula and the availability of books in K-12. In some states, it's not only high school AP (advanced placement) courses in African American studies being targeted. Postsecondary education is also being adversely affected by these debates and related shifts in policy. Teaching and scholarship on race and racism as systemic and that address white privilege and supremacy as problems needing to be unsettled, dismantled, and abolished are being contested and delegitimated within contexts where ultraconservatives wield power.

AISHA BELISO-DE JESÚS: This a helpful segue into the next question, which is about how your work is connected to race and political economy. We've noted how, more recently, a broad theoretical and cultural analysis has pervaded anthropological work that is not connected to political economy. We wanted to ask you, how has this move opened up or foreclosed the study of racism and white supremacy by anthropologists?

FAYE HARRISON: That's an excellent question, because the turn away from political economy, broadly conceived, deprives the social sciences of some of the useful tools that should be honed for explaining past and present formations and workings of structural racism, whose dominant form is white supremacy in its multidimensionality, materialist moorings, and globality. Understanding the power-mediated interplay among sociocultural forces, political economy, and, I would also add, political ecology, we are better able to think about white supremacy's place within a shifting yet enduring matrix of power and structural violence. This is the context within which modernity, coloniality, and restructured imperial formations are implicated as capital accumulation propels the race to the bottom. This race is reflected in forms of dispossession, displacement, and disposal that disproportionately jeopardize the lives, well-being, and human dignity of Black and Indigenous people on landscapes fractured and eroded by settler-slaver states.

The systemic character of white supremacy is harder to discern and corroborate with a focus on, for instance, the prejudice and discrimination of individuals—particularly the so-called bad apples—when we should seek to understand the workings of wider social forces whose dynamics exceed the sum total of individuals. Without situating patterns of bigotry within wider material contexts, there is the risk of succumbing to psychological and cultural determinism, or other kinds of reductionism.

The global, systemic character of white supremacy operates overtly and covertly across a diversity of sociocultural and institutional contexts. There are cases in which white people predominate in demographic terms, others in which they are small minorities, and still others where white supremacy is sustained despite the absence of an appreciable population of whites. In the absence of an appreciable population of whites, nonwhite proxies embrace the values and principles of capitalist modernity and its accompanying coloniality of power or, as Gustavo Lins Ribeiro (a leading world anthropologies proponent) emphasizes, the imperiality of power, which operates at the expense of the majority of the world's peoples.

By the time I finished my PhD, the shift away from political economy had already occurred in anthropology and across much of academia. I studied under Bridget O'Laughlin and St. Clair Drake, who had their different approaches to anthropological political economy. I never formally studied economics, but during my first year at Stanford I was part of an interdisciplinary seminar that economist

Don Harris, [US vice president] Kamala Harris's father, led. That experience had a profound effect on my thinking.

O'Laughlin, a Marxist economic anthropologist, introduced me to the seminar, where there were historians, sociologists, maybe geographers, and a few anthropologists, who outnumbered the economists present. I don't think any of us were there for a grade, but the work we did was serious and set the stage for what would become my approach to anthropology, which examined the interplay of culture, social organization, and political economy. When I finished my degree and went out into the job market, I found that nobody was interested in political economy. Academics seemed to presume that it meant economism or economic reductionism. But that was not the way I understood the methodological and analytical application of its principles.

When I searched for my first academic position, I was also at a disadvantage because that was before diaspora and Caribbean studies became "sexy" and a priority even in many Black/African American studies programs and departments. Although many of the jobs I applied for were in Black studies, I wasn't Black studies enough. Moreover, my work didn't appear to be focused enough on race, although my analysis of the color-coded class dynamics of urban poverty, informal sector participation, and underdevelopment in Caribbean peripheral capitalism had the makings of an intersectional approach on race, class, and gender before there was a name for that kind of perspective. Unfortunately, the compartmentalized frameworks of that time and the bias against Marxist and neo-Marxist-informed research made it hard to find a comfortable space where I fit.

My job talks didn't seem to stimulate the kinds of engaged discussions that could inspire me to rethink my interpretation of Jamaica's urban informal economy. I can see now how my project was amenable to a reinterpretation from a lens of racialization, white supremacy, and also cisheteropatriarchy in global capitalist accumulation. I came to that perspective in time. However, in the 1980s, conversations on those sorts of questions were less likely in most university settings—unlike those in which Cedric Robinson, one of the leading progenitors in theorizing racial capitalism, found himself. But even his historicized political economy was not widespread in Africana studies at that time. His approach has only recently inspired a resurgence of interest beyond the small community of scholars who specialized in modern world systems or who sustained their interest in the relationship between race and capitalism.

My first job offer was actually from a small Pan-African studies department where my interests were welcomed. I did not accept it because of my concern that I would be lost to anthropology. I was aware of the peripheralizing experiences of St. Clair Drake and his mentor Allison Davis, who were not employed in anthropology departments for most of their careers. Most people assumed that Drake was a sociologist. When he was recruited to Stanford from Roosevelt, he was brought there to direct African and African American studies. His tenure home was in anthropology where he was perceived as too sociological and too ethnic and area studies in his orientation. He was an "outsider within."

Somehow, I naively assumed, or maybe it was wishful thinking, that because of the generational difference, I wouldn't face a problem finding employment and advancing my career in academic anthropology. I found out that I had to struggle around the question of where I belonged. Especially during my junior years, though, support from colleagues in and allied to the ABA helped me ground my professional identity and find opportunities for stimulating exchanges that I couldn't have with most colleagues in my home department.

AISHA BELISO-DE JESÚS: You touch on a very important dynamic that is still with us today. It speaks directly to the white supremacy of the discipline of anthropology itself. Can you discuss a little more on how you see that working? Hearing about St. Clair Drake not being really considered part of anthropology at Stanford is an important point for us to understand here.

FAYE HARRISON: I've written about Drake's situation in a number of places, including in *Outsider Within* (2008) and, initially, in a 1988 special issue of *Urban Anthropology* that was a festschrift in his honor. There is also a 2013 symposium on his scholar-activism in the *Journal of African American History*. The articles reveal how he confronted and resisted the obstacles of white supremacy in his career.

Most anthropologists don't know who he is. This was evident when I discussed applying for graduate school in anthropology with professors at Brown. Where should I apply? Where should I go? I ended up at Stanford, but I don't remember anyone being able to tell me anything about Drake. I went to Stanford because Michelle (Shelly) Rosaldo was there. She and Louise [Lamphere] had coedited *Women, Culture, and Society* (1975). During my first year in graduate school, Drake was assigned to advise me. It was the year before his retirement. He was a self-deprecating person whose vast knowledge was awe-inspiring. When I first met him, he told me, "I don't know why they assigned you to me. I'm on my way out of here." Then he spent the next two hours talking to me about the internal racial politics of the department, which had implications for anthropology as a discipline and for academia on the whole. He offered insights into the institutional ambivalence toward students and scholars of color, even when it appears we are being embraced.

Professor Drake's lesson, along with those that would come later, on the power dynamics of institutions of higher learning and academic careers made a difference. I realized from almost day one that taking courses and performing well were necessary but insufficient. I needed a strategy and tactics for *political organizing* to ensure my success by establishing alliances and cultivating appropriate relationships with faculty in a department that had never, before me, graduated a Black woman PhD.

Before he retired, Professor Drake mainly taught undergraduate courses. He wasn't assigned graduate seminars, because his griot, storytelling style was not seen as conducive to teaching theory. As he put it, he wasn't a "theory man." Yet, I learned much of what I know about theory through his counter-story-telling pedagogy. He often spoke about methodology, theory, ideology, and utopia from a sociology of knowledge perspective influenced by Karl Mannheim. Through his captivating narratives, he helped me understand multiple levels and facets of knowledge production. Over years of ruminating about things he said, I realize how his erudition and encyclopedic breadth and depth of knowledge were peerless.

Drake's colleagues in the Pan-African anticolonial movement and Africana studies along with the many students and activists he influenced over the course of his life understood his significance. Cedric Robinson acknowledged his debt to him in *Black Marxism*. Robinson considered him a figure in the Black radical tradition on par with the individuals featured in his book: W. E. B. DuBois, CLR James, and Richard Wright. Those intellectuals as well as others such as George Padmore, Kwame Nkrumah, and in the context of childhood influences, Marcus Garvey, figured prominently in Drake's life of a scholar-activist who viewed colonialism, neocolonialism and global capitalism through a lens of racial domination and liberation-seeking responses to it among Black folk across time and space.

AISHA BELISO-DE JESÚS: You weave a wonderful tapestry for us to understand the struggles of Black anthropologists. The insights gleaned from Drake's teachings are very much still in practice—especially the feeling of being an outsider, of not being respected as "theoretical," these are all key ways the discipline maintains its whiteness.

This discussion also helps move us into the last question. The last decade has seen the growth of a number of social movements both in North America and worldwide that identified what we might call the racial violence and brutality in the policing and militarization of white supremacy. These movements have borrowed from yet gone beyond the radical liberation struggles of the 1960s, and they have launched the concept of white supremacy into the public debate in ways that are new but also seemingly old. How do you understand the role of global solidarity movements and other transformative approaches in anthropology in the struggle against racism and white supremacy?

FAYE HARRISON: Great question. White supremacy, accumulation by dispossession and expropriation, and the ecological crises of environmental injustice and climate change are global problems that cannot be dealt with simply within nation-states. We have to build multilevel and multilateral bridges that will permit activists to combine forces in greater measures of unity despite the differences and distances between us. There's the motto, "Act locally, think globally." It doesn't go far enough. Also needed are ways to think extralocally and "glocally" to inform how movements can have multiplicative effects across global terrain and seascapes. Can we design appropriate strategies and tactics to enable us to think and act glocally in a more sustained manner? This is the challenge for transformative praxis—symbiotically mutual theory and practice—at this conjuncture. There are a great deal of promising things happening, but the challenges are truly daunting.

New movements have the advantage of mobilizing and organizing in the local and global contexts of compressed time and space that new computer-mediated technologies make possible to navigate. The antiracist praxis that feminist and queer struggles have engendered expand opportunities for enacting alternatives to cisheteropatriarchal leadership. The vision and agenda of more of today's organizations are more explicitly intersectional; however, they are indebted to precedents from the past. These can be important sources of inspiration, but also of instruction. There are lessons still to be learned. The sankofa principle! Each new generation has to analyze its historically specific conditions to determine how to move forward. But there is also the need to look back at past struggles, especially those aspects that have been neglected or silenced.

Moving forward can benefit from lessons we can learn about past movements—the more radical trends during moments of the long struggle for freedom and civil/human rights. Today's global movements were foreshadowed in earlier internationalisms, particularly those that placed white supremacy, colonialism, and imperialism at the center of their agenda.

Learning more about life stories of publicly engaged, antiracist anthropologists can provide perspectives on the interplay among critical anthropological praxis, local agency, and global solidarity. Anthropologists work all over the world and have a repertoire of skills. Those committed to working toward an anthropology for liberation have the potential and opportunities to serve as emissaries, translators, and bridge builders across the horizontal and vertical boundaries of movements whose agendas prioritize combating white supremacy.

Anthropologists have already set important precedents in elucidating white supremacy's variegated forms, overt and covert, marked and unmarked. There is a rich record of documenting the dynamics of social movements and the conditions responsible for their rise, demise, routinization, and neoliberal capture. Insights from multisited and comparative knowledge can be instrumental if appropriately applied. Anthropologists need to take advantage of opportunities to practice what we preach and to demonstrate their sincerity and accountability as accomplices. Paul Farmer (cofounder of Partners in Health) wrote of pragmatic solidarity, direct forms of action and accompaniment. These are necessary if more anthropologists are to become active and expose the limits of armchair and bandwagon claims to being allies.

As individual scholar-activists but especially as participants in wider collectivities and coordinated webs of connection, anthropologists have the capacities to align themselves with, become accomplices with, and advocate on behalf of sociopolitical processes aiming to effect meaningful, substantive change. We often find ourselves at crossroads of knowledge and power that are relevant to (trans)national movements. It is beneficial for movements to enlist people with the skills and the will to bring disparate knowledges, even incommensurate perspectives, into respectful conversation and to establish partnerships to build the necessary networks that constitute movements as they ebb and flow. There are many cases, both exemplary and instructive cautionary tales, in the literature and the record of orally transmitted stories that shed light on how anthropologists have navigated or failed to navigate the contact zones where coalitions are built from the interactions and mutual objectives of academics, organic intellectuals, and civil society practitioners. Through their cooperative endeavors, diverse parties create conditions for imagining and implementing new designs for a world without white supremacy.

It is important to maintain a sense of the ideal, the long-term goal, and the enduring practices. We should also face the common problems and limitations. For instance, global solidarities are often constrained or undermined by the dynamics of differential power that shape relationships across class, race, gender, sexuality, nationality, and hemispheric locations. Solidarity networks are not level playing fields. Finding ways to work collaboratively along egalitarian, intercultural lines in an inegalitarian, imperial world is hard. It's imperative to practice an ethic of responsibility and accountability that entails that US and other western or northern activists decenter, listen to others more carefully, follow rather than lead, and facilitate the needed shift in the geography of reason, decision-making, and coleadership.

These objectives are easier said than done. There's an inadvertent tendency for northerners to exercise power and privilege in ways that reinforce western and anglophone hegemony. In these contexts, there's the danger that white supremacy will be reproduced despite good intentions. In transnational networks in which people of color are the principal actors, the effect of US hegemony can still rear its ugly head. It's important, therefore, to mobilize our skills and resources in ways that promote and advance the agendas that are collaboratively defined through egalitarian democratic processes.

Language is an axis of difference and power in a world in which English is the global lingua franca. Anthropologists can use their language competence to offset some of the problems of linguistic imperialism. Transnational and global movements benefit from shared bodies of knowledge. Facilitating engagement across language boundaries is important. Projects making significant authors and texts accessible to new constituencies of readers are something that anthropologists are undertaking, often partnering with others with complementary translation skills.

In the case of antiracist movements in Brazil and the United States and other anglophone settings such as the United Kingdom and South Africa, the writings of Brazilian and US Black feminists are being translated and circulated to expanded audiences. Afro-Brazilianists Kia Caldwell, Christen Smith, Keisha-Khan Perry, and others have made the thinking of Afro-Brazilian and Spanish-speaking Afro-Latin American feminists and anti-antiblack movement scholar-activists (e.g., Sueli Carneiro, Ochy Curiel) available in English, while the key works of major US Black feminists (e.g., Angela Davis, Patricia Hill Collins, and bell hooks) are now accessible to readers in Brazil, Lusophone Africa, and Portugal through Portuguese translations. Publishers are also introducing many Brazilian readers to book-length biographies and analyses of intellectuals such as Lélia Gonzalez and Beatriz

Nascimento, whose texts were marginalized in Brazil as well as in global circuits. The resurrection of "lost" intellectuals is an integral aspect of contemporary movements against all forms of racism, which are at once local, transnational, and, global.

Let me shift to the portion of your question concerning continuities and discontinuities between past and present movements in the United States. There are certainly features of, for instance, the Movement for Black Lives (M4BL) that are continuities from the 1950s and 1960s as well as from campaigns organized against racist repression in later decades (1970s–early 2000s). These seem to be forgotten in the wake of #BlackLiveMatter (BLM) and M4BL, a wide umbrella of fifty organizations. Before these new organizations and networks, the problems of racist policing and the prison industrial complex were addressed by, among others, Critical Resistance, and even before them the National Alliance against Racist and Political Repression, which grew out of the international campaign to free Angela Davis and other political prisoners in the early 1970s. After devolving into only two local branches, in 2019 NAARPR regrouped as a national network.

M4BL calls for the abolition of prevailing forms of social control, public policy, and problematic practices in government and civil society. This variant of antiracism demands more fundamental changes than the kinds of liberal reforms associated with the mainstream civil rights movement. The critique of liberal reforms is not new. I want us to think about the more radical social visions from left-of-center of the 1960s. They are not represented in dominant public commemorations of Martin Luther King Jr. King's radicalization over the course of his life is silenced. If we consult more than a single speech on his dream, we find that he envisioned a country and world without racism, poverty, capitalist materialism with its wealth disparities, and imperialist militarism. His liberation theology resonated with the transformational praxis of the Black Radical Tradition, its formal writings and vernacular expressions.

M4BL is rearticulating the thwarted goals of the more radical King, who in the last years of his life advocated for poor people, workers' unionization demands, and peace in the context of the Vietnam War. In many respects, the late King was aligned with contemporaries, including socialists, communists, and revolutionary workers who sought radical transformation. As a consequence, they were subjected to state violence along with being distanced by more moderate and conservative civil rights organizations—very similar to the treatment Paul and Eslanda Robeson received in the 1950s. The revolutionary social and economic visions of past Black radicals are being translated into the abolitionism of #BLM, M4BL, and related insurgencies and fugitivities. These movements, however, tend to depart from the prevailing masculinist bias and underestimation of gender as an axis of struggle that characterized much of the Black freedom movement. Despite this, we know that a rich archive of feminist consciousness and practice is being excavated. Those her-stories inspire today's visions of and for the future.

EDITORS' ACKNOWLEDGMENTS

THIS PROJECT BEGAN as a panel at the 2016 annual meeting of the American Anthropological Association (AAA) in Minneapolis, Minnesota (USA). It was soon after the election of Donald Trump to the presidency of the United States. Before Trump's ascent in US politics, many political and academic elites of the US and European countries seemed to be lost in the dream of a "postracial" era presumably ushered in by the election of the first Black president of the United States, Barack Obama. "Postracialism," however, has never been reflected in the material realities of nonwhite populations in Western countries. The year, 2016, was also the first AAA member vote to consider the academic boycott of Israeli academic institutions in solidarity with the Palestinian struggle for self-determination.

The AAA, and the discipline of anthropology more generally, has not always been a welcoming place from which to confront the facts of fascism, imperialism, settler colonialism, racism, and white supremacy. For the three editors, 2016 began our work to historicize, theorize, and act. We understood, moreover, that this work, more than anything, required recovery and celebration of the early scholarship of nonwhite anthropologists who grappled with the epistemological, ideological, and political impacts of the discipline. It was also a renewed call for decolonizing the discipline. This edited volume, *Anthropology of White Supremacy*, is one of the results.

As we embarked on this project, the two spaces that institutionally grounded us were the Association of Black Anthropologists (ABA) and AnthroBoycott. We want to first acknowledge the long tradition of Black radical critique in anthropology that has been placed on the margins of the history of the discipline, and the ABA as a grounding organization for this vital work. We also appreciate the organizers of AnthroBoycott who took on the difficult task of advocating for the recognition of and dismantling of settler colonialism in historic Palestine.

We are especially grateful to the participants of the 2016 panel who took up the challenge to help us name and theorize white supremacy as a historical, material, and ideological global system that has become so normalized as to seem invisible: Aisha Beliso-De Jesús, Faye V. Harrison, Keisha-Khan Perry, Jemima Pierre, and Junaid Rana. This panel led to a Special Section of the journal *American Anthropologist (AA)* in 2020. We are especially grateful to Deborah Thomas, whose leadership as the editor of the *AA* journal at the time, ensured that this important section came to fruition, despite a number of challenges from those who would not acknowledge the white supremacy in our discipline. This Special Section included essays not only from the original panelists, but also, Vanessa Díaz, Jonathan Rosa, Shalini Shankar, Shannon Speed, and Laurence Ralph. We are extremely grateful to all the contributors in this volume who answered our call with such analytically and methodologically rich contributions to the study of the anthropology of white supremacy.

Finally, we thank the Princeton University Press team for their patience and support in shepherding this book through. We especially thank Fred Appel for his enthusiasm for the project, and the production team, including Nathan Carr, James Collier, and Dawn Hall.

CONTRIBUTORS

SAMAR AL-BULUSHI is a political anthropologist and assistant professor of anthropology at UC Irvine who studies imperialism, race, militarism, and South-South solidarities. She is the author of the book, *War-Making as World-Making: Kenya, the United States, and the War on Terror* (Stanford University Press, 2024), which examines how Kenya emerged as a key player in the post 9/11 era of endless war.

OMOLADE ADUNBI is a political and environmental anthropologist, Professor of Anthropology and Afroamerican and African Studies, and the Director of the African Studies Center at the University of Michigan. His most recent book, *Enclaves of Exception: Special Economic Zones and Extractive Practices in Nigeria,* (Indiana University Press, 2022) interrogates the idea of Free Trade Zones and its interrelatedness to oil refining practices, infrastructure and China's engagement with Africa.

AISHA M. BELISO-DE JESÚS is a cultural and social anthropologist who studies race, religion, and police violence in the United States and Caribbean. She is the Olden Street Professor of American Studies, chair of the Effron Center for the Study of America, and co-directs the Center on Transnational Policing at Princeton University. Her most recent book, *Excited Delirium: Race, Police Violence and the Invention of a Disease* (Duke University Press, 2024), examines how the medicalizing of police violence covers up the deaths of Black and Brown people in the US. She is Editor-In-Chief of *Transforming Anthropology*, the flagship journal for the Association of Black Anthropologists.

MICHAEL L. BLAKEY is biocultural anthropologist and publicly engaged bioarchaeologist who is the National Endowment for the Humanities Professor at the College of William and Mary where he directs the Institute for Historical Biology. His work is at the intersection of biology, "nature," social inequality, and behavior; and the bioarchaeology of the African Diaspora. He directed the interdisciplinary analysis of the African Burial Ground in New York City. He has written a 3-volume book, *The Blinding Light of Race: Race and Racism in Western Science and Society* (Routledge Taylor Francis, 2025).

MITZI UEHARA CARTER is a cultural anthropologist and writer on Black/Asian connections. She is assistant teaching professor of Anthropology and Asian Studies in the Department of Global Sociocultural Studies and the Asian Studies Program at Florida International University. She also directs the Global Indigenous Forum. Her current book project traces her mother's journey from war torn Okinawa to a racially segregated US South as a lens for capturing Black Okinawan life (and afterlives) in the "Black Pacific."

VANESSA DÍAZ is an interdisciplinary ethnographer, filmmaker, and journalist trained in anthropology. She is associate professor of Chicana/o and Latina/o Studies at Loyola Marymount University. Díaz's book, *Manufacturing Celebrity: How Latino Paparazzi and Women Reporters Build the Hollywood Industrial Complex* (Duke University Press, 2020) focuses on race and gender in the production of media and popular culture.

CELINA DE SÁ is a social-cultural anthropologist working on the African diaspora. She is assistant professor of anthropology at the University of Texas at Austin. She is completing her first book, *Diaspora without Displacement: The Coloniality and Promise of Capoeira in Senegal*, under contract with Duke University Press.

SUBHADRA MITRA CHANNA is emeritus professor of anthropology at the University of Delhi. She studies marginalization through gender, caste and border communities. She has authored and edited eleven books, including, *Dhobis of Delhi: An Urban Ethnography from the Margins, 1974–2022* (Oxford University Press, 2024). She currently is co-editor of *Reviews in Anthropology*, chaired the Commission on Marginalization and Global Apartheid (IUAES), and was Senior Vice President of IUAES. She was awarded the S.C. Roy memorial gold medal by the Asiatic Society for lifetime contribution to cultural anthropology and awarded Best Teacher of Delhi University (2016).

BRITT HALVORSON is a social-cultural anthropologist whose research examines issues of religion, medicine and medical waste, colonialism, moral imagination, race and landscape in the US and Madagascar. She is associate professor of anthropology at Colby College and is the author of *Conversionary Sites: Transforming Medical Aid and Global Christianity from Madagascar to Minnesota* (University of Chicago Press, 2018).

FAYE V. HARRISON is a social and political anthropologist specializing in the study of social inequalities, the paradoxes of human rights, and intersections of race, gender, class, and (trans)national positioning. She is professor of African American Studies and Anthropology at the University of Illinois Urbana-Champaign. A past President of the Association of Black Anthropologists, she chaired the Commission on the Anthropology of Women, a unit of the International Union of Anthropological and Ethnological Sciences (IUAES), of which she served as president. Among her books and volumes, her most recent co-edited publication is *Visibilities and Invisibilities of Race and Racism: Toward a New Global Dialogue* (Routledge, 2024). She was the 2022 recipient of the Society for Applied Anthropology's Bronislaw Malinowski Award.

SARAH IHMOUD is a social-cultural anthropologist whose research interests lie at the intersections of Indigenous and decolonial feminisms, race and carcerality, and Middle East and Arab American Studies. She is assistant professor of Sociology and Anthropology in the Department of Peace and Conflict Studies at the College of Holy Cross. She is working on a book titled, *Almaqdasiyya: Palestinian Feminism and the*

Decolonial Imaginary, a feminist ethnography centering Palestinian women's resistance to colonial and patriarchal violence in occupied East Jerusalem.

ANTHONY R. JERRY is an associate professor of Anthropology and Black Study at the University of California Riverside. His research focuses on Blackness, racial value, and citizenship in Latin America, Mexico, and the US Southwest. He is the Founder and Director of The Empathy Archive, a digital education platform focused on increasing racial literacy and social and emotional learning competencies in the US. His book, *Blackness in Mexico: Afro-Mexican Recognition and the Production of Citizenship in the Costa Chica* (University Press of Florida, 2023) delves into the ongoing movement toward recognizing Black Mexicans as a cultural group within a nation that has long viewed the non-Black mestizo as the archetypal citizen.

DARRYL LI is an anthropologist and legal scholar examining questions of war, law, migration, empire, and racialization in the currents between the Middle East, South Asia, and the Balkans. He is associate professor of Anthropology and Social Sciences at the University of Chicago and associate member at the University of Chicago Law School. He is the author of *The Universal Enemy: Jihad, Empire, and the Challenge of Solidarity* (Stanford University Press, 2020), an ethnographic and archival study of "jihadist foreign fighters" in the 1990s war in Bosnia-Herzegovina.

KRISTÍN LOFTSDÓTTIR is a novelist and professor of anthropology at the University of Iceland whose work examines racism, colonialism, whiteness, and migrant precarity. She has done research in Europe (Iceland, Belgium, and Italy), as well as West Africa (Niger) and was a project manager on multiple important studies including: "Icelandic Identity in Crisis," "Mobility and Transnational Iceland," "Crisis and Nordic Identity," and "Decoding the Nordic Colonial Mind." She has written six monographs and two novels and co-edited nine volumes, most recently, *Creating Europe from the Margins* (Routledge, 2023), focusing on racism and borders in relation to Europe.

CHRISTOPHER A. LOPERENA is associate professor in the Ph.D. Program in Anthropology at the Graduate Center of the City University of New York. His research examines Indigenous and Black territorial struggles, land, environmental loss, extractivism, and the socio-spatial politics of economic development. He has also published on anthropological witnessing and cultural expertise. He is the author of *The Ends of Paradise: Race, Extraction, and the Struggle for Black Life in Honduras* (Stanford University Press, 2022). In addition to his scholarly work, he has provided expert testimony at the Inter-American Court of Human Rights and in support of US asylum claimants from Central America.

JEMIMA PIERRE is a social-cultural anthropologist of Africa and the African Diaspora. She is professor of Global Race in the Institute of Race, Gender, Sexuality and Social Justice (GRSJ) at the University of British Columbia and a research associate at the Centre for the Study of Race, Gender and Class at the University of Johannesburg. She has published widely with essays and articles examining the racial history of the discipline of anthropology, race and colonialism, Western resource extraction in Africa, and the history and politics of U.S. imperialism in Haiti and the Caribbean. She is the author of *The Predicament of Blackness: Postcolonial Ghana and the Politics of Race* (University of Chicago Press, 2013). She is the current president of the Association of Black Anthropologists.

KEISHA-KHAN Y. PERRY is an activist and Black feminist anthropologist who works on Brazil and the United States. She is the Presidential Penn Compact Associate Professor of Africana Studies at the University of Pennsylvania. Her research is focused on race, gender and politics in the Americas, urban geography and citizenship, intellectual history, and the interrelationship between scholarship, pedagogy and political engagement. She is the author of *Black Women against the Land Grab: The Fight for Racial Justice in Brazil*, (University of Minnesota Press, 2013).

JEAN MUTEBA RAHIER is professor of Anthropology and African & African Diaspora Studies at Florida International University (FIU). He is the author of three books, the editor and co-editor of four volumes, and has authored more than eighty articles and book chapters. His most recent book was *Blackness in the Andes: Ethnographic Vignettes of Cultural Politics in the Time of Multiculturalism* (Palgrave Macmillan, 2014). He was former Editor-In-Chief of the *Journal of Latin American and Caribbean Anthropology*, and is founder and director of the Observatory of Justice for Afrodescendants in Latin America (OJALA) at FIU. He is currently the Editor-In-Chief of the *Latin American and Caribbean Ethnic Studies* (LACES) journal.

RHEA RAHMAN is assistant professor of anthropology at Brooklyn College. Her research and teaching focus on transnational practices of racialization, human difference, systems of inequality and oppression, and practices towards liberation. Rahman is working on a book that frames international Muslim volunteerism, humanitarianism and development through intersecting logics of global white supremacy, anti-Muslim racism, and anti-Blackness. She is also beginning work on a second project that explores transnational links between Blackness and Islam in (West and South) Africa and the Caribbean.

LAURENCE RALPH is a writer, filmmaker, and medical anthropologist who studies gangs, masculinity, disability, and race in the United States. He is the William D. Zabel '58 Professor of Human Rights and professor of Anthropology and Public Affairs at Princeton University where he co-directs the Center on Transnational Policing. He is the recipient of numerous awards and fellowships including, the Andrew Carnegie Award, the Institute for Advanced Studies (IAS) Fellowship, a Harvard Radcliffe Fellowship, a John Smith Guggenheim Fellowship, and in 2023, was inducted into the American Academy of Arts and Sciences. He has written three books and numerous articles, most recently *Sito: An American Teenager and the City that Failed Him* (Hachette, 2024). He published an award-winning short, animated film, *The Torture Letters* (2020), based on his book with the same title. He is the Editor-In-Chief of *Current Anthropology* and a member of the advisory council for the Wenner-Gren Foundation.

RENYA K. RAMIREZ is a Ho-Chunk American anthropologist, author, and Native feminist. She is a professor of anthropology at the University of California, Santa Cruz. She has written two books on Native American culture, most recently, *Standing Up to Colonial Power: The Lives of Henry Roe and Elizabeth Bender Cloud* (University of Nebraska Press, 2018). Her work contributes to Native American studies and Native Americans and anthropology, cultural citizenship, expressive culture, and anti-racist education.

JUNAID RANA is a social-cultural anthropologist who writes about global capitalism, diaspora, racism, and social protest movements. He is associate professor of Asian American Studies at the University of Illinois at Urbana-Champaign with appointments in the Department of Anthropology, the Center for South Asian and Middle Eastern Studies, and the Unit for Criticism and Interpretive Theory. He is the author of *Terrifying Muslims: Race and Labor in the South Asian Diaspora* (Duke University Press, 2011).

JOSHUA RENO is a social-cultural anthropologist. He is the author of books on topics concerning contemporary American life, including landfills, the military industrial complex, fitness practices, and white supremacy. His most recent book is about non-verbal communication, entitled *Home Signs: An Ethnography of Life Beyond and Beside Language* (University of Chicago Press, 2024).

JONATHAN ROSA is a linguistic anthropologist who studies race, ethnicity, and language in the United States. He is associate professor in the Graduate School of Education and the Center for Comparative Studies in Race and Ethnicity at Stanford University. His research examines the co-naturalization of language and race as an organizing dynamic within modern governance, and he collaborates with schools and communities to understand and challenge the vulnerabilities they face. He is author of *Looking like a Language, Sounding like a Race: Raciolinguistic Ideologies and the Learning of Latinidad* (Oxford University Press, 2019). He is former president of the Association of Latino and Latina Anthropologists (ALLA).

SHANNON SPEED is a citizen of the Chickasaw Nation and a feminist Native anthropologist. She is Director of the American Indian Studies Center (AISC) and Professor of Gender Studies and Anthropology at UCLA. She has worked for the last two decades in Mexico and in the United States on issues of indigenous autonomy, sovereignty, gender, neoliberalism, violence, migration, social justice, and activist research. She has published numerous journal articles and book chapters in English and Spanish, as well as published six books and edited volumes, including her most recent, *Incarcerated Stories: Indigenous Women Migrants in the Settler Capitalist State* (University of North Carolina Press, 2019). She was the past President of the Native American and Indigenous Studies Association (NAISA).

MARIA DYVEKE STYVE is an Affiliate Scholar at the School of Social and Political Sciences at the University of Glasgow, Scotland and has been a Max Weber Fellow at the Department of History and Civilization at the European University Institute (EUI) in Florence, Italy. Her work revolves around the intertwined nature of anti-Blackness and capital accumulation in a historical perspective, and she has worked on mining finance in the City of London and South Africa. Her research interests span the history of anti-Black capital accumulation, the New International Economic Order, radical African economic thought, racial capitalism and economic history. Her work has been featured in the *Review of African Political Economy, The Extractive Industries and Society Journal* and the *Review of Political Economy*.

SHALINI SHANKAR is a social-cultural and linguistic anthropologist who has conducted ethnographic research with South Asian American youth, advertising agencies, and spelling bee participants in the US. She is professor of Anthropology and Asian American Studies at Northwestern University. Her work contributes to studies of race and ethnicity, diaspora and migration, youth, media, advertising, semiotics, South Asian diaspora and Asian diasporas in the United States. She is the author of two books, most recently, *Advertising Diversity: Ad Agencies and the Creation of Asian American Advertising* (Duke University Press, 2015). Her research has been funded by the National Science Foundation and the Wenner-Gren Foundation.

INDEX

Page numbers in italics refer to figures.

A NOTE ON THE TYPE

This book has been composed in Arno, an Old-style serif typeface in the
classic Venetian tradition, designed by Robert Slimbach at Adobe.

Printed in the USA
CPSIA information can be obtained
at www.ICGtesting.com
JSHW051943301124
74569JS00006B/18